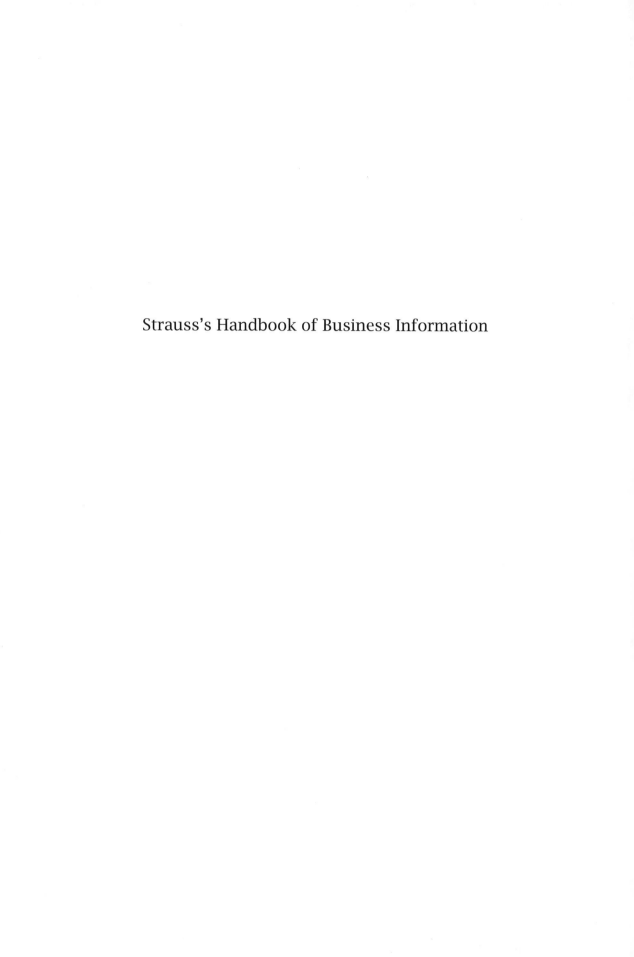

Strauss's Handbook of Business Information

Strauss's Handbook of Business Information

A Guide for Librarians, Students, and Researchers

Third Edition

Rita W. Moss and David G. Ernsthausen

LIBRARIES UNLIMITED

AN IMPRINT OF ABC-CLIO, LLC
Santa Barbara, California • Denver, Colorado • Oxford, England

Library of Congress Cataloging-in-Publication Data

Moss, Rita W.
    Strauss's handbook of business information : a guide for librarians, students, and researchers / Rita W. Moss and David G. Ernsthausen.
        p. cm.
    Includes bibliographical references and indexes.
    ISBN 978-1-59884-807-6 (acid-free paper) — EISBN: 978-1-61069-236-6 (ebook)
1. Business—Reference books—Bibliography—Handbooks, manuals, etc. 2. Business information services—United States—Handbooks, manuals, etc. 3. Government publications—United States—Handbooks, manuals, etc. 4. Business—Databases—Handbooks, manuals, etc. 5. Business—United States—Electronic information resources—Handbooks, manuals, etc. I. Ernsthausen, David G. II. Title.
Z7164.C81S7796 2012
[HF1010]
016.33—dc23   2011041547

ISBN: 978-1-59884-807-6
EISBN: 978-1-61069-236-6

16 15 14 13 12   1 2 3 4 5

This book is also available on the World Wide Web as an eBook.
Visit www.abc-clio.com for details.

Libraries Unlimited
An Imprint of ABC-CLIO, LLC

ABC-CLIO, LLC
130 Cremona Drive, P.O. Box 1911
Santa Barbara, California 93116-1911

This book is printed on acid-free paper (∞)
Manufactured in the United States of America

Contents

List of Figures. xv
Introduction xix

Part 1: Basic Resources, Print & Internet

Chapter 1: Basic Resources, Print & Internet. 3
  Guides 3
    Types of Business Guides. 4
  Bibliographies 9
  Dictionaries 12
    General Business Dictionaries 12
    Multilingual Business Dictionaries. 12
    Acronyms and Abbreviations Dictionaries. 13
  Almanacs 13
  Encyclopedias 14
  Handbooks. 15
  Internet Resources without Print Counterparts 15

Chapter 2: Selected, Consolidated Electronic Business Information 21
  Online Business Databases 22
    Database Producers, Vendors, and Aggregators 22
    Portals. 23
  Selected Commercial Products 23
    Selected Aggregators 24
  Periodicals and Newspapers 27
    Types of Business Periodicals 27
  Periodical Directories 35
  Newspapers 36
    Regular Daily Newspapers 37
    Business and Financial Newspapers 37
    Trade Newspapers 42
    Business Suites 42
    Resources "Free" on the Internet 44
  Notes. 46

Chapter 3: Company Information 47
  Questions 47
  Types of Information 48
    infoUSA. 48
    Bureau Van Dijk http://www.bvdinfo.com 49

Chapter 3: Company Information (*Cont.*)
    Standard & Poor's http://www.standardandpoors.com/ 50
    EbscoHost http://www.ebscohost.com/ 51
    ProQuest http://www.proquest.com 52
    Gale Cengage Learning http://www.gale.cengage.com/index.htm 52
    Mergent http://www.mergent.com/ 52
    Thomson Reuters http://thomsonreuters.com/ 53
    LexisNexis http://www.lexisnexis.com/ 53
    Other Publishers or Resources 54
    Industry Classification Codes 55
    Financial and Performance Ratios 55

Chapter 4: Industry Information 57
  Industry Classification Codes 57
    Things to Know about NAICS 58
    Why Is NAICS Used Instead of SIC? 59
  Examples of Other Industry Information 59
  Sources of Industry Information 60
    Government Resources for Industry 60
    Commercial Vendors Reports, Surveys, and Overviews 63
    Industry Trade Groups and Associations 71
    Industry Financial and Performance Ratios 72
    Notes 74

Chapter 5: Government Information and Services 75
  Federal Government Information 75
    Structure of the U.S. Federal Government 76
  Federal Government Publishers 81
    Government Printing Office 81
    National Technical Information Service 89
  Trends in Federal Publishing 93
  Commercially Published Guides, Bibliographies, and Periodicals 93
    Guides 93
    Bibliographies 95
    Indexes and Periodicals 96
  Federal Government Services to Business 97
    Federal Libraries 98
    Experts 98
    Grants, Loans, and Other Financial and Non-Financial Assistance 99
    Government Purchase of Goods and Services 99
  State Government Information and Services 100
    Published Information 100
    Services to Business 100
  Conclusion 101
  Notes 101

Chapter 6: Statistics 103
  Major Compilers and Publishers of Statistics 103
    Federal Government Agencies 103
    State Government Agencies. 109
    Trade Associations 109
    Commercial Publishers 110
    Other Organizations. 110
  Basic Statistical Concepts 110
    Sampling. 110
    Time Series Analysis. 111
    Forecasts and Projections. 112
    Index Numbers 112
  Economic Indicators 115
  Reliability of Statistics. 117
  Statistical Publications 118
    Dictionaries and Encyclopedias 118
    Guides and Indexes 119
    Statistical Compilations 121
  Compilations and Search Engines on the Web 125
  Free Resources for International Data on the Web. 126
  Notes. 129

Part 2: Fields of Business Information

Chapter 7: Marketing 133
  Marketing Basics 133
    Marketing Activities 133
    Market Segmentation 134
    Marketing Research 135
  Marketing Reference Sources 138
    Guides and Bibliographies 138
    Dictionaries and Encyclopedias 138
    Directories 141
    Periodicals 142
    Statistics 143
    Advertising Media 149
    Advertising Expenditures 155
    Geographic Information Systems. 156
    Web Sites. 157
  Marketing Associations 157
  Regulation of Marketing 158
    Federal Trade Commission 158
    Food and Drug Administration 160
    Federal Communications Commission 161

Chapter 7: Marketing (*Cont.*)
  Other Government Agencies. 162
 Notes. 162

Chapter 8: Accounting and Taxation 163
 Accounting Basics. 163
  Types of Accounting. 164
  Certified Public Accountants. 165
  American Institute of Certified Public Accountants (AICPA) 166
  Basic Accounting Concepts 167
 Sources of Accounting Information 174
  Guides and Dictionaries. 174
  Handbooks and Encyclopedias. 175
  Directories 176
  Periodical Indexes and Abstracts 176
  Periodicals 177
  Loose-Leaf and Electronic Services 178
  Government Documents 180
 Tax Basics 181
  Kinds of Taxes 181
  Internal Revenue Service 182
  Other Federal Government Agencies. 183
  Federal Tax Law and Administration 183
  U.S. State Governments 184
 Tax Publications and Information Sources 185
  Dictionaries 185
  Income Tax Guides 186
  Directories 188
  Periodicals, Newspapers, and Indexes 188
  Online and Loose-Leaf Services 190
  Government Publications and Services. 191
  Statistics 192
 Notes. 194

Chapter 9: Money, Credit, and Banking 195
 Money. 195
  Monetary System 196
  Monetary Measures 196
  Foreign Exchange 196
 Credit 198
  Creditworthiness. 198
  Interest 199
 Banks, Thrifts, and the Financial Services Industry. 200
  Commercial Banks 201
  Thrift Institutions 202

Other Financial Institutions. 203
Federal Reserve System 204
Organizational Structure 205
Services. 207
Monetary Policy 208
Other Federal and State Government Agencies 209
Federal Agencies. 209
State Agencies 210
Publications 211
Guides. 211
Dictionaries and Encyclopedias 212
Financial Manuals and Online Databases. 213
Periodicals, Newspapers, and Indexes 216
Government Documents 218
Statistics 219
Banking Tables. 222
Databases 222
Notes. 222

Chapter 10: Investments: An Introduction. .225
Investors and Their Information Needs. 226
Background Information Sources. 226
Encyclopedias and Handbooks 227
Dictionaries 229
Investment Advisory Services. 230
Securities Quotations 232
Notes. 232

Chapter 11: Stocks. 233
Introduction 233
Common and Preferred Stock. 233
Earnings per Share 234
Dividend Yield. 234
Price-Earnings Ratio 234
Warrants 235
Stock Exchanges 235
New York Stock Exchange Euronext 235
NASDAQ. 237
Regional Stock Exchanges 237
Over-the-Counter Market 237
International Stock Exchanges 238
Stock Prices. 240
Stock Tables 240
Stock Price Indexes 242

Chapter 11: Stocks (*Cont.*)
Dow Jones Industrial Average. 242
Standard & Poor's 500 Index 242
Other Indexes. 242
Stock Index Information Sources 242
Corporate Reports. 243
Registration and Prospectus 243
10-K Report 244
Annual Report to Shareholders 245
Other Reports 245
Comprehensive Investment Services 246
Investment and Research Information Services 247
Sources of Industry Information. 251
Industry Studies 251
Other Publications. 254
Notes 257

Chapter 12: Bonds and Other Fixed-Income Securities. 259
Bonds. 259
Interest 259
Prices. 260
Yield 260
Call Provisions. 261
Ratings 261
Secondary Bond Market. 262
Money Market Instruments. 263
Federal Government Securities. 263
Treasury Issues 263
Federal Agency Issues 266
Municipal Issues 267
General Obligation Bonds 267
Revenue Bonds 267
Sources of Information on Municipal Bonds 268
Corporate Securities 269
Types of Corporate Bonds 269
Trading of Corporate Bonds 270
Sources of Information on Corporate Bonds 270
General Information Sources. 271
Factual Sources 271
Advisory Services 273
For-Fee Databases 273
Web Sites. 274
Notes 275

Chapter 13: Mutual Funds and Investment Companies 277
Introduction 277
Types of Investment Companies. 279
Load and No-Load Funds 279
Investment Objectives 280
Portfolio Contents 280
Current Per-Share Information 281
Mutual Funds 281
Closed-End Investment Companies. 282
Information Sources 282
Prospectuses and Company Reports 282
Encyclopedias, Guides, and Factbooks 283
Subscription Databases 286
Directories 286
Periodical Lists and Ratings 286
Specialized Advisory Newsletters/Services 287
Notes 288

Chapter 14: Futures and Options 289
Derivatives 289
Guides. 290
Dictionaries 290
Futures 291
Commodities Futures 292
Futures Exchanges 293
Commodity Futures Trading Commission 295
Current Prices 295
Financial Futures. 295
Futures Information Sources 297
Handbooks, Manuals, and Guides. 297
Dictionaries 298
Periodicals, Newspapers, and Newsletters. 298
Statistics 300
Advisory Services 302
Databases 303
Options 303
Basic Features 304
Puts and Calls 304
Exchanges. 304
Listed Options Quotations. 305
Options Information Sources. 305
Guides. 306
Periodicals and Newspapers. 306
Statistics 306

Chapter 14: Futures and Options (*Cont.*)
    Dictionaries and Glossaries. 306
    Advisory Services 307
  Notes. 307

Chapter 15: Insurance. 309
  Insurance Basics. 309
    Characteristics of Insurance. 309
    Types of Insurance 311
    Insurance Associations. 319
    Regulation of the Insurance Industry 319
  Insurance Information Sources 320
    Guides and Dictionaries. 320
    Handbooks and Consumer Guides 320
    Directories 323
    Information about Insurance Companies 324
    Information about Insurance Policies 326
    Insurance Periodicals 327
    Periodical Indexes. 329
    Government Documents 329
    Statistics 332
  Notes. 334

Chapter 16: Real Estate. 335
  Basic Real Estate Concepts. 335
    Categories of Real Estate 336
    Real Estate Industry 338
    Government and Real Estate. 345
  Real Estate Information Sources 347
    Dictionaries, Encyclopedias, and Handbooks 347
    Directories 349
    Periodicals and Periodical Indexes. 350
    Government Documents/Resources. 351
    Statistics 352
  Notes. 360

  Appendix A: Business Acronyms and Abbreviations 361
  Appendix B: Federal Government Departments and Selected
      Agencies Relevant to Business. 365
  Appendix C: Federal Government Corporations and Independent
      Agencies Relevant to Business. 369
  Appendix D: Representative Types of Business Information
      Published by State Government Agencies. 371

Appendix E: Key Economic Indicators. 373
Appendix F: Selected Web Sites for Free Business Information 375
Appendix G: Finding Business Case Studies. 383
Title List. 385
Subject Index. 391

List of Figures

1.1. Front screen of Business 2.0 Business Books: Core Collections 5
1.2. Screen shot of the section: Financial Crises Books 6
1.3. Screen shot of Resource Shelf Blog 16
1.4. The DocuTicker DocuBase. 17
1.5. Economics & Finance FAQ (Princeton) 18
1.6. Company and Industry 19
2.1. Comparison of selected ProQuest and EBSCO databases. 26
2.2. Types of business periodicals. 28
2.3. Image of the Survey of Current Business. 33
2.4. Typical international data listing, Survey of Current Business 34
2.5. Newspapers of interest to the business community. 37
2.6. Interpreting a stock market table compiled for a fictional company XXX. 39
2.7. Typical listing, FedBizOpps. 41
3.1. Company count by region for select Bureau Van Dijk databases. 50
3.2. Coverage of "Moody's / Mergent Manuals" in Mergent WebReports. 53
3.3. Selected free company web sites. 55
3.4. Selected financial ratios. 56
4.1. U.S. Census Bureau Economic Programs and Surveys 60
4.2. U.S. Other Economic Programs of the U.S. Census Bureau 62
4.3. Partial list of industry reports available from IBISWorld 63
4.4. Example of IBISWorld Report 64
4.5. Passport GMID search menu. 65
4.6. Passport GMID statistics report 66
4.7. Example of Passport GMID analysis report 66
4.8. Mintel base page 67
4.9 Example of Mintel report 67
4.10. BizMiner main page 68
4.11. BizMiner Reports. 69
4.12. Example of a BizMiner industry Area Report. 70
5.1. Branches of the federal government. 76
5.2. Congressional committees especially important to business.. 77
5.3. Locate federal depository libraries 83
5.4. Official government information from FDsys. 84
5.5. Materials available from the *Federal Bulletin Board*. 84
5.6. Sample short entry from the *Catalog of U.S. Government Publications*. 85
5.7. New Titles Search from the *Catalog of U.S. Government Publications*.. 87
5.8. Sample entry in *U.S. Government Subscriptions Catalog for* Internal
        Revenue Bulletin. 88
5.9. NTIS—National Technical Information Service 89
5.10. Methods for ordering from NTIS 90
5.11. NTIS Product Search Page. 91
5.12. U.S. Patent Office web page. 92
5.13. U.S. Small Business Administration. 98
6.1. Some statistical organizations of the federal government. 104
6.2. Sample entry, *Census Blog*. 106

6.3. Selected News Release Schedules 107
6.4. Some agency listings for statistics 108
6.5. DATA.GOVraw data file 108
6.6. The Consumer Price Index for All Urban Consumers (CPI-U) 114
6.7. Part of a typical introductory section to a chapter, *Statistical Abstract
      of the United States* 122
6.8. Sample table from section 30, *Statistical Abstract of the United States* 123
6.9. Entry screen of OFFSTATS, Official Statistics on the Web 127
6.10. First country screen of OFFSTATS, Official Statistics on the Web 128
7.1. *American FactFinder* 145
7.2. Radio time slots 152
7.3. List of some of the business publications provided online by the FTC 160
7.4. Warning reproduced from the Consumer Updates section of the FDA
      web page 161
8.1. Balance sheet example 168
8.2. Income statement example 169
8.3. Description of three online tutorials from the SBA on financing
      your business 170
8.4. List of downloadable forms and other publications from the IRS 182
8.5. More forms and publications available from the IRS 187
8.6. Typical listing of charities from *Cumulative List of Organizations* 189
8.7. Sample page from *Statistics of Income Bulletin* (Winter 2011) 192
8.8. Listing of statistical tables provided by the IRS 193
9.1. Federal Reserve Bank of New York, sample of monthly exchange rates 197
9.2. The financial services industry 201
9.3. Structure and responsibilities of the Federal Reserve System 206
9.4. The 12 Federal Reserve Banks and Districts 207
9.5. Bank Data Guide 211
9.6. Search page for the Financial Institutions Directory 215
9.7. Example of publications available in the banking category 218
9.8. Representative list of publications on banks 219
9.9. Sample listing of commercial banking statistics available from FRED 220
9.10. Selected front screen links at FRASER 221
9.11. Part of report on securities of FDIC-insured savings institutions 221
10.1. Selected investment guides on the Web 228
11.1. U.S. stock exchanges registered with the SEC 236
11.2. Selected exchanges of the Mediterranean and Middle East 239
11.3. Extract of web page showing some regulators for Australasia 239
11.4. Hypothetical stock table 240
11.5. Search choices on the EDGAR database 244
11.6. The most widely used 1934 Act registration forms 246
11.7. *2007 Economic Census*: Schedule of releases 252
12.1. Bond rating categories 262
12.2. Table of Treasury auctions 264
12.3. Example of a newspaper quotation for a Treasury bill 264
12.4. Recent Auction Results: Treasury bonds and notes 265
12.5. Estimated ownership of U.S. Treasury securities 266
12.6. Example of a corporate bond table 270
13.1. Example of a daily online mutual fund table 281
13.2. Hypothetical listing of a closed-end fund 282

13.3. Checking on brokers and advisors showing links to FNRA.................284
14.1 Selected major commodity and financial futures traded in the
      United States. 291
14.2. Selected major U.S. commodities and futures exchanges. 293
14.3. Some corn futures trading conditions. 294
14.4. Example of a futures trading table 296
14.5. Image of the web page for minerals information .301
14.6. Screen of the USDA National Agricultural Statistics Service 302
14.7. Examples of exchanges and the options traded. .305
15.1. Major types of insurers. 311
15.2. Types of insurance sold by private insurers. 311
15.3. Selected government insurance programs 317
15.4. *Social Security Handbook*. Table of Contents 321
15.5. *Social Security Handbook*. Chapter Table of Contents 322
15.6. Sample entry, *Social Security Handbook* 322
15.7. Typical ratings assigned. 325
15.8. Example of the online help available from the Social Security
      Administration 330
15.9. Alternate languages available for some Medicare publications. 331
16.1. Types of real estate. 336
16.2. Data entry form for loan amortization table using a web calculator. 341
16.3. Sample loan amortization table using a web calculator 341
16.4. Selected mortgage calculators available on the Web. 342
16.5. Value of Construction Put in Place 352
16.6. Annual Construction Cost Indexes. 354
16.7. Sample listing of construction reports 355
16.8. Sample listing of housing reports 355
16.9. *Quick Report for Industry* entry form 356

Introduction

This book is aimed at librarians in both academic and public settings, students in either business schools or in library schools, general business researchers, and entrepreneurs. For this reason, to make access easier, the book is organized into two parts. The first six chapters are general areas of business while chapters 7 through 14 cover more specific topics such as marketing, investment, and real estate. There is some overlap between chapters and also some overlap of resources but that is the nature of business information. We hope the repetition, when it occurs, is not annoying but rather reinforces the fact that resources can be used for different research needs.

The decision to update the book was made because since the last edition there has been a transformation in the availability of business information. So many more resources are offered on the Internet either for free or for a fee, and this has changed the way libraries purchase or make business information available. Also many of the resources described in the earlier editions have either ceased publication, changed format, changed content, or disappeared. Also over the past years numerous librarians have asked when a new edition will be available.

At the same time we are all contending with shrinking budgets and rising prices. To find information freely available is a success that we share daily with colleagues. Simultaneously we do need to buy information that will help users and help ourselves to do our jobs well. We have tried in this book to mix together the information sources that we must pay for with those that are freely available. It is, for example, no longer really necessary for a small library to pay large sums of money for encyclopedias and guidebooks when much of the basic business information is freely available. There are often current newspaper and magazine articles accessible as well, although as we know there is always a price for an archive. We have tried in this edition to incorporate more free resources and to bring more analysis to the differences between the offerings from competing vendors. We do not intend to influence database choices but seek to describe the competing possibilities.

Sophisticated users of the Web are able to find much of the basic information that used to be provided in libraries simply by using a search engine. As a result librarians are working more closely with the less experienced user who "knows" that the information is "out there somewhere." It is often the librarian's lot to enlighten the users that just because they need the information does not mean that it is readily available without a price. The other side of the workload is finding complicated information that the user cannot find. One example is the professor who on skimming an article finds a reference to the "surprise index" and wonders why this is not in the library catalog. Public librarians are probably more involved with the users who want to develop or expand a business and work diligently to find the information needed and to point the user in the direction of other assistance that will help in the endeavor.

As we edited and reorganized this latest edition, publishers merged and resources changed, vanished, or improved. We hope that not too many more publications fade away before publication. If that occurs an Internet search may be necessary to determine the latest editions, new publishers, or new web addresses.

1

Basic Resources, Print & Internet

1

Basic Resources, Print & Internet

Accurate, timely business information is vital. Executives contemplating a plant relocation, for example, must consider such factors as corporate income tax rates, availability of and average weekly wages of workers, cost of living, climate, and community resources before making their decision. A marketing department will want to learn all it can about the economic and social characteristics of specific regions of the country so that it can decide how to boost sales or where best to launch a new product. Proprietors of new businesses may want to find out what kinds of financial assistance are available from government agencies and prospective investors, and to learn all they can about the recent successes (or failures) of related companies. Each of these situations illustrates the importance of information in business decision making, planning, and problem solving. As it has become easier, with the advent of the Internet, to find information, questions asked of researchers and librarians have become more complex and users have become more demanding. Users have become used to fast answers and also expect that everything they want to know is available somewhere. Librarians/ researchers are also used to finding much of their information on the Web, and this has affected the contents of collections housed within libraries.

Librarians and researchers seeking business information are confronted with an overwhelming number of books, periodicals, newspapers, government documents, databases, and web sources from which to choose. Examination of some of these sources will reveal that their quality varies considerably; some are superb, others are marginal at best. To succeed, the librarian or researcher must decide not only where to go for the desired information but also how to select the best sources from the many available. This chapter lists and describes selected business guides and other fact-finding aids that identify some of the most widely used sources of business information. Also included in this chapter are major reference sources—dictionaries, encyclopedias, and handbooks that may be available either in print or electronically.

Guides

Print bibliographic guides to business literature are no longer abundant. To find those that focus on specific business activities such as marketing and accounting, or management, it is often best to find a librarian or researcher who produces freely

3

available guides. Examples are those created by the business librarians at Rutgers, available at http://libguides.rutgers.edu/business and those compiled by the librarians at the Lippincot Library, listed at http://gethelp.library.upenn.edu/guides/business/. For people looking for guides that are less academic, those available at the Brooklyn Public Library can be checked at http://www.brooklynpubliclibrary.org/business/resources/guides.jsp and those from the Enoch Pratt Public library are listed at http://www.prattlibrary.org/research/subjects/. Most libraries produce guides, and these can be found through a simple web search. One of the advantages of using these resources is the constant updating so that new materials and links are included in a timely manner. They all tend to have something in common; they provide an overview of the area being covered; and they list, annotate, and sometimes evaluate relevant sources in a variety of formats. This section describes bibliographic guides that encompass the entire range of business activities.

Types of Business Guides

Business guides can be classified in a number of ways. They can, for example, be categorized by the breadth of coverage they provide. General guides cover many fields of business and may include handbooks and basic textbooks as well as reference sources. Selective guides, on the other hand, may include materials that point the user to only available commercial resources and another may include only free web sources. Dictionary guides are compilations of research materials in highly specialized areas such as robotics or corporate ethics. Although their level of subject specificity is valuable, dictionary guides lack the subject background provided by general and selective bibliographic guides. Finally, other guides are written with specific user populations in mind. They are written for managers and executives, researchers, women, business students, or novice library users. Each is written for a designated user group and describes the basic sources and research techniques most likely to be of interest to that group.

No single guide, no matter how thorough or well written, can possibly serve all needs. Therefore, representative examples of each type of guide may be essential sources in all but the smallest and most selective business reference collections. Some of the most important guides are described below.

General Guides

Business encompasses so many different activities and is characterized by such rapid change that a truly comprehensive, up-to-date printed guide to the core literature is impossible.

For this reason many researchers use web resources.

Mckay, Peter. **Business Books: Core Collections. University of Florida, George A. Smathers Libraries.**

http://businesslibrary.uflib.ufl.edu/businessbooks

The author and maintainer states on the introductory page, "It is my hope that you will find these bibliographies useful as reading lists, selection aids, guides to the literature, collection evaluation tools—whatever your purpose. The goal is to provide enhanced core collections in a broad cross section of business subjects. The collections are ongoing and updated as new essential titles are published."

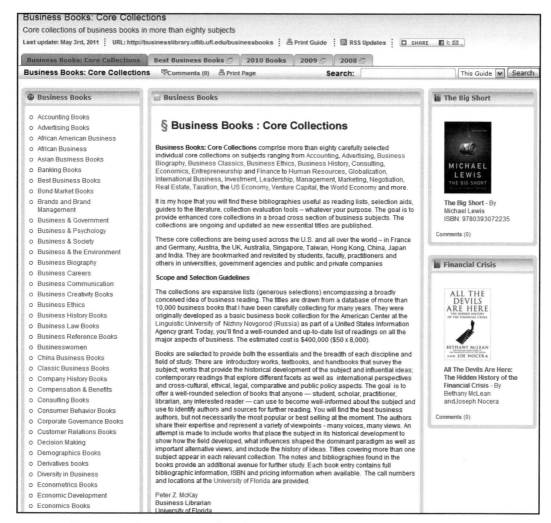

Figure 1.1. Front screen of Business 2.0 Business Books: Core Collections
http://businesslibrary.uflib.ufl.edu/businessbooks

The collections are divided into 87 categories ranging from Accounting to World Economy, and each section contains a list of books. The earlier compiled sections consist of a listed bibliography and some pricing information, but the later sections are fully annotated and link to buying information. Books are selected to show both the depth and breadth of a subject, and whenever possible the listings provide a variety of viewpoints. An extremely useful site intended to make the work of setting up or maintaining a business collection somewhat easier.

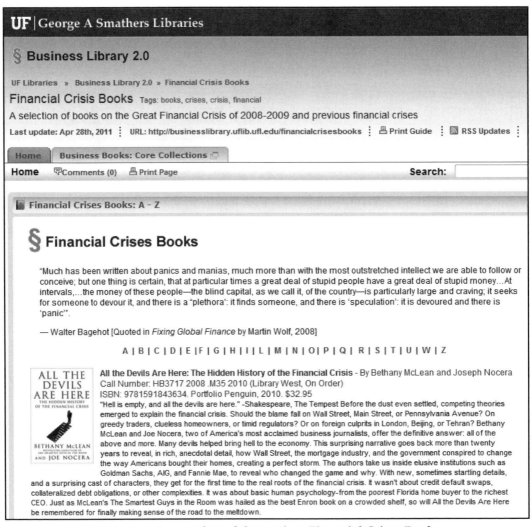

Figure 1.2. Screen shot of the section: Financial Crises Books
http://businesslibrary.uflib.ufl.edu/financialcrisesbooks

The distinction between general and selective business guides is an arbitrary one. Some limit their coverage by subject, information format, or type of library or information setting to which the listed source is appropriate. Guides emphasizing specific subject areas are included in many of the upcoming chapters. The titles listed below, however, selectively present sources relevant to several different fields of business.

Lavin, Michael. **Business Information: How to Find It, How to Use It.** 2nd ed. Phoenix, AZ: Oryx Press, 1992. 499p.

Although it is useful for identifying some resources appropriate to medium-sized business library collections, much of this information is very dated and has to be updated by the user's own searches for newer editions or publications, but the Lavin book is well known for its clear and well-written descriptions of basic research techniques and business concepts.

As its subtitle indicates, the guide emphasizes research techniques and basic business concepts as well as information sources. Lavin first introduces business information and basic finding aids, not only covering standard reference sources but also identifying major characteristics of business information and the organizations from which it typically is available. The various published sources of company data are also considered, with chapters on business directories; registered trademarks; corporate finance; and basic investment information, advice, and analysis. Another section focuses on statistical information. In addition to chapters that identify general economic and industry statistics with descriptions of many of the sources that contain them, it includes an extremely useful and interesting introduction to statistical reasoning in population estimates and projections. This is illustrated through an excellent discussion of the decennial Census of Population and Housing. Finally, four special topics—local area information, business and labor law, marketing, and taxation and accounting—are treated at length. Title and subject indexes are also included.

Business Information is different from other guides in many important respects. Each chapter begins with an outline of the topics to be covered and the major sources to be discussed and is followed by an explanation of the concepts necessary to understand each source. Although far fewer titles are covered than in most other guides, those that are included are treated more thoroughly. Annotations, which vary in length from a single paragraph to more than a page, are thorough and are sometimes supplemented with reprints from the sources being discussed. Finally, each chapter concludes with a brief, annotated list of titles for further reading. The second edition includes new topics and additions to those previously included in the first edition. Other changes include much updated and enlarged coverage of electronic products.

The Basic Business Library similarly seeks to identify business resources essential for small and medium-sized libraries. It presents an alphabetical, annotated list of core reference titles and a core list of business journals suitable for a small library. There is a bibliography on business reference and business librarianship and a series of essays on such topics as marketing business libraries, acquiring business books, developing a business reference collection, and evaluating investment and online resources. The overview of business librarianship and library practices and the several lists justify the retention of *The Basic Business Library* for most business reference collections.

The comprehensive and selective guides described above are most useful for descriptions of standard business publications and for general surveys of business literature. The librarian or researcher in quest of statistics on paper bag production or in need of information on the olive oil industry, however, will need to consult sources that provide more detailed subject indexing. Dictionary guides are particularly useful in such situations.

Dictionary Guides

A dictionary guide is a computer-generated list of publications, databases, and other information sources, usually arranged by very narrow and precise subject headings. The titles that follow are representative.

Woy, James, ed. **Encyclopedia of Business Information Sources**. 28th ed. Detroit: Gale Cengage Learning, 1970–. 2vs. Frequency varies.

Directory of Business Information Sources. 2011 ed. Lakeville, CT: Grey House Pub., 1992–.

Long the standard dictionary guide, the *Encyclopedia of Business Information Sources* lists a wide variety of published reference sources, databases, trade and professional associations, research centers and institutes, and other information sources on over 1,100 business-related subjects. It is arranged alphabetically by topic, from "Abbreviations" and "Abrasives Industry" to "Zinc" and "Zoning." Each topic is subdivided into types of information sources available (e.g., almanacs, abstracts, bibliographies, encyclopedias, handbooks, financial ratios, and price and statistics sources), with full bibliographic citations and prices for most of the items listed. E-mail addresses and web site URLs have been provided when they are available. Also included are the addresses and telephone numbers of publishers. This is also available electronically as part of the *Gale Directory Library*.

The *Directory of Business Information Resources*, covering 98 industry groups, is arranged alphabetically by category. It covers broad areas such as leather products, retailing, and wholesale services. The listings within each category begin, like the *Encyclopedia*, with the associations, although this publication does not limit the listings to those directly connected with the subject area but also lists those that are peripherally connected. For example, in Accounting an association that provides market information on the category is also included. Also included in the listings are newsletters, magazines and journals, tradeshows, and other directories and databases. This directory is also available via a database platform.

To this point, the guides that have been presented have been intended for an array of prospective users. Other guides are written with specific user populations in mind.

Guides for Specific User Groups

People who might benefit most from using a business library or consulting business information sources are often unaware of the range and availability of such resources. Accordingly, guides to sources of business information and to the libraries that contain them can serve an important function. Some are written specifically for businesspeople and business students, others for researchers. The following titles represent the guides intended for business professionals and students.

Abels, Eileen G., and Deborah P. Klein. **Business Information. Needs and Strategies.** United Kingdom: Emerald, 2008. 207p.

Maier, Ernest L., and others. **The Business Library and How to Use It: A Guide to Sources and Research Strategies for Information on Business and Management**. 6th ed. Detroit: Omnigraphics, 1996. 329p.

Business Information is intended to provide a guide to underlying information needs and the ways that the information can be found. The writers do not assume that users have an understanding of research procedures or any knowledge of sources. The book is arranged in eight sections, with the first two parts giving information on selecting and evaluating sources and then linking the needed information to a source that supplies the answer. Section C supplies sources to specific questions posed in two dozen business areas ranging from accounting and financial analysis to taxation. The format is columnar, with questions on the left of the page and suggested sources on the right. Frequently more than one source is suggested so that the user has a better chance of finding answers in a wide variety of libraries and information centers. Each entry in this section is cross-referenced to a descriptive profile of printed sources in Section D. Sections E and F follow the same plan for electronic resources.

The Business Library and How to Use It is a practical guide for librarians, students, and researchers. Divided into 16 chapters presented in four sections, the book presents a methodical approach to research in the library. The first section instructs readers in basic library skills, including the Library of Congress and Dewey Decimal Classification systems and the use of the card catalog, while sections two and three focus on specific information formats (periodical literature, databases, handbooks and yearbooks, directories, financial and investment services, and government publications). Chapters generally begin with a survey of the types of materials to be covered, followed by lists of relevant reference works with brief annotations. The fourth section provides some guidance and cites helpful sources for creating reports using the information gathered. *The Business Library and How to Use It* is not written with the sophisticated researcher in mind. Its annotations and introductory remarks, however, can be useful to librarians and general library users as well as to more specialized business clientele.

Although old there are still useful sections in this book, and it is generally held by most libraries.

Other guides are written for experienced researchers, who are already familiar with library materials and resources, and with many basic reference techniques. Coverage in these publications is usually more intensive, and often the focus will be on a specific aspect of business research rather than the whole gamut of available business information.

The above guides and others like them are invaluable. They provide readers with an introduction to basic business sources, concepts, and research techniques, and help to acquaint them with business information needs. They are not, however, intended to be nor should they be used as the sole sources of information about business publications and databases. Bibliographies are also important.

Bibliographies

Business bibliographies come in a variety of formats and serve an assortment of users. Some provide retrospective lists of significant publications in all languages. Others list only the most recent publications and are limited by country. Some cover relatively narrow fields, such as agribusiness or costs of living, while others include titles for all fields of business. This section focuses on bibliographies that present information on current English-language publications primarily issued by American publishers. Some are aimed at librarians and others at library users.

Of more practical benefit to small and medium-sized libraries are the bibliographies and resource guides that are available free of charge on many library web sites. Many of these bibliographies are annotated and can be used not only for instruction but as a collection tool. A good starting point would be the Business Reference Services at the Library of Congress (http://lcweb.loc.gov/rr/business/index1.html). As more libraries share their resources in this way and as more use is made of searching other institutions' online catalogs, smaller libraries with more limited budgets will be able to access the same bibliographic information as larger repositories. Furthermore, this information can be supplemented by accessing publishers' lists via the Web.

Other useful sources for annotated bibliographies include the following.

"Best Business Books [Year]," **Library Journal.** Annual feature, published in March.

Wynar, Bohdan S. **American Reference Books Annual**. Littleton, CO: Libraries Unlimited, 1970–. Annual.

BRASS Business Reference Sources Committee: **Outstanding Business Reference Sources: Yearly Selection of Recent Titles. Annual Feature. Reference & Users Services Quarterly. Also available at** http://www.ala.org/ala/mgrps/divs/rusa/sections/brass/brasspubs/publications.cfm

Every year, *Library Journal* lists and annotates some of the best books of the year in a survey of the past year's trends in business publishing. Written by a subject specialist, "Business Books" lists by subject both circulating and reference titles judged by the author to be superior or significant.

The emphasis is different in *American Reference Books Annual* (*ARBA*). First, only reference works are included. Second, whereas "Business Books" is a selective, subjective list of the most highly acclaimed titles, *ARBA* includes publications of varying quality. Some are first-rate; others are clearly inferior. What makes *ARBA* so useful are the detailed, critical reviews, some of which discuss the strengths and weaknesses of specific titles at considerable length. Each review is signed, and citations to earlier reviews in library journals are included. By including both so-called good and bad titles accompanied by thoughtful evaluations, *ARBA* allows librarians to make informed decisions about publications to avoid as well as those to collect. *ARBA* is one of the many publications that is also online. This service, available at http://www.ARBAonline.com, includes coverage from 1997 until the present and contains over 500 subject areas and titles from more than 400 publishers. Being available online makes an invaluable collection development tool more user-friendly and more current.

The Business Reference Sources Committee of BRASS (Business Reference and Services Section of RUSA/ALA) meets each summer at the Annual Meeting to select the best business reference sources published since May of the previous year. A short list (in 2010 it was 15) of the outstanding titles are chosen after discussion, and a full annotation is made for each book. These are books chosen by librarians as being good additions for any collection.

Although standard library publications such as *Library Journal, Choice,* and *Wilson Library Bulletin* publish reviews of current business publications, the following periodicals are particularly useful for tips on business research techniques and for information about relevant publications.

Guide to Reference. Kieft, Robert, ed. Chicago: American Library Association. 2008–. (http://www.guidetoreference.org/HomePage.aspx)

Special Libraries Association. Business and Finance Division. **BF Bulletin.** Los Angeles: The Division. 1988–. Triannual.

Business Information Alert. Chicago: Alert Publications, 1996–.

(Former title: *Business Information Alert: What's New in Business Publications, Databases, and Research Techniques,* by the same publisher)

Journal of Business and Finance Librarianship. United States: Routledge. 1989–. 4 issues a year.

The *ALA Guide to Reference* is a selective guide of resources organized by academic discipline that is now available only in electronic format. The first to eleventh editions were presented only in print and are held by most libraries. These older editions should be retained for historical research. The current edition, according to the selection procedures, will follow these guidelines: "Editors will comprehensively evaluate reference works, applying the same criteria to titles in all formats. Sources from governments, professional societies, commercial publishers, or other organizations with a publishing history will take precedence. If an Internet source not produced under these traditional auspices nevertheless meets selection criteria, an editor will weigh the creator's commitment to maintaining content and assess the permanence of the source. Generally, editors will prefer online sources if multiple formats are available. Annotations for online or print versions of a source will take into account alternate formats" (taken from the web page at http://www.guidetoreference.org/DynamicContent.aspx?ctype=21). The resource will be continually updated and so will be useful for most libraries although for many the subscription cost may be prohibitive.

The *BF Bulletin* is the official newsletter of the largest division of the Special Libraries Association. Like most such publications, it includes news of division activities and of its members, but what makes it most useful is its collection of articles, bibliographies, and suggestions for locating difficult-to-find information. An issue may, for example, explain business concepts such as market share and beta coefficients and then proceed to identify sources that contain them. The articles cover topics as diverse as a SOLO librarian describing her experience in holding an open house or the problems encountered and steps to be taken in setting up an information business. The emphasis throughout is on practical information.

Readers are encouraged to share their experiences, both good and bad, in looking for specific types of information or in using new business publications. The *Bulletin,* which is included with division membership and is available to nonmembers at a nominal price, is a forum where business and finance librarians from a wide range of library settings and many countries can share their common interests and concerns. It is well worth the subscription price.

Business Information Alert (http://www.alertpub.com/newsletters.html) has an intended audience of business information professionals and researchers and is as much a guide as a bibliography. Each issue is not long, but each page contains either analyses of sources, reviews of both electronic and hard copy information, or tips and techniques to help researchers. The regular columns include "From the Editor," as well as a leading article, which in the past has ranged from "Researching Unlisted Companies" to "Researching an IPO." The contributors are from a variety of companies, universities, and libraries, and the information shared is both timely and carefully researched. Subscriptions include an electronic transmission of the newsletter which allows for one download to help with routing. For an extra charge one can receive a print copy of the newsletter.

The *Journal of Business & Finance Librarianship* contains reviews of databases and books as well as articles on current topics of interest. A recent edition contained "Residential Real Estate Data on the Internet: Benefits and Limitations" while another discussed "Entrepreneurship Outreach: A New Role for the Academic Business Librarian." Aimed at the academic business librarian this publication still contains good information for any researcher. This journal is available both in print and online.

The titles described above are basic reference sources that enable librarians and researchers alike to identify business publications relevant to their interests. Equally important, however, are reference sources that provide quick, factual information.

This chapter concludes by examining five major categories of quick reference tools: dictionaries, almanacs, encyclopedias, handbooks, and subject web pages.

Dictionaries

Business vocabulary can at times be baffling to the uninitiated. The librarian confronted for the first time with such terms as *market segmentation, convertible debentures,* and *beta coefficient* or with such slang as *highlighting, Fannie Mae,* and *golden parachutes* may feel with some justification that standard English and business English are two different languages. Not only librarians but also most businesspeople need to be familiar with terms outside their usual areas especially as functions become blurred and management terminology becomes more cross-disciplined. Many standard dictionaries are, in fact, weak in their coverage of business jargon. As a result, specialized dictionaries are essential to all business collections and must be updated regularly as business terms change frequently. Dictionaries are available for each field of business. There are, for example, dictionaries of insurance, accounting, finance, and real estate, and some selected publications may be discussed in the chapters that follow.

General Business Dictionaries

Other business dictionaries provide more general coverage. Some of the best and most widely used general business dictionaries are listed in the earlier edition of this book. For many people now an online dictionary provides the fastest and most up-to-date method of finding the meaning of business terms.

Investorwords. WebFinance Inc. 1999–. http://www.investorwords.com/

Copyright © 2011 by WebFinance, Inc.

One of the best online dictionaries, this publication is available at no cost. The front page is clean and leads easily to other sections. One can easily search for a word or browse by subject. Business topics include accounting, banking, marketing, and real estate. The most popular words searched are available on the front screen. The true worth of the dictionary comes in the descriptions as words that may be difficult to understand are hot-linked to further explanation. A very well-thought-out and easy-to-use resource.

Multilingual Business Dictionaries

Although this book emphasizes U.S. business practice, this will often involve interaction with foreign companies and agencies, so it would be derelict to ignore dictionaries that present business terms in a variety of languages. Unlike their general business counterparts, these dictionaries do not include definitions. They are used instead by businesspeople who need to determine the English equivalent of a foreign term or the foreign version of an English phrase.

For those who are not satisfied using *Google translate*, there are other versions available.

Harrap's Five Language Business Dictionary. Bromley, Kent: Harrap Books Ltd., 1991. 448p.

Although old, *Harrap's Five Language Business Dictionary* is still a solid publication that brings together English, German, Spanish, French, and Italian business terms. Each page is arranged in six columns. In the first column are arranged the multilingual integrated alphabetical listings, and this is followed by a column for each of the five translations.

This enables the user to get all the translations for each word. The dictionary provides 80,000 translations based on 20,000 words and phrases.

For more intensive coverage of foreign business vocabulary, dictionaries that pair English terms with their equivalents in a specific foreign language are useful. A wide variety of such publications are available; there are, for example, English/German and English/Spanish dictionaries as well as similar works in other languages. A comprehensive collection of all such dictionaries in every language is generally impractical, but each library's collection should, of course, reflect the interests and needs of its own users. Robert Beard of Bucknell University began an excellent site devoted to dictionaries, which has now been transformed into a commercial site providing free dictionaries, language and language-related services, and links to translating services. This is available at http://www.yourdictionary.com/about.html.

Acronyms and Abbreviations Dictionaries

The language of business has its own unique vocabulary, filled with jargon and slang. It also makes frequent use of abbreviations and acronyms, and although some of these designations are commonly recognized, others can be baffling to the librarian or researcher new to the field. Offhand references by patrons to M1, NASDAQ, GNMA, or CFTC are not unusual, and often a librarian must refer to a list of acronyms or abbreviations to comprehend fully a request for assistance. A comprehensive list is available in the following standard reference work.

Bonk, Mary Rose, and Regie E. Carlton. eds. **Acronyms, Initialisms & Abbreviations Dictionary**. 44th ed. Detroit: Gale Cengage Research, 2010. 4v.
    Also available in e-book format through *Gale Virtual Reference Library*

Acronym Finder. 1988–2011. http://www.acronymfinder.com/ (August 18, 2003).

The *Acronyms, Initialisms & Abbreviations Dictionary* lists over 900,000 acronyms, initialisms, abbreviations, contractions, alphabetic symbols, and other condensed words or phrases. Although all disciplines and fields are represented in the *Dictionary*, many of the items listed are drawn from business and trade or are directly relevant to it. The *Dictionary* is issued in four volumes and alphabetically lists acronyms and abbreviations and the words or phrases that they represent. Any terms that are now historically obsolete are retained indefinitely. A companion volume to this title is the *Reverse Acronyms, Initialisms & Abbreviations Dictionary*. By consulting this most comprehensive of acronyms dictionaries, the full-text counterparts of most such business designations can be readily identified.

Acronym Finder is free on the Web at http://www.acronymfinder.com/. It contains about 100,000,000 terms, not all related to business, and is easily searchable by full or partial entry. For those libraries and individuals not able to afford the *Acronyms, Initialisms & Abbreviations Dictionary*, this may be an adequate substitute.

Almanacs

Almanacs are a solid part of any reference collection, making it possible to find quickly current information about a wide range of subjects. They may, for example, include summary country information, lists of award and prize winners, demographic and economic statistics, chronologies, and directories. The following entry may be especially good for those new to business and for public librarians who must answer a wide range of questions:

Almanac: Business and Finance. http://www.infoplease.com/bus.html
© 2000–2011 Pearson Education, publishing as Infoplease

The *Almanac* contains a compendium of business facts and statistics ranging from federal expenditures by state to the cost of eggs in 1996. There are five main sections: Business, Personal Finance, Taxes, Economy, and Consumer, but there are also links to other more general almanac information, including World Statistics and Associations. One can also search the Columbia Encyclopedia for more information.

Encyclopedias

Although there are some comprehensive, multivolume encyclopedias in business, such as the *International Encyclopedia of Business and Management* and the *Blackwell Encyclopedia of Management,* these quickly become dated and so the emphasis has often been on shorter works that deal with specific fields of business. Several specialized encyclopedias are discussed in later chapters, but it may be useful to consider here some titles that have more general applications.

Wankel, Charles, ed. **Encyclopedia of Business in Today's World**. Thousand Oaks, CA: Sage, 2009. 4vs. Also available online.

Kolb, Robert W, ed. **Encyclopedia of Business Ethics and Society**. Thousand Oaks, CA: Sage, 2008. 5vs. Also available online.

Dobson, John M. **Bulls, Bears, Boom, and Bust: A Historical Encyclopedia of American Business Concepts.** Santa Barbara, CA: ABC/CLIO. 2007.

"This encyclopedia is designed to include a vast range of different types of entries, including key companies, business policies, regions, countries, dimensions of globalization, economic factors, international agreements, financial instruments, accounting regulations and approaches, theories, legislation, management practices and approaches, ethical and social responsibility issues, legal and contractual structures, professional organizations, technologies, marketing and advertising topics, research and development practices, operations management, and logistics terms, with a global perspective" (taken from the introduction). With over 1,000 entries this publication covers much of the inter-connectivity of business in an international setting. The online edition is extremely easy to use either by searching or using the available subject index. In each topic there is at the left further links to related topics and a see-also list. This encyclopedia is a good solid reference to the many areas covered.

The second encyclopedia seeks to set out the key concepts in the connections between business, ethics, and society. It is, in both formats, an excellent, informative introduction to the key concepts in both business and ethics. There are approximately 1,000 well-written sections, and each has a bibliography of further readings. Many sections include graphs and tables but these are not, unfortunately, downloadable in the online version.

The final publication includes concepts, significant events, and biographies of selected business leaders. The book is divided into five sections: Colonial America 1607–1760; The New Nation 1760–1860; Industrializing America 1860–1900; Boom and Bust 1900–1940; and finally Recent American covers topics from 1940 until the date of publication. This is a very readable work that makes the subject matter understandable and interesting.

Handbooks

The difference between single-volume encyclopedias and business handbooks is often negligible. Both are good sources of quick, factual information, but as a rule handbooks tend to cover fewer topics at greater length than do encyclopedias and often presuppose a basic understanding of the subject. The following title represents handbooks that survey business activities. The availability of most handbooks in an electronic format is an added plus as it enables the user to retrieve only the chapters or sections that are of interest.

Free, Rhona C., ed. **21st Century Economics: A Reference Handbook.** Thousand Oaks, CA: Sage, 2010. Also available online.

There are 100 contributors to this reference, representing a wide array of academic fields and backgrounds, selected from universities and policy institutes around the globe. At this time interest in economics is high as we experience financial failures and government intervention. This publication includes summaries of theory and models in key areas of micro- and macroeconomics but all are presented in mostly non-mathematical form, which is useful for those who still remember calculus as a burden rather than a joy. For students an extra asset is that each entry has the correct citation at the end of the article.

Most handbooks focus on specific business activities such as insurance and accounting. Several specialized handbooks are discussed in chapters 9 through 18; still others can be identified by consulting standard business guides and available online catalogs.

Internet Resources without Print Counterparts

No one business Internet site will answer all questions, and despite the belief that "everything is on the Web," libraries and researchers still need print products. This section provides a description of several web sites that provide free information and links to other sources. The sites discussed here are search engines and blogs. Everyone can use a search engine like Google or Bing to find information, but the sites described below function more as guides as they are more directed in focus.

Resource Shelf. © 2003–2011 Free Pint Limited. http://www.resourceshelf.com/ (Accessed March 8, 2011)

DocuTicker DocuBase. © 2003–2011 Free Pint Limited. http://web.docuticker.com/go/ docubase/ (Accessed March 8, 2011)

The ResourceBlog contain daily posts from researchers and librarians who are willing to share the results of their search for information. This is the resource that you will want to check frequently as it links to free reports, statistics, and other quality information for business. It was originally founded in 2001 as "ResourceShelf" by noted information professional Gary Price, and it offers tens of thousands of sources, with more added every day. This was one of the first blogs made available to the research community, and each day one finds something new and useful.

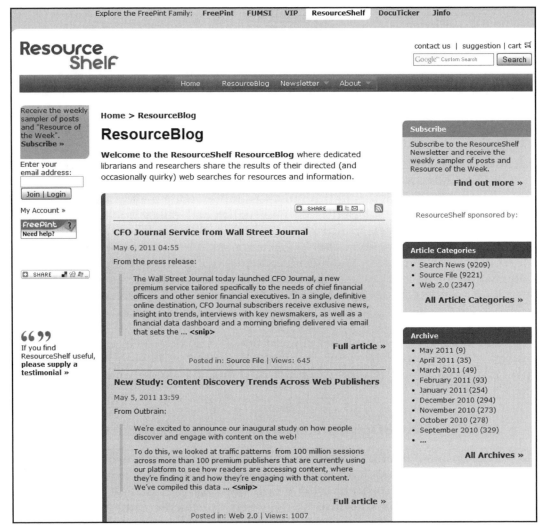

Figure 1.3. Screen shot of Resource Shelf Blog, at http://web.resourceshelf.com/go/resourceblog/. Reprinted with permission from Free Pint, Ltd.

DocuBase "offers a hand-picked selection of resources, reports and publications from government agencies, NGOs, think tanks and other public interest organizations." This is more focused on European sources, although both the United States and global organizations are also covered. Again the links are to materials freely available.

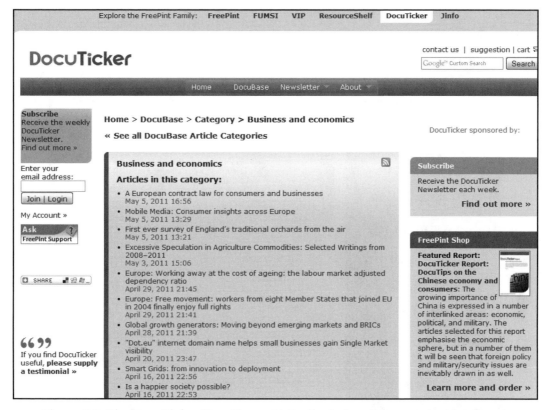

Figure 1.4. The DocuTicker DocuBase, at http://web.docuticker.com/go/docubase/.
Reprinted with permission from Free Pint, Ltd.

Blogs now make it easy for librarians and other researchers to share resources they have found and to contribute more to the learning experience of others.

Most university libraries have always prepared bibliographies and guides for their own students to use. Now almost all libraries in the world have a web presence, making it easier to find and use these materials. There are other options becoming available via these libraries, and these are the FAQs that one can check if a question is proving difficult to resolve. These lists point mainly to resources within the library providing the answers, but it is a simple task to check one's own collection to see if some of the materials are available. The staff of the library at the University of Pennsylvania have assembled a consortium of libraries that compile business FAQs using the software produced by the University of Pennsylvania Library, and the full list can be accessed at http://gethelp .library.upenn.edu/guides/business/BusinessFAQ.html. It is extremely useful to have a general idea of areas covered so that one can check on materials.

One example is listed below.

Economics & Finance FAQ. © Princeton University Library, based in part on software and content produced by the University of Pennsylvania Library and used by permission. http://faq.econlib.princeton.edu/recordList?library=princeton_ economics&institution=princeton (Accessed March 8, 2011).

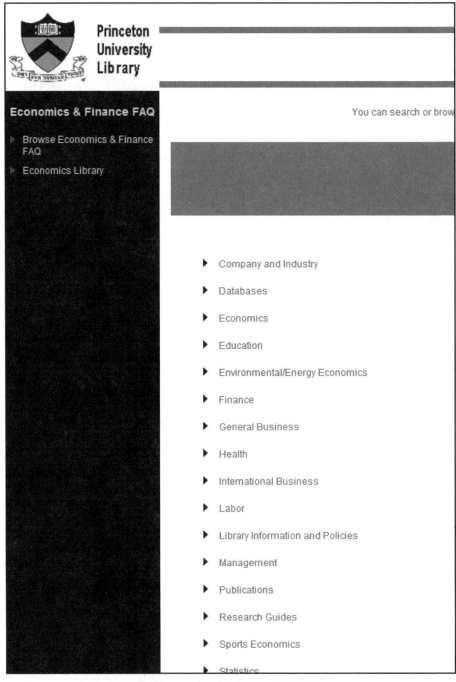

Figure 1.5. Economics & Finance FAQ (Princeton).
http://faq.econlib.princeton.edu/recordList?library=princeton_
economics&institution=princeton

By clicking on any of the headings one is linked to the questions in that area. This is especially helpful for researchers who are not familiar with the questions being asked or who are unsure of their knowledge of an area. The figure below shows questions in the Company and Industry section.

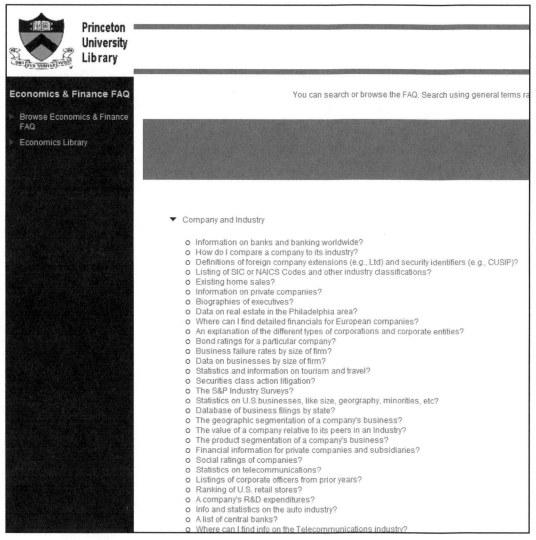

Figure 1.6. Company and Industry (copied from FAQ Princeton University)

Although the basic reference sources described in this chapter are important, they are by no means the only useful sources of business information. The next five chapters treat business information available in other formats, including directories, periodicals and newspapers, government documents, statistics, databases, and Internet resources.

2

Selected, Consolidated Electronic Business Information

Technology is now woven into the fabric of civilization in every corner of the globe. During the last 25 years, in the United States, computer usage has changed from a few researchers, scientists, and engineers using large mainframes to a general population in which more than one-third own at least one personal computer. In the fall of 1984, 7.9 percent of American households reported owning a computer, in contrast to 2010, when 76 percent reported owning one.[1] According to the May 2010 survey from Pew Internet & American Life, 79 percent of American adults use the Internet. By 2003, 55.5 percent of employees in the United States were using computers at work and 41.7 percent were using the Internet.[2]

Public interest in and enthusiasm for electronic information has increased tremendously along with familiarity with computers, and the Web has become the platform for innovation in information collection. End users have come to expect current information to be dynamic, fluid, and freely available. Academic and public libraries have purchased individual databases, and in some states there are statewide agreements with vendors to supply access to their databases via the Internet.[3] Business faculty and students, managers, small business people, market researchers, and individuals frequently log into online computerized databases and access the Internet to gather information for different projects. Publishers have also become part of the transformation by organizing access to information through a variety of customized interfaces that feature materials needed by companies, libraries, and individuals.

Online databases, offered through vendors such as Dialog, were at one time the type of electronic information with which librarians were most familiar, but this changed with the steady introduction of the CD-ROM and was revolutionized with the introduction of the Internet. This chapter examines electronic information in a variety of formats, ranging from CD-ROMs to suites of information available from vendors and free web portals, and discusses some publications that help in their identification.

This chapter also seeks to examine various types of business periodicals and newspapers as well as representative examples of each and the indexes, abstracts, online databases, and Internet resources that provide access to them.

At this time blogs, podcasts, and every type of access through computers and handhelds are also a means of accessing the needed information.

All different types of information and the means to access it will be interwoven in this chapter.

Online Business Databases

Online databases used to be stored on magnetic tape and required the use of mainframe computers housed at remote locations. When libraries and information centers began accessing these online databases they did so by using telephone lines and computer terminals or microcomputers with modems and telecommunications software. With the advances in technology most databases are now available through an Internet connection or, hard as it is to believe, many are still in a DVD format.

Database Producers, Vendors, and Aggregators

Organizations that are responsible for creating databases are known as database producers, although a broader term that has come into wide use is *content developer*. A database producer gathers information, edits it, and reproduces it in much the same way as traditional publishers do. Many databases, in fact, were preceded by and continue to have printed counterparts. As a result, most business publishers have also become business database producers. Dun & Bradstreet, Standard & Poor's, and Gale Research are major publishers of business materials and now offer both electronic and print versions of the data they collect. In the past, many producers did not market their databases to either libraries or the public; instead, they leased or sold them to database vendors such as Dialog or LexisNexis, which made them available. But in another major change in the industry, both traditional and nontraditional producers are offering their own products for lease or sale.

Database vendors used to be the suppliers of the necessary hardware and software, that is, the mainframe computers and the programs to run them. In addition, they provided a certain level of standardization among the databases they offered, marketing them to the public and supplying customers with database descriptions, instructions, and training in their use. Searching databases through a vendor meant paying for both the time spent online and the documents retrieved. While using a vendor service is still more economical for highly specialized databases or those that one uses infrequently, it is easier now for the end user to access information, without an intermediary, by using databases available on CD-ROMs and via the Internet. Database producers license their products directly to libraries and corporations, and as a result information is now more freely available.

Content aggregators compile listings from various sources into one database. Perhaps the best-known aggregated databases are those that provide selected full-text periodical content. Those well known in the library community are Dow Jones, EBSCO, Gale, LexisNexis, OCLC, and ProQuest; they provide some of the better- known aggregated databases such as *ABI/INFORM Global*, *LexisNexis Academic*, and *Business Source Complete*.

These aggregators are in many cases also database providers and vendors, and in fact the distinction among these terms is becoming blurred. One example of this is the option to choose the databases one wishes to license and have these appear on one screen as individual searchable units, with the choice also given to search all those purchased as a whole unit.

Not only have terms become blurred with the expansion of the Internet, but mergers between companies and services appear to be happening almost daily. Any business researcher or librarian who needs to keep abreast of current developments can do so by checking various publications, especially *Information Today*, *ONLINE*, *Econtent*, and *Searcher*.[4]

Business databases cover a wide range of subjects and can be categorized either by the type of information provided or by the vendors who supply them. Other chapters contain descriptions of some databases from commercial publishers, such as directories or periodicals and newspapers, so this chapter will concentrate on aggregated collections and what are being termed web "portals." Some of the portals described in this chapter are produced by commercial vendors and charge a fee, and some cover material available free on the Web.

Portals

The terms *portal, horizontal portal,* and *vertical portal* occur frequently in articles, but unfortunately there does not seem to be a consensus about what exactly each one means. Any dictionary will describe a portal as a "gateway," and this seems to be the general meaning accepted in the web world. Yahoo! (http://www.yahoo.com/) is a good example of a horizontal portal, as it provides access to a variety of information available in directory format and via search engine. Some articles also classify services such as Yahoo! as horizontal portals because they cover more than one subject area. One would then guess that a vertical portal covers only one subject area, as *cnnmoney* (http://money .cnn.com/) does, but perhaps a vertical portal could also cover only one aspect of business, such as mutual funds, rather than all business. A vertical portal can also exist within an organization to provide information only to its members.

One way of looking at the differences between the types of portals is to use a magazine analogy. *Newsweek* would be a horizontal portal as it covers all types of news, whereas *Business Week* would be a vertical portal because it concentrates on business news.

Selected Commercial Products

Electronic information has fundamentally changed since it was first used in the mid-1970s. Innovation has become the keyword. Electronic resources are now not only for business specialists but can also be used by the general consumer. Some of the major decisions that face researchers and librarians at this time are not only whether to buy or license a product but in which form it will be provided. Desktop delivery is popular in the business world, but this site licensing may be beyond the funding available to academic institutions, especially large institutions, when the pricing system is based on full-time enrollment (FTE). It is often difficult to convince vendors that only a small percentage of the students will be interested in highly specialized business databases, and that not everyone in the medieval history or comparative literature departments will be eager to access the specialized business information provided.

The following descriptions are divided into resources accessible "via" the Internet and those "on" the Internet. Because so often the Web is used as a vehicle for many commercial products, library patrons feel that they are getting the information at no cost and do not realize the price paid by the institution for value-added features such as full text and searchable indexes. Nevertheless the Internet provides access to a wealth of material that is freely distributed, and there are many sites that act as indexes and directories to this information.

Selected Aggregators

Serials are well represented online. Most fall into three categories: electronic versions of the serials themselves; collections of electronic versions of periodicals; and indexing, abstracting, and full-text services. Most publishers now offer the articles themselves in pdf format.

Like all major aggregators or vendors, EBSCO tailors its offerings to the client. One can choose from an extensive collection of business periodical databases, including *Business Source Elite, Business Source Premier, Business Source Complete,* and *Kiplinger Finance & Forecasts.*

Business Source Elite supplies cumulative full text for over 960 journals, including *Business Week, American Banker, Forbes, Fortune, The Economist,* and hundreds of peer-reviewed journals; full text for more than 40 regional business publications; and abstracts and indexing for 1,650 business journals. Offered in EBSCOhost, the online service, *Business Source Premier* provides the full text for more than 2,100 journals and provides indexing, abstracts and full text back to 1965.

Kiplinger Finance & Forecast is a continuously updated, fully searchable database of all Kiplinger personal finance and business publications dating from 1996. It includes content from *The Kiplinger Letter,* one of the nation's most widely read business forecasting newsletters; *Kiplinger's Personal Finance Magazine,* a leading magazine in the personal finance category; *Kiplinger's Retirement Report, The Kiplinger Agriculture Letter, The Kiplinger California Letter, Kiplinger.com, KiplingerForecasts.com,* and other Kiplinger periodicals and books.

The choices are designed to fit differing needs, but the search mechanisms and some searchable fields remain the same across databases so that switches can be made without users even being aware of the change. EBSCO also provides specialized services to corporate and special libraries.

Some full-text newspaper coverage is supplied by EBSCO in a separate database called *Newspaper Source.* This supplies the full text of *The Christian Science Monitor,* with coverage from January 1995; abstracts and indexing of the *New York Times,* the *Wall Street Journal,* and *USA Today,* all dating from 1995; and abstracts from the *New York Times Magazine* and the *New York Times Book Review* as well as 370 regional (U.S.) newspapers. In addition, full-text television & radio news transcripts are provided from CBS News, CNN, CNN International, FOX News, and NPR. As with most newspaper coverage in databases, obituaries (other than famous people), sports tables, classifieds, stock prices, and the weather are not included.

EBSCO offers a variety of periodicals and newspapers, with the option to download, print, or e-mail full-text articles.

Another well-known aggregator/vendor is ProQuest Inc., formerly known as Bell & Howell. Since the early 1990s, the name ProQuest has been associated with a suite of electronic databases serving the library and the educational community The major business databases available from Proquest are *ABI/INFORM, ABI/INFORM Global, Accounting & Tax Database, ProQuest Asian Business, ProQuest European Business, ProQuest Computing,* and *ProQuest Telecommunications.*

ABI/INFORM is especially useful for retrieving articles on strategic business and management issues as it provides extensive coverage of business conditions, management techniques, corporate strategies and trends, and product and competitor information. The database provides instructive indexing and extensive abstracts to articles from more than 1,000 principal business and management publications, including over 350 English-language titles from outside the United States. *ABI/INFORM* has always been available only in electronic format and has abstracts available from 1971. In its initial format one could search and retrieve abstracts via distributors such as Dialog, and then it became more widely available on CD-ROM. Now, on ProQuest, it provides entire articles, in full text, PDF, or in a text + graphics format for more than 1,000 of the most popular and significant sources.

ABI/INFORM Complete™ is one of the most wide-ranging business databases available. At this time it includes 5,745 journals, nearly 80% of which are full text. It provides much more than journal content, and the mix of content categories meets the varied needs of many researchers.

Accounting & Tax Database provides centralized access to top journals, reference reports, proceedings, dissertations, and more, including over 2,300 publications with hundreds in full text. The database includes all journals from the American Accounting Association and more than 7,800 Working Papers from SSRN (Social Science Research Network). Coverage is from 1905.

ProQuest Asian Business & Reference is designed for students and faculty at business schools, offering the latest business and financial information for researchers at all levels. It can be used as a standalone resource for regional Asian business news, or in conjunction with *ABI/INFORM Global*. Popular titles include *Far Eastern Economic Review, Asiaweek,* and *Fortune.*

ProQuest—"ABI/INFORM Trade & Industry is a source for major trade and industry news. It includes in-depth coverage of companies, products, executives, trends, and other topics for more than 2,290 publications, with over 2,110 in full text. With *ABI/INFORM Trade & Industry,* users can study and compare specific trades and industries, including telecommunications, computing, transportation, construction, petrochemicals, and many others" (Taken from the web page at http://www.proquest.com/assets/downloads/products/abi_product_overview.pdf).

One of the most useful newspapers provided by ProQuest is the *Wall Street Journal,* available in full-text format. Like all ProQuest full-text newspapers, it is fully searchable, with additional fields including section, page, and special feature. Subscriptions include full-text coverage from 1995 onward, with indexing available from 1989 to the present. More general full-text newspapers such as the *New York Times, USA Today,* and the *Washington Post* are also available.

There is considerable overlap between both publishers, but there are also unique materials.

ProQuest, for example, has full text access to the *Wall Street Journal, Financial Times,* and *MIT Sloan Management Review* while EBSCOhost has access to the full current and historical contents of *Harvard Business Review.*

In addition to journal content, *Business Source Complete* provides access to books and monographs, case studies, company profiles, conference proceedings, country reports, financial data, industry reports, investment research reports, market research reports, SWOT analyses, and trade journals. In addition to journal content, ABI/Inform provides access to the *Wall Street Journal* and *Financial Times,* working papers, business cases, annual reports, country reports, dissertations, and SWOT analyses.

While there appears to be much overlap of the added materials, the difference in content comes from the information providers. For example, the EBSCO databases contain SWOT analyses from Datamonitor while ABI contains these materials from several sources but not Datamonitor. EBSCO indexes the Harvard Business School cases while ProQuest indexes those from the Richard Ivey Business School case collection, the Darden Business Publishing case collection, and the Thunderbird case collection.

ProQuest	EBSCO*host*
ABI/Inform Complete Coverage varies (some back to 1923). Over 5,400 journals, 80% of which are full-text. Incorporates also the *Global, Trade & Industry* and *Dateline* databases. Includes over 3,000 full-text journals, 25,000 Business Dissertations, 14,000 *SSRN working papers*, key newspapers such as *The Wall Street Journal* and *The Financial Times*, as well as country-and industry-focused reports and data, SWOT analyses and selected business cases.	**Business Source Complete** Coverage varies (some back to 1922). Over 4788 journals of which 3680 are full text. Additional full-text, non-journal content includes financial data, books, conference proceedings, selected case studies, investment research reports, industry reports, country reports, company profiles and company SWOT analyses.
ABI/Inform Global Coverage varies (some back to 1923). Over 3,380 publications, with more than 2,380 available in full text. Includes scholarly journals, trade journals, and non-periodical content such as EIU ViewsWire, Business Dissertations, Author Profiles, and Business Cases.	**Business Source Premier** Coverage varies (some back to 1922). Features 3300 publications with full text for more than 2,200. Searchable cited references go back to 1998. Also includes industry and company reports form Datamonitor, EIU country reports and full text reference books including the PRS Political Risk Yearbook
ABI/Inform Research Coverage is 1971- present. Over 1,850 journals, with more than 1,230 available in full-text. It covers a variety of business-related subject areas including financial, pharmaceuticals, manufacturing, and more.	**Business Source Elite** Coverage is 1990-present. Over 1,797 journals with full text for over 1,000 and expanded PDF backfiles for 150 titles (back to 1985 or the first issue published for that journal). More than 10,100 substantial company profiles from Datamonitor are also included.
ABI/Inform Trade & Industry Coverage is 1975 – present. More than 1500 business periodicals with a trade or industry focus. 1340 are full text. Provides the latest industry news, product and competitive information, marketing trends, and a wide variety of other topics. Contains publications on every major industry, including finance, insurance, transportation, construction and more.	**Business Source Alumni edition** Coverage varies (some back to 2000). Provides access to 1,540 full-text business magazines and journals, of which over 750 are peer-reviewed. This database includes publications in nearly every area of business including marketing, management, MIS, POM, accounting, finance, econometrics, economics and more. Available to alumni who have purchased access through their associations.
ABI/Inform Dateline Coverage is 1982 – present. Over 240 journals, with more than 190 available in full text. It includes hard-to-find local and regional business publications with news about local companies, analysis, information on local markets, and more.	**Regional Business News** Coverage is 1990s to present for most resources. Provides full text for more than 80 regional US and Canadian business publications (including titles from Crain Communications).

Figure 2.1. Comparison of selected ProQuest and EBSCO databases

Another leading publisher of library materials is the Gale Group. Among its products are a variety of well-known and authoritative directories and the *InfoTrac* (IAC) family of online search and retrieval products, which are described in this section.

"General Reference Center Gold integrates a vast array of key business and general interest titles, from national news magazines and encyclopedias to core business journals, providing a comprehensive reference resource for general reference needs at all levels of research. Through an intuitive, easy-to-use interface, researchers have immediate access to a wide range of resources, including: more than 5,600 titles including more than 4,000 in full text and more than 20 reference books" (taken from the web page at http://www.large-print-books.com/PeriodicalSolutions/generalReference.htm).

It is not a full suite of business information, which will be discussed later in this chapter, but it incorporates the three sets of highly desirable information into one searchable unit and thus is an excellent place to start for company and industry information.

At the same time as producers and aggregators such as ProQuest, EBSCO, and Gale are refining and improving their products, they are also licensing their products to other nontraditional information services such as *Northern Light*.

Northern Light (http://www.northernlight.com) supplies information obtained from several sources, including ProQuest.

Indexing and abstracting services provide access to literally hundreds of general trade, scholarly, consumer, government, and regional business periodicals, enabling users to find recent information on a wide range of subjects. Some of the most popular business periodicals are also indexed in general indexes such as *Readers' Guide to Periodical Literature* and *Public Affairs Information Service Bulletin*. Even the smallest libraries often have access to databases that include some full-text business information even if they cannot purchase the more specialized resources.

Users may prefer to go directly to a newspaper or magazine that they have always used and with which they feel comfortable. Librarians and other users should also be aware of the information in certain individual publications and also on their web pages. The following section will describe some of the most popular publications.

Periodicals and Newspapers

The world of business is not static. In the course of a year, many things can happen. Interest rates may skyrocket and stock prices plummet; new technologies emerge and old products become obsolete. Executives may retire, be fired, or abscond with company funds. Companies themselves may be victims of hostile takeovers or may in turn acquire companies. As a result, although directories and other reference books provide valuable information about fixed points in time, they are seldom completely up-to-date. For current information, businesspeople turn to online databases, periodicals, and newspapers, and web sites. Of these, newspapers and periodicals are commonly used, either in hard copy or accessed via the Internet. This section seeks to examine various types of business periodicals and newspapers as well as representative examples of each.

Types of Business Periodicals

There are six main types of business periodicals: general business, trade, scholarly, consumer, government, and regional (see figure 2.2).

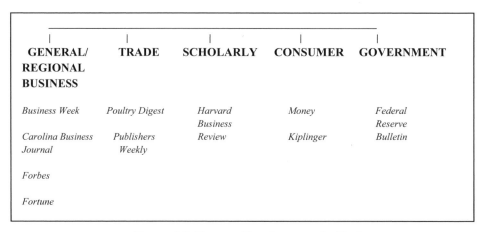

GENERAL/ REGIONAL BUSINESS	TRADE	SCHOLARLY	CONSUMER	GOVERNMENT
Business Week	*Poultry Digest*	*Harvard Business Review*	*Money*	*Federal Reserve Bulletin*
Carolina Business Journal	*Publishers Weekly*		*Kiplinger*	
Forbes				
Fortune				

Figure 2.2. Types of business periodicals

General Business Periodicals

General business periodicals provide broad coverage of the state of the economy and of commerce and industry. Although specific articles may treat different fields of business separately, the focus is broad, emphasizing overall trends and developments. *Business Week, Fortune*, and *Forbes* are general business periodicals. They are important and popular and can be used to supplement standard business reference sources. Many of these publications are available electronically. Some will appear full text in online databases, and all have a web presence with at least some of the information available at no charge. For back files of information generally one will need to use a database that contains the magazine contents or the older print copies or microfilm editions that are maintained by most libraries.

Bloomberg Business Week. New York: McGraw-Hill, 1929–. Weekly. Web version available at http://www.businessweek.com/.

Although *Business Week* may not, as its publishers advertise, show its readers how to "develop a silver tongue, a golden touch, and a mind like a steel trap," it does provide them with coverage of current conditions in national and international business and finance. It is the business manager's *Time* or *Newsweek*, with concise, interesting, and frequently entertaining articles supplemented by statistics, graphs, photographs, and illustrations. This publication was sold in 2009 to Bloomberg LLC and as a result has incorporated more information from the Bloomberg service.

Cover stories focus on subjects as diverse as artificial intelligence, capitalism in China, computer software, and baby boomers. Weekly news briefs include news with both analysis and commentary, international business, social issues, finance, management, information technology, media, marketing, and government. Also included each week are book reviews, editorials, and personal business advice. According to *Yahoo Finance*, *Business Week* enjoys tremendous popularity; with a readership of 4.8 million each week, in 140 countries, it is "the most widely read of all business periodicals."

Currently the first part of the print edition is divided into six recurring parts: opening remarks that generally discuss something from that week's news, Global Economics, Technology, Companies and Industries, Politics and Policy, and Markets and Finance. Occasionally an extra section is added which one week may be Enterprise and another week Green Enterprise. The Global Economics section always has a part labeled "Seven Days" that details major forthcoming events. This can be anything from projected earnings reports to upcoming trade shows or conferences. The Markets and Finance section has a Bid & Ask part which includes notes on offers, sales, or takeovers of companies.

Business Week also features a series of recurring articles and issues. Annual articles include:

Best Global Brands

Best Places to Launch a Career

Best Providers of Customer Service

Best Undergraduate Business Schools

Business School Rankings & Profiles

BW 50: Best Performing Companies

Top 100 IT Companies

Most Innovative Companies

The web site of Bloomberg *Business Week* offers a plethora of information. Like most web sites there are the sections designated at the top of screen and these include Management and Technology. Within the Management section is one of the hidden gems of the site—a link to company case studies and analysis. In the Finance section can be found company information that is provided by Standard and Poor's Capital IQ. Company information is fairly easy to find on many sites but *Business Week* also provides under the People tab a list of executives and board members that includes relationships with people in other companies.

Another special feature of Businessweek.com is at the bottom of the screen where one can link to the special reports available, the current lists and rankings and all the blogs and other social media that are supported.

For librarians facing difficult budget decisions, all these options should be explored as a means of acquiring essential information.

Fortune. New York: Time Inc., 1930–. Biweekly. Web version available at http://money .cnn.com/magazines/fortune/

Fortune is the glossiest of the general business periodicals. Its popularity in the business community is undisputed; it is a key source of current information on all aspects of management, business, finance, and the economy. Articles in *Fortune* are signed and generally longer than those appearing in *Business Week* but are less likely to contain statistical data. Also missing are regular business and financial statistics pages.

As does *Business Week*, *Fortune* publishes several special issues. Best known are the Fortune 500, 25 Most Powerful Businesspeople in Asia, World's Most Admired Companies, 100 Best Companies to Work For, and Global 500. Unlike *Business Week*, *Fortune* provides most of these special lists for no charge at its web site. Although *Fortune* is generally less useful than *Business Week* for answering statistical business reference questions, its profiles of up-and-coming executives and entrepreneurs, as well as of those elected to its business hall of fame, make it particularly useful as a source of current biographical information.

The web site of *Fortune* is not as well organized as it should be. Although there are many excellent topics and articles, finding them is not intuitive. The best parts of the web site are the tabs for Fortune 500 and Rankings, as these contain the information one would expect.

Forbes. New York: Forbes, 1917–. Biweekly. Web version available at http://www.forbes .com/.

Forbes is another important general business periodical. Like *Fortune* and *Business Week*, it includes regular columns and features such as management strategies and trends, profiles of prominent businesspeople, and investment commentary. Again, the scope is rather broad. However, whereas *Fortune* and *Business Week* are intended primarily for business professionals, *Forbes* is written with the investor in mind. As a result, the focus is somewhat different. Rather than a single column on personal investments, for example, *Forbes* features several such columns of commentary and advice, each dealing with a specific investment medium and each written by an acknowledged expert in the field. These recommendations are tracked annually, and the list of wins and losses is usually published in February.

Like *Business Week*, *Forbes'* articles are frequently supplemented with statistics, and it, too, contains regular features dealing with business and finance.

Forbes publishes several special issues. In addition to its list of largest companies, the Forbes' 500, it publishes a list of America's wealthiest individuals and families, and a special report on multinational corporations. The lists are available from the Web site under the Lists tab.

Taken together, *Business Week*, *Fortune*, and *Forbes* are among the three most important general business periodicals and are essential to business collections in all libraries.

Trade Periodicals

General business periodicals are useful because they provide an overview of current business and economic conditions, but they seldom provide the depth of coverage required by a business researcher seeking detailed descriptive and analytic data for a particular industry. Someone looking for statistics pertaining to the meat-packing industry, for example, or for the latest information on packaging and advertising of prescription drugs, would find little of value in *Fortune* or *Forbes*. In such situations, trade journals are often the best sources of information.

Almost every business endeavor is represented by at least one trade journal. "If there were just two guys in the world collecting and selling turkey buzzard eggs," writes Dick Levin, "you can be sure that one of the two would start a monthly *Turkey Buzzard Egg Dealers Journal* and start selling it to the other."[5] Although turkey buzzard eggs are not yet actually covered in depth by any trade journal, the poultry business is well represented by such publications as *Poultry Digest*, *News & Views* from the Poultry and Egg Association, *World Poultry Magazine*, and *Poultry Times*. There are, in fact, hundreds of trade journals, each one dealing with a specific business, industry, or profession. Some are issued by commercial publishers, others by trade and professional organizations. Most contain news of current developments in the field, reviews of past performance and forecasts for the future, descriptions of key companies and personalities, and buyers' guides and directories. They are, in short, veritable gold mines of highly specialized information, and can be invaluable to librarians and researchers seeking elusive statistics or information. Typical examples of trade journals are *Beverage World*, *Cosmetics and Toiletries*, *Pit and Quarry*, *Builder*, and *Sales & Marketing Management*.

Breadth and depth of trade journal hard copy collections vary considerably from library to library. Electronic access is becoming easier. Because of license agreements with companies such as EBSCO, Gale Group, and LexisNexis, many articles from trade journals appear full text on electronic databases shortly after publication. Associations may also feature at least part of their journals on their web pages, and there are meta web sites available for news and magazines, such as http://www.freetrademagazines.com/. A corporate information center may still subscribe to all of the trade journals that reflect its company's interests, and a public library may collect those relating to community industries and businesses, while an academic library may subscribe to those that support its curricula.

Scholarly Journals

Scholarly business periodicals focus on ideas rather than on the brief descriptions of present conditions, the recent past, or the near future found in general business periodicals and trade journals. Signed articles, based on research findings, are frequently lengthy and may include bibliographies. They may be theoretical or may suggest new ways of dealing with existing business problems. They are publications of substance, whose value endures long after the somewhat ephemeral information in trade and general business periodicals has ceased to be of widespread interest.

Scholarly periodicals are often published under the sponsorship of learned societies, professional associations, or colleges and universities. Academic libraries are the heaviest subscribers to scholarly publications. Although collections of these journals may be somewhat limited in special and public libraries, one such publication, the *Harvard Business Review*, is found in almost every library setting.

Harvard Business Review. Boston: Graduate School of Business Administration, Harvard University, 1922–. Bimonthly.

The *Harvard Business Review* is preeminent among scholarly business periodicals. Its popularity derives from the quality of its articles, authored by highly regarded scholars and business practitioners, and by their relevance to current business problems. Both its publisher and its readers view it as a continuing education tool for business executives. It is noted for the diversity of its articles, the eminence of its authors, and a combination of both the practical and the innovative. *The Harvard Business Review* is included in most of the business indexes and abstracts that are described later in this chapter. It can also be searched online and retrieved as full text, for the full run of the journal, through EBSCO, a major database vendor.

Consumer Periodicals

Consumer-oriented periodicals, also known as personal finance magazines, are aimed at the general public. Usually glossy, these periodicals court their readers with articles describing how to invest in stocks, bonds, and mutual funds; buy real estate; speculate in commodities; save money; and pay lower taxes. Often included are articles on successful investors, entrepreneurs, and self-made millionaires.

Although these periodicals are directed to the general public, they are particularly valuable to reference librarians because of regular articles that describe investment media and the mechanics of investing in nontechnical terms. They list major information sources, particularly investment advisory publications. *Kiplinger's Personal Finance Magazine* (http://www.kiplinger.com/magazine/contents.html) is one of the oldest of these periodicals, but perhaps the most popular of all is *Money*.

Money. New York: Time, 1972–. Monthly. Web version available at http://money.cnn .com/ or http://money.cnn.com/magazines/moneymag/

In addition to regular columns and features that include recent developments on Wall Street and a Fund Watch, *Money* includes articles describing the best brands of chocolates, ski gear, and other consumer goods as well as discussing subjects as diverse as computer software, facelifts, the latest automobiles, and advice from financial planners and investment analysts. Each issue of *Money* also monitors mortgage loan rates, credit card interest rates, and mortgage rates. In addition to its weekly features *Money* annually rates the "Best Mutual Funds and ETFs" and the "Best Places to Live."

The web version of *Money*, which is from the editors of both CNN and *Money* magazine, is one of the most comprehensive sites for the general investor. Articles are featured along with guides on budgeting and saving and *Money*'s popular features such as "Best Places to Live" and "Best Places to Retire." The Money 101 section includes 23 lessons for financial stability ranging form investing and planning for retirement to insurance and taxes.

Reading or checking *Money*, in any format, will help librarians anticipate user demand for specific information and, in some instances, will help to identify publications that should be added to the collection. *Money*'s explanation in lay terms of the newest investment media can also help librarians keep abreast of recent trends and developments.

Government Periodicals

Business periodicals published by the federal government may at first glance seem to be drab cousins of their colorful, commercially published counterparts. Appearances to the contrary, however, they contain a wealth of information and can be of significant reference value to librarians and researchers. However, the character of government publications has changed considerably in the last few years. Many of the publications have ceased or have been converted to web versions, so a researcher now needs to think in terms of sources of information rather than titles of publications. A few sources are described in this section, and many more are available. They can be identified by consulting the following booklets.

Geahigan, Priscilla C., and Robert F. Rose, eds. **Business Serials of the U.S. Government**. Chicago: American Library Association, 1988. 86p.

Key Business Sources of the U.S. Government. [Compiled by] Steven W. Staninger, Susan Riehm Goshorn, and Jennifer C. Boettcher. Chicago: Reference and User Services Association, American Library Association, 1998. 81p.

Business Serials of the U.S. Government lists and annotates over 180 titles, chosen for inclusion on the basis of their usefulness as business reference sources. Arrangement is by broad subject category. Each entry includes a standard bibliographic citation as well as Superintendent of Documents classification and serial numbers; the Library of Congress card number; and an annotation that includes the source(s) in which the title is indexed, pagination, the kinds of illustrations typically included, the sources of the data reported, and a description of scope and coverage. Some of the journals included in this listing are no longer published, and some are now only web publications. Much of the statistical information and some of the articles from federal publications are available on the appropriate agency web site. Many of the archival copies are available from FRASER at http://fraser.stlouisfed.org/cbt/browse.php?collection_id=23.

Key Business Sources of the U.S. Government originally started as an update to *Business Serials of the U.S. Government*, but because of unprecedented changes in the way the U.S.

government information was produced and circulated, it was difficult to confirm which items would continue and which would be eliminated. As a result, it was decided that the approach should be to include "key" sources of business information available from the U.S. government. This volume contains an annotated list of books, serials, CD-ROMs, microforms, and Internet sites and is a useful first step in finding essential information.

Both of these publications are very dated, but for the serious researcher looking for archival information they are still essential.

The following publications, which are among the most highly regarded and heavily used, are at this time still available in paper copy, although web versions also exist.

U.S. Council of Economic Advisers. **Economic Indicators.** Washington, DC: Government Printing Office, 1948–. Monthly. Web version available at http://fraser.stlouisfed.org/publications/ei/.

U.S. Department of Commerce. Bureau of Economic Analysis. **Survey of Current Business.** Washington, DC: Government Printing Office, 1921–. Monthly. Web version available at http://www.bea.doc.gov/bea/pubs.htm covers all issues from 1948 onwards.

The federal government is the world's largest collector and publisher of statistics, and many of them are published in government periodicals such as *Economic Indicators, Monthly Labor Review,* and the *Survey of Current Business.* Of these, the most widely used is the *Survey of Current Business,* published monthly by the Commerce Department's Bureau of Economic Analysis (see figures 2.3 and 2.4).

Figure 2.3. Image of the Survey of Current Business, http://www.bea.gov/scb/

Each issue is a comprehensive report on business activity and estimates and analyses of U.S. economic activity and includes, in addition to articles on the national, regional, and international economic accounts and related topics, a column describing the current business situation and statistical tables highlighting national income and product accounts. The statistical section consists of tables for about 270 series and charts for about 130 series.

Note: Beginning with the January 1998 issue, the Survey is available in PDF format free of charge on BEA's Web site at http://www.bea.gov/scb/. It is also once more available, since January 2002, as a print copy. Issues from 1994 to current are available at http://www.bea.gov/scb/date_guide.asp, and most of the issues from 1921 through 1997 are available in PDF format on the web site of the Federal Reserve Bank of St. Louis. The following link will allow you to go there directly: http://fraser.stlouisfed.org/publications/SCB/

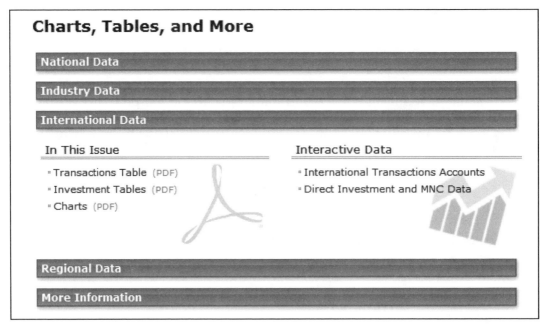

Figure 2.4. **Typical international data listing, Survey of Current Business,** copied from the web page (May 2011), http://www.bea.gov/scb/#chartsandtables

U.S. Department of Labor. Bureau of Labor Statistics. **Monthly Labor Review.** Washington, DC: Government Printing Office, 1915–. Monthly. Web version available at http://www.bls.gov/opub/mlr/.

The archive from 1981- is available at http://www.bls.gov/opub/mlr/archive.htm.

U.S. Board of Governors of the Federal Reserve System. **Federal Reserve Bulletin.** Washington, DC: Board of Governors of the Federal Reserve System, 1915–. Monthly. Web version available at http://www.federalreserve.gov/pubs/bulletin/ (articles only).

Other government periodicals are more specialized. The *Monthly Labor Review*, for example, includes articles and statistics on employment and unemployment, work stoppages, prices and price indexes, and wages. The *Federal Reserve Bulletin* concentrates on money and banking, featuring articles and detailed banking, financial, and monetary statistics.

The federal government is not the only government publisher of periodicals. Although space does not permit their inclusion, it should be noted that state, foreign, and international agencies also issue business periodicals and working papers that can be of considerable research value.

Regional Periodicals

The categories of periodicals previously discussed provide information on the national and international level. Economic statistics in government periodicals such as the *Survey of Current Business* are primarily for the United States. Corporations covered in general business periodicals such as *Fortune* are usually internationally prominent blue-chip companies.

Frequently, however, librarians are asked to provide information about small, private companies, or about state and local economic conditions. One valuable source of such information is the growing number of local, state, and regional business publications, categorized here as regional periodicals. Some, such as the *Boston Business Journal* and *New Orleans City Business*, focus on specific cities; others, such as *Business North Carolina* and *Texas Business*, provide statewide coverage. Such publications typically include profiles of locally prominent businesspeople, companies, and industries, and state and local economic indicators. At a minimum, a good business collection will include periodicals for the city and state in which it is located, and it may extend to regional periodicals as well. Links to many of the current issues of these magazines can be found at http://www.bibliomaven .com/citymags.html. Access to regional business periodicals is also available through such database vendors as EBSCOhost, Gale, ProQuest, and Dialog.

Periodical Directories

Literally hundreds of business periodicals are published every year. Some of the most popular, such as *Business Week*, *Money*, *Harvard Business Review*, and *Survey of Current Business*, are familiar to almost everyone. Others are not nearly so well known, and often librarians may be asked to help identify or provide information on such titles. For example, a businessperson may want to identify trade magazines in which he can advertise his new line of waterbeds, or he may want to find the source that will best enable him to keep up with the latest developments in the home heating industry. In these situations, librarians frequently turn to periodical directories; the following are used often.

Ulrich's International Periodicals Directory. New York: Bowker, 1932–. 5v. Annual. Also available online.

Gale Directory of Publications and Broadcast Media. Detroit: Gale Research, 1880–. Annual.

Ulrich's is the most commonly used periodical directory. The 36th edition contains information on over 156,000 periodicals from around the world, arranged in 856 broad subject classifications. In addition to a "Business and Economics" section, which includes listings for accounting, banking and finance, economic situations and conditions, and investment, as well as general business and economics publications, *Ulrich's* also includes categories for specific industries and trades, such as building and construction, the clothing trade, and paints and protective coatings. Other fields of business such as advertising and public relations and real estate are listed separately.

Each entry includes title, frequency of publication, the publisher's name and address, and Dewey Decimal Classification. In addition, the entry usually includes the ISSN (International Standard Serial Number), circulation, subscription price, year first published, language of the text, the presence of advertising and book reviews, and the names of the indexing and abstracting services in which the periodical is covered. A bullet symbol (•) is used to identify availability as an online database, and frequently the name(s) of the online vendor is listed as well. *Ulrich's* also includes, in volume 4, a cross-index to subjects, a list of periodicals that have ceased publication, a title index, a title change index, and an ISSN index. This publication is also available as *Ulrich's Online*.

The *Gale Directory of Publications and Broadcast Media*, formerly the *Gale Directory of Publications*, lists newspapers, magazines, and trade journals published in the United States, Puerto Rico, and Canada. Unlike *Ulrich's* the *Gale Directory* arranges serial titles by state and city rather than by broad subject classification. The beginning of each state entry includes a brief description of the state, with demographic and publishing statistics, and is followed by city listings. All periodicals published in each city are listed alphabetically regardless of subject content. The listing for Milwaukee, Wisconsin, for example, includes titles as diverse as the *Milwaukee Journal Sentinel*, one of the city's daily newspapers; *American Christmas Tree Journal*; *Building Operating Management*; *New Car Prices*; *Quality Management Journal*; *Sanitary Maintenance*; and *Spare Time*. The arrangement of the Gale Directory requires several cross-indexes. They include a master name and keyword index; separate subject lists of agricultural, college, foreign language, Jewish, fraternal, black, religious, and women's publications; newsletters; general circulation magazines; daily newspapers; daily periodicals, free newspapers, and shopping guides; and trade and technical publications.

Each of the directories mentioned above can be used to access major business and trade publications. Each has its strengths. *Ulrich's* includes more foreign-language titles and lists indexing and abstracting services in which specific periodicals are indexed, and *Gale* includes even more detailed information about advertising specifications and rates.

Newspapers

Sometimes monthly, biweekly, or even weekly periodicals are not recent enough to satisfy current information needs. Although most business developments are eventually described in periodicals, they appear first in newspapers. The categories to which newspapers can be assigned roughly parallel those for periodicals. They include regular daily newspapers with business sections or pages, and special business and financial, trade, government, and employment opportunity newspapers (see figure 2.5).

It is impossible to write about newspapers without discussing web-based products. As of July 19, 2002, NewspaperLinks.com listed, and linked to, all electronic versions of newspapers available worldwide. Internet versions of newspapers give researchers access that was never before possible to international, national, and local news. Most news sites are value added, with links not only to news on business and technology but also to stock quotes, information on mutual funds, and investment research. The Internet has revolutionized how people receive and process information, and newspapers will continue to offer online access to compete with other media.

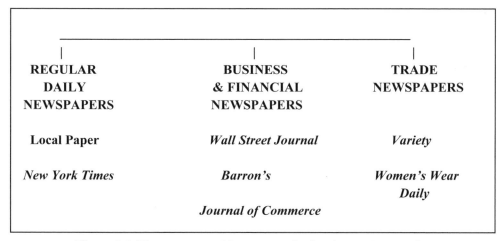

Figure 2.5. Newspapers of interest to the business community

Regular Daily Newspapers

Even the most modest daily newspaper includes a page or two of business information, usually consisting of news and feature articles about local businesses and tables of trading and price statistics for selected stocks, bonds, mutual funds, and commodities. Coverage is selective, with greatest emphasis being given to businesses and companies headquartered in the area. Some of the larger daily newspapers, such as the *Chicago Tribune* and the *Washington Post*, have excellent business sections. Coverage in the *New York Times* is outstanding. In addition to its lengthy business section in Sunday editions, the *Times* also publishes in its daily editions a compilation of news, features, tables, and advertisements that fills most of the paper's second section. Coverage ranges from brief statements of corporate and executive news to detailed analyses of major financial developments and specific industries. In many instances, the *New York Times* fills the need for news on industry trends, stock prices, and corporate developments. It is a resource that should not be overlooked.

Business and Financial Newspapers

In addition to regular daily newspapers, most libraries subscribe to papers that specialize in providing in-depth coverage of current business, economic, and financial conditions. The *Wall Street Journal* is the best known and most important of these business and financial newspapers.

Wall Street Journal. New York: Dow Jones, 1889–. Daily, except Saturdays and Sundays. Some free information available at http://online.wsj.com/home-page.

Investor's Business Daily. Los Angeles: Investor's Daily, 1984–. Daily, except Saturdays and Sundays. Some free information available at http://www.investors.com/.

The *Wall Street Journal* is considered indispensable by most people looking for information. Its coverage of political, social, economic, and financial news makes it required reading for executives, businesspeople, investors, and business reference librarians. With an estimated readership of over 2 million, the *Journal* is an integral part of the daily business scene; every reference librarian should be familiar with it. The *Wall Street Journal Interactive Edition* provides not only the entire contents of the print *Journal* but also a "Personal Journal," where one can set up a personalized news profile and portfolio, which can include stock, bond, and mutual fund quotes. Once the profile is set, whenever the *Journal* publishes news or columns that meet the criteria, these will be included in the personalized edition. The criteria may be updated as needed. This is a fee-based service, with a reduction in price to those who receive the paper copy. At this time the service is free to those with an educational subscription.

Regularly scheduled sections in the newspaper are:

> Section One—every day; corporate news, as well as political and economic reporting and the opinion pages

> Marketplace—Monday through Friday; coverage of health, technology, media, and marketing industries (the second section was launched June 23, 1980)

> Money and Investing—every day; covers and analyzes international financial markets (the third section was launched October 3, 1988)

> Personal Journal—published Tuesday through Thursday; covers personal investments, careers and cultural pursuits (the section was introduced April 9, 2002)

> Weekend Journal—published Fridays; explores personal interests of business readers, including real estate, travel, and sports

> Pursuits—formerly published Saturdays; section was originally introduced September 17, 2005, with the debut of the paper's Weekend Edition; focused on readers' lifestyle and leisure, including food and drink, restaurant and cooking trends, entertainment and culture, books, fashion, shopping, travel, sports, recreation, and the home. The Pursuits section was renamed Weekend Journal beginning with the September 15, 2007, publication.

Also included in the *Journal* are a series of special reports for each day of the week: Monday is "Americas," Tuesday is "Global View," Wednesday is "Business World," Thursday is "Wonder Land," and Friday is "Potomac Watch."

The third section contains statistical tables for stocks and other investment media. Among the statistics covered are the following:

> Dow Jones averages

> New York Stock Exchange (NYSE)

> NASDAQ national market issues

> Dow Jones global indexes

> Futures

> Foreign currency

> Options

> Bonds

To the uninitiated, many of these tables can seem overwhelming. The print is small, numbers dense, and explanations cryptic (see figure 2.6). Fortunately, many secondary sources provide detailed explanations of the most important of these tables. For example, chapters 11 through 15 of this book include lengthy descriptions of stock, bond, mutual fund, futures, and options tables. In addition, the *Journal*'s publisher, Dow Jones, makes available a series of explanatory and promotional brochures describing information contained in the *Journal*.[6]

1	2	3	4	5	6	7	8	9	10
High	Low	Stock	Div	PE	Vol 100s	High	Low	Last	Change
51.25	27.69	XXX	1.02	14.5	6412	47.99	47	47.54	+0.24

Columns 1&2	represent the highest and lowest price over the past 52 weeks.
Column 3	shows the stock name
Column 4	shows the annual rate of dividend based on the company's most recent declaration XXX company is showing 1.02 which means for every 100 shares owned the payout will be $102.
Column 5	represents the price earnings (P/E) ratio. This is the stock price divided by declared earnings-per-share for the last 4 quarters. A low P/E can indicate a flat stock (possibly with declining profits), while a high P/E can be a sign of rapid growth or volatility.
Column 6	represents the volume of shares (in 100s) traded the day before.
Column 7 & 8	shows the highest and lowest trading price the previous day.
Column 9	shows the price per share at closing the day before
Column 10	shows the difference in the closing price (per share) to the last trade of the preceding day.

**Figure 2.6. Interpreting a stock market table compiled for a fictional company
XXX**

The fourth section of the revamped *WSJ* is "Personal Investing." This the part that now contains the mutual funds listing as well as columns on subjects such as home equity loans and personal taxes. Dow Jones established an Educational Service Bureau in 1947 to promote the use of the *Wall Street Journal* by college educators. Since then, the Educational Service Bureau and the publications it offers have grown significantly. There are now five regional offices, each making pamphlets available to librarians and educators. (Address information is available at http://info.wsj.com/college/.) A guided tour of the *Journal* is available on the Web under the title "How to Read the Wall Street Journal," at http://info.wsj.com/college/guidedtour/index.html.

Although the *Wall Street Journal* remains the undisputed favorite, a relatively new business daily continues to enlarge its popularity. The *Investor's Business Daily*, which began publication in 1984, was conceived to provide both succinct and thorough coverage of business, financial, economic, and national news. It features potential successful stocks before they receive broad attention and offers evaluative tables, screens, and graphs (also available online at http://www.dailygraphs.com/).

In libraries in which neither user demand nor the materials budget is sufficient to accommodate two daily business newspapers, the *Journal* is still the best choice. The *Investor's Business Daily*, however, is a worthwhile addition to larger business collections. Other newspapers or services that are as useful are listed below.

Barron's National Business and Financial Weekly. New York: Dow Jones, 1921–. Weekly. Web version available at http://online.barrons.com/

Just as the *Wall Street Journal* is the most widely read business daily, so its sister publication, *Barron's*, is the most popular business weekly. Aimed primarily at investors, *Barron's* focuses on various investment media and covers political, economic, and social news as it affects investments.

Barron's is divided into three main parts. The first consists of articles and regularly featured columns. The articles may include interviews with prominent financial analysts, investment officials, executives, or government leaders, or they may analyze the prospects for specific companies. The second part of *Barron's*, titled "Market Week," consists of statistics for the past week's market transactions. These weekly statistics are one of the most comprehensive collections of current statistics available. The second section contains not only weekly statistics for traditional investments but also regularly featured columns. The columns, written by specialists, deal with different aspects of finance and investment. They include:

"Up and Down Wall Street": Focuses on trends in finance and investment

"The Trader": Summarizes the past week's stock market activities

"The Asian Trader": perspectives on Asian markets

"European Trader": perspectives on European markets

"Commodities Corner": Discusses one or two specific commodities

"Current Yield": Covers capital markets

"The Striking Price": Discusses options and financial futures

The final part of *Barron's* provides news and analysis of the "Mutual Fund" section.

Wall Street Transcript. New York: Wall Street Transcript, 1963–. Weekly. Web version available at http://www.twst.com/ (subscription)

Quite a different approach is offered by the *Wall Street Transcript*, a weekly that consists of transcripts of roundtable discussions of specific industries and selected reports on individual companies prepared by brokers and securities analysts. Although no tabular statistics are included, many of the reports on specific companies include tables, charts, and statistics.

Journal of Commerce. New York: Twin Coast Publishers, 1827–. Daily except Saturdays and Sundays. Web version available at http://www.joc.com/.

The *Journal of Commerce* is a specialized business newspaper. Emphasis in the *Journal* is on news and statistics pertaining to commodities such as coffee or fuel oil and on foreign trade and freight transport. Although the *Journal* is not common to all libraries, those that subscribe to it should make full use of it for its detailed data on shipping and specific commodities. Listings of inbound and outbound ships and their scheduled ports of call, for example, and the weekly shipping timetable to world ports make it particularly useful for the businessperson who is interested in international trade. The web site, at this time, includes free information on logistics, shipping, and trade.

FedBizOpps. n.d. [January 2002?]. https://www.fbo.gov/ (accessed February 23, 2011)

This is an online service that was once the print newspaper *Commerce Business Daily*. It offers opportunities to business firms seeking to sell products or services to the federal government. Each day, it lists government procurement invitations, subcontracting leads, sales of surplus government property, and foreign business opportunities (see figure 2.7).

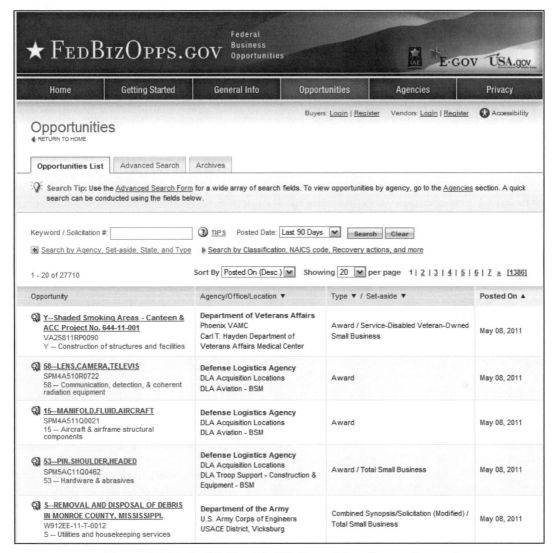

Figure 2.7. Typical listing, FedBizOpps, https://www.fbo.gov/

The above business and financial newspapers, although important, are but a sample of such papers presently being published. Others can be identified by consulting bibliographic guides and directories and by conducting a web search.

Subscription to any newspapers will, of course, be determined by the scope of the library's business collection, its users, and, not incidentally, the size of its materials budget.

Trade Newspapers

Trade papers, like their trade magazine counterparts, include news, statistics, and descriptions of developments in particular industries and trades that may be virtually impossible to locate elsewhere. Two of the best known are *Variety* (http://www.variety .com), the entertainment industry's trade paper, and *Women's Wear Daily* (http://www .wwd.com), which covers retailing of women's and children's apparel and accessories. As can trade magazines, many can be identified by using the *Gale Directory of Publications* and *Broadcast Media*.

Business Suites

Every database has a producer that is distributing files in a variety of ways. They may be available directly from the producer, or they may be available to be searched via a commercial vendor such as LexisNexis. In other cases, like that of Gale, publishers are becoming their own online vendors and amalgamating various products into suites of information. This section provides information on some of the largest online collections of business information. It is in some ways becoming difficult to differentiate these suites of information from other databases such as Business Source Complete and ABI/ Inform Complete. These databases also contain more than articles as they strengthen their offerings with company, industry, and country information as well as books. The two suites below, however, have added value and interactive features that enhance their offerings.

Factiva. 2000– (updated several times daily). Dow Jones Reuters Business Interactive LLC. Trading as Factiva. (Producer). http://djinteractive.com (accessed January 17, 2011)

LexisNexis. 1998– (updated several times daily). LexisNexis. (Producer) http://www .lexisnexis.com (accessed January 17, 2011)

Factiva.com is a customizable, enterprise-wide business news and research solution that includes content from top national newspapers, Dow Jones & Reuters newswires, business journals, market research reports, analyst reports, and web sites. With *Factiva*, one gets content from 118 countries, written in 22 languages. This encompasses information from 8,000 sources, including local and regional newspapers, trade publications, business newswires, company profiles, television and radio transcripts, business journals, and over 10,000 web sites.

Using the basic search screen, one can run one search across the entire *Factiva.com* collection, which includes print sources, newswires, web sites, pictures, and company reports. All content is universally indexed, with company, industry, geographical, and news subject codes from *Factiva*'s "Intelligent Indexing," which includes over 300,000 company codes, 720 industry codes, 340 news subject codes, and 370 geographical codes. The indexing is set up so that the user can choose the desired terms; after clicking on "Done" they will appear in the search box. Additional words or terms can be added to the search box before clicking on "Run Search." A "Company Quick Search," which will pull together both news and financial reports, is also available.

Some of the special features are both company and news tracking, the ability to build a personalized source list, and the option to store information in a briefcase for up to 30 days. The intelligent indexing provides a thesaurus approach to searching that guarantees a meaningful result with useful information. Boolean operators are supported, plus additional power searching connectors such as **w/n, at least, near,** and **same**.

The Lexis service, which began in 1973, was the first commercial, full-text legal information service, available to help legal practitioners research the law. The companion service Nexis, which covers news and business information, was launched in 1979. Since that time, the Nexis service has grown to become one of the largest news and business online information services and includes comprehensive company, country, financial, demographic, market research, and industry reports. Access is provided to worldwide newspapers, magazines, trade journals, industry newsletters, tax and accounting information, financial data, public records, legislative records, and data on companies and business executives. The online version of *LexisNexis* (http://www.lexisnexis.com) available via the Web contains more than 13,500 sources, including regional, national, and international newspapers, newswires, magazines, trade journals, business publications, and public records.

LexisNexis Academic, a subset of the full-blown LexisNexis service, is increasingly used by university students all over the world. No other comparable system offers the breadth and depth of business, news, and legal information from one service. One of the most crucial aspects of the contract offered to subscribers is the content loss threshold clause. The database has experienced significant fluctuations in level of content since it was set up. Some of the most significant deletions were made in August 1998, when 443 titles from *Business Dateline* and 345 titles from *ABI/INFORM* were removed, a 13.7 percent reduction in titles, a number of which were scholarly journals. Also in August 1998, *Ulrich's International Periodicals Directory*, *Books in Print,* and the *Encyclopedia of Associations* were no longer available. In the summer of 1999, 1,923 titles were removed by the Gale Group, including titles like *The Academy of Management Review,* the *Public Relations Quarterly,* the *International Journal of Advertising,* and the *British Medical Journal.* Titles have been added to replace some of the lost material. A content advisory board, consisting exclusively of librarians from selected universities, has been created to monitor the database's content quality and to examine guidelines for quality content. Major deletions are also announced, and monthly additions and deletions lists are published at http://amdev.net/rpt_download.php.

In the company section one can search a single name and then link to general company information, mergers, lists of executives, filings, legal actions, patents, and current news. For someone who needs to tackle all these areas in researching a company, this is an excellent resource. The interface has been recently updated and is much easier to navigate.

Despite its innovations and technical changes, LexisNexis must be fighting a rearguard action against free web news feeds, web directories, and the wealth of financial information available free on the Internet; however, its strength lies in ease of use and the consolidation of information, including substantial backfiles, within one service.

Traditional publishers and vendors have not vanished; they have instead followed the maxim "evolve or die," and they appear to have done this well. As long as they follow the criteria put forward by Bob Littell for evaluating web sites of "consolidate; filter and simplify; prioritize; content; categorize; convenience and cost," they should remain competitive.[7]

Resources "Free" on the Internet

Business Collections

How big is the Web, really? One calculation, from *WorldWideWebSize* (http://www .worldwidewebsize.com/, estimates that there are more than 13.71 billion pages. It is hardly a secret that there is all kinds of free information on the Internet. It used to be that librarians and researchers were wary of much of that information, and although it is true that there is an awful lot of "junk" still cluttering the Web, many companies and librarians have taken up the challenge of arranging some of this vast array of "information" into usable bites. Business researchers have been most fortunate with the amount of "free" information issued by reputable publishers and producers. There are web versions of newspapers, journals, product reviews, stock research, white papers, working papers, and statistics as well as guides to business information and even web pages created by professors for their students. Although the Internet appears at times to be a huge, unstructured morass, the improvement in search engines and the numerous collections of data have made data collection somewhat easier. Included here are short descriptions of some consolidated sites and portals that concentrate on business information and also provide a fair amount of free information or links.

Most portals of choice are the customizable search engines such as Yahoo! (http:// www.yahoo.com), which has over 20 country-specific sites and allows users to assemble their own pages using their own favorite sites. A good place to start is with *Yahoo! Finance.*

Yahoo! Finance. © 2003. Yahoo! Inc. (Producer). http://quote.yahoo.com/ (accessed February 18, 2011).

Often regarded as the most customizable page on the Web, *Yahoo! Finance* enables the user to create multiple portfolios, customize news, check weather and traffic, and set up an address book. By entering a stock symbol one can receive a company capsule, charts, financials, headlines, upcoming events for the chosen company, and useful web links. Yahoo! includes on the front page of this site updates on the stock market, with direct links to the exchanges and indexes, a quick quote search, and the subject divisions of information. *Yahoo! Finance* supplies not only links to its own services and to others on the Web but also information to advise and inform the user.

Another subject area site that can be customized by selecting what is wanted, removing what is not, and adding favorite links that are missing is *CEOExpress,* http:// www.ceoexpress.com.

CEOExpress. © 1999–2003. CEOExpress Company (Producer). http://www.ceoexpress .com (accessed February 18, 2011).

CEOExpress was first developed by a busy CEO, Patricia Pomerleau, who believes in the "80/20 rule."[8] In 1996 she founded AlphaSight Online Strategists, a consulting company focused on helping senior executives understand and utilize the Internet for strategic advantage. Out of this experience came *CEOExpress,* which gathers on a single page links to daily news, search engines, stock and business research, and references. It logically organizes most major classes of resources so that they look uncluttered and are easy to read. This is an excellent quick reference tool to easily access frequently used sites for news, financial quotes, business, technology, travel, and much more. The list is highly selective, and the resources found here are tested to ensure their substance and quality. Some categories on this site are Daily News, Business Magazines, Newsfeeds, Business News, Tech Magazines & News, International News, Financial Markets, Quotes and Market News, Online Investor Services, and Company Research. Another much appreciated feature is the emphasis on information and not on slow-loading graphics. There are subscription services also available, and for information on these check the web page.

cnnmoney.com. © 2003. CNN America, Inc. (Producer). http://money.cnn.com/ (accessed February 18, 2011).

The *CNN financial network* site is the home of much information about money and business. News is a big part of this site. But the site goes beyond just the news, with numerous articles on the world of finance. There's a strong focus on personal money management, along with many references and tools to help make that management easier. For surfers in "cyberwaters," the staff at *CNNfn* have charted a course through what they feel are the essential web sites. As well as being able to track stocks and get information on bonds and mutual funds and breaking news, one can open an online account with the broker Morgan Stanley Dean Witter. There are also available free tools and information that deliver to your e-mail a complete roundup of each day's trading activity from all the major stock and commodities exchanges, as well as breaking business news and feature stories.

There are many ways to try to keep track of changes in electronic offerings. These range from continually checking the web pages of publishers to reading specialized journals such as *Searcher* and *E-Content*. There are also some reference books available in most large libraries, of which the most comprehensive is the *Gale Directory of Databases*.

Gale Directory of Databases. Farmington Hills, MI: The Gale Group, 1993–. 2v. (Also available electronically through the *Gale Directory Library*.)

Gale Directory of Databases was formed by the merger of *Computer-readable Data Bases, Directory of Online Databases,* and *Directory of Portable Databases*. It profiles almost 14,000 databases available worldwide in a variety of formats. Entries include producer name, contact information, a description of the database, where it is available, the update frequency, and the cost. The first volumes describe online databases, with both Internet and dial-up access information. Volume II covers CD-ROM, diskette, magnetic tape, batch access, and handheld products. The *Directory* also includes full contact and contents information on more than 3,600 producers and 2,500 online services, vendors, and distributors. The *Directory* is for librarians looking to enhance their database offerings and other information providers seeking the best sources for competitive intelligence.

Exploring the Web can be frustrating, but there are many useful guides and services to help one solve problems or simply choose the engine that is most comfortable. The choice in searching is whether to use a directory such as Yahoo! or Business.com or a search engine, which creates its lists by crawling the Web. In the latter case one must decide which engine is best for the intended inquiry. This choice is made simpler by Search Engine Showdown (http://searchengineshowdown.com), developed to share information about search engines, and which now includes a search engine chart to help with evaluation, reviews, statistical analysis, and strategies. Search engines are constantly changing and upgrading, so it is useful to be able to keep abreast of developments by checking this site.

Another possibility is to use one of the many books available that list business web sites. This is much more problematic than using a search engine or Internet directory because of the lag time between writing or compiling and publishing print publications.

Notes

1. Pew Research Center, *Pew Internet & American Life Project,* http://www.pewinternet.org/Reports/2010/Gadgets/Report/Desktop-and-Laptop-Computers.aspx.

2. United States Department of Labor, Bureau of Labor Statistics, *Employed persons who used a computer or the Internet at work by selected characteristics, October 2003,* http://www.bls.gov/news.release/ciuaw.toc.htm.

3. Examples:

   GALILEO, http://www.galileo.usg.edu/welcome/

   NCLIVE, http://www.nclive.org

   OhioLINK, http://www.ohiolink.edu/

   TexShare, http://www.texshare.edu/

4. Tables of content and some free full text are available at

   Information Today, http://www.infotoday.com/

   ONLINE, http://www.onlinemag.net/

   Econtent, http://www.ecmag.net/

   Searcher: The Magazine for Database Professionals, http://www.infotoday.com/searcher/

   All are also available full text in aggregators.

5. Dick Levin, *The Executive's Illustrated Primer of Long-Range Planning* (Englewood Cliffs, NJ: Prentice-Hall, 1981), 182.

6. Educational publications from the *Wall Street Journal* are available at http://info.wsj.com/college/teaching/index.html. *Wall Street Journal* educational representatives are listed at http://info.wsj.com/college/sales.html.

7. Robert S. Littell, "Information Management," *Journal of Financial Service Professionals* (March 1999): 24–26.

8. Vilfredo Pareto, a 19th-century economist, found that 80 percent of production volume generally comes from only 20 percent of the producers. This rule has been applied by *CEOExpress* dynamic to the World Wide Web. Information on the Pareto principle is available at http://www.wikipedia.org/wki/Pareto_principle.

3

Company Information

Questions

There are several questions a researcher must answer when searching for information on a company. The first is whether the company is publicly traded or privately held.

The difference is that the public company has sold ownership shares that trade on one or more of the stock exchanges that exist in the United States and around the world. As a general rule publicly traded companies must at specified intervals, usually at least annually, or when specific events happen, file documents with some controlling agency that detail the company's financial state. These can include any changes in the capital structure, names and salaries of top-tier executives, any sales of stock in the company that the executives may have made along with other reports. A listing of the various reports a public company must file in the United States can be found at the Internet site for the U.S. Securities and Exchange Commission (SEC), http://www.sec.gov.

Private companies are not required to make filings with the SEC (there are exceptions) and information, particularly financial information, is usually much harder if not impossible to find.

Another question that must be answered is, does the company exist as a subsidiary of, or is it owned by another company? For example, Land's End and Kmart, along with a dozen or so others, are subsidiaries of Sears Holdings Corporation. Again because companies are not required to report financials for their subsidiaries individually, subsidiaries can sometimes be difficult to find financial information on.

What is the real name of the company? Sometimes companies can be known by a name that is not their true name.

Commonly called	Real Name
GE	General Electric
GM	General Motors
Kodak	Eastman Kodak

Types of Information

There are many types of information available for companies:

Directory or contact, including: company name, street address, phone numbers, email addresses, web page URL, names and biographies of executives and board members.

Descriptive including: ownership structure, industry classification codes, lists of subsidiaries, business descriptions, company history, and qualitative or quantitative reports about the company.

Financial, including: financial statements and performance ratios and stock pricing information.

There are hundreds if not thousands of resources for information on companies, and most of them can be used to find several types of information. Some resources are free to anyone with an Internet connection; others might provide information for free if you register with a web site, and still others cost thousands or even tens or hundreds of thousands of dollars to access. Vendors / sources include:

infoUSA

ReferenceUSA. Infogroup, infoUSA Library Division, Omaha, NE. http://www .referenceusa.com/

ReferenceUSA's multiple databases can be purchased separately. There are 4 databases with residential numbers. The *U.S. Standard White Pages* includes some 89 million U.S. households; and a *Canadian White Pages* directory has 12 million households. There are also 2 databases classed as residential that have potential to be very useful for business researchers; one is a databases of *U.S. New Movers / Homeowners* containing some 300,000 listings with 100,000 added each week. This database is updated weekly. This information would be useful to anyone wanting to know who the new homeowners are in a particular area to maybe target with "welcome marketing material." The other database in this grouping that has potential is the *U.S. Consumers / Lifestyle* database that contains information including median home values and median home income.

There are also 5 databases that are directly related to business in the United States and Canada. The *U.S. Business* database provides directory information on more than 14 million U.S. businesses, the *U.S. Healthcare* database covers 850,000 doctors and dentists, a *Canadian Business* database has 1.5 million listings, and a database of *U.S New Businesses* has 4 million listings and 50,000 listings added each week and a database. Each of these databases offers a number of different search points, including company name, yellow page headings, SIC and NAICS codes, executive names, sales volume, number of employees, and stock exchange ticker symbols. It also provides full corporate linkage and family tree information, mapping capability, Fortune 1000 rankings, and links to company web sites. The mapping capability allows for users to see via Google Maps where the business is physically located. There is also a capability for users to draw irregular geographic areas around a given location and determine what businesses are present.

There is also a database called *One Source* that contains "in-depth" company profiles containing company name, executive names, sales volume, company assets, number of employees, and more.

The data in all the databases is collected continuously from 5,000 public sources and verified with phone calls. According to their web site the company makes more than 26 million calls each year.

Bureau Van Dijk http://www.bvdinfo.com

Another major provider of company information is Bureau Van Dijk (BVD), http://www.bvdinfo.com/home.aspx. Bureau Van Dijk's large family of databases covers a range of geographies from individual countries to regions to the whole world. There are also databases for specific types of companies such as insurance companies (Isis) or financial institutions (Bankscope). There is also a database that covers Mergers & Acquisitions (Zephyr) and one for economic data. Depending on your subscription you can add on modules of Datamonitor reports, Edgar filings, and the ktMINE Royalty Database.

A nice feature is that many of the databases are linked to related BVD databases. For example, if you subscribe to both Osiris and Zephyr both databases link to the information that is available in the other. As with most families of databases the DVB databases all have a similar look and feel, and all provide the same searching and reporting mechanisms.

Some common feature of BVD databases is that they all can be searched by any data element that is in the database. The databases all contain graphing capabilities and integrated analysis software that allows users to compare companies against each other and produce tables and graphs to illustrate results, and the tables and charts can be downloaded into various word processing and spreadsheet formats. Selected Bureau Van Dijk databases are described below.

ORBIS. Bureau Van Dijk, Amsterdam, Netherlands, http://www.bvdinfo.com/Products/Company-Information/International/ORBIS.aspx

ORBIS has information on more than 80 million companies, both publicly quoted and privately held, in about 203 countries around the world. For a full count of companies covered by region see figure 3.1. For the more than 65,000 publicly quoted companies, the nearly 30,000 banks, and more than 11,000 insurance companies, information includes: typical directory facts, detailed or summary financial and ownership information, listings of subsidiaries, names and titles for executives and directors, and more. For the privately held companies, summary information includes much of the information that is included for the public companies except for the financial information.

Osiris. Bureau Van Dijk, Amsterdam, Netherlands, http://www.bvdinfo.com/Products/Company-Information/International/OSIRIS.aspx

Osiris contains information on more than 65,000 listed (publicly traded) companies, banks, and insurance companies from about 200 countries around the world. For a full count of companies covered by region, see figure 3.1. In addition to up to 20 years of income statements, balance sheets, cash flow statements, and ratios, Osiris provides ownership, subsidiaries, stock and bond ratings from Fitch Moody's and Standard & Poor's, country risk ratings from the EIU, earnings estimates, and stock data. In addition to the existing ratios you can create your own that you can display in the reports and also use in your searches and analyses. Osiris contains specific report formats for industrial companies, banks, and insurance companies and also has reports that reflect accounting procedures in the major world regions. Both standardized and "as reported" financials are provided.

Bankscope. Bureau Van Dijk, Amsterdam, Netherlands, http://www.bvdinfo.com/ Products/Company-Information/International/BANKSCOPE.aspx

Contains information on more than 30,000 banks around the world, including more than 13,600 US banks. For a full count of banks covered by region, see figure 3.1.

Information includes: up to 16 years of detailed accounts (country specific "as reported" and standardized), ratios, ratings and rating reports, ownership, and country risk and country finance reports.

Region	Orbis	Osiris	Bankscope
North America	22,000,000	19,000	13,700
Western Europe	32,000,000	13,000	8,200
Eastern Europe	12,300,000	1,400	1,900
Middle East	160,000	1,800	375
Far East & Central Asia	7,400,000	20,000	2,800
Oceania	79,000	2,800	190
South & Central America	6,900,000	5,000	1,600
Africa	660,000	2,000	1,400
	81,499,000	65,000	30,165

Figure 3.1. Company count by region for select Bureau Van Dijk databases

Zephyr. Bureau Van Dijk, Amsterdam, Netherlands, http://www.bvdinfo.com/Products/ Economic-and-M-A/M-A/ZEPHYR.aspx

Zephyr has global coverage and strives to be comprehensive. It includes mergers and acquisitions, initial public offerings, private equity, and venture capital deals and rumors. Coverage goes back to 1997. Users can search by hundreds of different deal elements including company financials and multiples. Users can display data using any of 12 currencies. There is a very nice alert service that users can set up to receive email when events meeting specified criteria occur. As of January 2011 there was information for more than 820,000 transactions. Up to 100,000 new deals are added per year..

Standard & Poor's http://www.standardandpoors.com/

Standard & Poor's is another publisher of business information that all business librarians should be aware of. There are several major products that are of particular interest.

Capital IQ. https://www.capitaliq.com/home.aspx

Capital IQ allows users to search for and screen for in-depth information on companies, investment firms, corporate professionals, and merger and acquisition transactions in both the public and private capital markets by a very wide range of company identification data, financial statement data, executive's biographical characteristics, and deal or transaction specifics. Information can be exported to Excel.

The Capital IQ platform, in various forms, is deployed at many investment banks, hedge/mutual funds, PE/VC firms, management consultancies, and Fortune 500 corporations.

Compustat. http://www.compustat.com/compustat_data/

Compustat Global provides annual and quarterly of data for hundreds of data items, ratios, and concepts. Authoritative financial and market data covering publicly traded companies in more than 80 countries, representing over 90 percent of the world's market capitalization, including coverage of over 96 percent of European market capitalization and 88 percent of Asian market capitalization. Data sets have been designed to reflect the varieties of actual reporting practices used across the globe, while allowing for minimal normalization and establishing consistency on an item-by-item basis for non–North American companies. Data sourcing through alliances with leading, local information providers in the Asia-Pacific region enhances Compustat Global coverage in this region.

Compustat North America's data includes more than 20 years of annual and 84 quarters of financial data, ratios, and concepts for more than 10,000 companies that are currently in business. The database also includes 20 years of annual financial data for 8,500 companies that are bankrupt, went private, no longer report, or were liquidated. Data elements are pulled directly from statements companies file with the SEC. The more than 900 Canadian companies listed in the database have similar information pulled directly from company filings with SEDAR.

ExecuComp. http://www.compustat.com/myProductDetail.aspx?id=305

ExecuComp contains current and historical compensation data for executives of publicly traded companies. The database also provides details on executive stock and option awards and pension plans. The inclusion of selected financial data allows users to compare executive compensation to a company's performance.

NetAdvantage. http://www.netadvantage.standardandpoors.com

This database is the online counterpart for several important S&P print publications including the *Register of Corporations, Directors and Executives, Daily Stock Price Record,* the *S&P Industry Surveys,* and much more. For public and large private companies, NetAdvantage provides company name, address, phone number, industry identification codes (NAICS and SIC.), and executive and director names and biographical notes when available. For public companies NetAdvantage provides financial statement information, stock, and corporate bond data. You will also find mutual fund information, current market and S&P indices information, business news and analyst commentary, screening tools, and a directory of information on security dealers. Some data is downloadable in Excel format.

EbscoHost http://www.ebscohost.com/

Business Source family of databases

In addition to the business news material mentioned in chapter 2, and industry reports mentioned in chapter 4, the Business Source family of databases also includes company reports and SWOT (strengths, weaknesses, opportunities, and threats) analyses for thousands of public companies and larger private companies from around the world. The reports typically are in the 12- to 20-page range and include a brief description of the company, a short company history, list of key executives and a short biography, an analysis of the company's revenue stream, lists of locations and subsidiaries, and a list of "top" competitors. These reports are usually very useful for obtaining a lot of information in a short time.

ProQuest http://www.proquest.com

Factiva

In addition to the business news information discussed in chapter 2, Factiva also contains information on thousands of companies from around the world. Users may search by company name, ticker symbol, DUNS number, or registration ID. Information available includes the typical directory information, stock pricing and split information, some graphs of financial performance data, a SWOT analysis, and links to recent news stories about the company. These reports are also very useful but have the advantage of having links to current news about the company that reports from *Business Source* or *ABI/Inform* do not have.

ABI/Inform family of databases

Along with the indexing and full-text articles that were described in chapter 2, ABI/Inform also has company profiles from a variety of vendors including Hoover's. These reports have much the same information as the *Business Source* reports (addresses, executive bios, SWOT analysis, company history, and summary to extensive financial information depending on the public or private nature of the company) but are usually from different data providers.

ProQuest Historical Annual Reports

A collection of more than 42,000 annual reports covering more than 800 companies, with some reports dating back to 1884. Each report is reproduced in full and is fully searchable.

Gale Cengage Learning http://www.gale.cengage.com/index.htm

Business & Company Resource Center

Like its counterparts from Ebsco and Proquest, Gale Cengage's Business & Company Resource Center provides access to a variety of information on companies in addition to articles. Information typically includes basic directory information including addresses and executive bios, as well as descriptive SWOT analyses and company histories. There is also a summary to extensive financial information depending on the public or private nature of the company.

Mergent http://www.mergent.com/

Mergent WebReports. http://www.mergent.com/productsServices-desktopApplications-web.html

Mergent Web Reports provides a comprehensive history of corporate America for almost 100 years. It includes corporate histories, brief financial statements, lists of subsidiaries, descriptions of long-term debt and stock offerings, officers and directors, and so on. Much of the historical data is available in PDF format from the print resources that were once known as the Moody's and Mergent Manuals. See figure 3.2 for a list of years covered. Users can search within and across manuals, by company name, manual year, or type. Additional resources in the archive include: corporate annual reports, industry reports, and equity reports.

Manual	coverage
Transportation	1909-present
Public Utility	1914-2007
Industrial	1920-present
Bank and Finance	1928-present
OTC Industrial	1970-present
International	1981-present
OTC Unlisted	1986-present
Municipal and Government	1955-present.

Figure 3.2. Coverage of "Moody's / Mergent Manuals"
in Mergent WebReports

Thomson Reuters http://thomsonreuters.com/

Thomson Reuters is a major player in the company and industry information business. They sell dozens if not hundreds of databases in a nearly mind-numbing array. Their focus ranges from financial to health care to legal to media to tax and accounting to science. Only a very small fraction will be mentioned here.

Investext Thomson Research. http://research.thomsonib.com/

Investext contains research/analyst reports on companies, 30,000+, and industries as well as the annual statistical reports of many industry trade associations. It delivers full-text reports in their original published formats, complete with charts, photographs, and graphics. The reports are written by expert analysts from more than 900 of the world's investment banks. There are currently more than 7.5 million company reports and more than 1 million industry reports dating back to 1982. More than 4,000 reports are added each week. Reports are generally added 1 to 2 weeks after initial publication.

SDC Platinum. http://thomsonreuters.com/products_services/financial/financial_products/a-z/sdc/

SDC Platinum is a collection of database modules covering Merger & Acquisitions, joint ventures, syndicated loans, global new issues or IPO data, bankruptcy, poison pills, and more. The search and report mechanisms are very flexible, allowing users to search for very specific information and download a report containing only the data elements of interest.

I/B/E/S http://thomsonreuters.com/products_services/financial/financial_products/a-z/ibes/

I/B/E/S. provides both summary and detailed analyst forecasts of company earnings, cash flows, and other important financial items, as well as buy-sell-hold recommendations for more than 60,000 companies in 67 countries.

LexisNexis http://www.lexisnexis.com/

LexisNexis is a well-known provider of news and information to the business, media, and legal worlds. Several of its databases that are most useful for business researchers are described below.

LexisNexis Academic

LexisNexis Academic as discussed in chapter 2 contains articles from a vast array of news sources including journals, newspapers, and wire services. But like Factiva it also contains a great deal of company information using its "Company Profile" search or the "Company Dossier" search. Users can access the full text of reports from organizations including Disclosure, Hoover's, Institutional Shareholder Services, Standard & Poor's, and Worldscope. You can also search the SEC's Edgar Filings by clicking on the SEC Filings link on the right side of the screen.

Another database provided by LexisNexis separate and apart from *LexisNexis Academic* is

Corporate Affiliation. http://www.corporateaffiliations.com/

Corporate Affiliations contains information on more than 65,000 major US and non-US corporations and their 135,000+ subsidiaries, divisions, and affiliates. It covers companies on the New York and American stock, NASDAQ, and various non-US exchanges; companies with affiliates that are traded over-the-counter; and major private companies and their affiliates. Information provided will typically include some or all of the following: company name, address, telephone number, stock exchange, ticker symbol, SIC and NAICS codes, business description, corporate hierarchy, key personnel, directors, competitors, net worth, total assets and total liabilities, a summary of merger activity, and lists of outside service firms such as advertising agencies, auditor, legal counsel, and major banking relationships.

Other Publishers or Resources

International Directory of Business Biographies. Edited by Neil Schlager; Schlager Group Inc. Detroit: St. James Press, 2005

Contains short biographies. Most are a few pages long of more than 600 business and corporate leaders, mostly from Fortune 500 and Global 500 companies, but also includes prominent entrepreneurs and other notable businesspeople. Each biography looks at the career paths, business achievements, leadership styles, business strategies, and industry impact of the profiled businessperson. Most biographies also some personal information such as marital status, birth year, birthplace, and education. This resource is also available through the Reference for Business website at http://referenceforbusiness .com/biography/.

International Directory of Company Histories. Editor, Thomas Derdak; associate editor, John Simley; editorial assistants, Anne Morddel, Stephanie Wasserman; writers and researchers, Gretchen Antelman . . . [et al.]. Chicago: St. James Press, 1988.

A continuing series started in 1988 and now totaling 118 volumes. Entries usually run 2 to 10 pages and may be organized by time or events. The entries also include company's legal name, mailing address of its headquarters, ownership status—public, private, or state controlled. Many entries also include a bibliography of additional sources of information on the company. Companies may have entries in multiple volumes as new events occur. This resource is also available through the Reference for Business website at http://referenceforbusiness.com/.

Annual Reports at Academic Business Libraries. Judith M. Nixon, Purdue University. http://gemini.lib.purdue.edu/abldars/

A very useful database of historical annual report holdings of 12 major collections of corporate annual reports Columbia University, Cornell University, Harvard University,

Massachusetts Institute of Technology, Purdue University, Stanford University, University of Alabama, University of California–Berkeley, University of Pennsylvania, University of Western Ontario, Yale University, and the Science/Industry/Business Library of the New York Public Library. The database includes the loan policies of the libraries. Most do not lend but will allow onsite use by users.

Bloomberg / Businessweek	Free company information from Capital IQ http://investing.businessweek.com/research/company/overview/overview.asp
Hemscott.com	Free UK financial information http://www.hemscott.com/companies/company-search.do
Kompass	Search company names, products and services, etc. 23m product and service references in 53,000 classes and 1.8m companies in 75 countries http://us.kompass.com
ThomasNet	Information on manufacturers, distributors and service providers http://www.thomasnet.com

Figure 3.3. Selected free company web sites

There are dozens to hundreds of other free sources of company information available on the Internet. See Appendix D for a list of some of them.

Two pieces of company information that will be very useful in chapter 4 are the industry classification codes and the financial ratios.

Industry Classification Codes

One piece of company information that is extremely important is the industry classification code assigned to the company. This is because many information sources described in chapter 4 on industry information use NAICS, SIC, or one of the other industry classification codes. Knowing this code helps you pull together information on other similar companies that may be competitors. Many electronic databases are searchable using the codes. This makes knowing a company's industry code(s) very useful. Most if not all of the sources discussed above contain one or more industry classification codes as part of the company information that is available.

Financial and Performance Ratios

Sometimes managers, executives, government officials, investors, and others use financial information just as it is presented in financial statements. Frequently, however, they convert it into ratios to facilitate comparison. A ratio is simply one number expressed in terms of another. Ratio analysis is the study of relationships between and among various items on financial statements. Each ratio relates one item on the balance sheet (or income statement) with another or, more often, relates one element from the balance sheet to one from the income statement. Financial ratios are measures of corporate performance and are particularly useful when compared with similar ratios for earlier years or, as will be discussed in chapter 4, with ratios for other companies in the same industry, or are used to compare a company to the industry as a whole.

As shown in figure 3.4, a number of financial ratios are in common usage, each serving as a yardstick against which a company can compare one aspect of current performance to earlier years or to the industry norm. When historical standards are used, the company's ratios are compared from one time period, year, quarter, or month, to another. By looking at changes over time, it is possible to identify trends and to appraise current performance in the light of historical relationships. Data used in historic ratio analysis for a specific company can be obtained from its annual reports or from commercially published sources, such as those issued by Standard & Poor's, Bureau Van Dijk, Mergent (Moody's), and Value Line.

Examples of Financial Ratios

Liquidity—measure the company's capacity to pay its debts as they come due.

Current Ratio: ratio between all current assets and all current liabilities.

$$\frac{\text{Current Assets}}{\text{Current Liabilities}}$$

1:1 means that the company has equal assets and liabilities. A better liquidity ratio would be higher than 1:1 say 1.25:1.

Quick Ratio: ratio between assets QUICKLY convertible to cash (i.e., Excludes Inventory) and all current liabilities.

$$\frac{\text{Cash} + \text{Accounts Receivable}}{\text{Current Liabilities}}$$

Shows if current liabilities can be met without sale of inventory or fixed assets. Usually a ratio of 1:1 indicates the bills can be met.

Safety—Show or measures a business's resistance to risk

Debt to equity: ratio between money invested by the owners and the money borrowed.

$$\frac{\text{Debt}}{\text{Equity}}$$

The higher the ratio the higher the risk to the creditors

Figure 3.4. Selected financial ratios

Included in this chapter are some of the more selective databases that contain company information. In other chapters, especially the one that details stock information, other resources are mentioned. Although many print directories still exist, the main request from users is for electronic information, so it was decided to concentrate on those resources. For those who need detailed descriptions of print resources we suggest checking those in the earlier edition as, for the most part, the descriptions are still worthwhile.

4

Industry Information

As with companies there is potentially a wide variety of information available on industries. The key is how you define the industry. The more narrowly you define the industry the less likely you are to find lots of information without resorting to the purchase of a specially done report. So how do you define or describe an industry? You use an Industry Classification Code.

Industry Classification Codes

Industry Classification Codes describe or define in consistent manner what the industry does and how it does it. The codes are one important piece of company information in many of the company information sources discussed in chapter 3. Industry codes are used by resources discussed later in this chapter to help present data collected from companies which have been assigned that code.

There are several different codes in use around the world to define or classify industries.

- NAICS—North American Industry Classification System

- SIC—Standard Industrial Classification (superseded by NAICS and now not being updated)

- GICS—Global Industry Classification Standard

- ISIC Rev. 4—International Standard Industrial Classification

- NACE—Nomenclature statistique des activités économiques dans la Communauté européenne

The United Nations has a well-designed web page that lists many of the activity- and product-based classifications systems used around the world at http://unstats.un.org/unsd/cr/ctryreg/ctrylist2.asp (accessed April 15, 2011).

The two industry codes most commonly used in the United States are:

Standard Industrial Classification (SIC). United States Department of Labor, Occupational Safety & Health Administration, http://www.osha.gov/oshstats/sicser .html (accessed April 15, 2011)

Originally developed in the 1930s to classify establishments by the type of economic activity in which they are primarily engaged and to promote the comparability of establishment data within the U.S. economy. Over the years, it was revised periodically to reflect the economy's changing industry composition and organization. The Office of Management and Budget (OMB) last updated the SIC in 1987.

North American Industry Classification System (NAICS). US Economic Classification Policy Committee (on behalf of the OMB), Statistics Canada, and Mexico's INEGI (Instituto Nacional de Estadística, Geografía e Informática), http://www.census.gov/ epcd/www/naics.html (accessed April 15, 2011)

Things to Know about NAICS

NAICS replaced the Standard Industrial Classification (SIC) system on January 1, 1997. US federal government agencies that collect statistics are required to use NAICS instead of SIC. Commercial publishers are free to use any industry code system they want to, and many use more than one.

Who Assigns NAICS/SIC Codes?

Lots of people and organizations! Each statistical agency in the government assigns the codes for its own publications, based on the answers provided by companies to surveys and questionnaires. In addition, the companies themselves choose their own NAICS codes when submitting their filings to the SEC. Commercial publishers have a variety of strategies: some use the codes they find in corporate documents (e.g., SEC filings), and others assign codes themselves.

Guiding Principle

NAICS retains the same guiding principle as SIC: to group together industries that have similar production processes.

Five- and Six-Digit Codes

The NAICS code system uses up to six digits to identify an industry. The first five digits are standardized in the United States, Canada, and Mexico. The sixth digit in the codes is specific to the individual countries. This allows each country to describe its economy according to its own needs.

Two-, Three-, and Four-Digit Codes

While the most specific and focused NAICS codes are five or six digits, as with the SIC and other industry codes, sometimes you'll see shorter codes that are used to describe broader sectors of the economy.

Primary NAICS (or SIC) Codes

A company's primary NAICS code is for the line of business that generates the most income for the company. Since large companies often have several lines of business, they also have several NAICS codes. For example, car manufacturers obviously have the NAICS code 336111 (automobile manufacturing). Because many of them also offer financing for car buyers, they also have NAICS code 522298 (All other non-depository credit intermediation). Some companies will have half a dozen or even more codes.

Updates

The NAICS code is reviewed and updated as necessary every five years.

Time Series Data Implications

The transition to NAICS from SIC means that, for some industries, time series will be broken. A web page with more detail on this question is http://www.census.gov/epcd/www/naicsusr.html#BREAKS (accessed April 15, 2011).

Why Is NAICS Used Instead of SIC?

NAICS classifies over 350 more industries than SIC does. Most of these new industries are in services sectors and manufacturing sectors that either were not around or were very small when the SIC was being developed. For example, NAICS includes industries that manufacture semiconductor machinery and fiber optic cable, reproduce software, and provide satellite telecommunications, paging, cellular, and other wireless telecommunications. Warehouse clubs and superstores, telemarketing bureaus, hazardous waste collection, and casinos are also new in NAICS.

NAICS is more consistent than SIC, and the NAICS gives special attention to new and emerging industries, service industries in general, and industries that produce advanced technology. As noted above, the SIC system, which was last revised in 1987, does not include many of these industries, or at least does not describe them well, and it will not be updated or changed.

With all the different codes in use and with the cost that would be incurred with trying to unify them being very high, it is very important to have good concordances to map between the codes. Once again the U.N. has a good web page, http://unstats.un.org/unsd/cr/registry/regot.asp?Lg=1 (accessed April 15, 2011), as does the U.S. Census Bureau, http://www.census.gov/epcd/naics/concordances/ (accessed April 15, 2011).

Examples of Other Industry Information

Once an industry has been defined by determining the appropriate industry classification code, researchers can move on to searching for information about the industry. The amount and type of information, at least for free or low cost, depends on the industry.

- Lists of companies in an industry
- Descriptions of where the industry has been
- Forecasts for where the industry is going
- Description of how the industry is segmented
- Description of what forces are driving the industry
- Industry averages for financial measurements and performance ratios
- Industry or market size in unit sales and or monetary units
- Regulations that apply to the industry

Sources of Industry Information

As with information on companies, there are hundreds of suppliers of industry information. Generally speaking, suppliers fall into one of three groups:

- government
- nonprofit organization (think trade and professional associations)
- profit commercial

Some vendors do not charge for the information, and others may charge tens of thousands of dollars for a single report on an industry.

Government Resources for Industry

As will be seen in this section and in chapter 5, governments, especially the U.S. government, can be an extremely valuable source of information.

The U.S. Census Bureau

Most everyone has heard of the U.S. Census Bureau (http://www.census.gov/). It is responsible for the Decennial Census of the U.S. population that gets so much attention. But the U.S. Census Bureau conducts other programs and surveys and "censuses" that are equally and perhaps in some ways more important for business researchers.

Descriptions of all the current economic statistical programs and some "discontinued programs of continuing interest"are available from the Census Bureau at http://www .census.gov/econ/progoverview.html (see figure 4.1).

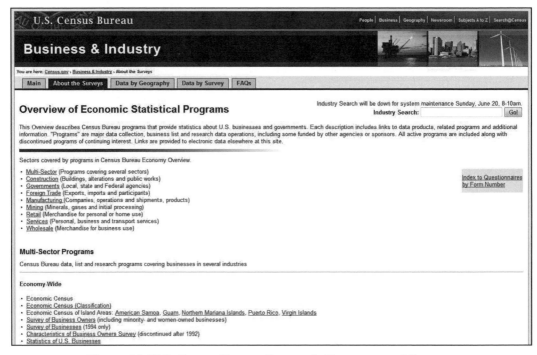

Figure 4.1. U.S. Census Bureau Economic Programs and Surveys

The following is a sample of some material that is available.

Economic Census. United States Department of Commerce, Bureau of the Census. February 15, 2011. http://www.census.gov/econ/census07/ (accessed April 15, 2011)

The Economic Census provides a detailed portrait of the nation's economy once every five years, in years ending in "2" and "7". The Economic Census presents statistics for the nation, states, metropolitan areas, counties, places, and ZIP codes, but that coverage varies from sector to sector. Economic Census statistics are collected and published primarily by "establishment." An establishment is a business or industrial unit at a single physical location that produces or distributes goods or performs services—for example, a single store or factory. By collecting separate information for each establishment, the Economic Census can include detailed data for each industry and area.

The Economic Census is a wonderful resource, but it is only conducted every five years. What about the years in between Economic Censuses? The U.S. Census bureau also conducts other surveys in the in-between years. Some of the surveys are conducted annually, some are conducted quarterly, and some are even conducted monthly. Several of the surveys are described below.

Annual Survey of Manufactures (ASM). United States Department of Commerce, Bureau of the Census. December 3, 2010. http://www.census.gov/manufacturing/asm/index.html (accessed April 15, 2011)

The ASM is conducted annually, except for years ending in "2" and "7", at which time ASM data are included in the manufacturing sector of the Economic Census. It provides statistics on employment, payroll, worker hours, payroll supplements, cost of materials, value added by manufacturing, capital expenditures, inventories, and energy consumption. It also provides estimates of value of shipments for over 1,800 classes of manufactured products. It includes manufacturing companies with one or more paid employees. (Taken from http://www.census.gov/econ/overview/ma0300.html.)

Service Annual Survey (SAS). United States Department of Commerce, Bureau of the Census. March 14, 2011. http://www.census.gov/services/index.html (accessed April 15, 2011)

Services industries account for 55 percent of economic activity in the U.S. Most of these industries are surveyed in the Service Annual Survey. Like the ASM, the SAS is conducted every year except for years ending in "2" and "7". Collected data include operating revenue for both taxable and tax-exempt firms and organizations, sources of revenue and expenses by type for selected industries, operating expenses for tax-exempt firms, and selected industry-specific items. In addition, starting with the 1999 survey, e-commerce data were collected for all industries, and export and inventory data were collected for selected industries. (Taken from http://www.census.gov/econ/overview/sas0500.html.)

Monthly & Annual Retail Trade Survey (ARTS). United States Department of Commerce, Bureau of the Census. March 31, 2011. http://www.census.gov/retail/index.html (accessed April 15, 2011)

The Annual Retail Trade Survey is also conducted annually except for years ending in "2" and "7". ARTS provides national estimates of total annual sales, e-commerce sales, end-of-year inventories, inventory-to-sales ratios, purchases, total operating expenses, inventories held outside the United States, gross margins, end-of-year accounts receivable for retail businesses, and annual sales and e-commerce sales for accommodation and food service firms located in the United States.

Monthly & Annual Wholesale Trade Survey (AWTS). United States Department of Commerce Bureau of the Census. March 23, 2010. http://www.census.gov/wholesale/index.html (accessed April 15, 2011)

The AWTS provides detailed industry measures of sales and inventories for wholesale trade activities. These include companies and wholesalers that take title of the goods they sell such as jobbers, industrial distributors, exporters, importers, and manufacturer sales branches and offices (MSBOs).

County Business Patterns. United States Department of Commerce, Bureau of the Census. 1964–. Annual. http://www.census.gov/econ/cbp/

This name is actually a misnomer; County Business Patterns does not focus just on counties. Users can also find data on metropolitan areas and ZIP codes. *County Business Patterns* provides subnational economic data by industry for most of the country's economic activity. The series excludes data on self-employed individuals, employees of private households, railroad employees, agricultural production employees, and most government employees. The series is useful for studying the economic activity of small areas; analyzing economic changes over time; and as a benchmark for statistical series, surveys, and databases between economic censuses. Businesses use the data for analyzing market potential, measuring the effectiveness of sales and advertising programs, setting sales quotas, and developing budgets. Government agencies use the data for administration and planning. The *County Business Patterns* program has tabulated on a North American Industry Classification System (NAICS) basis since 1998. Data for 1997 and earlier years are based on the Standard Industrial Classification (SIC) System.

A list of the other statistical programs from the US Census Bureau can be found at http://www.census.gov/econ/other_econ.html (see figure 4.2).

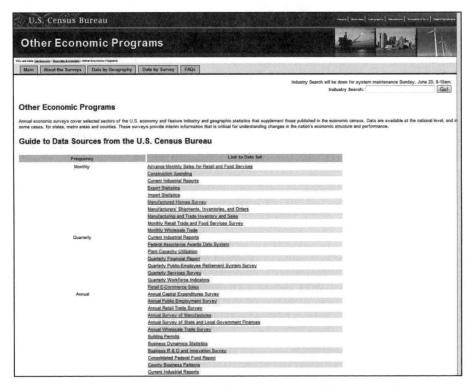

Figure 4.2. U.S. Other Economic Programs of the U.S. Census Bureau

Many departments and agencies other than the U.S. Census are also important sources of industry information. For a list, see Appendix B.

Commercial Vendors Reports, Surveys, and Overviews

IBISWorld Industry Reports. IBISWorld. http://www.ibisworld.com/

Covers more than 700 U.S. industries, as defined by 5-digit NAICS (North American Industry Classification System) codes. Each 30- to 40-page report covers industry conditions and performance, key sensitivities and success factors, segmentation, size, and outlook. Each IBISWorld report is updated every four months. Other products from IBISWorld are the *Industry Risk Rating Reports*, the *Global Industry Research Reports*, the *Company Research Reports*, and the *Business Environment Reports* (see figures 4.3 and 4.4).

US Industry Reports Available:

Agriculture, Forestry, Fishing and Hunting (28 Reports)

11111 - Soybean Farming	11192 - Cotton Farming	11251 - Fish & Seafood Aquaculture
11112 - Oilseed Farming	11193 - Sugarcane Farming	11291 - Apiculture & Honey Production
11115 - Corn Farming	11199 - Hay & Other Crop Farming	11292 - Horse & Other Equine Production
11117 - Wheat, Barley & Sorghum Farming	11211 - Beef Cattle Production	11311 - Timber Services
11120 - Vegetable Farming	11212 - Milk Production & Dairy Cattle	11331 - Logging
11134 - Orange & Citrus Groves	11221 - Hog & Pig Farming	11411 - Fishing
11135 - Fruit & Nut Farming	11231 - Chicken Egg Production	11421 - Hunting & Trapping
11142 - Nursery Plants & Flower Production	11235 - Chicken & Turkey Meat Production	11511 - Crop Support Services
11191 - Tobacco Farming	11241 - Sheep Farming	11521 - Livestock Production Support Services
11531 - Forest Support Services		

Mining (10 Reports)

21111 - Oil Drilling & Gas Extraction	21223 - Copper, Nickel, Lead & Zinc Mining	21232 - Sand & Gravel Mining
21211 - Coal Mining	21229 - Molybdenum & Other Metal Ore Mining	21239 - Phosphate & Other Mineral Mining
21221 - Iron Ore Mining	21231 - Stone Mining	21311 - Mining Support
21222 - Gold & Silver Ore Mining		

Utilities (10 Reports)

22111a - Coal & Gas Power Generation	22111e - Solar Power Generation	22131 - Water Supply & Irrigation Systems
22111b - Nuclear Power Generation	22112 - Electric Power Transmission, Control & Distribution	22132 - Sewage Treatment Facilities
22111c - Hydroelectric & Renewable Power Generation	22121 - Natural Gas Distribution	22133 - District Steam Heating & Air Conditioning
22111d - Wind Power Generation		

Construction (33 Reports)

23311 - Land Development	23492 - Transmission Line Construction	23552 - Flooring Contractors
23321 - Single-Family Home Building	23493 - Heavy Industrial Facilities Construction	23561 - Roofing Contractors
23322 - Multi-Family Home Building	23499 - Heavy Infrastructure Construction	23571 - Poured Concrete Contractors
23331 - Industrial Building Construction	23511a - Heating & Air Conditioning	23581 - Water Well Drilling
23332a - Commercial Building Construction	23511b - Plumbing	23591 - Steel Structure Contractors
23332b - Municipal Building Construction	23521 - Paint Contractors	23592 - Glass & Glazing Contractors
23411a - Road, Street & Highway Construction	23531 - Electrical Contractors	23593 - Excavation Contractors
23411b - Road, Street & Highway Maintenance	23541 - Brick, Stone & Masonry Contractors	23594 - Wrecking & Demolition Contractors
23411c - Road, Street & Highway Services	23542 - Drywall Contractors	23595 - Elevator, Millwright & Machine Rigging Contractors
23412 - Bridge & Tunnel Construction	23543 - Tile Contractors	23599 - Fence & Swimming Pool Contractors
23491 - Pipeline Construction	23551 - Carpentry Contractors	

Figure 4.3. Partial list of industry reports available from IBISWorld

Figure 4.4. Example of IBISWorld Report. Reprinted with permission of IBISWorld Inc.

Gartner.com Web Portal. Stamford, CT, Gartner Inc. http://www.gartner.com

One of the premier research and advisory firms for the information technology and telecommunications industries. Publications analyze a broad range of technology areas such as new media, computing, software, networking, telecommunications, and the Internet, and project how technology trends will affect businesses, consumers, and society.

Frost & Sullivan. http://www.frost.com/

Frost and Sullivan offers the full text including charts, tables, and other graphical material of technical reports, economic reports, and market analyses on emerging high-technology and industrial markets in 50 countries. Reports are from primary and secondary research from 1998 to present with many current reports available. Categories or industries covered include: Aerospace and Defense, Automotive and Transportation, Chemicals, Materials, Food, Electronics and Security, Energy and Power Systems, Environment and Building Technologies, Healthcare and Medical Devices, Measurement and Instrumentation, Information and Communication Technologies, and Industrial Automation and Process Control.

Passport GMID (Global Market Information Database). Euromonitor International.
http://www.euromonitor.com/

Passport GMID contains a great variety of information, including:

- Industry data—multicountry relational database of market and category sizes, market shares, distribution patterns, sales forecasts, and other measurements relevant to each sector.

- Country reports—in-depth analysis reports on both developed and emerging national markets. Each report provides qualitative commentary on sales trends, new product and marketing developments, consumer preferences, national company and brand competition and market strategies, and the views and assumptions underlying national sales forecasts.

- Global reports assessing the key issues affecting international market performance, with a focus on important developments by product sector and big-picture competition strategy.

- Company profiles—analytical profiles of the top international players in the industry, compiled in a standardized format for cross analysis.

- Comment—articles and presentations on key themes and discussion topics around the dynamics of the category.

Users can search for data using a menu approach or a text search. Users may select a product, then select countries (see figure 4.5).

Figure 4.5. Passport GMID search menu
Reprinted with permission from Euromonitor International.

Figures 4.6 and 4.7 show examples of the statistical reports and the analytical reports that can be found using Passport GMID.

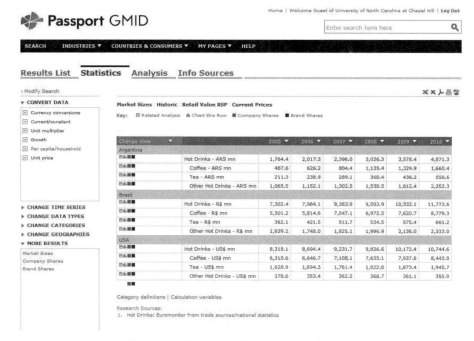

Figure 4.6. Passport GMID statistics report
Reprinted with permission from Euromonitor International

Figure 4.7. Example of Passport GMID analysis report
Reprinted with permission from Euromonitor International

Mintel Reports. 1990 – Mintel, http://www.mintel.com

Mintel is a leading provider of competitive media, product, and consumer intelligence. The company produces market research reports for Europe, the UK, and the US. Reports cover a variety of sectors including consumer goods, travel and tourism, financial industry, Internet industry, retail, and food and drink. Reports discuss market drivers, market size and trends, market segmentation, supply structure, advertising and promotion, retail distribution, consumer characteristics, and market forecasts. Mintel also offers a brief digest of relevant recent events in the News section as well as demographic and economic surveys and product launches for the U.S. and UK in the Databases section (see figures 4.8 and 4.9).

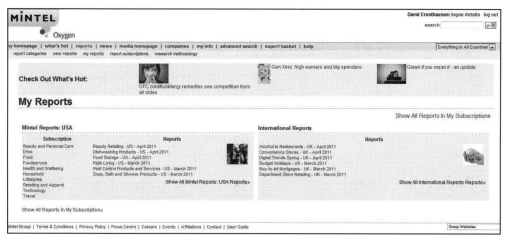

Figure 4.8. Mintel base page. Reprinted with permission Mintel Group

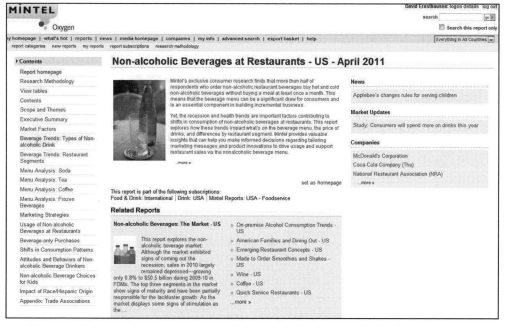

Figure 4.9. Example of Mintel report. Reprinted with permission Mintel Group

BizMiner. 1990 – The Brandow Company Inc., http://www.bizminer.com/

Provides detailed industry analysis and market research reports on more than 16,000 lines of business, based on SIC code, in national and local markets. Search or Drill down through industry reports available as PDF, HTML, or CSV files. Users can limit the results by geography or by firm size.

Several different types of reports are available:

- Industry Financial Profiles
- Market Research Reports
- Area Demographic Profiles
- Business Failure Rate Index
- Sole Proprietor/Startup Profit & Loss
- Local Market Vitality Profiles

Note : BizMiner was planning a change from SIC codes to NAICS codes for industry definitions in May or June 2011, so exact examples may not exist any longer.

Figures 4.10, 4.11, and 4.12 illustrate the drilldown process and show an example of the first page of a report generated by BizMiner.

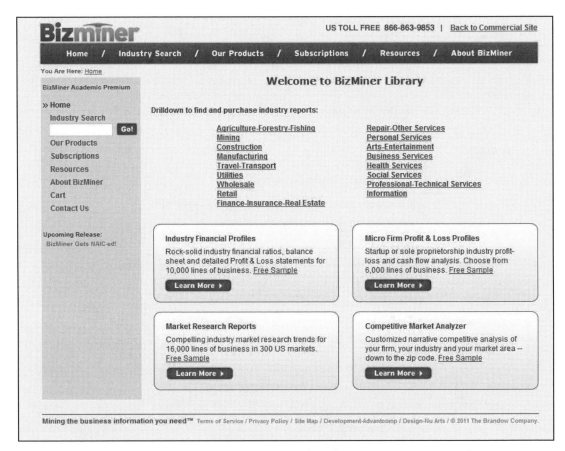

Figure 4.10. BizMiner main page. Reprinted with permission Bizminer Group

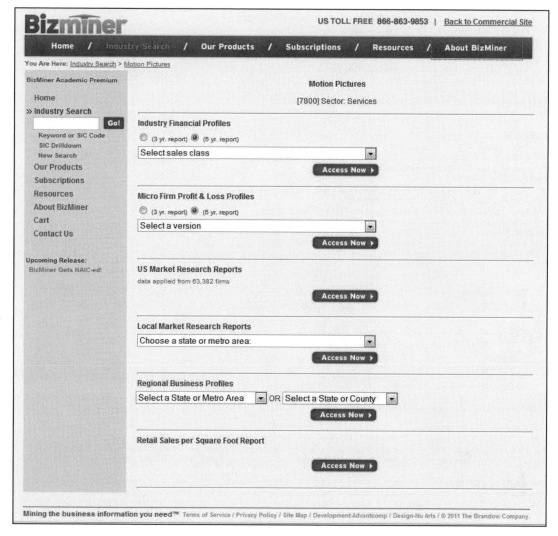

Figure 4.11. BizMiner Reports. Reprinted with permission Bizminer Group

Datamonitor 360. Datamonitor, http://360.datamonitor.com/

Until recently this source was known as *Business Insights Interactive*. It provides you with access to a library of more than 700 strategic management reports of various industries. Each report is based upon unique market research and provides detailed analyses of major markets. The reports are generally in excess of 100 pages in length. It provides accurate, up-to-date, incisive market and company analysis, and therefore is able to provide a single, off-the-shelf, objective source of data, analysis, and market insight. *Business Insights* works in association with leading industry experts to produce a range of reports across a wide range of industry sectors including: pharmaceuticals, healthcare, consumer goods, energy, finance, and technology.

Local Market Research Report
release date: November 2010

Raleigh-Durham-Chapel Hill, NC Metro Area

Motion Pictures

[128-800] Sector: Services

For non-commercial academic use only by authorized users

Contents
P1: Industry Population, Time Series
P2: Failure Rates (US industry)
P3: Industry Market Volume, Average Company Sales
P4: Company Sales Class Trends
P5: Market Share by Sales Class, Average Annual Company Sales by Class
P6: Market Share by Segment, Sales Per Employee
P7: Facility Employment Class Trends, Average Employment Trends
P8: Entrepreneurial Activity, New Branch Development, Sales-Employment Growth Indices
P9: Industry Concentrations, Consolidation Trends, Emerging Vitality Chart
P10: About the Data

Time Series Coverage:
2007
2008
2009
June 2010

Industry Population Analyzed as of:	2007	2008	2009	June 2010
Firms:	349	311	326	328
Establishments:	394	349	367	365
Small Businesses:	330	296	312	314
Startups:	34	16	7	7
Branches:	45	38	41	37

The **Industry Population** table displays the number of firms in the industry for five groups:

Establishments: Firms plus Branch operations.

Firms: Independent companies.

Small Businesses: In order to focus the analysis on the small businesses of greatest interest to our users, the analysis defines small businesses as single site firms with fewer than 25 employees. All small businesses are also "firms".

Startups: In order to reduce distortion and focus the analysis on the startup population of greatest interest to our users, the startup sales and employment analysis limits the definition of startups to single site firms with fewer than 50 employees, with less than $10m annual sales and reporting one year or less of operation. All Startups are also "firms"; The overwhelming majority are also "small businesses".

Figure 4.12. Example of a BizMiner industry Area Report.
Reprinted with permission BizMiner Group

Business Source family of databases. Ebsco Publishing, http://www.ebscohost.com/

In addition to the business news material mentioned in chapter 2, and company reports mentioned in chapter 3, the Business Source family of databases also includes industry and market research reports from a variety of publishers including Datamonitor. The reports typically include information on market value, market segmentation, market rivalries, competitive landscape, market forecasts, market share, and more. The reports are usually 15 to 40 pages in length.

Standard & Poor's Industry Surveys (via NetAdvantage). Standard & Poor's, http://www.standardandpoors.com/home/en/us

NetAdvantage features full text of Standard & Poor's Industry Surveys and S&P Global Industry Surveys. Most industries are fairly broadly defined. Each survey is available as HTML or PDF. Each survey includes some of the major current trends, a list of the major companies, and selected financial statement information and selected financial ratios for selected companies in the industry as well as industry averages. Each survey also includes a section titled "How to Analyze a . . . Company in This Industry" that is very useful. Another useful item is a short list of additional sources of industry information. S&P Industry Surveys are also available in print.

TableBase. Detroit: Gale Cengage Learning. 1996–. Daily updates. http://search.rdsinc .com/help/suite_about.html

TableBase is one module of the RDS Business Suite from Gale Cengage. TableBase specializes in indexing and extracting tabular data on topics such as market share, company and brand rankings, industry and product forecasts, production and consumption statistics, imports and exports, usage and capacity, number of users/outlets, trends, and demographics. It features indexing with concept terms, such as Ad budget, Consumption, Market Share, and Generation Y; industry terms like Broadcasting; and marketing terms like Community Advertising. Special features include the custom written unique titles that describe content and precise indexing at the table level as well as full-text searching. TableBase was originally introduced by Responsive Database Services Inc.

Industry Trade Groups and Associations

Industry, trade, and professional associations exist for almost every imaginable industry trade and profession. These associations can be a good source of information on specific groups of people or industries. The associations will often collect statistics and news stories about their area of interest. The association may or may not charge for the information they collect, and they may or may not provide information to non-members. Some will provide information to their members for free but charge non-members; others will charge everyone. A few examples of trade associations are: PHARMA, http:// www.phrma.org/; Consumer Electronics Association, http://www.ce.org/; American Manufacturer's Association, http://www.nam.org/. You can find industry trade groups and associations in many ways, including a basic Internet search.

ASAE Trade Association Directory. American Society of Association Executives, http:// www.asaecenter.org/Community/Directories/AssociationSearch.cfm?navItem Number=16581

Provides links to Internet homepages of more than 6,500 associations. Search by association name and/or words in the association name. You can also limit by city, state, or country. Information available is very basic and includes Name, Address, telephone number, and sometimes a web address. ONLY associations that have chosen to be listed are included, so this is not a comprehensive listing of all associations.

The sources below are just a few of the many commercial resources that are available.

Encyclopedia of Associations International Organizations: Gale Cengage 1989–. Annual.

Available in print and online. A directory of associations and interest groups of all kinds including but not limited to professional and trade groups. Each entry typically includes contact information, founding year, publication list, and brief description of the group.

Encyclopedia of Associations: National Organizations of the U.S.: Gale Cengage. 1961–. Annual.

Available in print and online. A directory of associations, interest groups, and nonprofit American membership organizations of national scope, including but not limited to professional and trade groups. Covers more than 23,000 organizations in categories such as trade, business, and commercial; legal, governmental, public administration, and military; cultural; educational; veterans, hereditary, and patriotic; athletic and sports; fan clubs, and many more. Information available varies but typically includes contact information, founding year, publication list, annual budget, and brief description of the group.

Encyclopedia of Associations: Regional, State and Local Organizations. Gale Cengage. 1987–. Annual.

Available in print and online. Provides information on more than 100,000 associations and societies that are organized and function at the regional (both interstate and intrastate), state, county, city, neighborhood, and local levels. Coverage includes all 50 states, the District of Columbia, and the U.S. territories of Guam, Puerto Rico, and the Virgin Islands. Information available varies but typically includes contact information, founding year, publication list, annual budget, and brief description of the group.

Industry Financial and Performance Ratios

As was discussed in chapter 3, one use of financial and performance ratios is to compare how well or poorly a company is doing today with how it was doing in the past. Another use is to compare how a given company is performing when compared with other specific companies in the same industry, or compared to the industry as a whole. Industry average or standard ratios are available in several different sources, some of the most well known of which are discussed below.

The following print sources below are among the most useful for comparing a company to the industry it participates in.

RMA Annual Statement Studies Financial Ratio Benchmarks. Philadelphia: Risk Management Association, 1923–. Annual.

Financial Ratio Benchmarks contains composite financial and operating ratios data on manufacturing, wholesaling, retailing, service, and contractor industries. Arrangement is by broad category, such as manufacturing, and then by line of business. More than 750 lines of business or industry groups appear, as determined by the 2007 NAICS codes. In addition to the data presented for each industry, the book includes explanations of balance sheet and income data, definitions of ratios, a listing of SIC/NAICS codes covered, and a bibliography of sources of composite financial information for industries not included.

Risk Management Association is now producing a companion volume to the *Annual Statement Studies*. This new volume, *Industry Default Probabilities and Cash Flow Measures*, now includes "average probability of Default Estimates, Cash Flow Measures, and Change in Financial Position information categorized by industry for more than 700 industries." The data are also available in print, on the Web, and via individual NAICS downloads.[1]

Troy, Leo. Almanac of Business and Industrial Financial Ratios. Englewood Cliffs, NJ: Prentice-Hall, 1971–. Annual.

The *Almanac of Business and Industrial Financial Ratios* is another basic source. Compiled annually from data collected by the Internal Revenue Service, the *Almanac* provides 50 performance indicators on more than 190 different lines of business as defined by NAICS codes and divided into 13 groups by amount of company assets. Compared to the *Annual Statement Studies*, the *Almanac* covers fewer businesses and presents fewer ratios. Further, where *Annual Statement Studies* presents three different values (upper quartile, median, lower quartile), the *Almanac* includes only the industry average for each ratio. Finally, although both the *Almanac* and *Annual Statement Studies* are published yearly, data in the *Statement Studies* are more current. In contrast, information in the *Almanac* may be as much as four years old. Data is available on an included CD.

If these were the only differences between the publications, the *Almanac* would be of negligible value. However, although the *Annual Statement Studies* covers more industries in greater depth, it lacks some of the features available in the *Almanac*. First, a greater number of companies in each line of business are represented in the *Almanac*, which is based on tax returns rather than on financial statements submitted to banks. The industry composite for manufacturers of apparel in *Annual Statement Studies*, for example, is based on data from 66 firms, while the composite in the *Almanac* is based on tax returns from 861 companies. In addition, the *Almanac* uses a greater number of asset size categories. The *Almanac* also distinguishes between profit-making companies and those that are not. Each entry is two pages long, with the first page presenting composite data for all companies in the industry, and the second page limited to companies that earned a profit for the year being reported. In many instances, these features result in even greater precision than is possible with *Annual Statement Studies*. Consequently, most business libraries subscribe to both publications.

Dun & Bradstreet Credit Services. **Industry Norms and Key Business Ratios: Desktop Edition.** New York: Dun & Bradstreet, 1982/1983–. Annual.

Contains tables of selected financial and operating ratios for over 800 lines of business. Most but not all 4-digit SIC codes are included in this work, so this is a good place to start looking for financial and/or operating ratios.

A third basic source, *Industry Norms and Key Business Ratios: Desktop Edition*, presents composite financial information for over 800 different lines of business, arranged by SIC. Based on data collected by Dun & Bradstreet for its credit reporting service, entries for each business include balance sheet and income statement information and 14 financial ratios. Although *Industry Norms and Key Business Ratios* does assign the same values to ratios as *Annual Statement Studies*, it does not categorize companies by asset size and generally includes less information for each line of business than either *Annual Statement Studies* or the *Almanac of Business and Industrial Financial Ratios*. Its real strengths are its timeliness and the wide array of industries it covers.

Only general data are supplied in the *Desktop Edition*. Although Dun & Bradstreet also publishes a series of industry volumes that include detailed geographic and asset-size breakdowns and offers multiple formats, they are costly and are not available in most libraries.

The three titles discussed above are among the most important sources of composite financial information, but they are by no means the only ones. Others include the Census Bureau's *Quarterly Financial Report for Manufacturing, Mining and Trade and Selected Service Industries* (http://www.census.gov/prod/www/abs/qfr-mm.html). The composite industry sources listed above are not inclusive. Not every industry is covered. "If," as Dick Levin writes, "you manufacture corrugated steel pipe, maple flooring, or fabricated roof trusses, or if you install ceiling tiles,"[2] the composite sources may not be particularly useful. In such instances, the best recourse is to identify sources of financial and ratio information for a single industry or group of related industries. Trade associations, accounting firms, large corporations, government agencies, and universities commonly issue such publications. Of these, trade associations are perhaps the most important providers of financial data, covering businesses and industries that are not included elsewhere. For example, the National Automatic Merchandising Association offers *Key*

Indicators to Success: Operating Ratio Report. Most trade associations have a web presence and can be found using a Google search or through the listings on Yahoo! at http://dir .yahoo.com/Business_and_Economy/Organizations/Trade_Associations/.

As discussed in Chapter 3, many of the company information resources, including Osiris and NetAdvantage and Compustat, contain financial ratios as part of each company record and by searching sfor companies in a specific industry code. Users can create industry averages or easily compare one company against another.

Notes

1. Description and ordering information available from Risk Management Association at http://www .rmahq.org/Ann_Studies/asstudies.html.

2. Dick Levin, *Buy Low, Sell High, Collect Early and Pay Late: The Managers Guide to Financial Survival* (Englewood Cliffs, NJ: Prentice-Hall, 1983), 102.

5

Government Information and Services

Governments, governing bodies, and agencies serve many roles, including regulator, overseer, and advisor of many commercial activities. The value of such government support cannot be overestimated. Agencies compile and publish data, supply personal expertise, and, in some instances, provide financial assistance to individuals and organizations. The aim of this chapter is to provide an overview of the major types and sources of business-related information and services provided by international, multinational, federal, and /or state governments, governing bodies, or agencies. There are also commercial publishers who recompile and in some cases add value to the basic government-collected information and sell it in a variety of formats.

Federal Government Information

The U.S. federal government is widely acknowledged to be one of the world's largest gatherers and publishers of information. Once primarily available in paper copy, information is now published in other formats as well, including microfiche, computer tape, CD-ROM, and especially on the Internet. In fact, some publications are available only on the Internet. Whatever the format, much of this information can be tremendously useful to the business community. In fact, there are many business fields in which government documents are the most comprehensive information source available; no private, commercial publisher, for example, can possibly match the detailed demographic and socioeconomic data routinely gathered and published by the Census Bureau. Government documents play an indispensable role in answering business-related inquiries, whether they are about the cost of living in Chicago, or forecasts for the steel industry, or the number of families in Memphis living in air-conditioned houses. There are Department of Labor publications on the outlook for specific occupations; congressional hearings on trade regulations and the national debt; Interstate Commerce Commission statistics on trucking; and Small Business Administration documents on how to establish, operate, and promote small businesses. There are, in fact, very few subjects about which the federal government has not issued publications. Unfortunately, except for a few standard reference works such as the *Statistical Abstract of the United States* and the *United States Government Manual*, government publications are often overlooked by patrons and sometimes even by librarians as important information sources.

Structure of the U.S. Federal Government

Effective promotion and use of federal documents begins with an understanding of the organizational structure of the government. The U.S. Constitution created three branches of government: legislative, executive, and judicial. In addition, although not set forth in the Constitution, an unofficial "fourth branch" of the U.S. federal government, comprising independent agencies and government corporations, is commonly recognized (see figure 5.1).

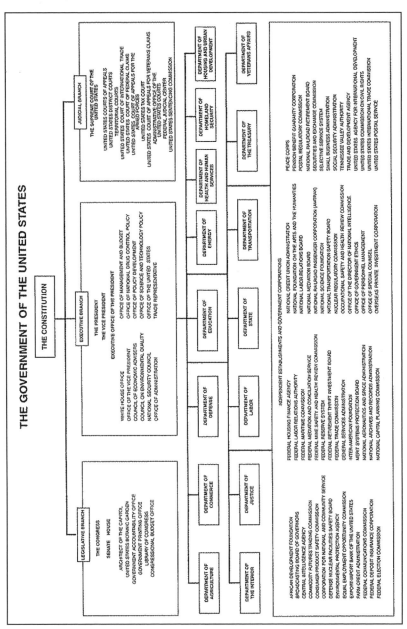

Figure 5.1. Branches of the federal government. Reproduced from page 21 of the *United States Government Manual* at http://www.gpo.gov/fdsys/pkg/GOVMAN-2009-09-15 (accessed December 15, 2010)

Legislative Branch

The legislative branch consists of both houses of Congress and various support organizations, such as the Congressional Budget Office, the Office of the Architect of the Capitol, the U.S. Botanic Garden, the Government Accountability Office (formerly the General Accounting Office), the Library of Congress, and the Government Printing Office. The publications of each organization reflect their varying purposes. The support organizations with most relevance to business are the Government Accountability Office, the Government Printing Office, the Library of Congress, and the now defunct Office of Technology Assessment.

Congressional documents, for example, provide a record of information gathered, opinions shared and debated, as well as laws enacted. The work of preparing and considering legislation is done largely by committee, and congressional committee publications such as committee prints (background information and studies prepared by staff for committee use), committee reports, and hearings testimony transcripts contain a wealth of information. While there are few congressional committees whose activities do not affect business in one way or another, many committees, particularly those listed in figure 5.2, are important.

House	Senate
Agriculture	Agriculture, Nutrition & Forestry
Energy & Commerce	Banking, Housing & Urban Affairs
Financial Services	Commerce, Science & Transportation
Science	Environment & Public Works
Transportation & Infrastructure	Finance
Ways and Means	Health, Education, Labor & Pensions
	Small Business and Entrepreneurship

Figure 5.2. Congressional committees especially important to business

Copies of current and recent committee prints, hearings testimony, and reports can usually be obtained via Thomas [http://thomas.loc.gov/], an Internet service of the Library of Congress. Thomas includes a searchable index of reports, bills, and a calendar of committee meetings back to the 104th Congress. It may also be possible to obtain committee reports by contacting the Senate Document Room or by writing or calling the documents clerk of the committee itself. Since congressional documents are printed in limited supply, it may be necessary to borrow older materials (prior to the 104th Congress) from nearby depository libraries or to acquire reprints from commercial publishers.

The **Government Accountability Office (GAO)** is an independent, nonpolitical agency responsible for auditing government agencies and for making recommendations to Congress on how to improve the efficiency and effectiveness of government programs. The GAO generates reports in response to legislation that specifically directs it to analyze and evaluate specific programs, and also to requests for assistance from congressional staff. Its findings are published in reports to Congress. All publications issued since 1971 are available with some availability back as far as 1922 at the GAO web page (http://www.gao.gov/). Reports can cover broad topics, such as foreign investment in the

United States and the financial condition of American agriculture, or they may focus on narrower topics such as income security and corporate financial audits and standards.

Although the **Library of Congress**, the world's largest, was established to serve the information needs of Congress, its considerable resources are also available to the public. The resources include print, electronic, and other format collections and access to a number of services, some of which are listed later in this chapter.

The **Government Printing Office (GPO)** executes printing and binding orders placed by Congress and by other government agencies. In addition, it produces and distributes federal government information publications, and provides public access to government information online. Its activities are more fully described in the section on federal government publishers.

The now defunct **Office of Technology Assessment (OTA)** was created by the Technology Assessment Act of 1972 to "help Congress anticipate and plan for the consequences of technology." Its basic function was to provide congressional committees with studies that identified the social, economic, and physical consequences that may accompany various policy decisions relating to the use of specific technologies, such as nuclear power and alternative fuels. This office was closed in September 1995, but an archival Internet site is maintained by the Woodrow Wilson School of Public and International Affairs at Princeton University (http://www.princeton.edu/~ota/).

Executive Branch

The executive branch consists of the president, the Executive Office of the President, the vice president, and 15 cabinet departments. While the duties of the president and vice president themselves require no discussion, the other executive agencies merit examination.

The Executive Office of the President is composed of various advisory and administrative support agencies. Those that are particularly important to business are the Council of Economic Advisers, the Council on Environmental Quality, the Office of Management and Budget, and the Office of the U.S. Trade Representative. For a full list of agencies and information about them, go the White House web site at http://www.whitehouse.gov/administration/eop/.

The **Council of Economic Advisers** (http://www.whitehouse.gov/administration/eop/cea/) is responsible for analyzing the economy and for advising and recommending policies to the president that promote economic growth and stability. It also assists in the preparation of two very important recurring documents: *Economic Indicators*, a monthly compilation of economic statistics prepared for the Congress's Joint Economic Committee, and the annual *Economic Report of the President*.

The main purpose of the **Council on Environmental Quality** (http://www.whitehouse.gov/administration/eop/ceq/) is to formulate and recommend national policies to improve the environment. These recommendations are based on a continuing analysis of the environment, and the changes or trends that affect it, as well as a review and appraisal of the ways in which government programs and regulations contribute to sound environmental policy. Nearly all federal activities affect the environment in some way, and before federal agencies make decisions they must have information about the potential impact of their actions on the quality of the environment. Many of these findings are published, and in recent years Council documents have covered such topics as urban sprawl, energy alternatives, forging conservation partnerships with farmers, blocking offshore oil drilling, and clean water. Like that of the Council of Economic Advisers, its annual report is filled with an impressive array of information and statistical data, ranging from the pollutant standard for urban air quality to the status of whale stocks. As are most other Council on Environmental Quality publications, the annual report is available from the Government Printing Office.

The **Office of Management and Budget** (http://www.whitehouse.gov/omb/) is charged with several responsibilities. They include reviewing the organization and management of the executive branch, developing and promoting interagency coordination and cooperation, helping the president prepare the budget, and supervising and controlling its administration. In addition, OMB is responsible for planning program performance evaluations and for keeping the president informed of work proposed, initiated, and completed by government agencies. Although it produces documents on a wide range of subjects, the most heavily used title is probably the *Budget of the United States Government* (http://www.whitehouse.gov/omb/budget/).

The **Office of the U.S. Trade Representative** (http://www.ustr.gov/) is responsible for administering trade agreements, coordinating trade policy, and explaining the benefits of international trade. The office publishes a variety of documents, including the text of multilateral and bilateral trade agreements to which the United States is a party.

Although the Departments of Commerce, Labor, and Treasury are particularly important, each of the 15 executive or "Cabinet" departments affects business in some way. Each department publishes a wide array of reports, periodicals, statistics, and information for the general public, most of which are available from their individual department web sites or the Government Printing Office. Each department also employs a complement of subject specialists who are generally quite willing to share their expertise, and in addition, each department has at least one public affairs or information office. Many departments also have regional or field offices, established to provide assistance to designated regions of the country. The Department of Labor's Bureau of Labor Statistics, for example, has regional offices in 8 different cities (http://www.bls.gov/bls/regnhome .htm), the Census Bureau in 12 (http://www.census.gov/regions/). One of the easiest ways to determine the location of the closest field office is by consulting the department's web page, or if one does not have access to the Internet, the *United States Government Manual*.

In addition to the agencies and departments mentioned above, the president can also establish ad hoc or temporary commissions, committees, boards, and task forces to conduct fact-finding missions. Most publish their findings, and many relate to business and the economy. Some examples would be the President's Economic Advisory Board, the White House Council on Community Solutions, and the 9/11 Commission.

Appendix B lists the cabinet departments, their primary responsibilities relating to business, and selected sub-cabinet agencies.

Judicial Branch

The judiciary is composed of the Supreme Court, the U.S. Courts of Appeals, and District and Territorial Courts. In addition, it includes national courts such as the U.S. Tax Court and the U.S. Court of International Trade. Finally, two support agencies, the Administrative Office of the U.S. Courts and the Federal Judicial Center, complete the roster of organizations in this branch.

Compared to the legislative and executive branches, the judicial arm of the government is not a prolific publisher. The documents it issues are primarily court decisions. While these decisions can have tremendous impact on how business is conducted, requests for the legal information they contain are generally handled by law libraries and in documents departments rather than in more general library settings. This may be changing because of the availability of federal court's decisions from such services as (http://thomas.loc.gov/) and the accessibility of state court's decisions and information through the Internet.

Independent Agencies and Government Corporations

The *United States Government Manual* (http://www.gpo.gov/fdsys/browse/collection .action?collectionCode=GOVMAN) lists more than 100 different independent government organizations authorized by the president or by Congress. Some, such as the Federal Trade Commission and the Nuclear Regulatory Commission, are regulatory agencies. In many instances, the activities they oversee and regulate are commercial ones; as a result, these agencies touch on business in a very real and constant way. Others, such as the Federal Deposit Insurance Corporation, are government-established corporations. Whatever their designation, these agencies, comprising an unofficial "fourth arm of the government," routinely gather and publish statistics, research findings, and agency regulations and decisions. They can be prolific publishers. Many of the agencies and government corporations with greatest impact on business activities are listed in Appendix C.

This overview of federal government structure attests to its complexity and diversity. There are literally hundreds of government departments, committees, bureaus, commissions, and agencies. Most are described in the official directory of federal organization, the *United States Government Manual.*

U.S. National Archives and Records Administration. Office of the Federal Register. **United States Government Manual**. Washington, DC: Government Printing Office, 1935–. Annual. Web version available at http://www.gpo.gov/fdsys/browse/ collection.action?collectionCode=GOVMAN

The *United States Government Manual* provides comprehensive information on legislative, executive, judicial, and independent agencies. The address and telephone numbers for each agency and district office are provided, as well as a brief description of its history, programs, activities, and a list of its principal officials. In addition, each entry features a section that lists the names and telephone numbers of departments responsible for public information, contracts and grants, publications, and employment. Organization charts for major departments and agencies are included, and a list of abolished and transferred agencies is appended. Name, subject, and agency indexes complete the *Manual*. This inexpensive directory is, in fact, a treasure trove of information, an indispensable guide to the federal government and, although much of the information is now available on the Internet, a print copy still belongs in every reference collection. In early 2011 the GPO announced that the *United States Government Manual* would only be produced as an Internet document.

Although the *Manual* provides an overview of the legislative branch, it is not the most comprehensive congressional information source. That distinction belongs to another federal publication, the *Congressional Directory*.

U.S. Congress. Joint Committee on Printing. **Congressional Directory**. Washington, DC: Government Printing Office, 1809–. Annual. Web version available at http://www .gpo.gov/fdsys/browse/collection.action?collectionCode=CDIR

Prepared for the use of members of Congress and their staff, the *Congressional Directory* is useful to anyone who requires information about the legislative branch of the government or about executive, judicial, independent, and private organizations whose activities affect Congress. It includes a listing of congressional committees and subcommittees, their staff, and the members of Congress who serve on them; a biographical section arranged by state; and an alphabetical listing of legislators, their office addresses and telephone numbers, and the names of their administrative and executive assistants. Information on embassies, diplomats, and international organizations is also included. Using the *Directory*, one can find the name of the ambassador to Botswana, determine when a senator's term of office will expire, and compile a list of OECD member countries. Like the *United States Government Manual*, the *Congressional Directory* is an inexpensive directory and is an indispensable guide to the federal government. Although much of the information is now available on the Internet, a print copy still belongs in every reference collection. Together they provide detailed and comprehensive access to most U.S. government organizations.

In government as in business, however, change is commonplace. Programs and responsibilities are reassigned, new departments and agencies are created, and old ones are reorganized or even abolished. Thus, as with many annual business directories, these government directories sometimes lag behind. One solution is to supplement them with commercially published directories issued more frequently. Following are two of the most commonly used commercial publications.

Carroll's Federal Directory: Executive, Legislative, Judicial. Washington, DC: Carroll Publishing, 1980–. Quarterly. http://www.carrollpub.com/index.asp

Federal Yellow Book. New York: N.Y. Leadership Directories, 1976–. Quarterly. http://www.leadershipdirectories.com/products/fyb.html

Carroll's Federal Directory and the *Federal Yellow Book* provide directory access to federal agencies and key executives. Although much of the information is garnered from federal telephone directories and the *United States Government Manual,* the commercial products' advantage is their relative currency. Both are updated quarterly, and as a result they sometimes reflect more accurately current government organization and staffing than do the government annuals. Both are also available electronically either as a CD-ROM or through the Internet; the Internet product from Leadership Directories is updated daily. Some of this information is free, at http://www.leadershipdirectories.com/. Subscriptions to these books, or to the online services, cost several times the purchase price of the *United States Government Manual* and the *Congressional Directory*.

Federal Government Publishers

The federal government, as we have seen, is complex and diverse, and each government agency produces documents for public information and use. Documents take many different forms, and their intellectual content varies widely, but most are made available (in print, CD-ROM, and/or Internet versions) through the two major government publishers, the Government Printing Office and the National Technical Information Service. With the continuing growth of the Internet, more and more information is being made available in an electronic format by the issuing agencies, although print versions may still be available from the GPO. Consideration of these and of the other federal publishers is in order.

Government Printing Office

Although it began as the printer for Congress and is officially an agency of the legislative branch, the Government Printing Office's activities have long since expanded to make it the primary source for printing, distribution, and sale of federal government documents. Each year it publishes thousands of items and makes many of them available through a network of depository libraries and a sales program.

Today the GPO is at the vanguard in providing government information through a wide range of formats, including printing, microfiche, CD-ROM, and especially online through *Federal Digital System FDsys* (http://www.gpo.gov/fdsys). Until March 2011, FDsys was known as *GPO Access* (http://www.gpoaccess.gov). The GPO Access site is still open but is no longer being updated.

Depository Libraries

The GPO distributes many of the documents it publishes, in various formats, to nearly 1,225 depository libraries. Generally speaking there is at least one depository library in each congressional district. The depository system was created to ensure public access to documents, and each depository library "is designated to receive, without charge on a deposit basis, government publications issued by governmental agencies, except those determined by the issuing agencies to be required for official use only or for strictly administrative or operational purposes . . . [or] classified for reasons of national security."[1] Four points should be emphasized. First, depository libraries do not pay for the documents they receive. Second, although housed in the library, the documents do not really belong to the library; they are there "on deposit." The federal government has the right to ask for their return at any time. Third, the depository program exists to make documents available to the public. Although definition of public availability varies from one depository library to another, at a minimum it means that anyone has the right to use, on site, any document held by the library. Fourth, not all GPO-published documents are sent to depository libraries; a distinction is made between nondepository documents, which are not sent to depositories, and depository documents, which are.

There are two types of depository libraries, regional and selective. The country's 49 regional depositories are required to receive and keep permanently all documents that have been designated as depository items. In addition, regional depository staffs are expected to provide interlibrary loan and reference service and other types of assistance, both to the public and to other libraries in their region. Many, but not all, regionals are hosted by major research universities or by major public libraries. Many regionals have been depositories since the late nineteenth or early twentieth centuries. As a consequence of their extensive collections and their strong service orientation, they are usually excellent providers of information, advice, and assistance.

Selective depository libraries can choose the documents that they want to receive; unlike the regionals, they are not required to accept and house every depository document published by the Government Printing Office. In addition, with the approval of the regional depository library in their area, they can discard unwanted documents. As a result, there is considerable variation in the breadth and depth of selective depository collections. Some selective libraries rival regional depositories in size and scope; others are considerably more focused in their collection. There are presently some 1,173 selective depository libraries in the United States, and like their regional depository counterparts, they provide access to and assistance in the use of their documents collections.

Although most nondepository library business reference collections include a core of basic business sources published by the federal government, depository libraries provide access to more specialized sources and to GPO titles that are no longer in print. Library staff and users would do well to become acquainted with collections, service policies, and documents librarians at nearby depository libraries. They constitute a rich information source, one that can be of particular benefit to business librarians and researchers. A complete list of selective and regional depository libraries can be obtained by checking the eeb page at http://catalog.gpo.gov/fdlpdir/FDLPdir.jsp (see figure 5.3).

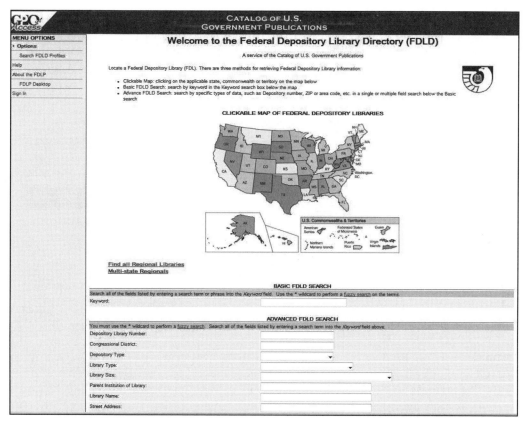

Figure 5.3. Locate federal depository libraries by state, area code, or by a variety of other criteria. http://catalog.gpo.gov/fdlpdir/FDLPdir.jsp

GPO Sales Program

Nondepository libraries wishing to build documents collections of their own or to acquire specific government publications usually purchase them from the Government Printing Office's U.S. Government Bookstore Internet site, http://bookstore.gpo.gov/. In addition, librarians can acquire federal documents through commercial book dealers, jobbers, and document delivery services.

Many libraries no longer buy print editions of documents but use the online products provided by the GPO. Public Law 103–40, known as the Government Printing Office Electronic Information Enhancement Act of 1993, stated that free electronic access should be provided to information products produced by the federal government. *GPO Access* was established by this law and began operations in 1994. It provided easy, one-stop, no-fee access to information from all three branches of the government. The information provided is the official, published version, and the material retrieved from *GPO Access* could be used without restriction, unless specifically noted. *GPO Access* provided free online use of more than 1,000 databases ranging from the *Budget of the United States Government* to the *Federal Register* (see figure 5.4). In 2004 the GPO reaffirmed its commitment to provide "perpetual, free, and ready public access to the printed and electronic documents . . . of the Federal Government." In 2009 the GPO started to transition to the new interface with the new name *Federal Digital System FDsys* (http://www.gpo.gov/fdsys). The transition was to be completed in early 2011.

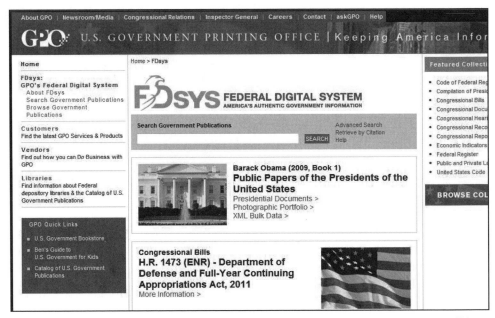

Figure 5.4. Official government information from FDsys. http://www.gpo.gov/fdsys

The *Federal Bulletin Board* (FBB) [http://fedbbs.access.gpo.gov/] is another component of the GPO. Federal agencies use the *FBB* as a means to distribute electronic files in various file formats to the public. Information is available from the White House and executive branch agencies, including independent agencies, such as the Department of State and Treasury and the Federal Labor Relations Authority. Data vary from *Daily Treasury Statements* to *Free National Export Strategy Documents* (see figure 5.5).

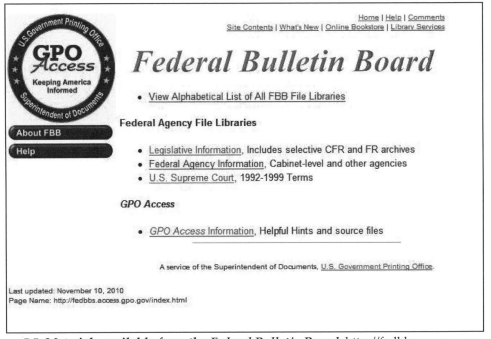

Figure 5.5. Materials available from the *Federal Bulletin Board*. http://fedbbs.access.gpo.gov/

GPO Bibliographies and Lists

Consulting one or more of the GPO's bibliographies and lists, available in differing formats, can identify documents published by the Government Printing Office. Among the most important are the *Catalog of U.S. Government Publications (CGP)*, *U.S. Government Books*, *New Products Catalog*, and *U.S. Government Subscription*. Each merits attention.

U.S. Superintendent of Documents. **Catalog of U.S. Government Publications**. Washington, DC: Government Printing Office, updated daily (http://catalog.gpo.gov/.)

The *Catalog of U.S. Government Publications* (CGP) records and indexes documents received by the Government Printing Office from all arms of the federal government, legislative, judicial, and executive branches, and the independent and regulatory agencies as well. The CGP was originally the online counterpart of the *Monthly Catalog of United States Government Publications*, which had been printed since the passage of the Printing Act of 1895. The print version of the *Monthly Catalog* was discontinued with the December 2004 edition. The CGP is now the finding tool for federal publications. It includes descriptive records for historical and current publications and provides direct links to those that are available online. Users can search by authoring agency, title, subject, and general key word, or click on "Advanced Search" for more options. More than 500,000 records generated since July 1976 are contained in the CGP, and it is updated daily (see figure 5.6).

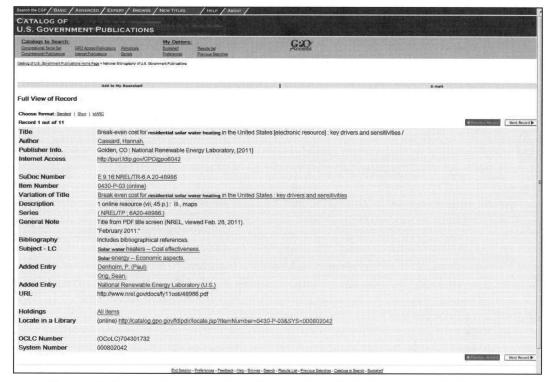

Figure 5.6. Sample short entry from the *Catalog of U.S. Government Publications*

The catalog will grow to include records for publications dating back to the late 1800s, making the CGP the central point for locating new and historical government publications. For publications issued prior to 1976, the printed *Monthly Catalog of United States Government Publications* should be consulted.

U.S. Superintendent of Documents. **Monthly Catalog of U.S. Government Publications**. Washington, DC: Government Printing Office, 1895–2004. Monthly, with monthly and annual indexes

"The Monthly Catalog," writes Yuri Nakata, "is to government publications what the Cumulative Book Index is to general book publications."[2] Arrangement of documents included in the *Monthly Catalog* is by issuing agency. All Department of Commerce publications, for example, are grouped together regardless of subject, as are those of the Department of Labor, the Federal Trade Commission, and other agencies. Entries are brief, and the publications that are depository items include heavy black dots, or bullets, in the main listing next to the item number. The preliminary pages of each issue of the *Monthly Catalog* describe its contents and use in some detail.

One should be aware of three additional pieces of information before calling upon depository libraries for assistance. As mentioned earlier, not all GPO-published documents are designated as depository documents. Regional depository libraries, required to receive and keep all depository documents, should have all of these bulleted documents. Selective depository libraries, on the other hand, may have only a limited number of such publications. In addition, many documents formerly published in paper copy are now available only in microfiche or via the Web. Finally, it is never safe to assume that a particular document, simply because it is not a depository item, will be unavailable at depository libraries. Many depositories have extensive holdings of nondepository documents collections purchased from commercial publishers such as Readex and Congressional Information Service, which was recently purchased by Proquest.

When the choice is to acquire documents rather than to borrow them from another library, other information is necessary. In many instances, documents can be ordered from the Superintendent of Documents; their availability from the GPO at the time of printing is usually indicated in the main record by an entry stating "For sale by the U.S. G.P.O., Supt. of Docs., Congressional Sales Office." Mail order forms are included in the preliminary pages of each issue of the *Monthly Catalog,* or one may order at the Online Bookstore at http://bookstore.gpo.gov/.[3] A document's inclusion in the *Monthly Catalog* does not guarantee its availability from the Government Printing Office. Some must be ordered from the issuing agencies themselves or may be freely available on agency web pages.

Having online access to the *Catalog of U.S. Government Publications* on the Web is great. But having online access to the U.S. Government publications in your own collection is perhaps even better. The Marcive company (http://www.marcive.com) has worked consistently with libraries to make the *Catalog of U.S. Government Publications* from 1976 available in electronic format. Many institutions choose to load the data from Marcive directly into their online catalog to make available an integrated collection of all library holdings, but there are also available both web versions and CD-ROMs. More information is available at the company web page.

Although the *Catalog* is the most comprehensive listing of GPO publications, it is not always the best source for building business reference collections, particularly in small and medium-sized libraries. In these settings, other sources, such as the *New Products Catalog,* may be more helpful.

New Products Catalog. Washington, DC: U.S. Government Printing Office, Superintendent of Documents, 1994–. Irregular.

New Products, formerly *New Products from the U.S. Government*, is a catalog of popular government books, periodicals, and databases. Entries are arranged by government agency and include title, date of publication, formats available, number of pages, GPO stock number, and price. Also included are lists of bestsellers and new releases. This publication is available free from the Superintendent of Documents. Another easy way to get the most recent new publications is to click on the New Titles tab in the CGP (see figure 5.7) then select the time period you want, from last 7 days to last 3 months. You can do this for both "tangible" (print) and electronic or just electronic publications. Finally you can sign up for an email alert service that will send you an email when a new publication is available in the areas you select [http://bookstore.gpo.gov/alertservice.jsp].

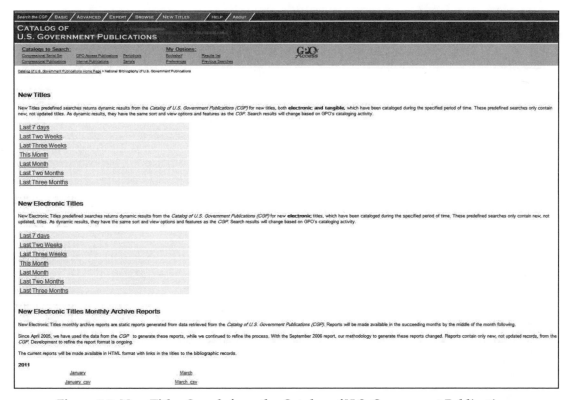

Figure 5.7. New Titles Search from the *Catalog of U.S. Government Publications*

U.S. Government Subscriptions. Washington, DC: Government Printing Office, 1974–. Web version available at http://bookstore.gpo.gov/subscriptions.jsp.

U.S. Government Subscription Catalog is an online list of periodicals, serial titles, and subscription services available from the Government Printing Office, including such titles as *Economic Indicators, Monthly Labor Review,* and *Internal Revenue Bulletin.* Entries are arranged by title and usually include current prices, stock numbers, Superintendent of Documents classification, and, date (see figure 5.8).

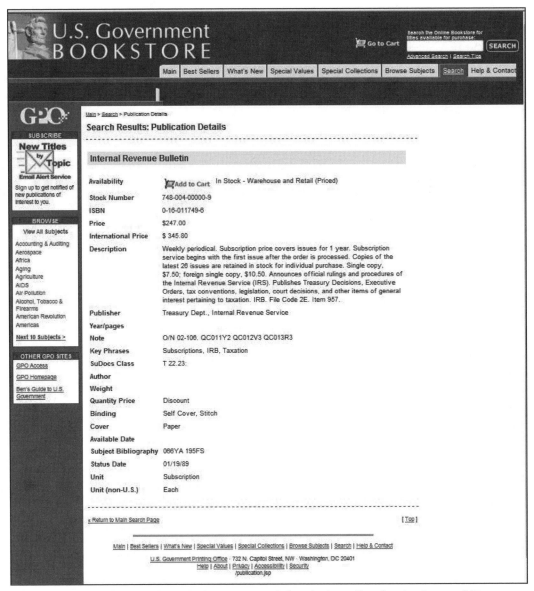

Figure 5.8. Sample entry in *U.S. Government Subscriptions Catalog* **for Internal Revenue Bulletin,** at http://bookstore.gpo.gov/actions/GetPublication.do?stocknumber=748-004-00000-9

The availability of most of this information via *Federal Digital System FDsys* (http://www.gpo.gov/fdsys) has made collection of and quick access to materials easier for people without easy access to a depository library. Once again the *Catalog of U.S. Government Publications* can easily be used to search for subscription publications; simply click on the "Periodicals" or "Serials" link and limit your search to that type of publication.

The *Catalog of U.S. Government Publications* can also be useful when searching for bibliographies. When doing a search simply add the term "bibliography" to your search terms.

Although the Government Printing Office is the principal printing agency of the federal government, it does not publish and sell all federal documents. Other government agencies are also involved in the publication of documents, usually more specialized than those available through the GPO. One of the most important of these agencies is the National Technical Information Service.

National Technical Information Service

The National Technical Information Service (NTIS) (http://www.ntis.gov/), an agency of the Department of Commerce, is the central source for public sale of government-sponsored research, development, and engineering reports, and technical reports prepared by foreign governments and by local government agencies (see figure 5.9).

Figure 5.9. NTIS—National Technical Information Service

When compared to the GPO, the NTIS has a much narrower focus. No congressional hearings or government regulations or consumer-oriented publications are included. There are other differences between the agencies. The GPO sells only current titles. The possibility of obtaining a 10- or even 5-year-old document from the GPO is remote. The National Technical Information Service, on the other hand, offers access to all of the documents received since its inception. Another difference is that the GPO subsidizes the printing and sale of its documents, which are very inexpensive. The NTIS, in contrast, is required by law to operate on a cost-recovery basis. As a result, there is considerable difference between the prices of NTIS and GPO documents. Finally, whereas the Government Printing Office has established a network of designated depository libraries, there is no NTIS equivalent. Although many research and technical libraries comprehensively collect NTIS documents, their collections are not part of a government-sponsored system.

NTIS documents are available in a wide variety of formats, including paper copy, microfiche, and microfilm, and various electronic and online formats. Orders can be placed online, by email, by mail, by fax, or by voice telephone (see figure 5.10).

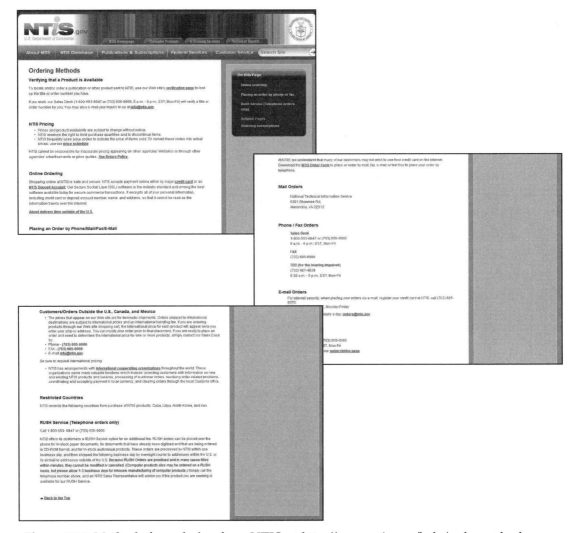

Figure 5.10. Methods for ordering from NTIS, at http://www.ntis.gov/help/ordermethods.aspx

NTIS has an electronic search engine (http://www.ntis.gov/search). The NTIS database includes 3 million records of government publications as well as data files, CD-ROMs, and audiovisuals. The complete electronic file dates back to 1964. On average, NTIS adds over 30,000 new records per year to the database. Many records include abstracts. All orders are electronic or print on demand, so no returns are allowed (see figure 5.11).

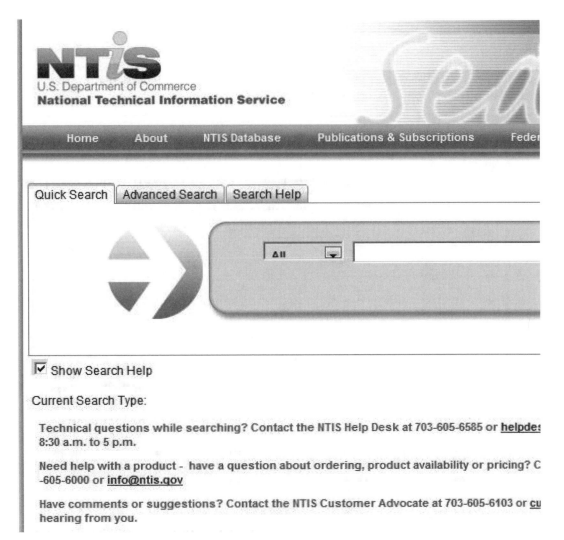

Figure 5.11. NTIS Product Search Page

There are also lists of NTIS bestsellers, audiovisual business products, computer business products, and online databases.

Both the Government Printing Office and the National Technical Information Service have extensive and wide-ranging publishing programs. Although the GPO is the government's major publisher and the NTIS the major information clearinghouse, they are by no means the only collectors and disseminators of government information. There are hundreds of additional federal information clearinghouses, information centers, and depository programs. Most focus on specific research or program areas, such as energy, aging, or education, and many collect and print both government and private sector publications. Two of the best-known clearinghouses are the Educational Resources Information Center (http://www.eric.ed.gov/) and the National Criminal Justice Reference Service (http://www.ncjrs.gov/); two of the best-known depository programs are those administered by the Patent and Trademark Office and the Census Bureau.

Of particular interest to business is the information available from the U.S. Patent and Trademark Office at http://www.uspto.gov/. Included at this web site are booklets such as *Basic Facts about Trademarks, General Information Concerning Patents,* and the *Examiner's Handbook.* There are also downloadable forms and instructions for patent and trademark applicants and a searchable database of registered patent attorneys and agents. The USPTO also offers free searchable databases to trademarks and patents. The patents, available from 1976 on, are offered in full image format (see figure 5.12).

Figure 5.12. U.S. Patent Office web page

Trends in Federal Publishing

Publishing activities of the federal government change from year to year and, more notably, from one administration to the next. Emphasis in recent years has been on reducing federal expenditures, which has been reflected in the government's publishing program. Many documents formerly available in paper copy, for example, are now available only on the Internet or in microfiche, or have been discontinued. In the April 2000 edition of *Administrative Notes* (http://www.access.gpo.gov/su_docs/fdlp/pubs/adnotes/), the now ceased newsletter of the Federal Depository Library Program, there is an update on the published formats of government information. This details the fact that the most popular dissemination medium in the Federal Depository Library Program is now online. According to the Government Documents Round Table (GODORT) of the American Library Association, "The FDLP is increasingly electronic. In Fiscal Year (FY) 2004, the percentage of **electronic-only** publications was 65%. In FY 2004, 32,348 new titles were disseminated through the FDLP; GPO Access makes more than 275,000 federal titles available to FDLP users as well as the public; and more than 32 million documents are downloaded each month" (http://0-www.ala.org.sapl.sat.lib.tx.us/ala/mgrps/rts/godort/godortfactsheets/fdlpfactsheet.cfm).

Many other titles have been "privatized." This means that commercial publishers bear the brunt of publishing costs and are also entitled to earn profits from the government titles they publish. Understandably, documents librarians are concerned about such changes, which mean that many formerly available documents are priced for profit rather than to cover costs.

Commercially Published Guides, Bibliographies, and Periodicals

Guides

The volume and scope of published federal information can overwhelm the uninitiated at times. One good way to begin the quest for such information is by consulting a guide to federal documents. A proper understanding of documents and documents librarianship begins with an understanding of the structure of the government and federal publishing programs. Although both have been covered briefly in this chapter, the sources noted below treat them in greater depth. They describe the publications and activities characteristic of each branch of the government as well as the history, responsibilities, and role of the Government Printing Office and the Superintendent of Documents. Depository libraries and legal and technical report literature are also covered. The guides focus on sources available on the Internet, but print resources are covered as well.

Forte, Eric J. Cassandra J. Hartnett, and Andrea Sevetson. **Fundamentals of Government Information: Mining, Finding, Evaluating, and Using Government Resources.** New York: Neal-Schuman Publishers, 2011. 396p.

Especially interesting in this new work is a chapter titled "How to Think Like a Government Documents Librarian" that gives insights into the thought processes of documents librarians. Others chapters titled "Business, Economic, and Consumer Information" and "Census" will also be important to business researchers. At the end of each chapter are sections on "Sources Mentioned in This Chapter" and "References."

Garvin, Peggy. **The United States Government Internet Directory.** Lanham, MD: Bernan Press, 2011. 627p. Annual.

Previously titled *E-Government and Web Directory: U.S. Federal Government Online* (2009) and *The United States Government Internet Manual* (2004–2008). The current edition like its predecessors focuses on web-based publications from the U.S. government, especially those that do not require payment or registration. It is organized into 20 subject-oriented chapters, rather than by agency or branch of government. Chapter 1 titled "Finding Aids" and the 4 indexes and sections on "what to watch for" and the "Economic recovery web sites" are sure to be useful.

Hernon, Peter, Robert E. Dugan, and John A. Shuler. **US Government on the Web Getting the Information You Need.** Westport, CT: Libraries Unlimited, 2003.

Available in print and as an e-book. According to the publisher's website (http://www.abc-clio.com/products/productFactSheet.aspx?id=2147496679) this resource is intended to be a "cardinal pointer through the labyrinthine structure and the myriad information resources available to the public, giving users a clearer understanding of U.S. government agencies and the online publications."

Three older titles are still useful, especially for historical work

Morehead, Joe. **Introduction to United States Government Information Sources**. 6th ed. Englewood, CO: Libraries Unlimited, 1999. 491p.

Introduction to United States Government Information Sources provides an authoritative overview of federal production and distribution of documents, in all available formats, as well as of the types of publications issued by specific government agencies.

Robinson, Judith Schiek. **Tapping the Government Grapevine: The User-Friendly Guide to U.S. Government Information Sources**. 3rd ed. Phoenix, AZ: Oryx Press, 1998. 286p.

Tapping the Government Grapevine is a highly readable text that explains the intricacies of government information and how to find sources that meet specific research needs. Chapters feature search and access tips, tables and illustrations, and detailed coverage of Internet resources and directories of World Wide Web addresses. Addresses for agencies, web sites, and lists of free publications appear at the end of relevant chapters.

Sears, Jean L., and Marilyn K. Moody. **Using Government Information Sources: Print and Electronic**. 3rd ed. Phoenix, AZ: Oryx Press, 2001. 536p.

Using Government Information Sources focuses more on practical search strategies and research techniques used to locate documents on specific subjects. Each chapter deals with a different topic; those particularly relevant to business include Foreign Countries, Occupations, Selling to the Government, Business Aids, Tax Information, Economic Indicators, Business and Industry Statistics, Income, Earnings, Employment, Prices, Consumer Expenditures, Foreign Trade Statistics, Projections, Budget Analysis, Technical Reports, Patents and Trademarks, and Standards and Specifications. Each chapter is grouped into subcategories of similar or related material, each with a checklist of titles providing full bibliographic information and Superintendent of Documents classification numbers. Narrative descriptions of the titles are included in each section, and many chapters are enhanced by the use of sample pages from the documents cited. Relevant indexes, databases, and other specialized sources are also listed.

Using Government Information Sources and *Tapping the Government Grapevine* are particularly helpful to librarians and researchers confronted for the first time with inquiries about subjects with which they have only limited familiarity; *Introduction to United States Government Information Sources*, on the other hand, is most useful for developing a sense of the types of publications that are available from the government, of the basic indexes used to identify them, and of the history and development of various federal publishing programs. Taken together, they provide an outstanding introduction to documents and to the types of business-related reference and research inquiries that documents can answer.

Bibliographies

Commercial publishers also publish documents bibliographies. Three of the most popular are the *Guide to Popular U.S. Government Publications*, *Government Reference Books*, and the *Subject Guide to U.S. Government Reference Sources*.

Hardy, Gayle J., and Judith Schiek Robinson. **Subject Guide to U.S. Government Reference Sources**. 2nd ed. Englewood, CO: Libraries Unlimited, 1996. 358p. Also available through NetLibrary.

The *Subject Guide to U.S. Government Reference Sources* selectively lists and annotates key government reference sources, regardless of format, available through depository libraries, the Internet, and occasionally as free copies from either the GPO or individual agencies. Arrangement is by broad subject category, such as social sciences or science and technology, and each entry includes full bibliographic information; an annotation; and when applicable, Superintendent of Documents, Library of Congress, and Dewey classifications.

Hoffman, Frank W., and Richard J. Wood. **Guide to Popular Government Publications**. 5th ed. Englewood, CO: Libraries Unlimited, 1998. 300p.

Guide to Popular Government Publications provides information about documents by topics. Those of special interest to business include Business and International Trade; Consumer Information and Protection; Copyrights, Patents and Trademarks; and Labor and Employment. Each annotated entry includes Superintendent of Documents classification, stock numbers, and prices.

Government Reference Books. Littleton, CO: Libraries Unlimited, 1968/1969 1993. Biennial.

Government Reference Books is a biennial listing of key reference sources issued by the Government Printing Office, an annotated guide to atlases, bibliographies, catalogs, dictionaries, directories, guides, handbooks, indexes, manuals, and other reference publications issued during the two-year period covered. Most titles are grouped together by subject; the section on economics and commerce, for example, includes titles categorized by such subject designations as employment and labor and government assistance and procurement. In addition to the bibliographic citation and annotation, each entry includes the Superintendent of Documents classification, *Monthly Catalog* entry number, stock number, and price. Most of the titles listed are depository documents.

The federal government is committed to providing public access to its information. In addition to being one of the world's largest publishers of printed sources, the federal government is also one of the world's largest producers and suppliers of electronic information, either through the Internet, as CD-ROMs, as magnetic tape, or as diskettes. Some federal databases are available through standard online database vendors. Still others can be accessed through government agencies, their contractors, or designated centers, or they can be purchased outright from the federal government. One way to identify such government-produced data files is through use of the *Federal Data Base Finder*.

Lesko, Matthew. **Federal Data Base Finder**. 4th ed. New York: Gale Research, 1995. 1253p.

The now-ceased *Federal Data Base Finder* gave information about databases, computer tapes, and microcomputer disks available from the government and private contractors. Each entry includes the name of the database; a description of its contents and scope; price; and contact information including the agency address, telephone number, and, in many instances, the name of an information or subject specialist. One way to update information in Federal Data Base Finder was to use the *Government Information Locator Service* (GILS) (http://www.gpoaccess.gov/gils/index.html/). A GILS was a decentralized collection of agency-based information locators that directs users to relevant information resources within the federal government. Not all agencies provided information on the location of their GILS records, so it cannot be considered a comprehensive database. In the years since GILS was issued, however, advances in technology made the standard obsolete that enable agencies to avoid the ongoing, resource-intensive cataloging efforts mandated by the GILS. As a result the GILS application on GPO Access is no longer being updated, and an archive is available. The archive database spans from December 7, 1994, through September 2, 2008.[4]

Indexes and Periodicals

Although periodicals published by the Government Printing Office are listed in the *Catalog of U.S. Government Publications*, their contents are not. Accordingly, many documents departments and large research libraries subscribe to a commercially published index to federal serial titles.

Index to U.S. Government Periodicals. Chicago: Infordata International, 1970–1987. Quarterly, with annual cumulations.

LexisNexis Government Periodicals Index. Bethesda, MD: LexisNexis, 1988–. Quarterly updates. http://www.lexisnexis.com/academic/1univ/govper/default.asp

The online source *LexisNexis Government Periodicals Index* is a continuation of the now-ceased print source *Index to U.S. Government Periodicals* and covers articles in approximately 170 current federal publications. It includes retrospective coverage from 1988 to the present of over 70 additional federal publications that have major research, reference, or general interest value. The *Index* provides detailed access by subject and author. The discontinued hard-copy *Index* lists articles by author and subject, with each entry featuring a standard bibliographic citation. As the online versions only begin coverage in 1988, the print volumes are still needed in collections to trace older articles.

Some of the most popular government periodicals, such as the *Federal Reserve Bulletin*, *Survey of Current Business*, and *Monthly Labor Review*, are also included in standard indexes such as *ABI/INFORM*, *Public Affairs Information Service* (*PAIS*), and *Business Source Premier*.

In addition, there is a specialized documents periodical that identifies important new documents and trends in government publishing. The final issue of the year contains a list of notable documents.

Government Information Quarterly. New York: Elsevier, v. 1–. 1973–. Quarterly.

Government Information Quarterly is a quarterly scholarly journal devoted entirely to international, foreign, federal, state, and local documents; their production and distribution; and documents librarianship. (Formerly titled *Journal of Government*

Information: An International Review of Policy, Issues and Resources and also *Government Publications Review.*) Tables of contents from 1973 to 1999 are available electronically at http://www.lib.auburn.edu/madd/docs/jgi/contents.html.

DttP: Documents to the People. College Park, MD: American Library Association, Government Documents Round Table (GODORT) v. 1–. 1972–. Quarterly.

DttP: Documents to the People is the official publication of GODORT and features articles on local, state, national, and international government information resources, government activities related to information, and other aspects of managing, maintaining, and using government information.

For up-to-date information on government documents and information one should access the ALA Government Documents Round Table (GODORT) web page at (http://www.ala.org/ala/mgrps/rts/godort/index.cfm).

To this point this chapter has focused on published information sources. Equally important, however, are the large number of government services available to business-people, many of which are described in the following section.

Federal Government Services to Business

The federal government spends billions of dollars annually, much of it for the accumulation of information and specialized expertise. The budget for publicizing the availability of such information and knowledge, however, is negligible. As a result, information and services that might contribute to productivity and profit are underutilized. There are literally hundreds of special programs and services available to business, ranging from counseling to special loans.

The government is often viewed, with some justification, as a vast, bureaucratic maze, complicated, confusing, and intimidating. For librarians and researchers in search of special information or assistance, the first question often is not where to find it, but rather how to find out where to find it, preferably with a minimum of telephone calls or web searches. Sometimes it is difficult to determine just which agency to contact. In such a situation it may be best to begin with the Small Business Administration at http://www.sba.gov/ (see figure 5.13).

The U.S. Small Business Administration is intended to be a one-stop electronic link to all the information and services a small business needs to comply with laws and regulations and to take advantage of all the services various levels of government provide for the small business community. Through a series of links one may access information on business development, financial assistance, taxes, laws and regulations, international trade, workplace issues, and buying and selling. Buying and selling, for example, is a good place to start if one wants to sell goods to either federal or state government agencies or needs to check on property for sale.

SBA.gov provides access not only to business information but also to electronic transactions; education, training, and online counseling; and networks of buyers and suppliers. Much of this information is also available at http://www.usa.gov/.

Figure 5.13. U.S. Small Business Administration

Federal Libraries

The government also offers specialized assistance through federal libraries. These libraries represent a tremendous information asset, offering unique collections and resources and highly skilled staff. Most routinely answer email, mail, and telephone inquiries, and many are open to the public. Particularly important to businesspeople and business librarians are the Commerce Department, Census Bureau, Labor Department, and Treasury Department libraries, and the Library of Congress. A listing of web sites of federal libraries is available at http://www.loc.gov/flicc/community.html.

Experts

"For any problem that you may face either professionally or personally," writes Matthew Lesko, "there is likely to be a free expert on the federal payroll who has spent years studying the very same subject."[5] These experts provide special assistance that, were it being sought from a private consultant, might cost hundreds or even thousands of dollars. Their areas of expertise range from stratospheric research to health care; for business, the most frequently consulted experts are those specializing in industry analysis, foreign markets, and the collection and analysis of statistical data.

Many industry analysts are employed by the Census Bureau; others are employed by the Commerce Department's International Trade Administration. At this time the easiest and most up-to-date method to find a contact is either to check the agency web page or to seek out experts by using the list at http://www.census.gov/contacts/www/contacts.html.

Although experts can be found in almost every government agency, the ones most often consulted by businesspeople are found in the Department of Commerce, the International Trade Administration, and the Bureau of Economic Analysis, as well as in the Departments of Labor, Agriculture, and the Treasury, and in the Small Business Administration.

Grants, Loans, and Other Financial and Non-Financial Assistance

More than 2,000 different federal assistance programs are available to individuals and organizations; many are intended to promote the development and continued financial well-being of business enterprises. These include loans from the Small Business Administration, grants from the Economic Development Administration, and insurance from the Overseas Private Investment Corporation. Such programs are listed and described in the following sources.

U.S. Office of Management and Budget. **Catalog of Federal Domestic Assistance.** (http://www.cfda.gov/ accessed December 15, 2010).

The most comprehensive listing of federal assistance programs is contained in the *Catalog of Federal Domestic Assistance*. The *Catalog* is the basic reference source for financial assistance programs, including grants, loans, loan guarantees, scholarships, mortgage loans, insurance, and nonfinancial assistance and services. The *Catalog* describes more than 2,000 federal domestic assistance programs. It contains information on all financial and nonfinancial assistance programs administered by the departments and establishments of the federal government. The free web site is the main means of access to the *Catalog of Federal Domestic Assistance*, but the GPO and General Services Administration (GSA) will continue printing and selling print copies through the GPO bookstore (http://bookstore.gpo.gov).

Other sources of loan and grant information include: *SBA.gov* (http://www.sba.gov/), where one can obtain information about loan guarantees, equity capital, trade financing, and surety bond guarantees; *GovLoans.gov* (http://www.govloans.gov/); and *Grants.gov* (http://www.grants.gov/), a central storehouse for information on more than 1,000 grant programs and providing access to approximately $500 billion in annual awards.

Government Purchase of Goods and Services

In 1955, the U.S. government adopted a policy of relying on private industry whenever possible to supply needed goods and services. Agency requirements vary tremendously, ranging from high-technology weaponry to painting and dry cleaning. There are two main categories of government purchasing. The first includes general items, such as office equipment and janitorial services, items for which the General Services Administration is the main purchaser. The second category consists of special, mission-oriented goods and services required by individual agencies.

Again the main place to gain information on opportunities to do business with the government is the web site *SBA.gov* formerly called *Business.gov* and *U.S. Business Advisor* (http://www.sba.gov/category/navigation-structure/contracting).

State Government Information and Services

State government agencies, like their federal counterparts, are key providers of information and services to business. They publish statistical compendia, research findings, market surveys, annual reports, and other documents; provide access to information about locally based companies; and offer counseling and technical assistance to new and relocating businesses. Unfortunately, such sources and services are underutilized by those who might most benefit from them.

Published Information

Publishing programs and policies regarding document distribution and sales vary from state to state. Most, however, publish a wide range of titles. Blue books, legislative handbooks, and statistical abstracts are the most commonly used state document reference sources, but others can make equally valuable contributions to business reference. Most states generally publish employment and unemployment statistics and economic indicators monthly or at least several times a year. In addition, glossy brochures designed to lure prospective businesses and tourists combine propaganda with useful information, and directories provide access to government officials, state manufacturing industries, and trade and professional associations. Although there is significant variation from one state to another, most have designated specific libraries as state document depositories. Often the state library is named the official depository, and it distributes duplicate copies of the documents it receives to other in-state depository libraries, usually large research and public libraries. In addition, some of these same libraries collect documents from other states.

One of the ways in which documents used to be chosen by libraries was by using the *Monthly Checklist of State Publications* issued by the Library of Congress. This long-standing serial title was discontinued in 1994, and its mission was taken up by librarians at the University of Illinois at Urbana-Champaign. This group produces *StateList: The Electronic Source for State Publication Lists,* accessible at http://www.library.illinois.edu/doc/researchtools/guides/state/statelist.html. The Internet site offers centralized access to state checklists and/or shipping lists that are currently available on the Internet for a total of 37 states.

Meta-indexes for state and local governments and a complete listing of all states with links to their first level of web pages are available via the Library of Congress at http://www.loc.gov/rr/news/stategov/stategov.html. Piper Resources maintains a directory of official state, county, and city government web sites called *State and Local Government on the Net* at http://www.statelocalgov.net/. The criterion for inclusion is that servers must be controlled and managed by state agencies or local government agencies.

Services to Business

Services offered to business by state agencies parallel those offered by the federal government.

Although not perhaps thought of as a service, there is much state statistical information available from state agencies and also from the federal government. One way to begin the search for statistics is to use http://www.fedstats.gov/. More than 100 agencies in the U.S. federal government produce statistics of interest to business and the public. The Federal Interagency Council on Statistical Policy maintains this site to provide easy access to the full range of statistics. One can search by state and deepen the search to individual counties.

State regulation of business activities requires that many businesses and corporations file reports with the government. Although many of these reports are not published as documents, they are available to the public at the state agency that collects them. Each state, for example, requires that a company file articles of incorporation that include information about the company, its location, and the nature of its business in order to incorporate. Other government filings include insurance company financial reports, complaints about companies or specific consumer products, environmental impact studies, and franchise information. Facilities for reading and often for copying some of these unpublished documents are available. Although some corporate directories are appearing on various state web pages, the majority of the information just mentioned is still only available after a personal visit to an agency.

Information from and about the states is becoming easier to access. Many business librarians work in settings in which only a few key documents reference sources are collected, but with electronic access the level of service provided can be as complex as that of any large research library. One can retrieve tax documents for all states, check on licensing regulations, and eventually even be able to check on all state filings. In addition, although not covered in this chapter, international, foreign, and local government documents can provide information that is unique, timely, and relevant to business research.[6]

Conclusion

Government information continues to be one of the major resources used by business librarians. We may use the raw data produced by the agencies or opt for a repackaged format from a vendor such as Gale, but whatever we use, the numbers have been compiled by either federal, state, or local governments. Moreover, it is becoming easier to access at least current information because of the Internet. The main problem that could arise is the loss of older materials as these are dropped from web pages by agencies. There must be some provision for this information to remain accessible in whichever format is appropriate.

Notes

1. Yuri Nakata, *From Press to People: Collecting and Using U.S. Publications* (Chicago: American Library Association, 1979), 15.

2. Ibid.

3. You may submit your order to the Government Printing Office via the Internet, phone, fax, postal mail, or teletype. Payment must accompany your order.

Internet	*GPO Access* Online Bookstore
Phone	(202) 512-1800 between 7:30 A.M. and 4:30 P.M., Eastern Time
Fax	(202) 512-2250
Mail	Superintendent of Documents
	P.O. Box 371954
	Pittsburgh, PA 15250-7954
Teletype	(710) 822-9413; ANSWERBACK USGPO WSH

4. Taken from Government Information Locator Service (GILS): About (http://origin.www.gpoaccess .gov/gils/about.htm).

5. *Information USA* (New York: Viking, 1983), 38.

6. Links to 220 world governments on the Web are at http://www.gksoft.com/govt/en.

6

Statistics

Statistics are vital to decision making. They are particularly important in management, accounting, marketing, finance, and any field of business where there is a need to assess past performance, compare and appraise current activities, and make predictions about the future. Market researchers, for example, use statistical data to compare sales of one brand with another and to predict consumer demand for new products. Union leaders use them to justify a case for increased wages to keep up with spiraling living costs, and personnel managers use them to measure labor turnover and absenteeism. Statistics are, in fact, so essential to business that the ability to identify, provide access to, and, in some instances, assess the relative merits of statistical data is fundamental to good business reference service. This chapter considers basic business-related uses of statistics, some of the major compilers and publishers of statistical data, key types of business and economic statistics, and the sources that contain them. In addition, it examines some of the pitfalls common in using such data.

Major Compilers and Publishers of Statistics

The cost of collecting primary statistical data, particularly on a large scale, is so great that usually only the largest or wealthiest organizations can afford to do so. Most businesses depend on secondary statistical data generated by government agencies, trade associations, commercial publishers, and private research firms. Each of these organizations regularly compiles, analyzes, and publishes statistics. Familiarity with their statistics-gathering programs and representative publications is an important first step in providing statistical reference assistance.

Federal Government Agencies

The federal government is the greatest single supplier of statistics. The 90-plus agencies (inclusive of organizational units that in official nomenclature are institutes, centers, services, and offices) that compile and publish statistical data report expenditures of at least $500,000 per year in statistical pursuits.[1] These data provide information on the population, agriculture, energy and the environment, employment and earnings, money supply, foreign and domestic trade, industrial activity, health, education, and many other subjects. Responsibility for collecting and analyzing such data is assigned to several different agencies within the government. Some major statistical analyses, such as labor force statistics, are carried out by agencies such as the Bureau of Labor Statistics, whose sole missions are statistical. In other cases, agencies have developed statistical programs that support their operational planning and evaluation functions as an outgrowth of their administrative responsibilities. Federal statistical organization, in essence, is decentralized, with the diverse statistical activities of all agencies coordinated by the Office of Management and Budget's Office of Information and Regulatory Affairs. The full report *Statistical Programs of the United States Government*, prepared by the OMB, is available at http://www.whitehouse.gov/sites/default/files/omb/assets/information_ and_regulatory_affairs/11statprog.pdf.

Earlier years are listed at http://www.whitehouse.gov/omb/regulatory_affairs/ reports_previous_yrs/.

Agencies fall into three broad categories according to their principal statistical activities and responsibilities (see figure 6.1).

GENERAL PURPOSE STATISTICAL AGENCIES	ANALYTICAL AND RESEARCH AGENCIES	ADMINISTRATIVE AND REGULATORY AGENCIES
Bureau of the Census	Bureau of Economic Analysis	Environmental Protection Agency
Bureau of Labor Statistics	Council of Economic Advisers	Federal Trade Commission
National Center for Education Statistics	National Agricultural Statistics Service	Securities & Exchange Commission
National Center for Health Statistics		Internal Revenue Service
Bureau of Justice Statistics		

Figure 6.1. Some statistical organizations of the federal government

Statistical Agencies

More than 90 agencies in the U.S. federal government produce statistics of interest to the public. The Federal Interagency Council on Statistical Policy maintains a web site, *FEDSTATS* (http://www.fedstats.gov/), to provide easy access to the full range of statistics and information produced by these agencies for public use.

These agencies collect, compile, and make available statistics in specific fields for general use. Businesses, private organizations, government bodies, and individuals in many different settings use the data they supply. Demographic statistics published by the Census Bureau, for example, enable companies to gauge future demands for their products based on the race, age, sex, occupation, and educational levels of different segments of the population. They are also used to help companies decide where to relocate, to measure population growth and decline in different parts of the country, and to document significant changes in the composition of the population.

The Bureau of the Census is the largest agency responsible for the collection, compilation, and publication of demographic and economic statistics. Its statistical programs fall into two main categories: (1) current programs, which produce the monthly, quarterly, and annual data contained in such publications as the *Current Population Reports* series and *County Business Patterns,* and (2) periodic censuses and programs mandated by law.

As a rule, data contained in the periodic censuses, which can be as much as 5 or even 10 years old, are updated by current Census Bureau publications. The *Economic Census,* for example, is brought up to date by annual and quarterly statistical releases.[2] Although useful, the current publications lack the detailed geographic, product, and demographic coverage common to censuses. In addition to censuses and surveys, the bureau also publishes such basic statistical compilations as the *Statistical Abstract of the United States* and the *County and City Data Book.*

Keeping up with census publications, the types of statistics they contain, and the formats in which they are available is no easy task. For current information one can access the Census Bureau information through the major subject areas or through the A–Z listing. Information ranges through the full array of economic, industrial, and international resources and many other products useful to the business researcher. Publications are mostly in PDF format although generally data can be retrieved using the supplied interactive tools and then can be downloaded into Excel. There are links to other federal agencies that provide data and to international statistical agencies. For the latest news, activities, and releases regarding the Population Census 2010 and 2007 Economic Census, the web page at http://www.census.gov should be monitored.

For the latest updates see http://blogs.census.gov/. For older materials the following publications are useful:

U.S. Bureau of the Census. **Census Catalog and Guide.** Washington, DC: Government Printing Office, 1946– 1999. Annual. Web version available at http://www.census .gov/prod/www/abs/catalogs.html.

U.S. Bureau of the Census. **Monthly Product Announcement.** Washington, DC: Government Printing Office, 1981–2000. Monthly. Web version available at http:// www.census.gov/mp/www/mpa.html. (Replaced by *Census Product Update* and ultimately the census blog (http://blogs.census.gov/)

U.S. Bureau of the Census. **Catalog of Publications, 1790–1972.** Washington, DC: Government Printing Office, 1974. 591p.

U.S. Bureau of the Census. **Guide to the 2007 Economic Censuses.** Washington, DC: http://www.census.gov/econ/census/guide/index.html (accessed February 3, 2011)

The annual *Census Catalog and Guide* lists and annotates data products in all formats. Web page availability is also cited. The latest edition (1998) is designed to be a companion to the 1997 edition. The main section contains abstracts of products issued by the Census Bureau from October 1996 through December 1997 (see figure 6.2). The products are grouped first by media and then by subject. The special section of the 1997 *Catalog* lists key sources of data and assistance whereas that of the 1998 *Catalog* leads users through the Internet programs and services of the Census Bureau. This reflects the strong public use of the Census Bureau Internet site.

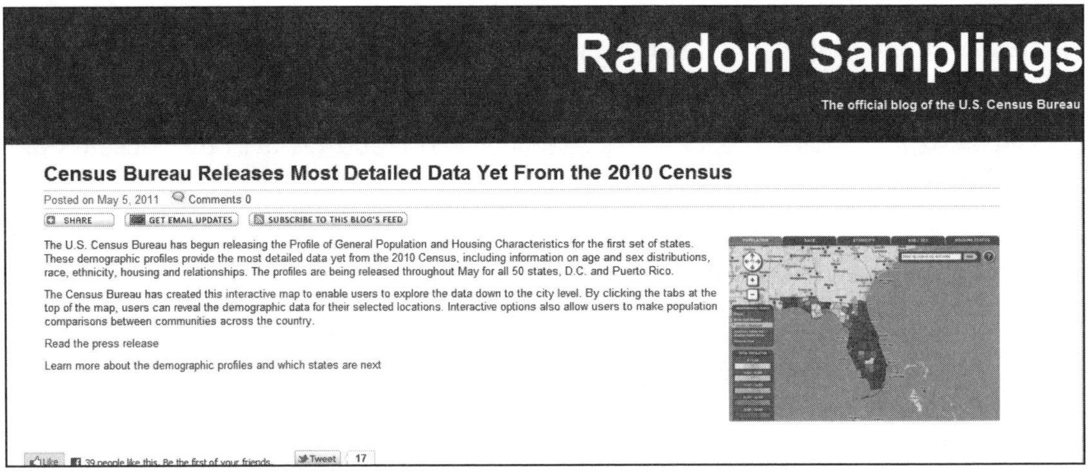

Figure 6.2. Sample entry, *Census Blog.* http://blogs.census.gov/
(accessed May 5, 2011)

The *Monthly Product Announcement* was a free list of recently released publications and data. Arrangement is by format, then by subject. Each listing included the title, series number, price, and, when available, the correct URL to access the document. This information is now available at http://www.census.gov/mp/www/cpu.html.

The first census publications were issued almost 200 years ago. Since then, the breadth and depth of census enumerations have increased considerably. In addition, titles and frequency of census data collection have changed, and specific items have been added to or deleted from successive census questionnaires. Statistics about American agriculture, for example, were once included as part of the Census of Population; today, they comprise a separate census. Similarly, data on religious affiliation included in early censuses are no longer gathered and published. The retrospective *Catalog of Publications, 1790–1972* is useful for identifying specific publications and what they contain.

Finally, the Census Bureau also publishes guides to specific censuses. One of the most useful for business librarians and researchers is the *Guide to the Economic Censuses*, which contains descriptions of the censuses that, taken together, comprise the Economic Census. A new edition is published for each census. The latest guide is available only on the Internet.

At this time the best source for information on census programs, publications, and statistics is the web page maintained by the Bureau at http://www.census.gov.

The Bureau of Labor Statistics (BLS) (http://www.bls.gov/) is the principal source of information on labor economics, and, as does the Census Bureau, the BLS makes its statistics available in a wide range of formats; much of the data now appears on its web page. Available from this site are statistics on employment and unemployment, prices and living conditions, compensation and working conditions, productivity and technology; links to surveys and programs; background papers on *Issues in Labor Statistics*; *BLS Research Papers;* and other publications such as the *Occupational Outlook Handbook* and *Bulletins and Reports*.

The Bureau of Economic Analysis is an agency of the Department of Commerce and along with the Census Bureau and *STAT-USA* is part of the Department's Economics and Statistics Administration. The mission of BEA is to produce and circulate accurate, timely, relevant, and cost-effective statistics that provide a comprehensive, up-to-date picture of economic activity. BEA's economic accounts present basic information on such key issues as U.S. economic growth, regional economic development, and the United States' position in the world economy. This information is released online through BEA's web site at http://www.bea.gov/. For a detailed description of BEA's economic programs, consult the *BEA Customer Guide* at http://www.bea.gov/agency/pdf/BEA_Customer_Guide.pdf, which is linked at the left of the BEA web page. Working Papers (released since 2000) and other publications are also linked to from the main page. For those who need to keep up to date on the exact time and date of economic releases, these are listed on the web page. One can also register for email notifications (see figure 6.3).

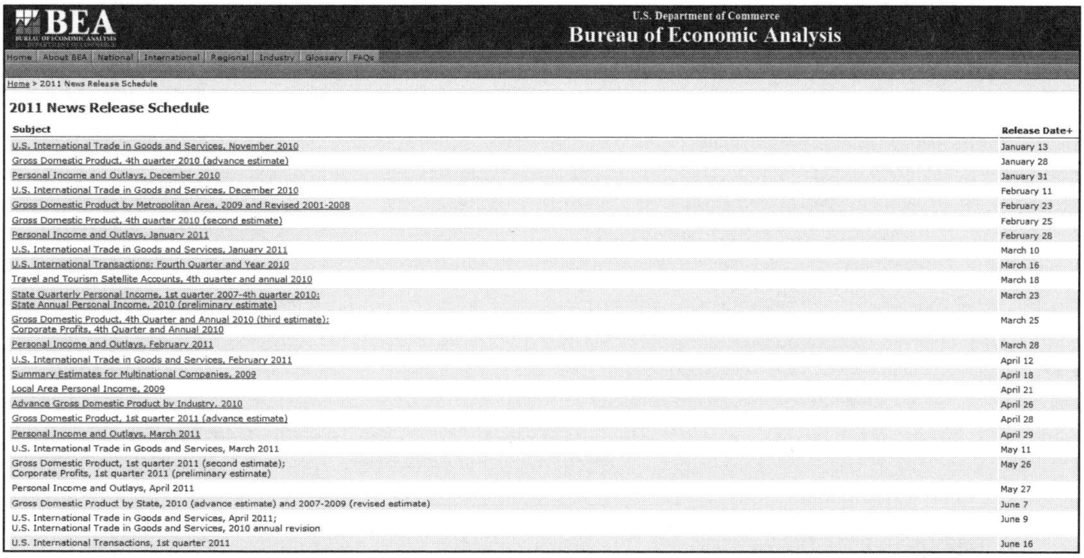

Subject	Release Date+
U.S. International Trade in Goods and Services, November 2010	January 13
Gross Domestic Product, 4th quarter 2010 (advance estimate)	January 28
Personal Income and Outlays, December 2010	January 31
U.S. International Trade in Goods and Services, December 2010	February 11
Gross Domestic Product by Metropolitan Area, 2009 and Revised 2001-2008	February 23
Gross Domestic Product, 4th quarter 2010 (second estimate)	February 25
Personal Income and Outlays, January 2011	February 28
U.S. International Trade in Goods and Services, January 2011	March 10
U.S. International Transactions: Fourth Quarter and Year 2010	March 16
Travel and Tourism Satellite Accounts, 4th quarter and annual 2010	March 18
State Quarterly Personal Income, 1st quarter 2007-4th quarter 2010; State Annual Personal Income, 2010 (preliminary estimate)	March 23
Gross Domestic Product, 4th Quarter and Annual 2010 (third estimate); Corporate Profits, 4th Quarter and Annual 2010	March 25
Personal Income and Outlays, February 2011	March 28
U.S. International Trade in Goods and Services, February 2011	April 12
Summary Estimates for Multinational Companies, 2009	April 18
Local Area Personal Income, 2009	April 21
Advance Gross Domestic Product by Industry, 2010	April 26
Gross Domestic Product, 1st quarter 2011 (advance estimate)	April 28
Personal Income and Outlays, March 2011	April 29
U.S. International Trade in Goods and Services, March 2011	May 11
Gross Domestic Product, 1st quarter 2011 (second estimate); Corporate Profits, 1st quarter 2011 (preliminary estimate)	May 26
Personal Income and Outlays, April 2011	May 27
Gross Domestic Product by State, 2010 (advance estimate) and 2007-2009 (revised estimate)	June 7
U.S. International Trade in Goods and Services, April 2011; U.S. International Trade in Goods and Services, 2010 annual revision	June 9
U.S. International Transactions, 1st quarter 2011	June 16

Figure 6.3. Selected News Release Schedules. Reproduced from the http://www.bea.gov/newsreleases/2011rd.htm (accessed February 10, 2011)

Government-produced statistics are used frequently by business researchers. Although data collected by the other statistical agencies may be used less widely, they also have direct business applications. At the web page of *FEDSTATS.gov* (http://www.fedstats.gov/) users may list agencies by the subject area in which they produce statistics. This listing provides users a link to the agency web page as well as to statistical lists and contacts, complete with telephone numbers or email addresses (see figure 6.4).

Another powerful web site available to all is *Data.gov* (http://www.data.gov/), which was launched in 2007. This includes searchable catalogs that provide access to "raw" datasets and various tools. In the "raw" data catalog, one can access data in XML, Text/CSV, KML/KMZ, Feeds, XLS, or ESRI Shapefile formats. According to the web page, "Data.gov increases the ability of the public to easily find, download, and use datasets that are generated and held by the Federal Government. Data.gov provides descriptions of the Federal datasets (metadata), information about how to access the datasets, and tools that leverage government datasets. The data catalogs will continue to grow as datasets are added. Federal, Executive Branch data are included in the first version of Data.gov." Though some agencies have done a great job of getting data and documents online, the accessibility and usability of government data overall can be improved and standardized. With attention to detail and metadata, Data.gov appears to be a step in that direction.

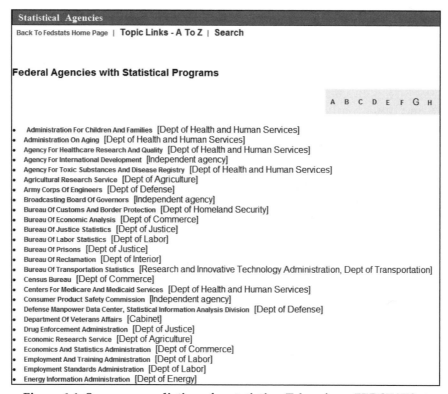

Figure 6.4. Some agency listings for statistics. Taken from *FEDSTATS* at http://www.fedstats.gov/agencies/

Figure 6.5. DATA.GOVraw data file, http://www.data.gov/catalog/raw (accessed March 10, 2011)

Administrative and Regulatory Agencies

Finally, although statistics gathering and dissemination are not their primary functions, almost every administrative or regulatory agency produces valuable statistics as a byproduct of its administrative operations. The *Statistics of Income* series published by the Internal Revenue Service, for example, is extremely useful to market researchers attempting to assess corporate and personal income. The Statistics of Income (SOI) program now has its own web page at http://www.irs.ustreas.gov/prod/tax_stats/, where one can consult data files compiled from tax and information returns on subjects such as corporations, partnerships, or sole proprietorships.

The statistical resources of the federal government are extensive and varied. Although once difficult to access, their identification has been considerably simplified by their widespread availability via the Internet using such search engines as *FEDSTATS*, Search. USA.Gov (http://search.usa.gov/), and of course, http://www.google.com/unclesam.

State Government Agencies

State agencies generally operate independently of the federal government in determining and carrying out their statistical programs. As a consequence, there is considerable variation in the scope of state statistical programs. Much information is, in fact, collected by state and local government organizations and then submitted to the federal government for compilation and publication.

Still other statistics-gathering and publishing activities remain the sole province of state agencies. Although state publishing programs vary, at a minimum most publish statistical compendia as well as specialized statistics focusing on industrial development, employment and unemployment, and the state's economy. *State and Local Government* on the Web links to all state and local government sites at http://www.statelocalgov.net/. This provides convenient access to a wide variety of links to information from specific states. Another link, http://www.usa.gov/Agencies.shtml, directs users to all federal, state, tribal, and local government web pages.

Trade Associations

Charged with keeping their members apprised of industry trends and developments, trade associations constitute another major supplier of statistics. These data are usually collected from association surveys or from reports submitted by member firms and are published as annual, monthly, and even weekly statistical compilations. Although coverage varies, most include information on industry production, inventories, shipments, sales, and prices. The Association of Home Appliance Manufacturers (http://www.aham.org/), for example, issues occasional reports on specific appliances, performance standards, and spec books, and has a blog that reports the latest things of significance in the appliance world. Many trade associations also include free statistical information on their web sites and so are excellent sources of industry information.

Although these publications are intended primarily for association members, they can be invaluable to librarians and researchers in need of detailed industry data. Although a few association publications are distributed only to members, some are available free of charge to educational institutions, and many can be purchased from the associations themselves, trade publishers, or other sources. Not all association statistics are published, however. When printed sources fail to provide the information being sought, the association staff should be contacted for assistance.

To find out if associations have a web presence one can use a subject directory such as Yahoo!, which has a listing of web addresses at http://dir.yahoo.com/Business_and_Economy/Organizations/Trade_Associations/ or perform a simple web search.

Commercial Publishers

Commercial publishers issue a wide range of statistical data, some gathered through original research, but most culled from government agencies and trade associations.

Trade journals are important sources of such information, often including both general business and economic statistics and highly specialized industrial data. *Beverage World*, for example, features annual rankings of soft drinks, beer, and bottled water at its web site, http://www.beverageworld.com/. One can access, among other things, statistics on top brands, regional consumption, and beverage category breakdowns. As well as statistics there is also a daily news roundup, news archives, and classifieds of interest to those involved in the industry. *American Banker* (http://www.americanbanker.com) publishes lists of the largest banks, credit unions, and foreign banks operating in the United States. Users must be aware that some of these business publications only operate correctly when using the Explorer browser. A selective list of trade journals can be accessed at http://dir.yahoo.com/Business_and_Economy/Business_to_Business/News_and_Media/Magazines/Trade_magazines/.

As America has become increasingly statistics-conscious, the market for popular statistics sources has also grown. Most of these sources draw on statistics generated and originally published by government agencies. Some repackage the government data, making them simpler to use by providing explanations and tables that are easier to understand. Others use these data to publish guides to high-paying jobs, safe cities, and locations where quality of life is better than average.

Finally, some commercial publishers make detailed and highly sophisticated economic and business information available to their customers, either in print or, more commonly, as online databases.

Other Organizations

In addition to data gathered and published by federal and state government agencies, trade associations, and commercial publishers, statistics are also published by university research centers, independent research organizations such as the Conference Board (http://www.conference-board.org/), the Tax Foundation (http://www.taxfoundation.org/), and business organizations such as stock and commodity exchanges, banks, accounting firms, and publicly traded companies.

Basic Statistical Concepts

Familiarity with key statistical concepts enables librarians to understand more clearly requests for specific kinds of statistical information and to anticipate problems that may arise when seeking or supplying such information. This section considers four statistical concepts—sampling, time series, forecasts and projections, and index numbers—that are basic to business statistics.

Sampling

Data about the population or some designated segment of it are tremendously important to business researchers, government agencies, and others. Ideally, such data should accurately reflect information collected from examination of each person in the population being studied. Surveying an entire population, however, is generally too time consuming, difficult, and costly to be practical or even effective. As a result, researchers usually select a smaller, representative segment of the population for studies and analysis and use the data gathered to make inferences about the entire population. This process is called sampling, and the representative segment of the population being measured is known as a sample. Sampling is not confined to demographic study; it is used whenever the universe being measured is too large to lend itself to analysis of each of its constituent units. Sampling techniques are often employed in the study of production, wages, sales, and other business-related activities as well as in analysis of the population.

The Census Bureau employs sampling as a means of gathering detailed information about the social and economic characteristics of the population. Every 10 years, for example, it sends questionnaires about population and housing to every household in the country. Most receive brief questionnaires, but others receive a lengthier document that solicits additional information. Thus, while some portions of the Census of Population reflect enumeration or counting of almost every household in the United States, other parts are statistical inferences based on the results of the Census Bureau's sample of households.

Other census publications are completely based on samples—for example, *American Housing Survey*,[3] a special study issued periodically as part of the *Current Population Reports* series. When a sample is being used, reputable statistical publications will describe its composition and, in many instances, point out its limitations. Thus, the Census Bureau's overview of the *American Housing Survey* includes the following information:

> Provides a current and ongoing series of data on the size, composition, and state of housing in the United States and changes in the housing stock over time. Collects housing statistics that the U.S. Department of Housing and Urban Development (HUD) uses to evaluate and develop its federal housing programs.

As with all types of statistical information, careful perusal of the introductory textual matter and footnotes is essential to determine the scope and limitations of the data being presented.

Time Series Analysis

Sometimes statistics are gathered and published on a one-time basis. A market research firm, for example, may be commissioned to collect data on consumption of and preferences for different types of bottled water. Such data meet specific needs, reflecting conditions at a fixed point in time. They result from a single research effort and are not updated on a regular basis.

Most situations call for regularly collected statistical data that reflect changes over time. Such numbers are called time series and are used to analyze changes in business conditions and the economy, including such items as income, prices, production, and consumption. Most time series consist of monthly, quarterly, or annual observations, and many are produced by the government. Such data are analyzed to identify patterns and, in some instances, to make forecasts about the future.

Many time series that are published weekly, monthly, or quarterly reflect predictable seasonal changes, caused by such factors as climate and school openings and closings. Building construction, for example, regularly shows a slowdown in winter months due to adverse weather conditions and increases during temperate months. Retail sales are influenced by such holidays as Christmas and Valentine's Day, and unemployment rates generally increase during the summer when school is closed and decrease when school reopens.

Time series that are subject to such predictable seasonal variations are often presented in two different ways: unadjusted and seasonally adjusted. Unadjusted time series present data as they are collected without regard to fluctuations caused by regular seasonal changes. Seasonally adjusted time series, on the other hand, are "deseasonalized" so that, as near as possible, predictable seasonal changes are eliminated through statistical manipulation. The resulting seasonally adjusted data reflect changes not caused by normal seasonal variation, changes that are sometimes difficult to identify using unadjusted data.

Many statistical publications present both unadjusted and seasonally adjusted time series. The *Survey of Current Business*, for example, includes both. To be effective, librarians must be clear about which type of information is being sought and label the time series data they supply as either seasonally adjusted or unadjusted.

Forecasts and Projections

Informed speculation about the future is essential for business executives, who must regularly decide whether to increase production of existing products, develop new ones, or otherwise prepare for anticipated changes. Thus, while they often consult time series to assess recent trends and developments, they also use them to make predictions about the future, in the form of forecasts and projections. Although these terms are often used interchangeably, there is a difference between the two. Forecasts are short-term predictions based on the recent past, generally extending no more than two years into the future. Since they draw on information about current conditions, which often do not change appreciably over a two-year period, forecasts can be quite accurate. Projections are predictions made about the distant future. The Census Bureau, for example, has already published population projections for the year 2100. Projections cover a greater time span, which may include technological developments, man-made and natural disasters, and other events that may not have been anticipated at the time the projections were made. As a result, projections are more speculative and prone to error than forecasts:

> Extrapolations are useful, particularly in that form of soothsaying called forecasting trends. But in looking at the figures or charts made from them, it is necessary to remember one thing constantly: The trend-to-now may be a fact, but the future trend represents no more than an educated guess. Implicit in it is "everything else being equal" and "present trends continuing," and somehow everything else refuses to remain equal, else life would be dull indeed.[4]

Business forecasts and projections are published by a wide variety of sources, including government agencies, private research organizations, corporations, commercial publishers, and others, and are contained in many of the publications that are described later in this chapter.

Index Numbers

One way in which researchers can consider changes over time is by comparing statistics for one time period with another. They can, for example, compare the number of automobiles manufactured in the United States in 2008 with the number for 1988, or they can contrast the cost of a haircut or rent or groceries or other consumer goods for one period with another. One way to do this is to count the actual number of units being measured, dollars spent for rent, or number of cars rolling off the assembly line. Often, however, index numbers are used instead.

In its simplest sense, an index number is the ratio of one quantity to another, expressing a given quantity in terms of its value relative to a base quantity. Index numbers frequently are used to compare percent change over time, to measure relative changes in quantity, price, or value of an item or series of related items compared with a designated time, known as the base period or base year. The base period has a value of 100, and any changes from it represent percentages. Upon consulting the *Statistical Abstract of the United States*, the researcher learns that the Consumer Price Index uses 1982–1984 as the base year, and that the index in 2009, for all items, was 214.5. This means that the CPI rose 114.5 percent from the base year. In other words, any number over 100, the number assigned to the base year, reflects an increase; anything less than 100, a decrease. Had the CPI been 90, it would have meant that costs had declined by 10 percent since the base year. Although months or groups of years are sometimes used for base periods, the most commonly used base period is a year. Base years are chosen to provide a good basis for comparisons and are thus relatively stable years economically. In the example used above, 1982–1984 is the base period, and government tables showing this and other consumer prices include this notation: [1982–84 = 100]. Base years sometimes change. Librarians comparing index numbers for 1977 with 2006 must first determine that the base year being used for both sets of data is the same. *Historical Statistics of the United States*, described later in this chapter, presents data using constant base years.

The index number consulted most frequently in libraries is the Consumer Price Index (CPI). This is a composite of indexes relating to the prices of specific consumer goods and services, used as a primary measure of inflation. Since some misunderstanding on the part of library users about the nature and application of the CPI exists, further discussion of this important index is in order.

The Consumer Price Index is a monthly measure of the change in average prices over time of a fixed list (usually called a market basket) of goods and services. It is based on the average prices of different items purchased for daily living, items such as shoes, fuel, dairy products, bus fares, newspapers, and dental services. Each item is assigned a weight to account for its relative importance in consumers' budgets. New cars, for example, may account for 4 percent of the index, whereas shoes may be less than 1 percent.

Each month, BLS data collectors visit or call thousands of retail stores, service establishments, rental units, and doctors' offices all over the United States to obtain price information on thousands of items used to track and measure price change in the CPI. Roughly 80,000 prices are recorded each month, and these represent a scientifically selected sample of the prices paid by consumers for the goods and services purchased. The Bureau of Labor Statistics now publishes two official Consumer Price Indexes, known as the CPI-U and the CPI-W.[5] Each month, BLS releases thousands of detailed CPI numbers to the media. However, the media usually focus on the broadest, most comprehensive CPI. This is "The Consumer Price Index for All Urban Consumers (CPI-U) for the U.S. City Average for All Items, 1982–84=100." These data are reported on either a seasonally adjusted or not seasonally adjusted basis. It is possible now by accessing the Bureau of Labor Statistics data series at http://bls.gov/cpi/home.htm#data to retrieve selected data and thus to compile tables only for the data needed. Figure 6.6 displays monthly data from the Consumer Price Index-All Urban Consumers, Medical Care Services, from 2002 until 2011. This data is also downloadable into Excel.

```
Series Id:      CUUR0000SAM,CUUS0000SAM
Not Seasonally Adjusted
Area:           U.S. city average
Item:           Medical care
Base Period:    1982-84=100
```

Download: 📊 .xls

Year	Jan	Feb	Mar	Apr	May	Jun	Jul	Aug	Sep	Oct	Nov	Dec	Annual	HALF1	HALF2
2001	267.1	268.9	270.0	270.8	271.4	272.5	273.1	274.4	275.0	275.9	276.7	277.3	272.8	270.1	275.4
2002	279.6	281.0	282.0	283.2	284.1	284.7	286.6	287.3	287.7	289.2	290.5	291.3	285.6	282.4	288.8
2003	292.6	293.7	294.2	294.6	295.5	296.3	297.6	298.4	299.2	299.9	300.8	302.1	297.1	294.5	299.7
2004	303.6	306.0	307.5	308.3	309.0	310.0	311.0	311.6	312.3	313.3	314.1	314.9	310.1	307.4	312.9
2005	316.8	319.3	320.7	321.5	322.2	322.9	324.1	323.9	324.6	326.2	328.1	328.4	323.2	320.6	325.9
2006	329.5	332.1	333.8	334.7	335.6	336.0	337.0	337.7	338.3	339.3	340.1	340.1	336.2	333.6	338.8
2007	343.510	346.457	347.172	348.225	349.087	349.510	351.643	352.961	353.723	355.653	357.041	357.661	351.054	347.327	354.780
2008	360.459	362.155	363.000	363.184	363.396	363.616	363.963	364.477	365.036	365.746	366.613	367.133	364.065	362.635	365.495
2009	369.830	372.405	373.189	374.170	375.026	375.093	375.739	376.537	377.727	378.552	379.575	379.516	375.613	373.286	377.941
2010	382.688	385.907	387.142	387.703	387.762	388.199	387.898	388.467	390.616	391.240	391.660	391.946	388.436	386.567	390.305
2011	393.858	397.065	397.726												

Figure 6.6. The Consumer Price Index for All Urban Consumers (CPI-U) Dec. 1999 = 100: Medical Care Services. http://data.bls.gov/cgi-bin/surveymost

The CPI affects the income of about 100 million persons as a result of statutory action: 54.5 Social Security beneficiaries, about 41 million food stamp recipients, and about 4.1 million military and federal civil service retirees and survivors. Changes in the CPI also affect the cost of lunches for 26.7 million children who eat lunch at school, while collective bargaining agreements that tie wages to the CPI cover almost 2 million workers.

However, using the CPI to compare one city's cost of living with that of another is virtually meaningless. This is because each measures price change only in the designated area. So if the 1999 CPI for New York is 177, this means that prices have increased by this amount in that area only since 1982–1984. Only the increase is measured, and this does not reflect the prices for 1982–1984. It could still cost more to live in a different city even if the CPI is lower. Fortunately, another source permits comparisons between cities.

American Chamber of Commerce Researchers Association. **ACCRA Cost of Living Index.** Louisville, KY: ACCRA, 1992–; ACCRA, 1981–. Quarterly.

Available online with pricing information at http://www.coli.org/

The *ACCRA Cost of Living Index*, formerly known as the *Inter-City Cost of Living Index* and the *Inter-City Cost of Living Indicators Project*, measures current prices for consumer goods and services in 310 urban areas. This empowers researchers to compare living costs in one city with another or to compare the actual dollar amounts paid for specific items, such as hamburger, haircuts, and apartment rent in several locations. Since the *ACCRA Cost of Living Index* is published specifically to permit comparison between cities, it is extremely useful to companies and individuals contemplating moving to another part of the country.

Three important differences between the *Consumer Price Index* and the *ACCRA Cost of Living Index* should be noted. First, the CPI measures change over time, with the base year equaling 100. The *Cost of Living Index*, on the other hand, measures change between locations rather than change over time, with a national city average of 100 used as the base for comparison. A CPI of 250, in other words, means that it now costs 150 percent more to buy the same goods and services as it did in 1982–1984 (or in any other base year designated), while an *ACCRA Cost of Living Index* of 116 means that it costs 16 percent more than the current national average to live in a specific city or town.

Second, while comparison of Consumer Price Indexes between specific cities is impossible, comparison of two or more cities to the national average using the *Cost of Living Index* is simple. Using it, a researcher can determine that Huntsville's index of 93.2 means that it would cost 6.8 percent less than the national average to live there, and that Flagstaff's index of 112.3 represents living costs 12.3 percent above the national average. Further, someone moving from Huntsville to Flagstaff could expect to pay approximately 19.1 percent more for consumer goods and services.

The *Inter-City Cost of Living Index* is not without its flaws. One of the most significant is that many large urban areas are not represented, but a list of geographies included is accessible through the web page. In addition, the list of cities represented does not always remain constant from one year to the next. Thus, simply because a city is included in one issue, it is not safe to assume that it will be listed in subsequent issues. Despite these drawbacks, the *Index* is a popular, much-used, and generally reliable source that belongs in most business reference collections.

In addition to indexes that permit comparison between cities, the *ACCRA Cost of Living Index* includes a section that lists actual dollar amounts paid for specific consumer goods, ranging from the average cost of a movie and a pizza to a six-pack of beer and a bottle of aspirin. Sample pages are available at the web site.

Another important BLS index, the *Producer Price Index*, is used to measure price changes in goods at various stages of production, ranging from raw materials such as logs and timber to finished products, such as furniture. Like the Consumer Price Index, the Producer Price Index appears in many different statistics sources, including the *Survey of Current Business* and the *Statistical Abstract of the United States*, and also at www.bls.gov.

Other privately produced price indexes are considerably more fanciful. The Big Mac Index, for example, is based on the theory of purchasing-power parity, the notion that a dollar should buy the same amount in all countries. The Big Mac purchasing power parity is the exchange rate that would mean hamburgers cost the same in America as abroad. The Big Mac Index can be found at http://www.economist.com in the economics section. Comparing actual exchange rates with purchasing-power parities indicates whether a currency is under- or overvalued. The Christmas Price Index (http://www .pncchristmaspriceindex.com/) measures changes from one year to the next in the prices paid for items mentioned in the popular "Twelve Days of Christmas" carol, including partridges, turtle doves, and gold rings.

Economic Indicators

In business libraries, some of the most frequently requested statistics are those used to assess the state of the national economy. Dozens of statistics are commonly used for this purpose, but among the most important are the Gross Domestic Product, Industrial Production, Leading Indicators, Personal Income, the Consumer and Producer Price Indexes, Retail Sales, Employment, and Housing Starts. All are issued on a regular basis by the government and are reported in newspapers, periodicals, statistical reference sources, online news services, and online government releases. The economic indicators listed above, however, are by no means the only ones. Keeping abreast of such statistics, their frequency of issuance, and the sources in which they appear is not always easy. Fortunately, in recent years several fine directories to economic time series data have been published. Some are listed below. Many indicator data sets have moved to the Web, and those sites that may be more permanent are listed at the end of this section.

Johnson, David B. **The Black Book of Economic Information: A Guide to Sources and Interpretation**. Sun Lakes, AZ: Thomas Horton and Daughters, 1996. 512p.

Guide to Economic Indicators. 6th ed. London: Economist, 2006. 244p. (also available as electronic text)

O'Hara, Frederick M., Jr., and F. M. O'Hara III. **Handbook of United States Economic and Financial Indicators.** Rev. ed. Westport, CT: Greenwood Press, 2000. 395p.

Lehmann, Michael B. **The Irwin Guide to Using the *Wall Street Journal*.** 7th ed. New York: McGraw-Hill, 2005. 368p.

The *Black Book of Economic Information* is a mixture of handbook and encyclopedic dictionary written for anyone who is "overwhelmed, bored or bedazzled" by economic data. Although dated it is still useful and if already part of a collection can still be used. Each topic or series covered begins with a "snapshot" about the data, including the correct name, the agency or institution that issues the series, the publications that carry the information, publication frequency, and a telephone number for further inquiries. This is followed by a short explanation of the series and then, for those who need it, there is a more detailed explanation. Some data sets are included, but as these can readily be found on federal web sites, they are not the main focus of the publication. It is an inexpensive volume that is available in most libraries.

The *Guide to Economic Indicators* (previous published as *The Economist Guide to Economic Indicators* (Princeton, NJ: Bloomberg, 2003) is written for the non-specialist, and as a result is a highly accessible guide that explains how to understand and interpret all the main economic indicators. The *Guide* is divided into a number of chapters discussing issues and examples related to, for example, consumer indicators, such as disposable income or consumer confidence and their significance, and prices and wages, like the effect of oil price changes, among others.

The *Handbook of United States Economic and Financial Indicators* lists 284 different time series, ranging from "Advisory Sentiment Index" to the "Wiltshire Small-Cap Index." Although entries are not long, they include a definition, an explanation of the derivation of the statistic, and comments on its applications, and list its frequency, publisher, and the publication(s) in which it is announced. Indicators published by trade associations, consulting firms, financial publishing companies, and other private organizations are also included. An appendix of non-quantitative indicators is also provided and is particularly helpful to librarians confronted with questions about such purported measures of economic and financial well-being as the "Short-Skirt Index," which holds that rises and falls in women's hemlines are accompanied by similar actions in the stock market; the "Surly Waiter Index"; and the "Drinking Couple Count."

Many economic statistics are first issued in government news releases. After the initial release, many are subsequently published in the Wall Street Journal, a good source of current economic indicators. The *Irwin Guide to Using the Wall Street Journal* focuses on some of the key statistics reported, describing what they measure, how they are computed, and when they appear in the *Journal*. In addition, the *Guide* provides information on how each statistic is used to track the economy and includes excerpts from *Wall Street Journal* articles that illustrate the context in which specific statistics are used. First published in 1984 this is still one of the most popular and useful publications for demystifying information.

Government periodicals such as the *Survey of Current Business* (http://www.bea.gov/scb/index.htm) and *Monthly Labor Review* (http://www.bls.gov/opub/mlr/mlrhome

.htm) are prime sources of economic statistics. *Economic Indicators* (http://www.gpo.gov/fdsys/), a monthly publication prepared by the Council of Economic Advisers for the Congress's Joint Economic Committee, includes historic as well as current data. The State of the Nation section of *STAT-USA* provides current and historical economic and financial releases and economic data.

FRASER (Federal Reserve Archival System for Economic Research) has PDF files for the *Survey of Current Business*, the Monthly Labor Review, Economic Indicators, and most other government periodicals at http://fraser.stlouisfed.org/cbt/browse.php?collection_id=23, or simply click on "Periodicals" at the home page.

Reliability of Statistics

Users, writes Joe Morehead, sometimes attribute "the power and value of holy writ"[6] to statistics. No statistics, whatever their air of authority, deserve unquestioning acceptance. Some, in fact, are deliberately misleading. The advertising cliche, "Nine out of 10 doctors surveyed prefer Brand X," is a good example. Clearly, sampling techniques were employed. The advertisers, however, do not document sample size in their commercial, nor do they describe how the sample was selected. Although the advertisement implies that a preponderance of all doctors prefer Brand X, it is entirely possible that the sample consisted of only 10 doctors, all of whom were employees of or stockholders in the company manufacturing Brand X. Further, the advertisers do not list the options the doctors could choose from when selecting Brand X. They might have been given alternate brands of the same product, or they might have been presented with choices that clearly were unacceptable. The numbers themselves are suspect, with the mention of doctors lending an air of credibility and respectability by flaunting what Darrell Huff, author of *How to Lie with Statistics*, calls the "O.K. name":

> Anything smacking of the medical profession is an O.K. name. Scientific laboratories have O.K. names. So do colleges, especially universities, especially ones eminent in technical work. . . . When an O.K. name is cited, make sure that the authority stands behind the information, not merely somewhere alongside it.[7]

The Pentagon's body counts during the Vietnam War and public opinion polls commissioned by politicians are also examples of statistics that are deliberately misleading. These examples lead to the first questions that astute librarians and researchers ask when reviewing statistical data: Where did the data come from? Is the source unbiased, or does it have a vested interest in supplying data that will lead to one conclusion rather than another? Are the statistics self-serving?

When, as near as possible, statistical objectivity has been ascertained, methodology must be examined. Most librarians are not statisticians, but by reading the table headers, footnotes, data dictionaries, and any additional documentation, they can learn about some of the more obvious limitations of the data being presented:

> It is important that users, whether primary or secondary users, know just how the data for a particular table were collected and analyzed, what was included, and what was omitted. For instance, firms with under a certain number of employees may be omitted from tables of production or employment statistics, and certain industries may for one reason or another be omitted from more general tables. In regular tables the content or classification may change at

some time; and errors or later information may mean that some regular tables (foreign trade statistics, for instance) are corrected in the cumulated figures published in the next or even a later issue. A new base year for time series will mean that one cannot use earlier tables of index numbers in the same context. Figures may be rounded up or rounded down in a table or series of tables, and if these figures are added together they can result in an inaccurate figure. Time series may be amended to allow for seasonal or other variations. Misinterpretations can be avoided if care is taken to read the explanatory notes or other matter which statisticians usually take trouble to provide in an effort to overcome these and other dangers.[8]

Statistics, in short, require careful scrutiny to determine both their reliability and their applicability to the research situation at hand. Such assessment presupposes the existence of statistical data, and this chapter concludes with consideration of some of the most important sources of statistical information.

Statistical Publications

Statistical inquiries are an intrinsic component of the driving force of business reference. More and more they comprise the bulk of day-to-day business reference work in most libraries. Many statistical reference questions are simple to answer, requiring only the use of an almanac or some other basic reference source. Others are considerably more difficult, calling for perseverance and ingenuity. A few are impossible to answer, either because the data do not exist or because they are inaccessible to libraries. Privately commissioned market research studies, usually because of high prices, fall into the last category, although more are becoming available to those libraries that can afford them. In most instances, though, statistics are available and can be identified by consulting the following sources.

Dictionaries and Encyclopedias

Theory has it that a good reference librarian can answer inquiries in any field without benefit of the appropriate educational background or even rudimentary knowledge of the subject being studied. No reference librarian, however, can answer an inquiry unless he or she understands the question being asked. This is particularly true in the area of business and economics statistics, where jargon is commonplace and terminology foreign to the uninitiated. Fortunately, several dictionaries and other sources define basic terms and concepts and are useful for definitions of less commonplace terms and concepts. Many of these publications are available, and almost any of them will be useful. Three favorite publications are listed below.

Marriot, F.H.C. **A Dictionary of Statistical Terms**. 5th ed. New York: John Wiley, 1989. 223p.

Shim, Jae K., and Joel G. Siegel. **Dictionary of Economics**. New York: John Wiley, 1995. 373p.

Vogt, Paul W., and R. Burke Johnson. **Dictionary of Statistics & Methodology: A Nontechnical Guide for the Social Sciences**. 4th ed. Thousand Oaks, CA: Sage Publications, 2011. 456p.

Since the publication of the first edition in 1957, *A Dictionary of Statistical Terms* has gained widespread acceptance as the standard dictionary of current statistical terminology. Nearly 3,500 entries are included, featuring brief definitions and, in many instances, equations and formulas. The focus in *A Dictionary of Statistical Terms* is on terms in current usage. The *Dictionary of Economics* is more general in coverage and designed for laypeople who want to understand terminology in publications such as *Business Week* and the *New York Times*. The explanations are clear and frequently illustrated. The *Dictionary of Statistics & Methodology* is also designed to give, as far as possible, nontechnical explanations of terms and concepts. The emphasis is on understandable terms and definitions that may be easily appreciated by the non-practitioner. Any of these publications will give the librarian or researcher a fair grounding in unfamiliar terms or concepts.

For those who prefer to do their searching electronically, the International Statistical Institute has a multilingual dictionary available online at http://isi.cbs.nl/glossary/. About.com also has a useful guide and glossary at http://economics.about.com/od/economicindicatorinfo/u/econ_indicators.htm.

Guides and Indexes

Some of the publications described in previous chapters can be particularly helpful in identifying and locating statistical data. Michael Lavin's *Business Information: How to Find It, How to Use It* includes a whole section on statistical information, with chapters on statistical reasoning, the Census of Population and Housing, population estimates and projections, general economic statistics, and industry statistics. The *Encyclopedia of Business Information Sources* offers a greater level of subject specificity, listing published sources of statistics pertaining to such topics as honey and zinc production, carpet imports, and peanut stocks. In addition, *Data Sources for Business and Market Analysis*, described in chapter 8, devotes considerable attention to both government and privately generated statistics sources. In addition to the titles listed above, several specialized statistical guides and indexes are also available. Although space does not permit consideration of them all, some of the most useful are listed below.

American Statistics Index. Washington, DC: Congressional Information Service, 1973–. Monthly, with annual cumulations.

Statistical Reference Index. Washington, DC: Congressional Information Service, 1980–. Monthly, with annual cumulations.

Index to International Statistics. Washington DC: Congressional Information Service, 1983–. Monthly, with annual compilations.

ProQuest Statistical Insight. 1987–. Ann Arbor, MI: ProQuest.

This is a series of statistical indexes published by Congressional Information Service, which is now owned by ProQuest. All contact information is now available at the ProQuest web page, but as of 2011 no new cataloging information is available.

The first of these, the *American Statistics Index*, made its debut in 1973, considerably simplifying work for documents and business librarians and for researchers seeking federal statistical data. The *American Statistics Index*, or *ASI*, is a master guide to statistical publications of the federal government. The print version is published in two parts, an Index Section and an Abstracts Section.

The *ASI* Index Section contains a variety of separate indexes. The main index lists sources by subject and name. Index entries include brief notations of content, frequently cite the title of the publication in which the statistics are presented, and always provide an accession number for reference to the *ASI* Abstracts Section and to microfiche reproductions of those publications sold by Congressional Information Service. Numerous cross-references to related index terms are also included.

In addition to the main subject index, the *ASI* Index Section also features an Index by Categories, which includes references to all publications that contain comparative tabular data broken down into designated geographic, economic, and demographic categories. Although the main subject index provides more detailed subject access, the Index by Categories is useful when more specific information is being sought. General information on the national labor force, for example, is identified more easily through the Subject Index, whereas the Index by Categories is more helpful to identify publications pertaining to women in the workforce.

Once publications and their corresponding accession numbers have been identified, the Abstract Section can be consulted. Entries are arranged by accession number and include many of the features common to entries in the *Monthly Catalog of United States Government Publications*, such as Superintendent of Documents classification, item number, and when applicable, the *Monthly Catalog* entry number and/or the NTIS number. As in the *Monthly Catalog*, depository documents are designated by a bullet.

Information in *ASI*'s Abstract Section, however, is considerably more detailed than that in the *Monthly Catalog*. Every publication is annotated and, in many instances, specific tables or articles are listed and described separately. Each annotation provides full bibliographic data, describes the publication, and lists tables and articles.

Microfiche copies of publications listed in *ASI* are available from the publisher. Libraries can order *ASI* Microfiche Library collections that include all of the publications indexed. Alternatively, they can select fiche copies of non-depository publications only.

Finally, each volume of the *American Statistics Index* includes a lengthy introduction that describes the types of publications that are indexed, explains their arrangement, and presents search strategies highlighting effective use of this index.

Arrangement is similar in the second major Congressional Information Service index, the *Statistical Reference Index* (*SRI*). As is the *American Statistics Index*, *Statistical Reference Index* is divided into index and abstract sections, with subject and category indexing provided in the Index Section, and publication descriptions in the Abstract Section. The *SRI*, however, indexes and abstracts statistics contained in publications not issued by the federal government. It includes statistics published by 1,000 private concerns such as trade associations, corporations, commercial publishers, and independent and university-affiliated research organizations, as well as approximately half of all state governments in the United States. Each entry includes an accession number, bibliographic information, a description of contents, and information for requesting or purchasing copies from the issuing source.

As with *ASI*, many of the publications listed in *SRI* are available from the publisher. However, while *ASI* documents are copied in their entirety, not all SRI publications are. Some are limited to designated statistical excerpts, and some are not available as part of the SRI Microfiche Library and must be ordered directly from the original publisher. However, in spite of these limitations, the *SRI* Microfiche Library permits access to many publications that otherwise would be difficult or time consuming to acquire.

A third Congressional Information Service index, the *Index to International Statistics*, provides abstracts and indexes of some 2,000 indispensable titles from 100 international intergovernmental organizations, including the United Nations, the European Union, and the Organization for Economic Cooperation and Development, and descriptions of statistical publications of international intergovernmental organizations. Before the advent of easy web searching, this was an indispensable way to find statistics for countries other than the United States.

ProQuest Statistical Insight brings together the *American Statistics Index, Statistical Reference Index,* and *Index to International Statistics* and links them to available full-text documents from 1995 to the present. Libraries can subscribe to one, two, or all three components, and there are also options to subscribe to part of each component. Many full-text statistical tables are linked to within the publication record or by using the "Find a Table" search option. Other key documents will always be available, as they are stored in permanent data archives by the company. Abstracts link directly to individual tables, figures, and charts.

ProQuest Statistical Insight comprises several modules that can be purchased individually and added to as the budget allows.

Statistical Compilations

One of the best ways to begin the search for data is by consulting a statistical compilation. Comprising data culled from many other sources, such publications can provide direct answers to many statistical reference inquiries and indirect access to sources that will answer others. International, foreign, federal, and state government agencies; commercial publishers; and other organizations publish statistical compendia. The following such compilations are basic to business reference.

U.S. Department of Commerce. Bureau of the Census. **Statistical Abstract of the United States.** Washington, DC: Government Printing Office, 1878–. Annual. Web version available at http://www.census.gov/compendia/statab/

Historical Statistics of the United States, Colonial Times to the Present. New York: Cambridge University Press, 2006. 5vs. (Also available as a web-based publication from Cambridge University Press)

Mitchell, B. R. **International Historical Statistics: Africa, Asia & Oceania, 1750–2005.** 5th ed. Basingstoke: Palgrave Macmillan Reference, 2007. 1175p.

Mitchell, B. R. **International Historical Statistics: the Americas, 1750–2005.** 6th ed. Basingstoke: Palgrave Macmillan, 2007. 875p.

Mitchell, B. R. **International Historical Statistics: Europe, 1750–2005.** 6th ed. Basingstoke: Palgrave Macmillan, 2007. 1068p.

At every minute of every working day, hypothesizes one writer, a librarian somewhere is using the *Statistical Abstract of the United States.* Although this observation falls into the realm of an unsubstantiated statistic, there is no doubt that the *Statistical Abstract* is one of the most heavily used reference sources in any business or general reference collection. Published since 1878, the *Statistical Abstract* is the standard summary of social, political, and economic statistics for the United States. It is a compendium of data collected from over 220 different government and private agencies, with information grouped together by broad subject categories such as "Population," "Labor Force, Employment, and Earnings," and "Business Enterprise." Each chapter begins with a description of the data being presented, definitions of key terms and concepts, and, in many instances, consideration of the limitations and the general reliability of the data being presented. Although the *Statistical Abstract* is available in electronic format, it is much easier and more efficient to use in hard copy.

Section 25
Banking, Finance, and Insurance

This section presents data on the nation's finances, various types of financial institutions, money and credit, securities, insurance, and real estate. The primary sources of these data are publications of several departments of the federal government, especially the U.S. Treasury Department, and independent agencies such as the Federal Deposit Insurance Corporation, the Board of Governors of the Federal Reserve System, and the Securities and Exchange Commission. National data on insurance are available primarily from private organizations, such as the American Council of Life Insurers and the Insurance Information Institute.

characteristics of U.S. families. The survey also gathers information on the use of financial institutions. Since 1992, data for the SCF have been collected by the National Organization for Research at the University of Chicago. Data and information on the survey are available on the Federal Reserve Board's Web site at <http://www.federalreserve.gov/pubs/oss/oss2/scfindex.html>.

Banking system—Banks in this country are organized under the laws of both the states and the federal government and are regulated by several bank supervisory agencies. National banks are supervised by the Comptroller of the Currency.

Figure 6.7. Part of a typical introductory section to a chapter, *Statistical Abstract of the United States.* Reprinted from the 2011 *Statistical Abstract of the United States,* http://www.census.gov/compendia/statab/

Since the chapters are usually several pages long, the most efficient way to identify the specific table needed is to consult the subject index. Unlike subject indexes in many government publications, that of the *Statistical Abstract* is superb. Using it, tables can be located that provide statistics on shipments and value of microwave ovens, volume of trading on the New York Stock Exchange, prices received by fishermen for tuna and cod, and hundreds of other subjects. When a fairly broad subject is being presented, subheadings are frequently used for greater precision.

The tables themselves provide basic statistics and, as shown in figure 6.8, frequently include definitions of terms or concepts as well as the source from which the statistics were derived.

The appendixes include a guide to sources of statistics, a list of state statistical abstracts and foreign statistical abstracts, a description of metropolitan areas, and a list of current metropolitan areas and their components.

Most tables present information for the past 5 or 10 years; historical information is seldom presented. Someone who wanted to show how prices paid for consumer goods in 1888 compared with those paid in 1988, for example, would find that the *Statistical Abstract* lacked the necessary historical information. It would be found, however, in *Historical Statistics of the United States, Colonial Times to the Present.* Previously issued by the Census Bureau, now by Cambridge University Press, as a supplement to the *Statistical Abstract, Historical Statistics* also serves as a reference source and finding aid. Like the *Statistical Abstract,* it footnotes the sources from which tables are compiled and includes introductory remarks in most chapters that describe methodology employed and limitations, if any, of the data as presented. Data later than 1970 are presented for some of the series in the annual issues of the *Statistical Abstract,* and there is a special historical appendix beginning with the 1975 issue.

Table 1362. Household Net Saving Rates by Country: 1995 to 2008

[As a percentage of household disposable income. Household savings are estimated by subtracting household consumption expenditure from household disposable income, plus the change in net equity of households in pension funds. Households include households plus nonprofit institutions serving households. Net saving rates are measured after deducting consumption of fixed capital (depreciation), with respect to assets used in enterprises operated by households, as well as owner-occupied dwellings. The household saving rate is calculated as the ratio of household savings to household disposable income (plus the change in net equity of households in pension funds). Minus sign (–) indicates an excess of expenditures over income]

Country	1995	2000	2002	2003	2004	2005	2006	2007	2008
United States	**5.7**	**3.0**	**3.7**	**3.8**	**3.4**	**1.5**	**2.5**	**1.7**	**2.7**
EU-27 [1]	(NA)	6.6	7.4	7.3	6.6	6.4	5.8	5.5	5.8
Australia [2]	6.4	2.2	–2.7	–3.2	–2.1	–0.2	0.8	(NA)	(NA)
Austria	11.8	9.2	8.0	9.2	9.4	9.7	10.9	11.4	12.0
Belgium	16.4	12.3	12.9	12.2	10.8	10.0	10.9	11.2	11.5
Canada	9.4	4.8	3.5	2.7	3.2	2.2	3.6	2.6	3.8
Chile	(NA)	6.5	6.8	6.4	7.2	7.1	7.7	7.7	(NA)
Czech Republic	10.0	3.3	3.0	2.4	0.5	3.2	4.8	6.3	5.8
Denmark	1.3	–1.9	4.1	4.1	0.7	–1.5	0.4	–1.0	–0.3
Finland	3.9	–0.1	0.6	1.4	2.5	0.7	–1.4	–1.2	–1.0
France	12.7	11.8	13.7	12.5	12.4	11.4	11.4	12.0	11.6
Germany	11.0	9.2	9.9	10.3	10.4	10.5	10.5	10.8	11.2
Greece	(NA)	–6.0	–8.0	–7.3	–7.2	–8.0	–7.3	(NA)	(NA)
Ireland	(NA)	(NA)	5.4	5.4	8.3	5.6	3.8	2.7	4.1

Figure 6.8. Sample table from section 30, *Statistical Abstract of the United States.* Reproduced from the 2011 *Statistical Abstract of the United States,* http://www.census.gov/compendia/ statab/2011/tables/11s1362.pdf

The *International Historical Statistics* series is an attempt to pull together in one place all the major statistical series for all countries for which information is available. The series provides the researcher with mainly economic statistical data, with the sources of information identified and an extensive set of explanatory footnotes. These are very detailed statistics, enabling one to identify information anything from the output of wheat in Estonia in 1919 to the English Consumer Price Index for 1781. This is a worthwhile series for most collections but especially for any institution that supports an interest in economic history. The compilation is also available electronically from Cambridge University Press, and special pricing for the print copy is available when an electronic subscription is bought.

Although important, the above sources are by no means the only collections of statistical data. Other more specialized sources are equally important. Although space precludes listing them all, some important representative examples of more specialized statistical compilations are described below. Other sources are included in the subject-oriented chapters that follow.

Strawser, Cornelia J. **Business Statistics of the United States: Patterns of Economic Change** 15th ed. Lanham, MD: Bernan Press, 2010. 395p.

County and City Extra: Annual Metro, City, and County Data Book Lanham, MD: Bernan Press, 1992–. Annual. (available electronically through ebrary)

Gaguin, Deidre A., and Richard W. Dodge, eds. **Places, Towns and Townships**. 2nd ed. Lanham, MD: Bernan Press, 2007. 1047p.

Handbook of U.S. Labor Statistics: Employment, Earnings, Prices, Productivity, and Other Labor Data. 13th ed. Lanham, MD: Bernan Press, 2010. 546p.

U.S. President. **Economic Report of the President**. Washington, DC: Government Printing Office, 1947–. Annual. Web version available at http://www.whitehouse .gov/administration/eop/cea/economic-report-of-the-President

Historical reports (1947–), http://fraser.stlouisfed.org/publications/ERP/

Business Statistics of the United States: Patterns of Economic Change is a wide-ranging and useful data collection that echos the nation's economic performance since 1929. Up to 80 years of annual data is provided for industrial and demographic data. The data is both national and regional. Especially useful are the Notes and Definitions provided with each chapter, and the expanded notes and articles on special topics and issues. Data provided includes gross domestic product, personal income, spending, saving, employment, unemployment, capital stock, and more.

Data on state, city, and metropolitan areas were available in two Census Bureau publications issued periodically as supplements to the *Statistical Abstract*: the *County and City Data Book* and the *State and Metropolitan Area Data Book*. Unfortunately the *County and City Data Book* is published infrequently, the last edition appearing in 2007 and available at http://www.census.gov/statab/www/ccdb.html. The *State and Metropolitan Area Data Book* is also published intermittently, last appearing in 2010, and print publication has been taken over by Bernan Press. There are tables freely available at http://www.census .gov/compendia/smadb/. Bernan is also now the publisher of such well-known favorites as *Business Statistics of the United States*, *Agricultural Statistics*, *Housing Statistics of the United States*, and the *Handbook of U.S. Labor Statistics*. Freely available government reference resources are listed at Uncle Sam's Reference Shelf (maintained by VSU Library) at http://library.vsu.edu/government/unclesam.htm.

The *County and City Extra* is a compilation of statistics taken from government and private agencies. Data are arranged by subject in five tables according to the geographic designations shown below.

Table	Geographic Coverage
A	Includes state level data
B	Includes state and county level data
C	Includes data for metropolitan areas
D	Data for cities with a 1990 population of 25,000 or more
E	Data for congressional districts of the 106th Congress

County and City Extra is a convenient collection of frequently looked-for local and state data. Information is clearly organized and well presented, making the book useful for reference collections in public, college, and university libraries. Each table represents a different geographic area but covers a wide range of subjects, including population, health, housing, the labor force, income and personal taxes, wholesale and retail trade, and federal funds and grants. At this time the *County and City Data Book* is fairly current but in subsequent years one should check to see if the *Extra* is being published more frequently.

A companion volume, *Places, Towns and Townships*, provides data on smaller communities of the United States. It presents population and housing statistics for every city, town, village, and township covered by the 2000 census, with population updates for 2005. It includes data on manufacturing, trade, services, employment, construction, crime, and government finances.

Someone seeking statistics for a specific state, county, or city would be well-advised to consult the statistical handbook or abstracts issued by the appropriate states and also to check the appropriate state web pages. Although many contain data derived almost exclusively from the statistical compendia described above, others offer statistics that are not available elsewhere.

As has already been shown, one way in which statistical compendia can reflect specialization is by limiting the data to specific geographic areas. Another type of specialization is by subject. Many government agencies and departments as well as commercial publishers issue statistical handbooks and yearbooks reflecting their special interests and responsibilities. One of the most useful of such publications for business research was the *Handbook of Labor Statistics*, last published by the Bureau of Labor Statistics in 1989 and since 1997 issued by Bernan Press under the title *Handbook of U.S. Labor Statistics: Employment, Earnings, Prices, Productivity, and Other Labor Data*.

The *Handbook*, which contains data from many BLS and Census Bureau publications, includes information on employment and unemployment, hours and earnings, occupation employment statistics, worker productivity, compensation, prices and living conditions, work stoppages, occupational injuries and illnesses, and foreign labor and price statistics. It also includes special labor force data on such subjects as work experience, educational attainment, alternative work arrangements, and marital and family characteristics of the labor force. Technical notes are included for each of the subjects covered, and footnotes are appended to most tables. Those needing more recent information should refer to such BLS periodicals as the *Monthly Labor Review*, the web page of the Bureau of Labor Statistics, or the *Economic Report of the President*.

In addition to the president's annual message to Congress on the state of the economy and an accompanying report by the Council of Economic Advisers, the *Economic Report of the President* includes detailed tables of supplementary statistics on national income, production and business activity, prices, money stock, government finance, corporate profit and finance, agriculture, and international economic activity. Sources are cited, and many of the figures date back 40 years or more.

The titles described above cover fairly broad subject areas. Other compendia, particularly those issued by trade associations and commercial publishers, focus on narrower subject fields. Many are discussed at length in later chapters on marketing, accounting, banking, and investments.

Compilations and Search Engines on the Web

Knowing that the statistics one may need are out there somewhere on the Web is often as frustrating as the search and time taken to find them. Fortunately there are shortcuts to much of this information. Listed below is just a sampling of major statistics finding aids.

American Fact Finder, http://factfinder2.census.gov/main.html. Demographic and economic information. Legacy information is available at http://factfinder.census.gov/

DATA.GOV, http://www.data.gov/. Datasets that are generated and held by the federal government

FEDSTATS, http://www.fedstats.gov/index.html. Official web site for statistics from federal agencies.

Economagic.com: Economic Time Series Page, http://www.EconoMagic.com/. Meant to be "a comprehensive site of free, easily available economic time series data useful for economic research, in particular economic forecasting." There are approximately 200,000 time series. Charts are included. Downloading requires a subscription.

FRED, http://research.stlouisfed.org/fred2/. Database of 27,086 economic time series. With FRED® you can download data in Microsoft Excel and text formats and view charts of data series: economic and financial data, including daily U.S. interest rates; monetary and business indicators; exchange rates; balance of payments; and regional economic data.

Also available through this web page are other other data collections including FRASER (Federal Reserve Archival System for Economic Research) and ALFRED (Archival Federal Reserve Economic Data)

National Bureau of Economic Research, http://www.nber.org/data_index.html. The National Bureau of Economic Research is a private, nonprofit, nonpartisan research organization dedicated to promoting a greater understanding of how the economy works. Information at the Web site includes macro, industry, and individual data.

ECONData, http://inforumweb.umd.edu/econdata/econdata.html. A source of economic time series data from Inforum, at the University of Maryland. Several hundred thousand economic time series, produced by a number of U.S. government agencies, can be found here. These series include national income and product accounts (NIPA), labor statistics, price indexes, current business indicators, industrial production, information on states and regions, and international data

Free Resources for International Data on the Web

Much of the information in the preceding sections has concentrated mainly on national statistics, but with the acceleration in the growth of international business this is often not enough. International business is a loose term used to describe transactions that are both private and government sponsored. It refers to all activites that involve the exchange of goods, services, and resources between two or more countries. The statistics that may need to be gathered include economic resources, capital, and production as well as information about the population and probably political factors.

Much of this information can be found in subscription databases such as *IHS Global Insight, Global Market Information Database,* and *IMF International Financial Statistics.* Few of these commercial resources are inexpensive, and so for this reason the next section will concentrate on free resources for international statistics. Naturally many of these sources also include information on the United States.

eurostat, http://epp.eurostat.ec.europa.eu/

Eurostat is the statistical office of the European Union situated in Luxembourg. Its task is to provide the European Union with statistics at European level that enable comparisons between countries and regions. One can search for data at http://epp .eurostat.ec.europa.eu/portal/page/portal/statistics/search_database either by using a keyword or the data navigations tree. There is a wealth of information for European countries, and one example is the economy and finance section that includes national accounts, exchange rates, interest rates, prices, and balance of payments.

International Macroeconomic Data Set, http://www.ers.usda.gov/Data/Macroeconomics/

Provides data from 1969 through 2020 for real (adjusted for inflation) gross domestic product (GDP), population, real exchange rates, and other variables for the 190 countries and 34 regions that are most important for U.S. agricultural trade. Real per capita income, for example, begins in 1969 and includes both decade averages and decade average annual growth.

NationMaster, http://www.nationmaster.com/

A compilation of data from such sources as the CIA World Factbook, UN, and OECD. Motto is "Where Stats Come Alive!" Covers a wide range of statistics that are not only economic. A wide range of demographic indicators are covered including literacy rates, taxation levels, and murders per capita. These are also available in pie charts, scatterplots, and correlation graphs. One can begin on the first screen or by clicking on the statistics tab, which reveals the list of topics covered. If one then clicked on lifestyle, the list reveals countries ranked by happiness level, cannabis use, or whether or not there is financial satisfaction. The type of information offered is wide but could be exacltly what a businessperson wants.

OFFSTATS, http://www.offstats.auckland.ac.nz/

This amazing resource is from the Business & Economics Information Services team at the University of Auckland Library, and provides access to free statistics from official sources on the Web for every country in the world, arranged alphabetically by region, region and subject, country, country and subject, subject and region, and subject and country.

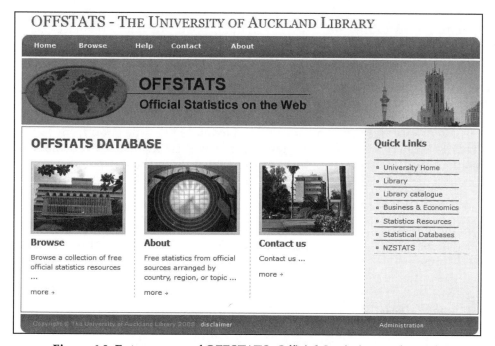

Figure 6.9. Entry screen of OFFSTATS, Official Statistics on the Web

University of Auckland Library, http://www.offstats.auckland.ac.nz/

After clicking on the browse button one can choose how to search the entries. If one chooses first country and then Afghanistan one will find links to data from the Central Statistics Office and Ministry of Finance and also from the World Bank, Asian Development Bank, and United Nations Children Fund.

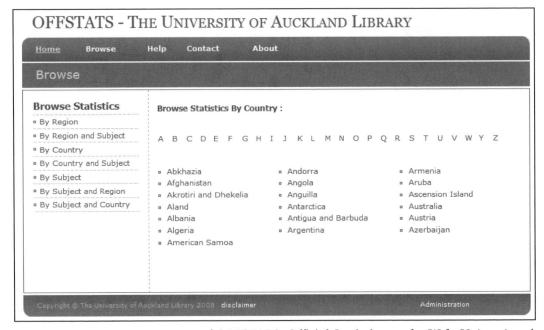

Figure 6.10. First country screen of OFFSTATS, Official Statistics on the Web. University of Auckland Library. http://www.offstats.auckland.ac.nz/browse/country/

Penn World Tables, http://pwt.econ.upenn.edu/php_site/pwt_index.php

The *Penn World Table* (PWT) is a set of national-accounts data developed and maintained by scholars at the University of Pennsylvania to measure real GDP (per capita) from the corresponding relative price levels across countries and over time.[1] Successive updates have added countries (currently 188), years (1950–2004), demographic data, and capital-stock estimates. A new version 7.0 will be ready shortly, and this increases the number of counties and territories to 189 and extends the time span from 1950 to 2007 with 2005 as a reference year. This new edition will be available from the same web site. People using this data set should always check with the variable lists as they are sometimes re-named between series.

World Development Indicators, http://data.bank.worldbank.org/

From the above web link choose the Databank tab to access the World Bank collection of development indicators which are compiled from officially recognized international sources. It presents the most current and accurate global development data available, and includes national, regional, and global estimates. One can select numerous variable ranging from adjusted net national income to worker's remittances. Previously a subscription database this has now been made freely available.

Other databases available from the same link, given above, include *Africa Development Indicators*, *Joint External Debt*, and *Worlwide Governance Indicators*.

UNSD Statistical Databases, http://unstats.un.org/unsd/databases.htm

The *UN Statistical Database* provides a global center for data on international trade, national accounts, energy, industry, environment, transport and demographic and social statistics gathered from many national and international sources. Not all data is free, but two databases that are most linked with business—Commodity Trade Statistics (COMTRADE) and National Account Main Aggregates—are free.

In a time of shrinking budgets and increasing prices from many commercial vendors it is important that librarians and researchers seek information that is freely available. Hopefully the resources included here will help.

Notes

1. Reported on the *FEDSTATS* web page at http://www.fedstats.gov/.

2. Examples of statistical updates:

> Economic Census: Manufacturing Sector, http://www.census.gov/mcd/

> Annual Survey of Manufactures, http://www.census.gov/manufacturing/asm/index.html

> Current Industrial Reports, http://www.census.gov/manufacturing/cir/index.html

> Manufacturers' Shipments, Inventories, and Orders, http://www.census.gov/manufacturing/m3/index.html

> Quarterly Survey of Plant Utilization, http://www.census.gov/manufacturing/capacity/index.html

3. U.S. Bureau of the Census, *American Housing Survey: 1997* (Washington, DC: Government Printing Office, 1997). Also available at http://www.census.gov/hhes/www/ahs.html.

4. Darrell Huff, *How to Lie with Statistics* (New York: Norton, 1954), 140.

5. Until 1978, when the Consumer Price Index for All Urban Consumers, or CPI-U, was introduced, the Consumer Price Index was limited to prices paid by urban wage earners. The pre-1978 Consumer Price Index, in other words, is roughly analogous to the Consumer Price Index for Urban Wage Earners and Clerical Workers, or CPI-W.

6. Joe Morehead, "The Uses and Misuses of Information Found in Government Publications," in *Collection Development and Public Access of Government Documents* (Westport, CT: Meckler, 1981), 62.

7. Huff, *How to Lie with Statistics,* 123.

8. Joan Harvey, "Statistical Publications for Business and Management," in *Information Sources in Management and Business,* 2nd ed. (London: Butterworths, 1984), 136.

2

Fields of Business Information

7

Marketing

Marketing Basics

Marketing is a mix of activities, beginning with estimating the demand for products and progressing to their development, pricing, distribution, and promotion. These activities can be reduced to four broad categories: product, price, place, and promotion.

Marketing Activities

Product planning involves the product itself as it is designed to appeal to a predetermined group of users or potential users. It includes decisions about package design, brand names and trademarks, warranties, and the development of new products. In 1995, for example, Kraft began test marketing a new product to see if user response merited full production and distribution. The product was DiGiorno pizza.

The test results were positive, and the pizza became an official product that, by 1996, was available in about 80 percent of the United States.

Marketers must also make a series of decisions relating to *pricing,* setting profitable and justifiable prices for their products. Other factors are at work here as well. The product's image is important and may be affected by its price. It would not do, for example, to set too low a price for a perfume intended for affluent consumers; they might ignore it or think it inferior and turn instead to more costly brands. Market demand and competitors' prices must also be considered. Finally, pricing is closely regulated and is subject to considerable public scrutiny.

Promotion involves personal selling, sales promotion, and advertising using print, broadcast, and other media. Even as DiGiorno, the pizza, was being test marketed, decisions were being made about how to promote it. Marketers settled on "It's Not Delivery, It's DiGiorno" as the advertising campaign slogan, and the target market for the product was men and women, ages 25 to 54, who bought carry-out pizza.

Place refers not only to the geographic area in which the product is marketed but also to the channels and marketing intermediaries through which the product moves, as well as the transportation employed en route to the final user.

Marketing has grown increasingly important in the current competitive environment, and marketing activities are undertaken by manufacturers of both industrial and consumer products and by companies that sell services. Importantly, marketing is increasingly commonplace in nonprofit organizations such as libraries, art museums, charities, and political parties. Whatever the nature of the product or service, good marketing helps.

Small businesses also depend on effective marketing to keep ahead. They, even more than large corporations, can ill afford costly errors based on faulty marketing decisions or inadequate information. Good marketing does not guarantee business success, but it reduces or eliminates unnecessary gambling and improves the odds of success.

Market Segmentation

Not all people need, want, or can afford all products or services. Someone in the restaurant supply business, for example, would be as disinclined to buy an industrial lathe as an adolescent would be to buy a Barbie doll, and while that same teenager might yearn for a Ferrari, it is unlikely that he or she would be able to buy one. Marketers define their markets by attempting to identify particular segments of the population that are likely to want to buy the product. Moreover, these should be people with "purchasing power and the authority to make purchase decisions."[1] This process is called *market segmentation*—that is, dividing a larger, somewhat diverse market into smaller markets in which demand for a particular product or group of products is likely to be greater:

> Firms that can identify buyers with similar needs may be able to serve those market segments quite profitably. The market consisting of people who use toothpaste (almost everyone), for example, can be divided into a number of smaller segments, each consisting of people who have more in common: children who want a toothpaste that tastes good, parents who want one that will reduce cavities, young adults who seek sex appeal and so on. The smaller, more homogeneous submarkets and serving those submarkets with your product, is called market segmentation.[2]

Although any characteristic that describes and distinguishes buyers may be useful for market segmentation, those most commonly used are geographic, demographic, psychographic, and sociographic.

Geographic

Consumers in different geographic regions may exhibit different buying behavior. Market research by automobile manufacturers has shown that certain styles and colors are more popular in some parts of the country than in others. Tastes may also vary. Campbell Soup Company, for example, makes its nacho cheese soup spicier for Texas and California than for other parts of the country. Campbell has, in fact, placed considerable emphasis on geographic segmentation.

Climate, political boundaries, and population density are some of the factors considered in geographic market segmentation.

Demographic

Demographic information is of key importance to marketers, who often segment their markets using such demographic variables as age, sex, race, income, marital status, and family size. A real estate developer considering sites for an exclusive retirement community, for example, would be particularly interested in the number of affluent adults aged 65 and older. Although current data would be important, so also would be historical statistics and projections for the future, reflecting past and anticipated trends. If statistics for the last 10 years showed an absolute decline in the number of adults 65 and older in a particular region, the developer would probably eliminate that region from the list of prospective sites for the retirement community.

Advertisers use demographic information to segment their markets as well. They identify the demographic characteristics of the people most likely to buy their products and then direct their advertising to these people through the media that will most effectively reach them:

> Therefore, if demographic analysis shows that the heaviest usage for our product is by women who are married and under 35 years of age, with 2 or more children under 8 and a blue collar occupation by the head of the household, then we know who our market is and from this we can determine what appeals in our advertising will be most effective. Finally, we can find out those advertising media with similar demographics to reach our market most effectively with our message.[3]

Psychographic

Psychographic segmentation looks at the values, activities, interests, and opinions of the population, what we often call lifestyle. As with geographic and demographic segmentation, the variables are quantitatively measured, but unlike them, the numbers are not as easily (or as inexpensively) available. According to Marvin I. Mandall, its value is in its ability to overcome deficiencies in both demographic and geographic data:

> For some purposes, geographic and demographic market segmentation may leave something to be desired. For example, age is a commonly used demographic classification. From it, advertisements have defined the "youth market." However, the youth market may need a new definition. Is it really an age group, or is it a state of mind? The youth market overflows the traditional age brackets and today can be defined more meaningfully in terms of those who think young in any age bracket—that is, in terms of youthfulness, not youth. Even among youth within the demographic age bracket there is a wide range of differences.[4]

Sociographic

Finally, sociographic segmentation looks at the social environment, including social class and culture, peer and reference groups, and family structure and decision making.

Usually marketers use a mix of geographic, demographic, psychographic, and sociographic factors to identify their market segment. As a result, marketing research, which gathers and analyzes such data, is extremely important.

Marketing Research

Marketing research, a close cousin to the industry research discussed in chapter 4, covers a whole gamut of activities but, in essence, is the process of systematically gathering and analyzing information about marketing problems and potentials for use in making marketing decisions.

Marketing research includes various subsidiary research: product research, which involves market testing for new products (such as DiGiorno pizza); studies of package effectiveness; and identifying new markets for existing products. It also includes market analysis, the study of the size, location, and other characteristics of the markets themselves. In measuring markets, market share analysis, which compares sales for one product brand against total sales for all brands of the product, is particularly important. Sales research is another important component of marketing research and includes such activities as evaluating sales policies, setting sales quotas, and measuring the effectiveness of the sales staff. Consumer research documents consumer attitudes, reactions, and preferences, and advertising research evaluates the advertising program used to promote products, including copy and media research as well as the evaluation of advertising effectiveness. Finally, corporate and economic research programs are used to consider the relevance of the product in the context of the company itself, which in turn is examined in the context of the economy as a whole.

Primary, Secondary, and Hybrid Data

Researchers use both primary and secondary data. Primary data are original and gathered for the specific problem being considered. Although the fit between data and problem is good, this advantage may be offset by the time, cost, and skill it takes to collect primary data. Techniques used for gathering primary data include surveys, observations, and field experiments:

- **Surveys.** Answers to questions are sought through telephone or personal, face-to-face interviews, or through the mail. Generally, a specific list of questions or a questionnaire is prepared and mailed. Validity and reliability of these surveys are vital considerations.

- **Observation.** Here the consumer is observed in the act of purchasing. Sometimes films are taken and analyzed. Candid camera is actually an observation technique.

- **Field experiments.** These may involve the survey method, the observation method, or both. The main characteristic is a more rigorous research design, often using sample control groups and sophisticated statistical techniques.[5]

The Internet is a relatively new, powerful, and sometimes controversial tool in the collection of data on potential customers. Market researchers can use the Internet to conduct surveys, such as when an Internet user is given a choice or invited to fill out a survey. Survey Monkey (http://www.surveymonkey.com/) and Qualtrics (http://www.qualtrics.com/) are two of many Internet survey companies. The Internet can also be used to monitor which links a user clicks on and how long a user stays on a specific web site.

Although large companies with highly skilled marketing staff may elect to do their own primary marketing research, often companies hire other companies to do it for them. A. C. Nielsen (http://www.acnielsen.com/) and Frost & Sullivan (http://www.frost.com/) are two well-known groups that compile reports in a variety of areas ranging from automobiles to pharmaceuticals.

Secondary data, on the other hand, is data that already exist "out there," often on the Internet. It is useful because the data might be free or inexpensive and easy to obtain. It can be expensive but usually less so than primary data. Secondary data is provided by trade organizations and associations, by the government, and by commercial publishers.

Many library collections are particularly strong in these areas and constitute a rich source of secondary marketing information. Secondary data does have drawbacks. The fit between marketing problems and secondary data may be none too good. The data may be outdated, or collected in an unreliable or biased manner. This may call in to question the validity of the data. Keeping these warnings in mind, market researchers will find secondary information is the more cost-effective data in most cases. Some major secondary data sources are described later in this chapter and in chapter 4.

"Off the shelf" market research reports are a hybrid, more specialized than the rather general secondary sources listed below and less specific than wholly original data collection. Although not tailor-made to meet a particular company's specific market research needs, they are often highly specialized and can be extremely useful, particularly to companies not prepared to embark on expensive primary research. Several types of off-the-shelf studies can be identified, including standard research reports, reports produced by securities analysts, and off-the-shelf surveys and audits.

Standard commercial market research reports are generally produced from secondary information sources available at many libraries—census data and trade publications, for example—and from primary data gathered from interviews and investigation. The reports, which are generally 50 to 200 pages long, may cost as little as $200 or as much as $15,000 or more, depending on depth of coverage, data used, and expertise required to compile the reports. Clearly, the cost of these publications will preclude their addition to most libraries. Even though these reports mostly fall outside the scope and budget of collections, librarians should be able to help patrons identify them. Some trade publications and periodical indexes list selected reports, but one of the most comprehensive listings is *MarketResearch.com*.

MarketResearch.com, MarketResearch.com, Rockville, MD (http://www.MarketResearch .com/)

MarketResearch.com is one of the leading providers of global market intelligence products and services. Presently it is offering more than 300,000 research publications from more than 700 top consulting and advisory firms. One of the attractions of this commercial web site is the ability to search the database at no charge, after free registration, and then buy information "by the slice." One is no longer obligated to purchase full reports but can select only the chapters or sections that are of interest and so cut costs. A full list of market research publishers, complete with a description of their activities and links to their web sites, is available from the MarketResearch.com site.

The company also provides academic subscriptions, via *MarketResearch.com Academic*.

MarketResearch.com Academic, MarketResearch.com, Rockville, MD (http://academic .marketresearch.com/)

MarketResearch.com Academic provides students, faculty, librarians, and administrators with access to the same reports, covering a wide range of industries, used by corporate executives and business professionals around the world. The reports are a balance of quantitative and qualitative data including: industry interviews, competitive analysis, market trends, product innovations, buyer behavior, market share, and more. Depending upon access purchased, users have access to the same full-length reports, containing up-to-date, real-world case studies as worldwide business leaders. Users can browse or search by keywords, and the reports are fully downloadable.

Marketing Reference Sources

Marketing reference sources are abundant. They include many different types of materials: guides and bibliographies, dictionaries and encyclopedias, directories, periodicals, statistical sources, and databases. Two of the places to identify these items are the bibliographic sources listed below.

Guides and Bibliographies

There are several guides to the literature and resources of marketing, including the following.

Ganly, John V., **Data Sources for Business and Market Analysis**. 4th ed. Metuchen, NJ: Scarecrow, 1994 (reprinted 2003). 475p.

The fourth edition of *Data Sources for Business and Market Analysis* lists virtually all of the major sources of external secondary marketing information. It includes chapters arranged by issuing organization (e.g., Census Bureau, professional and trade associations) and by publication type, such as services and directories. Though a bit dated the work remains a valuable annotated bibliography of a wide range of market research and statistical data sources. Publications of the federal government make up a major portion of the book, but regional and local sources, foreign publications, professional and trade association publications, and periodicals are also included. There are indexes by title, issuing agency, subject, and geographic area.

With the fast pace of globalization and communication growth it has become increasingly important to be able to locate sources of advertising and marketing information worldwide. The following publication provides a guide to international sources in the advertising and marketing arenas.

World Directory of Marketing Information Sources. London: Euromonitor plc, 2010. Biennial.

The *World Directory*, also known as Source:Euromonitor, provides a summary of more than 22,000 business research organizations in 82 countries, alphabetically listed. Included is full contact information for official organizations, trade development bodies, libraries and market research companies, trade associations, publications, and databases. Entries are compiled by Euromonitor researchers, who contact the organizations included. This is an excellent resource that provides information on countries as diverse as Sri Lanka and the Ukraine.

Dictionaries and Encyclopedias

Although most standard business dictionaries include definitions of key marketing terms, there are special dictionaries that focus solely on marketing or on some aspect of marketing, such as advertising.

There are many glossaries or dictionaries available on the Web for free. Some are general in nature and others focus on a specific area of marketing. AlphaDictionary .Com (http://www.alphadictionary.com/directory/Specialty_Dictionaries/Marketing/) is a great resource for links to online dictionaries both specialized and general. You can also use a general search engine to find other dictionaries.

Dictionary of Marketing (http://www.medialine.de/english/know-how/dictionary-of-marketing.html)

Wolfgang Koschnick, the responsible party for *The Dictionary of Marketing* web site, is an acknowledged leader in the area of marketing encyclopedias and dictionaries, having authored more than 40 of them. This online version is a very extensive marketing dictionary containing thousands of terms.

Internet Marketing Dictionary (http://www.marketingterms.com/dictionary/)

The Internet Marketing Directory is what its name implies, a concise dictionary of marketing terms related to Internet marketing. It is easy to use and navigate.

Rosenberg, Jerry Martin. **The Essential Marketing and Advertising Dictionary**. Naperville, IL: Spinx Pub, 2008. 770p.

The *Essential Marketing and Advertising Dictionary* is a new entry that has very good coverage including more than 5,000 terms. But the really interesting thing is it is available as an iPhone and iPad touch app.

Brace, Ian. **Questionnaire Design: How to Plan, Structure and Write Survey Material for Effective Market Research** 2nd ed. London: Kogan Page, 2008. 305p, also available as an eBook

Covers the design of questionnaires for market research, describes their role in the survey process, the different types, and how and when they should be used. Also covers objectives, layout, and writing of questionnaires. Ethical issues, social desirability bias, and international surveys are covered as well. New to this edition is information on online questionnaires.

Cavusgil, S. Tamer, Michael R. Czinkota, and Gary Knight. **Conducting Market Research for International Business**. New York: Business Expert Press, 2009. 127p, also an eBook

This short, concise book is intended to provide a basic understanding of the fundamentals of international market research. It offers coverage of the research issues that international business managers face when contemplating entry into international markets, including: market entry, engaging buyers in foreign markets, maintaining and growing market share, and expanding to newer opportunities abroad. Also includes a list of international internet sites for obtaining secondary data.

Market Research Handbook. 5th ed. Edited by Mario van Hamersveld, and Cees de Bont. Chichester: John Wiley & Sons. 2007. 627 p, also available as eBook

Formerly known as the *ESOMAR Handbook of Market and Opinion Research*, this edition has been completely revised to reflect the changes in marketing research. It is aimed at the professional rather than the novice and takes a very detailed and scientific look at all aspects of market research.

McQuarrie, Edward F. **The Market Research Toolbox: A Concise Guide for Beginners** 2nd ed. Thousand, Oaks, CA: Sage Publications, 2006. 205p

As the subtitle suggests this is a good book for the novice market researcher. It covers what market research is, why it is important, and how to do it. There are several chapters describing different methods of market research data collection that cover procedures, costs, strengths and weaknesses, and do's and don'ts for that method. There are also chapters on what to do with the data once you have collected it.

The Web, social media, and smart mobile devices are changing marketing in previously unimagined ways. The following sources are just a few of the growing number of guides and encyclopedias offering advice and explanations on how, when, where, and why one should make use of these new channels of communication with customers and potential customers.

Miller, Michael. **The Ultimate Web Marketing Guide**. Indianapolis, IN: Que, 2011. 618p.
　　Also available as an eBook.

Covers using the Web for marketing yourself or products or services, includes chapters on using Search Engines, Email, Blogs, Social Medias, Multimedia, and Mobile Devices. Also includes chapters on planning, establishing, and managing your or your company's web and online marketing efforts.

Reece, Monique. **Real-Time Marketing for Business Growth: How to Use Social Media, Measure Marketing, and Create a Culture of Execution**. Upper Saddle River, NJ: FT Press, 2010. 372p. Also available as eBook

This is an extensive work covering all aspects of using social media to support and expand marketing efforts that uses a mix of narrative and case studies to illustrate marketing issues, especially using social media to achieve and expand marketing objectives. The author presents a phase process for marketing Purpose, Research, Analyze, Implement, Strategize, Execute and Evaluate or PRAISE as a framework for making decisions.

Dushinski, Kim. **The Mobile Marketing Handbook: A Step-by-Step Guide to Creating Dynamic Mobile Marketing Campaigns**. Information Today, 2009. 218p.

Given the explosive growth of "smart phones" and other mobile devices, this guide to mobile marketing is greatly needed. Organized in two parts: "Mobile Marketing Strategy and Implementation" and "Mobile Marketing Toolbox: Tactics, Campaign Ideas and Resources." Topics discussed include: development of text-messaging campaigns, web promotions, and social networking. Also covered is how different industries may have different strategies. The book is updated by a web site reachable by entering a URL at the end of each chapter. This is a clever way of being sure that only those who purchase the book get the benefit of the updates.

Baker, Michael John. **The IEBM Encyclopedia of Marketing.** London: International Thomson Business, 2001. 865p.

Global in scope, the *IEBM Encyclopedia of Marketing* contains essays that explain the theoretical foundations of marketing. This work covers both marketing theory and practice.

McDonough, John, and Karen Egolf, eds. **The Advertising Age Encyclopedia of Advertising.** Chicago: Fitzroy Dearborn, 2003. 3v.

An international group of more than 200 advisors and contributors have compiled the 600 entries in *The Encyclopedia of Advertising*. Subject areas include the history of important advertising agencies and biographies of the people who worked in them; a history of major marketers and the campaigns they conducted; and important issues affecting advertising such as brand building, the commission system, and mass communications theory.

Information about successful marketing campaigns is useful to researchers aiming to target customers and prospects.

Encyclopedia of Major Marketing Campaigns. Detroit: Gale Group, 2000. 2063p.

Encyclopedia of Major Marketing Campaigns, Volume 2. Detroit: Thomson Gale, 2007.
1947p. Also available as an eBook

The *Encyclopedia of Major Marketing Campaigns* looks at 500 major marketing and advertising campaigns of the twentieth century. Each chapter looks at the campaign from a historical perspective, then explores the target market, competition, marketing strategy, and finally the outcome. In this volume one can read about the debacle of "new Coke" or find out why "snap, crackle, pop" became such a generational pleaser. 475 additional major marketing campaigns are covered in the *Encyclopedia of Major Marketing Campaigns Volume 2.*

Major Marketing Campaigns Annual. Farmington Hills, MI: Gale Research, 1998–1999.
Annual.

Major Marketing Campaigns Annual presents more recent campaigns in the same format as the *Encyclopedia* and is an excellent addition to it. Both titles contain campaign illustrations and interesting snippets of information such as why the mysterious "33" is featured on the back of the Rolling Rock beer bottle.

Directories

Since standard business directories were discussed at length in chapter 2, this section focuses on titles that deal specifically with marketing and advertising.

American Marketing Association. New York Chapter. **Green Book: Worldwide Directory of Marketing Research Companies and Services.** New York: The Association, New York Chapter, 1963–. Annual.

American Marketing Association. New York Chapter. **Green Book: Worldwide Directory of Focus Group Companies and Services.** New York: The Association, New York Chapter, 1992–. Annual.

GreenBook. The Guide for Buyers of Marketing Research Services. American Marketing Association. New York Chapter (http://www.greenbook.org)

One of the best known of these publications is the *Green Book: International Directory of Marketing Research Houses and Services*. The *Green Book* lists and describes services offered by major marketing firms. Foreign as well as U.S. marketing research firms are entered alphabetically in a single listing. Each entry includes the firm's address and telephone number, email address, web site URL, the names of its key officers, and a brief description of the services it offers. The directory contains listings by company name, research services offered, market specialties, industry specialties, computer programs, trademarked products and services, geographic location, and key personnel.

The *Green Book: Worldwide Directory* lists and describes organizations that offer facilities, recruiting, moderating, and transcription services. The listing is by city within state and identifies firms involved in marketing research, direct marketing, merchandising, audiovisual communications, and health-care marketing. Each entry includes the firm's address and telephone number, email address, web site URL, the names of its key officers, and a brief description of the services it offers. The directory contains listings by company name, research services offered, market specialties, industry specialties, computer programs, trademarked products and services, geographic location, and key personnel.

The web site (www.greenbook.org) also produced by New York AMA is the online equivalent of the two print volumes. It has a user-friendly interface that one can browse by category or search by key words, and limit by category and geography. A search will result in a list of companies that meet the criteria set out. Like the print volumes each entry includes the firm's address and telephone number, email address, a link to the company's web site, the names of its key officers, and a brief description of the services it offers. Each entry also has a MapQuest.com link to the company's location.

The Advertiser Red Books. New Providence, NJ : LexisNexis, 1917–2002, 2003–. Annual. http://www.redbooks.com/

The Agency Red Books. New Providence, NJ: LexisNexis, 1917–2002, 2003–. Annual. http://www.redbooks.com/

The Advertising Red Books. International Advertisers & Agencies. New Providence, NJ: LexisNexis, 1992–2002, 2003–. Annual. http://www.redbooks.com/

Agency Red Book, also known as *The Standard Directory of Advertising Agencies*, contains current information about 9,000 American advertising agencies and their branches, including their names and addresses, specialization, major accounts, and over 59,000 key staff members. The listing criteria are national and regional advertising agencies, spending a minimum of $200,000 annually on paid media.

In addition to the main section, which is arranged alphabetically by advertising agency, the directory has geographical listings of agencies by states and by foreign countries, a list of the largest advertising agencies, and a special market index, which lists agencies in special fields such as the African American and Hispanic markets, business to business, food service, and entertainment. It is an essential resource for those directly involved in advertising and can be found in many business reference collections.

Equally important is *The Advertiser Red Books*, also known as *The Standard Directory of Advertisers*, a companion directory that focuses on companies and other organizations that advertise, and includes trade names, the types of media used for advertising, the advertising agencies employed, and, frequently, annual advertising budgets. An online subscription service that includes the international as well as the U.S. information is also available at http://www.redbooks.com/.

Periodicals

Marketers turn to periodical literature to keep current with news about specific industries of interest to them, with developments in marketing and allied fields, and with the economy generally. Some may subscribe to one or two key publications, while others have extensive periodical collections at their disposal. This section begins by mentioning some of the databases used to identify relevant articles and concludes with a discussion of some of the major periodicals in the field.

For the most part, American marketers and librarians seeking articles on specific marketing topics will need to consult general business indexes (see chapter 2) such as *Business & Company Resource Center, ABI/INFORM Global, Business Source Premier*, or *Factiva*.

A similar product is *Business & Industry*, part of Gale Cengage's RDS Business Suite, which also has a strong global focus on product and industry information. *Business & Industry* is available only online (http://www.gale.cengage.com/rds/index.htm).

Marketing periodicals are abundant. Some deal with specific aspects of marketing, such as *Journal of Consumer Research* (http://www.journals.uchicago.edu/JCR/home .html) and *Direct Marketing News* (http://www.dmnews.com/). Some, such as the *Journal of Marketing Research* (http://www.marketingpower.com/) and *Marketing Science* (http://mktsci.journal.informs.org/), are scholarly journals, and others, such as

Advertising Age (http://www.adage.com/), *Sales & Marketing Management* (http://www.salesandmarketing.com/content/about-us), and *Women's Wear Daily* (http://www.wwd.com) are trade publications.

Advertising Age. Chicago: Crain-Communications, 1930–. Weekly. http://www.adage.com

Advertising Age is a newspaper that provides current coverage of advertising and marketing news. It includes descriptions of current advertising campaigns and trends in advertising, news of decisions by government regulatory agencies, consumer trends, and personnel changes in the industry. *Advertising Age* is particularly useful for the special issues it publishes, including those with information on leading ad agencies and market research firms. The web page contains some freely available features and articles. But much more information is available only to subscribers. These include special reports such as that on the history of television, or advertising at the Super Bowl, and a weekly report on web traffic and advertising from *Nielsen/NetRatings* and *Ad Age*. There is also a searchable database of 400 advertisers that will give the names and countries of agencies representing a product.

Sales & Marketing Management. New York: Bill Communications, Inc., 1918–2010. Bimonthly. http://www.salesandmarketing.com

SalesForce XP Xtra Performance for Sales Management. Excelsior, MN: Mach1 Business Media, 2003. 6 issues a year. http://www.salesforcexp.com/

Sales & Marketing Management covers all aspects of marketing, product development, packaging, place decisions, promotion, and pricing. It is a major publication and includes articles on specific marketing activities and on individual companies as well as personnel changes and trade news. Free resources accessible from the web page at http://www.salesandmarketing.com/ include an archive of past articles. In July 2010 *Sales & Marketing Management* was absorbed into *SalesForce XP*.

As with many magazines and newspapers, even if the library or individual does not hold a subscription, it is well worth checking the Internet site of the publication for any free information that might be there.

Statistics

As mentioned earlier, good marketing research is based on current and reliable statistical data. Market segmentation, for example, requires the use of statistics to define geographic, demographic, psychographic, and sociographic boundaries for market segments. The selection of a new plant site will be influenced by statistics on population and labor conditions, while the final decision about the location of a new business such as a pizza franchise or a computer store may in large part be based on statistics regarding the location of other, similar businesses in the area and the age, income, and educational levels of the population. Effective marketing strategies are based on planning. Planning involves assessing historical and current market conditions, setting objectives, developing marketing programs, and analyzing the results. Collection and analysis of data about markets and customers is an important part of the process. Factors such as sales trends, size and growth of a market, product life cycles, market share data, seasonality, profits, and industry capacity can be analyzed to develop marketing strategies. Using primary and secondary data, researchers can identify marketing opportunities. Statistics are, in short, vital for effective marketing research.

Marketing statistics fall primarily into two main categories: demographic and economic. Although trade associations and commercial publishers make statistical data available, the major producer of statistics is the federal government.

Federal Government Statistics

Almost every statistic that the government publishes is significant for research relating to industrial and consumer markets. The ones that will be most consistently useful and most heavily applied fall into four main categories: population, income, employment, and sales.

Population statistics, gathered, compiled, and published by the Bureau of the Census, are available in great detail and are basic to most marketing research. The Census Bureau, both in decennial census publications and in special reports and studies, also makes available income statistics, which indicate the buying power of consumers. *Series P-60* of the *Current Population Reports* (available online at http://www.census.gov/prod/www/abs/popula.html), for example, deals solely with consumer income, while *Series P-23* frequently includes studies that feature income and socioeconomic data. The most detailed information, however, is published in the decennial censuses.

The Bureau of Labor Statistics, the Internal Revenue Service, and the Bureau of Economic Analysis all publish income data as well. The Bureau of Labor Statistics and the Census Bureau primarily produce federal employment statistics, and sales statistics are most frequently taken from the *Economic Censuses*, the *Survey of Current Business*, and related reports. Sales and employment statistics are indicators of company performance and market size and can be put to many uses, such as the measurement of sales effectiveness.

One of the best ways to identify and locate federal statistical data, which are made freely available on the Web, is by using *FEDSTATS* (http://www.fedstats.gov/) or *American FactFinder* (http://factfinder2.census.gov/).

FEDSTATS provides access to official statistics collected and published by more than 100 federal agencies without the user having to know in advance which agency produces them. It provides linking and searching capabilities down to the county level within states. Information includes statistical profiles to the county level, published collections of statistics available online, and a subject listing.

American FactFinder is designed to make information easily accessible. The opening screen contains links to "Basic Facts," where one can find Quick Tables and Geographic Comparison Tables for Population and Housing data, Quick Reports for Economic data, and predefined Thematic Maps. It also contains search functions to help quickly locate any type of information that's available in *FactFinder* (see figure 7.1).

Commercial Statistical Publications

Government publications are unrivaled for their depth and breadth of statistical information; no commercial publisher comes close to matching them. However, some of the needed information simply may not be available from the government. Commercially published marketing guides, based on government statistics, are often supplemented with publisher-generated statistical estimates, which are extremely useful. Many are available, but the titles listed below are particularly important and can be found in most business reference collections.

Editor & Publisher Market Guide. New York: Editor & Publisher, 1924–. Annual.

The *Editor & Publisher Market Guide* is an annual that gives detailed statistical data for U.S. and Canadian cities publishing one or more daily newspapers. It is divided into six main sections. The first section is a compilation of market ranking tables, based on publisher estimates for the current year, showing population, disposable income, total retail sales, total food sales, and income per household. Within each category, entries are arranged by size. Thus, by consulting the "Disposable Income per Household" table, it is possible to identify those metropolitan statistical areas estimated by *Editor & Publisher* to have the highest disposable income (personal income less taxes) per household.

Figure 7.1. *American FactFinder* (http://factfinder2.census.gov/)

The second section is individual market surveys for U.S. cities, arranged alphabetically by state and then by city. A state map introduces the survey for each state and pinpoints the location of daily newspaper cities, the state capital, county seats, and metropolitan statistical areas. The city market data, however, are most heavily used.

It is easy to see why this publication is so popular. Not only does it collect and present statistical data from many government publications, but it also includes data gathered and prepared by the publisher, for example, the names of specific retail stores and shopping centers. Sections follow for population, sales, income population, and income. The publication concludes with a list of Canada's provinces and newspaper cities and some abbreviated surveys for that country.

Another publisher, ESRI Business Information Solutions, also issues both county and ZIP code demographic data.

Sourcebook of County Demographics. Redlands, CA: ESRI Business Information Solutions. 2008–.

Sourcebook of ZIP Code Demographics. Redlands, CA: ESRI Business Information Solutions. 2008–.

Sourcebook America. Redlands, CA: ESRI Business Information Solutions. 2008–.

All products include 2009 updates and 2014 forecasts and spending potential indexes for 20 product and service categories. *County Demographics* also includes 80 demographic variables for each U.S. county, while the *ZIP Code* edition contains dominant Tapestry lifestyle segmentation type for each ZIP code. Tapestry classifies U.S. residential areas into 65 market segments based on socioeconomic and demographic characteristics. There are 11 summary groups based on geographic, physical, and income features, and 12 summary groups based on lifestyle and life stage characteristics. Tapestry segmentation can be used to distinguish the spending patterns and lifestyle choices of consumer behavior. For more information on Tapestry segmentation, see ESRI's *Tapestry Segmentation Reference Guide* available online at http://www.esri.com/library/brochures/ pdfs/tapestry-segmentation.pdf. *Sourcebook America* combines the printed county and *ZIP code* editions with ArcReader and Zip*Search software on a CD that allows users to use mapping software to explore and view data in map form and to perform ring studies.

The Lifestyle Market Analyst. Wilmette, IL: Standard Rate & Data Service, 1989–2008. Annual.

One can search for market profiles using the abovementioned publications, but to find a lifestyle market one would need to check in *Lifestyle Market Analyst*. This volume correlates demographic characteristics with consumer behavior patterns and can be used to learn more about the interests, hobbies, and favorite activities of consumers so that market plans can be better targeted. Interests, as defined by *LMA*, include a wide variety of activities: bicycling, fishing, grandchildren, gambling, dieting, motorcycles, and Bible reading are included. *LMA* combines lifestyle, demographic, and geographic data to provide comprehensive profiles by market, lifestyle, and consumer segment. Each profile provides comprehensive demographic information about the defined market segment. It also includes a list of the top 10 lifestyle interests for the market and a ranking and index for 60 lifestyle interests. This publication ceased in 2008 and is succeeded by the following title.

SRDS Local Market Audience Analyst. Des Plains, IL: Standard Rate & Data Service and Nielsen Claritas, 2009–. http://www.srds.com/portal/main?action=LinkHit&fra meset=yes&link=ips

Lifestyle Market Analyst ceased publication in 2008 and was succeeded by *SRDS Local Market Audience Analyst*, an online-only service. *SRDS Local Market Audience Analyst* contains data on 210 DMAs and 3,000 U.S. counties Data is segmented by more than 200 Experian Simmons lifestyles and by Nielsen Claritas PRIZM segments, making this a very powerful market research tool.

Consumer Americas. London: Euromonitor, 2011–. Annual.

For more specific buying habits one should investigate *Consumer Americas*, formed by the merger of *Consumer USA and Consumer Latin America*. This volume, like so many others, contains an overview of the U.S. economy and market and trends in retailing and personal finance. But unlike other marketing publications, this will provide sales statistics (and forecasts) on much narrower product divisions. Examples of these are hard cheese, soft cheese, sugarless gum, mineral water, watches, personal care items, televisions and even financial or personal business software. Euromonitor (http://www .euromonitor.com) operates internationally to produce the same marketing information for many countries ranging from Asia to the Middle East. All carry the consumer designation, such as *Consumer Asia Pacific and Australia* and *Consumer Europe*.

Euromonitor also produces the online data resource Passport GMID, which provides more than 8 million internationally comparable market statistics including volume and value sales statistics for hundreds of consumer product categories from countries around the world. There are also more than 18,000 full-text market, company and country reports containing expert analysis of market, industry, and consumer trends. None of these publications is inexpensive, but any large library that serves an international business community will have some of them.

New Strategist is a publisher that specializes in publications on market segments. A full list of the books, complete with tables of contents, is listed at (http://www .newstrategist.com/store/). Subjects covered by this publisher include demographics of consumer demand, home ownership, attitudes, and information on different generations.

There are several products available that allow one to explore buying habits of people based on their media habits. GfK MRI (http://www.gfkmri.com/), formerly Mediamark Research, conducts audience samples that are then offered in reports containing comprehensive demographic, lifestyle, product usage, and advertising media information. With these reports one can target an audience that watches a certain television program and buys a certain food. If one wants to know who watches *Friends* and eats Hershey kisses, these are the reports to check. Once again, these are very expensive, but the company does allow academic libraries to purchase reports that are two to three years old at a much reduced price. These are now available only on Similar reports from Simmons (previously issued in book form as *Simmons Survey of Media and Markets* and are available as *Simmons Choices 3*.

Zenith Media (http://www.zenithmedia.com) issues several publications for the advertising sector. These are international in scope and include a series of market and media fact books. Typical data included are household penetration of television channels, advertising revenue over time, peak-time advertising rates and ratings, and total television advertising spending. Countries covered include those of Eastern and Western Europe, Latin America, Asia, the Pacific, and the United States.

Market Share

One of the statistical requests that business reference librarians regularly encounter is for information on the market share for a particular product or company. "What is the market share for Coca-Cola?" a patron may ask, or "What is Kellogg's share of the market for cold cereals?" Market share is, quite simply, the ratio of sales for one company's product or product line to the total market sales of that product or product line, expressed as a percentage of the market. Market share can be for a specific brand, Froot Loops versus Cheerios, for example, or for one company's product line, Kellogg's share of the market for cold cereals, versus General Foods' market share. The concept is not a difficult one; market share can be calculated whenever total sales and specific product (or company) sales information are available. Sales can be in the form of units sold or in dollars. Market share can be computed for local, state, national, and even international markets as long as the necessary sales information is at hand. A similar question is "What are the top X companies or brands of Y?"

Off-the-shelf market studies described earlier in this chapter frequently contain detailed market share data, but the latest publications are usually too expensive for most libraries. Other sources, more likely to be found in libraries, contain only selective market share information. *Advertising Age*, for example, regularly features market share data for some nationally advertised brands. *Ward's Business Directory of U.S. Private and Public Companies* and *D&B Business Rankings: Public and Private Businesses Ranked within Industry Category and State* include sales data by NAICS and SIC codes for some public and private U.S. companies. Although these directories do not give actual market share, it can be calculated easily by dividing the sales figure for a specific company into the total sales for the NAICS or SIC category of which it is a part. Researchers should be forewarned, however, that this is an approximate figure at best.

Many large companies are involved in the sale of a multitude of products and services, and sales figures presented are for the company as a whole rather than for the product(s) assigned the SIC code under which a company is listed. In addition, many companies too small to be included in the directories may also sell the same product or service. As a result, market shares derived from these publications are really little more than ballpark estimates. Although the sources mentioned above are useful, they have some drawbacks. Market share data are given for only a limited number of products and brands in *Advertising Age*, and the directories do not include market share for specific brands or for the market as a whole.

Market share for specific products or brands may also be included in periodical articles, which can be identified using some of the indexes already discussed and may also be available in the following publications.

Business Rankings Annual. Farmington, MI: Gale Group, 1989–. Annual.

International in scope, *Business Rankings Annual* lists the top business companies and provides information on such topics as "top cable programs by ad revenue." The comprehensive index is excellent.

Market Share Reporter. Farmington, MI: Gale Group, 1991–. Annual.

The most well known and widely available of these items is the *Market Share Reporter*, which is a compilation of reports from periodical literature such as *Advertising Age*, *Appliance Manufacturer*, and *Supermarket Business*. The basic arrangement of the chapters is by two-digit SIC codes and then within the chapters the arrangement is by four-digit SIC. Each of the more than 2,000 entries is also given a number. For example, entry 985 in the 2001 volume tells us that Sony is the top producer of CD players. The table of contents is arranged by SIC number, and accompanying this is a table of products. The several indexes include listings by company and product and refer the user to an entry number. *Market Share Reporter* covers companies and products in Canada, Mexico, and the United States.

These two publications along with several dozen other company directories are available through the online service *Gale Directory Library* (http://www.gale.cengage .com/DirectoryLibrary/), which allows for easy searching and downloading.

Global Market Share Planner Market Share Tracker. 6th ed. London: Euromonitor, 2010. 916p.

Euromonitor, a major international provider of marketing information, provides information for the top 15 consumer segments across 30 countries in the *Market Share Tracker*. Products ranging from alcoholic drinks to soft drinks are ranked within each country. If one needed to know the top-selling snack in Argentina, this would be a good source to check. All the information in this publication and much more is in an online product from Euromonitor (http://www.euromonitor.com/) called *Passport GMID*, formerly called *GMID Global Marketing information Database*.

TableBase. Detroit: Gale Cengage Learning. 1996–. Daily updates.

TableBase specializes in indexing and extracting tabular data on topics such as market share, company and brand rankings, industry and product forecasts, production and consumption statistics, imports and exports, usage and capacity, number of users/outlets, trends, and demographics. It features indexing with concept terms, such as Ad Budget, Consumption, Market Share, and Generation Y; industry terms like Broadcasting; and marketing terms like Community Advertising. Special features include the custom-written unique titles that describe content and precise indexing at the table level as well as full-text searching. *TableBase* was originally introduced by Responsive Database Services Inc.

Market share for a specific brand or product is influenced significantly by the effectiveness of the advertising that promotes it. Selection of the appropriate medium in which to advertise is an important part of the marketing process. The next section considers various advertising media and the sources relating to them.

Advertising Media

Selection of the best media in which to advertise is no simple task. Each medium has special characteristics that the advertiser must keep in mind. However, before these characteristics are considered and an advertising plan drawn up, the following questions should be answered:

- *What do I want my advertising to accomplish?* The objects of advertising should be to increase awareness of a business and to attract new customers.

- *What is the target audience?* Determine the demographics of the intended audience and the products and services that may be useful to them.

- *What is the advertising message?* The message must be targeted to the demographic group that must be attracted

- *What advertising medium should be used?* The basic choices are television, radio, magazines, outdoor, direct mail, and the Internet.

The prospective advertiser, in other words, needs to segment his or her market and then consider the best way(s) of reaching it.

Descriptions of four main categories of advertising media follow: print, broadcast, direct to home, and the Internet.

Print Media

The two main types of print media are newspapers and magazines. Both are used heavily by advertisers, but newspapers lead magazines and all other media in terms of advertising dollars spent. In 2011 Global Ad Spend in magazines was 6.4% and that in newspapers was 1%.[6]

Prospective newspaper advertisers usually want to know two things: the characteristics of the newspaper readers and/or the area in which they live, and the cost of advertising in specific newspapers. Both types of information are readily available.

Characteristics of newspaper readers in a city are likely to be similar to the population as a whole. Although this is somewhat less true of cities in which more than one newspaper is published, it is axiomatic that the socioeconomic and general demographic characteristics of the population served by a newspaper will be of great interest to those who are considering advertising in it.

Such local information may be closer at hand, either in government publications or in such statistical guides as the *Editor & Publisher Market Guide*, which gives demographic and trade information for daily newspaper cities. The other main factor affecting a marketer's decision to advertise in a specific newspaper is the cost of advertising in that newspaper. Since newspaper circulation is the basis for advertising rates and a major consideration in selecting a newspaper, credible circulation figures are essential. As a result, many newspaper publishers belong to the Audit Bureau of Circulations (http://

www.accessabc.com/), a nonprofit association whose purpose is to audit and ascertain the veracity of circulation figures for newspapers and magazines published by its members. The letters "ABC" in the *Editor & Publisher Market Guide* and other publications indicate that the circulation figures presented have been verified by the Audit Bureau of Circulations. There are two other groups, the Business Publications Audit of Circulation, or BPA Worldwide (http://www.bpaww.com/), and the Verified Audit Circulation Corporation (http://www.verifiedaudit.com/), that audit circulation figures and delivery of direct-to-home advertising in print and digital formats.

General circulation and readership statistics can be found at the web page of the Newspaper Association of America (http://www.naa.org/). This site also provides links to information on advertising expenditures, media usage habits, and industry forecasts. Newspaper circulation figures can also be found in many publications, but coverage is most complete in the following source.

Circulation. Wilmette, IL: Standard Rate & Data Service, 1957–. Annual.

Circulation covers the circulation of 1,300 dailies, over 190 newspaper groups, and 25 consumer magazines, organized by metro area, TV market, and county penetration. Although some general market area and demographic data are included, it is the circulation analysis that makes this a useful reference source. Entries include daily and Sunday circulation figures, by MSA or county, for each newspaper. In addition, market data (households, consumer spending income, retail sales, and circulation) are featured. Although some advertising rates are included, an advertiser would be well advised to turn to the following companion publications for more detailed information. A sample listing is available at http://www.srds.com/portal/main?action=LinkHit&frameset=yes&link=ips.

Newspaper Advertising Source. Wilmette, IL: Standard Rate & Data Service, 1919–. Semiannual. Also available online through SRDS Media Solutions interface (http://www.srds.com/portal/main?action=LinkHit&frameset=yes&link=ips)

Newspaper Advertising Source is a monthly SRDS publication that includes rates for daily and weekly newspapers as well as for individual ethnic groups, colleges and universities, and international newspapers, comics, and newspaper magazines. A sample page is available at http://www.srds.com/portal/main?action=LinkHit&frameset=yes&link=ips.

Magazines, the other print medium, can be divided into three main categories: consumer, farm, and business publications. Each of these, in turn, has many different subdivisions. Standard Rate & Data Service, for example, lists 80 classification titles for consumer magazines and 190 classifications for business publications.

As with newspapers, circulation, characteristics of the reader population, and advertising costs are the major factors considered. Advertising rates vary widely, based on the magazine selected and the type of advertisement to be placed; a full-page, four-color ad will, naturally, cost more than a 14-line black-and-white ad. A nationally circulated periodical with many readers will charge more than one with more limited circulation or more limited subject interest. In 2011, for example, it cost approximately $370,500 to place a full-page color ad in *Sports Illustrated*, which has an ABC-verified circulation of over 3 million, but only $14,033 to place a similar ad in *Bass Times*, which has a more limited readership. For local magazines, advertising rates are often comparable to those for newspapers.

Standard Rate & Data Service also publishes two main titles covering consumer, farm, and trade magazines.

SRDS Consumer Media Advertising Source. Des Plains, IL: Standard Rate & Data Service, 1919–. Annual. Also available online as Business Publications Media through SRDS Media Solutions interface (http://www.srds.com/portal/main?action=LinkHit&fr ameset=yes&link=ips)

SRDS Business Media Advertising Source. Des Plaines, IL: Standard Rate & Data Service, 1919–. Annual. Also available online as Consumer Magazine Media through SRDS Media Solutions interface (http://www.srds.com/portal/main?action=LinkHit&frameset =yes&link=ips)

Both *Consumer Magazine* and *Business Publication* provide detailed information about magazines, including circulation, advertising rates, mechanical requirements, special issues, and advertising deadlines.

While advertising rates are significant and will be a major consideration in magazine selection, equally important is choosing one in which reader characteristics most closely match the target market identified for the product. The decision made to advertise a new line of cosmetics in certain women's magazines rather than, say, in automotive or fishing magazines may be a fairly simple one, but the next step must be to select the most appropriate women's magazines. Would *Vogue* or *Redbook* be better, or *Cosmopolitan* or *Working Woman*? To help advertisers decide, many magazines survey their readers for information about their income, occupations, education, and geographic location as well as about their attitudes toward and use of specific products.

Broadcast Media

Radio and television are highly effective advertising media. Broadcast advertising offers several advantages over print advertising. Radio and television programs are aimed at specific segments of the population, and the advertising that accompanies them can be aimed at these audiences. Broadcast media are also more flexible than print media, being more responsive to quick changes.

The human voice, with its capacity to establish rapport with listeners and to convey urgency, is sometimes more persuasive than print. Finally, broadcast advertising is, in a sense, more democratic, making it possible for small as well as big businesses to establish the images they want to present.

Broadcast advertising is not without its disadvantages, however. Frequent repetition of advertisements is necessary, since potential customers can be reached only during the few seconds the message is being transmitted. Copy must be both brief and effective. Finally, planning for broadcast advertising is somewhat more difficult than for print since there is little standardization between broadcast stations. Nevertheless, these disadvantages are offset by the potential that broadcast ads offer for reaching a market and for saturating it with promotional messages.

Broadcast advertisers attempt to reach prospective buyers by selecting the media, station, program, and time most likely to reach the most appropriate audience. When considering a station, advertisers look at its coverage and its audience. Coverage refers to the geographical area where the station's signal can be heard, and audience refers to the number of people who actually watch or listen to that station or to a particular program on that station.

Just as verified circulation figures are crucial for print advertisers, so also are accurate audience statistics for broadcast advertisers. Several firms offer audience measurement services; key among these are the Arbitron Ratings Company and the A. C. Nielsen Company.

Advertisers distinguish between network and spot announcements, or spots. Network announcements require buying air time from the network; spot announcements are bought on a station-by-station or market-by-market basis.

Radio advertising is appealing for many different reasons. It is less expensive than television, and because radio programming is designed to segment audiences, a much more closely defined audience can be reached than when using print media, particularly newspapers.

Radio rates are based partially on radio coverage and audience. Another factor affecting rates is time of day. Radio is primarily a daytime and early-evening medium, and categories, based on when most people are likely to be listening, have been assigned to different parts of the day. Although these categories are not standardized among all stations, the classification shown in figure 7.2 is typical, with highest rates being charged for AA time slots, and lowest for D.

Class	Description	Time
AA	Morning Drive	6:00 A.M to 10:00 A.M.
B	Home worker	10:00 A.M. to 4:00 P.M.
A	Evening Drive	4:00 P.M. to 7:00 P.M.
C	Evening	7:00 P.M. to midnight
D	Nighttime	midnight to 6:00 A.M.

Figure 7.2. Radio time slots

The most current information on radio stations is available from the following source.

Radio Advertising Source. Wilmette, IL: Standard Rate & Data Service, 1929–. Annual. Also available online through SRDS Media Solutions interface (http://www.srds .com/portal/main?action=LinkHit&frameset=yes&link=ips)

This publication profiles more than 9,600 stations. Each issue includes SRDS's usual estimates of state, county, city, and metro area market data as well as profiles of the individual stations themselves. A sample page is available at http://www.srds.com/ portal/main?action=LinkHit&frameset=yes&link=ips.

Television advertising is big business. According to the 2011 *Statistical Abstract*, in 2008 more than 98.2 percent of homes in the United States have at least one television set, and people watch TV an average of 8.2 hours per day. Small wonder that advertisers turn to TV to promote their products.

Obviously knowing one's market and the shows that reach the designated audience is extremely important. *TelevisionAdvertising.com* at http://televisionadvertising.com/ offers some guidance for the small business person on choosing types of advertising. As in radio, television stations divide their broadcasting day into parts, based on when people are most likely to be watching. The categories and terms they employ, however, are different; they generally call their classifications daytime, early news, early fringe, prime, late news, late fringe, and weekend.

Time of day is one of the variables determining television advertising rates. Another has to do with the station's coverage and its audience. Broadcasters and advertisers may refer to a station's rating or to its audience share. Both are measures of its effectiveness and are based on the households using televisions index, or HUT. The HUT is simply the percentage of households in a designated area with the television set turned on. In a sample of 2,000 households with television, if 800 of these sets are turned on, the HUT would be 40. A station's rating is the percentage of households in a sample turned to a specific station at a specific time. If 400 households out of the sample of 2,000 reports turn to a particular station during the specified time period, that station would have a rating of 20 percent, usually expressed as 20.0 rating points. Finally, a station's share of audience, or share, is calculated by dividing the individual station's rating by the HUT. Thus, using the above example, dividing the station's rating of 20.0 by the HUT of 40.0 yields an audience share of 50 percent for the station. These concepts are employed for specific programs as well as for stations, with prime-time network programs ranked by rating and audience share.

One of the most heavily used listings of commercial television stations and broadcasting services is from Standard Rate & Data Service, one of the leading providers of all types of media rates and data to the advertising industry.

TV and Cable Source. Wilmette, IL: Standard Rate & Data Service, 1947–. Triannually. Also available online through SRDS Media Solutions interface (http://www.srds. com/portal/main?action=LinkHit&frameset=yes&link=ips)

TV and Cable Source profiles individual television stations, state networks and groups, and national networks and groups. Also included are sections on sports networks listings for Latin America, and a section on public television. A sample page is available at http://www.srds.com/portal/main?action=LinkHit&frameset=yes&link=ips.

Broadcasting & Cable Yearbook. New Providence, NJ: R. R. Bowker, 1935–2010. Annual.

The *Broadcasting & Cable Yearbook* includes sections that survey the broadcasting industry; profile television and cable stations; and focus on programming, professional services, technology, advertising and marketing, and satellites.

The television section of *Broadcasting & Cable Yearbook* lists all U.S. and Canadian television stations. In addition to these individual station entries, the *Yearbook* includes metro area maps showing in which counties metro area stations are viewed and a listing of television systems, including Spanish-language and independently owned. The technology section lists equipment manufacturers and distributors. Using it, one can identify manufacturers of studio monitors, cameras, and lighting systems. Similarly, by consulting the "Brokers & Professionals" section, one can find television brokerage services, research specialists, consultants, and attorneys specializing in communications law.

Direct Mail

Direct mail, which includes all forms of advertising sent through the mail, has certain advantages over other media. One of the most important is that it offers the advertiser the potential for selling to individuals, identifiable by name and address and possibly other characteristics, rather than to broad groups of potential buyers having certain demographic or psychographic characteristics in common. Using carefully chosen mailing lists, compiled by the advertiser or purchased or rented from mailing list brokers, one can target the advertising to specific individuals. Print and broadcast advertising are scattergun media; direct mail, in contrast, is a pinpoint medium.

Greater selectivity in a target audience is not the only advantage. Another is greater flexibility: Direct mail advertising does not have the same limits on space or format as other media and can be mailed at any time. The advertiser is not constrained by publishing deadlines or broadcast schedules. Finally, some claim that direct mail advertising receives more attention since it is a single message rather than one in a series of competing messages in print or broadcast media.

Effective direct mail advertising begins with a good mailing list. Although some prefer to compile their own, many others use lists supplied to them by mailing list companies or mailing list brokers. For example, although a local, independently owned hardware store might construct its own mailing list, composed of previous customers and neighborhood residents, the manufacturer of a line of hardware supplies intended for national distribution might purchase or rent a mailing list of hardware wholesalers. The manufacturer might limit the list further to directors of purchasing or sales managers working for hardware wholesalers. Many libraries provide access to products such as *ReferenceUSA* (http://www.referenceusa.com/) or *InfoUSA* (http://www.infousa.com) with which one can compile mailing lists.

When the decision is not to compile an in-house mailing list, advertisers must then consider outright purchase of a list from a mailing list company that compiles and sells its own list, or rent it from a mailing list broker who offers lists compiled by other organizations. These may include lists of subscribers, for example, and membership lists. For businesspeople interested in direct mail advertising, one publication is particularly important.

Direct Marketing List Source. Wilmette, IL: Standard Rate & Data Service, 1967–. Triannually. Also available online with the title **SRDS: DirectNet** through SRDS Media Solutions interface (http://www.srds.com/portal/main?action=LinkHit&frameset=yes&link=ips)

Mailing list compilers and brokers can be identified using *Direct Mailing List Source*, which profiles detailed descriptions of more 70,000 lists in some 230 market classifications. Relevant lists can be more quickly found in the online version, where one can search by keyword or classification system, list source, and gender selection. Information provided in the service includes a description of the list and contact information. A sample page is available at http://www.srds.com/portal/main?action=LinkHit&frameset=yes&link=ips.

Internet

Online advertising is becoming a revenue generator. More and more homes have access to the Internet, and time spent on it is rising. Although most Internet sites have some advertising, it is apparent that there is still an untapped potential audience. The company or person who needs information about this advertising medium will most likely search online for data and news. There are many sites that are excellent starting points. Some are listed below.

ClickZ (http://www.clickz.com/). Once known as CyberAtlas, ClickZ gathers online research from the best data resources to provide a complete review of the latest surveys and technologies available. Contains a section on web advertising and statistics.

Digital Media. Des Plaines, IL: Standard Rate & Data 1996–. Semiannual.

Digital Media (formerly *Interactive Advertising Source*) provides contact information and profiles of digital marketing and media and advertising opportunities. Sample page is available at http://www.srds.com/frontMatter/ips/interactive/sample.html.

Compete, Boston. Compete, a Kantar Media company (http://www.compete.com)

This resource provides site profiles, statistics, and analysis for almost 3 million websites. Data elements collected include: website traffic over time including number of visits, number of unique visits, ranking of referring sites and destination sites, average length of stay, and more. Users have the ability to compare data elements across websites. So one could compare forbes.com with fortune.com. Data can be downloaded to spreadsheet software via CSV format file, and graphs can be downloaded as an image or embedded into word processing documents.

There are many other SRDS publications including: the *Out of Home Advertising Source*, which details 25 nontraditional settings such as the cinema, taxis, bus shelters, and billboards. For a full description of these products the researcher should check the publisher's web page at http://www.srds.com. Accompanying each SRDS print subscription is one password to access the product online. The online products are updated daily. There are some licensing restrictions with its use, so not every library will have access to the electronic product.

Advertising Expenditures

Data on advertising expenditures by companies with big advertising budgets are readily available. Some of the sources already described include such information. *Advertising Age*, for example, lists leading national advertisers and their annual advertising expenditures, and the *Standard Directory of Advertisers* often includes figures on media expenditures for each company. One very good source for how much money companies are spending on which advertising media in the United States is Ad$pender.

Ad$pender. Kantar Media, http://www.kantarmediana.com/ or http://kantarmediana .com/intelligence/products/adspender.

Find dollars spent on advertising by companies and brands in up to 18 categories of advertising spending including: Network TV, Cable TV, Syndication TV, Spot TV, Spanish Language Network TV, Magazines, Sunday Magazines, Local Magazines, Hispanic Magazines, B-to-B Magazines, National Newspapers, Newspapers, Hispanic Newspapers, Network Radio, National Spot Radio, Local Radio, Outdoor, and US Internet. One can create as many reports as needed and can customize those reports to the layout that would work best for the user. Reports can be output to both PDF and CSV (MS Excel editable) spreadsheets. Note you will not be able to determine specific publications, stations, or networks, just the broad category totals. Five rolling years of data are available.

Ad$pender replaces the print resources.

Company/Brand $. New York: Competitive Media Reporting, 1974–. Quarterly.

Class/Brand $. New York: Competitive Media Reporting, 1974–. Quarterly.

Ad $ Summary. New York: Competitive Media Reporting, 1973–. Quarterly.

The first of the titles in this series is *Company/Brand $*, which lists company (and some brand) expenditures for advertising in 10 different media: consumer magazines, Sunday magazines, newspapers, outdoor, network television, spot television, syndicated television, cable TV networks, network radio, and national spot radio. The criteria for inclusion are brands that spend $25,000 or more per year in the 10 media measured. For companies that advertise several different products, there may be separate listings for each product.

The second title, *Class/Brand $*, provides quarterly and year-to-date expenditures per medium and the 10-media total for each brand, company, and classification. Media include magazines, newspapers, television, radio, and outdoor. In this publication, brands are grouped alphabetically within each of the Leading National Advertisers' (LNA's) product classes, showing brand expenditures for each medium. *Class/Brand $* is particularly useful when one wishes to compare advertising expenditures for different brands of the same product.

Arrangement in *Ad $ Summary* is alphabetical by brand name. Whereas its companion volumes, *Company/Brand $* and *Class/Brand $*, list advertising expenditures for each medium as well as total media expenditures, *Ad $ Summary* lists only total media expenditures. Types of media used to advertise each product, however, are designated. The publication includes listings of the top 100 companies in each of the 10 media.

Many libraries will not purchase the quarterly publications but instead will have the annual YTD volumes. These old volumes are indispensable for historical research outside the *Ad$pender* rolling coverage window. The publisher, Competitive Media Reporting, is one of the leaders of strategic information provided mostly to advertising agencies. Information about the company and its products is available at http://www.cmr.com/.

Geographic Information Systems

More and more enterprises are using geographic software to analyze business trends and to make key decisions about locating new branches and designing marketing programs. GIS allows users to analyze data in spatial terms and so create a map of potential users within, for example, 10 miles of a possible new store location. Strategies such as target marketing, micromarketing, and relationship marketing require more and more information about consumers that GIS can provide. Firms such as Arby's, Burger King, the Olive Garden, Popeyes, Red Lobster, and others use GIS for market analysis, franchisee selection and placement, site location analysis, and demographic profiling.[7]

Many libraries now contain collections of GIS data and software packages, and the researcher should be aware of its potential in the marketing area. One of the most popular desktop packages, *ArcView*, is produced by Environmental Systems Research Institute Inc. (ESRI) (http://www.esri.com/index.html). ESRI also conducts a virtual campus (http://training.esri.com/gateway/index.cfm/) where one can register for free and fee-based courses on using *ArcView GIS* for successful marketing. From the home page, one can also access several free publications on GIS, available services, and free and fee data downloads. For anyone just beginning to use or think about using GIS, the ESRI online site contains much useful information and assistance.

Another GIS tool is *Simply Map* from Geographic Research Inc. (http://www.geographicresearch.com/simplymap/). Simply Map is targeted to the non-technical user. Data comes from many sources including: the U.S. Census Bureau, Applied Geographic Solutions (AGS), D&B, Easy Analytic Software (EASI), Mediamark Analytics, Experian, Nielsen, and Simmons Study of Media and Markets. Data can be purchased in modules so you only have to buy the modules you want.

Simply Map and ESRI are only two companies involved in the expansion of GIS into the marketing field, but they are the services most often available in libraries and are also the services used by local many governments.

There are many books available on GIS business applications, and the simplest way to find these is to search an online service such as amazon.com (http://www.amazon.com). To learn more about GIS and how it might be used, the librarian or researcher can also check the *About.com Geographic Technology* page (http://gis.about.com/science/gis/cs/learninggis/), which has links to tutorials, software, data, and courses available through universities and other institutions.

Web Sites

Marketing activities are so pervasive that there are few bibliographic and full-text business databases in which the subject is not covered. General business indexes such as *ABI/INFORM* and *Business Source Premier* contain a wide range of articles, both general and scholarly, relating to the field.

If you need serious information about advertising and want to use the Web as a resource, one of the best ways to begin is to use *Advertising World* from the University of Texas at Austin (http://advertising.utexas.edu/world/). It is billed as "The Ultimate Marketing Communications Directory," and this claim is easy to understand when one scans the index. It appears as if every marketing and advertising link that exists is there. The Web sites are concisely annotated and are organized in alphabetical order.

For an excellent site on the history of advertising, including advertisements that can be downloaded, the researcher should check the Advertising Collections digital archive at Duke University (http://library.duke.edu/digitalcollections/advertising/). The collections include *Emergence of Advertising in America: 1850–1920* (http://library.duke .edu/digitalcollections/eaa/). Included in this collection are the J. Walter Thompson Company "House Ads" from 1889 to 1925. The collection contains more than 9,000 images that represent the emergence of the advertising industry in the United States. Ad*Access (http://library.duke.edu/digitalcollections/adaccess/) is a complementary collection that includes more than 7,000 advertisements from 1911 to 1955.

Marketing Associations

Marketer researchers are interested in the activities of two major types of associations: trade and professional.

Trade associations represent diverse and wide-ranging industries. The Advanced Medical Technology Association (http://www.advamed.org/), for example, serves manufacturers of medical devices; the Brick Industry Association (http://www.gobrick .com/default.aspx) represents manufacturers, distributors, and dealers of bricks and other clay products; while the Real Diaper Industry Association (http://www .realdiaperindustry.org/) is composed of owners of diaper manufacturers, retailers, and diaper rental and laundry services. What these associations have in common is, in addition to the other services that they provide their members, they commonly collect and compile data from their members that are extremely useful to market researchers. Sometimes the information collected is published and made available commercially, as in the *Annual Statistical Report* published by the American Iron and Steel Institute as both a download and in print.

Often large trade associations have divisions or sections that focus on marketing, and then there are some industries represented by associations whose sole function is marketing. Some of these associations are the ABA Marketing Network (http://www.aba .com/MarketingNetwork/default.htm), and the Automotive Market Research Council (http://www.amrc.org/).

Professional marketing associations promote advertising and marketing, conduct research, set standards, and, in many instances, publish journals, directories, and bibliographies. Among these associations are the Marketing Science Institute, the Business/Professional Advertising Association, and the Association of National Advertisers. Two of the most important are the American Marketing Association and the Advertising Research Foundation.

The American Marketing Association (http://www.marketingpower.com/) has some 45,000 members in 100 countries, including educators, marketing and marketing research executives, advertisers, and sales and promotion specialists. It offers conferences and seminars to its members, fosters research, and promotes the interests of its members. In addition, it publishes several periodicals, including the scholarly *Journal of Marketing Research;* the *Journal of Marketing,* which includes both scholarly and applied research; the *Journal of International Marketing;* and a biweekly newsletter, *Marketing News.* It also publishes occasional books, monographs, and pamphlets on marketing as well as a series of bibliographies on key marketing topics such as marketing distribution, selling, and small business marketing. The AMA, the leading professional marketing association, includes 400 U.S. chapters and over 400 worldwide collegiate chapters, in addition to the activities conducted at the national level.

The Advertising Research Foundation (http://www.thearf.org/) is a nonprofit organization whose membership is composed of advertisers, advertising agencies, the media, and colleges and universities. Its purpose is to promote the highest-quality research in business and consumer marketing, advertising, and the media by developing guidelines and standards and by providing objective and impartial technical advice and expertise. The Foundation organizes conferences, compiles statistics, and publishes the *Journal of Advertising Research* as well as bibliographies, monographs, and reports.

Founded in 1938, the International Advertising Association (http://www.iaaglobal .org) is an international partnership of advertisers, agencies, the media, and corporations. Its purpose is to advocate for freedom in advertising.

Trade and professional associations provide unique and highly specialized information about specific industries and should not be overlooked by the conscientious market researcher or the librarian seeking to build a comprehensive collection in a particular industry or group of industries. Since standard bibliographic works do not ordinarily include these publications, it may be necessary to identify issuing associations using the *Encyclopedia of Business Information Sources* or the *Encyclopedia of Associations.* Many trade associations now have a web presence, so another alternative source for locating them is to use a web search engine.

Regulation of Marketing

Marketing is regulated at the federal, state, and local levels. Federal laws prohibit price fixing, false or misleading advertising, and deceptive packaging and labeling. Several agencies administer these laws and exercise some measure of control over marketing. Prime among these are the Federal Trade Commission (FTC), the Food and Drug Administration (FDA), and the Federal Communications Commission (FCC).

Federal Trade Commission

The Federal Trade Commission (http://www.ftc.gov) was established in 1914 as an independent administrative agency:

> The FTC deals with issues that touch the economic life of every American. It is the only federal agency with both consumer protection and competition jurisdiction in broad sectors of the economy. The FTC pursues vigorous and effective law enforcement; advances consumers' interests by sharing its expertise with federal and state legislatures and U.S. and international government agencies; develops policy and research tools through hearings,

workshops, and conferences; and creates practical and plain-language educational programs for consumers and businesses in a global marketplace with constantly changing technologies.[8]

The FTC issues advisory opinions, sets industry guidelines, and establishes trade regulation rules. It has jurisdiction over false and misleading advertising and has a number of ways of dealing with advertisers involved in deceptive advertising:

> A simple procedure without formal complaint and hearings is to obtain a letter of voluntary compliance from an advertiser stating that the advertisement in question will be discontinued. After a formal complaint has been issued by the Commission, a consent order may be published in which the advertiser agrees to stop the practice without an admission of guilt. If, through formal hearings, the FTC finds the advertiser guilty of deception, the FTC may issue an order to cease and desist from such practice. The Commission also publicizes the complaints and cease and desist orders it issues. This adverse publicity for the advertiser proves to be an important weapon for the FTC. When dealing with alleged deception in advertising, the FTC considers a number of questions. At each point, a decision is made to either drop the matter or to proceed to another decision point until the matter is finally settled.[9]

In 1997, for example, the FTC issued a consent order to William E. Shell, M.D., who was at that time chairman of the board of Interactive Medical Technologies Ltd. and Effective Health Inc. The complaint involved the product Lipitrol, which was advertised as a weight control substance. Advertising implied or represented that:

- Lipitrol provides weight loss benefit.

- Lipitrol lowers blood cholesterol levels.

- Lipitol reduces, or reduces the risks associated with, high cholesterol, including clogged arteries, high blood pressure, diabetes, breast cancer, and heart disease.

- Lipitrol can be used, beneficially and safely, in amounts or with frequency sufficient to cause diarrhea.

It was further ordered that such claims be corroborated by competent and reliable scientific evidence that substantiated the representations.[10]

The FTC publishes a number of consumer guides and guidelines for business-people to use. The FTC Businesses series (http://business.ftc.gov/), for example, includes guidelines on franchise and business opportunities, appliance labeling rules, and advertising policy statements and guidance. The business publications section contains a link to consumer education, business education, guides, policy statements, and rules and acts related to advertising. Some of these publications are listed in figure 7.3.

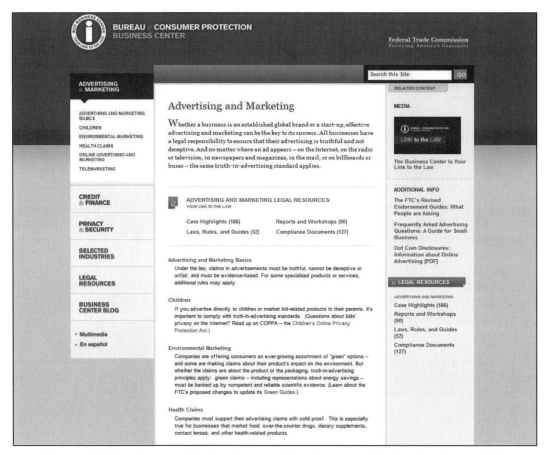

Figure 7.3. List of some of the business publications provided online by the FTC,
http://business.ftc.gov/advertising-and-marketing/

Food and Drug Administration

The Food and Drug Administration (http://www.fda.gov) is a scientific regulatory agency that acts to ensure consumer protection against a broad range of products, primarily food, drugs, cosmetics, and medical devices. As is the Federal Trade Commission, the FDA is concerned with preventing deception through misrepresentation of these products. The FDA, however, concentrates on false labeling and misrepresentation, whereas the FTC focuses on false advertising. Labeling includes not only the physical label but also any printed material accompanying the product. For example, in June 2011 the FDA issued new information relating to the marketing and labeling of sunscreen products (http:// www.fda.gov/Drugs/ResourcesForYou/Consumers/BuyingUsingMedicineSafely/ UnderstandingOver-the-CounterMedicines/ucm239463.htm). The FDA approves labeling for prescription medicines to ensure that physicians are fully informed about the drugs they prescribe and, in recent years, has issued regulations requiring nutrition labeling on many foods. In addition, the FDA now requires that the ingredients used in cosmetics be listed on the product labels. It also requires that warnings be included on the labels of products that are potentially hazardous. In 1979, for example, it required that warnings be included on the labels of permanent hair dye products containing an ingredient found to cause cancer in laboratory animals. Compliance guides and manuals are available at http://www.fda.gov/ora/compliance_ref/default.htm, while listings of recalls and safety alerts are available at http://www.fda.gov/Safety/Recalls/IndustryGuidance/default.htm.

Although the FDA will not take action to correct individual complaints, it will attempt to correct the situation that causes them and will post information on its web page warning consumers of potential dangers. The following is a warning released by the FDA about "Fraudulent Dietary Supplements":

Figure 7.4. Warning reproduced from the Consumer Updates section of the FDA web page, http://www.fda.gov/ForConsumers/ConsumerUpdates/ucm246744.htm

The FDA has an informative web site that contains primary information and publications, including reports, studies, pamphlets, and guides for its primary constituency: consumers, businesspeople, physicians, and others involved in the production, prescription, and consumption of drugs, medical devices, food, and cosmetics.

Federal Communications Commission

The Federal Communications Commission (http://www.fcc.gov) was established in 1934 as an independent federal agency. The Act charges the Commission with establishing policies to govern interstate and international communications by television, radio, wire, satellite, and cable. There are seven operating bureaus and eleven offices within the organization. The bureaus' responsibilities include processing applications for licenses and other filings, analyzing complaints, conducting investigations, developing and implementing regulatory programs, and taking part in hearings. The offices provide support services and advice.

The Media Bureau (MB) ensures that consumers have access to interference-free radio and television services that operate in the public interest. Specifically, it concerns itself with the quality of advertising and seeks to prevent obscene, profane, fraudulent, and deceptive advertising, all of which are obviously not in the public interest, convenience, or necessity. For the same reason, it also concerns itself with the quantity of time devoted to advertising.

The FCC may fine or suspend the license of any radio or television station that is transmitting profane or obscene words or images. This severe threat largely eliminates any violation of this sort, but it should be noted that profanity and obscenity are constantly subject to redefinition as social mores change. Fraudulent and deceptive radio and television advertising, on the other hand, is generally handled by the FTC's taking action against the advertiser. When the FCC receives complaints against advertisers, it notifies the station, and the station usually sees that the advertiser corrects the situation. If the station ignores the complaint, the FCC takes this fact into consideration when the license comes up for renewal.

Other Government Agencies

Although the FTC, FDA, and FCC are the major agencies involved in the direct regulation of marketing activities, other federal agencies are involved as well. The Postal Service (http://www.usps.com/), for example, not only regulates "obscene, scurrilous, or otherwise offensive" mail but also regulates against the use of the mails to defraud.

The Alcohol and Tobacco Tax and Trade Bureau (http://www.ttb.gov/) of the Treasury Department reviews proposed advertisements and labeling of alcoholic beverages for its approval or disapproval. If advertisements that raise its disapproval are not corrected to the Bureau's satisfaction, it can revoke the producer's license to sell alcoholic beverages. In addition, considerable adverse publicity can be attached to these activities.

State and local laws also regulate marketing activities. These laws vary considerably from one locale to another in their content, quality, and depth of coverage, and as a result can be confusing. They are important, however, because most federal laws come into effect only when interstate commerce is involved.

Notes

1. Louis E. Boone and David L. Kurtz, *Contemporary Marketing* (Hinsdale, IL: Dryden Press, 1974), 112.

2. Frederick A. Ross and Charles A. Kirkpatrick, *Marketing* (Boston: Little, Brown, 1982), 109.

3. Marvin I. Mandall, *Advertising*, 4th ed. (Englewood Cliffs, NJ: Prentice-Hall, 1984), 146.

4. Ibid., 147.

5. William T. Ryan, *A Guide to Marketing* (Homewood, IL: Learning Systems Company, 1981), 12.

6. Taken from Nielsen Global Ad Spend Media Type available at http://www.marketingcharts.com/television/global-ad-spend-rises-9-in-q1-2011-18273/nielsen-global-ad-spend-by-media-type-q1-2011-jul11gif/.

7. C. Battista, "Competition in the Food Chain," *Business Geographics* 3, no. 3 (1995): 32–34.

8. Taken from the FTC mission statement at http://www.ftc.gov/ftc/about.shtm.

9. Mandall, *Advertising*, 92.

10. U.S. Federal Trade Commission, Federal Trade Commission Actions, http://www.ftc.gov/os/.

8

Accounting and Taxation

This chapter introduces basic concepts and terminology in accounting and taxation that apply to the use of publications, databases, and other sources in libraries and information centers. Although they are covered in separate sections, it should be noted that accounting and taxation are closely related, and that the study of one almost inevitably requires consideration of the other. Both have profound and long-lasting effects on the daily conduct of business and, as a result, are of interest to business and laypeople as well as accountants and tax professionals.

Accounting Basics

Accounting provides information used to assess the financial status of businesses and other economic entities, including government agencies and nonprofit organizations. Although it is frequently confused with bookkeeping, the latter is but one aspect of the entire accounting process. Accounting is, in fact, a financial information system. It begins with determining the raw data to be collected; proceeds to gathering, recording, analyzing, and verifying them; and culminates in communicating the data to interested parties. An important aspect of accounting is the objectivity with which the information is presented:

> The essence of accounting is its special quality of neutrality. Accounting is financial map-making. It organizes, maps, and presents complex transactions and financial interrelationships in a reliable fashion. Not all information is necessarily useful. Of equal or greater importance is the accountant's assurance that the information is verifiable, objective, accurate, and has been compiled in an unbiased way.[1]

Accounting information is used within an organization to make decisions about finance, resource allocation, production, and marketing. It is also used externally by creditors, other businesses, investors, and government agencies charged with monitoring business activities and organizations. Accounting, which has been called the language of business, is quantitative and is usually expressed in monetary terms.

Types of Accounting

The three major fields of accounting are private, public, and government accounting. *Private accounting* is carried out within a single organization, such as a corporation. It includes such specialties as managerial, financial, and tax accounting. Managerial accounting develops, produces, and analyzes data to be used for internal management decisions. It includes cost accounting, which concentrates on determining various unit costs, and internal auditing, which checks for fraud and waste and helps to ensure that proper accounting procedures are being followed. Financial accounting gathers and reports information for inclusion in published financial statements such as balance sheets and income statements. These are included in corporate annual reports to shareholders, stock exchanges, and the Securities and Exchange Commission. Finally, tax accounting refers to recording and reporting corporate income tax and tax liability. It is a complicated specialty that requires knowledge of current and past tax legislation, court rulings, and administrative decisions, as well as accepted financial accounting practices that will minimize corporate tax liability.

Although private accounting is essentially for the benefit and under the purview of a single organization, *public accounting* is, either directly or indirectly, for the benefit of the public. It offers independent professional accounting assistance to the public and consists of three main specialties: auditing, management services, and tax services.

Private accountants employed by companies and other organizations are responsible for preparing and documenting financial statements. It is the responsibility of the independent public accountant to examine these financial statements and verify their accuracy, completeness, and compliance with generally accepted accounting principles. This process, called auditing, includes several different steps. In addition to checking figures for accuracy, it may also involve reviewing contracts, agreements, minutes of directors' meetings, and other corporate documents. In addition, it may require interviewing or corresponding with bankers and other creditors or conducting inventories. Upon completion of this process, the public accountant reaches a conclusion that becomes the auditor's report, expressed as an opinion. These opinions, more fully described in the section on basic accounting concepts, are accepted as authoritative by executives and managers within the company, and by creditors, stockholders, investors, and other interested parties. Only certified public accountants (CPAs) are allowed to conduct external financial audits for their clients.

Management services, another public accounting specialty, offer independent reviews of clients' accounting and management systems, with suggestions for their revision and improvement. Accountants may assess the availability and prudent use of financial and statistical information within the client's organization, monitor internal control systems devised to prevent losses through theft or waste, review internal accounting procedures for efficiency and effectiveness, consult on how to manage cash resources more profitably, or install or modify computerized accounting systems.

Finally, just as private accountants provide tax advice and assistance to the organizations for which they work, public accountants offer similar services to their clients. They prepare income tax returns and consult on tax problems. In addition to providing professional assistance with income taxes, public accountants also offer services pertaining to other types of taxes and tax-related issues, including property, foreign, and franchise taxes, and estate planning.

Public accounting firms range in size from sole practitioners to huge, multinational companies employing thousands of workers. The largest of these firms, now known as the Big 4, dominate the accounting marketplace and enjoy high visibility and prominence.

The largest companies at this time are Deloitte, Ernst & Young, PricewaterhouseCoopers, and KPMG (Klynveld Peat Marwick Goerdeler).

The third field of accounting is government accounting. Government agencies at all levels employ accountants in a wide range of positions. Their responsibilities parallel those of private and public accountants: They may prepare financial statements; audit the records of their own or other government agencies, contractors, or private citizens; or gather and present data that will help managers decide how best an agency should operate to meet its mandated responsibilities. At the federal level, for example, accountants in the Internal Revenue Service (IRS) audit personal and corporate income tax returns, while those employed by the Defense Contract Audit Agency examine the records of private defense contractors. The Government Accountability Office (GAO)—until July 7, 2004, the General Accounting Office—assists in investigations to determine the compliance of federal agencies with government policies and regulations and monitors the expenditure of public funds. Similar accounting activities are carried on at the state and local levels.

In summary, private, public, and government accounting are the three broad fields into which the profession is distributed. Although there is some overlap between the work performed in these areas, each has its own specialties. For all three fields, however, in the United States the generally acknowledged indication of professional competence is the CPA certificate, which is described in the following section. Not all CPAs are employed by Big 4 accounting firms or practice as public accountants. Many work as private accountants for corporations and nonprofit organizations, and still others are employed by the government. CPA status, in other words, designates a certain level of competency and adherence to professional standards and ethics and does not necessarily mean that an accountant works in the field of public accounting.

Certified Public Accountants

The right to practice as a CPA is governed by individual state boards of accountancy. Although the rules vary, particularly as they relate to minimum educational and experiential requirements, all require that candidates must pass the Uniform CPA Examination. The exam is given by computer 5 or 6 days a week at authorized test centers located throughout 55 U.S. jurisdictions. Testing is available in January & February; April & May; July & August; and October & November. Testing is not available in March, June, September, and December.

The test is prepared by the Board of Governors of the American Institute of Certified Public Accountants (AICPA) (http://www.aicpa.org/). The exam has 4 parts Auditing and Attestation, Business Environment and Concepts, Financial Accounting and Reporting, and Regulation. Total testing time is 14 hours. Each section, however, is graded separately, and candidates are permitted to take subsequent examinations until passing grades are achieved for all parts. See the AICPA's web page for more information: http://www.aicpa.org/BecomeACPA/CPAExam/Pages/CPAExam.aspx (accessed May 10, 2011).

Libraries can assist prospective CPAs by acquiring publications that will help them prepare for and pass the examination or by knowing where to direct them to find resources. Some of the most useful sources are those published by the American Institute of Certified Public Accountants. Others are commercially published.

American Institute of Certified Public Accountants. **Information for Uniform CPA Candidates**. 17th ed. New York: AICPA, 1970–. Annual.

American Institute of Certified Public Accountants. **Uniform CPA Examination: Official Questions and Unofficial Answers.** New York: AICPA, 1972–. Semiannual.

American Institute of Certified Public Accountants. **Uniform CPA Examination: Selected Questions and Unofficial Answers Indexed to Content Specification Outlines 1900s–2000.** New York: AICPA, Annual.

Many candidates begin their preparation for the Uniform CPA Examination by consulting *Information for Uniform CPA Candidates,* a booklet that discusses the format and focus of each section of the exam.[2] In addition, it includes a statement on the purpose and general objectives of the Uniform CPA Examination, describes how the exam is compiled and graded, and suggests how to prepare for it. The current edition also includes some sample questions.

Uniform CPA Examination: Official Questions and Unofficial Answers consists of all questions included in a specific exam, accompanied by unofficial answers and study references. *Uniform CPA Examination* includes detailed instructions for candidates taking the test and lists future examination dates. An index by content specification, which enables readers to identify by number all of the questions dealing with a specific subject, is also included.

The American Institute of Certified Public Accountants publishes a cumulative subject index to topics covered in earlier exams, *Uniform CPA Examination: Selected Questions and Unofficial Answers Indexed to Content Specification Outlines.* The index is particularly useful to candidates who are weak in certain areas and would like to improve their skills by studying the questions that focus on their weaknesses. It also helps candidates to determine topics emphasized during past exams and to anticipate the direction future exams might take.

As of about 2005 the AICPA has shifted to online publishing for its exam information, preparation, review, and practice material. It can be accessed at http://www.aicpa.org/BecomeACPA/CPAExam/Pages/CPAExam.aspx (accessed April 8, 2011). The print sources have all ceased.

Whittington, O. Ray, and Patrick R. Delaney. **Wiley CPA Examination Review.** New York: John Wiley, 1983–. 4v. Annual.

In addition to the publications issued by the AICPA, several commercially published sources are available. Typical of these is the *Wiley CPA Examination Review,* an annual, four-volume work that includes study guides, suggestions for test taking, and other information in addition to the CPA questions and unofficial answers.

Gleim **CPA Examination Review.** Gainesville, FL: Gleim Publications. 1975–. Annual.

Gleim is another system, a combination of print and online material, for preparing for the CPA exam.

Libraries in which there is heavy demand for materials relating to the Uniform CPA Examination can make a good case for acquiring one or more of the commercially published sources in addition to the official AICPA publications. In libraries where the demand is not so great, however, the AICPA titles should receive first consideration.

American Institute of Certified Public Accountants (AICPA)

The American Institute of Certified Public Accountants (http://www.aicpa.org/index.htm) is the oldest and largest association of professional accountants in the United States. Governed primarily by boards and committees composed of AICPA members, it promotes and maintains high professional and ethical standards; supports research; and represents the public accounting profession to government, the business community, and the general public. As was mentioned in the preceding section, it also prepares the uniform examination given to all CPA candidates. In addition, the AICPA publishes a wide range of professional accounting materials, including the *Journal of Accountancy*, which is indexed online in full text from 1997 at http://www.journalofaccountancy.com/ (accessed April 8, 2011). Also online at the AICPA web site are various newsletters and exposure drafts from different AICPA groups and committees (http://www.aicpa.org/ PUBLICATIONS/Pages/publications.aspx) (accessed April 8, 2011).

Basic Accounting Concepts

Although it is beyond the scope of this book to delve deeply into accounting principles, practices, and procedures, three accounting concepts and their application to business reference service should be considered. These are the basic financial statements included in corporate reports, the standards followed by the accounting profession in presenting and interpreting data, and the financial ratios used to assess and compare one company with others in the same industry.

Key Financial Statements

Although corporate annual reports and the financial statements extracted from them are common to library business collections, and ready access to them from the Web is established, not all librarians and researchers are familiar or comfortable with the data they contain. This section focuses on two basic financial statements, the balance sheet and the income statement, as well as on the notes and auditor's report that accompany them.

The balance sheet is a status report that describes the financial condition of a company at a fixed point in time. It is important to remember that the data being presented reflect conditions on the specified day only:

> As a snapshot on a certain day, it can be "managed." Companies will pick the best day in their year to take the snapshot, and always remember that they have 364 days notice of that day arriving! It may well be as like the business for the rest of the year as our passport photographs represent true and fair views of us![3]

Balance sheets present 3 broad "types of things": assets, or the company's financial resources, which include cash, buildings, property, supplies, and money owed to the company; liabilities, the debts and other corporate obligations and may include such items as long- and short-term debt and income tax; and stockholders' equity, the total interest that shareholders or owners have in a corporation. It is the company's net worth, derived by subtracting liabilities from assets, and is what stockholders would earn if the company were liquidated at its balance sheet value. (See figure 8.1 for an example of a balance sheet.)

Three points about balance sheets are worth noting. First, the assets and the liabilities and equity are equal; they always balance. Balance sheets are, in fact, based upon the following equation: Assets = Liabilities + Equity or, rearranging, Assets − Liabilities = Equity. Second, most balance sheets include information for the preceding as well as the current year. Third, the notes that follow the balance sheet are an integral part of it, and should not be overlooked.

Balance Sheets ($ millions)	2008	2009
Cash & Equivalents	492.47	366.81
Receivables - Total (Net)	205.68	215.25
Inventories	18.57	17.46
Current Assets - Other	3541.66	3577.04
Current Assets - Total	**4258.38**	**4176.56**
Plant, Property & Equip (Net)	274.53	267.58
Intangibles	509.95	484.82
Other Assets	19.36	24.87
Total Assets	**5062.22**	**4953.83**
Accounts Payable	37.33	37.30
Accrued Expenses	135.06	163.21
Other Current Liabilities	3437.76	3258.10
Total Current Liabilities	**3610.15**	**3458.61**
Long Term Debt	0.00	0.00
Deferred Income Taxes	12.76	7.80
Other Liabilities	71.27	76.48
Total Liabilities	**3694.18**	**3542.89**
Common Stock	482.83	504.07
Retained Earnings (Net of Other	885.21	906.87
Common Equity (Total)	**1368.04**	**1410.94**
Liabilities and Shareholders' Equity	**5062.22**	**4953.83**

Figure 8.1. Balance sheet example

The second basic financial statement is the income statement. Also known as the earnings report or the profit and loss statement, it shows how much money a company made, or lost, during the fiscal year being reported. Where the balance sheet highlights financial conditions on a given date, the income statement reflects the entire year's activities and frequently includes data from earlier years. Taken together, the historic and current information in an income statement can be used to assess the company's progress and to make predictions about its future. As a result, investors frequently consult income statements.

The two major items included in an income statement are revenues and expenses. Revenues consist of the money received or anticipated for goods and services sold by the company. Revenues can include sales or fees for a service, or interest received. Expenses usually consist of direct expenses such as salaries for employees and costs of materials, and indirect costs such as interest paid on loans, taxes, and other costs associated with the company's business (see figure 8.2).

Income Statements ($ millions)	2008	2009
Sales (Net)	2085.75	2000.82
less Cost of Goods Sold	594.74	567.14
equals Gross Profit	**1491.01**	**1433.68**
less Selling, General & Admin Expenses	597.45	622.44
less Depreciation, Depletion & Amortization	85.77	86.45
equals Operating Income	**807.79**	**724.79**
less Interest Expense	0.00	0.00
plus Non-Operating Income less (Expenses)	6.75	4.51
equals Pretax Income	**814.54**	**729.30**
less Income Taxes	278.53	252.31
equals Net Income	**536.01**	**476.99**

Figure 8.2. Income statement example

By comparing revenues with expenses, the income statement reflects net profit or loss for the company for the year being reported. In addition, net earnings per share of common stock is usually included.

Detailed notes that clarify, qualify, and supplement data presented in the balance sheet, income statement, and other financial statements are also included in annual reports and 10-K and 10-Q filings with the Securities and Exchange Commission. The notes offer information not contained in the text and should be examined carefully. Frequently they summarize significant accounting principles followed in preparing the financial statements, provide information on corporate operations and employee benefits, and describe pending lawsuits.

Following the notes that accompany the financial statements is a brief report submitted by the public accounting firm responsible for auditing the company's financial records.

Just as physicians presented with the same set of symptoms may diagnose different ailments, so also may public accountants auditing the same financial statements reach different conclusions. For this reason, auditors' reports are presented as opinions. Usually the opinion is that the financial statements are fair, and that they have been prepared in conformity with generally accepted accounting principles. If circumstances warrant, the auditors can qualify their opinions about an exception taken or state an adverse opinion. It is rare, however, for a report to be issued with an adverse opinion. External audits, as mentioned previously, are always conducted by independent CPAs in public accounting practice and, in the case of large, blue-chip companies, are usually conducted by one of the big accounting firms.

Corporate financial statements of publicly traded companies are included in annual reports, usually available on a company's web site, and in the 10-K, 10-Q, and other filings the company makes with the SEC (http://www.sec.gov/edgar/). Data from the reports are also reproduced in many of the commercially published Internet resources mentioned in chapter 3 including *NetAdvantgage, Osiris, Compustat, and Capital IQ.* Many print resources such as the *Mergent Manuals* also reproduce financial statement data for publicly traded companies.

As a result, familiarity with basic terms, concepts, and applications can be extremely helpful to librarians in understanding requests for assistance and in providing information to business researchers. One way to gain such familiarity is by studying tutorials provided by the Small Business Association for people starting a business (http://

www.sba.gov/content/online-courses-financing-your-business). The tutorials describe all aspects of starting a small business, including an "Introduction to Accounting" that covers the basics of accounting, including balance sheets and income statements, and explains their constituent parts and provides examples (see figure 8.3). Although it is designed for the small business operator, it is easy to understand and covers all the basic questions.

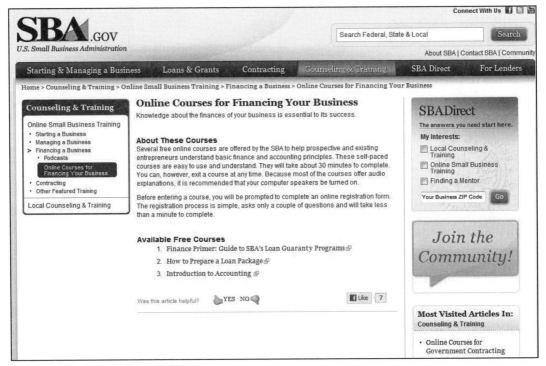

Figure 8.3. Description of three online tutorials from the SBA on financing your business, http://www.sba.gov/content/online-courses-financing-your-business

Another helpful online service, again directed to the small business owner, is the Toolkit provided by Commerce Clearing House at http://www.toolkit.cch.com/. The section "Managing Your Business Finance" (http://www.toolkit.cch.com/text/P06_0100 .asp) provides not only explanations but also Excel templates, which are useful for both business owners and students.

The Internet is full of free and for a fee material for help with understanding financial reports. Just do a search using the phrase "How to read a financial report." Also most libraries will have books on understanding financial statements, such as the Wiley publication *How to Read a Financial Report* or accounting handbooks and textbooks.

Accounting Principles and Standards

Accounting principles are human creations. They are not, writes Stephen Moscove, "like the immutable laws of nature found in physics and chemistry,"[4] but are instead rules developed by the accounting profession to serve the needs of the business community, investors, and government. Also known as *standards*, accounting principles are fundamental guidelines that help to determine whether specific choices of ways to record accounting information are acceptable. Their purpose is to ensure that the financial statements prepared by accountants are relevant, reliable, and comparable.

Accountants use the phrase *generally accepted accounting principles*, or GAAP, to refer to the body of conventions, rules, and procedures that define accounting practices at a particular time. Thus, an auditor's assurance that the financial statements examined present information fairly and in accordance with generally accepted accounting principles means that the financial accounting procedures followed reflect the consensus of accountants and officials regarding proper accounting practices at the time the report was prepared.

The inculcation of the principles and any changes to them is greatly influenced by government agencies; professional organizations in accounting and related fields; and academicians, securities analysts, bankers, other professionals, and major corporations.

Although many organizations have affected the formulation of accounting principles, the most important today are the Securities and Exchange Commission and the Financial Accounting Standards Board.

In 1934 the Securities and Exchange Commission (SEC) (http://www.sec.gov/) was established by Congress to regulate the nation's securities markets and to ensure that investors have adequate information on which to base their investment decisions. Among other things, Congress empowered the SEC to establish the accounting principles to be followed by publicly traded companies in reporting their financial condition. Although the SEC has chosen to delegate much of that responsibility to professional accounting organizations such as the Financial Accounting Standards Board, its role in helping to set and enforce those principles should not be underestimated.

Although the Securities and Exchange Commission has statutory authority to establish standards of financial accounting and reporting, it is the Financial Accounting Standards Board (FASB) (http://www.fasb.org) that is primarily responsible for setting generally accepted accounting principles for financial reporting. Established in 1973, the FASB consists of a substantial research staff and seven full-time board members appointed by the Financial Accounting Foundation. Like the foundation, the Financial Accounting Standards Board is independent of all other business and professional organizations. Its standards are recognized as authoritative and official by the SEC, the AICPA, and other organizations.

The FASB issues several types of accounting pronouncements. As of July 1, 2009 changes to U.S. GAAP, *FASB Accounting Standards Codification*®, are communicated through a publication called *Accounting Standards Update*. Prior to July 1, 2009, Statements of Financial Accounting Standards (SFAS) were authoritative statements that spelled out current accounting standards. One hundred sixty-eight SFAS were issued, each dealing with a specific accounting topic. SFAS 45, for example, dealt with accounting for franchise fee revenue, and SFAS 142 with goodwill and other intangible assets. A listing and summary of all statements can be found at http://www.fasb.org/st/.

In addition, the FASB issues *Concept Statements*, publications that describe ideas and concepts that will guide the development of future accounting standards and that may provide the groundwork for a philosophical framework for financial accounting and reporting.

Finally, as their name implies, Interpretations of Statements of Financial Accounting Standards explain, clarify, and sometimes amend previously issued statements of standards and reports in Accounting Research Bulletins and Opinions.

In addition, the FASB publishes Exposure Drafts, Discussion Memoranda, and special research reports. All can be purchased separately from the FASB or acquired through subscription plans. The FASB web page (http://www.fasb.org) provides summaries of much of the material and full-text downloads of Exposure Drafts and Bulletins.

Prior to the creation of the FASB in 1973, the AICPA (http://www.aicpa.org) was responsible for the promulgation of generally accepted accounting principles. From 1939 to 1959, the AICPA issued over 50 Accounting Research Bulletins (ARBs) and Accounting Terminology Bulletins through its Committee on Accounting Procedures. In 1960, the institute established the Accounting Principles Board (APB) to issue authoritative opinions and to publish research studies. Before its dissolution in 1973, the APB issued 31 Opinions, which were later adopted by the FASB as part of generally accepted accounting principles.

A wide range of publications is available to keep accountants apprised of FASB and AICPA official pronouncements. Some of the most widely used are listed and discussed below.

FASB. **Financial Accounting Research System (FARS).** Norwalk, CT: Financial Accounting Standards Board, 1996–. CD-ROM. Updates approximately 6 times a year.

FARS includes FASB and AICPA Pronouncements, FASB Statements, Interpretations, Technical Bulletins, and Concepts Statements; APB Opinions and Statements; and AICPA Accounting Interpretations and Terminology Bulletins. Also included is an abstract for each issue discussed by the FASB's Emerging Issues Task Force since its inception in 1984 and questions and answers from FASB Special Reports. The issuing of the CD made it easy for even the smallest library to now own a complete set of Standards for what is a very reasonable price. For full information on prices and subscriptions, check the web page at http://www.fasb.org.

Williams, Jan R. **GAAP Guide**. Chicago: CCH, 1974–. Annual. Also available on CD and several different online systems

The *GAAP Guide* has had many different names over its lifetime, including *Miller GAAP Guide, Miller Comprehensive GAAP Guide*, and others. It presents generally accepted accounting principles in current use. The *GAAP Guide* has been rewritten to minimize jargon and increase comprehension by using what its authors describe as "plain, understandable English."

Auditing Standards

Another acronym common to accounting is GAAS, or generally accepted auditing standards. While GAAP refers to rules and conventions followed in presenting financial information, GAAS refers to the rules followed by public accountants in auditing clients' financial records. Generally accepted auditing standards are developed by the Auditing Standards Board of the AICPA, the senior technical body of the institute, responsible for issuing pronouncements on auditing matters. All CPAs are required to follow the rules and procedures set forth by the Auditing Standards Board. Just as an auditor's report verifies that GAAP have been followed, so also does it indicate that the auditor preparing the report has followed GAAS when reviewing the statements for accuracy. Both GAAS and GAAP are important. The auditor's statement that a financial report has been examined in accordance with GAAS and has been found to conform to GAAP is, as one writer notes, "about as nice a compliment as you can pay a financial statement."[5] Publications dealing with auditing standards are abundant. Some that are widely used are listed below.

AICPA Professional Standards. Chicago: Commerce Clearing House, 1974–. Online subscription or 2v. Loose-leaf. Updated annually, or as paperback book.

U.S. Auditing Standards are in the first volume of *AICPA Professional Standards* and deal with auditing standards and guidelines. It includes Statements on Auditing Standards issued by the Auditing Standards Board, covering such subjects as the training and proficiency of independent auditors, adherence to principles, and the circumstances under which auditors may issue adverse opinions. A topical index and appendixes are also included.

GAAS Guide. Chicago: CCH, 1982–. Annual.

Like its *GAAP* counterpart, *GAAS Guide* has changed its title several times over the years. The most recent change occurred in 2007 when the title changed from *Miller GAAS Guide* to just *GAAS Guide*. *GAAS Guide* restates auditing standards in basic, jargon-free English. Arranged to correspond to the types of auditing or accounting services that CPAs provide to their clients, the annual paperback offers an inexpensive alternative to the more comprehensive and up-to-date service published by Commerce Clearing House.

International Accounting and Auditing

As the world's economies become increasingly more interconnected and dependent on each other, so too has the need for accounting and auditing standards to work well together. One international counterpart to the FASB is the IFRS Foundation (http://www.ifrs.org/) and its standards-setting body, the IASB (International Accounting Standards Board). IFRS and the IASB like the FASB produce many publications that detail various accounting standards for their areas of concern. Some of the material is available for free; other material requires a subscription. See the organization's web site (http://www.ifrs.org/IFRSs/IFRS.htm) for more details. Two commercial publications that are useful for help in understanding international accounting are:

Epstein, Barry J., and Abbas Ali Mirza. **Wiley IFRS: Interpretation and Application of International Accounting and Financial Reporting Standards.** Hoboken, NJ: J. Wiley & Sons, 2005–. Annual.

With the globalization of markets, a solid understanding of the accounting practices of other countries is needed, and this is supplied by the *Wiley IFRS: Interpretation and Application of International Accounting and Financial Reporting Standards.* In 2005, International Accounting Standards (http://www.iasb.org.uk/cmt/0001.asp) were enforced by the European Union, and already many other developing and emerging countries are adopting them. The *IAS Interpretation and Application* is a quick guide to all the standards issued and revised and includes examples and explanations.

Ordelheide, Dieter, and KPMG, eds. **Transnational Accounting (TRANSACC).** 2nd ed. New York: Palgrave, 2001. 3v. + supplement.

TRANSACC analyzes and describes what are regarded as the most important regulatory systems of accounting and financial reporting in the world. For each country covered, the information provided includes forms of business organization, general principles, special accounting areas, auditing and financial reporting areas, and national databases. This book is intended as a working tool for practitioners, academics, and students to compare accounting practices country by country.

In 2002 the IASB and FASB devised a Memorandum of Understanding on working together to close the differences in their two standards. As of April 2011 the boards issued a report detailing their progress and announced they expect to complete their convergence work in the second half of 2011.

Sources of Accounting Information

The literature of accounting is voluminous. It includes numerous handbooks, loose-leaf services, periodicals, documents, and online sources, some written for accounting practitioners and others for nonaccountants. This section considers many of the types of accounting information sources generally consulted and lists and describes representative publications in each category. Readers should, however, keep in mind that the literature of accounting reflects continuing and continuous changes. As accounting theories, practices, and principles change, so also do many accounting sources.

Guides and Dictionaries

For librarians and researchers confronted for the first time with an accounting research problem, one of the best ways to gain familiarity with the literature is by referring to guides and bibliographies.

Accounting Info.com. http://accountinginfo.com/

A concise, easy to use and navigate web page with links to sources of accounting standards and study guides for accounting topics, including, accounting for inventories, depreciation methods, present value and future value, accrual basis account, and more. There are also links to basic explanations of "intermediate" and "advanced" accounting topics.

The accounting profession has its own vocabulary and conventions. It includes many unique words and, in addition, uses familiar words in unique ways. As a result, most business reference collections supplement standard business dictionaries with specialized accounting sources. There are many different dictionaries available; some are more encyclopedic in scope and are usually available in academic libraries, and now there are also some available via the Web that may satisfy the needs of some researchers.

Clubb, Colin, ed. **Blackwell Encyclopedic Dictionary of Accounting.** 2nd ed. Oxford: Blackwell, 2006. 320p.

The *Blackwell Encyclopedic Dictionary* includes both definitions and explanations of major accounting terms. More than 100 contributors have compiled authoritative and comprehensive entries for terms ranging from "accounting for defeasance" to "warrants," many of which also include extensive bibliographies. The volume is extensively indexed and cross-referenced. This volume belongs in all libraries that support an accounting program.

Siegel, Joel G., and Jae K. Shim. **Dictionary of Accounting Terms.** 5th ed. Hauppauge, NY: Barron's Educational Series, 2010. 523p.

Less comprehensive in the length of its entries but also possibly less intimidating to casual users, the *Dictionary of Accounting Terms* offers clear and concise definitions of 2,500 accounting terms and concepts, both those regarded as standard and new expressions. In addition, if examples are required for clarity, they are included. The *Dictionary* provides cross-references when appropriate and a list of acronyms and abbreviations in the appendix. This is another dictionary that should be in all libraries.

Investorwords.com. **AccountingWords.** n.d. http://www.investorwords.com/cgi-bin/bysubject.cgi?1 (accessed April 10, 2011)

Investorwords began with an initial dictionary for investors but has since developed smaller web compilations by subject. For those needing to occasionally check words, *AccountingWords* is a handy, free tool. The company provides site licensing for a small fee.

AICPA. **Glossary of Terms, Acronyms and Abbreviations**. n.d. http://www.aicpa.org/ Press/DownloadableDocuments/Acronyms_and_Abbreviations.pdf (accessed April 10, 2011)

Although the *Glossary of Terms, Acronyms and Abbreviations* contains many terms internal to the organization, other more general terms are also included.

Handbooks and Encyclopedias

When more information is required than can be found in dictionaries, researchers frequently turn to handbooks and encyclopedias. Several such publications are available. Some deal with specialized fields of accounting and others are more general. Some are written for accountants, and some for managers, small business people, and others lacking accounting expertise.

Tracy, John A. **Accounting for Dummies.** 4th. ed. Hoboken, NJ: Wiley Pub, 2008. 382p.

Understanding basic accounting concepts, applications, and vocabulary greatly enhances the ability of managers and businesspeople to communicate with accountants and to assess corporate strength. *Accounting for Dummies* is not written for those who want to practice accounting but is an excellent aid for those who want to read and understand financial and accounting reports. Concepts are made easier to understand because of the many examples, templates, and worksheets.

Bragg, Steven M. **Accounting Reference Desktop.** New York: John Wiley, 2002. 615p.

Plank, Lois R. **Accounting Desk Book.** 19th ed. Chicago: CCH Inc., 2010. Various paging + CD-ROMs.

Handbooks for the professional accountant are equally abundant. Generally they come in two sizes: desk books, intended for quick reference, and detailed, comprehensive sources that are often published in more than one volume. The *Accounting Desk Book* and the *Accounting Reference Desktop*, for example, are two such ready reference sources, each highlighting topics of wide interest and appeal.

Coverage in these handbooks varies, but each treats in depth the theory and practice of accounting and their application to business problems and includes references to major accounting pronouncements, including those of the AICPA and FASB.

More specialized handbooks and encyclopedias are also available. Some deal with accounting practices as they relate to specific industries; others reproduce accounting forms, letters, and reports; and still others present mathematical tables and formulas. Two volumes available in most libraries are described below.

Plank, Tom M., and Lois R. Plank. **Encyclopedia of Accounting Systems.** 2nd ed. Englewood Cliffs, NJ: Prentice-Hall, 1994. 2v.

The *Encyclopedia of Accounting Systems* examines accounting practices and systems as they relate to specific industries, businesses, professions, and nonprofit organizations. Each chapter covers a separate industry and includes a general overview of the industry as well as a description of the basic design of the accounting system, data processing procedures, cost and payroll systems, plant and equipment records, and many other special features relating to the industry. The chapter on construction contractors, for example, includes a section on the functional peculiarities of the business, a chart of accounts for general contractors, and an example of a "percentage-of-completion" financial table. The *Encyclopedia* covers a wide assortment of industries and professions, ranging from aquaculture and funeral directing to scuba diving stores and real estate. It is one of the most comprehensive compilations of industry-specific accounting systems and is widely used.

Lipkin, Lawrence, Irwin K. Feinstein, and Lucille Derrick. **Accountant's Handbook of Formulas and Tables.** 3rd ed. Englewood Cliffs, NJ: Prentice-Hall, 1988. 627p.

Accountants are frequently required to draw upon tables, formulas, and computations in performing their work. Most accountants and financial managers will use computer programs for mathematical problems and calculations, but the *Accountant's Handbook of Formulas and Tables* is still useful for those who need to check on a formula before performing a calculation or incorporating it into a computer program. The *Handbook* includes examples for many formulae and presents data on many topics in 17 different tables, including present value, square roots and reciprocals, sample size, and random decimal digits. Although the book is now out of print, it is held by many libraries and is still a worthwhile item in collections.

Directories

Finding an accountant or a CPA firm is much easier now than even a few years ago. A simple web search ("cpa firms" and insert location here) using Google, Bing, or your other web search engine will often produce a good list. However, if you want something more comprehensive, try using one of the resources mentioned in chapter 2 or chapter 3. The ReferenceUSA U.S. Business database, for example, can be searched by SIC 8721 or NAICS 541211 code, then limited by geography as desired. Another source is Orbis; once again search by SIC or NAICS code, then limit geographically as desired.

Who Audits America. Menlo Park, CA: Data Financial Press, 1976–. Semiannual.

Who Audits America is a directory of publicly traded companies and the accounting firms that audit them. The first part of the directory focuses on the companies being audited. In addition to standard directory information, it provides the company's ticker symbol, the industry code for the primary product or service being sold, number of employees, corporate assets and sales, and the name of the accounting firm performing the audit for the period being covered. In addition, this section lists companies that have merged, been acquired, or changed their names since the last edition was published. The second part of *Who Audits America* focuses on auditors. It is arranged in several different parts, including a ranked listing of auditors by total sales of audited companies.

Periodical Indexes and Abstracts

Major accounting periodicals are either indexed or available full text in such standard business sources as *ABI/INFORM Global* and *Business Source Elite*. One specialized index, held in most major business reference collections, is also available.

ProQuest Accounting & Tax Index. Ann Arbor, MI: ProQuest, 1905–. http://www.proquest.com

Coverage consists of 2,300 accounting and tax publications, including government documents, published proceedings, dissertations, working papers from Social Science Research Network (SSRN), and official releases from the AICPA and FASB, as well as periodical articles. Fields covered include accounting, auditing, data processing, financial reporting, financial management, investment, and taxation. This database began life in 1921 when the AICPA Library published the *Accountants' Index*, an author, title, and subject index to English-language books and periodicals received by the library since

1912. Following publication of the original volume, supplements were issued every two or three years until 1971, when it became an annual. In 1992 this title was superseded by the print title *Accounting & Tax Index*, which was issued quarterly, with the fourth issue being the annual cumulation. In 1991 the electronic version was introduced as an alternative to the print titles.

Periodicals

The importance and pervasiveness of accounting in almost every facet of business is reflected in articles appearing in general business periodicals and newspapers. Accounting is also well represented by specialized periodicals, which are particularly valuable for their presentation of current accounting theory and practice.

Journal of Accountancy. New York: American Institute of Certified Public Accountants, 1905–. Monthly.

The official journal of the American Institute of Certified Public Accountants, the *Journal of Accountancy* serves as the principal medium for the exchange of information and ideas by and for accounting practitioners. It includes articles on accounting, auditing, management advisory services, taxation, and related fields. Regular features include columns on computer applications, recent tax developments, and government and professional news. In addition, the *Journal* prints the complete texts of official pronouncements issued by the AICPA and the Financial Accounting Standards Board. Although the *Journal* is included in most business and some general periodical indexes frequently with the full text of the articles, it is also available from 1997 onward at the web site, http://www.aicpa.org/pubs/index.htm. It is arranged by month and by year and is searchable in separate author and subject indexes at the site.

Other AICPA magazines and newsletters freely available from http://www.aicpa.org/pubs/index.htm are *The CPA Letter*, *CPA Exam Alert*, *In Our Opinion*, *The Practicing CPA*, *The Tax Advisor*, and recent accounting and auditing standards.

The Accounting Review [Sarasota, FL, etc.]. American Accounting Association. 1926–. Bimonthly.

One of the premier journals for reporting, explaining, and illustrating the results of accounting research. The intended audience is accounting academicians, graduate students in accounting, and others interested in accounting research. Manuscripts accepted for publication and articles that appeared in the journal from 1999 to date can be purchased individually on the journal's web site (http://aaapubs.aip.org/accr/).

Review of Accounting Studies. Norwell, MA: Springer, 1996–. Quarterly.

Another scholarly journal with articles on theoretical, empirical, and experimental aspects of accounting. Manuscripts accepted for publication and articles that appeared in the journal from 1996 to the present can be read online with a subscription or purchased from the journal's web page, http://www.springer.com/business+%26+management/accounting/journal/11142.

Journal of Accounting Research. Accounting Research Center U. of Chicago, 1963–. Quarterly + special Conference issue

The *JAR* publishes articles using analytical, empirical, experimental, and/or field study methods to explore any area of accounting research. Articles are available online with a subscription. For more information and subscription information, go to http://www.blackwellpublishing.com/journal.asp?ref=0021-8456.

Journal of Accounting & Economics. Elsevier. 1979–. Bimonthly.

JAE publishes articles that use economic theory to explain accounting phenomena and provides a forum for discussion of these issues. Topics such as the role of accounting within the firm, accounting's role in the capital markets, evolution of accounting standards, government regulation of corporate disclosure requirements, and other topics. More information on subscriptions can be found on Elsevier's web page, http://www.elsevier.com/locate/jae.

Loose-Leaf and Electronic Services

Frequent changes in accounting practices, which in turn reflect changes in laws, regulations, and professional standards, make this a field in which loose-leaf services are still abundant despite the proliferation of online services. Some deal exclusively with accounting standards and principles; key examples have already been discussed in the sections on generally accepted accounting principles and auditing standards. Others on taxation will be discussed later in this chapter. Many of the well-known online services, such as Commerce Clearing House (CCH) (http://www.cch.com), RIA (http://www.riahome.com/), and BNA (http://www.bna.com), provide both print and online products and services. It is impossible to mention more than a few of the products available, so for further information on the hundreds of products published it will be necessary for the researcher or librarian to check the product catalogs available at the company web pages.

SEC Accounting Rules. Chicago: Commerce Clearing House, 1968–. Loose-leaf, CD-ROM, and online.

Although the Securities and Exchange Commission has delegated much of its responsibility for setting the standards for financial reporting and accounting, it nonetheless remains active in this sphere, issuing several series that affect financial accounting practice. Some of its most important publications are those from the Division of Corporate Finance and the Staff Accounting Bulletins, all of which are included in the *Accounting Rules,* which continuously updates all SEC rulings. This product is also available as a CD-ROM or via the Internet.

CCH publishes many other services, aimed primarily at smaller accounting firms and individual practitioners, presenting practical information and advice and offering really the loose-leaf equivalents of handbooks.

Guide to Managing an Accounting Practice. Fort Worth, TX: Practitioners Publishing Company, 1975–. 3v. Loose-leaf, CD-ROM, and online.

The *Guide to Managing an Accounting Practice* is a three-volume loose-leaf service that provides practical guidance and articles on developing an accounting practice and on administration, personnel, keeping pace with technology, and management data. It includes forms, sample letters, worksheets, and other illustrations and, in addition, presents financial ratios, balance sheets, and financial statements about accounting firms of various sizes, so that performance and profitability can be evaluated. Practitioners Publishing Company (http://www.ppcnet.com/eCatalog) also produces more specialized guides for accountants, including *Preparing Financial Statements*, *Real Estate Taxation*, and *Estate and Trust Consultant.* All products are available in loose-leaf, on CD-ROM, or as a web service.

Technical Practice Aids. New York: American Institute of Certified Public Accountants, 1998–. 2v. Loose-leaf and online.

AICPA Technical Practice Aids, published by Commerce Clearing House for the AICPA, provides practical guidance for dealing with specific accounting and auditing problems in conformity with current standards and procedures. It covers financial statement presentation, assets, liabilities and deferred credits, capital, revenue and expense, audit fieldwork, auditors' reports, and specialized industry and organizational problems. The second volume includes Statements of Positions issued by both the AICPA Accounting and Auditing Standards Divisions and Lists of Issues Papers published by the AICPA Accounting Standards Division.

Behrenfeld, William, and Andrew R. Biebl. **Accountant's Business Manual.** New York: American Institute of Certified Public Accountants, 1987–. Loose-leaf and online.

The *Accountant's Business Manual* focuses on an array of general business, legal, and financial topics relevant to accounting practice rather than on accounting and auditing per se. Topics covered include individual and corporate tax changes, obtaining financing, investment vehicles, insurance, employment regulations, cash management, business plans, unemployment insurance, and human resources. With the manual comes a CD-ROM that contains worksheets, sample agreements, checklists, and other forms that can be tailored to fit the user's needs.

AICPA Online Professional Library. New York: American Institute of Certified Public Accountants, 199?–. Internet.

AICPA Online Professional Library contains AICPA's professional standards, technical practice aids, financial reporting trends, and standard-setting guidance. The titles included are *AICPA Professional Standards*, *AICPA Technical Practice Aids*, *Accounting Trends & Techniques*, all current AICPA Audit and Accounting Guides, and all current Audit Risk Alerts. The database is updated monthly. For information on pricing, check http://www.cpa2biz.com/, the online store for the AICPA. This resource was previously known as *AICPA reSOURCE ONLINE*,

BNA Tax Management. Washington, DC: Bureau of National Affairs, 1990s–. Internet.

BNA Tax Management covers U.S. income, estate, gifts and trusts, state, and foreign taxation. The service is divided into two libraries; the first covering foreign and U.S. and the second states. As with all the accounting resources online, content in *BNA* can be customized, and the areas for which there is no subscription paid appear in a lighter color. Subscription areas available in this service are *Portfolios Plus,* which provides practice tools and analysis for U.S. income, estate, gifts and trusts, and foreign income and journals and special reports; *Tax Practice,* which includes practice tools, analysis, and client letters for every area of taxation; and *State Tax,* which includes analysis, handbooks, legislation and regulation summaries, journals, and special reports for all U.S. state jurisdictions. Information on other products and prices is available at http://www.bna .com/. Some BNA material is also available through RIA Checkpoint (see below).

CCH Incorporated. **CCH Internet Tax Research Network.** Chicago: CCH, 1990s–. Internet.

CCH Internet Tax Research Network provides access to all of CCH's federal, state, and global products, which can be bought in modules and added on as the need arises or as money becomes available. As with all the online products guides, news, journals, and reporters are included, and all are searchable individually or as a group. Entries within search results are cross-linked, with the same symbol used in the loose-leaf files, and navigating within the service is relatively easy. Tax information is available, by year, from 1978 onward. Pricing and contact information is at http://www.cch.com. CCH is now owned by Wolters Kluwer.

RIA Group. **RIA Checkpoint.** New York: RIA, 1990s–. Internet.

RIA Checkpoint is a database of U.S. accounting and auditing material and U.S. federal, state, and global tax information. It contains primary federal tax resources such as the *Internal Revenue Code* and also a number of RIA full-text publications such as the *Federal Tax Coordinator 2d* and the *RIA Federal Tax Handbook*. It also includes Warren, Gorham, and Lamont financial reporting and management resources such as the *Handbook of SEC Accounting and Disclosure* and several BNA products. More information is available at http://www.riahome.com/.

Accounting is a discipline in which regular updates of materials are essential, and this has resulted in the proliferation first of loose-leaf products, and since the early 1990s, of CD-ROM and Internet-accessible products. The accountant is now provided with much more timely information in the form that it is needed. The growth of international accounting has also increased the demand for quickly available information.

It is impossible in a short description to include all the features of any database, and this is especially true of the collections summarized above. The web pages of each describe the wealth of materials included in each service and also give details about different subscription packages.

Most academic libraries that support an accounting degree program will subscribe to at least one of these services, but because of licensing agreements they may not be available to the public. For this reason some libraries may continue their subscriptions to some loose-leaf services.

Government Documents

Federal documents on accounting generally fall into three broad categories: "how to" booklets and pamphlets for small business people and non-accountants, procedural manuals for the audit of private government contractors, and studies and audits of government agencies themselves.

As we saw earlier in this chapter, one of the most prolific publishers of accounting aids for non-accountants is the Small Business Administration.

Companies doing business with the Department of Defense may be interested in publications issued by the Defense Contract Audit Agency, or DCAA.

U.S. Defense Contract Audit Agency. **DCAA Contract Audit Manual.** Washington, DC: Government Printing Office, 19uu–. Loose-leaf.

Established in 1965, the Defense Contract Audit Agency (http://www.dcaa.mil/) has the right to audit the books and records of any private contractor having a negotiated contract with the Department of Defense. Its *DCAA Contract Audit Manual* prescribes auditing policies and procedures and presents guidelines and techniques for DCAA personnel. Although the *Manual* is far too specialized for most library collections, librarians and researchers should be aware that such a publication exists and is available in most regional depository libraries and that some sections are available at the DCAA web site.

The General Accountability Office (http://www.gao.gov/), an agency of the legislative branch, is responsible for investigating and carrying out legal, accounting, auditing, and cost settlement functions of government programs and operations as assigned by Congress. Each year, it issues hundreds of reports and other publications that describe its findings. All publications issued since 1971 are available with some availability back as far as 1922 at the GAO web page (http://www.gao.gov/). GAO publications are also included in the *Catalog of United States Government Publications*.

Tax Basics

It probably could go without saying, but librarians should no more give tax advice (tell the seeker what the tax law or regulation means) than they would advice on any other legal or medical issue. However, librarians in almost every setting are called upon to provide information concerning taxation. This may range from supplying current federal and state income tax forms to stocking and providing access to, and assistance in the use of, loose-leaf or online services that present and analyze the most recent tax laws, rulings, regulations, and coexistence or amount of sales tax levied in another city or town. Whatever the nature of such requests for assistance, the librarian's ability to understand and communicate with researchers about them will be enhanced by an understanding of the tax system and some of the key tax reference resources. This section briefly describes major types of taxes collected in this country, the government agencies responsible, and some of the tax sources most frequently consulted by laypeople and tax professionals.

Governments levy taxes to promote certain economic and social objectives such as economic growth and full employment, to finance their operations, and to provide such public goods and services as education, a system of national defense, and a network of roads and highways. In the United States, taxes are imposed by state and local governments as well as by the federal government. As a result, there is considerable variety in the tax structures and tax rates levied in different places by different levels of government.

Kinds of Taxes

The following is a very simplified discussion of the different kinds or types of taxes. Taxes can be collected by one or more levels of government: federal, state, and municipal. And there several types of taxes that can be levied, including excise, sales, income, property, and more.

Excise taxes are directly imposed on the sale of a good. An excise tax is a fee that is levied regardless of the taxpayer's financial status or ability to pay. For example, everyone in the same tax district who buys a gallon of gasoline, a quart of whiskey, or a pack of cigarettes can expect to pay the same tax regardless of the price he or she paid for the item or because of his or her income level.

A sales or use tax is also charged on the sale of a good, but instead of a flat charge it is based on some percentage of the price of a good. At the present time the U.S. federal government does not charge a sales tax. Sales taxes can vary widely from state to state and in some cases municipality to municipality.

Property taxes are imposed on the basis of the value of certain property, whether it is real estate or personal property. Again at the present time the U.S. federal government does not charge a property tax. Property taxes can vary widely from state to state and in some cases municipality to municipality.

And nearly everyone knows individual or corporate income taxes are based on the annual income on the person or entity being taxed. Income tax rates are the same for all people of the same income level at the federal but vary widely at the state and municipal levels.

As mentioned earlier, the tax structures for state and local governments vary considerably. Some states tax personal income; others do not. Most depend on excise and sales taxes, but while one state may tax only luxury items, others will tax food and prescription drugs as well. Local governments impose different tax measures but usually draw upon revenues raised from taxing real and personal property. Although the federal government imposes gift, estate, and certain processing taxes, it's most productive sources of revenue are personal income and corporate taxes, both of which are collected by the Internal Revenue Service.

Internal Revenue Service

The Internal Revenue Service (IRS) (http://www.irs.gov), a bureau of the U.S. Treasury Department, is responsible for administering and enforcing federal tax laws and related statutes. Its activities include the determination, assessment, and collection of taxes; determination of pension plan qualifications and exempt organization status; and the issuance of rulings and regulations. In addition, it handles taxpayer complaints and provides taxpayer service and education. The IRS's service and education roles are particularly important to libraries, which may regularly acquire IRS forms and documents for their users and may occasionally refer them to regional and district offices for more specialized assistance.

The IRS issues all their forms via the Web at http://www.irs.gov/formspubs/index .html. Those forms marked "info copy only" are exclusively available directly from the IRS. Also accessible at this site are forms to download and use on personal computers and an easy-to-use help section for locating the correct forms (see figure 8.4).

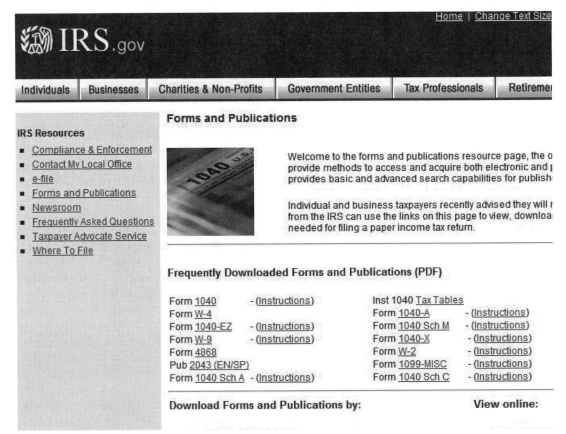

Figure 8.4. List of downloadable forms and other publications from the IRS, at http://www.irs. gov/formspubs/index.html

In addition, the IRS publishes the following annual document that offers access to even more forms.

U.S. Department of the Treasury. Internal Revenue Service. **Reproducible Federal Tax Forms for Use in Libraries.** Washington, DC: Government Printing Office, 1980–. IRS Publication 1132. Annual.

Reproducible Federal Tax Forms is a compilation of forms and accompanying instructions for libraries to lend to their users for photocopying. It includes different forms, or parts of forms, ranging from Form 1040EZ for single filers with no dependents to Form 9465 "Installment Agreement Request." Arrangement is by form number, with subject and title indexes. Certain specially printed forms are not included but may be ordered from the IRS forms distribution centers listed on the inside back cover of the volume.

Librarians would be well advised to retain superseded editions of *Reproducible Federal Tax Forms* as volumes for earlier years provide quick and convenient access to information and forms that might otherwise be difficult to find and are especially popular with patrons who need to file amended tax returns for previous years. These forms are also available from 1992 forward at the web site. In addition to forms, the Internal Revenue Service publishes manuals, regulations, statistics, and decisions, some of which are discussed later.

The IRS offers free consultation by telephone regarding tax questions and problems. Telephone lines are often busy, however, particularly during the height of the tax preparing season, and callers are advised to be patient and persevere.

Other Federal Government Agencies

Although the IRS is responsible for most of the federal taxes collected, another Treasury Department agency, the Alcohol and Tobacco Trade Bureau (http://www.ttb.gov/), is responsible for collecting revenues from the alcohol and tobacco industries.

Federal Tax Law and Administration

Taxes imposed in this country's early history were limited primarily to excise taxes, which were repealed whenever the government had enough money to meet its rather limited needs. During the Civil War, income as well as excise taxes were levied, but it was not until the early 20th century that income tax became a permanent part of our lives. In 1909, Congress passed the Sixteenth Amendment to the Constitution, permitting the imposition of federal income tax. In 1913, after ratification by three-fourths of the states, it became law.

All three branches of the federal government are actively involved in the enactment and administration of tax law. The Joint Committee on Taxation is composed of 5 members of the House Ways and Means Committee and members of the Senate Finance Committee, who are responsible for gathering information and holding hearings, which may eventually be reported to Congress and culminate in the passing of new or amended tax legislation. Federal tax laws are referred to collectively as the Internal Revenue Code, or Tax Code.

The Treasury Department, of the executive branch, is responsible for administering the Tax Code. It issues interpretations of the Tax Code, called Treasury Regulations, which are available in many regional depository and law libraries and through RIA Checkpoint, CCH, and other services.

The Internal Revenue Service, in addition to collecting taxes, enforcing tax law, and issuing rulings in response to requests for guidance, writes Treasury Regulations and negotiates disputes with taxpayers.

In the event that disputes between taxpayers and the IRS are not successfully negotiated, they can be taken to court. The Tax Court, federal district courts, and the Claims Court are empowered to hear cases involving the interpretation of tax law and its application in specific situations. Appeals are directed to U.S. Circuit Courts and to the U.S. Supreme Court.

The activities of these agencies of the federal government are important, because each is involved in amending or interpreting tax law. As amendments, rulings, regulations, interpretations, and court decisions are issued, they become part of the body of tax law and are in turn succeeded by rulings, regulations, interpretations, and court decisions pertaining to them. Such issuances are of vital concern to accountants, lawyers, and other tax professionals, who generally use either loose-leaf or electronic services to keep informed.

U.S. State Governments

In addition to federal agencies, each state has a department of taxation or revenue responsible for administering major taxes, including individual and corporate income taxes, and estate, sales, and other excise taxes. The names of state agencies, their tax rates, and the revenues they collect are included in several different sources, but one of the most convenient and readily accessible is *The Book of the States*. Even more detailed information is available in the *Multistate Corporate Tax Almanac*.

Council of State Governments. **The Book of the States.** Lexington, KY: The Council, 1935–. Annual. Also online at http://www.csg.org/

In addition to chapters on state constitutions, branches of government, elections, management, personnel, and administration, *The Book of the States* includes one on state finances. It provides an overview of the states' budget procedures, their revenue sources, expenditures, and debts. It also includes a summary of recent trends in state taxation; lists agencies responsible for administering different kinds of state taxes; and presents tables showing by state excise tax rates, sales tax exemptions, and rates and exemptions on individual and corporate income tax returns. A short descriptive segment follows several sections, including that listing state amnesty programs.

Multistate Corporate Tax Guide. New York: Aspen Publishers, 1990–. Annual.

The *Multistate Corporate Tax Guide* uses charts to compare different aspects of corporate taxation on a state-by-state basis, including such topics as S Corporations, Partnerships, Limited Liability Companies, and Limited Partnerships. In addition to charts, each section includes an analysis and description of trends. The *Guide* also features income, sales, and use taxation from the top state officials who interpret and apply the rules. This publication also includes a summary of key legislative and regulatory changes within states and charts that serve as a quick lookup service for questions on corporate taxation. This publication is also available on CD-ROM and via the Internet.

Just as taxes collected vary from one state to another, so also do services provided by state departments of revenue and taxation. At a minimum, however, most states compile and publish pertinent statistics and, like the IRS, will make multiple copies of tax forms and instructions available to libraries as well.

AccountantsWorld, LLC. **TAXSites.com.** 1995–. http://www.taxsites.com/ (accessed May 5, 2011)

TAXSites.com is a superior listing of web sites, with substantive information, in both accounting and taxation. The links range from the international to the local level. One can learn what the European Union means by "Value Added Tax" or which tax forms must be submitted to the state of North Carolina. Extremely valuable to every user is the link to all states and then within the state to all the agencies involved with taxation. Any librarian or user with access to the Internet can now access copies of tax forms from any state and also discover the filing regulations. *TAXSites.com* also links to local and municipal sites where available.

The taxes collected by county, municipal, township, and special district governments vary so much that it is difficult to generalize about them. Some information is contained in the Census Bureau's *Census of Governments*, which includes data on taxable property values and tax assessment and on the finances of school districts, special districts, county governments, and municipal and township governments. The Census Bureau also publishes some surveys of state and local finance. All publications of the *Census of Governments* are available at http://www.census.gov/govs/index.html.

Tax Publications and Information Sources

A wide range of frequently revised publications pertaining to taxation are available. Some are aimed at the general public, others at tax specialists. Clearly, the selection and inclusion of such publications in any library collection will reflect the interests and needs of its particular clientele. This section considers some of the main types of printed and electronic sources of potential interest to library users.

Dictionaries

In many libraries, the accounting and general business and economics dictionaries on hand will be sufficient to handle requests for definitions of tax terms. More specialized tax dictionaries do exist, however. The titles listed below are typical.

Minars, David, and Richard A. Westin. **Shepard's McGraw-Hill Tax Dictionary for Business.** New York: McGraw-Hill, 1994. 478p.

Shepard's McGraw-Hill Tax Dictionary for Business is an abridged version of a text widely used by tax attorneys, *Shepard's 1992–1993 Tax Dictionary*. It lists and defines 6,000 legal, technical, and accounting terms, with entries ranging in length from a single sentence to a paragraph or more. It is directed at both tax professionals and the layperson who wants to clarify tax concepts. References to the Internal Revenue Code, Treasury Regulations, and case law are frequently included, as are cross-references to related terms in the dictionary.

U.S. General Accountability Office. **A Glossary of Terms Used in the Federal Budget.** September 2005. http://www.gao.gov/new.items/d05734sp.pdf (accessed May 1, 2011)

Although not nearly as comprehensive as *Shepard's McGraw-Hill Tax Dictionary for Business*, *A Glossary of Terms Used in the Federal Budget* offers clear, brief definitions, intended for use by agencies, professionals, and the layperson. Although the primary scope is budget terms, accounting expressions are also defined. Terms are grouped by category, with cross-references from one section to another. In addition, the *Glossary* includes a brief description of the federal budget process, appendixes, and a solid index. It is available in PDF format from the web page and can be found by putting the title into the search box.

One can also find many dictionaries of tax terms by searching the Web with your favorite search engine for the phrase "tax dictionary." Such a search will yield sites like

Investopedia's Tax Dictionary (http://www.investopedia.com/categories/taxes.asp), Tax ACT's Tax Dictionary (http://www.taxact.com/tax-terms/tax-dictionary.asp), and Tax Definitions (http://www.taxdefinitions.com/), among many others.

Income Tax Guides

Issued annually to reflect current tax practice, income tax guides help individuals, accountants, lawyers, and others to identify, interpret, and prepare the necessary forms to be filed with federal and state agencies. Most are fairly general, summarizing federal income tax requirements as they apply to individuals, businesses, corporations, and organizations. Others have a narrower focus. They may be similar to those pertaining to federal tax but may deal with tax laws in specific states, or they may emphasize tax practices that apply to specific occupations or professions.

General guides fall into three categories: those published by the Internal Revenue Service itself, those issued by publishers of major online/loose-leaf tax services, and popular guides. Some are listed below.

Federal Government Guides

U.S. Internal Revenue Service. **Your Federal Income Tax.** http://www.irs.gov/pub/irs-pdf/p17.pdf (accessed May 4, 2011)

Your Federal Income Tax is an IRS booklet that describes the types of tax returns that can be filed by individuals, including for each return step-by-step instructions and comments. It explains the tax laws that cover salaries, interest and dividends, capital gains, and other types of income, and discusses itemized deductions. Sample forms and schedules are included, as are numerous examples showing how tax law applies in certain situations. In addition, the booklet briefly summarizes important tax law changes. The IRS prepares many similar booklets (see figure 8.5), and all are obtainable from the web site at http://www.irs.gov/formspubs/index.html. Libraries that supply tax information can now print any publication needed by patrons.

Commercial Online/Loose-leaf Publishers

Major publishers of loose-leaf tax services also issue tax guides. As compared to those mentioned above, they are more technical, and may include citations to their corresponding loose-leaf services or to the Tax Code itself. The two most commonly used guides are published by Commerce Clearing House, and the Research Institute of America.

U.S. Master Tax Guide. Chicago: Commerce Clearing House, 1943–. Annual.

Federal Tax Handbook. New York: Research Institute of America, 1975–. Annual.

Although there are some differences, these guides are quite similar in arrangement, format, and content. Each includes tax tables and schedules and a summary of recent developments. Like their loose-leaf counterparts, each uses numeric paragraph designation rather than page numbers to refer to specific topics, and each is arranged by broad topic. Each has detailed subject indexes and, in addition, includes footnotes citing references to more detailed information offered by the loose-leaf and online services. In addition, the *Federal Tax Handbook* includes editorial observations, notes, and warnings about specific tax practices. These guides are quite inexpensive and in many settings provide information sufficiently detailed to answer most tax-related inquiries. Libraries in which the need for information is more specific or highly specialized will, of course, need to subscribe to one or more of the loose-leaf or online services.

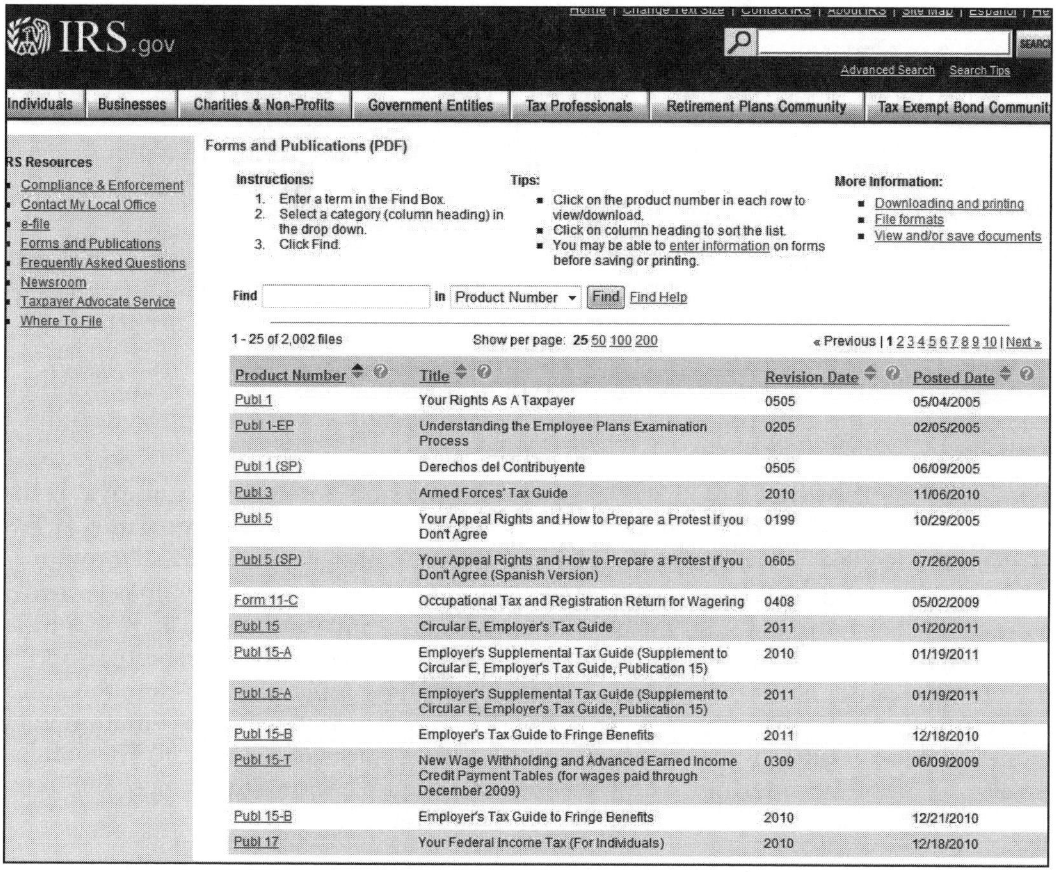
IRS.gov

Advanced Search | Search Tips

Individuals | Businesses | Charities & Non-Profits | Government Entities | Tax Professionals | Retirement Plans Community | Tax Exempt Bond Communit

RS Resources
- Compliance & Enforcement
- Contact My Local Office
- e-file
- Forms and Publications
- Frequently Asked Questions
- Newsroom
- Taxpayer Advocate Service
- Where To File

Forms and Publications (PDF)

Instructions:
1. Enter a term in the Find Box.
2. Select a category (column heading) in the drop down.
3. Click Find.

Tips:
- Click on the product number in each row to view/download.
- Click on column heading to sort the list.
- You may be able to enter information on forms before saving or printing.

More Information:
- Downloading and printing
- File formats
- View and/or save documents

Find [ ] in Product Number Find Find Help

1 - 25 of 2,002 files | Show per page: 25 50 100 200 | « Previous | 1 2 3 4 5 6 7 8 9 10 | Next »

Product Number	Title	Revision Date	Posted Date
Publ 1	Your Rights As A Taxpayer	0505	05/04/2005
Publ 1-EP	Understanding the Employee Plans Examination Process	0205	02/05/2005
Publ 1 (SP)	Derechos del Contribuyente	0505	06/09/2005
Publ 3	Armed Forces' Tax Guide	2010	11/06/2010
Publ 5	Your Appeal Rights and How to Prepare a Protest if you Don't Agree	0199	10/29/2005
Publ 5 (SP)	Your Appeal Rights and How to Prepare a Protest if you Don't Agree (Spanish Version)	0605	07/26/2005
Form 11-C	Occupational Tax and Registration Return for Wagering	0408	05/02/2009
Publ 15	Circular E, Employer's Tax Guide	2011	01/20/2011
Publ 15-A	Employer's Supplemental Tax Guide (Supplement to Circular E, Employer's Tax Guide, Publication 15)	2010	01/19/2011
Publ 15-A	Employer's Supplemental Tax Guide (Supplement to Circular E, Employer's Tax Guide, Publication 15)	2011	01/19/2011
Publ 15-B	Employer's Tax Guide to Fringe Benefits	2011	12/18/2010
Publ 15-T	New Wage Withholding and Advanced Earned Income Credit Payment Tables (for wages paid through December 2009)	0309	06/09/2009
Publ 15-B	Employer's Tax Guide to Fringe Benefits	2010	12/21/2010
Publ 17	Your Federal Income Tax (For Individuals)	2010	12/18/2010

Figure 8.5. More forms and publications available from the IRS. Taken from the web site at http://www.irs.gov/app/picklist/list/formsPublications.html

Popular Publishers

The third major type of general tax guide consists of popular guides written for laypeople. Such guides are in heavy demand at public and some academic libraries, particularly after major tax reform has been enacted. The quality of these guides can vary considerably, but one of the best is listed below.

Bernstein, Peter W., ed. **The Ernst & Young Tax Guide.** New York: Ernst & Young, 1992–. Annual.

The Ernst & Young Tax Guide is the only such guide issued by a Big 4 accounting firm. The *Guide* is well organized, and the information is comprehensive, including explanations, examples, tax-saving tips, and tax planning suggestions. A popular feature is a guide to the strategies to help plan the next tax year.

Specialized tax guides include those focusing on taxes levied by specific states or on tax practices most likely to be of interest to a specific professional or occupational group. The title that follows is typical.

CCH Tax Law Editors. **Guidebook to North Carolina Taxes.** Chicago: Commerce Clearing House, 1972–. Annual.

The *Guidebook to North Carolina State Taxes* is representative of commercially published state tax guides. Intended as a quick reference source, it describes general provisions of state tax laws, regulations, and administrative practice, and includes tax tables and explanatory paragraphs. References are made throughout the *Guidebook* to relevant sections in the state tax service, *CCH's North Carolina Tax Reports*. Included are "Highlights of Tax Changes," a detailed table of contents, "Law and Regulations Finding Lists," and a topical index. Similar guidebooks are published for other states.

Directories

Although there are few tax directories per se, many business, accounting, and government directories list tax practitioners and organizations. The *United States Government Manual*, for example, lists key officials and regional and district offices of the IRS.

There is, however, a special directory that is used whenever information on tax-exempt organizations is needed: the annual *Cumulative List of Organizations*, compiled by the IRS.

U.S. Department of the Treasury. U.S. Internal Revenue Service. **Cumulative List of Organizations Described in Section 170(c) of the Internal Revenue Code of 1986, Revised to 2006.** Washington, DC: Government Printing Office, 1954–. Annual.

The *Cumulative List* is a roster of organizations to which contributions are tax deductible. Each entry includes the organization's name and the city and state in which it is located. A coding system is also used that identifies each organization by type and the limitation on deductibility. Three cumulative quarterly supplements update the annual *List* by citing organizations to be added. The IRS also distributes this information via an online database at http://www.irs.gov/charities/article/0,,id=96136,00.html. The database can also be found by entering "Cumulative List of Organizations" into the search box at the home page of the IRS (http://www.irs.gov) (see figure 8.6).

Periodicals, Newspapers, and Indexes

Since professional tax assistance is most frequently provided by accountants and lawyers, many serials in those fields contain articles on tax law, theory, and practice. In addition, almost every type of periodical described in chapter 2 regularly features tax-related articles. These articles are most evident in January issues and whenever major tax reforms are enacted. Taxation also has special periodicals of its own, ranging from special-interest publications such as *Church Finance Today* and *Divorce Taxation* to serials with a much broader scope. Three such titles are discussed below.

National Tax Journal. Columbus, OH: National Tax Association—Tax Institute of America, 1948–. Quarterly.

The National Tax Association is an association of accountants, economists, attorneys, government tax officials, academicians, and others with an interest in taxation. One of its major goals is to promote the scientific, nonpolitical study of taxation, and one of the key publications that it uses to meet this goal is its quarterly periodical, the *National Tax Journal* (*NTJ*). The *NTJ* features articles by scholars and practitioners that report research; analyze and evaluate current national, state, and local tax policy; and treat other issues pertaining to government finance. Articles, which deal with topics as diverse as tax evasion by small businesses to corporate income and the impact of state taxation on infrastructure services, include abstracts and bibliographies and frequently contain formulas and graphs.

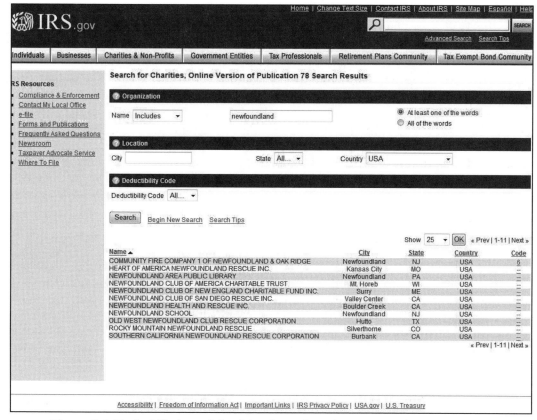

Figure 8.6. Typical listing of charities from *Cumulative List of Organizations*

The Journal of Taxation. New York: Warren, Gorham & Lamont, 1954–. Monthly.

The *Journal of Taxation* is written by and for tax practitioners and focuses more on technical and methodological concerns. It provides up-to-date information on the latest tax law changes, court decisions, revenue rulings, and administrative actions. Articles are grouped by broad topic such as "Accounting" and "Compensation & Benefits," and each issue includes new rulings. The *Journal of Taxation* is indexed in most business and many general periodical indexes. Details about the online version of this journal are available at http://www.riahome.com/estore/.

Tax Features. Washington, DC: Tax Foundation, 1957–2004. Monthly.

Although the publication ceased publication in April 2004 it may have value for historical research. *Tax Features* was published monthly by the Tax Foundation (http://www.taxfoundation.org/). It was a newsletter that presented news, semi-technical, and analytical articles on taxation and government spending policy. An archive back to 1976 is available for free online.

Tax Notes. Washington, DC: Tax Analysts, 1970–. Weekly.

Tax Notes is a great source for news, information, analysis, and commentary on federal taxation. Topics include changes in laws and regulations, special in-depth investigative reports on tax policy issues, and coverage of congressional and treasury actions. Other publications of interest by Tax Analysts are *State Tax Notes* and *International Tax Notes*.

Tax articles are included in *Business Source Elite*, *Business Source Premier*, *ABI/INFORM Global*, the *Wall Street Journal*, and most other business periodicals' online collections. In addition, Commerce Clearing House publishes a loose-leaf service that indexes and summarizes articles on federal taxation.

Federal Tax Articles. Chicago: Commerce Clearing House, 1968–. Loose-leaf, with monthly updates.

Federal Tax Articles is an annotated listing of articles, comments, and notes published in some 250 tax, accounting, legal, and other professional journals. The summary of each article includes the highlights of the main points plus citations to applicable cases, rulings, and regulations, which enables the user to quickly find primary materials. Only material dealing with some aspect of federal taxes is included. Articles are grouped together under the section(s) of the Internal Revenue Code to which they apply. Further access is provided by topical and author indexes.

Online and Loose-Leaf Services

Taxation is a complex field, made particularly so by the diversity of taxes collected at each level of government and by the voluminous and frequently changing laws, regulations, and other government issuances pertaining to them. As a result, it is an area in which online and loose-leaf services are abundant.

Although the nature and extent of these services will vary from one library to another, many business reference collections will include at least one of the comprehensive federal tax services listed below. These multivolume services present and analyze tax law, court cases and decisions, and IRS administrative rulings.

United States Tax Reporter. New York: Research Institute of America ThomsonReuters, 1970–. Loose-leaf, with weekly updates and online through RIA Checkpoint.

Standard Federal Tax Reporter. Chicago: Commerce Clearing House, 1913–. Loose-leaf, with weekly updates and online through *CCH Tax Research Network and IntelliConnect* (http://www.cch.com).

The overlap between the *United States Tax Reporter* and the *Standard Federal Tax Reporter* is considerable. Both are organized by code section, both include topical indexes, case tables, and numerical finding lists, permitting research by subject, case name, and numerical citation. Both services also include statutes, regulations, notes of court and administrative decisions, other administrative documents, some legislative history, and commentary. Finding aids include lists of Revenue Rulings, cases, Treasury Decisions, and Private Letter Rulings, all linked to the relevant paragraph numbers. Each has its own loyal following.

Federal Tax Coordinator 2d. New York: Research Institute of America ThomsonReuters, 1970–. Loose-leaf, with weekly updates and online through RIA Checkpoint.

The *Federal Tax Coordinator 2d* is a bit different. It is organized by subject and has thorough coverage of income, FICA, FUTA, estate, gift, and excise taxes. Each chapter deals with a fairly broad topic, such as income tax deductions or estate tax, and each occupies its own volume. Further, each chapter begins with a description of the taxes normally collected, followed by a detailed table of contents. It, in turn, is followed by descriptions of problems in the designated area. Frequently the tax explanations include illustrations, observations, recommendations, and cautions. Citations to supporting authorities are included in footnotes at the bottom of each page. Following the explanatory section is a verbatim reprint of all pertinent Tax Code and Treasury Regulation sections

Space does not permit detailed consideration of these services' respective contents, format, and arrangement, but such information is readily available in the descriptive information, and through the list of contacts and request for information tags available on the web sites of their publishers, RIA (http://ria.thomsonreuters.com/TaxResearch/) and CCH (http://www.cch.com).

In addition to the multivolume, comprehensive loose-leaf services described above, both CCH and RIA publish a number of smaller, more highly specialized tax services, including titles that focus on a specific type of tax, such as sales or estate and gift tax, or that present state tax law in all 50 states or in a single state.

Government Publications and Services

Federal tax publications generally fall into three broad categories: (1) income tax guides and instructional booklets published by the Internal Revenue Service; (2) statistics compiled from tax returns; and (3) congressional publications, tax laws, regulations, and court decisions.

The IRS offers the current and more comprehensive tax information at http://www .irs.gov. Many of the most important IRS guides and instructional publications have been discussed in earlier sections of this chapter. Compilations of tax statistics, the second major type of federal tax publication, are described in the section that follows. Finally, while discussion of the myriad of laws, regulations, and court decisions that comprise the third major type of federal tax information is more appropriate to a legal text, a few such publications should be noted.

U.S. Department of the Treasury. Internal Revenue Service. **Internal Revenue Bulletin.** n.d. http://www.irs.gov/app/picklist/list/internalRevenueBulletins.html (accessed April 8, 2011)

U.S. Department of the Treasury. Internal Revenue Service. **Internal Revenue Cumulative Bulletin.** n.d. http://www.irs.gov/app/picklist/list/internalRevenueBulletins.html (accessed April 8, 2011)

The *Internal Revenue Bulletin* lists and announces official IRS rulings and procedures, and publishes Treasury Decisions, Executive Orders, Tax Conventions, legislation, court decisions, and other items pertaining to taxation. Each issue is divided into four main parts: rulings and decisions based on the provisions of the 1986 Internal Revenue Code; treaties and tax legislation; administrative, procedural, and miscellaneous; and items of general interest. The highlights of each issue are described on its cover, and the first *Bulletin* for each month features an index to the preceding month's issues. Published in paper since 1954, all *Bulletins* since 1996 are now free on the Web.

Twice a year, the weekly issues of the *Bulletin* are consolidated into a permanent, indexed source, the *Internal Revenue Cumulative Bulletin*. Each *Cumulative Bulletin* follows the same general arrangement as the weekly *Bulletin* but also includes a subject index, finding lists, a cumulative list of announcements relating to Tax Court decisions published in the *Bulletin*, and a list of tax practitioners (primarily attorneys and CPAs) who have been disbarred from or voluntarily consented to suspend preparing tax returns for a specified time period. Published since 1969, the issues for 1995 onward are available on the Web. Much of the information is also available in RIA and CCH.

Statistics

Tax statistics generally fall into two main categories, those published by the government and those issued by other organizations, including trade associations, research organizations, and commercial publishers. Statistics published by the government are frequently summarized or presented in condensed form in the *Statistical Abstract of the United States* and many of the statistical compilations described in chapter 6. There are, however, sources compiled by the IRS's Statistics of Income Division that provide more detailed information on federal taxes. A listing of the publications is at http://www.irs.gov/taxstats/productsandpubs/index.html. Two examples are below.

U.S. Department of the Treasury. Internal Revenue Service. **SOI (Statistics of Income) Bulletin.** Washington, DC: Government Printing Office, 1981–. Quarterly.

The *Statistics of Income Bulletin,* http://www.irs.gov/taxstats/article/0,,id=117514,00.html, provides published annual financial statistics from various tax returns filed with the Internal Revenue Service. These statistics are presented in the *Bulletin*'s "Selected Statistical Series" section, which includes current and historic statistics on individual income rates and business tax returns, as well as returns submitted by sole proprietorships, partnerships, and corporations. Other tables highlight gross IRS collections and receipts, excise taxes, and projections of returns. In addition, the *Statistics of Income Bulletin* includes articles on a wide range of subjects, including demographic characteristics of taxpayers, high income tax returns, and environmental taxes (see figure 8.7).

Individual Income Tax Returns, Preliminary Data, 2009

Statistics of Income Bulletin | Winter 2011

Table 1. Individual Income Tax Returns, Tax Year 2009 Preliminary Data: Selected Income and Tax Items, by Size of Adjusted Gross Income

[All figures are estimates based on samples—money amounts are in thousands of dollars]

Item	All returns	Size of adjusted gross income						
		Under $15,000 [1]	$15,000 under $30,000	$30,000 under $50,000	$50,000 under $100,000	$100,000 under $200,000	$200,000 under $250,000	$250,000 or more
	(1)	(2)	(3)	(4)	(5)	(6)	(7)	(8)
Number of returns, total	**140,532,115**	**37,430,398**	**30,159,234**	**25,183,542**	**30,268,566**	**13,550,244**	**1,442,109**	**2,498,021**
Form 1040 returns	83,829,478	15,373,113	12,176,454	14,625,434	24,478,663	13,235,693	1,442,109	2,498,021
Form 1040A returns	39,872,098	12,393,000	13,961,185	8,238,770	4,978,197	300,948	0	0
Form 1040EZ returns	16,830,540	9,664,287	4,021,597	2,319,337	811,715	13,603	0	0
Electronically-filed returns [2]	99,012,015	25,110,843	22,042,531	18,273,495	21,493,858	9,548,129	965,701	1,577,458
Adjusted gross income (less deficit)	**7,648,676,270**	**106,375,907**	**663,562,563**	**983,479,617**	**2,147,895,336**	**1,805,900,040**	**320,046,293**	**1,621,416,514**
Salaries and wages:								
Number of returns	117,253,027	26,589,251	25,332,735	22,307,960	26,987,550	12,471,037	1,329,616	2,234,877
Amount	5,797,103,468	222,268,243	521,828,610	801,778,149	1,696,010,204	1,431,826,766	240,297,318	883,094,177
Taxable interest:								
Number of returns	57,980,811	9,268,249	7,575,955	9,351,252	17,578,030	10,582,642	1,276,193	2,348,490
Amount	148,292,561	15,793,973	11,741,558	15,146,271	31,325,780	26,770,246	5,955,965	41,558,769
Tax-exempt interest: [3]								
Number of returns	6,245,826	701,150	536,641	755,341	1,602,249	1,435,368	296,395	918,681
Amount	68,382,089	3,951,465	3,090,349	4,434,377	12,489,564	12,559,564	3,359,730	28,497,041
Ordinary dividends:								
Number of returns	29,239,484	4,614,818	3,259,482	3,868,918	8,394,319	6,233,881	932,279	1,935,788
Amount	147,144,977	8,688,868	7,003,334	9,218,677	24,007,484	26,071,666	6,948,428	65,206,522
Qualified dividends:								
Number of returns	25,397,334	3,910,569	2,734,289	3,318,390	7,220,926	5,544,347	862,566	1,806,249
Amount	112,590,344	5,288,669	4,181,748	5,866,597	16,828,379	19,572,986	5,506,785	55,345,180
State income tax refunds:								
Number of returns	23,711,859	678,055	1,513,765	3,679,405	9,855,268	6,534,328	607,199	843,841
Amount	28,528,315	918,854	911,229	2,503,631	8,641,143	8,239,733	1,223,671	6,090,054
Alimony received:								
Number of returns	431,210	63,165	96,168	118,463	113,060	33,348	1,816	5,192
Amount	8,356,158	466,810	1,024,754	1,718,605	2,719,280	1,596,904	129,682	700,123
Business or profession net income:								
Number of returns	16,466,708	5,608,854	2,808,850	2,200,299	3,287,095	1,833,357	245,911	482,340
Amount	295,277,183	41,774,365	34,503,512	28,234,076	53,316,836	56,101,590	17,028,700	64,318,104
Business or profession net loss:								
Number of returns	5,602,356	1,082,312	901,939	974,842	1,558,228	833,718	93,103	158,215
Amount	55,736,863	21,260,274	7,005,049	6,688,558	9,903,863	6,044,998	964,986	3,869,136
Net capital gain: [4]								
Number of returns	6,578,169	838,456	667,675	791,801	1,924,800	1,524,541	248,452	582,445
Amount	240,530,591	9,748,563	2,373,894	3,352,523	13,673,109	22,725,498	6,730,165	181,926,838

Figure 8.7. Sample page from *Statistics of Income Bulletin* (Winter 2011),
http://www.irs.gov/taxstats/article/0,,id=117514,00.html

U.S. Department of the Treasury. Internal Revenue Service. **Tax Statistics.** c2000. http://www.irs.gov/taxstats/index.html (accessed May 6, 2011)

Most of the information available from the IRS is contained in the Statistics of Income series, which includes separate sections for individual, partnership, and corporate income tax returns. The data, reports, and research studies are available from http://www.irs.gov from the *Tax Statistics* section (see figure 8.8).

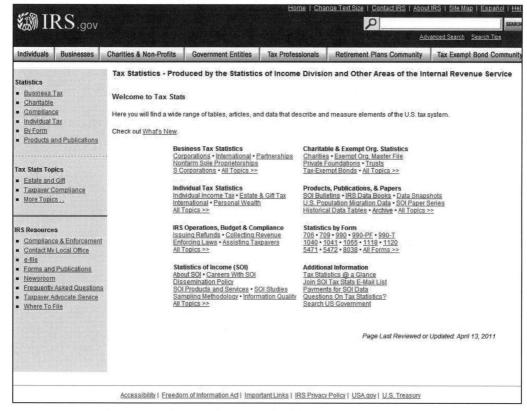

Figure 8.8. Listing of statistical tables provided by the IRS,
at http://www.irs.gov/taxstats/index.html

Privately published compilations of tax statistics include those made available in the *Book of the States*, the *Multistate Corporate Tax Almanac* mentioned above, and other commercially published sources. The Tax Foundation publishes a wide range of reports (http://www.taxfoundation.org/publications). One useful compilation is:

Facts and Figures on Government Finance. Washington, DC: Tax Foundation, 1941–2004. Biennial.

Facts and Figures on Government Finance contains about 300 tables providing current and historical data on government revenues and expenditures at the federal, state, and local levels. Each table cites the source(s) from which data were gathered and frequently date back for several years; some date back as far as 1902. A glossary and subject index are also included.

Many trade associations, particularly those representing industries that must pay special taxes, include relevant tax statistics in their publications or at their web sites.

Typical of these are the American Trucking Association (www.truckline.com/) and the Distilled Spirits Council of the United States (http://www.discus.org/). Such industry-specific data can usually be identified by consulting the *Statistical Reference Index*, or by searching the Web with a search engine using an industry name and the word "tax."

Notes

1. Martin Rosenberg, *Opportunities in Accounting Careers* (Lincolnwood, IL: VGM Career Horizons, 1983), 2.

2. Ordering information available at http://www.aicpa.org/edu/candpubl.htm.

3. Wendy McKenzie, *Financial Times Guide to Using and Interpreting Company Accounts* (London: Prentice Hall, 1998), 11.

4. Steven A. Moscove, *Accounting Fundamentals for Non-Accountants,* rev. ed. (Reston, VA: Reston Publishing, 1984), 7.

5. James E. Kristy and Susan Z. Diamond, *Finance without Fear* (New York: AMACOM, 1984), 45.

9

Money, Credit, and Banking

The availability of money and credit has a profound influence on the way business is conducted. Whether a company chooses to expand operations or lay off employees, whether retail stores maintain large or small inventories, or whether real estate sales soar or plummet is to a very large extent determined by money supply, interest rates, and the financial institutions and government agencies responsible for both. This chapter begins by considering briefly the basic characteristics of money, monetary measures, and foreign exchange. It next covers commercial and consumer credit, then proceeds to discuss such financial institutions as commercial banks, savings and loan associations, and credit unions, as well as such government agencies as the Federal Reserve System and the Federal Deposit Insurance Corporation. It concludes with the identification and description of key reference and research sources.

Money

One of the characteristics that distinguishes advanced cultures from more primitive ones is the widespread use of money, rather than barter, for the exchange of goods and services. Although one culture may designate wampum or fur pelts as money and another may choose gold and silver, money serves three major functions regardless of the forms it takes. First, money serves as the accepted medium of exchange; it is a tool to facilitate transactions. Second, it serves as a standard of value. In the United States, for example, librarians' salaries and television sets are priced by assigning dollar values to them. Finally, money serves as a store of value; it can be saved to permit future purchase of goods and services.

Money in the United States has evolved from such commodities as tobacco and gunpowder to the coins, paper currency, and demand deposits (checking accounts and other checkable deposits held by banks and thrift institutions) presently in use. Although most laypeople think of currency as comprising the bulk of our money supply, demand deposits are the most common form of money. Most payments today are made by check or by electronic transfer of funds from one account to another; few individuals or businesses use cash to pay for major purchases. Demand deposits and their role in the nations' money supply are discussed at length in the section on banks.

Monetary System

Most countries have a monetary system comprising the various kinds of money (for example, coins, currency, and demand deposits), the rules and regulations regarding their issuance and control, and the organizations responsible for them. The Constitution of the United States, for example, grants Congress the power to coin money and regulate its value. Congress has in turn delegated this money power to the Department of the Treasury and the Federal Reserve System and, through it, to commercial banks.

Monetary Measures

As economies become more complex, so also do their monetary systems, which is reflected in the way money is measured. The Federal Reserve System is responsible for collecting and publishing data on money supply in the United States. To do so, it has created a series of measures, M1 and M2, that it uses to determine just how much money there is. In March 2006, the Federal Reserve Board of Governors ceased publication of the M3 monetary aggregate. M3 did not appear to convey any additional information about economic activity that was not already embodied in M2. Consequently, the Board judged that the costs of collecting the data and publishing M3 outweigh the benefits.

Although this book does not delve deeply into the characteristics and uses of these alternative measures, please note that the measures progress from M1, the narrowest definition of money supply, to M2, the most inclusive, and that all are listed and defined in the Federal Reserves' release H.6, which is available at http://www.federalreserve.gov/releases/h6/.

Foreign Exchange

The growth of foreign trade and travel is reflected in the increasing number of questions that librarians and researchers must answer regarding foreign money and its value relative to the dollar. Although any number of sources list foreign currencies, one title is particularly useful for detailed information.

Cowitt, Philip P., ed. **World Currency Yearbook**. Brooklyn, NY: International Currency Analysis, 1955–1996. Annual. (Formerly *Picks' Currency Yearbook*)

Although dated and out of print, this series is still good for historical information. For each country listed in the *World Currency Yearbook*, a discussion of its currency's history, transferability, recent developments, and administration is included, supplemented by annual statistics covering the past decade for currency circulation and official, free market, and, when applicable, black market exchange rates. Annual exchange rates are useful for tracking changes over time.

Frequently, however, the need is for more current information. In such instances, the daily foreign exchange tables published in newspapers or on the Web are the best place to begin. Although not all countries are represented in such tables, those in which trading is heaviest are included. One of the best currency converters available on the Web is maintained by OANDA.com (http://www.oanda.com/currency/converter/). This site provides exchange rates for 164 currencies. Monthly exchange rates are also supplied by the Federal Reserve Bank of New York (see figure 9.1). Daily rates were discontinued on January 1, 2009, as there were so many other ways to obtain rates.

Federal Reserve Statistical Release

G.5

Foreign Exchange Rates (Monthly)

Release Date: February 1, 2011

Release dates | Dollar indexes, summary measures | Currency weights Data Download Program (DDP) | Announcements
Current release *Other formats:* Screen reader | ASCII

G.5(405)   February 1, 2011

FOREIGN EXCHANGE RATES

THE TABLE BELOW SHOWS THE AVERAGE RATES OF EXCHANGE IN JANUARY 2011 TOGETHER
WITH COMPARABLE FIGURES FOR OTHER MONTHS. AVERAGES ARE BASED ON DAILY NOON BUYING
RATES FOR CABLE TRANSFERS IN NEW YORK CITY CERTIFIED FOR CUSTOMS PURPOSES BY
THE FEDERAL RESERVE BANK OF NEW YORK.

(Currency units per U.S. dollar except as noted)

COUNTRY	MONETARY UNIT	2011 January	2010 December	2010 November	2010 January
*AUSTRALIA	DOLLAR	0.9962	0.9929	0.9889	0.9127
BRAZIL	REAL	1.6745	1.6955	1.7131	1.7817
CANADA	DOLLAR	0.9939	1.0081	1.0129	1.0438
CHINA, P.R.	YUAN	6.5964	6.6497	6.6538	6.8269
DENMARK	KRONE	5.5749	5.6366	5.4617	5.2177
*EMU MEMBERS	EURO	1.3371	1.3221	1.3654	1.4266
HONG KONG	DOLLAR	7.7803	7.7736	7.7546	7.7624
INDIA	RUPEE	45.3750	45.1000	44.9315	45.8944
JAPAN	YEN	82.6250	83.3376	82.5180	91.1011
MALAYSIA	RINGGIT	3.0595	3.1283	3.1132	3.3750
MEXICO	PESO	12.1280	12.3902	12.3376	12.8096
*NEW ZEALAND	DOLLAR	0.7656	0.7511	0.7723	0.7263
NORWAY	KRONE	5.8561	5.9833	5.9645	5.7402
SINGAPORE	DOLLAR	1.2863	1.3063	1.2987	1.3965
SOUTH AFRICA	RAND	6.9239	6.8237	6.9749	7.4631
SOUTH KOREA	WON	1118.8675	1145.4833	1129.6230	1138.1947
SRI LANKA	RUPEE	110.8200	111.0081	111.5155	114.3589
SWEDEN	KRONA	6.6673	6.8524	6.8201	7.1534
SWITZERLAND	FRANC	0.9565	0.9689	0.9847	1.0345
TAIWAN	DOLLAR	29.1105	29.9014	30.3180	31.8658
THAILAND	BAHT	30.5455	30.0857	29.8690	33.0274
*UNITED KINGDOM	POUND	1.5782	1.5595	1.5961	1.6158
VENEZUELA	BOLIVAR	4.2898	4.2893	4.2893	3.6137

Figure 9.1. Federal Reserve Bank of New York, sample of monthly exchange rates,
http://www.federalreserve.gov/releases/g5/20110201/

Credit

Credit, usually defined as the promise to pay in the future in order to buy or borrow in the present, is an integral part of our economy. Consumers, corporations, businesses, even governments use credit on a regular basis. This section examines credit from two different perspectives: What a bank or other creditor looks for when deciding whether to grant credit, and what the prospective recipient, or debtor, seeks.

Creditworthiness

One of the major elements in determining whether to extend credit is the creditworthiness of the individual or organization seeking it. The granting of credit, in other words, is based on the creditor's confidence in the debtor's ability and willingness to repay the loan in accordance with the terms of the agreement. To determine creditworthiness, the creditor begins by considering three factors, sometimes called "the three Cs": capacity, capital, and character.

Capacity is the debtor's present and future ability to meet financial obligations. In determining the capacity of a small business person to repay a loan, the creditor may take into account the applicant's business experience, general background, and demonstrated ability to operate a business profitably. Someone seeking a consumer loan, on the other hand, would be quizzed about his or her employment history and present level of debt.

The second factor is capital, the assets held by the debtor. Capital includes such items as savings accounts, securities portfolios, insurance policies, pension funds, and property, any of which might be used as collateral to secure the loan.

Capacity and capital help creditors to determine an applicant's ability to repay a loan. Equally important, however, is the applicant's willingness to repay, designated by creditors as character. Although character lends itself less easily to objective measurement than capacity or capital, certain factors such as the person's reputation, known associates, and credit history are considered to be important components of character. Of these, the most important to creditors is credit history.

Credit Reports

Creditors rely heavily on credit histories—records of how past debt obligations were handled—to make decisions about applicants. Such histories are contained in credit reports sold to banks and other organizations by credit bureaus and credit reporting services. Most credit bureaus are local. The credit reporting services, on the other hand, are large, national operations.

Dun & Bradstreet's *Business Information Reports* is one of a series of confidential ratings that presents credit histories and other information on companies and businesses. A report may range in length from 1 or 2 pages to 20 or more, but it includes the credit history, which notes outstanding debt, bills past due, late payments, and related data, as well as brief descriptions of the business and its key officers, current financial conditions, and banking information. In addition, special events such as burglaries or executive changes are noted, as are such public civil filings as lawsuits and tax liens. A credit rating assigned by Dun & Bradstreet is also included. An example of a report is available at http://support.dialog.com/searchaids/dialog/pdf/dnbbir.pdf.

Two points about the *Business Information Reports* and other, similar credit reports should be noted. The first, and most important for libraries, is that such reports are often sold only to financial organizations, businesses, and individuals with legitimate needs for them. They are not made available to business competitors, and they are not intended to be accessible to the public. As a result, except in libraries where access to the public is restricted, they are not a part of library collections. The D&B reports are available as File 519 for those that have a Dialog account.

The second is that while the credit history itself is based on data supplied by creditors, the company being rated supplies some of the remaining information, such as the description of current financial conditions, and is under no obligation to provide full or even accurate information.

There are also compilers of personal credit reports. Many of them are prepared or at least sold by local credit bureaus. Whether they are prepared locally or at some distant location, such reports generally include the person's name, address, and Social Security number; credit history; details concerning current and past employment; and such personal information as date of birth and number of dependents. Like their business counterparts, personal credit reports are intended primarily for financial institutions and other creditors and are not available in libraries. The two major companies that supply these reports are Experian (http://www.experian.com/) and EQUIFAX (http://www.equifax.com/). Consumers may access a free copy of their credit reports from these agencies. If the report is found to be in error, the issuing agency must amend it and submit the revised version to the creditor(s) or consumer who originally requested the report.

Interest

While creditors are most interested in culling creditworthy applicants from those who are not, those same applicants are concerned with getting the best terms possible. Although the terms of a loan may include such factors as loan fees and service charges, the single most important item is interest. Interest is the price that borrowers pay to lenders for credit over specified periods of time; it is, in effect, a rental fee paid for the use of money. The amount of interest paid is based on a number of factors: the amount of the loan, the length of time involved, the repayment schedule, the interest rate, and the method used to calculate interest.

Interest rates usually depend on the supply of loaned funds and the demand for those funds. In addition, the rates may vary depending on the borrower. Two rates that are frequently referred to in business publications and broadcasts are the discount rate and the prime interest rate. Neither is available to ordinary borrowers. The discount rate, described further in the section on the Federal Reserve System, is the interest charged on short-term loans made by Federal Reserve Banks to commercial banks that are members of the Federal Reserve System. The prime interest rate, on the other hand, is the rate commercial banks charge preferred customers, usually large corporations and business enterprises. Both discount and prime interest rates have an impact on the interest rates charged for all other types of loans, and both are regularly reported in the *Federal Reserve Release H15* (http://www.federalreserve.gov/releases/H15/data.htm).

By itself, however, the annual interest rate is not always an accurate indicator of what a loan really costs. More useful for comparative purposes is the annual percentage rate, or APR. The APR is the true cost of a loan and in some instances may be considerably higher than the annual interest rate. Suppose, for example, that someone wants to borrow $1,000 for one year at 6 percent interest. The most favorable terms for the borrower would be based on a single, annual simple interest payment; at the end of the year, the borrower would repay the creditor the $1,000 plus $60 interest. In this instance (and whenever the interest being paid is simple annual interest), the APR and the interest rate are identical.

If, however, the same person were offered a "discount" or an "add on" loan, the APR would exceed the annual interest rate. A discount loan is one in which the annual interest is deducted from the principal of the loan before the borrower receives it. The borrower, in other words, receives less than the principal but is being charged interest on the full amount:

> Let's borrow that same $1,000 for a year but this time from a bank. Say the annual interest rate is the same as you paid your friend, 6%. The bank would probably take out the $60 in the 6% annual interest—in advance. This is called a discount loan. Now, for openers, you receive only $940. Then you pay off $83 monthly to liquidate (pay off) the loan. Therefore, your true cost or APR is 11.8% on $1,000. Puzzled? Well, you were paying interest on $1,000 but had use of only $940, and not even that for the full year. Moreover, with your monthly payments reducing the principal amount of the loan, the average amount of your money at your disposal during the course of the year was $470.[1]

"Add on," another method of calculating interest, adds the annual interest to the principal at the outset and is thus somewhat more advantageous to borrowers than a discount loan, but less so than a simple interest loan. Once again, the APR is greater than the annual interest rate; the loan costs more:

> In this case, the 6% or $60 annual interest rate would be added to your principal sum of $1,000 at the outset. You pay back $88.30 a month, and your APR is 11.1%. Your monthly payments are a little bit higher, but your APR is slightly lower, and you have the use of more money—$1,000 versus $940—than you did with the discount loan.[2]

The point to be made here is not how to compute the APR but to stress its importance. Creditors are required by law to disclose the APRs for all prospective credit transactions so that borrowers can compare the terms offered by one financial institution with those extended by another.

Banks, Thrifts, and the Financial Services Industry

The various business organizations offering services relating to financial resources are generally referred to as the financial services industry (see figure 9.2). A number of these organizations—commercial banks, savings and loan associations, savings banks, and credit unions—serve as intermediaries, accepting the deposits of some and extending credit to others. They are classified as depository institutions. Although the distinctions between the different types of depository institutions and other components of the industry have become increasingly blurred, each was originally formed to serve different functions and still retains certain emphases. This section concentrates on two main types of depository institutions—commercial banks and thrifts—and considers briefly other financial service organizations.

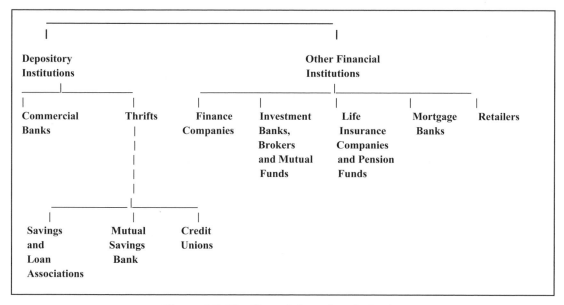

Figure 9.2. The financial services industry

Commercial Banks

In the year 2000 there were 8,315 FDIC-insured commercial banks in the United States, ranging from small, non-specialized operations to giant financial "department stores," with billions of dollars in deposits, and in 2011 there were 6,529. All, however, share certain characteristics. First, each is a business whose main goal is to achieve profit by lending and investing the funds placed at its disposal:

> The individual commercial bank has much in common with the business firms with which it deals. Like many of them, the bank is a corporation. It has applied for, qualified for, and received a charter from the proper national or state government agency, empowering it to do business as stipulated in the charter. The bank performs certain productive activities for which others are willing to pay; and in so doing, it incurs certain costs. In order to remain a going concern, it must experience a cash inflow from productive services rendered and from other sources that is sufficient for meeting all obligations as they become due, including all costs of doing business. Furthermore, its activities must provide an acceptable rate of return on investment. Usually a large fraction of a bank's income is in the form of interest on the claims it holds, particularly loans; while the two leading classes of bank costs are wages and salaries and interest paid on time deposits, that is, deposits not subject to check.[3]

Second, banks perform three functions: (1) They receive and hold deposits of funds from others, (2) they make loans or extend credit, and (3) they transfer funds by written orders of depositors.

Deposits of currency, checks, and bank drafts constitute the main source of funds available to commercial banks. Deposits are categorized as time or demand. A time deposit is one in which the funds deposited can be withdrawn only after a specified lapse of time or designated future date. Although a number of types of time deposits are available, the two best known are certificates of deposit and savings accounts.

Demand deposits, on the other hand, can be withdrawn at any time. They are available upon demand for immediate spending on goods and services and are thus considered to be part of the nation's money supply. Checking accounts are the most common type of demand deposit; a depositor simply writes a check on his or her account to transfer funds to the organization or person requiring payment. With depositors writing and depositing checks every day, funds continuously flow into and out of banks.

Banks are not, however, required to keep on hand the full amount deposited. Under what is known as the fractional reserve system of banking, they must keep only a designated percentage of their deposits in cash and reserve accounts. The remainder can be used for investments and loans, commercial banks' major profit-making activities. Such activities are important not only to banks but to the economy as a whole, because they permit the creation of new demand deposits and thus contribute to the money supply.[4]

> You deposit money into a bank account for safety, convenience, and the interest that banks pay on deposits. The bank accepts your deposits so it can loan out your money at a higher rate of interest than it paid you. The bank does not simply introduce lender to borrower and then collect a fee if the two decide to consummate the loan. Instead, the bank takes your deposit, according you the legal right to withdraw any or all your money whenever you want. Then the bank turns around and loans to a borrower who is under no obligation to repay the principal, much less the interest, until a specified date in the future.

Although banks can create new demand deposits by making loans, their ability to do so is greatly affected by the Federal Reserve System, which can increase or decrease legal reserve requirements (the percentage of total deposits that banks are required to keep available to make payments on demand) and can thus decrease or increase excess reserves available for lending and investing. This role is discussed further in the section on the Federal Reserve System.

Commercial banks traditionally have emphasized the credit and deposit needs of businesses rather than individuals. Further, since the bulk of a bank's money comes from demand deposits rather than savings accounts and other time deposits, the focus is on short-term loans rather than on long-term loans such as mortgages. Although commercial banks are now competing vigorously for individuals' business, other financial organizations have historically emphasized the banking and credit needs of individual consumers.

Thrift Institutions

Thrift institutions, or thrifts, received their name from the purpose for which they were originally established: to encourage thrift among the working class by providing places for them to deposit their savings and take out loans. Such organizations, accordingly, concentrated on savings accounts, residential mortgages, and other types of consumer credit. Three main types of thrift institutions evolved, each of which is considered briefly below.

Savings and Loan Associations

The savings and loan association, or S&L, is the predominant type of thrift institution. The first S&Ls, known as building and loan associations, were founded in the 19th century to help workers become homeowners. People formed an association and regularly deposited their savings. As deposits grew, the association's members bid for mortgage funds:

> In early associations, members agreed to purchase shares of stock in the amount that they wished to borrow. The shares were paid for by regular, mandatory payments. When enough money was collected to make a loan, the loan was auctioned off among the association's members. The loan carried a fixed rate of interest, usually 6%, and the member bidding the highest number of discount points got the loan. . . . Meanwhile, each member continued to pay for his shares and, with the interest from the first loan, another was soon made.[5]

Although they no longer require that borrowers be members, savings and loan associations remain a major lender for the purchase of homes and related types of real estate loans. The Office of Thrift Supervision (OTS) (http://www.ots.treas.gov/) supervises all federally chartered and many state-chartered thrift institutions, which include savings banks and savings and loan associations.

Mutual Savings Banks

Mutual savings banks are the oldest thrift institutions in the United States. Like savings and loan associations, they were established to promote financial security and thrift among workers and have been active mortgage and real estate lenders. Whereas savings and loan associations have developed throughout the country, however, mutual savings banks have been concentrated largely in the northeastern United States. Further, while S&Ls, like commercial banks, can be either federally or state chartered, until a few years ago all mutual savings banks were chartered solely by state agencies.

Credit Unions

Credit unions are similar in many respects to the other thrift institutions already described. Like them, credit unions came into being in the United States in the 19th century to meet the needs of workers. However, unlike savings and loans and mutual savings banks, credit unions will give loans only to members, who must share some common bond, such as place or nature of employment or institutional affiliation. Credit unions may be federally or state chartered, and most are also insured by federal or state agencies. Today, over 10,000 credit unions with over $480 billion in assets serve more than 79 million people in the United States.[6] The National Credit Union Administration (http://www.ncua.gov/) is an independent federal agency that supervises and insures about 7,950 active credit unions. There are almost 90 million members (89,854,941) with $679 billion on deposit ($679,416,086,824).

Other Financial Institutions

Depository institutions, however, are not the only components of the financial services industry. Other organizations include finance companies; investment banks, securities brokers, mutual funds, and investment companies; life insurance companies and pension funds; mortgage banks; and retailers.

Finance Companies

Finance companies fund both households and business firms and are, in fact, classified by the types of loans they make. Sales finance companies, for example, specialize in installment loans for the purchase of automobiles, home appliances, and other consumer durables; Global Automotive Services, a division of Ally Financial Inc. (formerly GMAC Financial Services, a General Motors unit), makes loans for the purchase of automobiles, and is an example of a sales finance company. Personal finance companies make personal loans, and business finance companies generally extend credit to business based on accounts receivable or sales of equipment. As a rule, loans made by finance companies are short term.

Investment Banks, Securities Brokers, and Investment Companies

Although the subject of investing is covered in the chapters that follow, it is worth noting here that three of the organizations most directly involved in investing are integral parts of the financial services industry.

Investment banks underwrite securities when they are first offered. When, for example, a corporation or government wants to raise money, it often issues stocks or bonds. These newly issued securities are then sold to investment banking firms, which in turn sell them to the public at a slightly higher price. Investment banks, in other words, buy large blocks of securities at wholesale prices and resell them at retail prices.

Securities brokers act as agents for clients interested in the purchase or sale of stocks, bonds, and other securities. In recent years, some brokers have begun to offer new services that compete with commercial banks. Large, full-service brokerage houses, for example, now offer financial products that combine the features and benefits of credit cards, checking accounts, money market funds, and traditional securities trading accounts. They have, accordingly, become an increasingly powerful segment of the financial services industry.

Investment companies and mutual funds are organizations that pool the funds deposited by individual investors to buy diversified securities portfolios. They have dramatically increased their business in recent years and are now frequently in direct competition with commercial banks, having siphoned off some of the business formerly handled by banks.

Life Insurance Companies and Pension Funds

The primary purpose of life insurance companies and pension funds is to provide financial security to individuals and households. Participants make periodic payments over long periods of time, in return for which they or designated beneficiaries will receive future payments. Insurance companies and pension funds, in turn, invest the money they receive in securities or use it to make loans.

Federal Reserve System

Although it is by no means the only government agency involved in the regulation of banking activities, the Federal Reserve System is the most important. This section examines its structure, the services it provides, and its impact on the economy.

Organizational Structure

The Federal Reserve System (http://www.federalreserve.gov/), often referred to as "the Fed," was established in 1913 by Congress to serve as the country's central bank. At the head is the chairman of the central governing body, the Board of Governors. Based in Washington, DC, the board consists of seven members appointed by the president with the advice and consent of the Senate. Each is appointed for a 14-year term and must represent a different Federal Reserve District, thus ensuring fair representation of regional interests. The president appoints one member of the board as chairman and another as vice chairman, each for four-year terms. Behind the scenes, financial experts, economists, and other support staff assist the Board of Governors (see figure 9.3).

The board's duties include overseeing the operations of the 12 Federal Reserve Banks, supervising state-chartered member banks, sharing the responsibility with the Reserve Banks for discount rate policy, and setting reserve requirements for member banks. In addition, the governors serve on the Federal Open Market Committee, described below. The board also regulates the implementation of certain consumer credit protection laws and carries on public information activities, including publication of the monthly *Federal Reserve Bulletin*, staff economic studies, and other materials.

The Federal Open Market Committee (FOMC) (http://www.federalreserve.gov/fomc/) is the Fed's most important policy-making body. Composed of all seven members of the Board of Governors and 5 of the 12 regional Federal Reserve Bank presidents, this committee has become the forum at which monetary policy matters are discussed and decisions made:[7]

> Before each regularly scheduled meeting of the FOMC, system staff prepare written reports on past and prospective economic and financial developments that are sent to Committee members and to nonmember Reserve Bank presidents. Reports prepared by the Manager of the System Open Market Account on operations in the domestic open market and in foreign currencies since the last regular meeting are also distributed. At the meeting itself, staff officers present oral reports on the current and prospective business situation, on conditions in financial markets, and on international financial developments. In its discussions, the Committee considers factors such as trends in prices and wages, employment and production, consumer income and spending, residential and commercial construction, business investment and inventories, foreign exchange markets, interest rates, money and credit aggregates, and fiscal policy. The Manager of the System Open Market Account also reports on account transactions since the previous meeting.[8]

The FOMC is, in fact, considered so important that committee members are not the only ones in attendance. The seven remaining Federal Reserve Bank presidents not serving on the committee, Board of Governors staff members, and senior staff economists regularly attend the meetings, which are held every five to eight weeks.

The next level of the Federal Reserve System consists of the regional Federal Reserve Banks and their branches (see figure 9.4). In all, there are 12 banks and 25 branches. Each bank serves a designated district of the country, providing banking services to member banks in its district. Like the Board of Governors, each bank also provides an assortment of information materials, ranging from sophisticated statistical studies to comic books and filmstrips intended for grade school students.

Chairman, Board of Governors	The President designates, and the Senate confirms, two members of the Board to be Chairman and Vice Chairman, for four-year terms.
Board of Governors	The seven members of the Board of Governors are appointed by the President and confirmed by the Senate to serve 14-year terms of office. The terms of each governor are staggered so that one governor's term expires every other year. The Board sets reserve requirements and shares the responsibility with the Reserve Banks for discount rate policy. These two functions plus open market operations constitute the monetary policy tools of the Federal Reserve System. In addition to monetary policy responsibilities, the Federal Reserve Board has regulatory and supervisory responsibilities over banks that are members of the System, bank holding companies, international banking facilities in the United States, Edge Act and agreement corporations, foreign activities of member banks, and the U.S. activities of foreign-owned banks. Another area of Board responsibility is the development and administration of regulations that implement major federal laws governing consumer credit such as the Truth in Lending Act, the Equal Credit Opportunity Act, the Home Mortgage Disclosure Act and the Truth in Savings Act
Federal Open Market Committee	The Federal Open Market Committee, or FOMC, is the Fed's monetary policymaking body. It is responsible for formulation of a policy designed to promote stable prices and economic growth. Simply put, the FOMC manages the nation's money supply. The voting members of the FOMC are the Board of Governors, the president of the Federal Reserve Bank of New York and presidents of four other Reserve Banks, who serve on a rotating basis. All Reserve Bank presidents participate in FOMC policy discussions. The chairman of the Board of Governors chairs the FOMC. The FOMC typically meets eight times a year in Washington, D.C. At each meeting, the committee discusses the outlook for the U.S. economy and monetary policy options.
12 Regional Reserve Banks	Federal Reserve Banks operate under the general supervision of the Board of Governors in Washington. Each Bank has a nine-member Board of Directors that oversees its operations.
Boards of Directors	Each regional Bank's board consists of nine members. Members are broken down into three classes: A, B, and C. There are three board members in each class. Class A members are chosen by the regional Bank's shareholders, and are intended to represent member banks' interests. Member banks are divided into three categories large, medium, and small. Each category elects one of the three class A board members. Class B board members are also nominated by the region's member banks, but class B board members are supposed to represent the interests of the public. Lastly, class C board members are nominated by the Board of Governors, and are also intended to represent the interests of the public. Each Director serves 3 years.

Figure 9.3. Structure and responsibilities of the Federal Reserve System

Finally, the last tier of the system is composed of commercial banks. All nationally chartered (that is, those with federal or national in their title) and most large state-chartered banks are members. Banks are required to comply with the Federal Reserve's regulations (http://www.federalreserve.gov/bankreg.htm) covering banking matters but are entitled to certain services as well.

For more information on the Federal Reserve, one can obtain a copy of the book *The Federal Reserve System: Its Purposes and Functions* at http://www.federalreserve.gov/pf/pdf/pf_1.pdf.

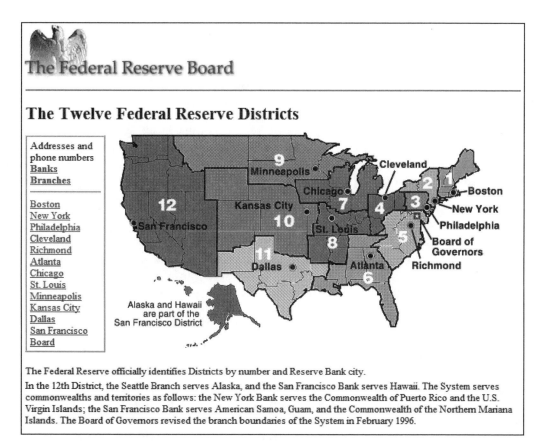

Figure 9.4. The 12 Federal Reserve Banks and Districts. Reproduced from the web page http://www.federalreserve.gov/otherfrb.htm

Services

The Federal Reserve System is a sort of "banker's bank," providing to member banks and the federal government services similar to those offered to the public by commercial banks. Federal Reserve Banks and their branches, for example, serve banks in their districts by holding their cash reserves and making short-term loans to them, charging the discount interest rate. The Reserve Banks also move currency and coin into and out of circulation:

> When Congress created the Federal Reserve System, it recognized that the demand for cash by the public and the banking system varies from time to time. This demand increases or decreases directly with the level of economic activity and with the seasons of the year. For example, consumers' demand for currency typically increases during holiday seasons, and farmers' demand increases during planting and harvesting seasons. The additional currency and coin put into circulation to meet seasonal demand is eventually returned to depository institutions by merchants and other business owners.[9]

Federal Reserve Banks issue Federal Reserve notes, the most common type of currency in circulation today. These notes are backed by assets held by Reserve Banks, which primarily consist of government securities and gold certificates.

The Fed also serves as a central check-clearing system. Each Reserve Bank receives checks from banks for collection, sorts them, sends the checks to the banks upon which they were written, and transfers payment for the checks through accounts at the Federal Reserve Bank.

Another service available to member banks is the national wire transfer of funds and securities using *Fedwire* (http://www.frbservices.org/), the Federal Reserve Communications System. In 2008, Fedwire processed an average daily volume of approximately 521,000 payments, with an average daily value of approximately $2.7 trillion (http://www .federalreserve.gov/paymentsystems/fedfunds_coreprinciples.htm#Use). The result of this legislation streamlined settlement and transportation of paper checks across the country, making check processing faster and more efficient. In 2004, federal legislation expanded the use of this technology, as well as the use of electronic deposit and presentment products, by making it possible for financial institutions to exchange electronic images of checks for settlement purposes.

The Fed provides financial services to the U.S. government as well. The Federal Reserve System, through district Federal Reserve Banks, accepts deposits and issues checks for the U.S. Treasury. Payroll withholding taxes, for example, are deposited into the government's checking accounts at Federal Reserve Banks, while redemption fees for such items as U.S. Savings Bonds and food stamps are paid by transferring funds from the appropriate government accounts to the commercial banks at which they originally were redeemed. Finally, Reserve Banks handle the clerical work involved in selling and redeeming government securities such as Treasury bills, notes, and bonds.

The Board of Governors and each Federal Reserve Bank employ research staff to gather and analyze economic data and interpret economic conditions and developments. Such data and the accompanying interpretations and projections are used by the Board of Governors, Federal Open Market Committee, and Federal Reserve Bank officers to make important administrative and policy decisions. They also serve to keep the public well informed. Most regional banks publish a monthly or quarterly journal devoted to basic research and analysis of current economic issues. Publications and statistics are available from the Federal Reserve Bank at http://www.federalreserve.gov/econresdata/ releases/surveysreports.htm.[10]

Monetary Policy

Even more important than the services it provides, however, is the Federal Reserve System's role in formulating monetary policy. By setting monetary policy, the Fed regulates the flow of money and credit, or money supply. Money supply is a key factor in economic stability. Too much money may lead to inflation; too little, to recession. As was mentioned earlier, the Fed continuously monitors economic conditions in the United States. Based on the data it gathers and analyzes, it recommends actions to encourage or discourage the ability of commercial banks to extend credit by increasing or decreasing the amount of credit available and by raising or lowering the cost of credit. To accomplish its goals, the Fed uses three main tools: reserve requirements, the discount rate, and the purchase and sale of government securities.

Reserves, it should be remembered, represent deposits not available for lending. Increasing or lowering the amount of reserves that member banks are required to keep, the Fed can significantly affect the amount of credit that is available. For example, if the reserve rate is set at 15 percent, it will enable banks to lend 85 percent of their deposits, but if reserve requirements are raised to 25 percent, the amount of credit available will decline to 75 percent. Increasing reserve requirements reduces the amount of money available for loans and results in higher interest rates. Decreasing reserve requirements, on the other hand, allows banks to lend more and usually results in lower interest rates.

The discount rate charged by Reserve Banks on short-term loans to member banks can also affect lending. Raising or lowering the discount rate will discourage or encourage banks' borrowing from the Fed, which will in turn affect commercial banks' lending practices.

Finally, the Federal Reserve System, along with other organizations and individuals, buys and sells government securities in the open market. Unlike the others, however, the Fed does this to affect the supply of credit rather than for investment purposes. To illustrate, the Fed buys securities to increase reserves and stimulate lending and sells them to decrease reserves and lending.

In summary, to stave off inflation, the Federal Reserve System usually raises reserve requirements and discount rates and sells government securities that it holds. To fight against recession, that is, to expand credit and increase borrowing, the Fed acts by taking the opposite actions. It lowers reserve requirements and discount rates and buys government securities. By making the policy decisions that result in these actions, the Fed contributes to the country's economic stability and growth.

Other Federal and State Government Agencies

The United States has a dual banking system. Banks and thrift institutions may be either federally or state chartered. As a result, both federal and state government agencies are involved in regulating and monitoring their activities.

Federal Agencies

The Office of the Comptroller of the Currency (http://www.occ.treas.gov/), part of the Treasury Department, is integral to the national banking system. As the administrator of national banks, the comptroller is responsible for chartering all national banks, for the conversion of state-chartered banks into national banks, and for the establishment of branches by national banks. The Office of the Comptroller also supervises national bank operations and is responsible for overseeing the regular examination of all national banks. It also supervises the federal branches and agencies of foreign banks:

> The OCC's nationwide staff of examiners conducts on-site reviews of national banks and provides sustained supervision of bank operations. The agency issues rules, legal interpretations, and corporate decisions concerning banking, bank investments, bank community development activities, and other aspects of bank operations. National bank examiners supervise domestic and international activities of national banks and perform corporate analyses. Examiners analyze a bank's loan and investment portfolios, funds management, capital, earnings, liquidity, sensitivity to market risk, and compliance with consumer banking laws, including the Community Reinvestment Act. They review the banks' internal controls, internal and external audit, and compliance with law. They also evaluate bank management's ability to identify and control risk.[11]

All banks belonging to the Federal Reserve System are required to be members of the Federal Deposit Insurance Corporation (FDIC) (http://www.fdic.gov). The FDIC is an independent, self-supporting government organization that helps to promote the stability and safety of the banking system by insuring the deposits at commercial and savings banks. Prior to the establishment of the FDIC, a bank failure meant that depositors lost all or part of their savings. Today, in the case of such failure, the FDIC takes over the bank. The claim of each depositor (up to $250,000) is paid, either as a result of the FDIC's sale of the bank's assets or its auction of the failed bank's assets and liabilities to the highest bidder, who then is responsible for operating the bank. Consumers and bankers can find additional information regarding the FDIC's deposit insurance coverage through the use of the FDIC's Electronic Deposit Insurance Estimator (EDIE) and deposit insurance publications at http://www.fdic.gov/deposit/deposits/index.html.

Another way in which the FDIC contributes to the safety of the banking system is by requiring the improvement of banks that examination shows to be improperly managed. If corrective action is not taken, the bank's insurance is terminated. Loss of FDIC insurance requires a national bank to give up its charter and a state bank to withdraw from the Federal System. Moreover, banks realize that public knowledge that they were no longer insured would be likely to lead to widespread deposit withdrawals and might culminate in bank failure.

Although commercial banks may be members of both the Federal Reserve System and the Federal Deposit Insurance Corporation, savings and loan associations, savings banks, and credit unions are excluded from membership. They are, however, served by other federal agencies patterned after the Fed and the FDIC.

The Federal Home Loan Bank System (http://www.fhlbanks.gov/) is to savings and loan associations what the Federal Reserve System is to commercial banks. Its primary purpose is to ensure that the banks remain adequately capitalized and able to raise funds in the capital markets. The system consists of three tiers: the Federal Home Loan Bank Board, 12 regional Federal Home Loan Banks, and some 8,000 member savings and loan associations.

The 12 regional Federal Home Loan Banks provide loans to member banks in their regions and help to stabilize the available supply of residential mortgage credit. Every federal savings and loan association and savings bank and every state-chartered savings institution insured by the FDIC is required to become a member of its regional Federal Home Loan Bank. Although the Home Loan Banks cannot regulate money supply as does the Federal Reserve System, they do lend funds, establish interest rates, and set other requirements for members. They are located in Atlanta, Boston, Chicago, Cincinnati, Dallas, Des Moines, Indianapolis, New York, Pittsburgh, San Francisco, Seattle, and Topeka.

Savings and loan associations and savings banks are covered by the Federal Home Loan Bank System, but credit unions are not. Federally chartered credit unions, however, are chartered, insured, supervised, and examined by the National Credit Union Administration (NCUA) (http://www.ncua.gov/).

It should be clear from this discussion that banks and thrifts are among the most heavily regulated and supervised institutions in the country.

State Agencies

State-chartered banks and thrifts come under the control of state authorities. Although the structure of banking agencies varies from one state to another, most are established as separate departments or are parts of state departments of finance or commerce. Like their federal counterparts, state banking agencies charter, regulate, and monitor the banks and thrifts under their control. In addition, each state has the right to prohibit certain kinds of banking activities, such as branch banking, within its borders.

Publications

The financial services industry is well represented by both print publications and other types of information sources. This section examines materials relevant to banking and credit. Other segments of the financial services industry are covered in the chapters that follow.

Guides

FDIC: Bank Data Guide. http://www.fdic.gov/bank/statistical/guide/index.html
(accessed March 3, 2011)

Perhaps one of the most useful parts of this site is the institutional directory that also links to financial reports for the banks included. Shown below is the segmentation of the page with the links.

Bank Find   http://www2.fdic.gov/idasp/main.bankfind.asp
- Find out if your bank is FDIC-insured
- Find the locations of your bank's branches
- Find out if your bank has merged or been acquired
- Review your bank's history

Institution Directory (ID)   http://www2.fdic.gov/idasp/index.asp
- The latest comprehensive financial and demographic data for every FDIC-insured institution.
- Create reports and downloads to analyze prospective mergers and classes of competitors
- Compare performance and condition data between individual institutions, peer groups and time periods

Call & Thrift Financial Reports   http://www2.fdic.gov/Call_TFR_Rpts/
FFIEC Central Data Repository (CDR)   https://cdr.ffiec.gov/public/
- Repository of the Report of Condition (call report) and Thrift Financial Report (TFR) filed since 1998 through FFIEC's Central Data Repository (CDR)

Summary of Deposits (SOD) / Market Share   http://www2.fdic.gov/sod/
- Annual survey of branch office deposits as of June 30
- Find a list of your institution's offices in Summary of Deposits (SOD)
- Create a Deposit Market Share Report that presents aggregates of each institution's deposits in any combined choice of states, metro areas, cities, counties or zip codes

Statistics on Depository Institutions (SDI)   http://www2.fdic.gov/sdi/
- Find individual and aggregate demographic and financial information (750+ items including balance sheets, income statements, performance ratios etc.) about banks and thrifts dated back to 1992
- Compare financial information between institutions based on common characteristics including size, financial performance, location, established date, status (open vs. inactive), charter type (state vs. national, commercial bank vs. savings institution), business specialty etc.
- Create custom peer groups, reports and downloads
- SDI Tutorial - http://www2.fdic.gov/sdi/Internet_tutorial.pps

Statistics at a Glance   http://www.fdic.gov/bank/statistical/stats/
- The latest quarterly statistics that define the banking industry and the most recent industry trends

Regional Economic Conditions (RECON)   http://www2.fdic.gov/recon/index.asp
- Standard graphs, tables and maps depicting economic conditions and how they changed over time for any state, MSA (Metropolitan Statistical Area) or county

Historical Statistics on Banking (HSOB)   http://www2.fdic.gov/hsob/index.asp
- Annual statistical information on the banking industry beginning in 1934
- Commercial bank, savings institutions and bank failure history

FDIC Quarterly   http://www.fdic.gov/bank/analytical/quarterly/index.html
- Timely analyses of economic and banking trends at the national and regional level
- Combines data from two retired publications-- the FDIC Outlook and the FDIC Banking Review

Quarterly Banking Profile (QBP)   http://www2.fdic.gov/qbp/index.asp
- Quarterly report card for the banking industry
- Summarized financial results in the form of analyses, graphs and statistical tables for all FDIC-insured institutions
- Results are published approximately 55 days after the end of each quarter beginning with December 31, 1994

FDIC State Profiles   http://www.fdic.gov/bank/analytical/stateprofile/index.html
- Quarterly data sheets of banking and economic conditions in each state

Center for Financial Research (CFR)   http://www.fdic.gov/bank/analytical/cfr/index.html
- Innovative research on topics that are important to the FDIC's role as a deposit insurer and bank supervisor
- CFR programs explore developments affecting the banking industry, risk measurement and management methods, regulatory policy, and related topics of interest to the FDIC

Figure 9.5. Bank Data Guide. Reproduced from the website, http://www.fdic.gov/bank/statistical/guide/bankdataguide.pdf

Other sources are considerably more specialized, focusing on specific types of publications or selecting materials intended for certain audiences.

Dictionaries and Encyclopedias

Dictionaries

Banking dictionaries can be divided into two main categories: those intended for practitioners and students and those written for consumers. Although a number of such dictionaries are regularly published, many users can now find sufficient information on the Web.

American Banker Online. **Glossary.** 2003. http://www.americanbanker.com/glossary .html

The American Banker *Glossary* is a handy online compilation of terms ranging from "ABO" to "zoning." Included are acronyms and cross-references.

Banking.Dictionary.com, http://www.bankingdictionary.com/

Easy-to-use free finance dictionary with over 8,000 definitions. Concise, clear, and comprehensive definitions of all terms used in the banking and finance industry.

Investorwords.com, http://www.investorwords.com/

Once again InvestorWords will be the web page to use for terms that are not understood or just need more clarification. One can perform a simple search or enter the banking subject area for browsing.

Handbooks

The following handbooks are a selection from the many that are currently available.

Oxford Handbook of Banking. New York: Oxford University Press, 2010. 994p.

Gregoriou, Greg N., ed. **The Banking Crisis Handbook**. Boca Raton: CRC Press, 2010. 569p.

Jackson-Moore, Elisabeth. **The International Handbook of Islamic Banking and Finance.** Cranbrook, Kent: Global Professional Pub., 2009. 300p.

The *Oxford Handbook of Banking* provides an overview and analysis of research in banking written by leading researchers in the field. The book strikes a balance between abstract theory, empirical analysis, and practitioner and policy-related material.

The handbook is split into five parts. Part I examines the role of banks, risk management, amalgamation, and diversification in banking. Part II discusses central banking, policy, regulation, and supervision, while Part III, Bank Performance, includes sections on globalization, innovation, and all aspects of lending from small business to the consumer. Part IV, Macroeconomic Perspectives, includes sections on economic activity and banking crises, while Part V looks at regional differences in banking. This last section scrutinizes banking in the United States, the developing nations of Asia, Japan, Latin America, and the EU-15 countries.

The first part of *The Banking Crisis Handbook,* which consists of thirteen chapters, describes how the crisis began. It scrutinizes the role of poor financial regulations, the U.S. mortgage crisis, shadow banks, unsuccessful risk management, the deleveraging of hedge funds, and their impact on the collapse of financial systems. The second section examines the crisis from the perspective of the global market as well as individual countries and regions. Areas included are Australia, Asia, Latin America, and Russia. In the final part, the book considers possible answers, including government intervention, regulatory rules, and methods to evaluate credit risk and the tools of credit risk transfer, including credit default swaps and mortgage-backed securities.

The *International Handbook of Islamic Banking and Finance* fills one of the needs for a readable and easily understood work on Islamic finance. It provides a thorough view of the development and current practices in Islamic banking and finance to enable bankers and accountants, as well as students studying Islamic practices, to understand the major aspects of Sharia compliance in all monetary transactions. This volume also includes an overview of Islamic accounting standards and both equity and bond investment. Major institutions and organizations involved with Islamic finance are also described.

Financial Manuals and Online Databases

Banking directories generally reflect the divisions between commercial banks, thrifts, and other financial service institutions. *Mergent Bank & Finance Manual*, however, is an exception.

Mergent. **Mergent Bank & Finance Manual.** New York: Mergent. 1900–. 4vs. Annual, with semiweekly supplements. (Available electronically in *Mergent Online,* http://www.mergent.com/)

Comprehensive treatment of more than 3,000 publicly held U.S. banks, bank holding companies, savings and loans, funds, insurers, finance companies, real estate companies, real estate investment trusts, and credit agencies, as well as facts on more than 6,500 unit investment trusts. The manual contains information about the institution's long-term debt and capital debt as well as income statements, balance sheets, and statements of cash flow. The center blue pages contain listings of the largest banks (not limited to U.S. banks) and other statistical data on the industry. Updates are at News Reports and are compiled on a monthly basis in Mergent Corporate News Reports Monthly, available at http://www.mergent.com/downloads-newsReports.html.

This information is also included in *Mergent Online,* where one can search by NAICS code to get a list of certain types of banks within a state and then link to the full-text information. Many libraries have chosen to retain the historical collection of all *Mergent Manuals* in either the available microfiche collection or the online PDF collection named *Mergent WebReports.* For those libraries that are contemplating switching from microfiche to the archival *WebReports,* I suggest that the microfiche be retained until the online image is improved as at this time many images are of poor quality.

For standard directory coverage, other publications are generally consulted. Commercial banks, for example, are listed in the following titles.

BankScope. Amsterdam: Bureau van Dijk Electronic Pub. 1998–current.

The Bankers' Almanac. West Sussex, England: Reed Information Services, 1919–. 6v. Semiannual. (Now available at http://www.bankersalmanac.com/)

The Bank Directory. Skokie, IL: Thomson Financial, 2000–. 5v. Semiannual.

BankScope is a comprehensive, global database of banks' financial statements, ratings, and intelligence. It covers over 28,600 (13,600 U.S.) banks around the world, including 16 years of detailed accounts and ratings from Fitch, Moody's, Standard & Poor's, and Capital Intelligence. The database contains stock data for listed banks, directors and contacts, original filings, detailed bank structures, business and related news, and M&A deals and rumors.

The Bankers' Almanac provides information on over 4,000 major international banks in 211 countries and 84,000 towns. To be included, the banks must hold a full banking license issued by the central bank or monetary authority in the country of domicile and must be able to supply a fully audited annual report and balance sheet. The first three volumes alphabetically list the banks by name, volumes 4 and 5 list the banks geographically, and volume 6 contains a brief alphabetical listing of over 18,000 other authorized banks. For each full listing in volumes 1, 2, and 3, information includes full addresses; the Telerate; bank code; web address; Fitch, Mergent, and S&P ratings; corporate structure; merger information; a listing of directors; a list of correspondents; standard settlement instructions; and information from the consolidated balance sheet. Indexes are included. The *Almanac* is expensive, and it is unusual for any but the largest, most specialized, or most affluent libraries to have a subscription.

The Bank Directory, formerly *Thomson Bank Directory,* profiles banks and their branch offices. Volumes 1 and 2 provide information for the United States, and volumes 3 and 4 cover the rest of the world. The arrangement in the first volumes is by state and town; in the world volumes it is by country and town. A number of entries provide some balance sheet information and principal correspondents. Most contain officer information. Various tables are listed, including the top 500 U.S. banks listed by assets, key financial information by state, credit ratings, and international offices of U.S. banks. This is one of the most popular directories and is held by most libraries. This publication is included in the *Thomson Global Banking Resource* (http://www.tgbr.com/), which is available online. These directories are also included in the full LexisNexis service.

Although the *Thomson Bank Directory* provides good coverage of commercial banks, it excludes savings and loan associations and credit unions. For listings of such institutions, other directories must be consulted.

Thomson Savings Directory. Skokie, IL: Thomson Financial, 1991. Annual.

Directory of Federally Insured Credit Unions. http://www.ncua.gov/DataServices/
Directory/cudir.aspx (accessed March 3, 2011)

The Thomson directory listed above provide a comprehensive listing by state and city for all active S&Ls, building and loan associations, cooperative banks, and savings banks in the United States. Although most entries lack the detailed financial data contained in the banking directories described above, they do include standard directory information and the location and addresses of branch offices.

The *Directory of Federally Insured Credit Unions* provides contact information and financial snapshots for all 10,366 credit unions in the United States. Best of all, the price fits all budgets, as it is free.

The FDIC issues a free online directory. The *Financial Institutions Directory* (http://www2.fdic.gov/idasp/index.asp) allows one to search for a holding company, an institution, or an office. It provides the latest comprehensive financial and demographic data for every FDIC-insured institution, including the most recent quarterly financial statements, with performance and condition ratios. For those who do not require a comprehensive global directory, this free online service probably contains much of the information that is needed.

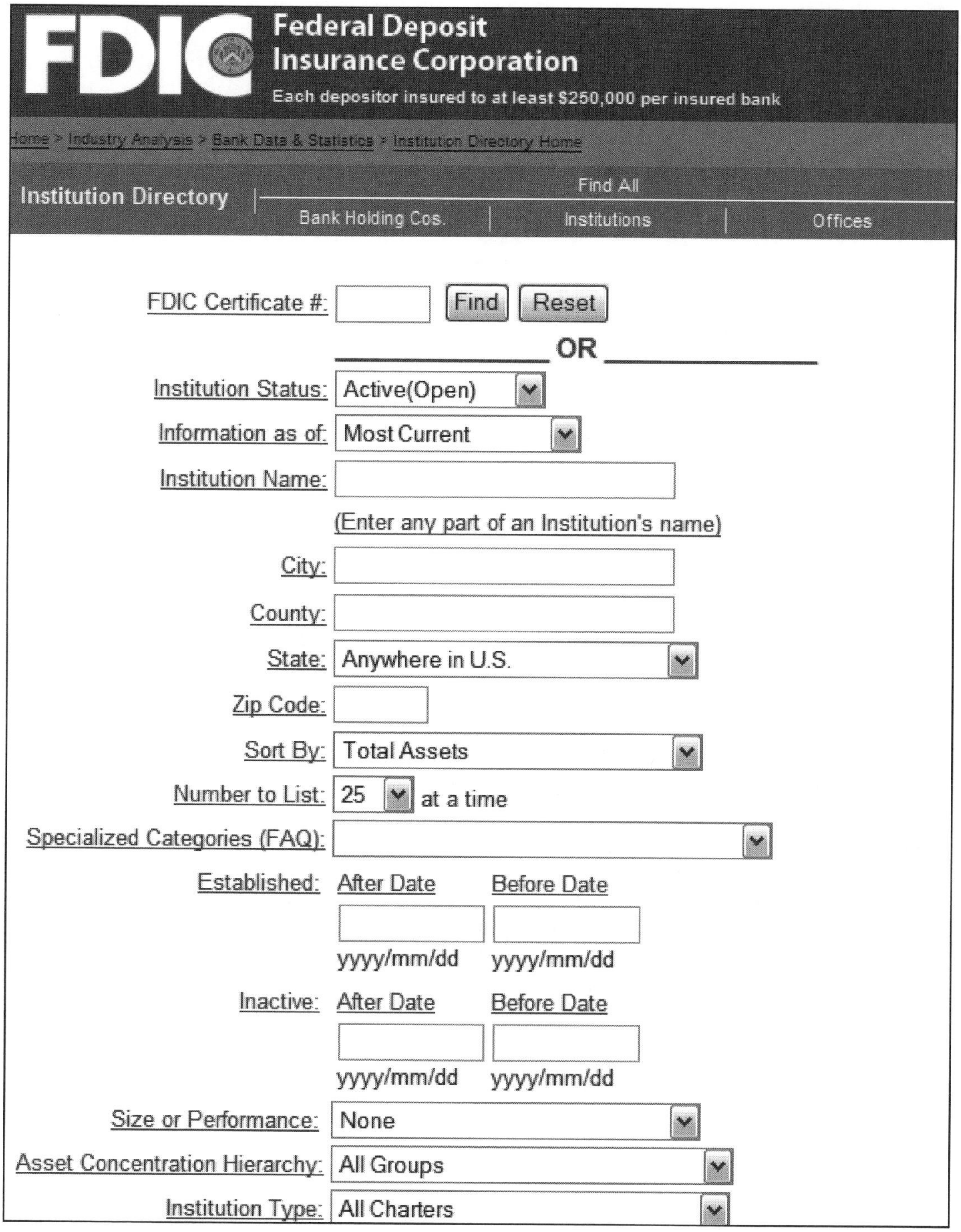

FDIC

Federal Deposit Insurance Corporation

Each depositor insured to at least $250,000 per insured bank

Home > Industry Analysis > Bank Data & Statistics > Institution Directory Home

Institution Directory

| | Find All | |
| Bank Holding Cos. | Institutions | Offices |

FDIC Certificate #: [____] [Find] [Reset]

_____ OR _____

Institution Status: [Active(Open) ▾]

Information as of: [Most Current ▾]

Institution Name: [_____]

(Enter any part of an Institution's name)

City: [_____]

County: [_____]

State: [Anywhere in U.S. ▾]

Zip Code: [_____]

Sort By: [Total Assets ▾]

Number to List: [25 ▾] at a time

Specialized Categories (FAQ): [_____ ▾]

Established: After Date _____ Before Date _____
[_____]   [_____]
yyyy/mm/dd   yyyy/mm/dd

Inactive: After Date _____ Before Date _____
[_____]   [_____]
yyyy/mm/dd   yyyy/mm/dd

Size or Performance: [None ▾]

Asset Concentration Hierarchy: [All Groups ▾]

Institution Type: [All Charters ▾]

Figure 9.6. Search page for the Financial Institutions Directory,
http://www2.fdic.gov/idasp/main.asp

Periodicals, Newspapers, and Indexes

Periodicals

Although personal finance magazines such as *Money* and general business periodicals such as *Business Week*, *Fortune*, and *Forbes* regularly report on the banking industry, most specialized banking periodicals are written for practitioners and scholars. Their number is impressive; over 350 banking and finance titles are listed in the *Standard Periodical Directory*. Although comprehensive coverage is impossible in a work of this sort, the titles that follow are standard banking periodicals.

ABA Banking Journal. Washington, DC: American Bankers Association, 1908–. Monthly. (Web version at http://www.ababj.com/)

The Banker. London: Financial News Ltd., 1926–. Monthly. (Some free information available at http://www.thebanker.com/)

Journal of Money, Credit, and Banking. Columbus: Ohio State University Press, 1969–. Quarterly. (Earlier volumes are available through *JSTOR*; later publications are online through MUSE and in the Wiley-Blackwell full collection)

US Banker. New York: General Banking Division of Faulkner & Gray, 1977–. Monthly. Web version available at http://www.americanbanker.com/usb_issues/

The *ABA Banking Journal* is the official publication of the American Bankers Association, the premier association for the commercial banking industry. It emphasizes current operations and practices in banking, recent developments, bank management, government regulation and legislation, and ABA-sponsored activities and services. Interviews with banking executives and government officials are frequently featured, as are reports on the implications of legislation enacted or being considered. Other articles cover the introduction of new financial products and such management-related issues as personnel, customer relations, bank marketing, and security.

The *Banker* is a premier magazine for banking professionals. Each monthly issue covers a number of countries and topics such as banking services, markets, and global securities services. At the web site http://www.thebanker.com/ are some free articles and a database of rankings where one can retrieve top banks in different regions and countries. Like the *ABA Banking Journal, The Banker* emphasizes practice rather than theory.

The *Journal of Money, Credit, and Banking* is scholarly and international in scope. The editors and contributors are usually university professors. Each author must provide any data and programs used in compiling the articles, and these are made available for researchers at http://webmail.econ.ohio-state.edu/john/IndexDataArchive.php. Recent articles have covered such topics as money supply, interest rates, and commercial credit.

US Banker covers more everyday and undoubtedly more popular subject matter. Topics covered recently include women and mortgages and the misdeeds of top executives. For those looking for a very readable glossy journal that will nonetheless keep them up-to-date with banking issues, this is probably an excellent choice.

The government's role in regulating and influencing financial activities is reflected in its periodical literature. The *Survey of Current Business* (http://www.bea.gov/scb/), for example, publishes selective statistics on banking, credit, and money. Other government periodicals provide even more comprehensive coverage.

U.S. Board of Governors of the Federal Reserve System. **Federal Reserve Bulletin.** Washington, DC: Government Printing Office, 1915–. Monthly. (Web version available at http://www.federalreserve.gov/pubs/bulletin/)

FDIC Quarterly. Washington, DC: Federal Deposit Insurance Corporation, 1988–. Quarterly. (Web version at http://www.fdic.gov/bank/analytical/quarterly/index .html)

The *Federal Reserve Bulletin* combines articles on the Fed and banking with the texts of reports and statements made by the Board of Governors to Congress; summaries of policy actions of the Federal Open Market Committee, staff research studies, and current legal developments; and announcements of Fed policy changes. Its "Financial and Business Statistics" section is an excellent source of current data on money, bank reserves, Federal Reserve and commercial banks, financial markets, federal finance, securities markets and corporate finance, mortgages, consumer credit, and related domestic and international banking activities. This section is, in fact, one of the best sources in which to locate information on monetary and financial conditions.

In addition, each issue of the *Bulletin* publishes a guide to special tables and statistical releases and the issues in which they appear, as well as lists of current members and official staff of the Board of Governors, the Federal Open Market Committee, and two advisory councils. Other lists contain the names and terms of people appointed to the Board of Governors since its beginning in 1913, and the locations, addresses, and officers of Federal Reserve Banks, branches, and offices. Articles but not statistical tables are available online at http://www.federalreserve.gov/pubs/bulletin/default.htm.

The *FDIC Quarterly* (formerly the *FDIC Banking Review*) provides original research on issues related to banking and deposit insurance. It supplies a comprehensive summary of the most current financial results for the banking industry, along with feature articles. These articles range from timely analysis of economic and banking trends at the national and regional levels that may affect the risk exposure of FDIC-insured institutions to research on issues affecting the banking system and the development of regulatory policy. The *FDIC Quarterly* brings together data and analysis that were previously available through three retired publications—the *FDIC Outlook*, the *FDIC Banking Review*, and *FYI: An Update on Emerging Issues in Banking*. Past issues of these publications are archived online under their original publication names.

Newspapers

Although major daily newspapers such as the *New York Times*, the *Wall Street Journal*, and the *Financial Times* devote considerable attention to money, credit, and banking, another daily is even more important.

American Banker. New York: American Banker, 1836–. Daily, Monday through Friday.

The *American Banker* (http://www.americanbanker.com/) is basic reading for most professionals in the financial services industry. It covers current news and developments; analyzes trends; and profiles key companies, executives, and officials. All aspects of the industry are covered. Many issues include special sections focusing on such topics as marketing or technology and financial networks. Ranked lists of the largest financial institutions are published regularly. A listing of the available special reports and rankings is available at http://www.americanbanker.com/specialreports.html.

Government Documents

Government involvement in regulating and monitoring banking activities is reflected in its documents output. The diversity and sheer number of documents on banking and the financial services industry are immediately apparent to anyone scanning through the subject index of the print *Monthly Catalog of United States Government Publications* or using the free online catalog at http://www.gpo.gov/fdsys/. Titles range from guides for consumers, to shopping for loans, to congressional hearings on bank deregulation and third-world debt, from periodicals and news releases to statistical compendia. Although the need for such publications will vary considerably from one library to the next, the web links that follow point to those found useful in many library settings.

The Federal Reserve System issues publications on actions taken by the board, its staff, and the Federal Reserve Banks; enforcement actions; regulations; and legal interpretations, all available from http://www.federalreserve.gov/bankinforeg/default .htm. The Fed also provides information for consumers, such as "Consumer's Guide: Credit Reports and Credit Scores" (http://www.federalreserve.gov/creditreports/) and "Showbusiness: The Economics of Entertainment" (http://www.bos.frb.org/ entertainment/index.htm). These and other publications are available by checking the web site at http://www.federalreserve.gov/publications.htm. Not all are on the Web, but instructions for ordering print copies are included.

There is also a catalog of publications at https://www.newyorkfed.org/publications/. By checking on one of the subjects at the left of the screen a list of publications in that category will appear. One may order copies online (see figure 9.7).

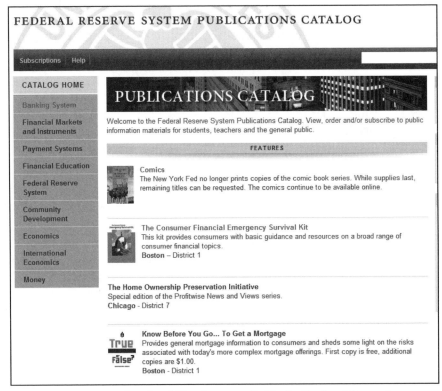

Figure 9.7. Example of publications available in the banking category,
at https://www.newyorkfed.org/publications/

The other agency much concerned with money and banking is the FDIC (http://www.fdic.gov/). Again, the web site contains an important accumulation of information. The researcher can link to information on deposit insurance, regulations for bankers, electronic banking procedures, and more.

Much of the information that a researcher needs is now available on the Web. Not only the resources from the Fed and the FDIC but also bills, committee reports, and prints that involve the banking industry can be located online. The representative list of publications in figure 9.8 was retrieved by entering "banking" as a keyword at http://thomas.loc.gov. Each document is retrievable in PDF format by clicking on the House or Senate number.

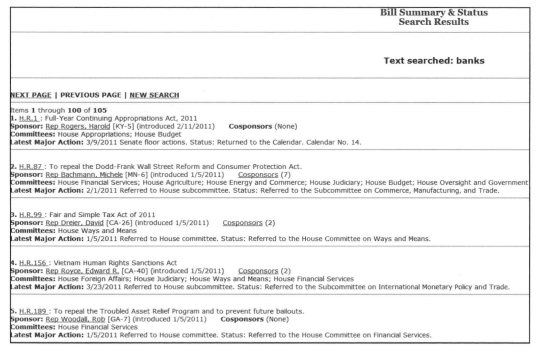

Figure 9.8. Representative list of publications on banks from http://thomas.loc.gov

Statistics

Government-issued publications, in a variety of formats, are some of the best sources of current statistical information. As was mentioned previously, the *Federal Reserve Bulletin* contains detailed monthly statistics on money, credit, and banking. Each of the Federal Reserve Banks publishes a monthly economic review and other titles as well. They are particularly useful for an overview of regional business and economic conditions. Similarly, each of the 12 regional Federal Home Loan Banks publishes information at its web site that features analysis of area economic conditions as they relate to mortgage loans and the thrift industry. Articles in the *Bulletin* and in the Federal Reserve periodicals that contain statistics are indexed in the *American Statistics Index* (*Statistical Insight*), which is one of the best sources of information on the statistical output of independent federal agencies. Links to each Federal Reserve District are at http://www.federalreserve.gov/otherfrb.htm, and the link to the Federal Home Loan Banks is at http://www.fhlbanks.com/.

Twenty-four-hour access to regional and national financial and economic data is provided by *FRED®* (http://research.stlouisfed.org/fred2/). This site provides historical U.S. economic and financial data, including daily U.S. interest rates, monetary and business indicators, exchange rates, balance of payments, and loans. The *FRED®* data files are grouped into 12 categories, including one for commercial banks and one for monthly reserves data. "All files, except those that are compressed, are in ASCII format. Compressed files are in .zip or self-extracting .exe formats. The compressed files contain all of the ASCII files within that category of data."[12] The "Commercial Banking" section has at least 50 years of monthly or weekly data on topics such as Bank Credit of all Commercial Banks, Consumer Loans at all Commercial Banks, and Total Automobile Credit Outstanding. For these large data sets there are excellent instructions for downloading and converting into Excel spreadsheets (see figure 9.9).

This is an excellent source of statistical information on money and banking.

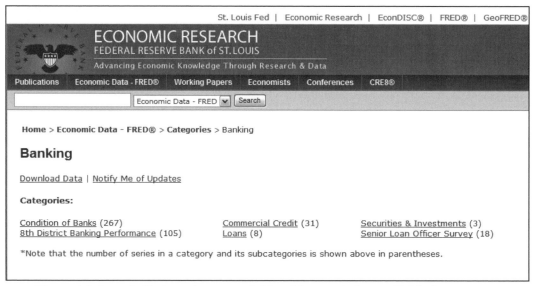

Figure 9.9. Sample listing of commercial banking statistics available from FRED,
at http://research.stlouisfed.org/fred2/

Another excellent source of information on the Federal Reserve System is *FRASER* (http://fraser.stlouisfed.org/), where one can link to archival reports and statistics (see figure 9.10).

FDIC Statistics on Banking (http://www2.fdic.gov/SDI/SOB/) is a quarterly publication that provides detailed aggregate financial information as well as number of institutions and branches for all FDIC-insured institutions. Aggregate statistics are retrievable from the fourth quarter of 1991 on balance sheets, income statements, and loans for commercial banks and savings institutions (see figure 9.11).

Figure 9.10. Selected front screen links at FRASER at http://fraser.stlouisfed.org/

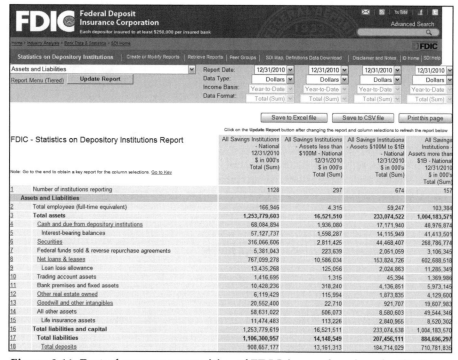

Figure 9.11. Part of report on securities of FDIC-insured savings institutions, generated from the web site at http://www2.fdic.gov/SDI/SOB/

According to the web site, "The FDIC has introduced a new feature that provides users with most of the financial information contained in the *Statistics on Banking* and allows them to dynamically generate customized reports for analysis. For instance, users can create reports that consist of any combination of single institutions or bank holding companies, standard peer groups of institutions, and custom peer groups of institutions and bank holding companies." This system is available at http://www2.fdic.gov/SDI/SOB/.

Other statistical compendia and guides are published by professional and trade associations. Following is a representative list with web addresses. All list available publications, and some free information is provided.

American Bankers Association	http://www.aba.com
ATM Industry Association	http://www.atmia.com/
Bank Administration Institute	http://www.bai.org
Consumer Bankers Association	http://www.cbanet.org
Independent Community Bankers of America	http://www.icba.org

Banking Tables

Basic to any banking reference collection is the presence of at least one compilation of banking and financial tables. A number of such sources are available, but one of the most comprehensive and popular works is listed below.

Thorndike, David, and Donald S. Benton. **Thorndike Encyclopedia of Banking and Financial Tables.** 4th ed. Austin, TX: Thomson Financial/Pratt, 2001. 1v. (various pagings)

The *Thorndike Encyclopedia of Banking and Financial Tables* groups tables by six broad categories. A general explanation precedes each table and describes its use, and each table begins with a summary of the rates, terms, payments, and yields that are shown in the table. A dictionary of financial terms is also included. A yearbook brings the *Encyclopedia* up to date.

Databases

Many of the databases mentioned in previous chapters are relevant to the banking industry. *Business Source Complete*, *ABI/INFORM Global*, and *LexisNexis*, for example, provide full-text articles from banking journals, many of them complete with graphs and statistics. There are, however, other databases whose main emphasis ranges from banking regulations to bankruptcies. These databases are listed in directories such as the *Gale Directory of Databases*.

Notes

1. Robin Gross and Jean V. Cullen, *Help! The Basics of Borrowing Money* (New York: Times Books, 1980), 41.

2. Ibid.

3. Thomas E. Van Dahm, *Money and Banking: An Introduction to the Financial System* (Lexington, MA: D. C. Heath, 1975), 48–49.

4. For simple descriptions of banking and credit, check the educational publications of the Federal Reserve Bank of Chicago at http://www.chicagofed.org/consumerinformation/index.cfm.

5. William Gobble and Bruce Harwood, *North Carolina Real Estate*, 2nd ed. (Reston, VA: Reston Publishing, 1984), 245–46.

6. Taken from the web page of the National Credit Union Administration at http://www.ncua.gov/indexabout.html.

7. The president of the Federal Reserve Bank of New York serves as a permanent member of the FOMC. For the remaining four memberships, which carry a one-year term, a rotating selection is taken from the presidents of the 11 other Reserve Banks.

8. Taken from the web page at http://www.federalreserve.gov/pubs/frseries/frseri2.htm.

9. *Reserve Bank Studies* in PDF format are at http://www.federalreserve.gov/pubs/staffstudies.

10. Details of publications from 12 Federal Reserve District Banks are available at:

Boston	http://www.bos.frb.org/genpubs/
New York	http://www.newyorkfed.org/research/index.html
Philadelphia	http://www.phil.frb.org/publications/
Cleveland	http://www.clevelandfed.org/research/
Richmond	http://www.richmondfed.org/index.cfm
Atlanta	http://www.frbatlanta.org/pubs/econresearch/
Chicago	http://www.chicagofed.org/webpages/publications/index.cfm
St. Louis	http://stlouisfed.org/publications/research_and_data.cfm
Minneapolis	http://www.minneapolisfed.org/publications_papers/
Kansas City	http://www.kc.frb.org/publications/
Dallas	http://www.dallasfed.org/pubs/index.html
San Francisco	http://www.frbsf.org/economics/

11. Taken from the web page of the OCC at http://www.occ.treas.gov/aboutocc.htm.

12. Taken from the web page at http://research.stlouisfed.org/fred2/.

10

Investments: An Introduction

As Americans become increasingly concerned with financial security, a growing number are seeking to find it through careful investment. Sponsored by the Federal Reserve Board, the Survey of Consumer Finances (SCF) is a triennial survey of the balance sheet, pension, income, and other demographic characteristics of U.S. families. Some of the latest information from the survey reveals that in 2007, direct and indirect stock ownership by families was holding relatively steady at 51.1 percent. This was slightly higher than the 50.2 percent listed for 2004 but lower than 2001 when it was 52.2 percent. One ongoing trend is the rapid growth of indirect methods of share ownership, such as ownership through investments in equity mutual funds or through 401(k) plans or defined contribution pension plan accounts. But stocks are not the only investment medium:

> Investment has many facets. It may involve putting money into banks, Treasury bills or notes, or common stocks, or paintings, or real estate, or mortgages, or oil ventures, or cattle, or the theater. It may involve speculating in bull markets or selling short in bear markets. It may involve choosing growth stocks, or blue chips, or defensive stocks, or income stocks, or even penny cats and dogs. It may involve options, straddles, rights, warrants, convertibles, margin, gold, silver, mutual funds, money market funds, index funds, tax exempt bond funds, and result in accumulation of wealth or dissipation of resources. Diversity and challenge characterize the field.[1]

In fact, as more people choose to invest, Wall Street has become increasingly ingenious in introducing new investment vehicles to the public. As a result, there are a myriad of investment opportunities for small, private investors. This chapter and the four that follow deal with the most common types of investments—stocks, bonds, mutual funds, futures, and options—and the basic types of information sources relevant to each.

Investors and Their Information Needs

Investors fall into two main categories: institutional and individual. Institutional investors include banks, insurance companies, mutual funds and investment companies, college endowment funds, corporate profit-sharing plans, and pension funds. They are organizations with considerable money to invest and large securities portfolios to manage. Frequently they have one or more departments that include securities analysts, portfolio managers, economists, and other experts to supply data and help make investment decisions. Individual investors, on the other hand, are private investors, people making their own, and comparatively small, personal investments. Generally they lack the expertise available to institutional investors and are not usually full-time investors.

To be successful, such investors must be well informed. The astute investor who is considering a purchase of stocks, for example, will attempt to learn not only as much as possible about the company itself but also about the industry of which it is a part, the economy generally, and all of the factors that affect it. Some will look to their brokers to supply the needed information. Many others, however, will take a more active role, reading financial newspapers, business periodicals, and advisory newsletters, and now gathering information from the Internet.

Investment information can be categorized in many ways. It can, for example, be classified as either descriptive or analytical. Descriptive investment information is factual; statistics comprise a large part of the data presented, and the focus is on the recent past or on the historical performance of the company, industry, or economic development being considered. Analytical investment information, on the other hand, does not limit itself to historical data but includes projections for future performance as well as investment recommendations. Both descriptive and analytical information sources belong in most business reference collections.

Before consulting these sources, prospective investors often need to learn more about specific types of investments. As a result, publications such as guides, encyclopedias, handbooks, and even textbooks are important because they provide broad coverage of the field.

Background Information Sources

Publications in this category introduce novice investors and librarians to specific types of investments, supply answers to quick reference questions, and often include lists and aids to further investigation. Although there are literally hundreds of such publications and Internet sites, the ones that follow are among the most highly regarded.

One good way to begin to understand the basics of investing in each of the major investment mediums is by consulting a personal finance guide.

Quinn, Jane Bryant. **Smart and Simple Financial Strategies for Busy People**. New York: Simon & Schuster, 2006. 242p.

Kansas, Dave. **The Wall Street Journal Complete Money and Investing Guidebook.** New York: Wall Street Journal Books, 2005. 224p.

In the first paragraph of Quinn's book are the sentences that sum up her philosophy of personal finance and what is available to the average reader: "When you really study this subject, as I have, you learn that what's on offer is mostly mediocre and sometimes downright bad. The products are expensive, which wastes your money. They're often complicated, with risky angles that you didn't know about. If you pick your own investments, you may choose things that don't go together well, leaving big gaps in your security fence. If you buy from brokers and planners who earn commissions, you may find yourself trapped in a poorly performing product that you don't understand." This is a good book to start with for coverage of spending and saving, buying a house, saving for college, and the everyday worries that many people have about personal finance. It is an up-to-date, comprehensive, and authoritative all-in-one resource that is not only helpful but also very readable.

The Complete Money and Investing Guidebook contains ten chapters, including those that explain stocks, bonds, mutual funds, and retirement investing. This is a straightforward general book full of helpful charts, graphs, and illustrations and is an essential source for novice and experienced investors alike. This book joins a fairly long list of publications from the *Wall Street Journal,* all of which are designed to be easy to understand (see http://online.wsj.com/public/page/2_1150.html).

Although an experienced investor might consider these sources superficial or unsophisticated, they are a good starting point for librarians confronted for the first time with a reference question about the data contained in a stock quote or on commodities trading.

Encyclopedias and Handbooks

Handbooks and single-volume encyclopedias constitute still another source of background information. Usually each chapter deals with a different aspect of investing or with a specific type of investment and is often written by a specialist in the area being covered.

Downes, John, and Jordan Elliot Goodman. **Finance & Investment Handbook.** 8th ed. Hauppauge, NY: Barron's Educational Series, 2010. 1152p.

Encyclopedia of Busine$$ and Finance. 2nd ed. New York: Macmillan Reference USA, 2006. 794p.

Investopedia. Copyright © 2011, Investopedia US, A Division of ValueClick, Inc. (http://www.investopedia.com)

Updated to reflect the current investment climate, the *Finance & Investment Handbook* presents a financial dictionary with definitions of more than 5,000 terms, an analysis of various current investment opportunities, guidelines for non-experts on what to look for when researching corporate reports and reading financial news sources, an updated directory of hundreds of publicly traded corporations in the United States and Canada, and a directory listing the names and addresses of brokerage houses, mutual funds families, banks, up-to-date information on federal and state regulators, and other major financial institutions. It is an excellent resource that covers many facets of investing.

The *Encyclopedia of Busine$$ and Finance* is a two-volume reference designed for the non-specialist, covering five areas: finance and banking, accounting, marketing, management, and information systems. Representing practical professional expertise as well as that of noted scholars, the book's contributors include executives and government administrators from leading business programs around the United States. Glossaries and reading lists are also included. The Barron's *Finance & Investment Handbook* is useful for both the novice and the more advanced investor. It provides a thorough overview of almost every type of investment, including bonds, annuities, life insurance, real estate investment trusts (REITs), and option contracts. It also contains lists of major financial institutions, historical data on leading indexes, as well as sections on how to read an annual report or financial pages and a comprehensive glossary of investment terms. It is probably the authoritative volume on investing, which is to be expected from Barron's.

Bloomberg Businessweek **http://www.businessweek.com/**	Still commonly known as Businessweek although it is now owned by Bloomberg. The new ownership has enabled the addition of outstanding company information that includes financials, ratios, transactions and ownership. The financial information includes nicely formatted SEC filings. Other sections under the finance tab include a learning center, an investment blog and retirement planning. At this time this is one of the best inclusive sites.
YAHOO! FINANCE **http://finance.yahoo.com/**	The most visited investment /finance web site, according to Marketingcharts.com. As well as the usual stock, bond and mutual fund information this site has investment guides and a personal finance section that covers all basic and intermediate information needs. It also includes both revenue and earnings forecasts. Especially useful is the historical daily stock price data where several years of monthly, weekly or daily results can be downloaded to excel. Yahoo was one of the first sites to democratize financial information.
Fidelity Investments **https://www.fidelity.com/**	This site provides excellent research on stocks and mutual funds (you don't have to be a customer to use it). Has clearly-written articles on basic investing, retirement planning, estate planning, college expenses, taxes, how to build a bond ladder portfolio, and much more. Very good stock research and analysis tools. Also has tools for selecting, evaluating, and comparing mutual funds.
The Motley Fool **http://www.fool.com/**	An entertaining investment and educational resource with an abundance of articles as well as the latest market commentary, analysis and news. The website is easy to navigate. Using the CAPS feature individual investors predict whether specific stocks will outperform or underperform the S&P 500 and over what time frame this will happen. One can see the ratings on any stock, or lists of the highest and lowest rated stocks.
MarketWatch **http://www.marketwatch.com/**	A huge resource of market news, commentary, and opinion. MarketWatch.com is a major player in this niche, and a huge resource for anything stock market or finance related. The site is very easy to navigate and can easily become a top site to utilize on a day to day basis for stock market related topics. An excellent addition to other sites that specialize in investment research.

Figure 10.1 Selected investment guides on the Web

For those who prefer to work with an electronic site, *Investopedia* is the place to start. Founded in 1999, *Investopedia* started as an online investing dictionary. Today, the site includes over 7,000 terms and offers articles, tutorials, frequently asked questions, and several free newsletter subscriptions. In 2004, *Investopedia* launched the Investopedia Stock Simulator, "an online investment portfolio where investors can test their trading and investing skills by trading real stocks, up to $100,000 through a virtual stocks account." Widely quoted by investment media, *Investopedia* receives several million visits every month, and other investment sites often link to the articles created by the writers. There are many ways to use this site. One can search a term, but it is probably more useful to use the tabs at the top of the screen. The articles section sorts topics by subject areas and then links within each article lead to more information on interrelated topics. The tutorial section is especially useful for beginners and more advanced investors, covering areas such as "How to Read Financial Tables," "How to Analyze Earnings," and many other investment concepts. Also included on the site is biographical information on the world's greatest investors, basic information on industry sectors, a dictionary, and even "exam prep" for global professional examinations. One of the best investment sources you will never pay for.

Dictionaries

Many of the publications already described contain glossaries, but for more detailed definitions or for a more comprehensive listing of terms, it may be necessary to consult an investment dictionary.

Banks, Eric. **The Palgrave Macmillan Dictionary of Finance, Investment and Banking.** Basingstoke, UK: Palgrave Macmillan, 2010. 565p.

Peterson, Nora. **Wall Street Lingo: Thousands of Investment Terms Explained Simply.** Ocala, FL: Atlantic Pub. Group, 2007. 288p.

InvestorWords. 1996–2011. WebFinance, Inc. (d/b/a InvestorGuide.com) (Producer). http://www.investorwords.com/ (accessed April 2, 2011)

The *Dictionary of Finance, Investment and Banking* contains concise and clear definitions of well over 5,000 terms commonly used in the industry, covering the disciplines of accounting, banking, corporate finance, investment management, and insurance. It includes succinct but thorough definitions of new terminology, reflecting developments following the global financial crisis. *Wall Street Lingo* covers fewer terms, over 1,000, but is easier to navigate because of the way it is compiled. On top of dividing the over 1,000 defined investment terms into twenty-five logical chapters, with all terms relating to a topic in the same chapter, a full index at the back of the book makes for quick referencing.

InvestorWords is one of the most comprehensive online glossaries available, providing solid definitions for over 15,000 financial terms, and including links between related terms. One can search by letter or within the 29 subject areas that include bonds, stocks, mutual funds, and trading. Searching for the word "options," one is given an exact explanation of the word but also the alternative of checking over 90 terms that include the word. One of the terms listed is "collar," and it has as one of its three definitions, "A combination of put options and call options that can limit, but not eliminate, the risk that their value will decrease." Further links are provided for the underlined terms. Perhaps best of all, this dictionary is provided free, and subject glossaries can be downloaded to a personal web site. A new term is featured every day on the web site or can be emailed to those who prefer it. This is only one of the many dictionaries that is produced by WebFinance; others are listed at http://www.webfinanceinc.com/products.php. For libraries that need a variety of such resources this is well worth checking. *InvestorWords* has diversified its offerings and now contains excellent company information, including stock charts and annual and quarterly financial information.

Many different types of publications—handbooks, textbooks, personal finance manuals, dictionaries—and web pages provide needed background information for prospective investors. Similar information is also available in the pamphlets, booklets, and brochures published by brokers, stock and commodity exchanges, mutual funds, and investment companies, most of which are now available via the Web. Investment advisors are using new technologies to provide investment advisory services, to offer their services to prospective advisory clients, to obtain investment research, to facilitate portfolio management, and to communicate with their clients. It is therefore important to be able to identify these companies and to find their Internet addresses. To identify brokers and investment managers, one can consult the following publication.

Standard & Poor's Security Dealers of North America. New York: Standard & Poor's, 1922–. Semiannual.

Standard & Poor's Security Dealers of North America has much shorter entries in its listing of U.S. and Canadian securities firms and is aimed at a more general audience. Arrangement is geographical, and the information provided for each firm includes its address, telephone number, identification number, and chief officers; for the firm's headquarters, it also includes the names of the exchanges of which the firm is a member and the types of securities in which it specializes. Also included in this resource are the names and addresses of Canadian and U.S. exchanges and associations, major foreign stock exchanges, a listing of North American securities administrators by state and province, and a section listing firms that have been discontinued—that is, have gone out of business, moved, or changed their name—since the last issue of the directory was published. This is also available electronically through various platforms, including *NetAdvantage*, which is a product available to most libraries.

There are two main types of brokerage firms, full service and discount. A discount brokerage firm is one that concentrates solely on executing transactions for its clientele, on buying or selling securities at the client's direction. No research is conducted, no advice given, no informational literature published. In return for this "no frills" service, clients can expect to pay some 30 to 50 percent less in commission fees than they would pay to traditional full-service investment firms. People who use discount brokers tend to be thrifty do-it-yourself-ers, and they often turn to the library and now the Internet for investment information.

Investment Advisory Services

Investment advisory services provide current information on general market conditions and/or specific companies. Some of these services are factual, and some are interpretive, making recommendations on the purchase or sale of specific securities. Quality, particularly of the newsletters that sell investment advice, varies tremendously. Some are respectable, and others are no more than hucksters' appeals to the gullible and greedy. There are literally hundreds of these publications, some of which are quite expensive. Each has its own, often vocal, following. Clearly, libraries must be highly selective and somewhat conservative in placing subscriptions to these publications. The service in vogue with investors one season may languish the next:

> Each quarter and each year, there are stars among the investment advisors and security analysts. These are individuals with a better record of picking winners than almost anyone else. Each year there are winners in the Irish Sweepstakes and the New York and Illinois state lotteries. No one, however, ever suggested that the winner of a million dollar grand slam prize in the

Illinois state lottery had good insights. Few would pay for his advice on how to buy a winning ticket in the next year's lottery. The key question is whether the winners among the investment advisors have more skill and insight than the winners of the Irish Sweepstakes and the Illinois and New York Lotteries.[2]

The coverage in investment services varies. Some focus on particular types of investments, such as mutual funds or precious metals. Others use specific approaches or methods. Some rely on technical analysis, basing their recommendations on past patterns of market trading and price behavior. Some advocate "contrary opinion," theorizing that if all the other investment advisors are espousing a specific course of action, the sensible thing is to do the opposite. Perhaps one of the most unorthodox systems was that devised by Frederick Goldsmith, who based his recommendations on the actions of Jiggs, a character in the comic strip, *Bringing Up Father*:

> If Jiggs was pictured with his right hand in his pocket, the market was a buy. If he was shown with two puffs of smoke rising from his cigar, this meant that the market would be strong in the second hour of trading. . . . When the strip showed Jiggs at the theater observing, "The intermissions are the only good thing about this show," Goldsmith advised his subscribers to buy Mission Oil.[3]

Almost anyone can publish an advisory letter. No special qualifications or preliminary tests are necessary. In fact, all that is required is that the publisher has no record of fraud and that he or she register with and periodically report to the Securities and Exchange Commission. It is mandatory that an annual report be filed with the SEC on the service's financial condition. This must include a brief description of the investment strategy being followed, information sources used, and methods of analysis employed. Publishers of such services have included people from a wide range of backgrounds, many of whom are not particularly well trained, to give investment advice and who may not always hold their readers' financial well-being uppermost.

It is evident that library subscriptions to these services should be made with caution. Few publications, however, regularly list or evaluate advisory services. Articles can be found in some of the popular business journals, and descriptions are included in some of the periodicals and newsletter directories mentioned in chapter 2.

The most current and comprehensive source of information in this area is the *Hulbert Financial Digest* (*HFD*), a monthly that tracks the performance of 180 investment letters with more than 500 recommended portfolios. This publication contains the rankings of top-performing newsletters, a listing of stocks and mutual funds that currently are most heavily recommended or shunned, and articles. The four top-performing newsletters are profiled in each monthly issue of the *Digest,* and custom profiles of all newsletters can be ordered from http://store.marketwatch.com/webapp/wcs/stores/servlet/Premium Newsletters_HulbertFinancialDigest. These customized newsletters contain complete performance ratings and risk-adjusted ratings for the entire period for which the *Digest* has data and graphical analysis of each newsletter's average performance and of each of the individual portfolios the newsletter is recommending. There is a complete listing of all the newsletters included, and Internet links to each web page, at the site reached by clicking on "Premium Newsletters." Delivery is by print or email.

The cost, sheer volume, widely differing quality, and rapidly fluctuating popularity with the investing public of investment advisory services are some of the main reasons why most libraries do not support extensive collections of such materials. Factual services, that is, those focusing on past performance, both recent and historical, are likely to be better represented in library collections.

Other services, which have become available to investors because of the emergence of the Internet, are the monitored and unmonitored discussion groups. Many magazines and investment web sites have an "ask an advisor" link, and then there are the news groups and blogs where individuals can share information.

Securities Quotations

Investors turn to quotations, brief, numeric price reports, to attempt to determine the present market condition for specific securities. Although the amount of information included in quotations varies, usually most include closing (the last price paid on a particular trading day) and bid (the price someone is willing to pay) prices, the number of units traded, dividends, and high and low prices paid over a designated time period.

Basic to providing good business reference service is the ability to decipher the newspaper tables that contain quotations. Quotations within most tables are arranged alphabetically by company name or abbreviation. The following publication is an extremely useful, compact, easy-to-understand volume that has everything one needs to master the vital information available in newspapers, in business publications, and on computers.

Passell, Peter. **How to Read the Financial Pages**. New York: Warner Books, 1998. 176p.

How to Read the Financial Pages offers clear explanations of basic statistics and translations of daily financial listings for the New York and American Stock and Bond Exchanges, Treasury and other government bonds, money market and mutual funds, and foreign exchanges. It should be consulted by any librarian or investor seeking to better understand the data contained in these tables.

Although this text is old it covers the basic explanations that one needs. If a library has a older book like this it probably covers much of the same ground, and careful thought should be given to the need for a newer publication, especially with the plethora of guides available on the Web, including those mentioned earlier listed on *Investopedia*.

Another publication which is useful to both investors and librarians is the interactive tour "How to Read The Wall Street Journal," available at http://info.wsj.com/college/guidedtour/index.html.

Newspaper abbreviations are not the only alternative designations by which a company may be known. In addition, each company is assigned a ticker symbol, a one-to five-letter designation used by the exchanges on which a company is traded, in ticker quotations, and in some publications and databases. The ticker symbol for Cisco Systems, for example, is CSCO; for Microsoft Corporation, MSFT. Ticker symbols are included, with other information, in many directories, investment services, exchange reports, and other publications, but they are not used in newspapers. Quick lookup services for ticker symbols exist on many business web pages, including *YAHOO!FINANCE* (http://finance.yahoo.com/lookup).

Notes

1. Jerome B. Cohen, Edward D. Zinberg, and Arthur Zeikel, *Guide to Intelligent Investing* (Homewood, IL: Dow Jones-Irwin, 1977), 3.

2. Robert Aliber, *Your Money and Your Life* (New York: Basic Books, 1982), 107.

3. Myron Kandel, *How to Cash In on the Coming Stock Market Boom: The Smart Investor's Guide to Making Money* (Indianapolis: Bobbs-Merrill, 1982), 89–90.

11

Stocks

Introduction

In the preceding chapter, basic investment guides were discussed. Before specific stock-related publications can be examined, however, it is first necessary to consider stocks themselves, the markets on which they are traded, and some of the ways in which stock market performance is measured.

Most companies issue stock to raise capital. Each share of stock represents part ownership in a corporation. An investor, after buying stock in a company, may get a handsomely engraved certificate testifying that he or she has, in effect, become part owner. The share of the corporate pie may be small, but the investor has, with the purchase, obtained that same fractional stake in everything the company owns, its plants and equipment, its patents and trademarks, even its management. Because stocks represent ownership, they are also known as equity securities, or equities.

Common and Preferred Stock

Stocks are either common or preferred. If a company issues only one type of stock, it is usually common stock. Similarly, unless the abbreviation "pf" or "pfd" follows a stock listed in a newspaper stock table, one can assume that it is a common stock.

With common stock ownership comes the opportunity to vote on corporate matters such as the election of company directors. Ordinarily each shareholder has one vote for each share held. This voting right is one of the ways in which common stock is different from preferred stock.

The other major difference pertains to dividends. A dividend is a payment, usually in cash, but occasionally in stock, made by a firm to its shareholders. Dividends are usually paid quarterly or semiannually. Newspaper stock tables and Internet services include estimates of annual dividends, usually based on the most recent quarterly or semiannual payment, in stock tables for each common and preferred stock traded on the national and regional stock exchanges.

The boards of directors determine dividends on common stocks. They are often, although not always, a direct reflection of how well the company has done in terms of earnings. A significant increase in company profits may well be reflected in an increased dividend to common shareholders. On the other hand, if the board decides to plow its profits back into company expansion or increased research and development, or if business is bad, dividends may be reduced or even eliminated. With common stock, there are no guarantees. The potential for profit or loss is much greater than with preferred stock.

Preferred stock is given preferential treatment over common stock. Preferred stockholders are entitled to their dividends, if any are forthcoming, before common stockholders are paid. Preferred stock, however, pays dividends at a specified rate, determined at the time the stock is issued; a holder of a preferred stock can expect no more than the specified dividend even if the company enjoys a banner year. In most corporations, preferred stockholders do not have the voting, or participation, rights enjoyed by common shareholders.

Convertible preferred stock is basically the same as regular preferred stock except that it can be converted into a certain number of shares of the company's common stock, determined at the time the convertible shares were placed on the market. To the investor, this is having the best of both worlds. The holder of the convertible preferred is promised a fixed dividend on the stock as long as he or she holds it and at the same time enjoys the prospect of being able, at a later date, to convert the shares to take advantage of a rise in the value of the common stock. This conversion privilege, however, can only be exercised once.

Earnings per Share

Investors use a wide range of measures to help determine the value of a stock and to compare it with other stocks. One such measure is earnings per share, or EPS, which translates total corporate profits into profits on a per share basis. A simple formula is used to derive earnings per share:

$$EPS = \frac{\text{Net profit after taxes} - \text{preferred dividends paid}}{\text{Number of shares of common stock outstanding}}$$

Dividend Yield

Another measure is dividend yield, derived by dividing annual dividends paid per share by the market price per share of stock. Unlike earnings per share, which is expressed in dollars and cents, dividend yield is expressed in percentage points. A company that paid $3 per share in dividends to its stockholders, and whose stock was trading at $30, for example, would have a dividend yield of 10 percent, while one paying $2 in dividends and whose stock is traded at $25 per share would have a dividend yield of 8 percent. Dividend yield is an indication of the rate of current income earned on the investment dollar and is one of the items reported in newspaper stock tables and in other stock-related information sources.

Price-Earnings Ratio

The price-earnings ratio, also known as the price-earnings multiple, multiple, p/e ratio, or p/e, is one of the most commonly used measures of stock value, particularly in comparison with other stocks in the same industry. The price-earnings ratio of a stock is simply the price of the stock divided by its earnings, normally its earnings for the past 12 months. The formula for this is:

$$P/E = \frac{\text{Price of a share of stock}}{\text{Earnings per share of the stock for the most recent 12-month period}}$$

Thus, a share of XYZ, selling for $35, with earnings of $7 per share in the past 12 months, will have a p/e ratio of 5. In other words, the market is willing to buy a share of XYZ at a price five times greater than its current earnings.

Generally speaking, stocks in a given industry tend to have similar price-earnings ratios, and growth industries tend to have higher p/e ratios than more established industries. The p/e ratio is but one measure of stock value, but it is one of the most widely used. Price-earnings ratios are included in the newspaper stock tables for most exchanges.

Warrants

Warrants exist in a sort of financial netherworld. They are neither stock nor bond, have no book value, and pay no dividends. A warrant is a purchasable right that allows investors to buy corporate securities, usually common stock, for an extended time at a fixed price. When the designation "wt." follows a corporate name (or abbreviation) in a newspaper stock table, it indicates that the security in question is a warrant.

Stock Exchanges

A stock exchange is a central marketplace where shares of stock and other securities are bought and sold, using the auction system. There are national exchanges in this country as well as several regional exchanges (see figure 11.1).

Each exchange is a private organization that sets its own standards for the securities it will list (or trade); only securities that have been admitted to a specific exchange can be traded there, and then only by exchange members or their representatives. The largest exchanges are the national exchanges: the New York Stock Exchange and the NASDAQ Stock Market.

New York Stock Exchange Euronext

The New York Stock Exchange traces its origins back to 1792, when a group of 24 brokers gathered under a buttonwood tree on Wall Street to devise rules of conduct for the trade of stock, hitherto unregulated, and to take buy and sell orders for those who wanted to trade. From these modest beginnings, the New York Stock Exchange has become the world's leading securities exchange, with more than 800 million shares of stock traded daily.

The standards for the stocks that it lists are also the most stringent. The NYSE requires that a company have an aggregate market value of publicly held shares of $40 million for companies that list at the time of their initial public offerings and $100 million for other companies. They must also earn at least $2 million annually and have at least 1,100,000 shares of publicly held common stock.[1] It is on this exchange that "blue-chip" stocks are traded, companies like Bank of America Corp., IBM, and the Gap.

Exchanges

A "national securities exchange" is a securities exchange that has registered with the SEC under <u>Section 6</u> of the Securities Exchange Act of 1934.

There are currently fourteen securities exchanges registered with the SEC under Section 6(a) of the Exchange Act as <u>national securities exchanges</u>:

- <u>NYSE Amex LLC</u> (formerly the American Stock Exchange)
- <u>BATS Exchange, Inc.</u>
- <u>NASDAQ OMX BX, Inc.</u> (formerly the Boston Stock Exchange)
- <u>C2 Options Exchange, Incorporated</u>
- <u>Chicago Board Options Exchange, Incorporated</u>
- <u>EDGA Exchange, Inc.</u>
- <u>EDGX Exchange, Inc.</u>
- <u>International Securities Exchange, LLC</u>
- <u>The Nasdaq Stock Market LLC</u>
- <u>New York Stock Exchange LLC</u>
- <u>NYSE Arca, Inc.</u>
- <u>NASDAQ OMX PHLX, Inc.</u> (formerly Philadelphia Stock Exchange)

Figure 11.1. U.S. stock exchanges registered with the SEC

Membership on the exchange is costly and hard won. The number of "seats" or memberships on the exchange has been limited, since 1953, to 1,366, most representing brokerage firms. The price of a seat on the exchange fluctuates, but in November 2005 one seat sold for $3,250,000.[2] In addition, prospective members must be sponsored by two current members in good standing and must be approved by the board of directors.

In 2007 NYSE Euronext was formed out of the merger of NYSE Group Inc. and Euronext N.V. The merger marked a milestone for global financial markets, bringing together major marketplaces across Europe and the United States.

On February 15, 2011, NYSE and Deutsche Börse announced their merger to form a new company, as yet unnamed, wherein Deutsche Börse shareholders will have 60 percent ownership of the new entity, and NYSE-Euronext shareholders will have 40 percent.

The NYSE now includes: NYSE Arca, the electronic exchange; NYSE Euronext, the primary market in the Eurozone for large- and medium-sized companies; NYSE Alternext, a pan-European market designed specifically for emerging companies; and the NYSE Amex.

The New York Stock Exchange offers a broad range of informational and educational tools. Click on "About the NYSE" at http://www.nyse.com, and then enter the education section. Here are found educational publications, an interactive education center, available outreach programs, and the educational curriculum section, which provides lesson plans at multiple grade levels. Information is not easy to find but with some digging one can find not only facts and figures but biographies of officials, annual reports, and statistics. The statistical information includes, in the archive, daily share volume back to 1888 (http://www.nyse.com/financials/1022221393023.html).

A site that includes much of the information that used to be included in the now defunct NYSE Fact Book is listed below.

New York Stock Exchange. **Facts & Figures.** New York: The Exchange, 1956–. http://www.nyse.com/about/newsevents/1091545088140.html

Also available by clicking on Media and then Media Resources.

Facts & Figures is a compilation of current and historical statistics. It is an ideal quick reference source for people seeking answers to questions on the volume of shares traded, lists of stocks with largest market value, and the exchange's history.

NASDAQ

The NASDAQ (http://www.nasdaq.com) is the world's first electronic-based stock market and has become the model for developing markets worldwide. Today small, growing companies, as well as many large corporations that have become household names, trade their securities on this electronic market. It is a registered national exchange rather than a stock market. To qualify for listing on the exchange, a company must be registered with the U.S. Securities and Exchange Commission (SEC), have at least three market makers (financial firms that act as brokers or dealers for specific securities), and meet minimum requirements for assets, capital, public shares, and shareholders.

Regional Stock Exchanges

In addition to the national stock exchanges, there were seven regional exchanges in the continental United States, but major changes have occurred over the past several years: the Boston Exchange was merged with NASDAQ; Cincinnati is now a wholly electronic exchange headquartered in Chicago; Intermountain (Salt Lake City) is closed; Pacific (San Francisco and Los Angeles) is now merged into the NYSE; Philadelphia merged with NASDAQ; and Spokane, which is closed. The only one still operating is the Chicago Exchange (formerly the Midwest) (http://www.chx.com/). These exchanges were formed originally to help finance local corporations; because their standards are not as strict as those of the NYSE, many smaller companies are traded on the regional exchanges. At the same time, some stocks listed on the national exchanges are also listed on regional exchanges. These stocks are said to be dually traded.

Over-the-Counter Market

The over-the-counter market (OTC) is unlike any of the stock exchanges. It is a decentralized, informal market, a network of thousands of dealer-brokers across the country who do most of their business by telephone and computer. Although NASDAQ stocks are frequently referred to as "over the counter," NASDAQ is not the U.S. over-the-counter (OTC) market.

Over-the-counter securities are issued by companies that either choose not to, or are unable to, meet the standards for listing on the NASDAQ or any other stock exchange. Often stocks traded on the OTC market are said to be unlisted, that is, not traded on any of the national exchanges. It is on the OTC market that many small corporations sell shares to the public for the first time, and, as a result, investment in OTC-traded shares of these unproven companies tends to be more speculative than investment in companies listed on the organized exchanges.

The Financial Industry Regulatory Authority (FINRA) monitors the OTC market and sets standards for the ethical conduct of its members in much the same way the exchanges do. OTC Markets Group Inc., formerly known as Pink OTC Markets Inc., operates OTC Link, an electronic quotation system that displays quotes from broker- dealers for many OTC securities. Market makers and other brokers who buy and sell OTC securities can use the OTC Link to publish their bid and ask quotation prices. Prior to that, dealer quotations were disseminated by paper copy only. These copies were printed on pink-colored paper, and so the securities became known as "Pink Sheet" stocks.

International Stock Exchanges

Many publicly owned companies are increasingly international in both their operations and their ownership, so many investors need to find information on international investment. There are now available more resources, in both print and electronic format, which can guide the researcher in seeking out information on stock exchanges and their regulation.

Global Stock Markets Factbook. New York: Standard & Poor's, 2003–. Annual.

World Stock Exchange Fact Book. Round Rock, TX: Meridian Securities Markets LLC, 1995–. Annual.

The *Factbook* provides details of the performance and characteristics of world stock markets for the last ten years as measured by S&P Developed BMI Indices, S&P's Emerging Markets Database (S&P EMDB), and local stock market indices.

By contrast, the *World Stock Exchange Fact Book* is a reference source that includes up to 25 years of data from more than 45 of the major stock markets worldwide. Arrangement is alphabetical by exchange, and each entry contains a mixture of text and statistics. The text includes information on clearing and settlements, commissions and fees, listing requirements, and investor protection, including regulatory agencies. The statistical information consists of historical tables containing as much as 25 years of data on number and value of shares traded; market indicators, including liquidity; the market value index reported monthly; as well as the much-sought-after market capitalization. A useful appendix contains details about the calculation of various indexes and other performance measures. This publication is expensive and so may be beyond the reach of smaller libraries.

There are available on the Internet many web sites with direct links to international exchanges. Using these one can audit whether companies are listed and check stock prices. One site that is very logically arranged is compiled and edited by Jonathan E. Halsey, and is sponsored by Arch International Group. The exchanges page (http:// www.compliance-exchange.com/ex.htm) is by region and then by country, with direct links to stock markets and other exchanges (see figure 11.2). This web site links not only to stock exchanges but also to associations, regulators, selected investment companies, and educational resources, all complete with active links (see figure 11.3). This is one of the easiest ways to get links to both exchanges and regulators. It is well arranged, and the information is current.

Mediterranean and Middle East

Location	Exchange	Comments
Abu Dhabi	ADX	Abu Dhabi Securities Exchange
Bahrain	BSE	Bahrain Stock Exchange
Bahrain	BFX	Bahrain Financial Exchange
Cyprus	CSE	Cyprus Stock Exchange
Dubai	DFM DGCX NASDAQ	Dubai Financial Market Dubai Gold and Commodities Exchange NASDAQ Dubai
Iran	TSE	Tehran Stock Exchange
Iraq	ISX	Iraq Stock Exchange
Israel	TASE	Tel Aviv Stock Exchange
Jordan	ASE	Amman Stock Exchange
Kuwait	KSE	Kuwait Stock Exchange
Lebanon	BSE	Beirut Stock Exchange
Malta	Borza Malta	Malta Stock Exchange
Oman	Muscat	Muscat Securities Market
Qatar	DSM	Qatar Exchange
Palestine	PEX	Palestine Exchange
Saudi Arabia	TADAWUL	Saudi Stock Market
Syria	DSE	Damascus Securities Exchange
Turkey	ISE	Istanbul Stock Exchange
Turkey	IAB	Istanbul Gold Exchange

Regulators] [Governance] [Associations] [Exchanges] [Services] [AML] [Media] [Education]

Figure 11.2. Selected exchanges of the Mediterranean and Middle East.
Reprinted with permission of http://www.compliance-exchange.com/

Australia and New Zealand

Jurisdiction	Regulator	Full Name
Australia	ASIC	Australian Securities and Investments Commission
Australia	APRA	Australian Prudential Regulation Authority
Australia	ACCC	Australian Competition and Consumer Commission
Australia	AUSTRAC	AUSTRAC is Australia's anti-money laundering and counter-terrorism financing regulator and specialist financial intelligence unit
New Zealand	NZSC	New Zealand Securities Commission
New Zealand	RBNZ	Reserve Bank of New Zealand

[Home] [Regulators] [Governance] [Associations] [Exchanges] [Services] [AML] [Media] [Education] [Contact]

Figure 11.3. Extract of web page showing some regulators for Australasia.
Reprinted with permission of http://www.compliance-exchange.com/

Most newspapers also have web sites that include a business section from which one can access a quote server that will give the latest stock price information. The added advantage of using the Internet is that the quotes are usually only 15 to 20 minutes delayed, at the most, and these pages will often link to current news stories about the stock being checked.

Sometimes historical stock prices may be required. Brokers, accountants, tax lawyers, and serious investors who need such data or want to study trends in the prices of specific stocks over a period of time can use either online or printed sources.

Daily Stock Price Record. New York: Standard & Poor's. Quarterly. (Available in separate editions: American Stock Exchange, 1962–2011; New York Stock Exchange, 1962–2011; and NASDAQ, 1968–2011)

Now available only in electronic format through *NetAdvantage*.

Dow Jones & Co., Reuters Ltd. **FACTIVA.** New York: Factiva, 2002–. Updated continuously.

Silicon Investor. 1995. http://www.siliconinvestor.com/ (accessed April 2, 2011)

YAHOO! FINANCE. 1995. http://finance.yahoo.com/ (accessed April 2, 2011)

Each printed edition of the *Daily Stock Price Record* includes both daily and weekly stock prices and trading information for three-month periods. Separate volumes are issued each quarter for the American Stock Exchange, the New York Stock Exchange, and the NASDAQ. Although this publication may be too specialized for small and medium-sized libraries, librarians providing business reference service should know that it exists and that it provides a convenient alternative to online services. The electronic version includes several years of data but, as of this time, not the total print run, so the print will have to retained.

Historical quotes are included in the *Companies/Markets* section of *Factiva*, an online database that provides daily, weekly, monthly, and quarterly high, low, and closing stock prices for the past year, as well as stock trading volumes. The service also provides the ability to adjust for capital changes such as stock splits. The information can be produced in a formatted report, in an Excel spreadsheet, in a chart, or as a comma-delimited file.

For smaller libraries and researchers there is now available similar information free on the Internet from *Silicon Investor* (http://www.siliconinvestor.com). This service began as a discussion group forum but has evolved to provide research tools and resources that include company news, industry trends, and market commentary. Anyone can access the site, but to post to the discussion forum one must be a member. To get daily historical stock prices as far back as 1968, the user (after registration) first enters the stock symbol of the company for which information is being sought. The quote that appears is for current data, and then there is an option to link to, for example, historical prices, a company profile, and earnings estimates.

Another resource that is perhaps better known among librarians and investors is *YAHOO! FINANCE*. From the front screen one can search by ticker symbol to get the current pricing, but then one has the option of choosing "Historical" from the left to get prices (daily, weekly, or monthly) as far back as the 1970s. Especially useful is the opportunity to list historical dividends. All the data available is downloadable to spreadsheets. Included on the site are the usual message boards, news sections, and tutorials.

One drawback of these sites is that when a company is de-listed, the historical information also vanishes. For this reason *The Daily Stock Price Record* is invaluable.

Stock Price Indexes

Although investors are interested in the performance of specific stocks, they are also concerned with general stock market trends. Stock price indexes or averages give an overview of general stock market conditions. An index is a benchmark against which financial or economic performance is measured. There are several such market indicators, but the two best known are the Dow Jones Industrial Average and the Standard & Poor's Composite 500 Index.

Dow Jones Industrial Average

Anyone who watches network news has probably heard of the Dow Jones Industrial Average, which is given nightly along with other stock market information. The Dow Jones Industrial is a statistical compilation of the average prices of 30 well-known, blue-chip common stocks traded on the New York Stock Exchange. "For the sake of continuity, composition changes are rare, and generally occur only after corporate acquisitions or other dramatic shifts in a component's core business. When such an event necessitates that one component be replaced, the entire index is reviewed. As a result, multiple component changes are often implemented simultaneously" (http://www.djaverages.com/). Although Dow Jones compiles averages for transportation and utilities as well, it is the Industrial Average that is Wall Street's most widely quoted measure of stock market performance.

Standard & Poor's 500 Index

More inclusive than the Dow Jones Industrial Average is the Standard & Poor's 500 Index, which measures the activities of 500 stocks considered to be a benchmark of the overall stock market. This index is composed of industrial, transportation, utility, and financial companies, with a heavy emphasis on industrial companies,

Other Indexes

Other indexes commonly referred to by market analysts reflect the behavior of stocks on each of the major markets on which they are traded. The New York Stock Exchange Composite (http://www.nyse.com/about/listed/nya.shtml) includes all stocks listed on that exchange, and the NASDAQ Composite Index (http://www.nasdaq.com/) is composed of all stocks traded on NASDAQ. Another widely used index is the Russell 2000 (http://www.russell.com/US/Indexes/default.asp), which is one of the best-known of a series of market-value-weighted indexes published by the Frank Russell Company. The index measures the performance of the smallest 2,000 companies in the Russell 3000, index of the 3,000 largest U.S. companies in terms of market capitalization. The Wiltshire 5000 Equity index is a broad market-value-weighted index, and it is used to measure a wider variety of investment styles. There are now over 6,700 stocks in the index. Stocks selected for the Wilshire 5000 must be headquartered in the United States and have readily available pricing data.

Stock Index Information Sources

Information on stock price indexes is easy to find, particularly for the more popular indexes. It is contained in financial newspapers, at most financial web sites, and in sources that provide comprehensive stock market information. In addition to the standard statistical guides described earlier, a more specialized guide, useful despite its age, lists sources that contain stock price indexes and averages.

Bentley, Linda Holman, and Jennifer J. Kiesl. **Investment Statistics Locator.** Rev. ed. Phoenix, AZ: Oryx Press, 1995. 275p.

The *Investment Statistics Locator* lists by subject data available in 53 major investment serials. It cites the sources, for example, that publish half-hourly, hourly, daily, weekly, monthly, quarterly, and yearly versions of the Dow Jones Industrial Average. Less widely quoted market indicators and other types of investment statistics are also covered. This has in the past been an invaluable resource but it needs updating.

Each issue of the *Wall Street Journal Index* includes closing Dow Jones averages for the month or year being indexed, and Standard & Poor's *Daily Stock Price Record* series include three-month compilations of stock price indexes and averages in the first part of each volume. A brief explanation of each indicator is also provided.

When historical information is being sought, the following publication is helpful.

Pierce, Phyllis, ed. **The Dow Jones Averages, 1885–1995.** Chicago: Irwin Professional, 1996. 1v. Unpaged.

The Dow Jones Averages, 1885–1995 is useful for its description of the history and development of the indexes created by Dow Jones as well as for daily stock averages from January 16, 1885, through December 31, 1985. Each daily listing includes data on the Dow Jones Industrial, Transportation, and Utilities Averages as well as daily sales figures. Some of this data can also be found at several web sites, including http://finance .yahoo.com/q/hp?s=%5EDJI, which lists the averages back to January 1, 1928, and includes open, close, high, low, and volume data. The information here is also more current.

Corporate Reports

Astute investors require more than stock price and dividend information about the companies in which they are interested. They also want to know about company management, the products manufactured, and prospects for the future. Corporate reports, particularly those submitted to stockholders and the U.S. Securities and Exchange Commission, provide this information and are the primary data sources on which most published financial and investment advisory services are based.

Registration and Prospectus

The Securities and Exchange Commission (SEC) (http://www.sec.gov), established by the Securities Exchange Act of 1934, serves as the government watchdog over the securities industry. Two of its major functions are to require that publicly traded companies make detailed financial reports to it and to make the information contained in these reports accessible to the public so that it can make informed investment decisions. This begins with the company registration.

Before most companies can make a public offering of new securities, they must file a registration statement with the SEC.[3] This document includes general business information such as corporate history, products, sales, number of employees, and an assessment of competition. It also includes detailed financial statements and balance sheet information, a description of the security being offered, and information about management.

The prospectus, a document intended for prospective investors, contains the highlights of the registration statement. The SEC is careful to point out that while the information contained in the prospectus is accurate, its approval of the document does not imply that the security being offered is necessarily a wise and prudent investment choice. Four key areas in the prospectus deserve the would-be investor's concentration: (1) "Company Business," (2) "Recent Developments," (3) "Use of Proceeds," and (4) "Litigation." The prospectus is a very useful source of information on officer compensation.

A copy of the prospectus can be obtained from the company itself, from brokers selling the stock, and from the SEC database *EDGAR* (http://www.sec.gov/edgar.shtml).

10-K Report

The 10-K report, so called because it is submitted on form 10-K, is a detailed annual report that all publicly traded companies must submit to the SEC. It is the most exhaustive source of current corporate information. The report is divided into two sections, financial data and supporting data. The financial section includes a statistical summary of operations for the last five years, financial statements for each line of business, legal proceedings, and a list or diagram of parents and subsidiaries. The supporting data in the second section of the report include a list of principal stockholders, security holdings of management, and a list of directors with specific background information and term of office for each.

The information contained in 10-K reports is basic to investment analysis. Major business reference collections may include microfiche copies of 10-K reports for all publicly traded companies, for Fortune 500 companies only, or for some specially designated category (perhaps by industry or state). These reports are also available electronically from the SEC through the *EDGAR* (Electronic Data Gathering, Analysis, and Retrieval) system (see figure 11.5). Companies were phased in to *EDGAR* filing over a three-year period, ending May 6, 1996. As of that date, all public domestic companies were required to make their filings on *EDGAR*, except for those filings made in paper that had been given a hardship exemption. It should be noted that companies that have fewer than 500 investors and less than $10 million in total assets are not required to file annual and quarterly reports with the SEC.

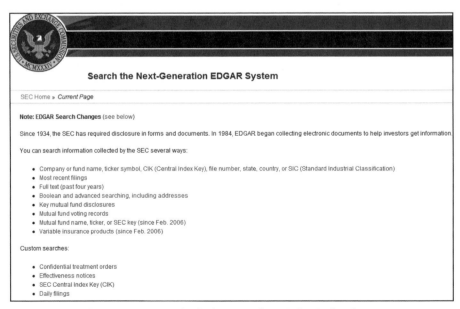

Figure 11.5. Search choices on the EDGAR database,
at http://www.sec.gov/edgar/searchedgar/webusers.htm

Comprehensive investment services routinely include information extracted from these reports. And in some instances, the companies themselves duplicate the contents of their 10-K reports in their annual reports to shareholders (known as an ARK). Finally, many libraries have online databases, such as *Disclosure,* that extract data from the 10-K and other SEC reports. The information contained in 10-K reports is easily accessible to all libraries and researchers.

Annual Report to Shareholders

Annual reports are free and generally available to libraries upon request; the only costs involved are for the postcards to request them, the staff time to process them, and the file cabinets in which to store them. Many are also available from company web pages, although most companies only have current reports available. There are also services that will provide access to web versions and hard copies of some current reports, including the following:

> *Public Register Online,* http://www.annualreportservice.com/
>
> *Annualreports.com,* http://annualreports.com/
>
> *The Public Register (formerly PRARS),* http://www.prars.com/index.php

Not all companies participate in these services, but if the information is available a direct link to the report is provided, which negates having to search company sites, and in some cases if a print copy is preferred it can be provided.

Historic collections of annual reports are also included in LexisNexis as part of the *NAARS* section and more recent years in the annual reports module of *Mergent Online.*

Since annual reports to shareholders are not official SEC filings, there is considerable leeway in the depth of information they contain. One company's report may be little more than a glossy public relations effort; another's may essentially duplicate its 10-K report. Novice investors should be forewarned that annual reports do not always present the unvarnished truth.

Annual reports generally have two main parts. The first part summarizes the company's financial state, reviews its accomplishments for the past year, and discusses its plans and outlook for the future. The tone is positive, and problems or failures are seldom discussed. The second part of the report consists of the corporate financial statements or extracts from them, which are prepared by the company and verified by independent auditors. It is an excellent source of financial statistics, including current assets; property, plants, and equipment; liabilities; stockholders' equity; earnings; per share data; and for most companies, a 10-year summary of financial highlights.

The four reports that have been mentioned thus far—the registration statement, the prospectus, the 10-K report, and the annual report to shareholders—are rich sources of corporate information.

Other Reports

The reports described above are the most commonly consulted company filings, but they are not the only ones a company is required to make. Other reports must be filed with the SEC. The 8-K, for example, must be filed whenever unscheduled material events or significant corporate changes take place. Companies are also required to file listing application statements with national or regional stock exchanges whenever they propose to trade a new security on that exchange. A listing and description of these are available from the SEC web site. Figure 11.6 gives examples of explanations of basic filings.

Form 10K	Annual report pursuant to Section 13 or 15(d)
Form 10Q	General form for quarterly reports under Section 13 or 15(d)
Forms S1, S3 and S4	Registration statement under Securities Act of 1933
Form 13F	Information required of institutional investment managers pursuant to Section 13(f)
Form 20F	Generally used by foreign issuers. Registration statement / Annual report / Transition report

Figure 11.6. The most widely used 1934 Act registration forms

Finally, companies must file detailed reports with agencies of the state in which they are located. Three types of reports may be required:

1. *General corporate reports.* These will include the initial articles of incorporation (required in all states), notices of mergers and name changes, and, in most states, annual reports.

2. *Debt reports.* Under the Uniform Commercial Code, a company must file a report whenever it borrows against any of its assets. A separate statement is filed for each debt and will usually show the name and address of the debtor and the lender, along with a description of the property used as collateral and the maturity date of the loan.

3. *Security reports.* If a publicly traded company is listed on one of the national exchanges or if it is traded in more than one state, it must submit disclosure filings to the SEC. If its securities are traded in only one state, it is not required to report to the SEC but must file similar disclosure statements with the state in which it is being traded.

These state-filed reports are valuable information sources, particularly for smaller companies that are not traded on the national exchanges. Copies of these reports are usually available from the state agencies where they are filed.

Comprehensive Investment Services

Comprehensive investment services are used by people who want information about stocks and bonds and about specific companies and industries. Investment services fall into two categories. Some, which present facts and figures but contain no recommendations, are called investment and research information services. Others, which go one step further and advise readers regarding the investment outlook for the securities they list, are called investment advisory services. Investment and research information and advisory services, however, have several characteristics in common. Both are based on data compiled from the various SEC filings, annual reports, and other corporate releases, and may provide information on thousands of companies. Both are revised and updated on a regular basis. Finally, the cost of compiling these services is high, and as a result, subscriptions to them are expensive. Most are offered both as hard copy and electronic services.

Investment and Research Information Services

One product that most librarians and researchers know about is the collection of *Moody's Manuals*, now officially listed as *Mergent Manuals*. In 1998 Mergent Inc. (formerly Financial Communications Company Inc.) acquired the Financial Information Services division of Moody's Investor's Service. In this process it acquired "cornerstone" products that have traditionally been the *Manuals* and *Investment Guides*. Although Mergent has maintained these sources, it has focused its product development agenda on electronic technology and transfer of data. Both print copies and electronic products are described in this section.

Mergent FIS, Inc. **[Mergent] Moody's Manuals.** New York: FIS, a Mergent Co. Annual. (8 different titles, described below)

Mergent Online. New York: Mergent, 1998–. Computer file. http://www.mergent.com

Mergent Manuals on Microfiche. New York: Mergent, 1909–. Annual.

Mergent WebReports. New York: Mergent, 1909–.

Standard & Poor's NetAdvantage. New York: McGraw-Hill, 1999–. Internet resource. (Search http://www2.standardandpoors.com.)

Mergent Manuals is the collective designation for a series of publications. Together, they cover approximately 25,000 American and foreign companies traded on the national, regional, and OTC exchanges, and some 17,000 municipal and government securities. These listings are consolidated by type into the following eight manuals, issued annually.

1. **Mergent Bank & Finance Manual.** New York: Mergent, 1955–. Annual. (Updated by Mergent Bank & Finance news reports at http://www.mergent .com/downloads-newsReports.html, which are cumulated monthly in *Mergent Corporate News Reports*, July 1999–, 4v.) These volumes cover banks, insurance companies, real estate companies, real estate investment trusts, and miscellaneous financial enterprises.

2. **Mergent Industrial Manual.** New York: Mergent, 1954–. Annual. (Updated by *Moody's Industrial News Reports*, 1970–June 1999; by Mergent news reports at http://www.mergent.com/downloads-newsReports.html, which are cumulated monthly in *Mergent Corporate News Reports*, July 1999–, 2v.) Includes industrial companies traded on the New York, American, and regional stock exchanges. Although coverage varies, each company listing generally includes history and background, a description of the business, a list of subsidiaries and of principal plants and properties, and names and titles of officers and directors. Statistical data include income accounts, financial and operating statistics, and long-term debt and capital stock. The "Special Features Section," a blue paper insert in volume 1, includes a classification of companies by products and industries, a

geographic index, and several tables pertaining to industrial securities, many of which go back 40 years or more.

3. **Mergent International Manual**. New York: Mergent, 1981–. Annual. (Updated by *Mergent International News Reports* at http://www.mergent.com/downloads-newsReports.html, which are cumulated monthly in *Mergent International News Reports*, July 1999–). Provides financial and business information on more than 9,000 major foreign corporations and national and transnational institutions in 100 countries. The "Special Features" section includes a classification of companies by industries and products and selected financial statistics.

4. **Mergent OTC Industrial Manual.** New York: Mergent, 1970–. Annual. (Updated by *Mergent OTC Industrial News Reports* at http://www.mergent.com/downloads-newsReports.html, which are cumulated monthly in *Mergent Corporate News Reports*, July 1999–, 1v.) Information is very similar to that contained in the *Industrial Manual* except that the companies listed are those whose securities are traded over-the-counter.

5. **Mergent OTC Unlisted Manual.** New York: Mergent, 1986–. (Updated by *Moody's OTC Unlisted News Reports*, 1986–June 1999 and by *Mergent OTC Unlisted News Reports* at http://www.mergent.com/downloads-newsReports.html, which are cumulated monthly in *Mergent Corporate News Reports*, July 1999–, 1v.) A collection of over 2,200 companies not listed on national or regional exchanges.

6. **Mergent Municipal & Government Manual.** New York: Mergent, 1955–. Annual. (Updated by *Moody's Municipal & Government News Reports*, 1986–June 1999 and by *Moody's Municipal & Government News Reports* at http://www.mergent.com/downloads-newsReports.html, which are cumulated monthly in *Mergent Municipal News Reports*, 1999–.) Includes federal, state, and local government bond issues.

7. **Mergent Public Utility Manual.** New York: Mergent, 1954–. Annual. (Updated by *Moody's Public Utility News Reports*, 1986–June 1999 and by *Moody's Public Utility News Reports* at http://www.mergent.com/downloads-newsReports.html, which are cumulated monthly in *Mergent Corporate News Reports*, July 1999–.) Domestic and foreign public utilities are covered, including electric and gas utilities, gas transmission companies, and water and telephone companies

8. **Mergent Transportation Manual.** New York: Mergent, 1954–. Annual. (Updated by *Moody's Transportation News Reports*, 1986–June 1999 and by *Moody's Transportation News Reports*, http://www.mergent.com/downloads-newsReports .html, which are cumulated monthly in *Mergent Corporate News Reports*, July 1999–.) Includes railroads and airlines as well as other fields of transportation such as bus and truck lines; water transport; oil pipelines; private bridge, canal, and tunnel companies; and car and truck rental companies. Its coverage of the railroad industry is outstanding.

The focus of each *Manual* determines the kind of specialized information it contains. Each listing, however, includes a history of the company or institution, a description of its business, its address, a list of its officers and directors, and basic financial data.

In addition to company-specific information, each *Manual* includes a blue "Special Features" section, which provides a wealth of current and historical statistical data and other information. This section in the *Bank & Finance Manual*, for example, lists stock splits and stock dividends, while the one in the *Transportation Manual* includes a comprehensive statistical and analytical survey of the railroad industry.

Each of the *Manuals* is updated by a newsletter, which may include interim financial statements, merger proposals, litigation, personnel changes, description of new debt and stock issues, and announcement of new financings. These are available online.

Mergent is a comprehensive service, and as a result, bonds as well as stocks and other securities are listed. For both bonds and preferred stocks, it assigns ratings so that relative investment qualities can be noted. For bonds, nine symbols are used, ranging from Aaa (highest investment quality, least risk) to C (lowest investment quality, highest risk). A variation of the bond rating symbols is used for Moody's (Mergent) preferred stock ratings, with aaa the designation for a top-quality preferred stock and caa the symbol for an issue that is likely to be in arrears on dividend payments. The blue pages in the front of each manual describe these ratings in some detail.

Moody's Complete Corporate Index, an index that is included with a subscription to the *Manuals*, is a convenient alphabetical index to the companies listed in the seven manuals that Moody's classifies as its corporate manuals. (*Municipal & Government Manual* is not included.) This is available from 2004– at http://www.mergent.com/downloads-newsReports.html.

Moody's Manuals on Microfiche, which includes all former titles, is a useful collection for historical research. Also available at this time is the digitized WebReports database, which also provides a comprehensive history of American industry for almost 100 years. It includes corporate histories, financial statements, subsidiaries, long-term debt, officers and directors, etc. Specifically the database contains: Transportation Manual 1909–present; Public Utility Manual 1914–2007; Industrial Manual 1920–present; Bank and Finance Manual 1928–present; OTC Industrial Manual 1970–present; International Manual 1981–present; OTC Industrial Manual 1986–present; and Municipal and Government Manual 1955–present. Additional resources in the archive include corporate annual reports and equity reports. Users can search within and across manuals, by company name, manual year, or type.

Mergent incorporates into *Mergent Online* historical and financial information as reported by the companies for over 10,000 U.S. public companies traded on the NYSE, AMEX, and NASDAQ stock exchanges as well as historical and financial information for approximately 17,000 non-U.S.-based companies from over 100 countries. Financials for 10 years (which will expand to 15 years) are "as reported" and can be downloaded to spreadsheet software such as Microsoft Excel. Financial information is given in either local currency or U.S. dollars. It includes links to EDGAR filings from 1993 to the present for U.S. companies, and annual reports in image format, archived from 1996, are also available. One can also retrieve lists of institutional holdings and insider trades.

In the basic mode, one may search by company name or ticker symbol. In the advanced mode, one may search for companies meeting specified criteria, including selected SIC codes, geographical areas, revenues, and profits. The "build a report" function enables users to select, rank, and sort data items for companies. The database can be purchased in modules and added to as funds become available.

Standard & Poor's NetAdvantage includes electronic versions of several S&P publications providing company, industry, and market-specific information and data: the *S&P Bond Guides; Earnings Guide; Corporation Descriptions; Industry Surveys; Mutual Funds; S&P Outlook; Register of Corporations, Executives, & Directors; S&P Stock Guide;* and *Stock Reports* and from 2011 the *Daily Stock Price Record*. As with *Mergent Online*, the data can be bought in modules and added to as funds allow.

Like Moody's (Mergent), Standard & Poor's rates bonds for their investment safety. The highest rating is AAA, which indicates that the capacity to pay interest and repay principal is extremely strong. D, the lowest rating, indicates that the company is in arrears of paying interest and/or repaying the principal.

In contrast to the Mergent's and Standard & Poor's investment information services, Value Line Investment Survey is an investment advisory service.

Value Line Investment Survey. New York: Value Line, 1936–. Weekly.

Value Line Investment Survey (Expanded Edition). New York: Value Line, 1995–. Weekly.

Like the others, *Value Line* includes investment information, but it goes beyond presentation of factual material to include advice regarding the investment outlook for specific stocks and industries. "The operation is stumbling," the would-be investor may be warned, or, on a more hopeful note, "This stock is a worthwhile speculation." In addition, *Value Line* numerically ranks the stocks it lists for investment safety, probable price performance, and yield in the next 12 months, and for estimated appreciation potential in the next three to five years. These rankings are one of the reasons why *Value Line* is such a popular service.

There are three main parts to *Value Line*: an index and summary section, a newsletter, and the company and industry reports section. The index includes the page citations to the companies listed. It also features tables for best- and worst-performing stocks, stocks with high three- to five-year appreciation potential, high-yielding stocks, and lists of the companies whose stocks have been rated highest for safety and performance. Finally, for each company listed in the index, selected financial information, taken from the company reports section, is also included.

The second section, "Selection & Opinion," includes general stock market information, investment strategies, and an in-depth analysis of a specially recommended stock in its "Stock Highlight" feature.

The "Ratings & Reports" section, however, comprises the bulk of the service. In all, some 1,700 companies are covered in detail. Companies are grouped into broad industrial categories and then listed alphabetically. Particularly noteworthy for each company listing are the *Value Line* ratings; the "Insider Decision Index," which compares the purchase versus the sale of stocks in the company by its officers, directors, and other "insiders"; detailed statistical analyses, including historical data and projections; and beta. Beta, also known as the beta coefficient, is a measure of the sensitivity of a specific stock's price to overall price fluctuations in the New York Stock Exchange Composite Average. It is essentially an index of risk, in which the Composite Average is assigned a value of 1.0. Individual securities may be assigned betas that are less than, the same as, or more than the Composite Average. Generally, the higher the beta, the more volatile the stock. A high-risk stock thus has a high beta, a low-risk one a low beta. Although betas are included in a few other printed and online sources, *Value Line* is one of the most widely held publications containing betas.

Value Line, which is issued weekly, continuously analyzes the stocks it lists. Four times each year (or every 13th week), each stock is reevaluated, and a new analysis is printed. The *Expanded Edition*, which covers a further 1,800 stocks, follows, for the most part, the same layout, but the emphasis is on smaller and mid-cap stocks.

Unlike Moody's and Standard & Poor's, *Value Line Standard Edition* includes industry as well as company analyses. The listings for Coca-Cola and PepsiCo, for example, are preceded by a survey of the soft drink industry. Usually included in the industry analyses are a discussion of current political, economic, and technological developments that may affect the outlook for the industry, composite statistics, and *Value Line's* assessment of investment opportunities in the industry. It also includes explicit rankings of the industry investment prospects. In all, 93 different industries are covered, ranging from advertising to wireless networking.

Value Line is available on the Web, and both the standard and the expanded editors are available via the web as well as in print. For many individual investors, the printed *Value Line* offers economical access to investment information. For those who would like to sort, screen, and graph individual common stocks, industry groups, or portfolios, the electronic versions are a worthwhile alternative.

Sources of Industry Information

Information on specific companies is vital to investors, but it should be supplemented with industry-wide information. Someone contemplating a stock purchase in a large newspaper chain, for example, needs all available information about its financial well-being and the quality of its management but also needs to learn more about the outlook for the newspaper industry generally. Fortunately, there are many published industry studies. Depth of coverage varies but usually includes a review of the industry's recent performance, a description of the present situation, and projections for the future. A survey of the newspaper industry, for example, may discuss the effects that automation and consolidation of ownership have had on the industry, consider the implications of the shift of advertising dollars from newspapers to television, or speculate about the development of the Internet and whether electronic technology will fully replace print newspapers. Considerable statistical data may be included. More industry information can be found in chapter 4.

Industry Studies

The most comprehensive of all of the industry studies are the economic censuses published every five years by the federal government. The economic censuses are supplemented by monthly, quarterly, and annual surveys. Data from the 2007 census are published on the basis of the North American Industry Classification System. The census taken in 2007 is primarily available on the Internet (see http://www.census.gov/econ/census07/). 2007 Economic Data are released on a flow basis so some geographies and/or industries may not yet be available. One huge advantage of this method is that one may see quickly which reports are available, find the dates of publication for others, and link quickly to reports and tables. No longer does one have to check with a depository library to access the information.

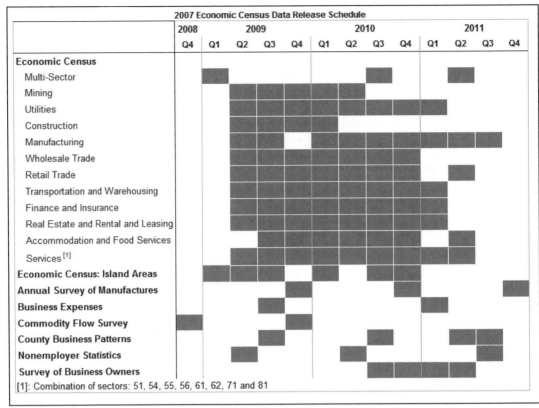

Figure 11.7. *2007 Economic Census:* **Schedule of releases**
http://www.census.gov/econ/census07/www/data_release_schedule/

In the preceding section, it was mentioned that *Value Line* contains industry as well as company analyses. Other sources, however, concentrate primarily on industry information.

Encyclopedia of American Industries. 3rd ed. Farmington Hills, MI: Gale Cengage, 2011. 6th ed. 3v.

Standard & Poor's Industry Surveys. New York: Standard & Poor's, 1973–. Weekly. (Supplemented monthly with *Monthly Investment Review* and *Trends Projections*)

Mergent's Industry Review. New York: Mergent, 1989–.

Standard & Poor's Analyst's Handbook. New York: Standard & Poor's, 1964–. Annual, with monthly supplements.

Encyclopedia of American Industries contains comprehensive information on a wide range of industries in every realm of American business. Volume 1 covers 1,000 manufacturing and service industry essays; volume 2 has approximately 320 essays including agriculture, mining, construction, wholesale, and retail, and volume 3 covers nearly 230 essays on the topics of finance, insurance, real estate, service industries, and public administration.. The volumes contain both an alphabetical and an industry index and a list of contributors. The information on each industry appears under uniform headings such as industry snapshot, background and development, and industry leaders, and each entry contains a bibliography of both print and Internet sources. The essays incorporate major historical events, the organization and structures of the industry, statistics, government regulations, technological advances, and information on the leading companies within the sector. This title has quickly become a favorite of both librarians and researchers.

One of the most heavily used and well-known titles in this area is *Standard & Poor's Industry Surveys.* This service includes, for 51 major industry categories, detailed analysis of each category and of the industries that it comprises. The categories are fairly broad and may include several subsets. In each survey, the investment outlook for the industry, comparisons of leading companies, and specific investment recommendations are featured, supplemented by statistical data, tables, and charts. A new *Survey* is issued weekly, so each industry should have a new publication at least once a year.

The surveys include, for each industry, a report on the "Current Environment," an "Industry Profile," and a "Company Comparative Analysis." The narrative descriptions are supplemented with numerous tables and graphs, frequently cite relevant trade publications and government documents, and include summary financial statistics for major companies. A monthly supplement, "Trends and Projections," is also included. It focuses on the current state of the economy, includes basic economic indicators, and presents industry and economic forecasts. Finally, both company and industry indexes are included. *Standard & Poor's Industry Surveys is* an excellent source of both factual and advisory information on many industries. This publication is available via the Internet as part of *Net Advantage* and other services maintained by Standard & Poor's. It will be necessary to contact the publisher to find which package is suitable for your institution's needs.

Mergent's Industry Review focuses on specific companies within designated industries rather than on the industries themselves. It contains financial information, operating data, and financial ratios for approximately 6,000 companies, arranged in 137 industry groups. Each industry listing includes comparative statistics, annual rankings of companies by revenue, net income, return on capital, yield, and other categories, as well as price scores for the most recent 12 months and for the past 7 years. A chart of composite stock price movements is also included.

For historical information, the *Analyst's Handbook* is useful. It contains financial statistics from 1967 from the Standard & Poor's industry group stock indexes. More than 200 industry categories are featured, including aerospace/defense, footwear, paper and forest products, and life insurance companies. Coverage for each industry includes approximately 20 financial statistics, most of them on a per share basis. In addition, the *Handbook* contains selected financial ratios and income statement and balance sheet items for the past six years for most industry categories.

Commercial publishers and government agencies are not the only organizations that issue industry studies. Securities analysts and brokerage houses frequently publish substantial analyses of specific industries and companies. The following sources are particularly useful for such information and are available at many libraries and organizations.

Investext. Boston: Thomson Reuters, 19uu–. Computer file. Updated continuously.

Datamonitor 360. London: Datamonitor Group, 19uu–. Updated continuously.

Investext is a full-text, online database that permits access to publications issued by investment houses, brokerage firms, and securities analysts. Although one can access *Investext* directly from *Thomson One Banker,* it is also available from a variety of vendors including LexisNexis and Dialog. *Investext* provides full-text company, industry, and geographic research reports (approximately 1.7 million) written by analysts from the leading worldwide investment banks, brokerage houses, and consulting firms. Coverage varies between vendors depending on the percentage of reports each one is allowed to access and on any time embargoes that may exist. There may be as long as a three-month time lag from some vendors. Thirty-Five analyst research firms distribute their reports exclusively through Thomson Reuters; these include Wachovia, Credit Suisse, and HSBC Global Research.

With *Datamonitor 360*, the product available to libraries, one can read and download the full-page image (PDF files) of market research reports on a wide variety of industries. Reports are generally very extensive and lengthy; most are well over 100 pages and have lots of charts, tables, and graphs. Reports are grouped into five broadly defined areas: Energy, Consumer Goods, Finance, Healthcare, and Technology. A very basic search engine built into the site looks for any of the words you type into the search field and looks through both the title and body text of publications in its archive. This database is also international in scope. *Datamonitor 360* includes an interactive reports search function which offers the ability to extract and download sections of the reports.

The federal government is a prolific publisher of industry studies. Government regulatory agencies produce detailed statistical analyses of the industries they monitor. Perhaps the most well-known publications from the government are the *Current Industrial Reports*, listed by subject, available at http://www.census.gov/manufacturing/cir/index.html. Another resource from the government is the *EPA Sector Notebooks* (http://www.epa.gov/compliance/resources/publications/assistance/sectors/notebooks/index.html), which provide an environmental profile along with regulatory requirements and pollutant release data.

There is also available on the Web a growing number of trade publications and trade associations that issue statistics, overviews, and articles. Information is also accessible from many of the periodical databases previously mentioned.

Other Publications

Published financial and investment information is a highly marketable commodity. The quantity, variety, and expense of material in this field is almost overwhelming. This chapter concludes by examining a few of the general categories of investment materials not yet considered. It should be emphasized that it is a representative and not a comprehensive listing.

Stock Reporting and Alert Services

Stock reporting services, although somewhat narrower in scope and less detailed than the comprehensive investment information services described previously, are useful for summary information and a quick overview of investments. Such publications are available in a variety of formats. Some are issued as loose-leaf services, others as paperback books or booklets. Stock reporting services are also available through an abundance of Internet sites.

Standard & Poor's Stock Reports. New York: Standard & Poor's, 1973–.

The *Stock Reports* provide current and background information on companies whose stock is traded on one of the national exchanges or on the OTC market. A few companies traded on regional exchanges are also included. In each service, a two-page company report highlights the company's business, its sales and earnings, per share data, beta, and related information. This service is also available through *NetAdvantage*.

Other stock reporting services are available in paperback and are considerably less expensive.

Handbook of Common Stocks. New York: Mergent, 1965–. Quarterly.

Handbook of Nasdaq Stocks. New York: Mergent, 1997–. Quarterly.

The *Handbook of Common Stocks* (formerly *Moody's Handbook of Common Stocks* from 1989 to 1998 and before that *Moody's Handbook of Widely Held Common Stocks* from 1965 to 1989) gives basic financial information on nearly 900 NYSE stocks with high investor interest. The reviews of company background, recent developments, and investment prospects, supplemented by financial and operating statistics, make it particularly useful for a quick survey of the most popular stocks. Stocks are evaluated and assigned a rating of "High Grade," "Investment Grade," "Medium Grade," or "Speculative."

Using any stock or newspaper quote service, one may link to the latest prices, but there are "alert" services that give any price changes, on designated stocks, as they occur. One free service, which only requires registration, is offered by Yahoo! at http://alerts .yahoo.com. One may activate the alert and receive alerts on any device that receives e-mail. Another service, with free registration, is Zignals, http://zignals.com/main/stock_ alerts/stock_alerts.aspx. One can build alerts around price moves, fundamentals, analyst estimates earnings and ratings, or trading volume with over 100 variables from which to choose.

Charting

Most of the reference sources that have been discussed in this chapter favor what is called the fundamental approach to investment analysis, that is, basing investment decisions on the financial analysis of a company and examination of its management, the products or services it sells, and the general well-being of the industry of which it is a part. These data are used to help the investor make judgments about the worth of a particular stock.

Not every investor uses the fundamental approach. Some favor technical analysis, in which the focus is on timing: when to buy and sell stocks. Technical analysts follow fluctuations in stock prices and volume of trading rather than the considerations mentioned above and depend heavily on charts to help make investment decisions. Charts, the technicians contend, make it possible to tell at a glance what a stock's past performance has been and to make informed judgments about its future prospects.

In some libraries, patrons who are technically oriented may consider a financial collection that does not include at least one charting service inadequate. Although charts are included in several of the publications already mentioned, *Value Line,* and the stock reporting services, there are some sources that confine themselves to graphic presentation of stock and industry data. Typical of these is *Standard & Poor's/Trendline Current Market Perspectives,* a monthly publication that includes charts for over 1,500 stocks. Free charts can also be accessed through the Big Charts web site at http:// bigcharts.marketwatch.com/ and through many of the web pages mentioned earlier that give the option of retrieving stock information in chart form.

Obsolete Securities

Occasionally, librarians are asked to help patrons determine the value of shares in companies that are no longer in business. Someone who has unearthed a yellowing stock certificate for 200 shares of Yum-Yum International Restaurant may want to know whether to plan a world cruise or use it as kindling. A search of the standard business directories and comprehensive investment services may fail to yield information on the elusive Yum-Yum Restaurant chain. There are, however, several sources of information on companies that are no longer in business.

Directory of Obsolete Securities. Jersey City, NJ: Financial Information, 1927–. Annual.

Robert D. Fisher Manual of Valuable and Worthless Securities. New York: Robert D. Fisher, 1938–1975. Frequency varied.

The *Directory* lists companies and banks whose original identities have been lost because of name changes, mergers, acquisition, dissolution, reorganization, bankruptcy, or charter cancellation. Yum-Yum International Restaurant is listed in the *Directory*. "Charter cancelled and declared inoperative and void for nonpayment of taxes," the listing indicates, and assesses the current value of Yum Yum common stock at one cent per share.

Volumes 5 through 15 of the *Fisher Manual* list companies whose securities may have value or may be worthless. This reference superseded the *Marvyn Scudder Manual of Extinct or Obsolete Companies,* which was published by Marvyn Scudder in four volumes and included stocks from 1926 to 1937.

Stock Services on the Internet

Over the years there have been many books and articles printed and Internet sites founded that deal with stock information. It is easy for the individual investor, librarian, and researcher to gather information, but the amount of information available can be a problem. There are a myriad of stock services on the Internet, and it is easy to become overwhelmed. Listed below are four places one can begin.

1. *YAHOO!FINANCE.* http://finance.yahoo.com/

   This site is good for getting a quick stock quote, or going deeply into a company's financial statements. The site has a great page of key statistics for each company, and has good industry comparison pages as well.

2. *The Street.* http://www.thestreet.com/

   Excellent commentary that can give one some good stock ideas.

3. *Schaeffer's Investment Research.* http://www.schaeffersresearch.com/

   Geared more to the advanced investor this site has some great information on popular stock screens, put/call ratios for options, and numerous technical indicators.

4. *Zack's.* http://www.zacks.com/

   The site does a good job of keeping track of brokerage analysts' latest estimates and notes, and has some interesting blogs with investment ideas that are updated regularly.

The electronic and print resources included in this chapter are only a fraction of those available. Along with publishers' catalogs, journals, and magazines, any researcher may need to frequently check online resources such as the *Free Pint* newsletter (http://www .freepint.com/issues/issues.htm) and *The Virtual Acquisition Shelf* (http://resourceshelf .freepint.com).

Notes

1. New York Stock Exchange, *Listed Company Manual,* available at http://nysemanual.nyse.com/LCM/.

2. New York Stock Exchange, *Facts & Figures.* Available at http://www.nyse.com/about/newsevents/ 1091545088140.html. Or click on Media and then Media Resources to find *Facts & Figures.*

3. A full description of major filings with the SEC, including registration and prospectus, is available at http://www.sec.gov/info/edgar/forms.htm.

12

Bonds and Other Fixed-Income Securities

The preceding chapter examined stocks, the markets on which they are traded, and the use of stock-related publications by investors. This chapter deals in a similar way with another broad category of investments: bonds and fixed-income securities.

How do these securities differ from stocks? Stocks are equity securities; they represent partial ownership in the issuing organization. Fixed-income securities, on the other hand, are debt securities, representing money lent to the issuing organization for a designated time period. They are, in effect, IOUs.

Usually, the issuing organization agrees not only to repay the principal at some future date but also to make regular, fixed interest payments for the use of the money. Some fixed-income securities are long-term loans, others are short term. Bonds fall into the first category.

Bonds

Bonds are long-term, fixed-income debt securities issued by corporations and governments to raise money. They can be as staid as U.S. savings bonds or as speculative as Mexican petro-bonds paid in pesos, but most share certain characteristics. Bonds usually mature 10 years after they are issued, and some are issued for as long as 30 years.

When a bond reaches maturity, the issuing organization is required to repay the principal, or face value, to the bondholder. Usually bonds are issued in $1,000 denominations or in multiples of $1,000. There are, for example, bonds with face values of $5,000 or even $10,000; others, called "baby bonds," have face values of only $100 or $500. Most, however, come in $1,000 denominations.

Interest

Bondholders are entitled to interest, usually paid semiannually. The amount of interest paid is determined in advance and is a fixed percentage of the face value of the bond. A 4.5 percent $1,000 bond will earn its holder $45 per year; a 5.5 percent bond, $55. The important thing to remember is that the rate of interest is set at the time the bonds are first sold to the public and remains fixed for the duration of the bond's life. While the prime interest rate may skyrocket or plummet according to the state of the economy, the rate of interest paid on a bond remains the same for its entire life span. As a result, bonds provide a steady, predictable income.

259

With certain bonds, interest is collected by clipping one of the coupons attached to the bond and presenting it for payment. Thus, the interest paid on a particular bond is often called its coupon rate or coupon, and bonds with coupons attached are called coupon bonds. They are also called bearer bonds because the holder of the bond is presumed to be its owner. If someone loses a bearer bond, the finder can sell it or hold it, collect interest on it, and redeem it at maturity.

In contrast, a registered bond is registered in the name of the bondholder, and only that person can sell it, receive semiannual interest payments on it, or redeem it. No coupons are attached to a registered bond; interest payments are automatically sent to the bondholder when they come due.

There are also adjustable rate bonds. The rate on these is changed periodically to reflect interest rate indexes, such as that on Treasury bills. Zero coupon bonds may be bought at less than the face value, but the bearer will not receive periodic interest payments. For example, a bond with the face value of $20,000, which will mature in 20 years, may be bought for about $7,000. The difference in the face value and price paid is 5½ percent interest compounded annually. Taxes must be paid on this annual interest although it is only paid at the end of the 20 years.

Prices

Although the interest rate is locked in for the life of the bond, the price of a bond fluctuates in much the same way as stock prices. What causes bond prices to rise or fall? Interest rates are the key.

When general interest rates rise, the interest rates on new bond issues must also be higher to attract investors. Interest rates on bonds already outstanding, however, are fixed and cannot be changed. As a result, an adjustment to the new interest rate takes place through a change in the prices of the outstanding bonds. When interest rates rise, the prices of outstanding bonds tend to decline. Conversely, if interest rates fall, bond prices rise.

If, for example, an investor paid $1,000 (face value or par) for an XYZ Corporation bond that paid 5 percent, and subsequently the XYZ Corporation offered 7 percent interest on its new bond issues, the resale market for the 5 percent bond selling at par (or $1,000) would be nonexistent. Why accept 5 percent interest when 7 percent is available? If, however, the 5 percent bond is offered for $850 instead of $1,000, the bond would be more attractive because the buyer would be earning annual interest of $50 on an $850 investment as well as a $150 profit when the bond matured.

Bonds selling for less than face value are said to be selling at a discount, while bonds selling at a premium are those selling for more than face value. Thus, investment advice to buy "deep discounted bonds" simply means to buy bonds selling for considerably less than their face value.

Yield

There are two different ways of expressing yield, or return on an investment. The first, current yield, measures the annual return on the price that the buyer actually pays for the bond. Current yield is derived by dividing the interest rate by the price paid for the bond. If the bond was bought at par ($1,000), the interest rate and current yield are the same. If, however, the bond was bought at premium or discount, the current yield will be different from the interest rate.

The 5 percent XYZ Corporation bond purchased for $850, for example, has a current yield of 5.88 percent (5 divided by 850), while a 9 percent bond bought at premium for $1,050 would have a current yield of 8.57 percent (9 divided by 1,050). Current yields are calculated and usually included in the bond tables in financial newspapers.

Yield to maturity, the other expression of bond yield, is the effective rate of return to the bondholder if the bond is held to maturity. It takes into account the amount paid for the bond, its par value, the interest rate, and the length of time to maturity. For a given interest rate, maturity, and price, yield to maturity can be determined by using tables from reference books commonly called basis books or yield books. Although libraries generally do not include these highly specialized sources in their collections, yield to maturity is one of the data elements included in major bond publications such as Standard & Poor's *Bond Guide* and Mergent's *Bond Record*, which are discussed later in this chapter.

Call Provisions

When an investor buys bonds, he or she takes the risk that the issuing organization may default on interest payments or on repayment of the principal, or that spiraling inflation and general interest rates may make the long-term, fixed-interest bonds a poor investment. The investor may also have to risk recall of the bonds by the issuing organization before they reach maturity. This may result from two kinds of recall provisions, known as call and sinking fund.

A sinking fund is a pool of money put aside by the issuing organization so that, each year, it can recall and retire a certain percentage of the bond issue in advance of the actual maturity date. The rationale behind a sinking fund provision is that it is easier to retire the bond issue gradually than it is to pay the entire amount at maturity. If a bond issue has a sinking fund provision, a certain portion of the issue must be retired each year. The bonds retired are usually selected by lottery. The issuer usually has the option of buying the bonds on the open market or recalling them from bondholders. If the market price of the bonds is higher than the sinking fund call price, the issuer is entitled to recall a certain number of bonds from the bondholders and to redeem them at the stated sinking fund price. Usually there is a 5- or 10-year grace period before the sinking fund provision goes into effect.

Although establishment of a sinking fund provision at least theoretically reduces the likelihood of default on repayment of principal, it can also work to the disadvantage of the investor whose bonds are redeemed before maturity, because the prospect of a steady source of fixed-interest income has been eliminated. As a result, one of the things that many prospective investors want to know about a particular bond is whether it contains a sinking fund provision. Many printed investment sources identify bond issues containing sinking fund provisions with the letters s.f.

Other bonds have call provisions that permit the issuer, after a lapse of 5 or 10 years, to redeem the bonds at any time prior to their maturity, at a set price. Such bonds are labeled, appropriately, as callable bonds. Generally the issuer will exercise the call provision whenever the fixed interest rate for their outstanding bond issues is significantly higher than the interest rate at which they could issue new bonds. Bonds that are called in under this provision are redeemed at face value plus a fixed payment, often equal to one year's interest rate. Call prices are included for callable bonds in Mergent's (Moody's) *Bond Record*, Standard & Poor's *Bond Guide*, and many other investment publications.

Ratings

Investors pay close attention to the credit ratings assigned to bonds. The ratings most commonly consulted are those prepared by Mergent (Moody's) and Standard & Poor's. They represent an assessment of the issuing organization's ability to pay interest and repay principal to bondholders. Not every bond is rated, but the major ones are.

Slightly different rating symbols are used by Mergent (Moody's) and Standard & Poor's, as evidenced by their rating categories shown in figure 12.1. Lists and explanations of the various bond rating symbols are contained in many of the Moody's and Standard & Poor's publications described later in this chapter.

General Description	Moody's	Standard & Poor's
Highest Quality	Aaa	AAA
High Quality	Aa1, Aa2, Aa3	AA+: equivalent to Moody's Aa1 AA: equivalent to Aa2 AA-: equivalent to Aa3
Upper Medium Grade	A1, A2, A3	A+: equivalent to A1 A: equivalent to A2
Medium Grade	Baa1, Baa2, Baa3	BBB
Somewhat Speculative	Ba1, Ba2, Ba3	BB
Low Grade Speculative	B1, B2, B3	B
Poor Grade, Default Possible	Caa1, Caa2, Caa3	CCC
Poor Grade, Partial Recovery possible	Ca	CC
Default, Recovery Unlikely	C	C

Figure 12.1. Bond rating categories

Although each publisher is highly respected, some claim that Mergent surpasses Standard & Poor's in the value of its rating of municipal bond issues, whereas Standard & Poor's is more highly regarded for its rating of corporate bonds. In most instances, though, both services either assign the same rating to an issue or are within one rating level of each other. Neither service claims to be infallible.

Nevertheless, the ratings are useful. They give prospective investors an indication of the risk attached to each bond and carry enough weight so that bonds with higher ratings (that is, those with less risk) have lower yields than bonds with lower ratings. New issues with the same maturity and face value may offer different interest rates, based on their ratings. A triple A bond will have a lower coupon rate than a double A bond, and so on. Ratings can change, and if they do, announcements are featured in financial newspapers and other publications. One can also check the web page of Standard & Poor's (http://www.standardandpoors.com), where recent changes are listed in the ratings section.

If the rating assigned to an outstanding bond changes, its price in the resale market (discussed in the next section) will reflect this change. A lower rating will usually result in the lowering of a bond's price, and vice versa.

Secondary Bond Market

Not all investors hold newly issued bonds to maturity. As a result, there is a secondary arena for bonds, with most of it centered in the OTC market, which is the primary market for the trading of outstanding government and municipal bonds, and for many corporate bonds as well. The New York Stock Exchange lists bonds, most of them corporate, although some government, international bank, and foreign bonds are also traded.

Price and related trading information for many of the bonds traded in these markets is included in financial newspapers, bond-related publications, and web sites. One example of a web site with a quote center is *bonds online* (http://www.bondsonline.com/). Registration is required.

Money Market Instruments

Bonds are long-term debt obligations. Corresponding short-term loans to various borrowers, federal and local governments, corporations, and banks are known collectively as money market instruments.[1] These short-term obligations are issued by organizations with high credit ratings, are highly liquid (easily convertible into cash), and are generally of less than one year's duration. Typical money market instruments include Treasury bills, commercial paper (short-term IOUs issued by corporations), and commercial bank certificates of deposit.

Many of these securities require a substantial cash outlay and are thus of greater interest to institutional investors than to all but the wealthiest individuals. Commercial paper, for example, is sold in minimum denominations of $100,000. When interest rates are high, however, there is widespread interest in money market funds, which are a type of mutual fund. For as little as $500, an investor can buy into a money market fund, which pools investors' money and buys these expensive short-term obligations. Money market funds are discussed briefly in the next chapter.

Federal Government Securities

The federal government issues a wide range of marketable securities. Some, known as direct government obligations, are issued by the Treasury Department. These include Treasury bills, notes, and bonds. Others, such as the issues of federal agencies and government-sponsored agencies, are not considered direct obligations but enjoy credit ratings almost as impressive as those assigned to Treasury issues. The rating given to government securities is based on the federal government's power to tax and print money. Risk of default on a U.S. government bond is considered nonexistent although in 2011 Standard & Poor's did downgrade the rating they awarded because of the burden of debt held by the U.S. government. Government securities usually offer lower interest rates than do corporate debt obligations, which compensate for their greater risk by offering higher interest rates.

Trading of government securities is active, with billions of dollars' worth of short- and long-term securities bought and sold during a normal business day. Bills, notes, and bonds can be purchased over the Internet or phone, or by mailing a tender to a *TreasuryDirect*[2] office. Treasury marketable securities can be resold through financial institutions and government securities brokers and dealers.

Treasury Issues

One of the ways in which the Treasury Department finances the nation's debt is by issuing marketable securities. Three main types of Treasury issues, distinguished by their varying maturities, can be identified: Treasury bills, Treasury notes, and Treasury bonds.

Treasury bills (T-bills or bills) are short-term securities, issued in maturities of 3, 6, and 12 months. T-bills are sold in denominations of $1,000 up to a maximum purchase of $5 million. They do not pay interest. Instead, they are issued at a discount of their face value. An investor may purchase a T-bill for $9,750, for example, and redeem it at maturity of one year for the full $10,000, thus earning $250. The price at which the bills are discounted is determined by the market, more specifically by the investors and dealers who submit competitive bids at weekly and/or monthly auctions of Treasury bills (see figure 12.2). The highest bids determine the discount. Most of the competitive bidders are dealers in government securities, commercial banks, and other institutional investors. For more information on types of Treasury issues, one should investigate the web page http://www.treasurydirect.gov/.

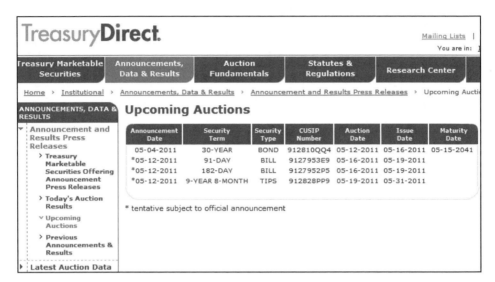

Figure 12.2. Table of Treasury auctions. Taken from http://www.treasurydirect.gov/RI/OFAnnce

There is an active secondary market for T-bills, and the *Wall Street Journal* and many other newspapers report the daily prices of Treasury bills. The quotations look like those in figure 12.3. Daily prices can also be found at http://www.investinginbonds.com and at http://www.bondsonline.com.

Mat. Date	Days to Mat.	Bid	Asked	Change	Ask/Yield
May 25 '11	160	5.59	5.55	-0.01	5.66
Explanation:					
Mat. Date	Date at which Treasury Bill matures—160 days to wait				
Bid	Bid is the yield that someone **selling** the bill will earn. **Selling** a $10,000 T-bill maturing May 25, 2012 will earn a yield of 5.59%				
Asked	The yield the **buyer** will earn				
Change	Shows that yesterday's bid price was $5.60				
Ask/Yield	The ask/yield is the return the buyer will get if the ask price is paid and the bond is kept until it matures				

Figure 12.3. Example of a newspaper quotation for a Treasury bill

The table in figure 12.3 indicates that the buyer of a bill maturing on May 25, 2011, for example, earns 5.66 percent; that is, the asked price provides a yield of 5.5 percent. The 5.59 in the bid column refers to the yield someone selling the bills would reap. Actual dollar prices are not quoted in this table but can be determined by using a formula that takes into account discount rate and the number of days to maturity.[3] The last column, Ask/Yield, is investment yield, the figure to be used in comparing the return on Treasury bills with other types of investments.

Treasury notes and bonds have longer maturities than T-bills and are interest bearing. Bonds and notes come in denominations of $1,000, $5,000, $10,000, $100,000, and $1 million. Treasury notes range in maturity from 1 to 10 years, most falling in the 2- to 5-year range; Treasury bonds, on the other hand, generally mature in 10 years or more.

The Treasury follows essentially the same auction procedures for new note and bond issues as it does for bills. An offering is announced in advance of the issue date, and investors submit either competitive or noncompetitive bids and await the results.

Treasury notes and bonds are traded actively in the OTC market, and OTC bond and note prices are included in the financial pages of most newspapers. One can also see quotes and buy directly from Treasury.Direct (see figure 12.4).

TreasuryDirect.

Mailing Lists |
You are in:

| Treasury Marketable Securities | Announcements, Data & Results | Auction Fundamentals | Statutes & Regulations | Research Center |

Home > Institutional > Announcements, Data & Results > Latest Auction Data > Recent Bill Auction Results

ANNOUNCEMENTS, DATA & RESULTS

Recent Bill Auction Results

- **Announcement and Results Press Releases**
- **Latest Auction Data**
  - ᵛ Recent Bill Auction Results
  - > Recent Note, Bond and TIPS Auction Results
  - > Additional Statistics (Historical)
- **Historical Auction Query**
- **TIPS/CPI Data**
- **Treasury BuyBacks**
- **SLGS Data**
- **Savings Bond Data**

Security Term	Issue Date	Maturity Date	Discount Rate %	Investment Rate %	Price Per $100	CUSIP
4-WEEK	05-12-2011	06-09-2011	0.015	0.015	99.998833	9127952U4
13-WEEK	05-12-2011	08-11-2011	0.025	0.025	99.993681	9127953D1
26-WEEK	05-12-2011	11-10-2011	0.065	0.066	99.967139	9127953T6
4-WEEK	05-05-2011	06-02-2011	0.005	0.005	99.999611	912795W64
13-WEEK	05-05-2011	08-04-2011	0.050	0.051	99.987361	9127953B5
26-WEEK	05-05-2011	11-03-2011	0.100	0.102	99.949444	9127953R0
52-WEEK	05-05-2011	05-03-2012	0.200	0.204	99.797778	9127953N9
4-WEEK	04-28-2011	05-26-2011	0.030	0.030	99.997667	912795ZS9
13-WEEK	04-28-2011	07-28-2011	0.065	0.066	99.983569	912795X63
26-WEEK	04-28-2011	10-27-2011	0.115	0.117	99.941861	9127953Q2
4-WEEK	04-21-2011	05-19-2011	0.030	0.030	99.997667	9127952R1
13-WEEK	04-21-2011	07-21-2011	0.060	0.061	99.984833	9127953A7
26-WEEK	04-21-2011	10-20-2011	0.110	0.112	99.944389	9127952K6
4-WEEK	04-14-2011	05-12-2011	0.025	0.025	99.998056	9127952Q3
13-WEEK	04-14-2011	07-14-2011	0.050	0.051	99.987361	9127952Z3
26-WEEK	04-14-2011	10-13-2011	0.110	0.112	99.944389	9127953P4
4-WEEK	04-07-2011	05-05-2011	0.050	0.051	99.996111	912795VE8
13-WEEK	04-07-2011	07-07-2011	0.050	0.051	99.987361	9127952X8
26-WEEK	04-07-2011	10-06-2011	0.130	0.132	99.934278	9127953M1

Figure 12.4. Recent Auction Results: Treasury bonds and notes,
http://www.treasurydirect.gov/RI/OFBills

The interest earned on Treasury securities is subject to federal income tax but exempt from state and local taxes. The same exemptions apply to federal agency issues.

Treasury securities are considered a "safe" investment and are actively traded. There is an abundance of information about them at the web site http://www.treasury.gov/, plus the ability to purchase the securities directly without using a broker. Each month the *Treasury Bulletin* (http://www.fms.treas.gov/bulletin/index.html) issues a list of the estimated amount of public debt securities held by private investors (see figure 12.5). Email updates are available for the *Bulletin*.

OWNERSHIP OF FEDERAL SECURITIES   41

TABLE OFS-2.—Estimated Ownership of U.S. Treasury Securities

[In billions of dollars. Source: Office of Debt Management, Office of the Under Secretary for Domestic Finance]

End of month	Total public debt [1] (1)	Federal Reserve and Intragovernmental Holdings [2] (2)	Total privately held (3)	Depository institutions [3,4] (4)	U.S. savings bonds [5] (5)	Pension funds [3] Private [6] (6)	Pension funds [3] State and local governments (7)	Insurance companies [3] (8)	Mutual funds [3,7] (9)	State and local governments [3] (10)	Foreign and international [8] (11)	Other investors [9] (12)
2001 - Mar......	5,773.7	2,880.9	2,892.8	188.0	184.8	153.4	177.3	109.1	225.3	316.9	1,012.5	525.5
June.....	5,726.8	3,004.2	2,722.6	188.1	185.5	148.5	183.1	108.1	221.0	324.8	983.3	380.3
Sept.....	5,807.5	3,027.8	2,779.7	189.1	186.4	149.9	166.8	106.8	234.1	321.2	992.2	433.1
Dec......	5,943.4	3,123.9	2,819.5	181.5	190.3	145.8	155.1	105.7	261.9	328.4	1,040.1	410.7
2002 - Mar......	6,006.0	3,156.8	2,849.2	187.6	191.9	152.7	163.3	114.0	266.1	327.6	1,057.2	388.8
June.....	6,126.5	3,276.7	2,849.8	204.7	192.7	152.1	153.9	122.0	253.8	333.6	1,123.1	313.8
Sept.....	6,228.2	3,303.5	2,924.8	209.3	193.3	154.5	156.3	130.4	256.8	338.6	1,188.6	297.0
Dec......	6,405.7	3,387.2	3,018.5	222.6	194.9	153.8	158.9	139.7	281.0	354.7	1,235.6	277.4
2003 - Mar......	6,460.8	3,390.8	3,070.0	153.6	196.9	165.8	162.1	139.5	296.6	350.0	1,275.2	330.2
June.....	6,670.1	3,505.4	3,164.7	145.4	199.2	170.2	161.3	138.7	302.3	347.9	1,371.9	327.8
Sept.....	6,783.2	3,515.3	3,267.9	146.8	201.6	167.7	155.5	137.4	287.1	357.7	1,443.3	371.0
Dec......	6,998.0	3,620.1	3,377.9	153.1	203.9	172.2	148.6	136.5	280.9	364.2	1,523.1	395.4
2004 - Mar......	7,131.1	3,628.3	3,502.8	162.8	204.5	169.8	143.6	172.4	280.8	374.1	1,670.0	324.8
June.....	7,274.3	3,742.8	3,531.5	158.6	204.6	173.3	134.9	174.6	258.7	381.2	1,735.4	310.1
Sept.....	7,379.1	3,772.0	3,607.1	138.5	204.2	174.0	140.8	182.9	255.0	381.7	1,794.5	335.5
Dec......	7,596.1	3,905.6	3,690.5	125.0	204.5	173.7	151.0	188.5	254.1	389.1	1,849.3	355.4
2005 - Mar......	7,776.9	3,921.6	3,855.3	141.8	204.2	177.3	158.0	193.3	261.1	412.0	1,952.2	355.5
June.....	7,836.5	4,033.5	3,803.0	126.9	204.2	181.0	171.3	195.0	248.7	444.0	1,877.5	354.4
Sept.....	7,932.7	4,067.8	3,864.9	125.3	203.6	184.2	164.8	200.7	244.7	467.6	1,929.6	344.3
Dec......	8,170.4	4,199.8	3,970.6	117.1	205.2	184.9	153.8	202.3	251.3	481.4	2,033.9	340.6
2006 - Mar......	8,371.2	4,257.2	4,114.0	113.0	206.0	186.7	153.0	200.3	248.7	486.1	2,082.1	438.1
June.....	8,420.0	4,389.2	4,030.8	119.5	205.2	192.1	150.9	196.1	244.2	499.4	1,977.8	445.6
Sept.....	8,507.0	4,432.8	4,074.2	113.6	203.7	201.9	154.7	196.8	235.7	502.1	2,025.3	440.3
Dec......	8,680.2	4,558.1	4,122.1	114.8	202.4	207.5	156.2	197.9	250.7	516.9	2,103.1	372.5
2007 - Mar......	8,849.7	4,576.6	4,273.1	119.8	200.3	221.7	158.3	185.4	264.5	535.0	2,194.8	393.2
June.....	8,867.7	4,715.1	4,152.6	110.4	198.6	232.5	159.3	168.9	267.7	580.3	2,192.0	242.7
Sept.....	9,007.7	4,738.0	4,269.7	119.7	197.1	246.7	138.9	155.1	306.3	538.5	2,235.3	332.0
Dec......	9,229.2	4,833.5	4,395.7	128.9	196.5	257.6	141.6	141.9	362.9	537.6	2,353.2	274.6
2008 - Mar......	9,437.6	4,694.7	4,742.9	125.3	195.4	270.5	142.0	152.1	484.4	531.0	2,506.3	336.3
June.....	9,492.0	4,685.8	4,806.2	112.7	195.0	276.7	141.8	159.4	477.2	519.9	2,587.4	336.3
Sept.....	10,024.7	4,692.7	5,332.0	130.0	194.3	292.5	143.9	163.4	656.1	503.2	2,802.4	449.1
Dec......	10,699.8	4,806.4	5,893.4	105.0	194.1	297.2	146.4	171.4	768.8	485.5	3,077.2	649.2
2009 - Mar......	11,126.9	4,785.2	6,341.7	129.1	194.0	330.9	150.2	191.0	716.0	516.9	3,265.7	849.1
June.....	11,545.3	5,026.8	6,518.5	140.7	193.6	353.4	159.9	200.0	695.7	514.4	3,460.8	800.0
Sept.....	11,909.8	5,127.1	6,782.7	199.3	192.5	398.1	167.3	210.2	644.9	504.4	3,570.6	890.5
Dec......	12,311.3	5,276.9	7,034.4	206.4	191.3	429.8	174.5	222.0	666.3	505.9	3,685.1	953.2
2010 - Mar......	12,773.1	5,259.8	7,513.3	274.4	190.2	462.2	179.7	229.8	649.7	506.4	3,877.8	1,143.2
June.....	13,201.8	5,345.1	7,856.7	270.1	189.6	531.9	184.5	240.0	634.5	511.8	4,002.9	1,291.4
Sept.....	13,561.6	5,350.5	8,211.1	337.5	188.7	587.5	187.8	254.5	607.9	508.7	4,257.1	1,281.3
Dec......	14,025.2	5,656.2	8,368.9	n.a.	187.9	n.a.	n.a.	n.a.	n.a.	n.a.	4,370.0	n.a.

Figure 12.5. Estimated ownership of U.S. Treasury securities,
from http://www.gpo.gov/fdsys/

Federal Agency Issues

Federal agency securities are debt obligations of various U.S. government-guaranteed or government-sponsored entities. Included among these are the Small Business Administration and the Federal Home Loan Mortgage Corporation. Among these agency issues, or agencies, as they are collectively known, are those issued by the following organizations:

Small Business Administration

Federal Home Loan Mortgage Corporation (FHLMC or Freddie Mac)

Federal Farm Credit Bank

Federal National Mortgage Association (FNMA or Fannie Mae)

Government National Mortgage Association (GNMA or Ginnie Mae)

Student Loan Marketing Association (Sallie Mae)

Mergent's (Moody's) *Municipal & Government Manual* describes agency issues in some detail. For each listing, fairly detailed financial and organizational information is given, including descriptions and ratings of outstanding debt obligations. Daily quotations for many agency issues are included in the *Wall Street Journal* and other newspapers as well as web sites. The format used for reporting is very similar to that used for Treasury notes and bonds.

Municipal Issues

Issuance of debt securities is not limited to the federal government. State, city, town, and other units of local government and political subdivisions also issue bonds, referred to collectively as municipals or munis. They are also known as tax exempts because the interest earned on them is exempt from federal income tax and often from state and local income taxes where they are issued. Because of this tax-exempt feature, municipals can pay a lower rate of interest and still be competitive with taxable bonds paying a higher rate of interest. The Bond Market Association has on its web page at http://investinginbonds.com/ a "Tax-Free vs. Taxable Yield Comparison Calculator." With this one can compare what one would need to earn on a taxable investment to match the tax-free yield of a municipal bond.

Municipal securities are issued to help finance new roads, highways, bridges, schools, hospitals, libraries, sports and convention centers, airports, sewers, utilities, and other facilities. Unlike federal government securities, municipals are not sold directly to the public. Instead, municipals are sold to investment bankers or underwriters who in turn make them available to investors. There are two basic types of municipal bonds, based on the source of revenue used to repay the bond.

General Obligation Bonds

General obligation bonds are secured by the full and unlimited taxing power of the government issuing the bonds. Also known as full faith and credit bonds, these securities are ranked second in safety only to federal government issues. This is because the issuer of a general obligation bond is required by law to exercise its taxing power so that bondholders can be paid. Income from property tax or other locally levied taxes is used to pay local general obligation bonds, while holders of state general obligation bonds are paid with revenues generated from income, sales, gasoline, tobacco, corporation, or business taxes. Theoretically, at least, general obligation bonds have first claim on the revenue of the state or local government issuing the bond. "By law," wrote *Wall Street Week* sage Louis Rukeyser, "such bondholders are right up there with the school teachers and the policemen in their claim on the community; in fact, in Chicago, during the Depression, municipal employees generally got scrip, bondholders got cash."[4]

Revenue Bonds

Revenue bonds, on the other hand, are backed only by revenues from a specific project, such as the tolls, fees, or rents paid by the users of the facility constructed with the proceeds from the bond. A typical example would be a bond issued to build a toll road, backed not by local taxpayers but by the income generated, in the form of tolls, from the motorists who use the road. Because payments to holders of revenue bonds are not guaranteed by the unlimited taxing power of the issuing government, revenue bonds are generally considered riskier than general obligation bonds, and usually the investor is compensated for the added risk by receiving a higher rate of interest. Clearly the investor contemplating purchase of revenue bonds should learn all he or she can about factors that might affect the profitability of the facility being constructed. Although not common, default on revenue bonds does occur.

Sources of Information on Municipal Bonds

Information on municipals is not always easy to locate, and in some instances may be completely unobtainable from the standard printed sources available in most libraries or from free Internet sources. Daily price quotations for municipal issues in the *Wall Street Journal*, for example, are limited to a few, select revenue bonds. The sheer volume and diversity of municipal bonds make it impractical for printed sources to list them all; the fact that many of them are serial bonds, each with a whole range of different maturities, makes it all but impossible. So, in many instances, an investor seeking current price and trading information for a specific municipal issue may well have to get it directly from a securities broker or a commercial bank.

Two major bond publications described later in this chapter, the *Mergent Bond Record* and *Standard & Poor's Bond Guide*, list many municipal issues, but the information given is limited to the rating assigned to each. Somewhat more detailed information is contained in the weekly bond advisory newsletter issued by Standard & Poor's. The publication is *Credit Week,* and it includes fairly detailed analyses of a few issues, as well as tables that briefly summarize new tax-exempt issues. Mergent also has an online resource called *Bond Viewer,* but it is not available to libraries.

The most comprehensive source of information that is widely available and affordable for libraries is *Mergent's Municipal & Government Manual*. Its arrangement is alphabetical by state, and then by city, town, and political subdivision. Information for each state includes a description of principal tax sources; financial, population, and industry statistics; a map of the state and its counties; and a list of outstanding issues.

After state government information is given, local government units are listed. The type of information provided varies according to the nature of the political subdivision. A town listing will include the name of the county in which it is located, date of incorporation, population in the most recent decennial census, assessed value of property, tax collected, the Mergent (Moody's) rating, overdue taxes, and the name of the bank making interest payments. A school district listing might include the district's location in the state, average school attendance figures, assessed valuation of property in the school district, the Mergent (Moody's) rating, and the name of the bank making semiannual interest payments to bondholders.

The main drawback to *Mergent's Municipal* is that the information becomes somewhat dated as the year progresses. This is offset by the publication of a newsletter that updates the *Manual*. It includes listings of new and prospective issues, securities whose ratings have been changed or withdrawn, and a list of call notices posted by international, federal, and municipal organizations that are calling in some of their securities.

There are also some excellent sources of information on the Web. One of these, mentioned previously, is maintained by the Securities Industry and Financial Markets Association and is available at http://investinginbonds.com/. The site includes *Learn*

More guides to all types of bonds. The guide to municipals describes the types of bonds and includes an explanation of safety factors, understanding market risk, calls, and taxes on the issues. The web site also includes the daily report of transactions.

Corporate Securities

Corporations also issue bonds and other debt securities. As with government securities, corporate securities can be classified by length of time to maturity. Short-term corporate debt obligations, discussed in the section on money market instruments, are called commercial paper. Generally, commercial paper has a maturity of from 2 to 270 days, and since it is traded in minimum denominations of $100,000, is only indirectly purchased by individual investors via money market funds.

Corporate bonds, on the other hand, are usually issued in denominations of $1,000 or $5,000, making them a more likely target for the individual investor. As on many government and municipal bonds, interest is generally issued semiannually. Corporate bonds usually have maturities of from 20 to 30 years, and many of them contain the sinking fund and call provisions described earlier in this chapter.

Types of Corporate Bonds

Corporate bonds can be categorized broadly by the type of collateral put up to secure the bond. Some bonds are unsecured, with no collateral pledged as security. Others may pledge specific equipment, facilities, or their own portfolios of stocks and bonds.

Debenture bonds or debentures are unsecured loans, backed only by the company's "full faith and credit." In other words, all that stands behind repayment of the loan is the company's own word that it will repay the principal and make the requisite number of semiannual interest payments. Obviously, the financial and managerial well-being of a company issuing debentures should be of prime interest to the prospective bond buyer, and careful attention should be paid to the ratings assigned by Moody's and Standard & Poor's.

Other bonds may be backed by some specific, tangible asset against the possibility of default. If the company fails to make interest payments or to repay the principal, the asset can be sold so that the bondholders will be paid. Mortgage bonds, for example, are secured by a specific piece of fixed property such as a company plant or laboratory. Still other bonds pledge movable equipment as security. They are called equipment trust certificates and are generally issued by airlines and railroads. Finally, collateral trust bonds are those bonds backed by securities held by the issuing corporation. The collateral must have a market value at least equal to the value of the bonds.

Some bonds can be converted at the holder's option into a designated number of shares of common stock. These bonds are called convertible bonds or convertibles and offer the investor the chance to do a little financial fence-straddling. If the company fails to prosper, the convertible bondholder can choose not to exercise the conversion privilege and can instead collect semiannual fixed-interest payments much as he or she would on any other bond. (The interest rate will be less, however, than for straight, nonconvertible bonds issued by the same company.) On the other hand, if the company should prosper, the investor has the option of converting the bond into common stock at a previously specified conversion price. Assume, for example, that Placebo, Inc., a pharmaceutical company, issues a $1,000 convertible bond, giving its holders the option of converting the bond into 20 shares of its common stock. The conversion price per share of common stock would be $50, or $1,000 (the price of the bond) divided by 20 (the number of shares into which the bond can be converted). Suppose further that at the time the bond was issued, Placebo common was selling for $30 per share. No one would trade the bond for stock. But if Placebo should discover a cure for the common cold and its stock should zoom to $75 per share, the convertible bondholder would be able to tap into company profits by converting the $1,000 bond into 20 shares of stock, now worth a total of $1,500. Convertible bonds can be identified by the letters cv following the name, interest rate, and maturity date of bond listings in financial newspapers and other publications.

Trading of Corporate Bonds

Although the bulk of trading of corporate bonds is done on the OTC market, some corporates are also traded on the New York Stock Exchange. Daily trading activity on the NYSE is reported in the *Wall Street Journal* and *New York Times*. A look at the information contained in the daily bond quotation tables may be helpful. The sample shown in figure 12.6 is typical.

Company	Coupon	Maturity	Rating	High	Low	Change	Yield
XXYY	7.875%	Nov '11	Baa2	118.05	117.797	0.017	4.445

Explanation:

Coupon   Interest rate that the issuer pays to the bondholder – can be fixed or variable.

Maturity   Date on which the bond's issuer will pay back the principal value to the bondholder.

Rating   Credit rating from a Nationally Recognized Statistical Rating Organization.

High   Highest trading price on the previous day.

Low   Previous day's lowest price at which the bond traded.

Change   Change in price from the previous price at which the bond traded.

Yield   The annual return until the bond matures or is called. Yield is calculated by the amount of interest paid on the bond, divided by the price.

Figure 12.6. Example of a corporate bond table

Sources of Information on Corporate Bonds

Various company-issued reports, such as the annual report to shareholders and the 10-K report, will be of interest to investors, as will the comprehensive investment services described in the preceding chapter. The various *Mergent Manuals*, particularly the *Industrial, OTC Industrial, Public Utility, Transportation,* and *Bank & Finance* manuals with their detailed financial statements, company histories, and descriptions and bond ratings, are basic corporate bond information sources. *Mergent Online* also includes a separate module, *Corporate Bond Portraits,* which can be added to the basic product as budgets allow.

Mergent Bond Record and *Standard & Poor's Bond Guide* include lengthy sections on corporate issues. The *Bond Guide* lists over 6,800 domestic corporates, more than 560

Canadian and other foreign issues, and over 320 convertibles. General information is provided on each company, including its industry code and limited balance sheet data, as well as on each bond issued by the company. For each issue listed, data include the type of bond, the rating assigned to the bond, interest payment dates, coupon and maturity, information on redemption provisions, both current yield and yield to maturity, and other financial data. All of this information is packed into a single line, so abbreviations and symbols are heavily used. Detailed explanations are given on the front and back inside covers of each issue.

Convertible bonds are listed separately from the other corporate issues in the *Bond Guide*. Information given for each convertible issue includes coupon rate and maturity, Standard & Poor's rating, expiration date of conversion privilege, number of shares of common stock into which each bond can be converted, the conversion price per share of common stock, and the dividend income per bond. In addition, current stock data — market price, price-earnings ratio, and earnings per share — are included.

Mergent Bond Record provides similar information in a slightly different format and includes Canadian provincial and municipal obligations and international listings, as well as domestic corporate bonds, in a single listing. Otherwise, the information is virtually identical, with coupon rate and maturity, dates of interest payments, ratings, current price, sinking fund and call provisions, yield to maturity, and other financial data given for each issue.

As in the *Bond Guide*, convertibles are listed separately in the *Bond Record*. Data include the Mergent rating, conversion period and price, number of shares of common stock into which the bond can be converted, and current stock and bond data.

The bond advisory newsletters, discussed briefly in the section on municipals and at greater length in the forthcoming section on general information sources, include periodic in-depth analyses of specific corporate issues as well as brief tabular summaries of others.

General Information Sources

On the whole, information on bonds is more difficult to find than information on stocks. This is because of the diversity and complexity of bonds, because some bonds are traded only locally or have limited distribution, and because much of the published information is directed toward securities dealers and institutional investors rather than individual investors. Some publications are available mainly to bond dealers.

This is not to say information sources are not available; they are. The *Encyclopedia of Business Information Sources* lists publications, in a variety of formats, dealing with bonds. Most can be categorized as either factual sources that provide summary statistical data or as advisory services. Both are deserving of attention, but it should be kept in mind that while the few titles mentioned below represent the types of publications available, they in no way comprise a comprehensive list. The *Encyclopedia of Business Information Sources* lists major bond publications, and the librarian attempting to build a collection in this area would do well to consult them.

Factual Sources

Financial newspapers provide concise statistical data on bonds and other fixed-income securities. The *Wall Street Journal* has fairly comprehensive daily information on trading of federal government and corporate debt obligations, as does the *New York Times*. Weekly trading information is available in *Barron's*, *Commercial and Financial*

Chronicle, and *Media General Market Data Graphics*. Two publications issued by Mergent and Standard & Poor's contain monthly trading information. Although each has been referred to in earlier parts of this chapter, an overview of both is useful.

Standard & Poor's. **Bond Guide.** New York: Standard & Poor's, 1938–. Monthly.

Mergent Bond Record. New York: Mergent, 1932–. Monthly.

The *Bond Guide* is a monthly pocket guide to corporate, foreign, and municipal bonds. The bulk of each issue is devoted to corporate bonds, with 6,800 domestic corporates, more than 560 Canadian and foreign issues, and over 320 convertibles. Information in these sections is condensed into one-line summaries, which include detailed information on both the issuing companies and the specific issues themselves. The municipal section, which is so densely packed that the print is difficult to read, is limited to the ratings assigned by Standard & Poor's to each issue.

The *Bond Guide* also includes a directory of underwriters of corporate bonds, a description of the S&P rating scheme, and a digest of investment security regulations. It briefly lists corporate and municipal bonds whose ratings have changed and recent issues registered with the Securities and Exchange Commission. Because of its compact format, abbreviations and symbols are heavily used, and the inner covers of each issue explain each item included in the table in some detail.

Mergent's offering is the *Bond Record*, another monthly. Like the *Bond Guide*, it provides most information on domestic, Canadian, and some foreign bonds as well as Canadian provincial and municipal obligations. Convertible bonds are listed separately. In addition, it lists and rates commercial paper issued by companies. Separate rating and listing sections are also assigned to preferred stocks, industrial revenue bonds, environmental control revenue bonds, and municipal bonds and short-term loans. Finally, the *Bond Record* includes several charts: corporate bond yields by rating categories, yields of U.S. government securities, and weekly money market rates, among others.

Most small and medium-sized libraries will not find it necessary to subscribe to both the *Bond Guide* and the *Bond Record*. Both are good, basic guides, each with its own special features. Mergent's *Bond Record*'s format is more attractive and the print easier to read than that in Standard & Poor's *Bond Guide*. In addition, the *Bond Record*'s scope is broader; it provides information on short-term debt securities and government and federal agency obligations, whereas the Standard & Poor's publication does not. On the other hand, the corporate listings in Standard & Poor's *Bond Guide* feature more information about the companies themselves, assigning industry codes and including balance sheet figures and other financial data. Furthermore, the *Bond Guide* lists corporate underwriters. Clearly, the choice of one or the other of these publications will be a reflection of the library's budget, its clientele and their preferences, and the type of information requests concerning bonds most commonly handled.

There are also several web pages on bonds. Perhaps one of the best is that of the Bond Market Association (http://www.investinginbonds.com), mentioned previously in this chapter. This contains descriptive guides for all types of bonds, a glossary of terms, a comparison calculator, and the ability to retrieve bond prices for the previous day and to sort them by CUSIP, ratings, issue, sector, coupon, maturity, yield, spread price, or size. This web page also links to other resources through an annotated subject guide that includes listings for the asset-backed securities market, money market instruments, federal agency securities market, corporate bond market, municipal securities market, mortgage securities market, and Treasury securities market. It is a well-organized site and up to this time the information is free.

Advisory Services

Like weekly stock advisory services, bond services provide their readers with general information about the economy, the investment climate, and market trends as well as analyses of specific issues. Typical of these publications is *Credit Week*.

CreditWeek. New York: Standard & Poor's, 1973–. Weekly.

Value Line Convertibles Survey. New York: Value Line, 1970–. Bimonthly.

CreditWeek combines economic and credit market commentary with reviews and analyses of short- and long-term corporate issues, international bonds, and municipals. The "CreditWatch" section lists bonds and other fixed-income securities under special surveillance for possible changes in S&P ratings. A company merger, for example, may positively or negatively affect the credit standing of a corporation, while a voter referendum reducing local property taxes would have the same effect on municipal obligations.

Standard & Poor's is not the only publisher of bond advisory services. Fitch Investors Service (http://www.fitchibca.com/), a New York–based credit rating firm, rates municipal and corporate bonds, while *Value Line Convertibles* rates convertible bonds and preferred stocks. *Value Line Convertibles* ranks over 600 convertibles for potential risk and return, showing which convertibles make the best buys and which should be sold. Approximately 80 warrants, which are like options and are very risky, are also followed and evaluated. This service is available in both print and CD-ROM formats.

Since many libraries subscribe to one or the other or both of the library investment "packages" offered by Mergent and Standard & Poor's, their publications are the services most likely to be found in business reference collections.

For-Fee Databases

Many of the databases described in the preceding chapter contain information about bonds and fixed-income securities as well as stocks. General financial information, for example, is available in files produced by Dow Jones and Mergent. Some of the more specialized databases are described below.

Bond Buyer Full Text. New York: Bond Buyer. 1982–. Daily updates. http://www .bondbuyer.com/ (accessed January 5, 2011)

Fitch IBCA Ratings Delivery Service. New York: Fitch, 1998–. http://www.fitchibca .com/ (accessed January 5, 2011)

RatingsDirect. New York: Standard & Poor's, ©1994–2003. http://www.ratingsdirect .com/ (accessed January 5, 2011)

Value Line Convertibles Securities File. New York: Value Line, 19uu–. http://www .valueline.com (Accessed January 5, 2011)

The *Bond Buyer* is the online, full-text version of the daily *Bond Buyer*, which is published five days a week. It focuses on fixed-income securities and includes statistics on bond yields, prices, and sales; articles on federal laws and regulations affecting tax-exempt financing; Internal Revenue rulings; and a complete record of municipal borrowings. Although the *Bond Buyer* is intended for institutional rather than private investors, the data it contains can be useful to scholars and researchers as well. There is a fair amount of free information available at the web site.

Fitch provides online, real-time ratings in the three sectors of corporate, asset-backed, and municipal bonds. These ratings, based on information obtained from issuers, underwriters, and their experts, are not recommendations to buy, sell, or hold any security. The web site allows free access to recent press releases, presale reports, criteria reports, and all current ratings maintained by Fitch. For details about the ratings service and fees, the user needs to check the web site at http://www.fitchibca.com/. Fitch ratings are also made available through third parties, including Dow Jones, LexisNexis, and Interactive Data.

Standard & Poor's provides an integrated online service, *RatingsDirect,* which covers more than 6 million ratings, 248,000 issues, and 71,000 reports. The content includes ratings of specific securities and research, and analysis related to the supplied ratings. Subscriptions are available to information on all of Standard & Poor's global ratings activities or to information about a specific sector or region of interest.

The *Value Line Convertibles* is one of the largest sources of information available on convertible securities. It covers over 600 convertible bonds, preferred stocks, and warrants, with approximately 150 fundamental and proprietary data items on each. *Value Line's* evaluations are included.

These fee-based services are expensive and are usually subscribed to by institutional investors, but librarians should be aware of them and the availability of the data for researchers.

Web Sites

Investing in Bonds.com. http://investinginbonds.com/

Geared toward many types of investors—from beginners to experienced equity investors who are new to bonds to sophisticated bond investors—*Investinginbonds.com* is a unique source of bond price information and includes a wide variety of market data, news, commentary, and information about bonds. The site, which has been ranked as a top investor site for bonds by *Money,* CNBC, *Forbes,* and others, was mostly recently named one of *Kiplinger's Personal Finance* magazine's two 2009 Best Investing Sites for its information for newcomers and data for experts. The site is continually enhanced and updated with new data, information, and features. (Taken from the web site)

Morningstar. http://www.morningstar.com/

Click on the "Bonds" tab to link to news, the investing classroom, corporate credit ratings, corporate bond data, and calculators. Amazing source of information, and it is all free.

BondsOnline. http://www.bondsonline.com/

Using this site one can obtain news, yield curves, and charts. Parts of the site designated by $$ are fee based.

Notes

1. The Federal Reserve Bank of Richmond issued in 1993 the seventh edition of *Instruments of the Money Market*. This book is no longer in print, but the chapters have been placed on the Web at http://www .richmondfed.org/publications/research/special_reports/instruments_of_the_money_market/?WT.si_ n=Search&WT.si_x=3.

2. *TreasuryDirect* is a program designed for investors who purchase Treasury bills, notes, and bonds and intend to hold them until maturity. Individual investors can establish a single *TreasuryDirect* account for all marketable Treasury securities with the same ownership and hold all their bills, notes, or bonds in the same account. Principal and interest payments are made electronically by direct deposit to an account at a financial institution designated by the investor.

More information can be obtained from
   http://www.treasurydirect.gov/write.htm
   http://www.treasurydirect.gov/email.htm

3. The formula for converting the yield column to dollar price is

$$\text{Price} = 100 - \frac{\text{Yield (Maturity)}}{360}$$

4. Louis Rukeyser, *How to Make Money in Wall Street* (Garden City, NY: Doubleday, 1974), 161.

13

Mutual Funds and Investment Companies

Introduction

Stocks and bonds are for those who prefer direct participation in the investment market. Investment companies—that is, companies that sell shares in the investments held in diversified securities portfolios acquired with the pooled money of shareholders—are for those who prefer to relinquish responsibility for selection of securities and portfolio management to professional investment managers. The investor's responsibility ceases after he or she makes the initial selection and purchase of shares in a chosen investment company, until such time as the investor decides to redeem the shares at current market value or switch to another fund.

The shares purchased may be in open- or closed-end investment companies. Open-end investment companies, known as mutual funds, are those that will sell an unlimited number of shares to all interested investors; they stand ready to issue new shares or redeem old ones on a daily basis. As the number of shareholders increases, the pool of money to be invested grows proportionally and the securities portfolio expands. The shares are sold, or repurchased, at prices reflecting the value of the underlying securities.

Closed-end investment companies[1] on the other hand, issue and sell a fixed number of shares only once, at the time they are established. If new investors want to buy into a closed-end investment company, they must purchase some of the existing shares from another investor, using a stockbroker as an intermediary. Shares in these companies, also known as publicly traded investment companies, are traded on the major stock exchanges and over the counter, and their prices move up and down with investor demand. Shares in open-end investment companies, on the other hand, are sold directly to the investor by the issuing company. This distinction is an important one to the librarian doing business reference, because information for both types of investment companies may not be given in the same place. Daily share price information, for example, is given separately for open- and closed-end investment companies in financial newspapers.

Mutual funds and closed-end investment companies, however, have two basic operating principles in common: They pool money from their investors to buy a broad range of stocks, bonds, and/or other investment vehicles, and they have professional investment managers who take full responsibility for all investment decisions.

Mutual funds and closed-end investment companies offer certain advantages to the investor with limited resources. Prime among these is diversification of investments. Although all investors routinely are counseled to minimize risk by diversifying their investments in a wide range of companies and industries, few individual investors can hope to achieve the variety found in most investment company portfolios. The Janus (JANSX) Mutual Fund is a case in point. Its investment portfolio recently featured stocks of 74 companies in 9 different industries. For an individual investor to research and then vigilantly maintain constant oversight of this amount of information would be a full-time occupation.

Professional management is another advantage, particularly for the inexperienced or anxious investor. The professional manager handles basic investment decisions. In addition, he or she takes care of all of the paperwork and administrative details, including the preparation and distribution of quarterly reports to shareholders. In return for these services, an annual management fee percentage of the total is deducted from the company's assets.

A third advantage is that fund performance is subject to frequent reviews by various publications and rating agencies, making it possible to conduct comparisons between funds.

Mutual funds are attractive because in most instances they require only relatively small minimum investments, and dividends earned can be automatically reinvested in additional shares. Thus, it is possible for the small investor to steadily increase his or her holdings in a way that is difficult to match in other kinds of investments. Another significant advantage is the ease with which most investment company shares can be redeemed. This is particularly true of open-end investment companies or mutual funds, which stand ready to redeem shares at any time the securities markets are open. Shares are redeemed at net asset value, the value of the company's holdings minus its debt, divided by the number of shares outstanding. Net asset value is determined daily, so that market fluctuations in the price of the securities held by the fund can be taken into account. Closed-end investment companies, on the other hand, are traded on the securities exchanges, and their price is a reflection of supply and demand in the marketplace as well as of their net asset value.

Finally, many investment companies offer special services to their investors, including check writing privileges, special withdrawal plans, and the opportunity to switch from one company fund to another.

This is not to say that investment companies are without flaw. Some charge substantial sales commissions, some charge redemption fees, all levy management fees, and, in some instances, the return on these investments is not as great as one might earn from direct investment in stocks and bonds. Another disadvantage is that the investor exercises no control over what securities are bought or when they are sold. Still, for many the advantages they offer outweigh their drawbacks.

A mutual fund alternative is the unit investment trust (UIT). This is a registered investment company that buys and holds a relatively fixed portfolio of stocks, bonds, or other securities. "Units" in the trust are sold to investors, who receive a share of principal and interest or dividends. Many are collections of long-term bonds and therefore may remain outstanding for 20 or 30 years. Investors who choose bond UITs receive regular monthly income, and those who hold stock UITs receive dividend income, paid out monthly, quarterly, or semiannually, plus long-term capital growth potential. Unit investment trusts have a stated date for termination, and when they are dissolved, proceeds from the holdings are paid to the investors.

Another alternative is a hedge fund, which is an unregistered private investment pool that is subject to far less regulatory oversight than a mutual fund. With the exception of anti-fraud standards, they are exempt from regulation by the SEC under the federal securities laws, unlike mutual funds, which are regulated by the Securities Act of 1933, the Securities Exchange Act of 1934, the Investment Company Act of 1940, and the Investment Advisers Act of 1940. Hedge fund managers are not forced to disclose information about the hedge fund's holdings and performance. Hedge funds are only open for investment to a limited number of accredited or qualified investors who meet criteria set by regulators. One drawback is that usually one must be prepared to invest $1 million or more.

Types of Investment Companies

Mutual fund investment companies, as we have seen, can be categorized as open- or closed-end. They can also be classified by the presence or absence of a sales fee, their investment objectives, and their portfolio contents. Each of these classifications merits further consideration.

Load and No-Load Funds

Some mutual fund shares are sold using stockbrokers or securities dealers as middlemen. They promote the funds, handle the paperwork, and make it convenient for the investor to buy shares. These services must be paid for, so for each transaction, a sales charge, or load, ranging from 1½ to 8½ percent is deducted from the initial investment. Thus, a $10,000 investment in a fund charging an 8½ percent load is really only a $9,150 investment; the remaining $850 goes to the salesperson. Further, an investor who puts $10,000 into a load fund from which the $850 load immediately is deducted must earn $850 on his or her investment just to break even.

Other funds must be purchased directly from the issuing investment company. Because no middlemen are involved, often no sales commission, or load, is deducted, and these funds are called, appropriately enough, no-load funds. The total amount of the investment goes directly into fund shares, which means that, over the long run and given the same initial investment, shareholders in no-load funds come out ahead.

Let's assume two $10,000 investments, one in a load fund and the other in a no-load fund. In the case of the load fund, 8½ percent or $815 is deducted; the remaining $9,150 is invested. If both funds grow at the same rate—10 percent per year, for example—the no-load fund will be worth $11,000 at the end of the first year, while the load fund will be worth only $10,065. The no-load investor is now $1,000 ahead; the load fund investor is about even. But let's look closer. Originally the no-load investor had $850 more working for him than did the load fund investor. Now the differential is $935 ($11,000 versus $10,065). What has happened is that the $850 paid out as commission in one case, but invested in the other, is also growing. And over the years this sum will continue to grow and compound, widening the differential. By the end of 20 years, the no-load investment will be worth $6,000 more.[2] This is not always the case, and an investor should also check for other possibilities and outcomes through article research and the Closed-End Fund Association web page.

In terms of quality of professional investment management, neither the load nor the no-load fund is intrinsically superior. There are good, bad, and mediocre funds in both categories. Purchase of no-load funds, however, requires more investor initiative, since it is the investor who must identify potential no-load fund investments, contact each company for additional information, and initiate the actual purchase of shares. Although securities brokers are not ordinarily forthcoming with information on no-load funds, the investor can find these funds advertised in financial newspapers and publications and listed in some of the basic sources described later in this chapter. Another way in which no-load funds can be identified is through the Mutual Fund Education Alliance Web page,[3] which has a searchable database of funds.

Investment Objectives

Investment companies can also be differentiated by their investment objectives. Some funds, which stress immediate income and invest primarily in corporate bonds or high-dividend-yielding stocks, are income funds. Growth funds, on the other hand, look for long-term capital or income growth. Still other funds seek to attain a balance between income and growth. These are balanced funds. Many basic reference sources classify the various funds by their investment objectives; another source of this information is the prospectus issued by the fund itself. The 2001 prospectus for the Red Oak Technology Select Fund, for example, states that it is a non-diversified mutual fund whose investment goal is long-term capital growth and whose investment focus is U.S. common stocks. The fund strategy is to invest in common stocks of companies that rely extensively on technology in their product development or operations, or which the adviser expects to benefit from technological advances and improvements. The fund is concentrated (invests at least 25 percent of its total assets) in "technology companies" that develop, produce, or distribute products or services related to computers, semiconductors, and electronics. In other words, this is for people who are willing to risk investing in a fund that invests in relatively few companies in one industry.

Portfolio Contents

Varying objectives necessitate the purchase of different types of securities for each investment portfolio. As a result, another way in which investment companies can be categorized is by the types of securities they hold. Although there are several variations, the basic categories are as follows:

1. Bond funds

2. Equity (stock) funds

3. Money market funds

4. Balanced funds

5. Index funds

6. Asset allocation funds

There is, of course, considerable variety within each of these categories. One bond fund, for example, may invest only in double and triple A-rated bonds, while another fund's portfolio may include a mix of high-, medium-, and low-rated bonds. Similarly, funds are often described by the kind of stocks they invest in. Funds that invest in growth stocks (stocks of companies with positive outlooks for growth) are described as growth funds. Funds that invest in value stocks (stocks of companies that are currently considered to be cheap based on fundamental data like earnings, revenue, and assets) are described as value funds. Some mutual funds invest only in stocks of foreign companies. These are called international funds, while global funds are those that invest in stocks of both foreign and U.S. companies. Sector funds are those that invest in stocks of a particular industry or area such as technology, real estate, or precious metals. Money market funds have relatively low risks compared to other mutual funds. They are limited by law to certain high-quality, short-term investments such as Treasury bills. Balanced funds mix some stocks and some bonds with money market instruments in an effort to provide growth, income, and conservation of capital. An index fund is a mutual fund that tries to mimic, as closely as possible, the holdings of a particular index. They are distinct from actively managed mutual funds in that they do not involve any stock picking by a fund manager; they simply seek to replicate the returns of a specific index, such as the S&P 500 or the Dow Industrial. Many of the basic reference sources give an indication of portfolio contents, and this information is spelled out in detail in individual investment company prospectuses.

As the economy changes, so also does interest in specific types of funds. In years of spiraling interest rates, for example, money market funds enjoy tremendous popularity, with a resulting proliferation of guides, directories, and advisory letters, many of which are in great demand by library users. Some of these titles are discussed later in the section on information sources.

Closed-end funds are divided into many of the same categories as mutual funds.

Current Per-Share Information

Mutual Funds

Mutual funds stand ready to redeem their shares at net asset value whenever the securities markets are open. Net asset value for each fund is determined daily and is listed in financial newspapers such as the *Wall Street Journal* and on various web sites. Compared to stock and bond tables, those for mutual funds are relatively easy to decipher, and figures are in dollars and cents. Web sites provide significantly more data about a given mutual fund than a fund table does. Yahoo! Finance, MSN Money, and all of the major mutual fund companies provide robust web sites filled with fund information.

52 Week High	Low	Fund Name	Week's High	Low	Close NAV	Wk's - Chg.	% Return - 1-Wk	YTD	3-Yr	Income+ Cap Gains	Ex Date	Inco. Divs	Cap Gain
31.14	23.90	XX	31.07	30.41	30.57	-0.57	-1.8	+5.0	**NS**	0.0160	12-22-10	0.0160	---

Explanations

NAV (Net Asset Value)
The market value of a fund share. In the case of no-load funds, the NAV, market price, and offering price are all the same figure, which the public pays to buy shares; load fund market prices are quoted after adding the sales charge to the net asset value. NAV is calculated by most funds after the close of the exchanges each day by taking the closing market value of all securities owned plus all other assets such as cash, subtracting all liabilities, then dividing the result (total net assets) by the total number of shares outstanding.

NS
Fund not in existence for whole period.

Figure 13.1. Example of a daily online mutual fund table

Thus, in the example shown in figure 13.1, the item listed, XYZ Fund, a load fund, could be redeemed for $30.57 per share, its current net asset value. The net asset value was down $.57 per share from the preceding trading day, which makes a –1.8 percentage point change.

Closed-End Investment Companies

The market prices of shares in closed-end investment companies are shown in the tables of most financial newspapers. Like stocks, each fund has a ticker symbol which is useful for locating data, especially when an electronic search can be performed (see figure 13.2).

Fund Name	Stock Exchange	NAV	Market Price	Premium/ Discount	52-Week Market Returns / 52-Week Yield
XYZ Fund	NYSE	17.18	19.5	+ 13.5	7.1

Column 1	Name of fund
Column 2	Exchange on which fund is traded
Column 3	Net asset value of a share. Calculated by taking the fund's total assets, securities, cash and any accrued earnings, less expenses and liabilities, and dividing the remainder by the number of shares outstanding
Column 4	Final price of stock at close of trading
Column 5	Plus or minus figures shows the percentage premium (+) or discount (-) above or below the fund's NAV per share, at which the shares last sold
Column 6	For stock funds this shows the 52-week percentage change in price plus dividends. For bond funds it shows the dividends paid during the 52 weeks as a percentage of market price.

Figure 13.2. Hypothetical listing of a closed-end fund

Information Sources

A wide range of printed and Internet sources exists to help investors select and monitor investment companies in which they are interested, ranging from prospectuses and reports issued by the companies themselves to guides, directories, and specialized advisory newsletters. Some major reference tools, representative of the various types of information sources available, are described below.

Prospectuses and Company Reports

Investment companies are required by law to submit a prospectus to all prospective investors. This document describes the fund's investment objective, portfolio, management, special services offered, assets and liabilities, and per-share income. This constitutes a summary of the registration statement filed with the Securities and Exchange Commission and provides an overview of a specific fund's investment philosophy and performance. Quarterly financial reports update the prospectus and pinpoint the company's current financial status.

These are readily available to anyone either from the SEC (http://www.sec.gov), from the web page of the mutual fund company, or for those who want a print copy, directly from the company. This information comprises the primary source on which most basic investment company reference publications are based.

Most web sites that give information on mutual funds and many government web sites offer tutorials on reading and understanding a prospectus. Among them are the sites listed below.

1. Missouri Secretary of State
    http://www.sos.mo.gov/securities/pubs/prospectus.asp

2. How to Read a Prospectus
    http://hawaii.gov/dcca/sec/publications/download/breg_securitieseducation_prospectus.pdf

3. (Motley Fool) How to Read a Prospectus
    http://www.fool.com/School/MutualFunds/Basics/Read.htm

Encyclopedias, Guides, and Factbooks

Many of the general investment guides discussed in chapter 12 offer basic introductions to mutual funds and investment companies. More specialized guides are also available. Some are inexpensive booklets aimed at readers new to mutual funds. Others focus on specific types of mutual funds, such as money market funds or foreign equity funds. The type of mutual fund investment in vogue one season, however, may not be in the next, and these specialized guides may remain unread on library shelves for years after a brief period of popularity. Although such publications can be useful for the short term, libraries with limited book budgets should first acquire a core collection of general mutual fund guides or a core listing of web sites that provide the same type of information.

Beginners' Guide to Mutual Funds: Online Publications at the SEC. 2009.

Available at http://www.sec.gov/investor/pubs/beginmutual.htm

Investment Company Institute. **Mutual Fund Fact Book.** Washington, DC: The Institute, 1966–. Annual. (Available in PDF format at http://www.ici.org/stats/mf/index.html)

The SEC guide is a series of links to information provided on the basics of mutual fund investment, questions and answers about everything from eligibility to rollovers, from investing to hardship withdrawals, how to check on advisors and brokers, and much more.

The *Mutual Fund Fact Book* is very different in that it provides an overview of the mutual funds industry, including its history, growth and development, composite industry statistics, and a glossary of key terms. It is extremely useful for the researcher who wants to learn about mutual funds generally and does not require information on specific funds. The web site for the Investment Company Institute (http://www.ici.org/) also contains information on the taxation of mutual funds, an investor education section, data highlights, and recent news.

Checking Out a Brokerage Firm, Individual Broker, Investment Adviser Firm, or Individual Investment Adviser

Information concerning brokerage firms and individual brokers is publicly available online through FINRA's Broker Check program or by calling toll-free at (800) 289-9999. Information about certain investment adviser firms is available through the SEC's Investment Adviser Public Disclosure (IAPD) Program. You may also obtain information about brokerage firms, individual brokers, and investment adviser firms, as well as information on individual investment advisers, through your state securities regulator. You can find out how to get in touch with your state securities regulator through the North American Securities Administrators Association, Inc.'s Web site.

FINRA's BrokerCheck Program

Information on brokerage firms. FINRA's BrokerCheck Program provides the following information on brokerage firms: the firm's address, legal status, types of businesses, and direct and indirect owners and officers; felony charges and convictions, and investment-related misdemeanor charges and convictions, for the past 10 years; disciplinary actions and proceedings initiated by regulators; investment-related civil court actions and proceedings for the past 10 years; bankruptcy proceedings; unsatisfied judgments or liens; summary information on arbitration awards; and (for former FINRA firms-registered firms) the date that the firm ceased doing business, and, as appropriate, certain information regarding funds owed to customers or other firms.

Information on individual brokers. BrokerCheck provides the following information on individual brokers: current employer; employment history for the past 10 years; other businesses outside of employment with the brokerage firm; approved licenses and registrations and qualification exams passed; criminal felony charges and convictions; investment-related misdemeanor charges and convictions; disciplinary actions and investigations by regulators; investment-related civil court actions and proceedings; consumer-initiated complaints, arbitration proceedings and civil law suits; unsatisfied judgments and liens, and bankruptcy proceedings; and employment terminations following alleged misconduct or failure to supervise subordinates.

Figure 13.3. Checking on brokers and advisors showing links to FNRA,
http://www.sec.gov/answers/crd.htm

There are numerous web sites, including those belonging to fund families, which include basic guides and information to the different funds. Several are listed below.

About.com Mutual Funds. 2003. http://mutualfunds.about.com/ (accessed January 11, 2011)

This site includes basic guides on the different types of mutual funds, guides to beginning investing in funds, and guides to asset allocation. This site is heavy on advice and guidance in all areas.

The Motley Fool Mutual Funds. 1995–2003. http://www.fool.com/mutualfunds/ mutualfunds.htm (accessed January 30, 2011)

For those who prefer a more irreverent but still extremely useful look at mutual funds, this is the site to use. Information ranges from the "The Truth" to the "Owner's Guide." There is also an interesting look at the cost of mutual funds, including loads, expense ratios, taxes, and turnover and cash reserves. With free registration a user may take part in the online discussion boards.

Mutual Fund Investor's Center. 1996–2003. http://www.mfea.com/ (accessed January 14, 2011)

Another very usable site designed to help investors reach their financial goals. It contains a large collection of mutual fund company listings, as well as links to planning, tracking, and monitoring tools available on the Internet. One special feature is a section designed for teen investors and the problems they may have. This is a site that librarians as well as investors should explore.

Morningstar. 2011 http://www.morningstar.com/ (accessed January 30, 2011)

This web site covers not only mutual funds but also closed-end funds, ETFs, stocks, and bonds. Morningstar, too, has lots of tools. Some of these are premium features (indicated by a plus-sign [+] immediately to the left of the corresponding link), but many are free. Morningstar is probably best known for its proprietary fund ratings. Funds are ranked from 1 to 5 stars "according to their risk-adjusted returns," with the best performers getting the highest number of stars.

YAHOO! FINANCE Mutual Fund Center. http://finance.yahoo.com/funds (accessed January 14, 2011)

Another well-laid-out site from YAHOO! that contains not only the expected guides, news, and message boards but also a fund screener. Using the screener it is easy for most users to generate a list of funds in which they feel comfortable investing.

This is only a short selection of accessible web sites. They were chosen because of the carefully written guides, the simplicity of the language, and the wealth of free information provided. There are many others available, and it is up to librarians to acquire or recommend those most useful for patrons.

For those who are interested in learning more about closed-end funds, an excellent source of information is the *Closed End Fund Center* web page (http://www.closed-endfunds.com/) maintained by the Closed-End Fund Association (CEFA), the national trade association representing the closed-end fund industry. The CEFA web page is a comprehensive collection of free information on the general composition of the funds, the advantages, and investment risk, as well as statistics, articles, and a fund tracker. Included on the page is information on buying and selling, dividends, discounts, and premiums, as well as the annual reports for over 200 closed-end funds and daily information on the industry's leaders. The information included encompasses both that needed by a beginner in investing and that needed by someone who has already invested in the funds.

Subscription Databases

Morningstar Investment Research Center. Chicago: Morningstar Library Services. 2011.

The Morningstar Investment Research Center is a subscription database aimed to appeal to institutions, individual investors, business students, faculty, and anyone trying to stay on track toward a financial goal. Many people associate Morningstar with its reports on mutual funds, but the Investment Research Center also covers stocks, bonds, exchange-traded funds (ETFs), and market indexes. It sorts financial information by stock sectors, indexes, investment style, fund category, and industry. The service analyzes portfolios, examines management effectiveness, establishes fair market value for stocks, describes "economic moats" enjoyed by companies, reports corporate credit rankings, and importantly assigns stars to stocks and mutual funds. The user can search for a stock or mutual fund by entering a name or ticker symbol. The database also has screens to help narrow a search within a certain area of interest or a user can create his own screens based on data or selected characteristics. Funds also have the Morningstar rankings and analyst reports.

NetAdvantage. New York: Standard & Poor's. 2011.

Reports on over 14,000 mutual funds and exchange traded funds—featuring Standard & Poor's proprietary STARS ranking system—are available by clicking on the "Mutual Funds" tab. One can use the search tool to retrieve a report on a specific fund or one can use the fund screener to identify a group of funds that match a common set of performance or descriptive criteria.

Directories

Many investors feel more comfortable with print publications but still want composite information about open- and closed-end investment companies as well as details on specific funds. For them, the following title will be particularly useful.

Mergent Bank & Finance Manual. New York: Mergent, 1955–. 4v. Annual. (Supplemented by *Bank & Finance News Report*, web version available at http://www.mergent.com/)

Mergent Bank & Finance Manual is another source of detailed information. Volume 2 lists major U.S. and Canadian investment companies. Its entries contain detailed listings of portfolio contents and thorough company histories. *Mergent* also includes a listing of money market fund ratings. Volumes 3 and 4 contain information on UITs.

Although *Mergent Bank & Finance Manual* provides information on both open- and closed-end investment companies, other publications are more specialized.

Although there are no widely held publications devoted specifically to closed-end investment companies, *Value Line* offers a quarterly summary of the investment company industry as well as detailed analyses of selected major closed-end investment companies whose shares are traded on national stock exchanges and over-the-counter.

Periodical Lists and Ratings

Many newspapers and periodicals regularly list and rate funds. One of the most comprehensive surveys is that offered by *Barron's*. *Barron's* includes a periodic pull-out section on mutual funds that consists of articles on specific types of funds, investment strategies, and interviews with fund managers, supplemented by tables showing the Lipper mutual fund performance averages and weekly financial tables. In addition, each quarter, with the assistance of Lipper Analytical Services, a fund-rating organization,

Barron's presents the *Lipper Mutual Funds Quarterly*, which includes "Leaders and Laggards," "Winners and Losers," as well as financial information for funds.

Other general business periodicals cover mutual funds as well as many web sites including those listed in this letter.

Specialized Advisory Newsletters/Services

In addition to the periodic coverage of mutual funds and investment companies in such standard sources as *Barron's*, several advisory services and newsletters specializing in mutual funds are published. Although a comprehensive collection of such material is impractical for most libraries, many will include one or two such sources in addition to mutual fund directories and guides. A good guide to the newsletters follows.

The Hulbert Financial Digest. Washington, DC: Hulbert Financial Digest, 19uu–. Monthly.

HFD rates for actual performance most of the investment newsletters available. If a subscription is contemplated the user should first check *HFD* for the quality of a newsletter's effectiveness. This publication checks on approximately 180 newsletters and gives subscription details. The full list of publications covered is at http://hulbert-digest. com/. This is a subscription site, but there are free trial details at the web page. Each month there are reports on the top-five-performing newsletters plus a section on mutual fund newsletters. The *HFD* features in-depth profiles of four of the top-performing letters, presenting detailed analyses of their track records, strategies, and techniques, with graphs of their performances as far back as 1980.

Moneyletter. Holliston, MA: PRI Financial Publishing, 1980–. Biweekly. (For more information, check http://www.moneyletter.com/)

Mutual Fund Prospector. Moline, IL: Mutual Fund Prospector, 1998–. Monthly. Web version available at http://www.ericdany.com/.

Value Line Mutual Fund Survey. New York: Value Line Publishing, 1993–. Monthly.

Moneyletter (http://www.moneyletter.com/) emphasizes funds likely to be of interest to individual investors and includes these in 10 model portfolios. Like the other services, it combines general information and investment advice with lists of top-performing funds, a fund scoreboard with recommendations, and coverage of specific investment companies.

Morningstar (http://www.morningstar.com), a Chicago-based fund-tracking company, provides data on more than 10,000 mutual funds and 8,000 stocks. The electronic products have already been described earlier in the chapter but many smaller libraries still subscribe to the print copies. Products are available in print, on the Internet, and on CD-ROM and can be customized for institutional or corporate clients. *Morningstar Mutual Funds* is one of the industry standards for rating funds, and uses a star (risk-adjusted) rating system for each bond or stock fund. Funds are assigned anywhere from one to five stars, one being the least attractive and five considered the best. To obtain these ratings the first number Morningstar checks is the fund's rate of return. First all sales charges and redemption fees are subtracted from the performance of the fund being measured. Then the T-bill's return is subtracted from the fund's load-adjusted figure. This will give by how much the fund return has exceeded the risk-free rate. A comparison is then made between that fund's return and other funds in its broad group. This is the return score. The groups used are U.S. stock, international stock, taxable bonds, and municipal bonds funds.

To get the risk score Morningstar analysts check the performance of a fund against the Treasury bill and compare this transaction against other funds in the group. The result is the risk score. The final part of the rating is to subtract the fund's risk score from its return. The results are then shown on a bell curve, with the top 10 percent given a five-star rating and the bottom 10 percent the one-star rating.

Many libraries buy *Morningstar* either as a print publication or as an online service, and individuals can take out a single premium subscription online at http://www .morningstar.com/. There is, however, a fair amount of free information at the web site. This includes the rating of the fund, its top investments, and links to news stories. For those libraries that have researchers who need to perform a deeper level of analysis, the best product is probably the CD-ROM *Morningstar Principia*.

The *Mutual Fund Prospector* offers investment advice, timely information, and a model portfolio, whose performance is followed each month and which is available on the Web at http://www.ericdany.com/model_portfolio_performance.htm. When available, links are provided on the web page to the funds that are followed in the newsletter.

Those researchers who have used the *Value Line Investment Survey* to follow stocks will be very comfortable using the *Value Line Mutual Fund Survey*. The first part of the *Survey* provides current rankings and performance data on 2,000 funds; the second part contains over 150 full-page reports on individual funds. Included are historical returns (up to 20 years), top portfolio holdings, ratings, and risk. More information and a sample newsletter are available at http://www.valueline.com/productsamples.html. *Value Line* also has an online service.

There are numerous services and newsletters available, and just about every financial web page has a section on mutual funds.

Notes

1. The Closed-End Fund Association (CEFA) is the national trade association representing the closed-end fund industry. Information about closed-end funds is provided at http://www.closed-endfunds .com/. The web site provides general information, a list of all funds, plus links to annual reports and statistics. Educational features are included.

2. Yale Hirsch, *Mutual Funds Almanac*, 11th ed. (Old Tappan, NJ: The Hirsch Organization, 1980), 54.

3. The Mutual Fund Education Alliance™ is the not-for-profit trade association of the no-load mutual fund industry. The web site at http://www.mfea.com/default.asp contains educational materials, a portfolio tracker, and listings of mutual funds with links to information.

14

Futures and Options

Stocks, bonds, and mutual funds are the most common investment mediums for individual investors, but they are by no means the only ones. This chapter focuses on other increasingly popular types of investments, specifically derivatives, examples of which are futures and options, and reviews of information sources relevant to them.

Derivatives

Derivatives are risk-shifting instruments. A derivative is a contract established by two or more parties where payment is based on (or "derived" from) some agreed-upon value, which is established on the future value of an underlying asset, typically a commodity, bond, equity, or currency. Simply put, derivatives are instruments whose return depends on the return of other instruments. A derivative is a promise to transfer ownership at an agreed-upon time in the future for an agreed-upon price. A common property of many derivatives is that the asset itself is not exchanged, only the change in value of the asset. Derivatives include a wide range of instruments including futures and options.

Derivatives are broadly classified as forward-based derivatives or "futures," "option"-based derivatives, and OTC or "over the counter" derivatives. OTC derivatives and futures are used by institutional investors for risk management and yield management of assets and liabilities. The average retail investor will be more involved in the options market.

The term most commonly associated with derivatives is *risk*. This is because most of us *associate with risk financial disasters* such as Orange County, California,[1] the collapse of Barings Bank,[2] and the subprime mortgage crisis of the late 2000s. Another failure, in the recent financial crisis, was the loss of US$18 billion through a subsidiary, trading in credit default swaps, by American International Group (AIG). The collapse of the company was averted by government intervention. Although the instruments themselves were blamed, it was more a lack of adequate internal and external controls that was to blame. As with all investments, risk is involved, but an understanding of the risks being taken and an organization's exposure to risk is needed.

Most general business and financial encyclopedias will give an overview of derivatives, but many specialized sources also exist.

Guides

There are hundreds of books available that will give an in-depth analysis of derivatives. To find them one can search any library catalog or web-based book service. Two titles that are useful and not too complicated are listed below.

McDonald, Robert L. **Fundamentals of Derivatives Markets.** Boston: Pearson Addison Wesley, 2009.

Chisholm, Andrew. **Derivatives Demystified: A Step-by-Step Guide to Forwards, Futures, Swaps and Options.** 2nd ed. Chichester. NY: Wiley, 2010.

Fundamentals of Derivatives Markets is an adaptation of McDonald's previous text *Derivatives Markets,* which has been a staple for students taking college financial courses. This is a briefer book and is useful also for anyone who wants to have a greater understanding of derivatives. Strategies and theories are discussed through real-life situations throughout the four main sections of the book.

The Chisholm publication, part of the Wiley series in finance, breaks down a complex subject into manageable units that do not overwhelm the novice reader. Descriptions of instruments and products are clearly set out, and the book also covers the responsibility and legal liability of companies and officers within the company. This book cuts through the jargon and the mystique surrounding derivatives. It explains the essentials in a very simple and intuitive way, with lots of examples and cases.

Both books are well written and laid out logically so that they are easy to understand for someone who wants to know more about derivatives.

For a more extensive listing of books on derivatives, check the web site at http://www.uflib.ufl.edu/cm/business/books/derivbks.htm.

Dictionaries

Most financial dictionaries contain at least some of the vocabulary of derivatives, but the following publication contains most of the specialized jargon as well as being a guide to the instruments in use. It is designed to provide more information, for each entry, than most typical dictionaries. The definition of "bull spread," for example, covers nearly two pages and contains diagrams.

Inglis-Taylor, Andrew. **Dictionary of Derivatives.** Basingstoke, UK: Macmillan, 1995. 444p.

The second part of the *Dictionary* includes articles on exchanges that give the basic data about each, including their histories, the instruments they trade, the contract months, and expiration dates.

Derivatives. ValueClick. Alberta, Canada. Accessed through Investopedia at http://www.investopedia.com/investing-topics/Derivatives/Term

The listing at Investopedia covers all major terms with links to both definitions and explanations, for example:

"*Investopedia explains Airbag Swap.* These swaps were created to hedge investments in areas where interest rate fluctuations have significant effects. Due to an increasing notional value, an asymmetrical payout schedule occurs whereby the swap's net payment with higher interest rates is greater than that occurring with lower interest rates."

This makes this site an extremely useful addition to anyone trying to fathom the mysteries of derivatives.

Futures

In the futures market, investors trade futures contracts, which are agreements for the future delivery of designated quantities of given products for specified prices. This market is meant to provide an efficient and effective mechanism to manage price risk. The market can be termed as a continuous auction market. Although futures trading in the United States began with agricultural commodities such as corn and wheat, items traded today are considerably more diverse. It is now possible to trade in precious and strategic metals, petroleum, foreign currency, and financial instruments as well as in such agricultural commodities as grain and livestock.

Futures are usually divided into two broad categories: commodities and financial (see figure 14.1).

COMMODITY FUTURES		FINANCIAL FUTURES	
Grains, Cereals, Oilseed		**Interest Rates**	
Barley	Canola	Treasury Bonds 30 Year	Euro Dollar
Corn	Soybean Meal	Treasury Notes 2 Year	Euro Yen
Rice	Soybean Oil	Treasury Notes 5 Year	Gilts Long
Wheat		Treasury Notes 10 Year	
Spring Red Wheat			
Livestock and Meat			
Broilers	Hogs	**Currencies**	
Feeder Cattle	Live Cattle	Australian Dollar	Japanese Yen
Frozen Pork Bellies		British Pound	Mexican Peso
		Canadian Dollar	Swiss Franc
Food and Fiber		New Zealand Dollar	Euro
Butter	Lumber		
Cocoa	Cotton		
Coffee		**Indexes**	
Orange Juice		Dow Jones Industrial Average	
Sugar		Russell 2000	
		S&P 500	
Petroleum and Energy		US Dollar Index	
Brent Crude	Natural Gas	NYSE Composite Futures	
Light Crude	Heating Oil	Nasdaq 100	
Ethanol		Libor 1 Month	
		London FT-SE 100	
Metals		Nikkei 225	
Gold	Uranium		
Copper			
Silver			
Platinum			

Figure 14.1. Selected major commodity and financial futures traded in the United States

Commodities Futures

Commodities are sold in two different ways. Someone can buy sugar or wheat or pork bellies and take immediate possession of the product, which must be in a basic, raw, unprocessed state. Such a purchase is commonly referred to as a cash, or spot, transaction. Frequently, however, commodities are bought and sold for delivery at a later time by means of futures contracts. A commodities futures contract is a legal agreement between buyer and seller that a specified number of units of the commodity being traded on a particular futures exchange will be delivered at a certain place, during a certain month, for an agreed-upon price. In July, someone who anticipates a rise in wheat prices, for example, may instruct his or her broker to buy one Kansas City Board of Trade (KCBT) (http://www.kcbt.com) wheat contract, to be delivered in December for $2.66 per bushel. If the market price of wheat rises from, say, $2.66 to $3.00 per bushel between the signing of the contract and the delivery date, the investor will make a profit. At this point, the purchaser of the wheat contract does not actually have physical possession of the bushels of wheat. The purchaser is not required to accept delivery; he or she can offset the transaction at any time before the delivery month. In fact, actual delivery occurs in less than 5 percent of all commodities futures transactions.

Someone who expects wheat prices to fall might instruct his or her broker to execute a contract to sell wheat at the current prevailing price. If prices fall, the seller of the contract to deliver will have earned a profit; if they rise, the buyer of the contract will come out ahead.

As indicated above, most traders choose to liquidate their contracts before delivery by arranging offsetting transactions to reverse the original actions. Buyers, in other words, liquidate their contracts by executing a similar number of contracts to sell the same commodity, and sellers offset theirs by purchasing an equal quantity of contracts to buy the product. The difference between the first transaction and the second transaction is the amount of profit or loss (excluding broker's commission and other expenses) accruing to the trader. Each commodities exchange has a clearinghouse that oversees all "buy and sell" transactions and stands ready to fulfill a contract in the event of buyer or seller default.

To this point, people who trade commodities have been referred to generically as investors. In fact, there are two main categories of commodities traders speculators and hedgers. Speculators are traders who voluntarily assume high levels of risk in anticipation of equally high profits. The difference between speculating and investing is worth emphasizing. Whereas investing offers the opportunity for making reasonable profit over the long term, speculating focuses on short-term trading and may involve considerable risk in the attempt to realize high profits.

The other main type of commodities trader is the hedger. Hedgers are often producers or major consumers of commodities who use futures contracts very conservatively to reduce risk and to protect themselves against adverse price fluctuations.

Commodities futures contracts appeal to individual investors who are willing to assume considerable risk in the hope of making a substantial profit in a short period of time. The risks should not be minimized: Commodities prices fluctuate, affected by such unpredictable factors as world economic conditions, the weather, political developments, and the supply of the commodity being traded. Additional risk is introduced by the purchase of commodities futures contracts on margin. Margin simply means that the contract is not fully paid for in cash. Instead, the trader deposits earnest money, usually 5 to 20 percent of the cash value of the contract, with the broker. Buying on margin greatly increases the impact of commodities price fluctuations. With a 10 percent margin, for example, the commodities trader will realize a gross return of 50 percent if the futures profits are 5 percent. If, on the other hand, the prices move in the wrong direction and losses are 5 percent, the holder of a contract with a 10 percent margin will suffer losses of 50 percent. As a result, even minor price fluctuations may have disastrous consequences for some. Individual investors are usually counseled to avoid commodities futures trading unless they can absorb the losses and have a high tolerance for risk.

Futures Exchanges

Trading in commodities and financial futures is mostly conducted in the United States on major exchanges. In many respects, commodities exchanges are similar to stock exchanges. Both are membership organizations. In commodities exchanges, most members are either individuals representing brokerage firms (through which non-members trade) or those who are directly involved in producing, marketing, or processing commodities.

Like the stock exchanges, each commodity exchange has its own governing board, which sets and enforces the rules under which the trading takes place, and like the stock exchanges, the commodities exchanges themselves do not buy or sell the product being traded or set prices.

Yet another similarity is the willingness of the exchanges to provide information to prospective investors about the mechanics of trading and about specific commodities. As a result, it is a fairly simple matter for a librarian wishing to build a comprehensive pamphlet collection to acquire an impressive number of publications from the exchanges, usually at no cost. The web pages of the exchanges also contain much of the information either in PDF or HTML format, and these are probably the easiest places to begin a search for information (see figure 14.2).

EXCHANGES	SAMPLE OF COMMODITIES TRADED
Intercontinental Exchange ICE [NYBOT] New York Board of Trade is now a unit of ICE. It did keep its trading floor as ICE trades only electronically. https://www.theice.com/homepage.jhtml	Crude oil, electricity, natural gas (ICE) Cocoa, coffee, cotton, ethanol, frozen concentrated orange juice, sugar (NYBOT)
Chicago Board of Trade (CBOT) http://www.cmegroup.com/company/cbot.html	Corn, ethanol, gold, oats, rice, silver, soybeans, wheat
Chicago Mercantile Exchange http://www.cmegroup.com/company/cme.html	Butter, milk, feeder cattle, frozen pork bellies, lean hogs, live cattle, lumber
Kansas City Board of Trade (KCBT) http://www.kcbt.com/	Wheat, Value Line Index
New York Mercantile Exchange (NYMEX) http://www.cmegroup.com/company/nymex.html	Aluminum, copper, crude oil, electricity, gasoline, gold, heating oil, natural gas, palladium, platinum, propane, silver

Figure 14.2. Selected major U.S. commodities and futures exchanges

Each exchange sets certain standards for the goods it trades; a Minneapolis Grain Exchange wheat contract is always for 5,000 bushels of spring wheat, while the NYMEX coffee "C" contract is always for 37,500 pounds. The exchange also specifies delivery site(s) and the months in which delivery may take place. Figure 14.3 summarizes the basic regulations set by the Chicago Board of Trade pertaining to corn futures contracts. Not included are the regulations for shipping. All CME (CBOT) regulations are available from http://www.cmegroup.com/market-regulation/index.html.

Contract Size 5,000 bushels

Deliverable Grade
#2 Yellow at contract price
#1 Yellow at a 1.5 cent/bushel over contract price
#3 Yellow at a 1.5 cent/bushel under contract price

Pricing Unit
Cents per bushel

Tick Size [1]
1/4 of one cent per bushel ($12.50 per contract)

Contract Months [2]
March May July September December

Daily Price Limit [3]
$0.30 per bushel expandable to $0.45 and then to $0.70 when the market closes at limit bid or limit offer.

Settlement Procedure
Physical Delivery

Last Trade Date
The business day prior to the 15th calendar day of the contract month.

Last Delivery Date
Second business day following the last trading day of the delivery month.

[1] Tick is the smallest allowable increment for a price movement for a contract
[2] Contract month is the specific month in which delivery may take place.
[3] Daily Price Limit is the maximum price set by the exchange.

Figure 14.3. Some corn futures trading conditions

Each exchange also sets limits on the amounts by which prices can either rise or fall during a single trading day. An exchange temporarily suspends trading of a particular delivery month in a commodity when it reaches the daily limit established by the exchange, thus controlling some of the wide swings that might otherwise develop in commodities prices.

Commodity Futures Trading Commission

Futures trading is regulated by the Commodity Futures Trading Commission (CFTC) (http://www.cftc.gov/), an independent federal regulatory commission established by Congress in 1974. The mission of the CFTC is to

> regulate commodity futures and option markets in the United States. The agency protects market participants against manipulation, abusive trade practices and fraud. Through effective oversight and regulation, the CFTC enables the markets to serve better their important functions in the nation's economy—providing a mechanism for price discovery and a means of offsetting price risk.[4]

The CFTC also serves as an important source of commodities futures information, issuing periodic statistical compilations and reports on the trade in various commodities. In addition, it offers several publications, including a glossary of terms, for the individual investor considering trading in commodities. These are all downloadable from the web page at http://www.cftc.gov/ConsumerProtection/EducationCenter/CFTCGlossary/index.htm.

Current Prices

Because of the volatility of the commodities market and its rapid price fluctuations, current price information is vital to traders. Professional investors may get up-to-the-minute information using tickers, wire services, and online databases. Small investors, on the other hand, may rely on the current daily price information found in the *Wall Street Journal*, *New York Times*, *Journal of Commerce*, and many local newspapers or may retrieve time-delayed (usually 15 minutes) data from sites on the Internet. A sample of the kind of information contained in daily futures tables is shown in figure 14.4.

Prices for major commodities are easy enough to locate in key financial newspapers and on the Internet.

Financial Futures

Although commodities futures trading has been practiced for generations, financial futures are relatively new. Financial futures trading began in the 1970s with the trading of futures contracts on selected foreign currencies and fixed income securities, such as Treasury bills. Since then, the diversity of products and trading volume has expanded considerably, and as with commodity futures contracts, traders can use financial futures for hedging.

Futures markets provide an arena in which companies that are dependent on prices of basic commodities, exchange rates, or securities markets can reduce the risk of unfavorable price swings. For example, if an importer needs to pay large bills three months into the future rather than take the risk that the currency markets will be favorable, then he could buy futures contracts to ensure that his prices will remain stable.

Financial futures can also be used for speculating. Someone who expects interest rates to increase can buy interest rate futures. If expecting the value of the Japanese yen to decline, the person can sell foreign currency futures. The most rapidly growing sector of the financial futures market, stock index futures, permits traders to try to profit from swings in the stock market by buying or selling futures contracts tied to such stock indexes as the Standard & Poor's 500 and the New York Stock Exchange Composite Index. Other index futures are tied to municipal bonds, the consumer price index, and commodity futures.

-GRAINS AND OILSEEDS-

Corn (CBOT) 5,000 bu.; cents per bu.

	Open	High	Low	Settle	Change	Lifetime High	Lifetime Low	Open Interest
May (this year)	252.00	252.75	250.75	278.00	-.25	285.00	228.00	4233
July	258.00	258.75	256.50	258.00	-.25	285.50	232.50	141648
Sept	262.75	263.50	261.50	262.00	.....	270.50	238.00	33922
Dec	266.25	267.50	264.75	266.75	.....	268.00	235.50	141307
March (next year)	272.50	273.50	271.00	272.75	.....	274.00	249.50	14723
May	276.25	277.00	275.00	276.75	.....	277.75	259.50	1352
July	278.25	279.25	277.25	278.75	.....	280.00	254.00	7351
Dec	253.75	253.75	252.75	253.50	.....	258.50	239.00	4373

Est. vol 38,000; vol Wed 38,592; open int 348,967 + 987

The third line of the table reads as follows: "Corn (CBOT) 5,000 bu; cents per bu." and means that the table applies to the Chicago Board of Trade (CBOT) corn contract and the contract size is 5,000 bushels. The prices shown in the table are in units of cents per bushel, so 252.75 cents means $2.52 and three quarters of a cent per bushel.

The **open** or opening price is the price or range of prices for the day's first trades, registered during the period designated as the opening of the market or the opening call. In our example, this year's May corn on the Chicago Board of Trade (CBOT) opened at $2.52 per bushel. Many publications print only a single price for the market open or close regardless of whether there was a range with trades at several prices.

The word **high** refers to the highest price at which a commodity futures contract traded during the day. The high price for this year's May corn was $2.52 and ¾ cents per bushel.

Low refers to the lowest price at which a commodity futures contract traded during the day. The low price for May corn was $2.50 and ¾ cents per bushel.

Some publications show a **close** or **closing price** in their tables. The closing price is the price or range of prices at which the commodity futures contract traded during the brief period designated as the market close or on the closing call—that is, the last minute of the trading day.

Because the last few minutes of trading are often the busiest part of the day, with many trades occurring simultaneously, the exchange computes a **settlement** price from the range of closing prices. The settlement price, which is abbreviated as **settle** in most pricing tables, is used by the clearing house to calculate the market value of outstanding positions held by its members. It is also frequently used synonymously with closing price; although they may, in fact, differ.

The **change** refers to the change in settlement prices from the previous day's close to the current day's close. The -.25 change for July corn indicates that the previous day's settlement price must have been 258.25 (i.e., 258 +).

The **lifetime high** and **low** refer to the highest and lowest prices recorded for each contract maturity from the first day it traded to the present.

Open interest refers to the number of outstanding contracts for each maturity month. Some newspapers do not include this information.

At the end of the table another line of information appears: Est. vol 38,000; vol Wed 38,592; open int 348,967 + 987. **Est. vol** indicates that the estimated volume of trading for that day was 38,000 contracts. **Vol Wed** means that the trading volume for the previous day was 38,592 contracts. **Open Int** refers to the total **open interest** for all contract months combined at the end of the day's trading session. The 348,967 open contracts represent an increase of 987 contracts from the open interest of the previous day at the close.

Figure 14.4. Example of a futures trading table. (From the U.S. Commodity Futures Trading Commission; (http://www.cftc.gov/ConsumerProtection/EducationCenter/howtoreadfuturespricetables.html)

Financial futures are traded on the Chicago Board of Trade, Chicago Mercantile Exchange, Kansas City Board of Trade, and ICE (https://www.theice.com/homepage .jhtml). Financial futures prices for major products are reported daily in futures price tables along with commodity price data and are also available on the Web from all of the commodity exchanges as well as private services.

Futures Information Sources

Futures traders require current information to help them make sound investment decisions. They may acquire this information through brokerage firms, by reading financial newspapers and magazines, or from commodity exchanges, government agencies, commercial publishers, and database vendors. While only the largest and most specialized institutions will have a comprehensive collection of relevant reference materials, virtually every library should include selected publications. This section examines certain basic works and some relevant web sites.

Handbooks, Manuals, and Guides

Finding information on how futures trading works is easy. There are virtually hundreds of "how to" books for would-be traders, ranging from flamboyant rags-to-riches overnight sagas to weighty academic tomes, and almost all of them include descriptions of the mechanics of futures trading. Sometimes, however, a patron may want a brief introduction to futures trading. The titles listed below are particularly useful.

Chicago Board of Trade. **The Chicago Board of Trade Handbook of Futures and Options.** New York: McGraw-Hill, 2006. 444p.

Previously published by the Board as the *Commodities Trading Manual*, the *Chicago Board of Trade Handbook of Futures and Options* provides information on everything from the uses and purposes of the futures market to nuts-and-bolts descriptions of day-to-day exchange operations.

For each of the commodities covered, the *Handbook* includes a summary of past production, performance, supply, and demand. It lists the exchanges on which each is traded (and includes each exchange's regulations pertaining to delivery months, trading units, price and position limits, grades deliverable, delivery sites, and exchange trading hours) and cites selected sources of commercial, government, and trade information. An extensive glossary is included, part of which is online at the web page of the Board in the Knowledge Center section (http://ww.cbot.com).

The Board issues many useful and free publications, which can be found at http://www.cmegroup.com/ under the education tab at the top right of the screen.

To find comprehensive information on exchanges, trading houses, and finance institutions worldwide, more specialized sources will be needed.

Handbook of World Stock, Derivative and Commodity Exchanges. Welwyn Garden City, UK: MondoVisione, 2000–. Annual.

Previously known as both the *Bridge Handbook of World Stock, Derivative & Commodity Exchanges,* and the *MSCI Handbook of World Stock, Derivative & Commodity Exchanges,* the strength of the *Handbook* lies in its brief descriptions, which provide trading, settlement, and organizational information on about 250 exchanges in over 100 countries and regions.

The information furnished includes a concise summary of exchange history, a summary of the organizational structure, and full addresses and contacts. Also included are the main indexes, aggregate trading data, and articles from industry figures. An online version of this book, with regular updates, is now available, although it is probably more useful, and affordable, for traders than libraries.

For students, researchers, and traders interested in finding out more about trading futures, detailed information will be needed on algorithms, indicators, and programs. One of the most detailed publications available on trading systems has been updated to contain information on the latest techniques.

Kaufman, Perry J. **New Trading Systems and Methods.** 3rd ed. New York: Wiley, 2005. 1174p.

Not intended for the casual reader, *Trading Systems and Methods* consists of in-depth analyses of both new and classical trading systems and techniques and incorporates detailed explanations, heavily interspersed with both calculations and graphs.

Dictionaries

Many of the publications that have already been described contain glossaries of key terms. In addition, the standard investment dictionaries listed in chapter 11 also include basic futures trading vocabulary. Another source is particularly useful for its coverage of commodities trading.

About.Com Commodities. New York: NYT Group, 2011.

Available at: http://commodities.about.com/od/glossary/Glossary_of_Commodities_ and_Futures_Terms.htm

Some terms are explained here; but it is not a full glossary. What it does have is basic explanations of commodities, commodity trading, and commodity types. Accompanying each section is an explanation of the terms used. This is more than a glossary but less than a full guide. There are also many other glossaries available on the Web, including those at the web sites of the various exchanges and the U.S. Commodity Futures Trading Commission.

Periodicals, Newspapers, and Newsletters

Futures trading is covered to a certain extent in such general business periodicals as *Business Week* and *Forbes*, but these will be too dated to be of much practical use to professional traders. Most traders need immediate, unfiltered information.

There is, however, one specialized commodity periodical that is popular with traders and researchers alike.

Futures. Chicago: Futures Magazine, 1972–. Monthly. Semimonthly in January, June, and September. (Online subscription and some free information are available at http:// www.futuresmag.com/)

Futures offers its readers a series of articles on different aspects of futures and options trading. An issue may contain as many as 20 different articles dealing with such subjects as trading techniques, government policy affecting trading, the economy, and developments at specific exchanges. It also includes a section on international markets and news. Although readers new to futures trading may find some articles difficult going, for the most part *Futures* is lively and well written and can be useful to novice investors as well as seasoned professionals.

There is also an excellent education section that guides one through the intricacies of futures. On the web page is also a link to the *SourceBook* (http://www.futuressourcebook .com/). The *SourceBook* contains the names and addresses of the major U.S. and non-U.S. brokerage, charting, computer, and advisory services, as well as publishers, consultants, and available software.

Although not as popular as *Futures,* another periodical contains data of interest to academicians and other researchers.

The Journal of Futures Markets. New York: John Wiley in affiliation with the Center for the Study of Futures Markets, Columbia University, 1981–. Monthly.

Published in affiliation with the Center for the Study of Futures Markets of the Columbia Business School, the *Journal of Futures Markets* contains articles written by scholars on the technical and methodological aspects of futures trading and analysis. Each issue includes between four and eight signed articles. This journal is also available on the Web, from 1981 onward, via the Wiley electronic journals collection.

Several financial newspapers contain information about commodities markets in addition to the price quotes that they regularly supply. The *Wall Street Journal*, for example, devotes at least some part of each issue to commodities, including features on specific products and the political, economic, industrial, and climatological factors that affect them, as well as summaries of significant developments in futures markets on the preceding trading day. *Barron's* column, "Commodities Corner," features analysis of recent developments in the trading of specific products, as well as more general information, including a listing of changes in the key commodity indexes.

It is the *Journal of Commerce*, however, that provides the most comprehensive financial newspaper coverage of commodities. The daily price tables it includes for both futures and cash markets list more commodities than comparable tables in other newspapers, with data on foreign markets, London metals, Tokyo gold, Singapore rubber, and Sydney steer, among others, as well as domestic markets. It also includes articles on individual commodities, reviews of past trading, and projections for the future, all of which are included in the first section of the paper and indexed on page 1. In addition, the *Journal of Commerce* covers all the major business and financial news that can affect commodities prices. Periodically, whole sections of the paper are devoted to specific industries, products, and commodities, or to special studies of supply and demand for each commodity. It is an important source of information for the serious commodities trader. This publication is available as a subscription web product at http://www.joc.com/ and is available from various database vendors including Dialog (as File 637) and LexisNexis.

Other newspapers and journals specialize in futures trading, but the one most favored by brokers and traders is *Consensus*.

Consensus. Kansas City, Mo.: Consensus, 1971–. Weekly.

Consensus focuses on commodities. Each weekly issue includes digests of current market letters, special studies, buy and sell recommendations issued by major brokerage firms, daily price quotations, and detailed price charts. Whether the cost of a highly specialized publication such as *Consensus* is offset by its anticipated use by library users must, of course, be determined by each library. There is a subscription web version of this publication with daily updates. From the site at http://www.consensus-inc.com, one can view a sample issue of the publication and also check on some of the other services offered, such as access to the "Bullish Index Hotline" and links to the web pages of other useful publications.

Commodities newsletters and weekly or monthly reviews of commodities trading and trends are issued by several sources. Many are free, particularly those issued by banks, brokerage firms, and commodities exchanges.

Statistics

A wide range of statistical publications is available, including those issued by commercial publishers, federal and state governments, and commodities exchanges. Some are highly specific, dealing with a particular commodity or group of commodities, such those provided by the U.S. Department of Agriculture, at http://www.fas.usda.gov/commodities.asp. Others are more general and cover the whole gamut of futures trading. Of these general sources, one of the most widely used and highly regarded is the *CRB Commodity Yearbook* (formerly *Commodity Year Book*), the single most important source of current and retrospective statistical data, which should be in most library reference collections.

CRB Commodity Yearbook. New York: John Wiley, 1939–. Annual. (Quarterly supplements)

The *Commodity Yearbook* provides detailed statistical data on over 100 commodities, ranging from alcohol to zinc. Coverage for each basic commodity generally includes a review of the past year's supply and demand and the conditions affecting both; a list of the exchanges on which the commodity is traded in the United States; and several tables on world production, domestic price support programs, domestic price supply, distribution, production, prices, exports, volume of trading, and other statistics. Most tables give information for at least 10 years, and some date back as far as 14 years. The *Yearbook* also includes charts of cash prices for many commodities, with prices plotted on a monthly basis for the past 10 years. Each edition also features special research studies. The 2001 edition, for example, included articles on the cocoa market and technotrading. The *Commodity Yearbook* is produced by Commodity Research Bureau, a division of BRIDGE Information Systems Inc. (Chicago), which is one of the country's largest resources for financial statistics, historical data, and charting services. Its information is available online, in CD-ROM format, and through newsletters, charting services, and wire reports. It is closely associated with the Chicago Mercantile Exchange and the Chicago Board of Trade and is regarded as one of the leading sources of information on international and domestic commodity movements.

The Chicago Board of Trade, at http://www.cmegroup.com/, makes freely available both historical and current agricultural, financial and metal, futures, and options data.

More specialized information is also available, often in publications from trade associations and the federal government.

Metal Statistics. New York: American Metal Markets, 1908–. Annual.

U.S. Department of the Interior. U.S. Geological Survey. **Minerals Yearbook.** Washington, DC: Government Printing Office, 1932/1933–. 3v. Annual.

Typical of these is *Metal Statistics*, which compiles trade and production data on over 27 different metals, and the *Minerals Yearbook*, issued in three volumes by the U.S. Geological Survey. Volume I contains chapters on approximately 70 metals and minerals, mining, and quarrying trends, while Volume II reviews the information by state. An annual review of mineral production and trade and of mineral-related government and industry developments in more than 175 foreign countries is provided in Volume III. The USGS also makes available at http://minerals.usgs.gov/minerals/ information from the

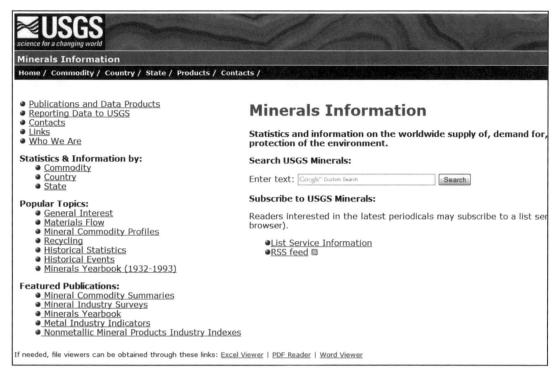

Figure 14.5. Image of the web page for minerals information,
at http://minerals.usgs.gov/minerals/

Minerals Yearbook, both current and historical (see figure 14.5). Also featured at this site is contact information by commodity, state, and country.

The U.S. Department of Agriculture is a major supplier of data on agricultural commodities. Much of this information is available through the USDA's *Statistics Service*, which, on the web page at http://www.nass.usda.gov/Publications/index.asp, makes available agricultural statistics and issues special reports on specific commodities (see figure 14.6). The Web has made this information accessible to librarians and researchers as soon as it is compiled.

Figure 14.6. Screen of the USDA National Agricultural Statistics Service,
http://www.nass.usda.gov/Publications/index.asp

Other sources of general and specialized commodities statistics are the *American Statistics Index, Encyclopedia of Business Information Sources, Statistical Reference Index, ProQuest Statistical Insight,* and *Statistics Sources.*

Advisory Services

Another source of market information is futures advisory services. There are many such organizations, most of which make their publications available on the Web because fast and current information is essential. As with all investment advisory services, cost and quality vary, as do user opinions about the merits of each. Major advisory services can be found using any web search engine.

For many librarians, however, the decision will not be which of the many commodities advisory services to subscribe to, but whether to subscribe to any. The infrequent use of commodities advisory services by patrons compared to other investment services may mean that a subscription to such a publication cannot be justified, particularly with a limited serials budget.

Databases

Like the other investment media, a number of the general business databases contain information relevant to futures traders. Such files as *ABI/INFORM Global* and *Business Source Complete*, for example, often yield valuable background information. News and general index information is also available at Thomson Reuters, but a subscription is needed to get information on the more than 300,000 stock options, commodities, futures, indexes, and currencies. Some academic business libraries will have a subscription to another service, *Datastream*, but this is not generally accessible for public use. To find out more about available services, the librarian or researcher can check in the *Gale Directory of Databases*.

Options

Options give their holders the right to buy or sell certain securities, traditionally common stocks in 100-share units, at a set price by a certain, predetermined date regardless of how high or low the price of the underlying stock may move during that time. An option holder may, for example, purchase the right to buy 100 shares of Acme Electronics for $60 per share anytime between date of purchase and, say, May. This means that, whatever the current market value of 100 shares of Acme may be, the holder can buy them for $6,000. If, for example, Acme shares soar to $106 (or $10,600 per 100 shares), the lucky option holder can either sell the option itself to another investor for a profit or can exercise the option and acquire Acme shares at a cost considerably below market value. If, on the other hand, the stock plummets to $50 per share (or $5,000 per 100 shares), the holder may choose not to exercise the option simply by allowing it to lapse; that is, by doing nothing until the contract expires in May. Why pay for the right to pay $6,000 for 100 shares of stock when it can be had for $5,000?

Holding an option is vastly different from owning the stock itself. Stock ownership represents part ownership in the issuing company, whereas an option merely gives its holder the right—which may or may not be exercised—to buy or sell stock at a predetermined price within a designated time period. An option holder has none of the rights of a stockholder; he or she cannot vote, owns no part of the company issuing the stock, and receives no dividends. Options are issued or written by individual investors and security dealers, who retain ultimate responsibility for carrying out the terms specified in the options contracts. They are not written by the companies issuing the underlying stock.

Options are attractive to many investors because they can be purchased for a fraction of the cost of the underlying stock and offer the opportunity for high profit with limited risk. Unlike the more speculative commodities trading, in options risk is limited to a predetermined amount, the amount paid for the option itself. If the market should go against an unlucky option trader, the worst that can happen is that the option will expire and become worthless. Finally, the action is fast. Most options expire at the end of three, six, or nine months.

Basic Features

Options contracts contain four basic features: (1) the striking price (also called the exercise price), or the price at which 100 shares of the underlying common stock can be bought or sold; (2) the exercise period, or the duration of the options contract; (3) the expiration cycle; and (4) the premium, or purchase price of the option itself. Each of these merits further attention.

The striking price is the price at which an option can be executed. In the above example, the striking price for a May option on Acme Electronics is $60 per share. (Note that while the striking price is listed on a per-share basis, the option contract itself is for 100 shares.) There are usually two or three different striking prices for options contracts expiring in a particular month.

The exercise period is the time during which an option can be executed. Listed options are written for periods of three, six, and nine months. For example, there are Acme options that expire in February, May, and August, and someone trading in Acme options could choose any of these exercise periods.

Closely allied to the exercise period is the expiration cycle. All options (other than LEAPS) are placed in one of three cycles created by the exchanges that list options. There is a January-April-July-October cycle, a February-May-August-November cycle, and a March-June-September-December cycle. Prices are quoted for only three of the months listed in any cycle. For Acme, the February-May-August expiration dates would be quoted until the February options expired, then the May-August-November dates would be quoted, and so on.

The striking price, exercise period, and expiration date are all set at the time an option contract is written and do not change for the duration of the contract. The premium, or cost of the option itself, however, fluctuates from day to day, reflecting the current market value of the underlying stock and investor expectations about its future value. Option premiums are quoted in option tables on a per-share basis. If, for example, the premium for Acme is listed at 30.5, the cost of an options contract would be $3,050 or $30.5 x 100.

Puts and Calls

There are two basic forms of options: puts and calls. A call gives its owner the right to buy 100 shares of common stock at a specified price (the striking price) within a given time (the exercise period) before the expiration date. A put, on the other hand, is an option to sell 100 shares of common stock for the striking price, exercise period, and expiration date designated in the contract. The purchaser of a put expects the value of the underlying stock to decline, while the purchaser of a call expects the stock's value to increase.

Exchanges

Prior to 1973, all options were traded in the OTC market, with each option written to meet the specific requirement of the buyer. These conventional options were, in fact, so specialized that the secondary market for them was almost nonexistent. Holders of these conventional options could choose to exercise them and buy or sell the underlying stock at the striking price, or they could let the options expire; very seldom were they able to sell the options to other investors.

In 1973, the Chicago Board Options Exchange (CBOE) was opened by the Chicago Board of Trade, and listed options came into being. Unlike the conventional options traded over the counter, listed options are standardized, with systematic procedures for trading. As a result, there is a brisk secondary market in listed options, and although conventional options are still available in the OTC market, trading in listed options is far more active.

Although it was the first, the CBOE is not the only exchange that lists options. Puts and calls are also traded on the selected U.S. exchanges listed in figure 14.7.

NYSE Amex Options http://www.nyse.com/futuresoptions/nyseamex/1218155409117.html	Stock, warrants, ratios
Chicago Board of Trade (CME) http://www.cmegroup.com	U.S. Treasury Bonds, Agricultural Futures & Options, Metals, and Finance Futures and Options
ICE/New York Board of Trade (NYBOT) https://www.theice.com/homepage.jhtml	Sugar, coffee, cocoa, cotton, currencies
Kansas Board of Trade http://www.kcbt.com	Wheat, natural gas, stock indexes
International Securities Exchange http://www.ise.com	Equity, ETF, index, FX products

Figure 14.7. Examples of exchanges and the options traded

Listed Options Quotations

Because options have such comparatively short life spans, and because the market for them can be extremely volatile, many professional traders follow price movements on an hour-by-hour or even a minute-by-minute basis. Smaller, private investors may find free options quotes, delayed by 20 minutes, at all exchanges, and a good place to start is the Chicago Board Options Exchange web page at http://www.cboe.com/. One can obtain detailed or multiple quotes. For a small monthly fee any investor can become a member of this service and obtain "real time" quotes. Reports on options and futures volume traded, along with other information, are available from the OCC (Options Clearing Corporation) at http://www.optionsclearing.com/.

Options Information Sources

Decisions to purchase and trade in options are based primarily on the investor's opinion of the underlying stocks. As a result, the types of information sources described in chapter 11 will interest the person who speculates in options as much as the investor who buys stocks outright. Both will want to consult corporate reports, financial newspapers and journals, industry reports, stock charting, reporting and advisory services, and comprehensive investment services. There are, however, other, more specialized publications.

Guides

Librarians and lay investors seeking to learn more about options trading can consult a wide assortment of introductory publications, ranging from pamphlets issued by brokers and exchanges to full-length texts outlining sophisticated trading techniques. In addition, sources that run the gamut of finance and investment often provide good basic information about options.

The Chicago Board Options Exchange (http://www.cboe.com/) includes free online tutorials, options basics, a bibliography of suggested reading, and a glossary. One may also download the "options toolbox," which allows one to simulate options strategies.

Exchange-issued information is revised fairly frequently and tends to more accurately reflect the constantly growing and changing options market. It is becoming necessary for all librarians to include web links to training materials such as these because books that are only a year old may fail to indicate the breadth or volume of options trading today. One can also receive a list of free publications from *Futures* magazine at http://www .futuresmag.com/. Included in this listing are pamphlets and books.

A specialized web site for options is http://www.optionetics.com/. In the education section one can learn "How Options Work," "How to Use Options," or "What Affects Equity Option Prices." It is becoming more and more apparent that the way to provide up-to-date information on this rapidly changing field is to maintain constantly monitored web links to instructional materials, tutorials, articles, and the relevant exchanges.

Periodicals and Newspapers

Options trading is covered periodically in *Business Week*, *Forbes*, *Money*, and other standard business serial titles. Some good current coverage of options trading can be found in *Barron's*. Along with articles that appear regularly is the column, "The Striking Price," which covers recent developments and trends in this fast-moving market. Articles on new developments, trading coups and fiascoes, and tax aspects of options trading are also regularly featured in the *Wall Street Journal*.

Statistics

Statistics on the options market are generally available from the exchanges on which they are traded. The easiest way to obtain these is to visit the web pages of the various exchanges, where there are various listings as well as access to the annual reports.

Dictionaries and Glossaries

Many of the available dictionaries and glossaries are online. Some are prepared by university professors to help their students; others are made available by traders or investment centers. Following is a small example of what is available.

> *Glossary*, http://www.riskglossary.com/. Prepared by Glyn Holtman, an independent consultant in financial risk management.
>
> **YAHOO! Finance.** http://biz.yahoo.com/opt/glossary1.html
>
> **Stock Options Trading.** http://www.stocks-options-trading.com/sitemap_glossary.asp

Other general financial dictionaries and glossaries, whether web-based or available in hard copy, will also describe many of the relevant terms needed.

Advisory Services

Although prospective options traders may be content with some of the standard stock advisory services described previously, others may wish to consult special options services. Although there are not as many options services as there are stock services, their number is growing, reflecting the increased interest in this area.

One service that may be available in many libraries is supplied by Value Line.

Value Line Options. New York: Value Line. 1981–. Weekly.

Value Line Options is a weekly that ranks options performance and evaluates risk levels for both writers and buyers of puts and calls. This information is also available through the online Value Line center.

There are other options advisory services, some similar in scope and content to *Value Line Options,* others that are more like newsletters in tone and format. Some of these publications are listed in *Futures* (http://www.futuresmag.com/), and the librarian seeking to build a representative collection of options advisory services would do well to consult it.

Notes

1. For more information, see Mark Baldassare, *When Government Fails: The Orange County Bankruptcy* (San Francisco: Public Policy Institute of California, 1998).

2. For more information, see Peter G. Zhang, *Barings Bankruptcy and Financial Derivatives* (Singapore: River Edge, NJ: World Scientific, 1995).

3. Taken from http://www.cmegroup.com/.

4. Taken from http://www.cftc.gov/.

15

Insurance

This chapter describes basic concepts and identifies key information sources in insurance. It is an area in which information is sought by consumers as well as by investors and businesspeople. Research inquiries may range from the investment performance of certain insurance companies to the computation of Social Security retirement benefits, from the number of unemployment insurance claims filed to the names of companies that insure against unusual risks. As a result, sources relevant to many different kinds of library users are examined.

Insurance Basics

We live in a world filled with risk. Headlines and news broadcasts daily announce disasters: explosions, droughts, floods, and crashes. Lives are lost, property destroyed. Modern technology brings with it a new array of real and potential disasters. To automobile wrecks and airliner crashes have been added nuclear reactor accidents, toxic waste, space shuttle explosions, and terrorist attacks. At the same time, many of our lives are touched by less dramatically newsworthy but equally devastating events: the untimely death of a spouse or family member, the loss of a job, floods or hurricane damage, or unexpected disease or disability. Almost all of these events have severe financial consequences for the afflicted. Many people turn to insurance to reduce such financial risk.

Characteristics of Insurance

Insurance is a social mechanism that allows individuals, businesses, and organizations to reduce financial risk by substituting a small but definite cost (the insurance payment, or premium) for a large, uncertain loss. Each of the insured pays a premium to the insurer for the promise that he or she will be reimbursed for losses up to the maximum amount indicated on the insurance policy.

Insurance, in other words, provides a certain measure of financial protection against major and minor catastrophes. It helps to protect against financial risk associated with death, disease, and property loss. It also may cover theft and embezzlement, professional malpractice, farm crops, ships' cargoes, satellite launches, movie stars, hijackings, product liability, and even the health of pets. Although different insurance companies (and government agencies) provide different types of insurance, certain characteristics are common to all.

The first of these is risk transfer. The insured pays premiums to the insurer, thus transferring financial risk within the limits stipulated by the insurance policy. The second is that of pooling. The premiums paid by all of the people cover the losses of the unlucky few to whom the insured-against event occurs.

Premium rates are in part based on the forecasts, made by insurers, regarding the number and severity of claims they will have to pay. Such forecasts are the responsibility of actuaries, experts in the mathematics of insurance. To determine premium rates, actuaries rely on the Law of Large Numbers and probability to predict the amount they will have to pay over a given period. The Law of Large Numbers is a mathematical principle that states that as the number of exposures increases, the actual results tend to come closer to the expected results; probability means that a given event will occur. For example, if one rolls a dice thousands of times, the number 1 will come up on the dice on the average of one out of every six times. So will the other numbers. In other words, according to the Law of Large Numbers combined with probability, the chances of a single event occurring, when there are six equal chances of it occurring, are one out of six:

> A practical illustration of the Law of Large Numbers is the National Safety Council's prediction of the number of auto deaths during a typical holiday weekend. Because millions of automobiles are on the road, the National Safety Council[1] has been able to predict with great accuracy the number of motorists who will die during a typical July 4th holiday weekend. Although individual motorists cannot be identified, the actual number of deaths for the group of motorists as a whole can be predicted with some accuracy.[2]

In the insurance industry, the Law of Large Numbers means that as the number of people and organizations choosing to insure against certain financial risks increases, the number and extent of loss claims filed with the insurer will more closely approach those predicted. Using statistical data from mortality tables, for example, actuaries are able to predict with reasonable accuracy the number of people in a given population who will die within a specified period and whose beneficiaries might be expected to file life insurance claims.

A fourth characteristic of insurance is that policies enable the insured to be indemnified (either fully or partially reimbursed) for insured losses, but not to profit from such losses. The intent of this principle of indemnity is to eliminate or at least reduce the likelihood of intentional injury or destruction of property for profit. While the principle of indemnity does not, for example, preclude the possibility of arson to collect fire insurance, it means that fewer will be tempted to do so because the motive for profit will be missing.

The four basic characteristics of insurance, then, are that it transfers risk, pools losses, relies on the Law of Large Numbers to predict future losses, and utilizes the principle of indemnity to limit claims to no more than the actual losses incurred.

The terms of agreement between the insurer and the insured are set forth in the insurance policy, a legal contract that specifies types of coverage, amount and frequency of premiums, maximum coverage and amount deductible from coverage, exclusions, and the like. Although policies were once written in language unintelligible to all but lawyers and insurance professionals, many are now written so that laypeople may understand them more easily.

Types of Insurance

Insurance can be classified in many different ways. One of the most common is by type of insurer. As shown in figure 15.1, there are two groups of insurers, private and public. Private insurers are primarily commercial insurance companies that sell policies; public insurers are government agencies that provide compulsory or voluntary insurance. Each of these kinds of insurers can, in turn, be categorized by the type of insurance they offer.

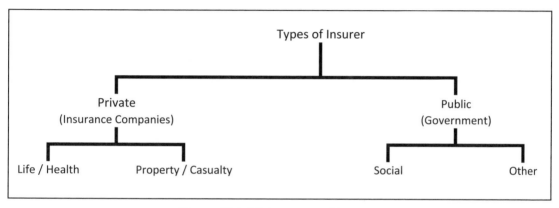

Figure 15.1. Major types of insurers

Insurance Sold by Private Insurers

Insurance sold by private insurers falls into two broad categories, life/health and property/casualty (see figure 15.2). Although some companies handle both types of insurance, many sell only one or the other. Life/health insurance and property/casualty insurance are, in fact, often treated as separate industries, as reflected in industry reports published in *Value Line* and Standard & Poor's *Industry Surveys.*

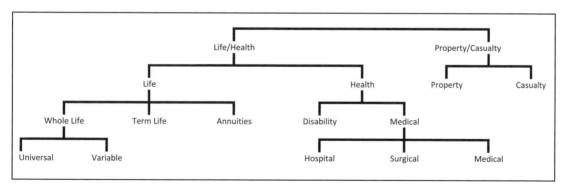

Figure 15.2. Types of insurance sold by private insurers

Life Insurance

Life insurance offers financial protection against the death of a family member, usually the major wage earner(s) and/or the person responsible for running and maintaining the home. Although coverage varies, all life insurance policies generally pay money to the beneficiary upon the insured's death.

There are two basic types of life insurance, term and whole. Term life, which is the least expensive type of life insurance, is often compared by insurance companies to renting, rather than buying, a house. In return for the payment of premiums, the insured is covered for a specified period, or term. The term may be as short as one year or may extend for as long as 20 years or more. During that period, the insured is covered by the policy. Should he or she die while it is in force, the insurance company will pay the beneficiary the face amount of the policy. Should the insured live beyond the term covered, he or she will have to negotiate a new term life policy with the insurance company.

If term life is the insurance equivalent of renting, whole life is analogous to buying a house. Unlike the temporary coverage provided by term insurance, whole life provides insurance coverage over the entire life of the insured. While the cost is determined by the insured's age at the time the policy is drawn up, based on actuarial tables that reflect the incidence and likelihood of death. Once the policy is in force, the premiums will remain the same, whatever the insured's health may be, or however long he or she may live.

Another difference between term life and whole life insurance is that the latter combines a forced savings plan with life insurance coverage. Part of each premium covers "pure" insurance, and part is diverted into a fund, called the cash value, which is similar to a savings account. The policyholder has two choices at any time: to continue paying the premiums at the rate originally agreed upon so that beneficiaries can receive death benefits or to terminate the policy and be given the cash value and its accumulated interest. The interest earned by the cash value in most whole life policies, however, is generally significantly less than the same money would earn in savings accounts, and consumers are frequently counseled to consider alternative forms of investment.

There are several other variants of whole life insurance. The first of these is universal or adjustable life, which offers adaptability in both premium payments and the death benefit a family receives. After the initial fixed payment, premiums can be paid in differing amounts, subject to certain rules fixed by the insurance company, and as a family's coverage, security, and asset accumulation needs change. Variable life provides death benefits and cash values that change with the performance of a portfolio of investments bound to the achievement of financial markets. As with any portfolio, the investor chooses the investment allocation from stocks, bonds, and other vehicles, and if the market does not perform well in the chosen segments the value of the policy may fall. This type of insurance policy will issue a prospectus. The final choice is a variable universal life policy, which combines features of variable and universal life policies. With this, the policyholder can have the investment risks and rewards attributed to variable life insurance, combined with the ability to adjust the premiums and death benefit, characteristic of universal life insurance.

Whereas the types of life insurance described above are intended primarily to cover the death of the insured and its financial consequences for the beneficiaries, life annuities focus on providing income payments to policyholders who have reached a certain age. Life insurance, in other words, provides protection for beneficiaries; life annuities are designed to provide income for old age. One increasing common example of an annuity is "Long-Term Care" insurance.

An annuity is a series of income payments guaranteed for a number of years or over a lifetime. There are two main types of annuities. An immediate annuity is one that is purchased with a single, lump-sum payment. The income starts one month from the purchase date if the income payments are to be made on a monthly basis, or one year from the purchase date if payments are made annually. Immediate annuities are usually purchased by the middle-aged or elderly who want annuity income to begin at once and to continue throughout the remainder of their lives.

A deferred annuity provides an income that begins at a future date. Although deferred annuities may be purchased with a single, lump-sum payment, more commonly they are paid for in installments over a number of years. The amount that the purchaser, or annuitant, receives is determined by the size of the premiums and the interest they earn as well as by the annuitant's age when payments to the insurance company began. The period of time between the first payment by the annuitant to the insurance company and the time the annuitant receives the first payment from the insurance company is known as the accumulation period. All interest earned on the accumulated payments during the accumulation period is currently tax-deferred; taxes are not levied on the interest until it is actually paid to the annuitant. This tax-deferred provision is one of the reasons that annuities are popular with many investors.

There are also two basic types of annuity contracts, fixed and variable. Money in a fixed annuity guarantees a fixed payment every month when withdrawals are begun. The equity indexed annuity is a variation of the fixed annuity. With this type of annuity, money accrues tax deferred at a minimum fixed rate of return, but the account also may earn additional interest based on the performance of an equity index such as the S&P 500. Money in a variable annuity promises no fixed payment, as it is invested in bond and stock funds, selected by the purchaser, and the value depends on how those funds perform. This type of annuity is also tax deferred.

Health Insurance

At the time this book was written, a major piece of legislation, the Patient Protection and Affordable Care Act (http://www.gpo.gov/fdsys/pkg/PLAW-111publ148/pdf/PLAW-111publ148.pdf) had just passed the U.S. Congress and been signed into law, bringing changes to the health insurance industry. Some of these changes affect preexisting conditions clauses, maximum coverage limits, the ability of insurers to drop or cancel coverage, and much more. However, some provisions are being challenged in the courts, and others are not yet in effect. Much of the following is subject, even likely, to change.

Just as the death of a family's key provider can cause severe financial hardship, so also can unexpected disease or disability. Health insurance deals with two major types of financial loss. The first helps to cover medical expenses, including the cost of hospital stays, surgery, regular medical bills, and the major medical expenses caused by catastrophic illness or injury. The nature and extent of coverage of such health insurance policies vary considerably; most have some restrictions, contain certain deductibles, and set limits on coverage. As a result, sources that permit some comparison between companies are vital.

The other major type of "health" loss is that caused by disability. Disability insurance provides periodic payments when the policyholder is unable to work owing to a covered injury, illness, or disease. Although disability insurance helps to replace lost income, the principle of indemnity is very much in force. Companies, in fact, generally limit the amount of disability income to no more than 70 or 80 percent of the insured's earned income.

Some health insurance policies provide both medical coverage and disability income payments; others offer only one or the other. Whatever the type of coverage offered, health insurance policies generally have certain provisions in common. The first of these is the continuance provision, which refers to the length of time that an individual policy may be in force and whether or not it will be renewed. A continuance provision may specify that the policy can be canceled by its holder or, alternatively, that the insurer can refuse to renew the policy. It can also specify that the policy must be renewed or that it cannot be canceled.

Many health insurance policies contain a preexisting conditions clause, which states that mental or physical conditions that existed in the insured prior to the issuance of the health insurance policy are not covered until the policy has been in force for a specified period, usually a year or two.

Some policies also have a probationary period immediately following their issuance, during which time sickness is not covered by the policy. The probationary period, which is intended to eliminate coverage for sickness that existed before the policy went into effect, does not extend to accidents, which are covered even during the probationary period.

Although much of the available health insurance is offered by private, commercial companies, they are by no means the only insurers in this field. Others include Blue Cross and Blue Shield and health maintenance organizations.

Blue Cross organizations are independent, membership corporations that provide protection against the cost of hospital care. Blue Shield organizations are similar in structure and membership but focus on medical and surgical costs. The Blue Cross and Blue Shield Association provides guidance and direction to the "Blues," setting and enforcing standards for their operation. Originally, Blue Cross and Blue Shield organizations were represented by separate associations. Following their merger into the Blue Cross and Blue Shield Association in 1982, many local Blue Cross and Blue Shield organizations also merged. Originally all were nonprofit organizations, but some have transformed themselves into for-profit companies.

Another alternative to traditional health insurance provided by profit and nonprofit insurance companies is the coverage offered through membership in health maintenance organizations. A health maintenance organization (HMO) is an organized system of health care that provides comprehensive health services to its members for a fixed, prepaid fee. By owning or leasing medical facilities, entering into agreements with hospitals and physicians to provide medical services, and hiring their own support staff, HMOs have greater managerial and financial control over the services offered. In return for a fee, usually paid monthly, HMO members are provided with a range of health services, most of which are covered in full, although coverage can be, and is, denied if an illness should need experimental medical treatments. All policies need to be carefully examined.

Another disadvantage is that although coverage is guaranteed to its members for the life of the HMO, not all health maintenance organizations survive. The membership in an HMO must be sufficient to support the cost of the services that are offered. When this is not the case (and sometimes, even when it is), HMOs may fail.

Another disadvantage is that members' selection of physicians and health care facilities is limited to those approved by the organization. Such limits to choice, some argue, destroy the traditional physician-patient relationship or result in poorer quality health care. In spite of these real and perceived disadvantages, HMOs have become a popular alternative to traditional health insurance.

Property/Casualty Insurance

While some private insurers specialize in life/health insurance, others protect against property damage or liability caused by negligence, and are categorized as property/casualty insurers. Although the distinction between property and casualty lines has become increasingly blurred, each has its own focus. Property insurance provides financial protection against loss of or damage to property caused by fire, theft, riots, natural disasters, or other calamities. It covers buildings, equipment, and inventories, as well as losses caused by interruptions in business operations. Casualty insurance is designed to protect the insured against legal liability for injuries to others or damage to their property. Property and casualty insurance are further divided into specific types of insurance, known as lines. Property insurance, for example, includes such lines as crop hail, ocean marine, and personal property insurance. Casualty insurance includes medical malpractice and product liability lines.

Property and casualty insurance can also be described as "first party" and "third party" insurance. Property insurance protects the policyholder, the first party, against damage to his or her property, whereas casualty insurance protects the policyholder from financial liability if he or she is held responsible because someone who is not a member of the household is injured on his or her property. Often both property and casualty coverage are provided in a single policy, as in automobile and homeowner's insurance.

Private insurers, as has been shown, can be classified according to the lines of insurance, life/health or property/casualty, written by them. Other classifications, based on the type of policyholder and the insurer's legal organization, are also possible.

Personal and Commercial Insurance

The first of these categories is insurance by the type of policyholder rather than by type of coverage, distinguishing between personal and commercial lines. Personal lines are sold to individuals; commercial lines, to businesses. Product liability insurance sold to a large pharmaceutical company is one of many commercial insurance lines. Many private insurers sell both personal and commercial lines.

Forms of Legal Organization for Private Insurers

Another way in which private insurers can be categorized is by form of legal organization. Most are either stock companies or mutual companies. Others are classified as fraternal benefit insurers, reciprocal insurance exchanges, and Lloyd's Associations.

Stock insurance companies are publicly traded corporations. Individual shareholders provide capital for the company in return for stock shares and the possibility of dividends. Most of the large property/casualty insurers are stock companies. The Travelers Insurance Corporation, for example, is traded on the New York Stock Exchange.

Mutual insurance companies, also known as mutuals, are owned by their policyholders rather than by shareholders. Just as shareholders earn dividends when stock companies have profitable years, policyholders benefit when mutuals have excess earnings, reaping benefits in the form of policyholder dividends or reduced policy renewal costs. While stock insurance companies are dominant in the property/casualty industry, mutuals are prevalent among life/health insurers.[3]

Although most private insurers are either stock companies or mutuals, there are also other forms of legal organization. They include fraternal insurers (originally formed in England as Friendly Societies), and fraternal benefit societies such as the Knights of

Columbus and Thrivent Financial for Lutherans, formerly Aid Association for Lutherans/ Lutheran Brotherhood, that write insurance for their members. A reciprocal exchange, on the other hand, is a form of cooperative insurance, an association in which members insure one another:

> To illustrate, assume each of ten business firms owns a building valued at $1 million. The ten firms could form an association and agree that each member would insure (and be insured by) each of the others in the amount of $100,000. If any of the buildings were damaged or destroyed, the loss would be shared by all of the association members, each paying 10% of the loss. The advantage of this arrangement would be that each firm's loss exposure would be spread among the ten locations. Instead of standing to lose $1 million in a single loss, each would be exposed to a maximum $100,000 loss at each of the various locations. If the association grew to include 100 members the exposure of each would be lowered to $10,000 at each of the 100 locations.[4]

Another characteristic of reciprocal exchanges is that they are managed by an attorney-in-fact, an individual or corporation responsible for such administrative duties as collecting premiums, investing funds, handling claims, and seeking new members.

Insurance is also available through Lloyd's Associations, organizations comprising individuals and corporations who underwrite insurance on a cooperative basis. The most well known of this type of insurance organization, in fact probably the most famous of all insurers, is Lloyd's of London (http://www.lloydsoflondon.co.uk), thus the name. Most of the insurance that is sold at Lloyd's falls into property/casualty lines, and while it is best known for its unusual policies (covering, for example, the legs of *Lord of the Dance* star Michael Flatley for £25 million, and Betty Grable's legs for £1 million), most of its policies are written to cover somewhat more mundane but specialized risks. Lloyd's of London is not an insurance company. It is an insurance market, roughly analogous to a stock exchange. Lloyd's provides a location and general set of rules for and services to its members who do write and sell insurance.

Lloyd's has a multi-tiered structure, composed of brokers, underwriters and insurance syndicates, and members. If someone wants insurance through Lloyd's he or she must approach a Lloyd's accredited broker, who in turn will present a "slip," which sets out the terms of the risk, to an underwriter. The underwriter, who is employed by a syndicate, will either accept the whole of the risk or a percentage. If he or she accepts a percentage the broker will carry the slip to other underwriters until the whole risk is covered. In 2011 there were 80 different syndicates, each specializing in certain insurance lines including casualty, marine, energy, aviation, product liability, and others. The members provide the capital to support the syndicates underwriting. Members can be corporations, limited partnerships, or individuals. Overseeing all of this is the Corporation of Lloyds.

> To illustrate in a simplified fashion how Lloyd's operates, consider the following example. Jack Wilhoft is going into business and wants $1 million of products liability insurance on a new roller skate that he is manufacturing. An agent locates a company in the United States that will sell him $100,000 of products liability insurance. Since another American company cannot be found to underwrite the remaining insurance, the agent contacts a surplus line broker who arranges to place the remaining $900,000 of products liability insurance with Lloyd's of London. Information about Jack's roller skating business is submitted to a Lloyd's broker, who then presents the proposal

to a syndicate specializing in high-risk products liability insurance. A lead underwriter then determines the initial premium rate. Let us assume that the lead syndicate takes $100,000 of the desired $900,000 of insurance. Each member of the syndicate will take his or her agreed-upon share. The Lloyd's broker will then contact the other syndicates as well. The second syndicate may take $50,000, the third, $10,000, and so on, until the entire $900,000 is placed. Each member of the various syndicates takes his or her share of the insurance, and pays his or her share of any loss. Finally, the policy is prepared, issued, and the insurance is in force.[5]

In 1989 the number of Names associated with Lloyd's was 31,329, and there were 401 syndicates. It was at this time that a number of catastrophic events began to take effect in the insurance industry. These included Alaska's *Exxon Valdez* oil spill, huge asbestos claims, hurricanes, and pollution claims, including the company held responsible for Love Canal. Lloyd's was involved in all these insurance claims. The Names were held responsible for losses of £8 billion between 1988 and 1992, and as a consequence many bankruptcies and suicides[6] occurred. As a result there have been reforms in the operation of Lloyd's. Corporations now account for about 80 percent of Lloyd's capacity, and the number of Names has diminished to 3,296 (figures taken from the web site). And as of March 6, 2003, no new Individual members with unlimited liability have been admitted as new members.

Insurance Provided by Public Insurers

Although the private insurance industry handles billions of dollars annually, it is by no means the only source of insurance coverage. Many federal and some state and municipal government agencies provide voluntary or compulsory protection against financial risk associated with unemployment, old age, death, and other perils. The insurance provided by public insurers falls into two broad categories: social insurance, such as Social Security, and other types of insurance, such as crop or flood insurance.

Many government benefit programs are listed at http://www.benefits.gov/benefits, and many insurance programs are included. Checking those listed by the Department of Health and Human Services, one finds not only Medicare and Medicaid but also the State Children's Health Insurance Program (see figure 15.3).

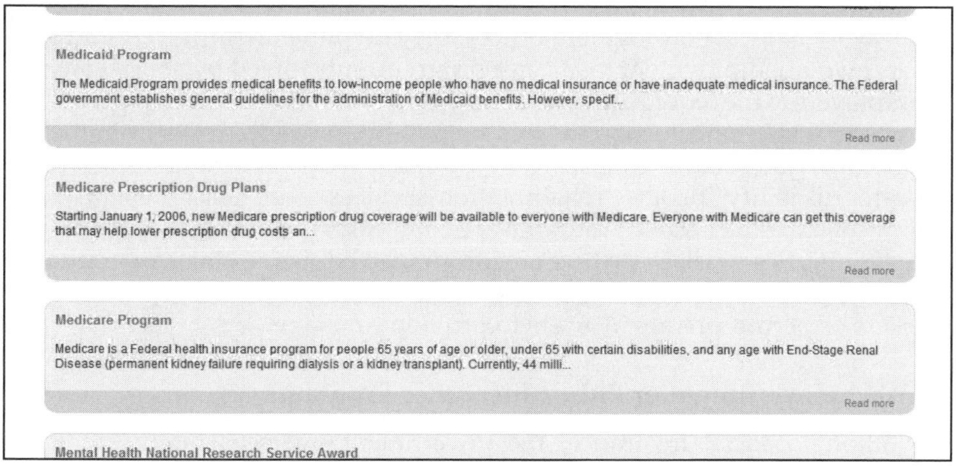

Medicaid Program

The Medicaid Program provides medical benefits to low-income people who have no medical insurance or have inadequate medical insurance. The Federal government establishes general guidelines for the administration of Medicaid benefits. However, specif...

Read more

Medicare Prescription Drug Plans

Starting January 1, 2006, new Medicare prescription drug coverage will be available to everyone with Medicare. Everyone with Medicare can get this coverage that may help lower prescription drug costs an...

Read more

Medicare Program

Medicare is a Federal health insurance program for people 65 years of age or older, under 65 with certain disabilities, and any age with End-Stage Renal Disease (permanent kidney failure requiring dialysis or a kidney transplant). Currently, 44 milli...

Read more

Mental Health National Research Service Award

Figure 15.3. Selected government insurance programs,
reproduced from http://www.benefits.gov/benefits

Social Insurance

Social insurance is publicly financed insurance, usually compulsory, enacted into law to achieve certain social goals or to provide coverage that private insurers are unwilling or unable to offer. Social Security, for example, came into existence as an attempt to deal with the widespread unemployment and poverty of the Great Depression.

Certain characteristics distinguish social from private insurance. First, social insurance is based on law rather than contract, with eligibility requirements and benefits prescribed by law. Second, coverage is compulsory for all people to whom the law applies. As a rule, social insurance covers only those who are or have been employed, their spouses, and their dependents. Third, social insurance programs are intended to be financially self-supporting, with specific payroll taxes designated to fund them. Fourth, social objectives are paramount. The purpose is to guarantee a minimum level of economic security, not to subsidize fully all living expenses:

> The philosophy is that, in an economic system that stresses free enterprise and individual initiative, people should not rely entirely upon governmental programs. Social insurance is designed to guarantee economic security at minimal levels; those who want more adequate benefits obtain them through personal savings and private insurance.[7]

Finally, benefits are paid as a matter of course to anyone who meets certain eligibility requirements; an eligible millionaire, for example, receives Social Security benefits whether or not he or she actually needs them.

The most important social insurance programs in the United States are the old age, survivors, disability, and health insurance programs, commonly known as Social Security, unemployment insurance, and workers' compensation.

Enacted into law as a result of the Social Security Act of 1935, Old Age, Survivors, Disability and Health Insurance provides most workers with retirement, survivor, disability, and Medicare benefits. Eligibility requirements for these benefits vary but are based to a very large extent on credit earned for the length of covered employment, with the amount of credit required in turn affected by the type of benefit being sought. Unemployment insurance programs, another example of social insurance, provide short-term financial protection to workers who are involuntarily unemployed. Such programs pay workers weekly cash benefits; in addition, by requiring applicants for benefits to register for work at local employment offices, they help the unemployed find jobs. Each state has its own unemployment insurance program, subsidized by special payroll taxes paid by employers to the federal government. Workers' compensation programs are state-authorized social insurance programs that help to protect employees from the financial consequences of job-related injuries and disease. Workers' compensation provides medical care, disability income, rehabilitation services, and death benefits. Coverage varies from state to state. Most programs are compulsory, cover most occupations, and are limited to injuries or diseases that are job connected. Some states operate their own workers' compensation funds, while others allow approved employers to self-insure their workers or permit private insurers to provide coverage.

Other Government or Public Insurance Programs

In addition to social insurance, the government oversees many other types of insurance programs. These include insurance on checking and savings accounts provided by the Federal Deposit Insurance Corporation (FDIC); federal crime insurance for property owners and businesses in high crime areas; and riot reinsurance, known as the Fair Access to Insurance Requirements (FAIR) plan, for property owners unable to obtain property coverage through private insurers. Further, the government offers some programs, such as life insurance for members of the armed forces and veterans, that are similar to coverage provided by private insurers.

Insurance Associations

The insurance industry is represented by several different associations. Some of the most important are Property Casualty Insurers Association of America (http://www .pciaa.net/) formed by the 2004 merger of the Alliance of American Insurers and the National Association of Independent Insurers. Another association is the American Insurance Association (http://www.aiadc.org/). In terms of the information they make available to the public and to libraries, however, two of the most important are the American Council of Life Insurance (http://www.acli.com/) and the Insurance Information Institute (http://www .iii.org).

The American Council of Life Insurance, the major trade association for the industry, serves more than 300 member companies, who handle more than 90 percent of the assets and premiums of the U.S. life insurance and annuity industry. (information from the web site). In addition to member services, this council lobbies legislators and government officials and collects and dispenses data about the life insurance industry. Its publications range from booklets for consumers to actuarial, economic, legal, social, and statistical research studies, most of which are available in PDF format from the web site.

The Insurance Information Institute is the property/casualty industry's counterpart. Supported by major companies, it focuses on public relations, research, and publishing. Many of the booklets, statistics, and reports it publishes are available to the public and contain very useful industry data. Available at the web site (http://www.iii.org/), for example, are links to an insurance glossary, industry statistics, industry financials, and special reports. A more general publication, *Financial Services Fact Book*, not only covers insurance but also provides information on other services, including securities and savings; it is made available by the Insurance Information Institute at (http://www2 .iii.org/financial/). Many resources are available for free downloading, but some require payment for downloading or for a print copy.

Regulation of the Insurance Industry

Government regulation of the insurance industry is intended to protect against insurer insolvency and fraud, to ensure reasonable premium rates, and to make insurance protection widely available. It is carried on at the state level by state insurance departments, usually under the direction of appointed insurance commissioners. In addition to the broad regulatory responsibilities outlined above, state insurance departments must review new kinds of policies, license insurance agents, and settle policyholder disputes. To find state insurance information, the Insurance Information Institute provides a directory with links to all state insurance departments, commissioners, and "Official State Organizations" at http://www.iii.org/directory/.

The National Association of Insurance Commissioners (NAIC) (http://www.naic .org/state_web_map.htm), a nonprofit association of state insurance commissioners, also provides a directory with links to state and other jurisdiction insurance regulators.

Insurance Information Sources

This section considers materials in a wide variety of formats, listing for each the key insurance information sources available.

Guides and Dictionaries

There is at this time no comprehensive guide to insurance. One source of fairly wide coverage is "Insurance and Real Estate," chapter 15 in *Business Information Sources.* In it, Daniells annotates key handbooks, textbooks, and services available in the fields of risk and insurance, and life/health and property/liability insurance, as well as bibliographies and indexes, law and legal services; sources of information about insurance companies; and statistics, periodicals, and directories. A list of insurance associations is also included. Unfortunately this publication has not been updated since 1993.

Insurance vocabulary can, at times, baffle those within the profession as much as those outside it. There are specialized dictionaries and glossaries available in many libraries, and there are also many glossaries on the Web.

Rubin, Harvey W. **Dictionary of Insurance Terms.** 4th ed. Hauppauge: Barron's, 2000. 573p.

Clark, John Owen Edward. **International Dictionary of Insurance and Finance.** Chicago: Glenlake Publishing Company, Fitzroy Dearborn Publishers, 1999. 342p.

The *Dictionary of Insurance Terms* defines terms and phrases as well as abbreviations and acronyms connected with all phases of the insurance industry. Arranged in alphabetical format, each term, concept, acronym, and proper name is clearly defined, often in great detail. Cross-references are included.

The *International Dictionary of Insurance and Finance* covers life, health, property, casualty, marine, disability, business interruption, and copyright and trademark protection, as well as other major insurance topics. Explanations are fairly short but contain many "see also" pointers. The explanations are weighted to the United Kingdom and United States rather than being "international" (as indicated in the title). This may also prove too expensive for small collections.

The Web is a great resource for dictionaries and glossaries covering all areas and insurance is no exception. One web glossary is from AM Best at http://www .ambest.com/resource/glossary.html. Another, Insurance Dictionary at http://www .insurancedictionary.org/ claims to have almost 200 terms and is aimed at consumers. The Insurance Information Institute has a glossary to go along with all the other information they provide at http://www2.iii.org/glossary/. Another that can be browsed or searched can be found at http://www.insure.com/glossary.cfm. There are dozens more out there. A simple web search with a phrase such as "insurance + [dictionary or glossary]" will produce a long list.

Handbooks and Consumer Guides

Insurance handbooks generally fall into two categories: those written for insurance professionals and those intended for laypeople. The following titles are representative of each.

Dionne, Georges. **Handbook of Insurance.** Boston: Kluwer Academic Publishers, 2000. 974p.

Online Social Security Handbook: Your Basic Guide to the Social Security Programs.
U.S. Department of Health and Human Services. Social Security Administration. February 9, 2011. http://www.ssa.gov/OP_Home/handbook/. (accessed March 31, 2011)

The *Handbook of Insurance* is volume 22 of the Huebner International Series on Risk, Insurance and Economic Security. It provides a single reference source that reviews the research developments in insurance that have occurred over the last 30 years. The *Handbook,* which begins with the history and foundations of insurance theory, contains peer-reviewed chapters, written by leading authorities on insurance, on such phases of insurance as volatility and underwriting cycles, fraud, monopoly, liability, and loss reduction. Included is an extensive index.

The *Social Security Handbook* is the basic reference for social insurance programs and benefits, as well as social assistance programs, made available through the Social Security Administration. It describes federal retirement, survivors, disability, and black lung benefits; supplemental security income programs; health insurance; and public assistance programs. It also stipulates the evidence necessary to establish rights for specific benefits, lists the procedures for applying for benefits or filing claims, and describes the appeals review process. Each chapter covers a specific program or set of procedures and is subdivided into numbered paragraphs (see figures 15.4 to 15.6). An index, with citations to paragraph numbers, is also included.

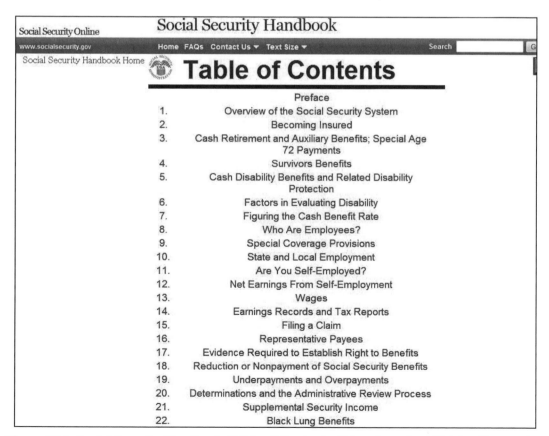

Figure 15.4. *Social Security Handbook,* **Table of Contents.** Taken from the official online version at http://www.ssa.gov/OP_Home/handbook/

Social Security Online

Social Security Handbook

www.socialsecurity.gov Home FAQs Contact Us Text Size Search

Social Security Handbook Home

Chapter 10: State and Local Employment

Table of Contents

1000.	Social Security Coverage for State and Local Government Employees
1001.	What type of work is excluded from mandatory Social Security and Medicare coverage?
1002.	Terms Defined for Section 218 Agreement Purposes
1003.	Social Security and Medicare Coverage Under a Section 218 Agreement
1004.	Absolute Coverage Groups
1005.	Retirement System Defined
1006.	Retirement System Coverage Groups
1007.	Social Security Coverage for Police Officers and Firefighters Under a Retirement System
1008.	Divided Retirement Systems
1009.	What are the procedures for conducting a referendum?
1010.	Effective Date of Section 218 Agreement
1011.	Can former employees be considered for retroactive coverage?
1012.	What types of work are not covered by Section 218 Agreements?
1013.	Public Transportation Systems
1014.	Does the State have the option of including or excluding certain types of services under a Section 218 Agreement?

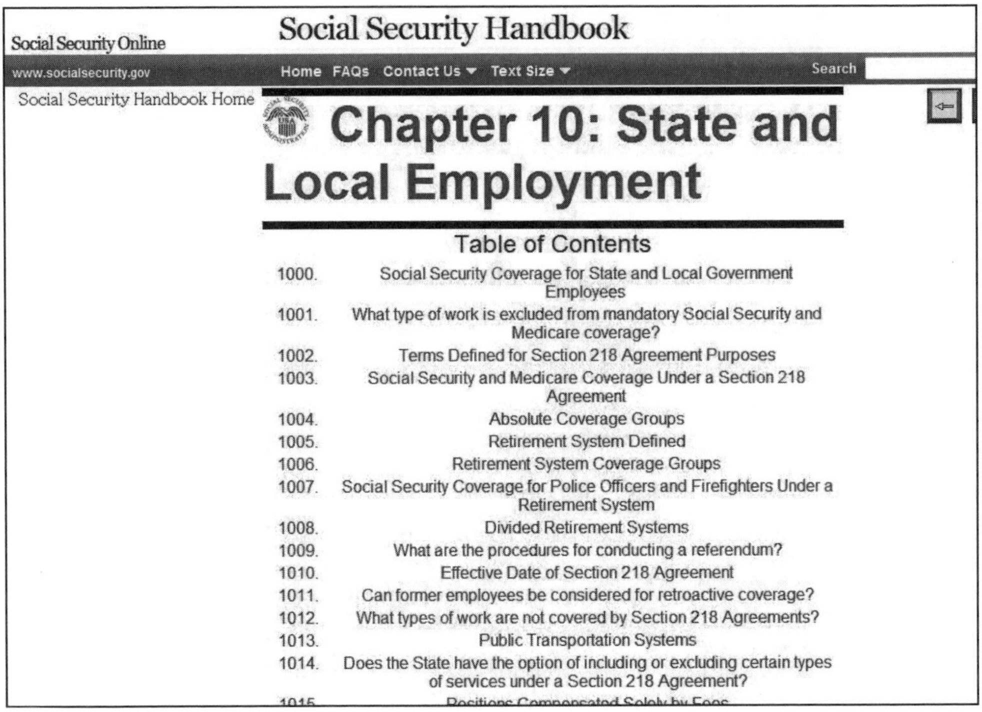

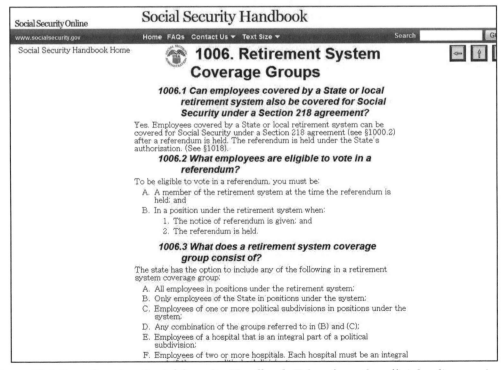

Figure 15.5. ***Social Security Handbook,*** **Chapter Table of Contents.** Taken from the official online version at http://www.ssa.gov/OP_Home/handbook/handbook.10/handbook-toc10.html /

Social Security Online

Social Security Handbook

www.socialsecurity.gov Home FAQs Contact Us Text Size Search

Social Security Handbook Home

1006. Retirement System Coverage Groups

1006.1 Can employees covered by a State or local retirement system also be covered for Social Security under a Section 218 agreement?

Yes. Employees covered by a State or local retirement system can be covered for Social Security under a Section 218 agreement (see §1000.2) after a referendum is held. The referendum is held under the State's authorization. (See §1018).

1006.2 What employees are eligible to vote in a referendum?

To be eligible to vote in a referendum, you must be:

A. A member of the retirement system at the time the referendum is held; and

B. In a position under the retirement system when:

1. The notice of referendum is given; and
2. The referendum is held.

1006.3 What does a retirement system coverage group consist of?

The state has the option to include any of the following in a retirement system coverage group:

A. All employees in positions under the retirement system;

B. Only employees of the State in positions under the system;

C. Employees of one or more political subdivisions in positions under the system;

D. Any combination of the groups referred to in (B) and (C);

E. Employees of a hospital that is an integral part of a political subdivision;

F. Employees of two or more hospitals. Each hospital must be an integral

Figure 15.6. Sample entry, ***Social Security Handbook.*** Taken from the official online version at http://www.ssa.gov/OP_Home/handbook/handbook.10/handbook-1006.html

In addition to the handbooks described above, consumer guides periodically are published to help laypeople make decisions about insurance coverage or about specific insurance companies. Although the number of companies in the insurance business and the types of policies they write are too numerous to lend themselves to more than brief coverage in such sources, consumer guidebooks can nonetheless be useful for simplifying and providing a basic introduction to insurance. The Web is also an invaluable source of up-to-date information.

Baldwin, Ben G. **The Complete Book of Insurance: The Consumer's Guide to Insuring Your Life, Health, Property, and Income**. Rev. ed. Chicago: Irwin Professional Publishing, 1996. 272p.

insurance.com. ©1998–2011. http://www.insurance.com/ (accessed March 31,2011).

Consumer Guides. America's Health Insurance Plans 2004–2011. http://www.ahip.org/content/default.aspx?bc=41|329

The *Consumer's Guide* explains in simple terms the importance of insurance and the many types available. Each chapter is dedicated to a different category of insurance, including disability, life, real estate, vehicle, and long-term care. Also included are chapters on the kinds of insurance available and how to choose appropriately. Throughout the book are sample letters and insurance tables, and glossaries are appended to each chapter. This book is useful for any library with a clientele interested in insurance.

Insurance.com organizes the site by type of insurance covered on auto, home and renters, life, health, and "other insurance." Each section incorporates quality descriptions of that type of insurance as well as articles on many topics, such as the insurance of rental cars. One must always remember that this is a commercial site, so quotes and quote comparisons are offered for those who are interested. It is, however, easy to use this as just an information site.

Consumer Guides from America's Health Insurance Plans provides links to the full text of the organization's publications aimed at the general public. The publications have titles including "Questions and Answers about Health Insurance," "Guide to Long-Term Care Insurance," and several others. It is important to remember that the association is both a trade group and a political advocacy group.

Directories

Two directories dominate the insurance field.

The Insurance Almanac: Who, What, When, and Where in Insurance, An Annual of Insurance Facts. Englewood, NJ: Underwriter Printing and Publishing, 1912–. Annual.

Who's Who in Insurance and Risk Management. Englewood, NJ: Underwriter Printing and Publishing, 1948–. Annual.

The Insurance Almanac is a compilation of lists by categories of insurance companies and practitioners. Insurance companies, for example, are listed by form of legal organization and lines of insurance written. The company entries are fairly brief, including company address and telephone number, date and state in which the company was established, officers' names, types of insurance coverage written, and territory covered. Most entries also include the names of the executives in charge of advertising and claims.

The Insurance Almanac also lists agents and brokers in principal cities; insurance adjusters; and insurance inspection, investigation, and software development services. Finally, the *Almanac* identifies organizations related to various types of insurance, assigned risk plans and rating bureaus, and state insurance officials. It is a basic insurance reference work and belongs in most business reference collections.

Who's Who in Insurance and Risk Management, until 2003 titled *Who's Who in Insurance*, provides biographical information on insurance officials, brokers, agents, and buyers. Each entry generally includes the person's address, educational background, positions held, club and association memberships, and other personal data.

Both *The Insurance Almanac* and *Who's Who in Insurance and Risk Management* are published by Underwriter Printing and Publishing, one of the firms dominating the insurance reference marketplace. Publications of two others, A. M. Best and National Underwriter, are discussed in the sections that follow on company and policy information.

Other biographical directories published by professional organizations related to insurance include the American Academy of Actuaries and the Society of Actuaries, who now share a directory at https://actuarialdirectory.org/SearchDirectory/tabid/242/Default.aspx. Such specialized lists of members are sometimes available free from the societies via their web pages.

Information about Insurance Companies

One of the major considerations in selecting an insurer is the company's financial strength. All other things being equal, it is better to insure with a company that is financially sound—and likely to be so at some unknown time in the future, when a claim may be filed—than it is to buy insurance from a company that lacks financial strength or stability. As a result, publications that document and permit financial comparison of insurers are vital. Most reflect the traditional industry division between life/health and property/casualty insurers, but one does not.

Mergent. **Mergent's Bank & Finance Manual.** New York: The Service, 1900–. 3v. Annual.

Volume 2 of *Mergent's Bank & Finance Manual* permits comparison of some of the largest U.S. and Canadian insurance companies. As with the other Mergent (Moody's) manuals, length of coverage varies and to a certain extent depends on the fee paid by the company to Mergent. At a minimum, however, a listing includes the corporate address, number of employees, officers and directors, types of insurance written, and states in which the company is licensed to operate. Each entry also features comparative financial statistics for the current and preceding year, as well as investment and stock ownership information. The center blue pages provide data on the distribution and dollar value of assets (government securities, stocks, bonds, mortgages, real estate, and policy loans) held by U.S. life insurance companies and an interim earnings and dividend section. As with all Mergent Manuals, this information is included in the electronic versions, Mergent Web Reports and Mergent Online.

Although *Mergent Manuals* provides useful financial and background information about many insurance companies, its coverage is neither as detailed nor as broad as that made available in more specialized sources. Some of the most widely used titles are described below.

A. M. Best Company. **Best's Insurance Reports: Life/Health.** Oldwick, NJ: A. M. Best, 1906–. Annual.

A. M. Best Company. **Best's Insurance Reports: Property/Casualty.** Oldwick, NJ: A. M. Best, 1976–. Annual.

Best's Insurance Reports are published annually in two editions, one for the life/health industry and one for property/casualty insurers. The latest *Life/Health* edition provides detailed information on some 2,300 U.S. and Canadian life and health insurance companies. The latest *Property/Casualty* edition features more than 4,080 companies. Each report summarizes the company's history and describes its management and operation. It also presents key balance sheet and income statement data and includes statistics on the value of new business issued, insurance in force, and company development. Although each company report focuses on the past year's performance, many of the statistical tables provide historical data as well. In addition, most companies are assigned a financial size category and are rated on the basis of their financial strength and ability to meet contractual obligations. Company performance is compared to industry norms established by Best in the areas of profitability, leverage, and liquidity. In addition, Best's evaluation includes a qualitative review, focusing on such factors as "the amount and soundness of a company's reinsurance, the quality and diversification of investments, the valuation basis of policy reserves, and the experience of management."

Based on these factors, most companies are assigned ratings like those in figure 15.7.

Rating	Meaning
A and A-	Execellent
B++ and B+	Very Good
B and B-	Fair
C++ and C+	Marginal
C and C-	Weak
D	Poor
E	Under Regulatory Supervision
F	In Liquidation
S	Rating Suspended

Figure 15.7. Typical ratings assigned

Companies not rated are assigned an NR in the report. Those that are excluded are usually either inactive, are too small, lack sufficient experience, or fall below minimum standards. In all, there are five main categories for exclusion, each of which is listed and described on the *Reports'* front cover and at http://www.ambest.com/ratings/guide.pdf.

People consulting *Best's Reports* for the first time are advised to read them with care. A certain amount of reading between the lines in company reports is necessary. Best seldom overtly condemns a company for bad management or investment policies. Either the comments are favorable, or none are included. As a result, Best's assessments must be interpreted with caution.

In addition to detailed reports, *Best's Insurance Reports: Life/Health* lists state insurance commissioners, guaranty fund provisions by state, retired life/health companies, and data on the distribution of assets of U.S. life insurance companies and the growth of life insurance in the United States from 1880 to the present. *Best's Insurance Reports: Property/Casualty* also includes a listing of state officials and guaranty fund provisions as well as a ranked list of the largest 250 property/casualty companies

The preface in both volumes describes Best's rating system and financial size categories in detail and explains each of the items contained in company reports. In addition, each edition includes the group affiliations of life/health and property/casualty insurers; lists legal reserve life insurance companies by state; and cites recent name changes, mergers, and dissolutions.

A. M. Best Company. **Best's Key Rating Guide: Life/Health.** Oldwick, NJ: A. M. Best, 1991–. Annual.

A. M. Best Company. **Best's Key Rating Guide: Property/Casualty.** Oldwick, NJ: A. M. Best, 1976–. Annual

Best's Key Rating Guides are intended primarily for insurance professionals. They present summary financial information, operating ratios, and Best's ratings for some 4,080 property and casualty insurers and 2,300 life/health companies in tabular format. Other tables list insurance groups, states in which companies are licensed to do business, and companies and associations that have retired.

The print versions of *Best's Reports* and *Best's Key Rating Guides* are available in many larger libraries that need to answer general insurance questions. For those who need more specialized information or the added functionality of an electronic version, most Best's products are available on CD-ROM that comes with the print subscription.

Many of Best's publications are also available through their *BestLink* or *Best Library Center* services via the web. And many of Best's subscriptions include access to *BestAlert Service,* a real-time e-mail notice of rating changes, news articles, and press releases for insurance companies of their choice, *Best's Review, and BestWeek:* publications that cover news and events in the insurance industry. Detailed information about A. M. Best's products is available from their web page (http://www.ambest.com). This page can also be used as a gateway to the web pages of insurance companies. Enter a name in the search box to get the address and web link to a company as well as news about the company. Registration is required for more information.

Financial ratings are also available from other companies, most notably Standard & Poor's and Fitch. The ratings awarded by these companies can be obtained free of charge from the web site of *insure.com* at http://www.insure.com/ratings/. An explanation of the ratings is on each page. For libraries with budget restraints this is an excellent site to gain information for patron questions.

Information about Insurance Policies

Requests for information about insurance policies generally fall into two categories: identifying companies that write policies offering special coverage and comparing policies written by different companies. An insurance agent, for example, may want to compile a list of companies writing ocean marine insurance or selling health coverage for hemophiliacs. The head of a family may want to compare the provisions of life insurance policies sold by Baltimore Life with those offered by Northwestern Mutual Life. Although precise comparison is impossible, the sources listed below provide a good base for identifying companies offering special coverage and for comparing the basic provisions of many insurance policies.

Who Writes What in Life and Health Insurance. Cincinnati, OH: National Underwriter.
(Continued as a series of articles in *National Underwriter Life & Health* 2001–2008)

The Insurance Marketplace. Indianapolis, IN: Rough Notes, 1962–. Annual.

Who Writes What in Life and Health Insurance was a listing of insurance companies and brokers that provide hard-to-place, unusual, substandard, or new types of life and health insurance coverage. This directory has been discontinued, but the information is now available as a series of articles in *National Underwriter Life & Health,* a weekly publication also available online with daily updates. For all National Underwriter product and subscription information check the web page at http://www.nationalunderwriter.com/.

The Insurance Marketplace identifies more than 640 categories of coverage and more than 800 providers that write policies for unusual or hard-to-place risks. This annual is a supplement to the December issue of *Rough Notes* magazine (http://www.roughnotes .com/); nonsubscribers can buy it separately or access it online from the company web page. Information is supplied by region: Northeast, Southeast, Midwest, Southwest, and Western.

There are also various rating guides published by A. M. Best (http://www.ambest .com) and National Underwriter (http://www.nationalunderwriter.com/). These are more specialized publications to which most libraries would not subscribe, but details are available on the companies' web pages.

Insurance Periodicals

Periodicals relating to the insurance industry are generally either trade publications aimed at insurance practitioners or scholarly journals focusing on the study of insurance, risk management, and actuarial science. The titles that follow are typical trade publications.

Best's Review. Oldwick, NJ: A. M. Best, 2001–. Monthly.

BestWeek. Oldwick, NJ: A. M. Best, 2001–. Weekly.

National Underwriter: Life & Health. Erlanger, KY: National Underwriter, 1897–. Weekly.

National Underwriter: P & C. Erlanger, KY: National Underwriter, 1896–. Weekly.

Each of the two major insurance publishers, A. M. Best and National Underwriter, publishes trade magazines for the insurance industries. Best's offering is *Best's Review*, an amalgamation of the *Life/Health* and *Property/Casualty* editions published since 1899. It contains news on industry and company developments and strategies, as well as prominent practitioners who have changed companies, been promoted, or retired. In addition, it covers regulation of the insurance industry, sales and marketing, and government policies as they affect insurance. Regular features include "Resources," which lists selected books, proceedings, software, and educational resources; "Statistical Studies and Special Reports," which indexes the reports and "top listings" published by *Best's Review* in the last twelve months; and "Ratings," which provides new or recently changed *Best's* ratings. Each edition of *Best's Review* also includes a "Technology" section, which features technological advancements in the insurance industry and how these are changing everything from back office operations to distribution channels.

Further, each monthly edition of *Best's Review* provides more specialized coverage. Recent issues have included articles on how the World Trade Center disaster has affected the industry and changes in the needs of people investigating long-term care insurance. Each January edition includes an index to the articles included in the previous year's issues. This publication is also available online at http://www.bestreview.com, and subscribers to the print edition may access it by using the password provided in the paper copy.

Also available from this company are *BestWeek* and *BestDay*. *BestWeek* is published both in print (also downloadable in PDF format on Friday afternoon) and on the Web at http://www.bestweek.com. The weekly provides coverage of recent industry developments, interviews, financial news, and federal and legislative activity. *BestDay*, on the Web at http://www3.ambest.com/bestdaynews/BestDay.asp, provides breaking news in the insurance industry. Some of the stories are free to any visitor to the site, and subscribers to *BestWeek* have access to all the news. These publications will rarely be found in libraries as they are targeted to the insurance practitioner.

Similar coverage is provided in both editions of the *National Underwriter*, a weekly trade paper that reports on recent developments in the insurance industry. Articles may focus on commercial or personal insurance, group and employee benefits, sales, management, current legislation, and regulation. Special reports include markets, rankings, and financial reviews. Both these and other journals are accessible via the Web from http://www.nationalunderwriter.com. Both journals have also had several slight title changes over the past few years so be aware of that when looking for older issues. The *National Underwriter* and *Best's Reviews* are the most widely read and circulated of all such trade journals.

Scholarly treatment is provided in several periodicals; two of the most highly regarded follow.

American Risk Insurance Association. **The Journal of Risk and Insurance.** Athens: The Association, Mount Vernon, NY, 1932–. Quarterly.

The Society of Financial Service Professionals. **Journal of Financial Service Professionals**. Bryn Mawr, PA: The Society, 1946–. Bimonthly.

The *Journal of Risk and Insurance* is the most scholarly and quantitative of all insurance periodicals. Articles are usually written by academicians rather than insurance practitioners and frequently include formulas, statistics, and lengthy footnotes. Typical articles are "Optimal Asset Allocation Towards the End of the Life Cycle: To Annuitize or Not to Annuitize?" and "Life Insurer Financial Distress, Best's Ratings and Financial Ratios." Each issue also contains "Recent Court Decisions," which briefly describes important legal actions, and "Book Reviews," which features lengthier, signed reviews.

The *Journal of Financial Service Professionals*, formerly the *Journal of the American Society of CLU & ChFC*, publishes applied research in all areas of financial planning, including retirement planning, health care, economics, and information planning for the industry. A typical issue includes articles on estate, financial, and tax planning; information management; economic trends; and current ethical, legal, and social issues relating to the profession. The articles themselves are written by insurance professionals as well as by academicians and are generally less theoretical and quantitative than those appearing in The *Journal of Risk and Insurance*.

The *Journal of Risk and Insurance* and *Journal of Financial Service Professionals* are available for their members online directly from their organizations at http://www.aria.org/ and http://www.financialpro.org/, respectively. The journals are also available from one or more of the periodical indexes and aggregators such as Ebsco and Proquest mentioned below.

Current information about the insurance industry is as important to consumers as it is to agents and brokers. Although no consumer-oriented serial is devoted entirely to insurance, some periodically describe or evaluate specific types of insurance coverage and insurance companies. *Consumer Reports, Business Week*, and *Money*, for example, frequently include articles intended to help consumers keep abreast of industry developments and make wise insurance decisions.

The above periodicals focus primarily on private, rather than public, insurance. One key government periodical, however, contains current information on social insurance programs provided by the federal government.

U.S. Department of Health and Human Services. Social Security Administration. **Social Security Bulletin.** Washington, DC: Government Printing Office, 1938–. Quarterly.

Each issue of the *Social Security Bulletin* includes summaries of recent research, notes and brief reports, and two or three articles treating some aspect of social insurance or public assistance. Recent issues, for example, have included articles on privatization of social security in Latin America, the pension status of divorced women at retirement, and a study on lifetime earnings patterns and the impact of pension reform. The articles are often written by the Social Security Administration research staff and usually include statistics, tables, and graphs. The *Bulletin*'s "Current Operating Statistics" section contains several pages of statistics pertaining to Social Security Administration programs as well as economic indicators relating to personal income and prices paid for medical care. An annual statistical supplement is included with the subscription. Articles from this publication are available at http://www.socialsecurity.gov/policy/docs/ssb/.

Periodical Indexes

Major insurance periodicals are indexed in such standard business sources as EBSCO*host*'s *Business Source Elite* or *Business Source Premier* and *ABI/INFORM* from ProQuest. In many instances, these sources will suffice. There are, however, more specialized sources available.

Insurance Periodicals Index. Ipswich, MA: Ebsco Publishing Ipswich, 2003–.
  Formerly by Chatworth, CA: NILS Publishing, 1964–2000. Annual.

The *Insurance Periodicals Index* is now part of the Ebsco family of databases. It provides indexing and abstracting for nearly 200 journals, magazines, and industry reports. Coverage is back to 1946 in some cases.

The *Insurance Periodicals Index* was originally compiled by members of the Special Libraries Association's Insurance and Employee Benefits Division from monthly lists in both editions of *Best's Reviews*. In 1982, the NILS Publishing Company joined with the division to help them develop the computerized database out of which the annual *Index* was then published. The contents of *IPI* are still a major source of information for the years that it covered.

Insurance & Employee Benefits Division (IEBD). **Guide to Insurance Research.** Washington, DC: Special Libraries Association, 2001–2004. Quarterly.

The *Guide to Insurance Research* was once prepared by members of the Insurance and Employee Benefits Division of SLA. Its aim was to selectively abstract journal articles, research reports, and books. The first issue contains reviews of 22 research studies from 2001. The division[8] may have more information about obtaining old copies of the publication.

Government Documents

Insurance is regulated at the state level. As a result, the federally published statistical compilations, consumer guides, and information sources so common to federally regulated industries are not generally available for private insurance. Congressional hearings regarding the insurance industry are held periodically and are subsequently published and distributed by the Government Printing Office. Most federal documents, however, deal with social insurance programs. Many are written for program beneficiaries. One such source, the *Social Security Handbook*, has already been described. Other booklets and brochures deal with specific types of social insurance coverage. Many of these publications are no longer issued in print form, but the information is available at the agency web sites.

From the site maintained by the Social Security Administration one can read the history of social security, check the trustee's report, find answers to most questions, print copies of needed forms or fill them out online, and even calculate Social Security benefits. In figure 15.8 are some of the frequently asked questions with links to the answers. Information on laws, regulations and rulings, research and data, and services for business is also directly available.[9]

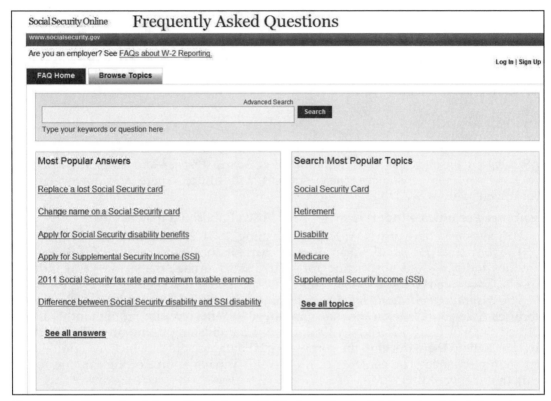

Figure 15.8. Example of the online help available from the Social Security Administration, at http://ssa-custhelp.ssa.gov/app/home

The Office of the Actuary, as part of its mission of monitoring the current and future soundness of the program, prepares reports on the financial outlook of Social Security and historical data on numbers of beneficiaries and average benefits. These can be requested from the web page at http://www.ssa.gov/OACT/NOTES/actstud.html. Some of the more recent studies and notes are available for immediate printing from the same site.

Medicare and You. Washington, DC: Government Printing Office, 1990–. Annual.

Medicare and You describes the Medicare program (http://www.medicare.gov) and the different plans available, lists medical care services and supplies included under or excluded from Medicare coverage, and includes a glossary of some of the words an individual may need to know. *Medicare and You* also focuses on situations in which it is advisable to obtain private insurance to supplement Medicare coverage, with tips for selecting insurers and supplemental insurance. These and other similar documents[10] are free from the web site at http://www.medicare.gov/Publications or can be ordered online or by telephone. At this time many of the publications are also available in Spanish and some are available in Chinese, Vietnamese, Korean, and Russian (see figure 15.9).

Figure 15.9. Alternate languages available for some Medicare publications,
at http://www.medicare.gov/multilanguage.aspx

Public and state-supported libraries can provide a useful service by providing access to patrons to the *Resource Locator* at http://www.medicare.gov/navigation/resource-locator/resource-locator-overview.aspx, a tool for finding doctors, hospitals, formularies, nursing homes, and other related Medicare resources. As more of these materials become readily available from the Internet, librarians will need to be guides to the information in this medium or will need to have copies on hand in their collections.

Although such consumer-oriented booklets are the most common type of federal document, other insurance-related sources are also available. Some present statistics relating to social insurance programs, others describe supplementary state programs, and still others, produced by the Small Business Administration, cover insurance as it relates to business. Again, most of this information is available from individual government web sites, or one can use a search engine such as http://www.google.com/unclesam to find the appropriate data or publication.

Many state government agencies also issue insurance-related documents. They range from guides such as *Alaska Insurance Consumer Guide* and the Maine *Coping with the Aftermath of Weather Related Disasters Bulletin* to statistical compilations, fact books, and manuals. Such publications are frequently produced by state insurance departments and can be identified by checking the agency web page. Some of the most detailed information on the insurance industry and on specific companies can be found in the annual reports issued by state insurance departments. The reports are available from the departments themselves, state document depository libraries, and through the SRI Microfiche Library. They are usually quite long, contain extensive statistical information, and are one of the primary sources from which data presented in the statistical sources listed in the following section are derived. A complete listing of the addresses and web links to state insurance departments is provided by the Federal Consumer Information Center (FCIC) of the U.S. General Services Administration at http://www.consumeraction.gov/insurance.shtml. These web pages are an excellent way of keeping current with changes in the industry, insurance alerts, and listings of companies operating within a state.

Statistics

Insurance statistics are plentiful. Many of the sources already described contain valuable statistical information. Such trade publications as *Best's Review* regularly publish annual surveys of company and industry financial performance, while federal publications such as the *Social Security Bulletin* present detailed statistics on social insurance programs and benefits. State insurance departments publish statistics as well, based primarily on the reports submitted to them by insurance companies. Many of these current statistics are available from both government and association web pages.

Although these sources are useful, they are by no means the only publications in which statistics are available. Although there is no single source that presents comprehensive information on all types of commercial and social insurance, several titles focus on specific insurance lines. Most reflect the traditional division between the life/health and property/casualty industries. Many libraries keep older editions of these publications so that historical statistics are obtainable.

The life/health industry is represented by several different sources. The two most widely consulted sources follow.

American Council of Life Insurers. **Life Insurance Fact Book.** Washington, DC: The Council, 1946–. Annual.

The *Life Insurance Fact Book* is a fundamental source. Based on data compiled from annual statements provided by life insurance companies, council surveys, and other organizations, it summarizes industry trends and developments, presenting information on life insurance purchases and ownership, annuities, life insurance and annuity benefit payments, pension and retirement programs, policy lapses and surrenders, life insurance assets, and other aspects of the life insurance business. For the most part it emphasizes the recent years, with data in tables, charts, and graphs supplemented by brief, narrative descriptions. Some historical data are presented. Additional sections identify key state insurance officials and present mortality tables, historic dates, and names and describe important trade and professional life insurance associations. A glossary and index are also included. The full text of the *Fact Book* and other statistical publications can be downloaded from the publications section of the council's web page (http://www.acli .com/.)[11]

Although the *Fact Book* is perhaps the most widely used statistical sources, others are also available.

The Life Insurance Marketing and Research Association (LIMRA) (http://www .limra.com/) is one of the most prolific international publishers of statistics and reports on the life insurance industry. It conducts research, produces a wide range of publications, and is a principal source of industry sales and marketing statistics. It regularly surveys life insurance companies, agencies, agents, and brokers, and publishes its findings in such studies as *Guaranteed Living Benefits Utilization: 2009 Data*, *Social Media and Financial Services*, *2011 Industry Projections*, and *Targeting the Hispanic Market in the U.S.*, but to view or download the information, a membership is required. The membership roster is freely accessible and is composed of financial services companies from around the world. By checking the "News Center" on the site, one may also find some of the latest statistics.

The property/casualty industry is also well represented by statistical publications. Two of the most useful are as follows:

Insurance Information Institute. **The Insurance Fact Book.** New York: The Institute, 2009–. Annual.

A. M. Best Company. **Best's Aggregates & Averages: Property/Casualty.** Oldwick, NJ: A. M. Best, 1976–. Annual.

The *Fact Book* is another association-published fact book. It was formed by the merger of *Fact Book: Property/Casualty Insurance Facts* and several other publications. Like the others, it includes detailed current and historic industry statistics, grouped under broad categories including the Dollars and Cents of the Business, Factors Affecting Costs, Losses by Category, and Laws Affecting Motorists. As a handy compilation of statistics, this publication is extremely useful and inexpensive. For those researchers needing to find free information, the statistics and research reports section of the Institute's web pages at http://www.iii.org/media/facts/ and http://www.iii.org/media/lateststud/ will provide some significant information.

Best's Aggregates & Averages: Property/Casualty includes composite industry data as well as information on specific companies. It is particularly useful for researchers who need to compare the performance of one company with others in the same line or with the industry aggregate. It presents consolidated industry totals as well as totals for companies categorized by type of organization and by predominant type of insurance written. Each of these listings presents aggregate balance sheet and operating statistics, showing assets and liabilities for the current and preceding year, average yield on company investments, premiums written, premiums earned and collected, commissions, expenses, and other operating data.

In addition, *Best's Aggregates & Averages* features time series data on industry resources and operating results, loss and expense ratios, and an extensive "Lines of Business" section that provides statistics on leading companies and insurance groups. Also included are lists of leading companies and of underwriting expenses by company. This resource is also available as an online subscription (http://www.ambest.com/sales/aggavgonlinepc/).

Other publications are more specialized. The Insurance Research Council (http://www.ircweb.org), an industry-sponsored organization, conducts research, publishes the findings, and makes them available to the public. *Uninsured Motorist*, for example, presents detailed demographic information on the characteristics of uninsured drivers and the cars they drive, accident claims, and state laws on uninsured motorist coverage. From the Council's web page one can access the news releases or the abstracts of the publications to find a few statistics free. If the full report is wanted, there is a fee. Two industry-sponsored organizations, the Insurance Institute for Highway Safety and the Highway Loss Data Institute (http://www.hwysafety.org/), jointly publish reports on theft, insurance losses, and collision coverage of automobiles, vans, pickup trucks, and utility vehicles, as well as on accident-related injuries. The organization makes all of its reports freely available from its web site.

For a librarian looking to improve a collection of materials on insurance it would be advisable to check all the web sites of associations, organizations, and commercial publishers, as the amount of free information now available is extensive. The smallest public library can now provide some free statistics and ratings of insurance companies.

Notes

1. Some National Safety Council statistics are available at http://www.nsc.org/lrs/statstop.htm.

2. George E. Rejda, *Principles of Insurance* (Glenview, IL: Scott, Foresman, 1982), 24.

3. Although most property/casualty insurers are stock companies, there are some exceptions. State Farm Insurance, a mutual insurance company, is perhaps the most notable.

4. Frederick G. Crane, *Insurance Principles and Practices* (New York: John Wiley, 1980), 427.

5. Rejda, *Principles of Insurance*, 505.

6. Adam Raphael, *Ultimate Risk* (London: Bantam Press, 1994), 11–16.

7. Crane, *Insurance Principles and Practices*, 303.

8. Insurance & Employee Benefits Division (IEBD)
   c/o Special Libraries Association
   331 South Patrick Street, Alexandria
   VA 22314-3501 USA
   Tel: (703) 647-490700, Fax: (703) 647-4901
   Web: http://units.sla.org/division/dieb/index.htm

9. Publications can be viewed or printed from the web site at http://www.ssa.gov/pgm/formspubs.htm. Contact information for local offices can be found by using the locator at https://secure.ssa.gov/apps6z/FOLO/fo001.jsp.

10. Publications can be viewed or printed from the web site at http://www.medicare.gov/Publications/Search/View/ViewPubList.asp?Language=English (or access this page by using the site map; language can be changed to Spanish, Chinese, Russian, Korean at this site) or by writing to: U.S. Department of Health and Human Services Centers for Medicare and Medicaid Services
    7500 Security Blvd.
    Baltimore, MD 21244-1850
    Phone: 1-800-MEDICARE

11. For more information on publications from the Council, check http://www.acli.com/, or write to:
    American Council of Life Insurers
    101 Constitution Avenue, NW, Suite 700
    Washington, DC 20001-2133
    Phone: 202-624-2000

16

Real Estate

Previous chapters covered such traditional and speculative investments as stocks, bonds, mutual funds, commodities futures, and options. This chapter examines another investment medium, real estate. Its importance is difficult to overestimate:

> Each of us uses real estate every day. Real estate provides shelter, protection, comfort, convenience, privacy, and many other things. Business firms need a place of business—a store, office, plant, or other parcel of real estate—in order to carry on operations. Farms and ranches, of course, rely heavily on real estate. Governmental, educational, religious, and cultural institutions all make use of real estate. Our real estate resources—the homes, factories, office buildings, stores, shopping centers, farms, rights of way, roads, streets, parks, recreational areas, and other kinds—represent more than half of our national wealth.[1]

This chapter explains basic real estate concepts and describes reference sources of potential interest to homeowners, business people, investors, realtors, and real estate practitioners.

Basic Real Estate Concepts

Real estate means land and the attachments to it that are intended to be permanent. Such attachments, also known as improvements, may include fences, landscaping, bridges, and pipelines as well as buildings. Automobiles parked on the land or possessions stored in the buildings, however, are personal rather than real property. The distinction is an important one. Personal property includes items of a temporary or movable nature, and real property includes land and its permanent structures. Land includes more than the earth's surface. It begins at the earth's center and continues through to the surface and beyond it into space; rights to the subsurface, surface, and airspace for the same plot of land may, in fact, be separately held.

According to a US Department of Agriculture report from 2002 (http://www.ers .usda.gov/Briefing/LandUse/majorlandusechapter.htm), the United States has a land area of about 2.3 billion acres, which can be categorized as:

- Rural (2.2 billion acres, or 97 percent) includes agricultural (range, cropland, pasture, farmsteads, and roads), forest, and other land.

- Urban (60 million acres; 3 percent) includes residential, commercial, utilities, mixed, transitional, and other urban land.

Categories of Real Estate

Real estate can be categorized in many different ways. It can, for example, be classed as urban or rural or as residential, commercial, or industrial. It can also be categorized as property purchased primarily for occupancy (a house, store, or factory) by its owner, or for investment purposes (an apartment building, a syndicated real estate partnership). A brief discussion of each of these classifications is in order.

As the population has grown and become increasingly urban, so also has the proportional increase of urban real estate. Even so, such real estate accounts for only about 2.9 percent of the total land area in the United States, according to a report issued by the Economic Research Service of the U.S. Department of Agriculture (http://www .ers.usda.gov/Publications/RCAT/rcat102/Rcat102k.pdf).

Most other land can be classified as rural. It includes not only farms, ranches, and the land they occupy, but also commercial forests, wildlife refuges, reservoirs, and recreational and wilderness areas. Finally, some real estate can be categorized as both urban and rural; interstate highways and railroad rights of way fall into this classification.

Real estate is often described by the uses for which it is intended (see figure 16.1). Owner- and renter-occupied housing, for example, is generally referred to as *residential property,* while real estate used for wholesale, retail, and service industries is considered *commercial property.* Shopping centers, office buildings, resorts, restaurants, and hotels and motels are all categorized as commercial property. Real estate used primarily for manufacturing or warehouses is referred to as *industrial property,* and includes factories, warehouses, and industrial parks.

	Types or Real Estate
Residential	Dwellings, usually owner occupied
Commercial	Shopping Centers, Stores, Office buildings, resorts, restaurants, hotels, motels, recreation facilities? rental housing??
Industrial	factories, warehouses, industrial parks

Figure 16.1. Types of real estate

All real estate ownership represents investment, some of it considerable. Not all real estate, however, is purchased primarily for investment purposes. Although the homeowner hopes that his or her property will appreciate in value, usually the primary goal is to enjoy other benefits, such as shelter, privacy, convenience, and status that home ownership may bring. The same is true for the small business person who owns the buildings and land occupied by his or her business. The emphasis in these situations is on ownership of real property for occupancy rather than for any immediate investment returns. Others, however, buy property primarily for investment. Land developers and contractors who routinely buy and sell real estate, and institutional investors, such as insurance companies that invest heavily in buildings and land, fall into this category. So also do a growing number of small, private investors. Some purchase real property directly; a person who has recently inherited money, for example, may choose to buy rental property rather than stocks or bonds. Other investors may buy a distressed property with the intention of quickly fixing it up and selling it, hoping to get more for the property on the resale than they paid for it. Still other investors share ownership of real estate through limited partnerships and real estate investment trusts.

A *real estate limited partnership* enables member investors to share ownership in more extensive and diverse real estate holdings than they would be able to afford individually. Membership in such syndicates consists of limited and general partners. Limited partners put up the capital. General partners seek the investors, make the investment decisions, and act as the syndicate managers. In addition, general partners assume greater risk than limited partners; although limited partners do risk the loss of capital, their liability is limited to the amount of their investment. General partners, on the other hand, must personally assume all other liabilities of ownership and financing. In return for their services and their assumption of greater risk, general partners receive fees from the limited partners, much as investment company managers receive them from shareholders.

The partnerships may be either private (that is, not open to the public) or public. Public real estate limited partnerships, also known as master limited partnerships or MLPs, are publicly traded on the major stock exchanges and in the OTC market. Like other publicly traded securities, master limited partnerships are under the regulation of the Securities and Exchange Commission and are required to report to it on a regular basis.

Real estate investment trusts (*REITs*) are related investment media. Like limited partnerships, real estate investment trusts pool the money of several investors for the purchase of real property (or mortgages on such property) and are generally considered long-term investments. Like MLPs, REITs are publicly traded. REITs, however, are organized and function as corporations rather than partnerships; REIT investors are exempt from the risk of liability that limited partners must assume. By law REITs must be widely held and must distribute almost all their taxable income as dividends to shareholders. The best source of free and substantial information about REITs is available at the web site of the National Association of Real Estate Investment Trusts (http://www.nareit.com/) Here one can obtain

- *About REITs* (http://www.reit.com/AboutREITs/AllAboutREITs.aspx)

- *Guide to REIT Investing* (http://www.reit.com/AboutREITs/GuidetoREITInvesting.aspx)

- Statistics on the industry (http://www.reit.com/IndustryDataPerformance/IndustryDataPerformance.aspx)

- A link to companies and ticker symbols (http://www.reit.com/AboutREITs/REITsbyTickerSymbol.aspx)

Prospective investors are counseled to learn all they can about specific MLPs and REITs before they invest.

Real Estate Industry

Discussion of real estate to this point has focused on the property holder—the homeowner, businessperson, or investor—rather than on the business of real estate. Real estate is, however, a major industry. It includes a wide variety of businesses, most of which can be categorized as marketing, producing, or financing enterprises. In addition, several related industries and professions are frequently directly involved in the real estate industry.

Marketing

Marketing enterprises include two main types of business: brokerage and property management. *Real estate brokerage* involves selling, leasing, buying, or exchanging property for others on a commission basis. Brokerage firms, or real estate agencies, may range in size from small, one- or two-person operations to large national firms. They may handle all types of real estate or may specialize in residential, commercial, industrial, or farm property. All, however, serve as intermediaries, and all charge commissions. Owners and partners of brokerage firms are usually referred to as *brokers,* while other employees assisting in marketing real estate are usually called *real estate agents* or *salespeople.* Both brokers and agents must pass examinations to be licensed to practice in the states in which they are located.

Often the term *realtor* is used by laypeople to designate both *brokers* and *salespeople.* Not all such real estate practitioners, however, are Realtors. A *Realtor* is a broker who is affiliated with a local real estate board that is a member of the National Association of Realtors (NAR) (http://www.realtor.org/). The term is copyrighted by the NAR, and only those with the stipulated membership ties are allowed to use it.

The National Association of Realtors first organized in 1908 and is the most important national real estate organization. The NAR performs many of the activities characteristic of trade and professional associations. It offers seminars and other continuing education opportunities, promotes the interests of the real estate industry, and has an active public relations program. The creation and support of its *Code of Ethics* (http://www.realtor.org/mempolweb.nsf/pages/code) is generally regarded as its most important contribution to the profession and to the public. In 1916, the NAR voted to use the term *realtor* to designate member brokers and to distinguish them from other brokers who, it was felt, might not always adhere to the high standards set forth in the *Code of Ethics.* From the Association web pages there are links for consumers, residential brokers, sales agents, and real estate specialties.

Property management is the other main type of real estate marketing enterprise. As the number of properties owned by absentee landlords and groups of people or organizations (including, for example, life insurance companies and pension funds, limited partnerships, and real estate investment trusts) increases, so also has the demand for professional property management. A property manager acts as the owner's agent, performing such duties as negotiating leases; collecting rent; supervising maintenance, repair, and upkeep of the property; and providing accounting and financial services. The property manager reports periodically to the owners and carries out any additional duties specified in his or her contract. These may include preparing and filing tax returns and arranging for insurance coverage. Although property management is available, usually through brokerage firms, for single-family dwellings, more often it is characteristic of larger properties such as condominiums and apartment complexes, shopping centers and stores, and office and industrial buildings. In return for such services, the property manager or the property management firm is usually paid a fixed percentage of rents collected from the occupants of the property.

Production

Another major functional division of the real estate industry is generally referred to as *production*. Production begins with land development, which consists of three phases: preliminary analysis, implementation, and evaluation. During the first phase, the developer attempts to determine the market for a proposed development. This will include consideration of local economic conditions, demographic factors likely to affect demand, the existence and occupancy rates of similar types of property, and the availability of land for development. During this phase, developers may seek information from local government agencies, chambers of commerce, and trade organizations. Although sometimes overlooked, libraries can also provide valuable information. The *Economic Census*, the *Census of Population and Housing, County Business Patterns,* and many other government, trade, association, and commercial publications can help developers analyze the local market. If market research indicates that conditions are favorable, further study is required. It will include identification and analysis of possible tracts of land, subsequent selection of the site to be developed, and analysis of local, state, and possibly even federal government regulations that may affect the project.

During the second phase, the developer negotiates with and secures the approval of various government agencies, purchases and finances the land, and, with the aid of engineers and other specialists, draws up a complete layout and design for the tract. Someone developing land for a shopping center, for example, will use topographic maps, surveys, and the results of soil and drainage tests to designate space for the building itself and for parking, access roads, and landscaped areas. Implementation also includes the establishment of land use restrictions for future occupants, acquiring the necessary liability insurance and performance bonds to ensure completion of site improvements, and the actual installation of improvements on the site. The final step in the implementation phase involves marketing the new development to prospective buyers.

The third phase is feedback and evaluation. It involves assessment of development costs, sales performance, and other factors that helped the project succeed or fail.

The building process follows the land development stage. Many of the builder's tasks parallel those of the developer. Both begin with preliminary analyses. Like the developer, the builder wants to be certain that there will be a market for the finished product. Accordingly, the astute builder will also be interested in learning as much as possible about local market conditions and can benefit from consulting Census Bureau publications and other library information sources.

The preliminary phase of the building process also includes drawing up the building design and engineering plans. Other steps in the building process include securing the necessary financing, constructing the building(s), and, finally, marketing the finished product.

Sometimes the same company handles both land development and building. Whether the operations are combined or separate, however, the phases most closely tied to library resources and research are the preliminary planning phase when economic and demographic information is being sought and the phase in which the finished project is about to be marketed to prospective buyers or lessees. Both are marketing research-oriented, and many of the sources described in chapter 7 will be useful.

Financing

Few purchasers of real estate, whether they are individuals or businesses, have the capital to purchase property outright. Most must borrow from banks, savings and loan associations, or other financial institutions. These institutions, in fact, comprise the third main type of real estate enterprise: organizations involved in the financing of real estate purchases.

Although many lending institutions and practices are covered at length in previous chapters, certain special characteristics of real estate financing are worth noting. First, most real estate financing is long term; home mortgage loans, for example, may be for 20, 25, or even 30 years. Second, real estate loans are typically made with the property itself as collateral. For this reason, such loans require that the property be evaluated by a professional appraiser so as to arrive at an objective estimate of its current market value. Finally, the amount and terms of credit available for real estate financing are based to a large extent on the state of the economy and general money market conditions. When, for example, money is tight, real estate financing, particularly for residential properties, is more difficult to obtain.

The mortgage loan is the most common form of real estate financing. A *mortgage* is a legal instrument that allows the borrower to pledge the real property as collateral to secure the debt with the lender. It consists of two separate documents: the mortgage agreement, also known as the deed of trust, which sets forth the terms of the loan and pledges the property as security; and the promissory note, or deed of trust note, in which the borrower is made personally responsible for the debt.

Although the number and types of mortgage loans have increased tremendously in recent years, the two most common are the amortized or fixed rate mortgage and the adjustable rate mortgage.

An *amortized loan* is one that is spread out over a period of time and repaid periodically in payments that include both principal and interest. The loan, in other words, is paid off gradually. The payment is a fixed amount, and interest has first claim on the disbursement. With each payment made the amount of interest owed is reduced and so the amount paid off the principal increases.

Loan amortization tables, schedules, or calculators are used to determine the size of the payments needed to repay a loan. A loan amortization table, or schedule, includes four main pieces of information: the amount of the loan, the rate of interest being charged, the length of time to maturity, and the amount of the periodic payments.

Since library users often request such information, an examination of the amortization table shown in figure 16.2 is in order. The table in figure 16.2, for example, shows the rates for a loan of $100.000 at 6.75 percent interest. The schedule is for monthly payments, and maturity is 15 years. This table was produced at http://www.hughchou.org/calc/mort .html. One can easily change mortgage amounts, years of the mortgage, and interest rates to see how much will be paid monthly. It must be noted that these tables do not include required insurance and property tax payments

Loan amortization schedules are also available at banks and thrift institutions, and most libraries include one or two in their business collections as well. Two representative print publications are listed below.

Estes, Jack. **Handbook of Loan Payment Tables.** New York: McGraw-Hill, 1976. 659p.

Although dated, the *Handbook of Loan Payment Tables* includes monthly amortization schedules for 329 interest rates from 5 to 25.5 percent, in increments of 8ths and 10ths of a percent. Terms are from 1 to 25 years in one-year increments, and then for 30, 35, and 40 years, and amounts covered in the *Handbook* range from $5 to $100,000. Many libraries still possess a copy in their collections.

Thorndike, David. **Thorndike Encyclopedia of Banking and Financial Tables.** 3rd ed. Boston: Warren, Gorham & Lamont, 1987. 1700p.

Also dated, the *Thorndike Encyclopedia of Banking and Financial Tables* contains a whole series of mortgage and real estate tables, including monthly and quarterly amortization schedules, constant annual percent tables, mortgage loan payment tables, percent paid off tables, and depreciation schedules.

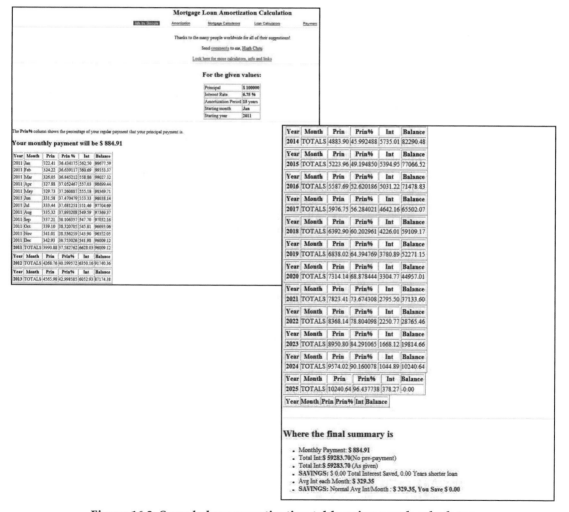

Figure 16.2. Data Entry form for loan amortization table using a web calculator.
Copyright © Hugh U. Chou, http://www.hughchou.org/hugh. Reprinted with permission

Figure 16.3. Sample loan amortization table using a web calculator,
Copyright © Hugh U. Chou, http://www.hughchou.org/hugh. Reprinted with permission

If the truth be told, books of amortization tables are now probably no longer a necessary purchase except perhaps as a backup for times when the Internet is not available for one reason or another, or if patrons prefer to use a printed resource instead of the Internet. There are dozens if not hundreds of web sites that will calculate a payment and display an amortization table given the inputs of principal, interest rate, number of payments per year, and number of years in the loan. Mortgage calculators range from those that do just the basic calculation of principal and interest to those that give you the option to account for extra payment of principal, include expected insurance and property taxes, and other embellishments. There are also mortgage calculators for your iPhone, iPad or Android-powered mobile device.

Listed in figure 16.4 are several free online calculators that can be used for mortgage computations.

Selected Mortgage calculators on the web	
Name	URL
Hugh Chou Mortgage Payment Table Calculator	http://www.hughchou.org/calc/flap.cgi
Bankrate.com	http://www.bankrate.com/calculators/mortgages/mortgage-calculator.aspx?ec_id=m1027724
Mortgage calculator list of calculator links	http://www.mortgagecalculator.com/calculatorshttp://www.mortgagecalculator.com/calculators/
Mortgage calculator	http://www.mortgagecalculator.org/
interest.com list of calculators	http://mortgages.interest.com/content/calculators/index.asp
interest.com calculator	http://mortgages.interest.com/content/calculators/mortgage_calculator.asp

Figure 16.4. Selected mortgage calculators available on the Web

Amortized mortgages are not the only types of mortgage loans that are made. Others are *variable rate* or *adjustable rate mortgages,* in which interest rates fluctuate within a specified range; *balloon mortgages,* in which payments are initially low and repayment of the principal is made in one lump sum at the date of maturity; and *flexible payment mortgages,* which enable borrowers to adjust their payments so that they will be less in the beginning and will become progressively greater, reflecting expected increases in the borrowers' incomes.

There are of course other forms of mortgages, but because of the financial (including home mortgages) crisis that started in 2008, there is a great deal of uncertainty how the mortgage financing industry will shake out. In July 2010 the Dodd-Frank Wall Street Reform and Consumer Protection Act was enacted as a partial response to the crisis. A great deal has been written and will continue to be written in the future about how the requirements of the law will change how a mortgage works.

Frequently points are attached to mortgage loans. In finance, a point is 1 percent of the amount of the loan. On a $50,000 loan, a point is $500; on a $100,000 loan, $1,000. Points are used in real estate financing to increase the return on loans.

Financing for the purchase of real estate is available from both private and public organizations. In the private sector, thrift institutions such as savings and loan associations have been important as sources of funds for the purchase of residential property, while commercial banks traditionally have provided commercial and industrial property loans. Since most commercial bank deposits come from checking rather than savings accounts, the emphasis is on short-term construction loans rather than on long-term mortgages. Life insurance companies also offer real estate financing, particularly for large-scale projects such as shopping centers, apartment complexes, and office buildings. Finally, two special organizations are involved in real estate financing. They are mortgage banking companies and mortgage brokers.

A *mortgage banking company* makes mortgage loans to borrowers and subsequently sells them as long-term investments to such institutional investors as life insurance companies, pension funds, savings institutions, and government agencies. The mortgage banking company handles the preliminaries: it assesses the creditworthiness of the borrower and the value of the property, prepares the necessary papers, and makes the loan. After it sells the mortgage, the mortgage banking company is usually retained by the purchaser to collect the monthly payments, handle additional paperwork, and deal with any borrower-related problems.

Mortgage brokers, in contrast, act as middlemen only. They neither lend money nor service the mortgages they help to arrange. Instead, they act as agents, bringing together prospective borrowers and lenders. In return, brokers are paid a fee, usually expressed in points, for each loan that they help to arrange.

In addition to the private organizations mentioned above, some federal government agencies are also either directly or indirectly involved in real estate financing. Although space does not permit consideration of all such agencies, two are particularly important to prospective home buyers: the Department of Veterans Affairs and the Federal Housing Administration.

The Department of Veterans Affairs (http://www.va.gov/) helps to finance home ownership by guaranteeing loans made by private lenders to eligible veterans. The Federal Housing Administration (FHA), a part of the Department of Housing and Urban Development (http://www.hud.gov/), insures mortgage loans made by private lenders against possible borrower default. By so doing, it lessens risk for private lenders and thus increases the supply of credit available for home financing. Veterans Administration– and Federal Housing Administration–insured loans are known respectively as VA and FHA loans; loans made by private lenders without government backing or insurance are called conventional loans.

Discussion of real estate financing to this point has focused on what is known as the *primary mortgage market,* consisting of lenders and borrowers directly involved in the financing and purchase of real estate. In addition to the primary market, however, there is an active *secondary mortgage market,* in which lenders sell existing mortgages to other investors. The secondary mortgage market helps to increase the amount of credit available for real estate loans in all parts of the country.

Three government or quasi-government agencies and one private corporation are actively involved in the secondary mortgage market. The oldest of these is the Federal National Mortgage Association, also known as the FNMA or "Fannie Mae" (http://www.fanniemae.com/). Established by the government in 1938, FNMA was rechartered as a private corporation in 1968 to provide secondary market support for the private residential mortgage market.

On September 6, 2008, Director James Lockhart of the Federal Housing Finance Agency (FHFA) appointed FHFA as conservator of Fannie Mae. In September 2008, we also entered into an agreement with the U.S. Department of Treasury that was most recently amended in December 2009. Under the agreement, Treasury will provide us with capital as needed to correct any net worth deficiencies that we record in any quarter through 2012. The agreement is intended to ensure that we are able to continue providing liquidity and stability to the housing and mortgage markets.[2]

Fannie Mae issues publicly traded stocks, bonds, and notes, and uses the funds from their sale to finance the purchase of FHA, VA, and conventional mortgage loans. FNMA encourages home ownership by buying more mortgages when money is tight, so that the original lenders can use the money from mortgage sales to issue new mortgage loans. It remains to be determined how if at all the Dodd-Frank legislation or future legislation related to the financial crisis will affect Fannie Mae.

The Government National Mortgage Association, also known as GNMA or "Ginnie Mae" (http://www.ginniemae.gov/), operates as a corporation within the Department of Housing and Urban Development. Ginnie Mae is known as much for what it does not do—make or purchase mortgages from mortgage lenders—as by what it does do: act as the guarantor of securities issued by approved lenders who participate in its programs.

Ginnie Mae guarantees Mortgage Backed Securities (MBS) originated by "approved" issuers (mortgage lenders who meet the requirements and are approved to issue Ginnie Mae MBS). In doing this, GNMA indirectly promotes home ownership. Each of Ginnie Mae's programs has its' own requirements (http://www.ginniemae.gov/guide/guidtoc.asp?Section=Issuers). In general, the MBS pass through to the investors' monthly payments of principal and interest on mortgaged property held in the pool. The MBS Programs' purpose is to increase the availability of mortgage credit by attracting new sources of funds for the mortgage market. Since its securities are backed by the full faith and credit of the U.S. government, the program has been successful in attracting both institutional and individual investors.

The Federal Home Loan Mortgage Corporation, also known as the FHLMC or "Freddie Mac" (http://www.freddiemac.com/), is a government-sponsored enterprise (GSE) chartered by Congress to stabilize the nation's residential mortgage markets and expand opportunities for homeownership and affordable rental housing.[3] It buys individual mortgages from savings and loan associations and banks that meet its requirements for loan applications and appraisal methods and that use standardized forms that it has developed. The loans are subsequently packaged into pools of several million dollars each and resold to institutional investors. Like Fannie Mae, Freddie Mac is currently under conservatorship that began September 6, 2008, but is continuing to operate. It again remains to be determined how if at all Freddie Mac will be affected by the Dodd-Frank legislation or future legislation related to the financial crisis.

The Mortgage Guaranty Insurance Corporation (MGIC) (http://www.mgic.com/) also buys and sells conventional loans. MGIC also sells home buyers mortgage insurance on their loan, which reduces or eliminates the loss to the lender should the borrower default. Unlike the FNMA, the GNMA, and the FHLMC, the MGIC has no direct ties to the federal government; it is a private corporation. It does, however, share a common purpose with the FNMA, GNMA, and FHLMC: it attracts investors who might not otherwise invest in mortgage loans.

In summary, the real estate industry consists of three main elements: marketing, land development and construction (production), and financing. Financing, as has been shown, consists not only of providing direct loans to borrowers but also of participating in the secondary mortgage market.

Government and Real Estate

Private ownership and control of real estate in this country is a right that is subject to certain government restrictions. Although private citizens have the right to own buildings and land, the government has certain property rights as well: taxation, police power, and eminent domain.

Property taxes are levied to help support community services and facilities such as roads, sewers, schools, and libraries. To encourage citizens to pay such taxes promptly and in full, the government has the power to seize any property for which taxes are delinquent and to sell it to recover the unpaid taxes. Property taxes are collected primarily at the local level local property tax rates and assessed value of real property are published in the *Issuer Financials* volume of the *Mergent* (Moody's) *Municipal & Government Manual*. Many cities, counties, and other taxing authorities also publish their local property tax rate online. One easy way to find the property tax rate for a given area is to do an Internet search using the name of the city, town, or county and the phrase "property tax rate."

Each state government has the right of police power, to enact and enforce laws and regulations for the common good. Such power can be exercised at the state level or delegated to local governments. Police power as it applies to real estate enables state and local governments to set building codes for minimum structural requirements for buildings, to decide what type of structures can or cannot be built by enacting planning and zoning ordinances, and to draw up other related regulations. These might, for example, include regulations relating to the maximum height of buildings or to the minimum distance houses must be set back from the street. Since the right of police power affects how land can be used, it has a significant impact on property values. Local zoning laws, for example, may decree that land in a certain area be excluded from commercial or industrial use and will thus affect the value of that land as well as the uses to which it can be put.

Another way government has "power" over property is eminent domain. Whenever the government or a public utility needs land for public use or for the construction of public facilities, it has the right to take ownership of privately held real estate. This right of eminent domain empowers the government to buy the property at fair market value whether or not its owner actually wants to sell it. Eminent domain laws vary state by state and have been a cause of much debate recently.

In addition to the activities tied to the rights of taxation, police power, and eminent domain, many federal, state, and local government agencies are involved with real estate. At the federal level, the Department of Housing and Urban Development (http://www.hud.gov/) is perhaps the best known of all such agencies.

The Department of Housing and Urban Development (HUD) was established in 1965 as the first cabinet-level department to oversee housing matters. It administers federal programs concerned with housing needs, fair housing opportunities, and community development. HUD also administers FHA mortgage insurance programs, facilitates construction and rehabilitation of rental units, and offers rent subsidy programs to low-income families. In addition, it oversees home buyer consumer protection and education programs and publications and supports neighborhood preservation and development programs. Many of the documents published by HUD are extremely useful to real estate researchers; some key titles are described later in this chapter.

Another important federal organization is the Federal Housing Finance Agency

(FHFA) (http://www.fhfa.gov/), which was created on July 30, 2008, when the president signed into law the Housing and Economic Recovery Act of 2008. The Act gave FHFA the authorities necessary to oversee vital components of—secondary mortgage markets—Fannie Mae, Freddie Mac, and the Federal Home Loan Banks. In addition, this law combined the staffs of the Office of Federal Housing Enterprise Oversight (OFHEO), the Federal Housing Finance Board (FHFB), and the GSE mission office at the Department of Housing and Urban Development (HUD). FHFA's mission is to provide effective supervision, regulation, and housing mission oversight of Fannie Mae, Freddie Mac, and the Federal Home Loan Banks to promote their safety and soundness, support housing finance and affordable housing, and support a stable and liquid mortgage market.

The Federal Financial Institutions Examination Council (FFIEC) (http://www.ffiec.gov) is a formal interagency body empowered to prescribe uniform principles, standards, and report forms for the federal examination of financial institutions by the various regulatory organizations of the U.S. government, including the Board of Governors of the Federal Reserve System (FRB), the Federal Deposit Insurance Corporation (FDIC), the National Credit Union Administration (NCUA), the Office of the Comptroller of the Currency (OCC), and the Office of Thrift Supervision (OTS). The FFIEC also makes recommendations to promote uniformity in the supervision of financial institutions.

The Council was also given additional statutory responsibilities by section 340 of the Housing and Community Development Act of 1980 to facilitate public access to, and the aggregation by census tract and each metropolitan statistical area (MSA) of the data that depository institutions must disclose under the Home Mortgage Disclosure Act of 1975 (HMDA) (http://www.ffiec.gov/hmda) and the Community Reinvestment Act of 1977 (CRA) (http://www.ffiec.gov/cra).

The CRA is intended to encourage depository institutions to help meet the credit needs of the communities in which they operate. Information is available on the regulation and its interpretation and information on of CRA examinations.

The HMDA requires depository institutions and certain for-profit, nondepository institutions to collect, report to federal agencies, and disclose to the public data about originations and purchases of home mortgage loans for home purchase, home refinancing, and home improvement. It also collects data on loan applications that do not result in originations—for example, loan applications that are denied or withdrawn.

Once the CRA and HMDA data are final, the FFIEC posts the data and the various data products to the FFIEC web site (http://www.ffiec.gov/reports.htm). HMDA data for a new year generally become available by September of the year following the calendar year (CY) of the data. Detailed descriptions of HMDA publications can be found at http://www.ffiec.gov/hmda/hmdaproducts.htm. Detailed descriptions CRA publications can be found at http://www.ffiec.gov/cra/craproducts.htm.

Other federal departments and agencies are also involved in real estate. The Departments of Agriculture (http://www.usda.gov/) and the Interior (http://www.doi.gov/), for example, include agencies responsible for the nation's system of forests and parks, and the GNMA and the FNMA, as stated, are active participants in the secondary mortgage market. Other agencies are less directly involved or focus on some narrower aspect of real estate activity. Researchers seeking information on government involvement in real estate are advised to begin by consulting the *Catalog of U.S. Government Publications* (http://catalog.gpo.gov) or by using a web browser such as http://www.google.com/unclesam.

State and local governments are similarly involved in promoting and protecting the public interest in real estate. Most states have agencies responsible for housing and land development programs, and many local governments have planning boards and related agencies. Much of this information is now available on the Web. One good place to start is the web page for each state's Department of Revenue.

Real Estate Information Sources

The literature of real estate ranges from pamphlets for prospective home buyers to valuation manuals for real estate practitioners. Some sources, especially databases, are so specialized that they are not widely available. Other, more frequently consulted titles can be found in many different library settings, and many others are available via the Web. The remainder of this chapter focuses on dictionaries, encyclopedias, handbooks, directories, government documents, and statistical compilations in all available formats that fall into this second category.

Dictionaries, Encyclopedias, and Handbooks

A wide range of general and specialized real estate dictionaries is available. Although space does not permit consideration of all of them, the following are typical.

Shim, Jae K., Joel G. Siegel, and Stephen W. Hartman. **Dictionary of Real Estate**. New York: John Wiley, 1996. 307p.

Useful for both practitioners and laypeople, the *Dictionary of Real Estate* defines over 3,000 terms in real estate and allied fields. In addition to standard real estate vocabulary, the *Dictionary* includes abbreviations and acronyms that are adequately cross-referenced. Tables commonly used in real estate transactions are also featured, including monthly installment loan payments. Especially useful is the inclusion of diagrams and examples.

Cox, Barbara, Jerry Cox, and David Silver-Westrick. **Prentice Hall Dictionary of Real Estate.** Upper Saddle River, NJ: Prentice Hall, 2001. 314p.

Although the *Prentice Hall Dictionary* and the *Dictionary of Real Estate* have many features and terms in common, there are enough differences that most libraries will hold both titles. Some terms are handled in detail in one book but not in the other, and although both contain tables and diagrams, these do not fully overlap. The appendixes in the *Prentice Hall Dictionary* contain a full diagram of the "Anatomy of a House" and a "Monthly Payment Matrix for a 30-Year Amortizing Loan," as well as instructions for various software packages; those in the *Dictionary of Real Estate* include "corner influence" and "present value of a dollar" tables.

Fisher, Jeffrey D., Robert S. Martin, and Paige Mosbaugh. **Language of Real Estate Appraisal.** Chicago: Real Estate Education, 1991. 290p.

The *Language of Real Estate Appraisal* is intended primarily for appraisers and other real estate professionals. Although the focus is on appraisal, terms in the areas of finance, statistics, and energy are also included. Definitions are generally brief, ranging in length from a sentence or two to an entire page. In addition, lists of acronyms, symbols, and abbreviations are included, along with tables for monthly and annual compounding. It features descriptions of and formulas for subdivision analysis, depreciation methods, and valuation models.

There are dozens of dictionaries available on the Internet, include some specifically for the real estate industry. These can be found using any web search engine, but the three listed below are especially useful.

Investopedia ULC, **List of Real Estate Terms.** 2011. http://www.investopedia.com/

categories/realestate.asp (accessed April 1, 2011)

Online Real Estate Dictionary Corp. **Real Estate Dictionary** Online Real Estate Dictionary Corp. 2005–2011. http://www.realestatedictionary.org/ (accessed April 1, 2011)

WebFinance Inc. **investorwords.com.** 1997–2011. http://www.investorwords.com/cgi-bin/bysubject.cgi?18 (accessed April 1, 2011)

All three dictionaries contain a short description of most real estate terms. Many of the definitions contain links to related terms for easier understanding. *Investorwords.com* also has a list of "see also" terms at the end of each definition. For libraries without a strong interest in real estate, these may provide adequate information.

Arnold, Alvin L., with the assistance of Eric Stevenson, Marshall E. Tracht, and Paul D. Lapides. **The Arnold Encyclopedia of Real Estate.** 2nd ed. New York: John Wiley, 1993. 610p.

The Arnold Encyclopedia of Real Estate lists, defines, and explains, in plain English, basic concepts in real estate, law, banking, and taxation. Arrangement is alphabetical, and the entries range in length from a sentence or two to several pages. Most, however, are one or two paragraphs long. Appended is a list of abbreviations.

Abbott, Damien. **Encyclopedia of Real Estate Terms.** 2nd ed. London: Delta Alpha Publishing, 2000. 1430p.

Roark, Bill, and Ryan Roark. **Concise Encyclopedia of Real Estate Business Terms.** New York: Best Business Books. 2006. 291p.

The *Encyclopedia of Real Estate Terms* is an excellent guide to the meaning, use, and significance of over 8,000 real estate words and phrases. This edition is weighted to the North American market, but this is compensated for by reference to materials from Europe, Australia, Canada, Hong Kong, India, and New Zealand.. These references include case law and bibliographic references. The inside cover contains an extremely useful "Guide to the Encyclopedia," which shows the layout of individual entries. The appendixes contain a wide array of additional information, including a 900-book bibliography listed by area; selected codes and laws; a listing of real estate organizations, complete with web locations; tables of measurement; financial formulae; and a nine-page listing of acronyms. This is probably the most comprehensive, fairly inexpensive one-volume work available in this field.

The *Concise Encyclopedia* is a smaller edition of the *Encyclopedia of Real Estate Terms* that contains only about 300 words in common use. The entries are typically a few paragraphs in length.

Real estate handbooks are commonplace. For general information, the following cover different areas and complement each other.

Jack C. Harris, Jack P. Friedman, and Barry A. Diskin. **Barron's Real Estate Handbook.** 7th ed. Hauppauge, NY: Barron's Educational Series, 2009. 777p.

Barron's Real Estate Handbook is a compilation of information, including the definitions of over 2,000 terms, some with illustrations; "How to Read an Appraisal Report"; federal legislation; information on REITs; and a collection of useful mortgage and measurement tables.

Irwin, Robert, ed.-in-chief. **The McGraw-Hill Real Estate Handbook.** 2nd ed. New York: McGraw-Hill, 1993. 641p.

The McGraw-Hill Real Estate Handbook presents 31 chapters, written by industry experts, classed under broad subject headings: Real Estate Taxation, Real Estate Business, Finance, and Buying and Selling. The *Handbook* is indexed.

Other guides focus on specific segments of the real estate industry. One area in which interest is particularly strong is the purchase and sale of real estate for investment.

Alvin, Arnold. **Real Estate Investor's Deskbook.** 3rd edition. St. Paul: West Group, 2002. Various paging.

Designed for use by both advisors and prospective investors, the *Real Estate Investor's Deskbook* is a comprehensive guide to all aspects of the process of investing in real estate. It is divided into 13 chapters that are further divided into sections. The chapters cover the strategies and techniques of acquiring, financing, and disposing of real estate. This is one of the most detailed sources available for investors and will probably be found in most libraries that cater to patrons interested in personal investment or to advisors who are helping them. The deskbook is published as a loose-leaf and is updated as needed by supplemental and substitute pages. It is also available as an electronic resource through WestLaw.

McLean, Andrew James, and Gary W. Eldred. **Investing in Real Estate.** 3rd ed. New York: John Wiley, 2001. 311p.

Investing in Real Estate is intended for use by prospective investors rather than seasoned professionals. Written for the layperson, it discusses real estate as an investment medium and describes how to find properties, assess worth, and improve the value. Techniques for the analysis of specific investments are explained, and tax information is included.

Directories

A wide range of general and specialized directories is available. This section lists and describes some of the most widely used specialized titles and points to web sites that list general Realtors.

U.S. Real Estate Register. Wilmington, MA: Barry Inc., 1985–. Annual.

The *U.S. Real Estate Register* is designed for the professional to be able to quickly find services and properties. The *Register* is divided into four sections to make information conveniently accessible. Section One alphabetically lists the largest 1,200 companies along with contact information; Section Two is an alphabetical listing of 9,000 companies involved in all aspects of real estate from finance to utilities; Section Three lists currently available commercial and industrial properties that are for sale or lease; and Section Four is a classified index by state of all the listings.

Nelson's Directory of Institutional Real Estate. Port Chester, NY: Nelson Publications, 1992–2005. Annual. Ceased publication in 2005.

Nelson's Directory of Institutional Real Estate, and slightly varying titles, ceased as a print publication in 2005, had separate sections covering real estate investment management firms, real estate service firms, pension funds and foundations that invest in real estate, the 2,000 largest corporations with active real estate operations, and real estate investment trusts. Each entry includes an overview of the firm, names of key executives, and contact information. It is searchable geographically and by type of service offered. Coverage is mainly for the United States, but there are some entries for foreign entities. The electronic service that supposedly "replaced" it does not appear to cover real estate as heavily.

There are many web directories of realty and appraisal companies. One aimed at individuals and corporations or other organizations contemplating relocation

in another part of the country is maintained by the Worldwide ERC at http://www
.worldwideerc.org/. Along with other information there is an online directory at http://
www.worldwideerc.org/Directory/. One can search by geography to find both agents
and appraisers who are members of ERC. Also featured is a listing of relocation service
companies by area of specialization. All listings include full contact information.

Other links to realty companies and agents can be found on the web at most major
real estate sites. Examples are REALTOR.com at http://www.realtor.com/ and HomeGain.
com at http://www.homegain.com.

Periodicals and Periodical Indexes

The diversity of the real estate industry is reflected in such periodicals as *Appraisal
Journal, Builder, Constructor, Journal of Real Estate Finance and Economics,* and *Journal of Real
Estate Portfolio Management.* Although a comprehensive collection of such serials is rare
in all but the largest or most specialized business collections, some real estate periodicals
are more commonly held. They include the following titles.

Real Estate Forum. New York: Real Estate Forum, 1946–. Monthly

Real Estate Forum is a commercially published trade magazine that focuses primarily
on recent developments in commercial and industrial real estate. A typical issue contains
one or two articles; recent issues, for example, have included articles on the corporate
sector and recovery. The bulk of each issue, however, consists of brief announcements
in such regular sections as "Market Pulse," "National Leasing," "Global Digest," and
"Finance." The February issue contains its annual "Deals of the Year," which examines
major sales and leases across the country and identifies residential, commercial, and
industrial markets that are unusually strong or weak.

Real Estate Review. St. Paul, MN: West Information Publishing Group, 1971–. Quarterly.

While *Real Estate Forum* is essentially a newsmagazine, *Real Estate Review* contains
more scholarly articles on a wide range of topics. Recent issues have included articles
on such subjects as liquidity risk, conservation easements, and damage valuations.
Contributors include real estate executives and practitioners as well as scholars, and the
emphasis is on practical information and problem solving.

National Real Estate Investor. Metcalf, KS: Primedia Business Magazines and Media,
1959–. Monthly, with an additional issue in July.

The *National Real Estate Investor* (http:www.nreionline.com) is another trade
publication. It covers construction, development, finance, investment, and management,
and combines news and announcements with articles. The magazine is divided into three
major sections: the first is "Developments," which provides the latest news; the second
section is more substantive and contains articles on the industry, the major players, and
emerging trends. Finally, the third section, "Strategies," covers case studies, noteworthy
problems, and regulatory issues. The web site features the "Best of the Best," a set of
regularly conducted surveys including "Industrial Trends," "Top Shopping Center
Owners," and "Office Trends."

Some periodicals are particularly useful for the statistics they contain. Representative
of these is *U.S. Housing Markets.*

U.S. Housing Markets. Detroit, MI: Hanley-Wood Market Intelligence , 1966–. Every
two months.

U.S. Housing Markets is issued in two parts, which can be subscribed to separately.
The first part is the *Flash Report,* in which is published permit detail and history on all

330+ metropolitan areas approximately six weeks after the quarter ends. The second part is the *National Review,* published 10 weeks after the quarter ends, which surveys housing for all metropolitan areas in nine regions and the United States as a whole. Data on private housing permits for single- and multifamily units are provided, along with additional information on multifamily housing units completed or under construction, rental vacancy rates, household formats, and U.S. households by age groups. Also included are selected local data on total permits issued and listings of the busiest builders. Sample pages of each part are available at http://www.hwmarketintelligence .com/v4/reports_ushm.asp.

Many real estate periodicals are indexed and available full text in standard sources such as *Business Source Premier, Business Source Elite,* and *ABI/INFORM Global.* This makes it easier for even some of the smallest libraries to provide information in such specialized areas.

Government Documents/Resources

Federal real estate publications are rich and diverse. They include hearings on real estate development and financing, GNMA manuals for institutional investors, reports on new housing technology, statistics, and market analysis. The field is so broad that it is all but impossible to list even selectively documents likely to interest real estate brokers and salespeople, developers, builders, financiers, and investors. Each library will want to collect documents or provide web links to sources that reflect its users' interests and needs.

One area in which there is widespread interest in most public and many academic libraries is the purchase of residential property.

U.S. Department of Housing and Urban Development. **100 Questions & Answers about Buying a New Home.** http://www.hud.gov/offices/hsg/sfh/buying/buyhm .cfm#Dear (accessed April 5, 2011)

100 Questions & Answers about Buying a New Home is a guide for prospective homeowners. Sections discuss the advantages and disadvantages of owning a home, selecting a house, purchase contracts, home financing, the closing process, money management, and mortgage insurance. A glossary is appended. Although some will find the language and information simplistic, for many first-time buyers the simple layout and question-and-answer format are ideal.

U.S. Department of Housing and Urban Development. **Buying Your Home: Settlement Costs and Information.** http://portal.hud.gov/hudportal/HUD?src=/program_ offices/housing/ramh/res/sfhrestc (accessed April 5, 2011)

Buying Your Home contains information on home buying, home financing, and the settlement process. Information includes items such as "Shopping for a Loan" and "Specific Settlement Costs." This booklet is available in PDF format or MS Word, so those libraries that prefer can have a print copy available for patrons.

U.S. Department of Housing and Urban Development **I Want to . . . Buy a Home.** http:// portal.hud.gov/hudportal/HUD?src=/i_want_to/buy_a_home (accessed April 5, 2011)

I Want to . . . Buy a Home sections on "How Much You Can Afford," "Buying vs. Renting," "Knowing Your Rights, and others offer great insights and information for especially for first-time home buyers.

U.S. Federal Reserve Board. **Consumer Handbook on Adjustable Rate Mortgages.** n.d. http://www.federalreserve.gov/pubs/arms/arms_english.htm (accessed April 5, 2011)

For those seeking to understand the basics of an ARM, a good source is the *Consumer Handbook*, a 27-page booklet, which will answer questions on what exactly they are and how they operate. Included are a mortgage checklist and a glossary.

Statistics

Statistics concerned with all aspects of real estate are abundant. They include data gathered and published by a wide range of sources and provide information on construction and sale of housing, growth of shopping centers and industrial plants, operating costs, and vacancy rates. In addition, general demographic, social, and economic statistics are of direct importance to real estate operations of all kinds. Although space does not permit coverage of every relevant statistic, some of the most important ones are discussed below.

On the most basic level, most people pay rent or monthly mortgage loan installments. Costs for housing are, in fact, one of the major components of the consumer price index, which presents data on rent, owners' equivalent rent, homeowners' or tenants' insurance, and maintenance and repair. Such information is included in the CPI *Detailed Report* and the *Inter-City Cost of Living Index*, both of which are described in chapter 6.

Data on construction and building costs are also compiled and reported. The information compiled by the government is issued in a *Value of Construction Put in Place*, now available at http://www.census.gov/const/www/totpage.html (see figure 16.5). Links are available to monthly and annual data on residential and nonresidential real estate as well as public utilities and farm construction. Statistics are downloadable as spreadsheets or as PDF files.

Value of Construction Put in Place - Seasonally Adjusted Annual Rate
(Millions of dollars. Details may not add to totals due to rounding.)

Type of Construction:	Mar 2011[p]	Feb 2011[r]	Jan 2011[r]	Dec 2010	Nov 2010	Mar 2010	Percent change Mar 2011 from - Feb 2011	Mar 2010
Total Public Construction[2]	292,788	292,803	296,889	297,852	306,742	299,604	0.1	-2.3
Residential	8,692	8,963	9,671	9,355	10,488	8,953	-3.0	-2.9
Nonresidential	284,096	283,841	287,218	288,496	296,254	290,651	0.2	-2.3
Office	11,995	11,749	12,055	11,663	12,864	13,457	2.1	-10.9
Commercial	3,172	3,196	3,180	2,917	3,096	2,739	-0.8	15.8
Health care	10,337	10,040	10,398	9,839	10,023	9,214	3.0	12.2
Educational	68,463	68,137	69,938	68,653	70,010	74,027	0.5	-7.5
Public safety	10,658	10,629	10,124	9,909	10,682	12,625	0.3	-15.6
Amusement and recreation	10,344	10,321	10,070	10,457	10,989	9,722	0.2	6.4
Transportation	30,530	29,845	29,533	29,479	29,075	34,358	2.3	-11.1
Power	11,479	12,032	11,969	14,497	13,237	10,198	-4.6	12.6
Highway and street	82,878	82,420	83,593	84,335	87,097	79,000	0.6	4.9
Sewage and waste disposal	22,301	22,700	23,207	24,266	24,973	24,208	-1.8	-7.9
Water supply	13,971	14,306	15,159	14,624	15,199	14,098	-2.3	-0.9
Conservation and development	6,708	7,132	6,871	6,504	7,803	6,094	-5.9	10.1

[p]Preliminary [r]Revised

[1]Includes the following categories of private construction not shown separately:
public safety, highway and street, sewage and waste disposal, water supply, and conservation and development.

[2]Includes the following categories of public construction not shown separately:
lodging, religious, communication, and manufacturing.

Figure 16.5. Value of Construction Put in Place.
Reproduced from http://www.census.gov/const/www/totpage.html

There are several major construction cost indexes, some produced by the government, others by private organizations. The Census Bureau, for example, issues the *Index of New One-Family Houses* (http://www.census.gov/const/price_deflator_cust.xls). The Federal Highway Administration publishes indexes relating to highway construction (http://

www.fhwa.dot.gov/ohim/nhcci/index.cfm), and the Department of the Interior issues the *Bureau of Reclamation Construction Cost Trends* (http://www.usbr.gov/pmts/estimate/cost_trend.html), which measures the costs of constructing dams and reclamation projects sponsored by the department. The Federal Energy Regulatory Commission (FERC) issues a Federal Energy Regulatory *Commission Pipeline Index* (http://www.ferc.gov/industries/oil/gen-info/pipeline-index.asp), which presents data on construction costs reported by pipeline companies regulated by the commission.

Some of the most widely cited indexes are issued by private sources. Key among these are the *Boeckh Indexes,* which cover 11 building types in 213 cities throughout the United States and 53 cities in Canada. It has costs for 115 elements in each location. These consist of 19 building trades, 89 materials, and 7 tax and insurance elements. The *Engineering News-Record* (http://www.enr.com/), a trade paper for the construction industry, publishes national cost indexes for construction and building, which are available to subscribers in the "Economics" section of their web site. Other sources are the *Turner Building Cost Index* (http://www.turnerconstruction.com/corporate/content .asp?d=20) and the *Handy-Whitman Indexes,* which present building costs for reinforced concrete buildings, gas plants, and electric light and power plants. Most of the indexes described are published annually on the Web by the U.S. Census Bureau at (http://www .census.gov/pub/const/C30/annindex.pdf) file is there but it is dated (see figure 16.6).

Other indexes supply information on industrial vacancies and office vacancies. These are compiled by CB Richard Ellis (http://www.cbre.com/EN/Pages/default.aspx). Included in the free reports are metropolitan downtown suburban areas with the highest and lowest vacancy rates and the methodology for compiling the index. The reports are available at http://www.cbre.com/EN/Research/pages/globalreports.aspx.

The most detailed and comprehensive statistics on the construction and housing industries are those published by the U.S. Census Bureau. Such data include a series of monthly, quarterly, and annual surveys. These are available only in electronic format. A sample listing is provided in figures 16.7 and 16.8.

Annual Construction Cost Indexes (1996 = 100)

Year	U.S. Census Bureau One Family		Turner	Federal Hghwy Adm Composite	Bureau of Reclamation	Handy Whitman Building	Handy Whitman Electric	Handy Whitman Gas	Handy Whitman Water	C.A. Turner Telephone	Engineering News Record Buildings	Engineering News Record Construction
	Fixed-Weighted	Price Deflator										
1964	18.0	18.0	18	19.7	20	20	19	21	19	29	19.1	16.6
1965	18.6	18.6	19	20.5	21	20	19	21	20	30	19.6	17.3
1966	19.5	19.5	19	21.5	21	21	20	22	20	32	20.3	18.1
1967	20.1	20.2	20	22.5	22	21	21	22	21	33	21.0	19.0
1968	21.3	21.2	21	25.3	23	22	22	23	22	34	22.5	20.5
1969	22.6	22.6	23	28.5	24	24	23	24	23	36	24.7	22.6
1970	23.2	23.2	26	30.2	26	26	24	25	25	39	26.1	24.6
1971	24.5	24.5	29	31.5	28	28	26	28	28	40	29.6	28.1
1972	26.2	26.3	30	31.6	31	31	28	30	31	41	32.7	31.2
1973	28.8	28.8	32	34.8	32	34	30	31	33	44	35.5	33.7
1974	31.7	31.7	38	47.5	36	41	36	35	39	51	37.6	35.9
1975	34.5	34.5	39	47.6	42	45	42	40	43	53	40.8	39.3
1976	36.7	36.7	40	46.1	45	46	44	43	45	56	44.5	42.7
1977	41.1	40.6	41	49.0	48	49	47	47	48	59	48.2	45.8
1978	46.2	46.1	44	58.0	51	53	50	51	52	63	52.2	49.4
1979	52.1	51.7	49	70.1	56	59	55	55	57	70	56.8	53.4
1980	58.0	57.0	54	79.7	62	66	60	60	64	79	60.6	57.6
1981	62.1	61.0	60	77.2	68	69	66	66	68	80	65.5	62.9
1982	63.3	62.8	64	72.5	72	69	69	71	70	82	69.7	68.0
1983	65.1	64.5	68	71.8	73	71	71	73	72	79	74.4	72.3
1984	68.1	67.0	71	75.9	74	74	73	76	75	76	75.5	73.7
1985	69.8	68.3	74	83.6	75	76	74	75	76	77	75.8	74.6
1986	73.4	71.4	76	82.9	76	78	74	73	78	76	77.5	76.4
1987	76.8	74.7	79	82.0	77	79	75	75	79	77	79.3	78.4
1988	79.5	77.7	82	87.4	79	82	80	80	81	78	81.1	80.4
1989	82.2	80.8	84	88.3	82	84	84	84	84	85	82.2	82.1
1990	84.6	83.4	87	88.9	85	85	86	86	85	87	84.4	84.2
1991	84.8	84.1	89	88.1	88	83	88	87	85	87	85.9	86.0
1992	85.8	85.6	89	86.1	89	84	89	89	87	87	88.5	88.7
1993	90.0	90.0	91	88.8	91	89	92	91	89	89	93.5	92.7
1994	94.1	94.0	94	94.3	94	94	95	97	95	90	97.1	96.2
1995	98.1	98.1	97	99.8	98	97	98	99	98	96	97.1	97.3
1996	100.0	100.0	100	100.0	100	100	100	100	100	100	100.0	100.0
1997	102.9	102.9	104	107.5	103	103	102	102	102	102	105.0	103.6
1998	105.6	105.6	109	105.2	105	104	104	104	104	102	105.8	105.3
1999	110.4	110.4	113	111.9	107	107	105	107	107	101	107.9	107.8
2000	115.4	115.5	118	119.3	111	110	109	111	112	103	110.5	110.7
2001	121.2	121.3	121	118.7	112	114	113	114	116	106	111.6	112.7
2002	124.4	124.4	123	121.2	114	116	116	116	120	108	113.1	116.3

Source: U.S. Census Bureau
Construction Expenditures Branch
Manufacturing & Construction Div.
Washington, DC 20233-6916

Annual Construction Cost Indexes as Reported by or Computed from Sources

Year	Fixed-Weighted (1996=100)	Price Deflator (1996=100)	Turner (1967=100)	Federal Hwy Adm. Composite (1987=100)	Bureau of Reclamation (1977=100)	Handy Whitman Building (1973=100)	Handy Whitman Electric (1973=100)	Handy Whitman Gas (1973=100)	Handy Whitman Water (1973=100)	C.A. Turner Telephone (1972-3=100)	Engineering News Record Buildings (1913=100)	Engineering News Record Construction (1913=100)
1964	18.0	18.0	91	24.0	42	58.3	63.0	67.3	58.0	70.3	612.0	936.0
1965	18.6	18.6	94	25.0	44	59.5	65.0	68.5	59.2	73.3	627.0	971.0
1966	19.5	19.5	97	26.2	44	61.1	66.7	70.0	61.0	76.8	650.0	1019.0
1967	20.1	20.2	100	27.4	46	63.3	69.3	71.7	62.8	79.9	672.0	1070.0
1968	21.3	21.2	106	30.9	48	66.7	72.2	73.7	66.0	83.0	721.0	1155.0
1969	22.6	22.6	117	34.8	51	71.6	76.3	77.2	71.0	86.6	790.0	1269.0
1970	23.2	23.2	129	36.8	55	76.1	81.8	82.3	76.2	94.6	836.0	1381.0
1971	24.5	24.5	144	38.4	59	84.0	88.5	89.3	84.0	96.1	948.0	1581.0
1972	26.3	26.3	153	38.6	64	91.3	93.7	95.5	92.3	98.8	1048.0	1753.0
1973	28.8	28.8	163	42.5	67	100.0	100.0	100.0	100.0	106.1	1138.0	1895.0
1974	31.7	31.7	190	57.9	76	120.8	119.4	114.0	117.4	123.2	1204.0	2020.0
1975	34.5	34.5	198	58.1	88	134.3	139.4	130.6	130.1	128.5	1306.0	2212.0
1976	36.7	36.7	202	56.3	94	137.1	148.5	140.7	135.1	135.0	1425.1	2401.1
1977	41.1	40.6	209	59.8	100	144.4	158.6	151.1	143.9	143.6	1544.5	2575.8
1978	46.2	46.1	222	70.7	106	158.1	168.1	165.0	157.4	152.4	1673.5	2776.0
1979	52.2	51.7	246	85.5	117	175.4	184.5	178.6	173.7	170.7	1819.1	3002.6
1980	58.0	57.0	273	97.2	130	195.0	201.5	193.5	192.8	191.1	1941.4	3237.1
1981	62.1	61.0	301	94.2	142	204.9	219.9	215.1	205.2	195.0	2097.2	3534.9
1982	63.3	62.8	325	88.5	150	205.0	232.3	230.7	211.4	198.7	2233.5	3825.1
1983	65.1	64.5	342	87.6	152	210.3	239.3	237.8	218.3	191.8	2384.0	4066.3
1984	68.1	66.9	360	92.6	154	220.2	244.5	245.0	225.8	184.6	2417.3	4145.7
1985	69.8	68.3	374	102.0	157	226.4	247.3	244.0	230.9	188.4	2427.8	4195.0
1986	73.4	71.4	384	101.1	159	231.0	249.5	237.4	235.2	185.8	2483.0	4295.0
1987	76.8	74.7	397	100.0	161	234.8	253.1	244.1	239.0	188.7	2541.3	4406.4
1988	79.5	77.7	412	106.6	166	243.4	270.1	259.1	246.4	189.0	2598.4	4519.4
1989	82.2	80.8	426	107.7	172	250.6	281.6	271.4	254.0	206.0	2634.0	4615.0
1990	84.6	83.4	441	108.5	178	253.1	290.0	277.0	258.4	210.4	2702.2	4731.9
1991	84.8	84.1	448	107.5	184	247.3	294.5	283.1	258.2	212.4	2751.3	4835.2
1992	85.8	85.8	450	105.1	186	251.1	298.5	288.2	263.2	212.0	2833.6	4984.8
1993	90.0	90.0	460	108.3	191	264.6	307.6	295.9	275.0	215.5	2995.9	5210.4
1994	94.1	94.2	474	115.1	197	280.6	319.1	313.1	287.9	219.2	3110.7	5407.6
1995	98.1	98.2	492	121.8	205	288.0	330.0	320.1	295.9	233.0	3111.5	5471.2
1996	100.0	100.0	505	122.0	209	297.4	335.7	323.6	302.4	243.2	3203.2	5622.2
1997	102.9	102.9	525	131.1	217	305.8	342.0	331.5	309.5	248.6	3364.4	5825.1
1998	105.6	105.6	549	128.4	219	310.0	349.1	337.1	314.9	248.5	3390.5	5920.4
1999	110.4	110.4	570	137.5	223	317.7	352.3	345.7	322.2	245.2	3455.6	6060.0
2000	115.4	115.5	595	145.6	231	328.6	366.5	360.8	339.0	250.1	3539.5	6221.2
2001	121.2	121.3	613	144.8	235	338.0	377.9	367.6	352.2	257.6	3573.6	6334.0
2002	124.4	124.4	619	147.9	239	344.4	389.2	375.1	362.8	261.8	3623.2	6537.9
Factor	1.000	1.000	5.048	1.220	2.090	2.974	3.357	3.236	3.024	2.432	32.032	56.222

Source: U.S. Census Bureau
Construction Expenditures Branch
Manufacturing & Construction Div.
Washington, DC 20233-6916

Figure 16.6. Annual Construction Cost Indexes.
Reproduced from http://www.census.gov/pub/const/C30/annindex.pdf

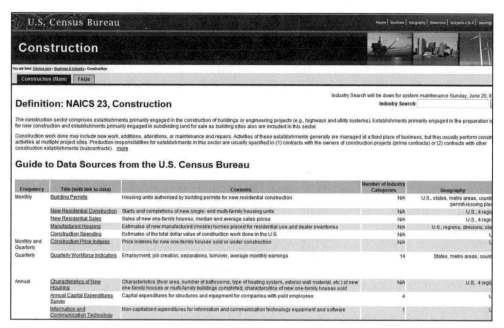

Figure 16.7. Sample listing of construction reports,
available at http://www.census.gov/econ/construction.html (accessed April 5, 2011)

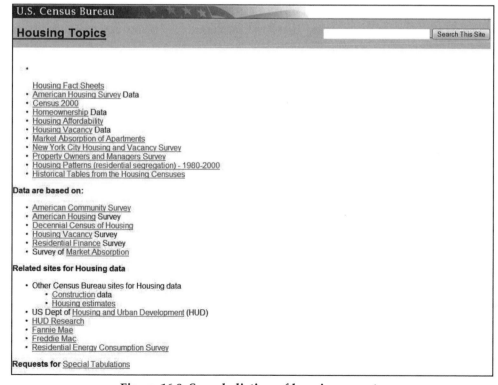

Figure 16.8. Sample listing of housing reports,
available at http://www.census.gov/hhes/www/housing.html (accessed April 5, 2011)

U.S. Department of Commerce. Bureau of the Census. **Factfinder for the Nation.** July 2000. http://www.census.gov/prod/2000pubs/cff-9.pdf (accessed April 3, 2011)

The *Factfinder for the Nation*, a free Census Bureau guide, lists and briefly describes construction reports published by the Bureau and the type of information included. This resource is a bit dated as it has data from the 2000 Census, but it is still available and may have uses in historical research.

U.S. Department of Commerce. Bureau of the Census. **Economic Census. Construction.** Washington, DC: Government Printing Office. Quinquennial, taken in years ending in 2 and 7.

The Economic Census (http://www.census.gov/econ/census07/) information enumerates construction establishments that operate as general and special trade contractors, builders, and land subdividers and developers. It consists primarily of two main series, an *Industry Series*, which includes reports on different construction industries, and the *Geographic Area Series*, which presents data for selected metropolitan areas, all 50 states, nine census divisions, and the United States as a whole. While *American FactFinder* (http://factfinder.census.gov/servlet/DatasetMainPageServlet?_program=ECN&_submenuId=datasets_4&_lang=en) is the sole issuing point for Economic Census 2007 data, it also has data from the 1997 and 2002 Economic Censuses.

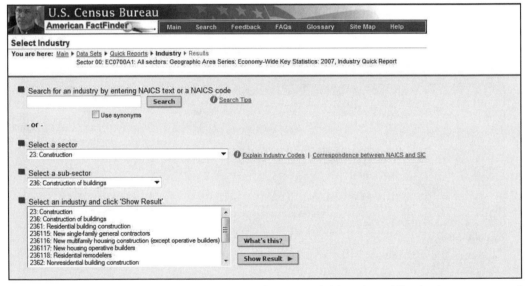

Figure 16.9. *Quick Report for Industry* **entry form,** available at http://factfinder.census.gov/servlet/IQRSelectIndustryServlet?ds_name=EC0700A1&_lang=en&_ts=320162836537

Once a sector, for example construction, has been chosen, the next step is to choose a sub-sector and finally an industry, The report that then appears contains industry and financial data for the industry segment being researched. This step-by-step approach makes it easy for even a novice researcher or librarian to find needed data.

Most libraries can now provide access to the complete *Economic Census* and the various construction reports and statistics, as these are freely available on the Web, but quick access to many of the statistics is still available using the *Statistical Abstract of the United States*.

The Census Bureau also issues a series of statistical publications relating to housing. Key among these are the *Census of Population and Housing, Current Housing Reports*, and the *American Housing Survey.*

U.S. Dept. of Commerce. **Census of Population and Housing.** Washington, DC: Government Printing Office, 1790–. Decennial. http://www.census.gov/prod/www/abs/decennial (accessed April 4, 2011)

Every 10 years, the Bureau of the Census collects detailed demographic and economic information about U.S. inhabitants and their dwellings. This decennial *Census* (http://www.census.gov/) presents housing and occupancy information. Both general and detailed housing characteristics are provided, supplemented by subject reports such as the *Survey of Market Absorption* (http://www.census.gov/hhes/www/soma.html), *Housing Vacancies and Home Ownership* (http://www.census.gov/hhes/www/hvs.html), and *Housing Affordability* (http://www.census.gov/hhes/www/housing/hsgaffrd/hsgaffrd.html). By using the *Census* and the reports, researchers can obtain valuable information about the physical and financial characteristics of housing units. They can, for example, determine the number of condominium- and renter-occupied units, housing vacant and for sale, and housing lacking complete plumbing facilities. Data are available for each state and for designated metropolitan areas, as well as for the United States as a whole. As with other *Census* material the fastest way to develop custom reports is by using *American FactFinder* (http://factfinder.census.gov/servlet/BasicFactsServlet). Using the "enter an address" option, one can obtain information down to the block and tract level.

Archival data for some *Current Housing Reports* is at http://www.census.gov/prod/www/abs/apart.html (accessed April 4, 2011) and http://www.census.gov/prod/www/abs/h121.html (accessed April 4, 2011).

The *American Housing Survey* supplements the *Census* by providing current information on housing characteristics.

U.S. Dept. of Commerce. Bureau of the Census. **American Housing Survey.** Last revised December 19, 2008. http://www.census.gov/hhes/www/ahs.html (accessed April 3, 2011)

> The *Survey* is conducted by the Bureau of the Census for the Department of Housing and Urban Development. The American Housing Survey (AHS) collects data on the Nation's housing, including apartments, single-family homes, mobile homes, vacant housing units, household characteristics, income, housing and neighborhood quality, housing costs, equipment and fuels, size of housing unit, and recent movers. The AHS conducts a national survey and a metropolitan area survey. Both surveys are conducted during a 3- to 7-month period. The national survey, which gathers information on housing throughout the country, interviews at about 60,000 housing units every 2 years, in odd-numbered years. For 2009, the metropolitan survey included five areas as part of the national survey: Chicago, Detroit, New York, Northern New Jersey, and Philadelphia. Additionally, two independent areas were also surveyed: Seattle and New Orleans.

The metro survey program has changed many times, mostly in response to changes in the AHS budget. In 2007, seven metropolitan areas were surveyed. Prior to that, during the period 1985–2004, the AHS surveyed 41 areas. During 1985–1995, there were metro surveys every year. During 1996–2004, the metro surveys were conducted in even-numbered years, although there was none in 2000. In addition, during that period, the six largest metropolitan areas (the five listed above plus Los Angeles) were surveyed every four years (that is, in 1995, 1999, and 2003) as part of the national survey. The AHS returns to the same housing units year after year to gather data; therefore, this survey is ideal for analyzing the flow of households through housing.[4]

The government issues other statistics as well. The Bureau of Labor Statistics' monthly *Producer Price Index* highlights changes in the cost of such building materials as plumbing fixtures, lumber, and mobile homes. In addition, the *Federal Reserve Bulletin* presents information on primary and secondary mortgage market activity and on outstanding residential, commercial, and farm mortgage debt. In some libraries, however, the "Construction and Housing Section" of the *Statistical Abstract of the United States*, which contains excerpts from many of the sources described above, will suffice.

Contractors who submit bids on all types of construction projects need statistics and costs. They are routinely asked to submit estimates of how much it will cost to erect the proposed structure or remodel an existing one. These estimates are usually based on past experience and reflect anticipated labor and building materials costs. Sometimes published building cost estimators are also used. An extremely useful online source is the F. W. Dodge web site (http://fwdodge.construction.com/), which provides analysis, forecasts, and trends for the construction industry. The construction owner can also find plans and specifications and be alerted by e-mail to new projects out to bid. These are subscription databases, and it is unlikely that many libraries will have access. But researchers and librarians need to know about this source so that they can direct patrons to what is an extremely useful source of information.

Other publications provide operating statistics for different categories of commercial, industrial, or residential property, showing income and expense data for each. By consulting these sources, building owners, property managers, developers, investors, and others can compare their operations to the national, regional, or local norms for that type of property.

Institute of Real Estate Management. **Income/Expense Analysis: Conventional Apartments.** Chicago: The Institute, 1954–. Annual.

Institute of Real Estate Management. **Income/Expense Analysis: Condominiums, Cooperatives, and Planned Unit Developments.** Chicago: The Institute, 1978–. Annual.

Institute of Real Estate Management. **Income/Expense Analysis: Federally Assisted Apartments.** Chicago: The Institute, 1986–. Annual.

Institute of Real Estate Management. **Income/Expense Analysis: Office Buildings.** Chicago: The Institute, 1976–. Annual.

Institute of Real Estate Management. **Income/Expense Analysis: Shopping Centers.** Chicago: The Institute, 1991–. Annual.

Each year, the Institute of Real Estate Management (http://www.irem.org) compiles and analyzes financial operating data contributed by its members for over 7,700 buildings and developments. Coverage varies, but each publication charts recent trends in building operations, covers income by source, and presents data for the type of building described in the title. The *Conventional Apartments* report, for example, features information on such expenses as utilities, security, repairs, grounds maintenance, and real estate taxes, and presents median income and operating costs as dollars per square foot of rentable area and as a percentage of gross possible income.

Building Owners and Managers Association International. **BOMA Experience Exchange Report.** Washington, DC: The Association, 1920–. Annual.

Operating statistics for U.S. and Canadian office buildings are also available in the annual *BOMA Experience Exchange Report*. The *Report* presents income and expenses for different types of private and public office buildings and also includes building occupancy rates, year-end rent, and space per tenant and worker. Data on selected areas by ZIP code are included. Beginning with 2010 the report is only available online at http://www.boma.org/Resources/benchmarking/Pages/default.aspx.

Urban Land Institute. **Dollars & Cents of Shopping Centers/the SCORE.** Washington, DC: The Institute, 1961–. Biannual.

Dollars & Cents of Shopping Centers reports on shopping center operations. Based on responses made by shopping centers to periodic surveys by the Urban Land Institute, *Dollars & Cents* includes operating receipts and expenses, sales, rent, and detailed tenant information. Data are by type of shopping center (super regional, regional, community, and neighborhood) and cover the United States and Canada. Also available on CD-ROM.[5]

Standard & Poor's; Fiserv Inc. MacroMarkets LLC. **S&P/Case-Shiller Home Price Indices.** www.homeprice.standardandpoors.com (accessed April 15, 2011)

S&P/Case-Shiller Home Price Indices is a family of 23 indices that track home prices in the United States. 20 of the indices cover specific MSAs, 2 indices are aggregations of the MSA indices—one of 10 MSAs and one of all 20 MSAs. The final index is a national index is a composite based on single-family home prices in the 9 U.S. Census divisions. The MSA and the two aggregations are calculated monthly using a 3-month moving average and published on a 2-month delay. The national index is calculated quarterly. For more details, click on the Methodology link on the web page.

Realty Trac. **Realty Trac.** http://www.realtytrac.com (accessed April 15, 2011)

Realty Trac is a subscription-based online marketplace of foreclosure properties. As of the spring of 2011 it covered more than 1.5 million properties including those in default, auction, and bank-owned, listing from more than 2,200 U.S. counties. There are also aggregated statistics and information that can be used for tracking trends in foreclosures and sales by specific property characteristics, including estimated market value, square footage, and number of bedrooms. There is some limited information for free. The "Learning Center" tab has links to publications on the foreclosure process, state foreclosure laws, how to avoid foreclosure, and more. Some of the publications are free; others must be purchased.

U.S. Department of Housing and Urban Development. **HUD USER.** http://www.huduser .org/portal/ (accessed April 4, 2011)

HUD USER includes reports, documents, and other sources dealing with affordable housing, housing finance, building technology, economic development, housing for special groups such as the elderly and disabled, energy conservation, assisted housing, and other topics. Although most of the titles are issued by the Department of Housing and Urban Development, documents from other government organizations and some journal articles are indexed as well. Most of the documents cited in *HUD USER* are available in PDF format and can be downloaded. For those few that need to be purchased, there are links to the online store.

U.S. Department of Housing and Urban Development. **Homes for Sale.** http://www
.hud.gov/homes/homesforsale.cfm (accessed April 4, 2011)

At this site one can link not only to HUD homes for sale but also to properties offered
by other agencies such as the FDIC and IRS. Most are searchable by geography, and most
of the information about the various properties is fully listed at the web site.

There are other databases offered by associations such as the Appraisal Institute and
Urban Land Institute, but these are very specialized and require subscriptions. Most
libraries will not have access to these, but librarians should be aware of them so that they
can direct patrons to them.

Notes

1. George F. Bloom, Arthur M. Weimer, and Jeffrey D. Fisher, *Real Estate*, 8th ed. (New York: John Wiley,
1982), 3.

2. Taken from the "About Us" section of the Fannie Mae web site, http://www.fanniemae.com/kb/
index?page=home&c=aboutus.

3. Taken from the "FAQ" section of the Freddie Mac web site, http://www.freddiemac.com/corporate/
company_profile/faqs/.

4. Taken from http://www.census.gov/hhes/www/housing/ahs/datacollection.html.

5. Pricing and ordering information is available at https://netforum.uli.org/eweb//DynamicPage.aspx?s
ite=ULIMC&webcode=ULIAllBooks&prd_name=. Or at the International Council of Shopping Centers
at http://www.icsc.org/cgi/displaybook/000300.

Appendix A

Business Acronyms and Abbreviations

AACSB   American Assembly of Collegiate Schools of Business
ABA   American Bankers Association
ABC   Audit Bureau of Circulations
ABI   *Abstracted Business Information* (variant name for the database, *ABI/INFORM)*
ACCRA   American Chamber of Commerce Researchers Association
ACE   Active Corps of Executives
ACH   Automatic Clearing House
ADR   American Depositary Receipts
AGI   Adjusted Gross Income
AICPA   American Institute of Certified Public Accountants
AID   Agency for International Development (U.S.)
AIRAC   All-Industry Research Advisory Council (insurance organization)
AMA   American Management Association
AMA   American Marketing Association
APB   Accounting Principles Board
APR   Annual Percentage Rate
ARB   *Accounting Research Bulletin*
ARBA *American Reference Books Annual*
ARF   Advertising Research Foundation
ARM   Adjustable Rate Mortgage
ARS   Annual Report to Shareholders
ASB   Auditing Standards Board (AICPA)
ASR   *Accounting Series Releases* (SEC)
ASI   *American Statistics Index*
ATM   Automated Teller Machine
B2B   Business to Business
B2C   Business to Consumer
BEA   Bureau of Economic Analysis (U.S.)
BLS   Bureau of Labor Statistics (U.S.)
BNA   Bureau of National Affairs, Inc.
BPA   Business Publications Audit of Circulation
BPI   *Business Periodicals Index*
BPI   Buying Power Index
BRASS   Business Reference and Services Section, American Library Association
BRS   BRS Information Technologies, formerly Bibliographic Retrieval Services, Inc.
CAGR   Compound Annual Growth Rate
CBOE   Chicago Board Options Exchange
CBT   Chicago Board of Trade
CCPA   Consumer Credit Protection Act
CCH   Commerce Clearing House, Inc.
CD   Compact Disk
CD   Certificate of Deposit
CD-ROM Compact Disk, Read-Only-Memory
CEA   Council of Economic Advisers (U.S.)
CEO   Chief Executive Officer

CFA	Chartered Financial Analyst
CFO	Chief Financial Officer
CFTC	Commodity Futures Trading Commission (U.S.)
CIO	Chief Information Officer
CIS	Congressional Information Service, Inc.
CIT	Commission on Insurance Terminology (of the American Risk and Insurance Association)
CLU	Chartered Life Underwriter
CME	Chicago Mercantile Exchange
CMX	Commodity Exchange, Inc.
COGS	Cost of Goods Sold
COLA	Cost of Living Adjustment
CPA	Certified Public Accountant
CPI	Consumer Price Index
CPI-U	Consumer Price Index for All Urban Consumers
CPI-W	Consumer Price Index for Urban Wage Earners and Clerical Workers
CRS	Congressional Research Service (U.S.)
CSCE	Coffee, Sugar & Cocoa Exchange
Cv	Convertible Security (i.e., convertible preferred stock or convertible bond)
D & B	Dun & Bradstreet, Inc.
DCAA	Defense Contract Audit Agency (U.S.)
DDA	Demand Deposit Accounts
DOD	Department of Defense (U.S.)
DOL	Department of Labor (U.S.)
D-U-N-S	Dun's Universal Numbering System
EBI	Effective Buying Income
ECI	Employer Cost Index
ECOA	Equal Credit Opportunity Act
EPA	Environmental Protection Agency (U.S.)
EPS	Earnings per Share
ERC	Employee Relocation Council
ERS	Economic Research Service (U.S.)
ESA	Employment Standards Administration (U.S.)
ETA	Employment Training Administration (U.S.)
FAA	Federal Aviation Administration (U.S.)
FAIR	Fair Access to Insurance Requirements
FASB	Financial Accounting Standards Board
FCC	Federal Communications Commission (U.S.)
FCRA	Fair Credit Reporting Act
FDA	Food and Drug Administration (U.S.)
FDIC	Federal Deposit Insurance Corporation (U.S.)
Fed	Federal Reserve System (U.S.)
FERC	Federal Energy Regulatory Commission (U.S.)
FHA	Federal Highway Administration (U.S.)
FHA	Federal Housing Administration (U.S.)
FHLB	Federal Home Loan Bank
FHLBB	Federal Home Loan Bank Board
FHLBS	Federal Home Loan Bank System
FHLMC	Federal Home Loan Mortgage Corporation (U.S.) (Freddie Mac)
FICB	Federal Intermediate Credit Banks (U.S.)
FIFO	First In First Out
FNMA	Federal National Mortgage Association (U.S.) (Fannie Mae)

FOMC	Federal Open Market Committee
FNRA	Financial Industry Regulatory System
FRB	Federal Reserve System (U.S.)
FRM	Fixed Rate Mortgage
FSLIC	Federal Savings and Loan Insurance Corporation (U.S.)
FTC	Federal Trade Commission (U.S.)
GAAP	Generally Accepted Accounting Principles
GAAS	Generally Accepted Auditing Standards
GAO	General Accounting Office (U.S.)
GDP	Gross Domestic Product
GNMA	Government National Mortgage Association (U.S.) (Ginnie Mae)
GNP	Gross National Product
GPO	Government Printing Office (U.S.)
GSA	General Services Administration (U.S.)
HBR	*Harvard Business Review*
HMO	Health Maintenance Organization
HUD	Housing and Urban Development Department (U.S.)
HUT	Households Using Television
ICC	International Chamber of Commerce
IMM	International Monetary Market
IPC	Individuals, Partnerships, and Corporations
IPO	Initial Public Offering
IRS	Internal Revenue Service (U.S.)
ISBN	International Standard Book Number
ISSN	International Standard Serial Number
ITA	International Trade Administration (U.S.)
ITS	Intermarket Trading System
KCBT	Kansas City Board of Trade
LIMRA	Life Insurance Marketing and Research Association
LLC	Limited Liability Corporation
LMS	Labor Management Standards Office (U.S.)
LOMA	Life Office Management Association
MBS	Mortgage-Backed Securities Program
MGEX	Minneapolis Grain Exchange
MGIC	MGIC Investment Corporation
MRDF	Machine-Readable Data File
MVMA	Motor Vehicle Manufacturers Association
NAIC	National Association of Insurance Commissioners
NAICS	North American Industry Classification System
NAR	National Association of Realtors
NAREIT	National Association of Real Estate Investment Trusts
NASD	National Association of Securities Dealers, Inc.
NASDA	National Association of State Department Agencies
NASDAQ	National Association of Securities Dealers Automated Quotations
NAV	Net Asset Value
NBS	National Bureau of Standards (U.S.)
NCHS	National Center for Health Statistics (U.S.)
NCUA	National Credit Union Administration (U.S.)
NLRB	National Labor Relations Board (U.S.)
NMS	National Market System
NTIS	National Technical Information Service (U.S.)
NYFE	New York Futures Exchange

NYME	New York Mercantile Exchange
NYSE	New York Stock Exchange
OASDI	Old Age, Survivors, Disability and Health Insurance
OBA	Office of Business Analysis (U.S.)
OCC	Office of the Controller of the Currency
OMB	Office of Management and Budget (U.S.)
OSHA	Occupational Safety and Health Administration (U.S.)
OTA	Office of Technology Assessment (U.S.)
OTC	Over-the-Counter
PAIS	*Public Affairs Information Service Bulletin*
P/E	Price/Earnings Ratio
PFD	Preferred Stock
P-H	Prentice-Hall, Inc.
PIT	Preferred Stock
PPI	Producer Price Index
R&D	Research and Development
REIT	Real Estate Investment Trust
RELP	Real Estate Limited Partnership
RMA	Risk Management Association
ROA	Return on Assets
ROC	Return on Capital
ROE	Return on Equity
ROI	Return on Investment
ROS	Return on Sales
RPI	Retail Price Index
S & L	Savings and Loan Association
S & P	Standard & Poor's Corporation
SBA	Small Business Administration (U.S.)
SBW	Small Business Workshop (IRS)
SCORE	Service Corps of Retired Executives
SCSA	Standard Consolidated Statistical Area
SEC	Securities and Exchange Commission (U.S.)
SF	Sinking Fund
SFAS	Statement of Financial Accounting Standards
SIC	Standard Industrial Classification
SLA	Special Libraries Association
SMSA	Standard Metropolitan Statistical Area
S/N	Stock Number (U.S. Superintendent of Documents)
SRDS	Standard Rate & Data Service
SRI	*Statistical Reference Index*
SUDOCS	Superintendent of Documents (U.S.)
T BILL	Treasury Bill
TCE	Tax Counseling for the Elderly
USDA	Department of Agriculture (U.S.)
VA	Veterans Administration (U.S.)
VITA	Volunteer Income Tax Assistance
WSJ	*Wall Street Journal*
WT	Warrant

Appendix B

Federal Government Departments and Selected Agencies Relevant to Business

Department or Agency	Function	URL
Agriculture	Works to improve farm income; develop markets for agricultural products; and help curb hunger, poverty, and malnutrition. Helps landowners protect soil, water, forests, and other natural resources. Through inspection and grading, ensures quality of daily food supply. Responsible for rural development, credit, and conservation programs.	http://www.usda.gov/
Economic Research Service	Provides economic information to aid in the development of agricultural policies and programs. Information made available through monographs, reports, situation and outlook periodicals, and databases.	http://www.ers.usda.gov/
National Agricultural Statistics Service	Prepares estimates and reports on production, supply, and prices of agricultural products.	http://www.nass.usda.gov/
Commerce	Advances economic growth and jobs and opportunities for the American people. It has cross-cutting responsibilities in the areas of trade, technology, entrepreneurship, economic development, environmental stewardship, and statistical research and analysis.	http://www.commerce.gov/
U.S. Census Bureau	The leading source of quality data about the nation's people and economy	http://www.census.gov/
International Trade Administration	Promotes world trade; strengthens U.S. international trade and investment position.	http://www.ita.doc.gov/
Patent and Trademark Office	Examines, registers, and administers national system of patents and trademarks.	http://www.uspto.gov/
Defense	Provides military forces needed to deter war and protect national security.	http://www.defense.gov/
Defense Logistics Agency	Works with current and potential suppliers of weapon systems and other DOD materials; administers defense contracts and other support services.	http://www.dla.mil/

Department or Agency	Function	URL
Education	Establishes policy for federal assistance to education; supports educational research.	http://www.ed.gov/
Institute of Education Sciences	Provides rigorous and relevant evidence on which to ground education practice and policy and share this information broadly.	http://ies.ed.gov/
Energy	Coordinates and administers the government's energy functions, sponsors energy technology research and development, and administers energy data collection and analysis programs.	http://www.energy.gov/
Energy Information Administration	Collects, processes, and publishes data in the areas of energy resources and reserves, as well as energy production, demand, consumption, distribution, and technology.	http://www.eia.doe.gov/
Health and Human Services	Administers government programs in the areas of health, welfare, and income security; collects, analyzes, and publishes data relating to them.	http://www.hhs.gov/
Food and Drug Administration	Works to protect against impure and unsafe foods, drugs, cosmetics, and other hazards.	http://www.fda.gov/
National Center for Health Statistics	Collects, analyzes, and disseminates health statistics; promotes and conducts research in health data systems and statistical methodology.	http://www.cdc.gov/nchs/
Social Security Administration	Administers national program of contributory social welfare; conducts research relating to poverty, financial insecurity, and health care for the aged, blind, and disabled.	http://www.ssa.gov/
Housing and Urban Development	Responsible for programs concerned with housing needs and assistance, community development, mortgage lending and rent subsidies, and encouraging private homebuilding.	http://www.hud.gov/
Interior	Responsible for nationally owned public lands and natural resources, protects fish and wildlife, assesses mineral resources, and works to ensure that their development is in the public interest.	http://www.doi.gov/
U.S. Geological Survey	Identifies the nation's land, water, energy, and mineral resources; classifies federally owned land for minerals, energy, resources, and water power potential; investigates natural hazards; and conducts the National Mapping Program.	http://www.usgs.gov/

Department or Agency	Function	URL
Justice	Enforces law in the public interest, including law relating to drugs, immigration, and naturalization. Promotes effective law enforcement, crime prevention and detection, and prosecution and rehabilitation of offenders.	http://www.justice.gov/
Federal Bureau of Investigation	Investigates all violations of federal law except those assigned to another agency.	http://www.fbi.gov/
Bureau of Alcohol, Tobacco, Firearms and Explosives	A law enforcement agency in the United States Department of Justice that protects the illegal use and trafficking of firearms, the illegal use and storage of explosives, acts of arson and bombings, acts of terrorism, and the illegal diversion of alcohol and tobacco products.	http://www.atf.gov/
Labor	Administers federal labor laws and monitors changes in employment, prices, and other measures of the national economy.	http://www.dol.gov/
Bureau of Labor Statistics	Collects, analyzes, processes, and disseminates data relating to employment, wages, and prices.	http://www.bls.gov
Employment and Training Administration	Fulfills DOL responsibilities relating to employment services, job training, and unemployment insurance.	http://www.doleta.gov/
Occupational Safety and Health Administration	Develops and promotes occupational safety and health standards, issues regulations, conducts investigations and inspections to determine compliance with safety and health standards, and issues citations and proposes penalties for noncompliance.	http://www.osha.gov/
State	Provides the president with advice in formulating and executing foreign policy.	http://www.state.gov/
Transportation	Establishes and administers national transportation policies and programs, including those relating to highways, mass transit, railroads, and aviation.	http://www.dot.gov/
Federal Highway Administration	Operates and administers highway transportation programs relating to highway development and travel, transportation needs, and engineering and safety aspects.	http://www.fhwa.dot.gov/
Federal Railroad Administration	Promulgates and enforces rail safety regulations, administers financial assistance programs, and conducts research and development.	http://www.fra.dot.gov/
Maritime Administration	Administers programs to aid in the development, promotion, and operation of the U.S. merchant marine.	http://www.marad.dot.gov/

Department or Agency	Function	URL
National Highway Traffic Safety Administration	Carries out programs relating to safety and performance of motor traffic vehicles, their occupants, and pedestrians.	http://www.nhtsa.dot.gov/
Bureau of Transportation Statistics	Administers data collection, analysis, and reporting and to ensure the most cost-effective use of transportation-monitoring resources. BTS brings a greater degree of coordination, comparability, and quality standards to transportation data, and facilitates in the closing of important data gaps.	http://www.bts.gov/
Treasury	Formulates and recommends economic, financial, tax, and fiscal policies; serves as the financial agent for the U.S. government; and manufactures coins and currency.	http://www.treasury.gov/
Alcohol and Tobacco Tax and Trade Bureau	Responsible for all inquiries in regards to regulating the alcohol and tobacco industries and Special Occupational Tax and for the collection of Firearms and Ammunition Excise Taxes imposed on manufacturers and importers of these products.	http://www.ttb.gov/
Internal Revenue Service	Administers and enforces internal revenue laws, excluding those relating to alcohol, tobacco, firearms, and explosives; determines, assesses, and collects taxes; and educates and advises the public.	http://www.irs.gov/
Veterans Affairs	"To care for him who shall have borne the battle, and for his widow, and his orphan" by serving and honoring the men and women who are America's veterans. Provide veterans the world-class benefits and services they have earned—and to do so by adhering to the highest standards of compassion, commitment, excellence, professionalism, integrity, accountability, and stewardship (taken from VA mission statement at http://www.va.gov/landing2_about.htm)	http://www.va.gov/
Homeland Security	Secure the nation from the many threats the United States of America faces	http://www.dhs.gov/
Customs and Border Protection	Assesses and collects customs duties, excise taxes, fees, and penalties due on imported merchandise; seizes contraband; and processes persons, carriers, cargo, and mail into and out of the United States.	http://cbp.gov/

Appendix C

Federal Government Corporations and Independent Agencies Relevant to Business

Organization	Functions	URL
Commodity Futures Trading Commission	Regulates and oversees the trading of commodity futures and Commission options.	http://www.cftc.gov
Consumer Product Safety Commission	Protects the public against risk of injury from consumer products, develops uniform safety standards, and promotes research and investigation.	http://www.cpsc.gov/
Environmental Protection Agency	Protects and enhances the environment by controlling and abating air, water, solid waste, radiation, and toxic substance pollution.	http://www.epa.gov
Equal Employment Opportunity Commission	Responsible for compliance and enforcement activities relating to equal employment opportunities among federal employees; promotes voluntary action programs by employers, unions, and community organizations.	http://www.eeoc.gov/
Export-Import Bank of the United States	Facilitates and aids in financing exports of U.S. goods and services.	http://www.exim.gov/
Federal Communications Commission	Regulates interstate and foreign communications by radio, television, wire, and cable.	http://www.fcc.gov/
Federal Deposit Insurance Corporation	Promotes and preserves public confidence in banks; protects the money supply through provision of insurance coverage for bank deposits.	http://www.fdiv.gov/
Federal Maritime Commission	Regulates waterborne foreign and domestic offshore commerce of the United States.	http://www.fmc.gov/
Federal Mediation and Conciliation Service	Provides mediators to help labor and management settle work stoppages and other disputes.	http://www.fmcs.gov/
Federal Reserve System	Central bank of the United States; responsible for administering and policy making for U.S. credit and monetary affairs.	http://www.federalreserve.gov

Organization	Functions	URL
Federal Trade Commission	Promotes the free enterprise system; ensures that it is not hindered by monopoly, restraints on trade, or unfair or deceptive trade practices.	http://www.ftc.gov/
General Services Administration	Responsible for providing the government with an economical and efficient system for managing its property and records.	http://www.gsa.gov
National Credit Union Administration	Charters, insures, supervises, and examines federal credit unions.	http://www.ncua.gov/
National Labor Relations Board	Administers federal labor law; prevents and remedies unfair labor practices.	http://www.nlrb.gov/
National Mediation Board	Resolves air and railway disputes that might disrupt travel or threaten the economy.	http://www.nmb.gov/
National Science Foundation	Promotes science and engineering through the support of research and education programs.	http://www.nsf.gov/
National Transportation Safety Board	Investigates accidents, conducts studies, and makes recommendations on safety measures and practices.	http://www.ntsb.gov/
Nuclear Regulatory Commission	Licenses and regulates U.S. commercial power plants and the civilian use of nuclear energy.	http://www.nrc.gov/
Securities and Exchange Commission	Protects investors and maintains the integrity of the securities markets.	http://www.sec.gov
Small Business Administration	Aids, counsels, assists, and protects the interests of small business.	http://www.sba.gov/
United States Agency for International Development	Responsible for policy planning, policy making, and coordination of international economic issues affecting developing countries.	http://www.usaid.gov/
United States International Trade Commission	Furnishes studies, reports, and recommendations involving international trade and tariffs to the president, Congress, and other government agencies	http://www.usitc.gov

Appendix D

Representative Types of Business Information Published by State Government Agencies

Department/Agency	Information Provided
Agriculture	Crop production and demand, agricultural statistics, market surveys, consumer guides
Commerce/Business	Business and economic statistics, directories, surveys and assessments, economic indicators
Economic Development/Planning	Promotional literature; directories; reports, forecasts, and projections
Education	Public and private education statistics, school enrollment, directories, reports
Energy	Energy statistics, alternative energy sources, energy conservation
Insurance	Annual reports, insurance statistics, lists of authorized insurance companies, consumer guides
Labor/Employment	Hour and wage statistics, cost of living, unemployment compensation, occupational safety and health, local labor market information
Taxation/Revenue	Income statistics, sales of certain taxed products, tax guides, statistical reports
Tourism	Guides and brochures, maps, calendars of events
Transportation	Traffic statistics, transit development plans, research studies, traffic safety

Appendix E

Key Economic Indicators

Indicator	Description	Government Agency	Frequency and URL
Balance of Payments	Difference in value of goods and services exported and imported by the United States.	Bureau of Economic Analysis	Monthly
Building Permits/ Housing Starts	Shows the number of permits issued and housing units begun. Used to check the economy, as construction is usually one of the first industries to show changes.	U.S. Bureau of the Census	Monthly http://www.census .gov/const/www .newreconstindex .html
Consumer Price Index (CPI)	The measure of prices for a fixed basket of consumer goods. Used to measure inflation.	Bureau of Labor Statistics	Monthly
Gross Domestic Product (GDP)	The dollar value of the goods and services produced and consumed in the private, public, domestic, and international sectors. It is the broadest measure of economic output and growth.	Bureau of Economic Analysis	Quarterly
Interest Rates	Interest is the charge for borrowing money; and interest rates are the price of money. The rate is the interest per year divided by the principal and expressed as a percentage.	Federal Reserve Board	Weekly http://www .federalreserve.gov/ releases/H15/
Personal Income	The income, from all sources, received by households. Used as a measure of purchasing power.	Bureau of Economic Analysis	Monthly http://www.bea .doc.gov/bea/dn/ nipaweb/SelectTable .asp?Selected=Y

Indicator	Description	Government Agency	Frequency and URL
Producer Price Index	An index of commodity prices; it measures the average price over time received by domestic producers for their output.	Bureau of Labor Statistics	Monthly
Retail Trade	Provides the first indication of the strengths and weaknesses of consumer spending.	U.S. Bureau of the Census	Monthly http://www.census.gov/ mrts/www/mrts.html
Unemployment	Percentage of the workforce that is involuntarily out of work.	Bureau of Labor Statistics	Monthly http://stats.bls.gov/ news.release/empsit.toc .htm

Appendix F

Selected Web Sites for Free Business Information

General Sites and Search Engines

AllTheWeb. http://www.alltheweb.com/

This search engine uses dynamic clustering based on Open Directory. Basic web search plus searching in real time news, pictures, videos, MP3s, and ftp files. This search engine is now powered by YAHOO!

BRASS Best of the Best Business Web Sites. http://www.ala.org/ala/mgrps/divs/rusa/ sections/brass/brassprotools/bestofthebestbus/bestbestbusiness.cfm

A subject index to the "Best of the Best" created by members of the BRASS (Business Reference and Services Section of ALA) Education Committee.

Other resources maintained by the business librarians of ALA contain presentations, newsletters, and subject guides. All are available from the main screen at http://www.ala .org/ala/mgrps/divs/rusa/sections/brass/index.cfm.

Global Risk Management Network @ BRINT. http://www.brint.org/

BRINT is short for Business Research in Information and Technology. The site links to 10 research centers, including news, management, and finance. Within each section there are further links and information. One cannot adequately describe the breadth and depth of information on this site so the only recommendation can be to explore.

Google. http://www.google.com/

A simple search in *Google* returns web pages that contain all the words in the query, so narrowing the search is as easy as adding more words to the search terms. *Google* ignores common words such as "how." If the word is essential to the search add + (+how) or make the whole search a phrase. To limit searches to PDFs add the words "filetype:pdf". Search areas include sets of images, news groups, and a directory.

Searches can also be limited by the type of site preferred.

e.g. search term site:org

    search term site:edu

    search term site:gov

Librarian's Index to the Internet. http://www.ipl.org/

A directory of web links. Sites are selected, indexed, and annotated by librarians.

From the front screen click on "subject" and then choose "business." At this time 523 resources are listed but using the site is made easier by the further listing of subjects at the left, e.g., Industry.

Yahoo. http://www.yahoo.com

Browsable directory of web sites. One can search the whole Web or search within topic and region. If nothing is found in *Yahoo*, the search defaults to *Google*.

Acronym Database. http://www.acronymfinder.com/

"The web's most comprehensive database of acronyms, abbreviations, and initialisms. 229,000+ definitions!"

Investorwords.com. http://www.investorwords.com/

Over 6,000 business definitions, each with appropriate cross-referencing.

Accounting and Taxes

CPA Directory. http://www.cpafirms.com/Firmlist/firmlist.cfm

A listing of U.S. CPA firms by region, state, or area code. This directory also contains about 300 international firms.

CPA JOURNAL Home Page. http://www.cpaj.com/

Table of contents of the current journal is available. There is also a link to archives of the journal available from the New York State Society of Certified Public Accountants web site. These archives when last checked covered 1989–2011.

CPAnet. http://www.cpanet.com/

The online community and web site resource for accounting professionals. Links include news, directories, articles, associations, and software.

Tax and Accounting Sites Directory. http://www.taxsites.com/

Inclusive site, with links to forms, associations, publishers, rates and tables, and career and legal information. International, federal, and state links.

Banking

AAAdir Bank Directory—US and International Banks. http://www.aaadir.com/

A directory links to a short directory listing and the web pages of the world's banks. Also contains statistical information and links to stock exchanges, central banks, organizations, and dictionaries. One must check the "useful information" tab to find some of the extra material.

Bank Rate Monitor. http://www.bankrate.com/

Rates for mortgages, home equity loans, car loans, CDs, credit cards, etc. Search by state and type of loan needed. Includes calculators.

Central Bank Hub—Bank for International Settlements. http://www.bis.org/cbanks.htm

Links to all central banks.

FDIC Data. http://www.fdic.gov/bank/index.html

Analytical, statistical, and historical information on banks from the Federal Deposit Insurance Corporation.

Yahoo—Banks. http://dir.yahoo.com/business_and_economy/shopping_and_services/ financial _services/banking/banks/

Alphabetical listing of banks, with links to the web sites.

Bankruptcy

American Bankruptcy Institute World. http://www.abiworld.org/

The premier site for bankruptcy information on the Web. Contains statistics on both business and consumer filings.

Bankruptcy Resources for Consumers. http://consumer.abi.org/

InterNet Bankruptcy Library. http://bankrupt.com/

Information on conferences, local rules, books, and periodicals. News section contains free articles from specialized periodicals embargoed for 90 days.

Bonds

Bonds Online. http://www.bonds-online.com/

Includes explanations of different types of bonds as well as quotes, yields, calculators, and outlook. A subscription is required for the more specialized information.

Standard & Poor's Rating Services. http://www.standardandpoors.com/

Information on all areas covered by S&P, but bond information is available under "ratings" and "fixed income."

T-bills, Notes & Bonds Online. http://www.treasurydirect.gov/sitemap.htm

Information on T-bills, notes, and bonds, including how to buy them online. Information on interest rates and expenses, STRIPS, security liquidations, and current and historical public debt statistics. It is easier to begin the search for information by using the site map.

MunicipalBonds.com. http://www.municipalbonds.com/

Basic membership is free and with this one gets pricing and ratings on all Municipal bonds.

Codes

Harmonized Tariff Schedule of the United States. http://www.usitc.gov/tariff_affairs/

The *HTSA* provides the applicable tariff rates and statistical categories for all merchandise imported into the United States; it is based on the *International Harmonized System*, the global classification system that is used to describe most world trade in goods.

NAICS. http://www.census.gov/eos/www/naics/

The *North American Industry Classification System* (*NAICS*) has replaced the *U.S. Standard Industrial Classification* (*SIC*) system. *NAICS* was developed jointly by the United States, Canada, and Mexico to provide new comparability in statistics about business activity across North America.

Schedule B Export Codes. http://www.census.gov/foreign-trade/schedules/b/index.html

Trade transactions are classified under approximately 8,000 different products leaving the United States. Every item that is exported is assigned a unique 10-digit identification code. Every 10-digit item is part of a series of progressively broader product categories.

SIC (lookup system). http://www.osha.gov/oshstats/sicser.html

Search the 1987 version SIC manual by keyword to access descriptive information for a specified four-digit SIC.

Company Directories/Company Financial

Annual Report Service—The Public Register online. http://www.annualreportservice .com/

Choose to view the online annual or to request a free hard copy. Free registration is required.

Bloomberg Businessweek http://investing.businessweek.com/research/company/overview/ overview.asp

Use the above link or go to businessweek.com, click on the finance tab, and choose companies. Information includes news, charts, financials, earnings, people, and options. Contains 4 years of annual data and 1 year of quarterly. For those who do not have a subscription to Hoovers', this sight might work well in its place.

EDGAR Database of Corporate Information. http://www.sec.gov/edgar.shtml

Official Securities and Exchange Commission web site. Financial filings from public companies.

Kompass—International Directories. http://www.kompass.com

Worldwide search by company name or product. Basic directory information on 1.6 million companies is free; enhanced reports can be bought.

Manta.com. http://www.manta.com/

Online directory of 60 million small businesses. Not as much information as subscription databases but is a good option for those with no other access.

SearchSystems.net. http://publicrecords.searchsystems.net/

Useful to check state sites to find the names of corporations that file only in that state.

Thomas Register of American Manufacturers Online. http://www.thomasnet.com/

Searching is by company or product. Directory information plus links to online catalogs are supplied. More than 72,000 product headings and over 170,000 companies listed.

Futures, Options, Commodities

Commodity Futures Trading Commission. http://www.cftc.gov/

Contains information on "how to trade," a listing of trader's commitments, consumer advisories, and enforcement bulletins.

TFC Commodity Charts. http://tfc-charts.w2d.com/

Extensive free source of daily commodity futures and financial charts and quotes.

Futures and Options Resources on the Web. http://ofor.ace.illinois.edu/resource.htm

Exchanges, Prices & Outlook, Research, Government Resources, and other futures and financial sites. Maintained by Department of Agricultural and Consumer Economics, University of Illinois at Urbana-Champaign. This is a mega site for all types of information.

Options Industry Council (OIC). http://www.optionseducation.org/

Includes guides to all aspects of futures and options as well as quotes, volume data, links to SEC filings, and contract adjustments and product specifications.

USGS Minerals Information. http://minerals.usgs.gov/minerals/

Statistics and information on the worldwide supply, demand, and flow of minerals. For some of the commodities, data are reported as far back as 1900.

Industry

2007 Economic Census. http://www.census.gov/econ/census07/

Latest economic census data. Use the legacy American FactFinder, which will provide Geography Quick Reports, Industry Quick Reports, and Data Sets. factfinder.census.gov

Country Analysis Briefs. http://www.eia.doe.gov/emeu/cabs/

Some country overview information and in-depth energy information.

County Business Patterns. http://www.census.gov/econ/cbp/index.html

Provides county, state, ZIP, and national-level business data from 1977 to the most recent year available. Statistics include number of establishments, payroll (annual and first quarter), number of employees, and number of establishments by size class for two-digit SIC industry groupings.

Current Industrial Reports—US Census. http://www.census.gov/manufacturing/cir/index .html

Newspaper Industry—Newspaper Association of America. http://www.naa.org/

Basic facts on newspaper distribution and sales as well as advertising data.

Pharmaceutical Industry—P*h*RMA. http://www.phrma.org/

Useful industry information, but remember that PHRMA represents the country's leading research-based pharmaceutical and biotechnology companies.

Polson Enterprises Industry Home Pages. http://www.virtualpet.com/industry/mfg/ mfg.htm

Links to publications and other sites for most major industries. There is also a link to a "How to Learn About an Industry or a Specific Company" site, which is a useful guide on how to conduct industry and company research.

Initial Public Offerings (IPOs)

IPO Central—Hoover's Online. http://www.hoovers.com/ipo-central/100004160-1.html
Lists latest IPOs with company details.

Insurance

A.M. BEST. http://www.ambest.com/
News on all aspects of the insurance industry. Some general reports are free, as is information on the ratings system. Individual ratings can be retrieved after free registration.

Insurance Information Institute. http://www.iii.org/
Information on all types of insurance. Includes industry statistics, financials and outlook, hot topics, research studies, and a glossary.

insure.com. http://www.insure.com/
Basic guides to all types of insurance and company information, including ratings from S&P and Fitch. Directory listings by state of insurance agents. Includes a lawsuit library. Free quotes.

International Links

Governments on the Web. http://www.gksoft.com/govt/
A comprehensive database that includes parliaments, ministries, offices, law courts, embassies, city councils, public broadcasting corporations, central banks, multinational organizations, political parties, etc.

Country Analysis Briefs. http://www.eia.doe.gov/countries/
Substantive reports on individual countries and special topics provided by the Department of Energy.

US Commercial Service. http://www.export.gov/about/eg_main_016806.asp
This page is the jumping-off spot for *Country Commercial Guides* (often known as "Doing Business In") and the international *Market Research Library*.

Mutual Funds

MORNINGSTAR. http://www.morningstar.com/
Lots of free information about individual funds; ratings are included in the free information.

Mutual Fund Investor's Center. http://www.mfea.com/
An excellent site for general information, educational materials, and links to mutual funds.

Mutual Funds Facts & Figures—Investment Company Institute. http://www.ici.org/stats/
Site includes facts and figures, statistical reports, and the latest factbook.

Periodicals and Newspapers

Bizjournals. http://www.bizjournals.com/
Business news from 41 local markets.

NewsLink. http://newslink.org/biznews.html
Links by state to business dailies and business magazines.

OnlineNewspapers.com. http://www.onlinenewspapers.com/
Listings, by country, of thousands of available newspapers.

Real Estate

Directory of Real Estate Centers. http://www.cba.uc.edu/getreal/center.html
List of real estate centers compiled by the University of Cincinnati.

Fannie Mae. http://www.fanniemae.com/
Information about mortgages and applications. Scroll down the screen and on the left find a link to the database of Fannie Mae properties for sale.

FDIC Owned Real Estate. http://www.fdic.gov/buying/owned/index.html
FDIC properties for sale. Also calendars of special sales.

Mortgage Calculators. http://www.bankrate.com/calculators.aspx
Find the monthly payment for a particular loan and calculate discount points.

Small Business

FedBizOpps. https://www.fbo.gov/
Buying from and selling to the federal government.

MoreBusiness.com. http://www.morebusiness.com/
Articles, guides, software downloads, and calculators.

U.S. Small Business Administration (SBA). http://www.sba.gov
Everything for the small business owner. Advice, forms, legal information, sample business plans. The place to start for those opening a new business.

Statistics

Bureau of Labor Statistics. http://stats.bls.gov/
Links to federal economic indexes, productivity and employment statistics, and publications.

FEDSTATS. http://www.fedstats.gov/

The gateway to statistics from over 100 U.S. federal agencies.

OFFSTATS. http://www.offstats.auckland.ac.nz/browse/

Browsable site from the Library of the University of Auckland. Links are provided, and maintained, to every country and its major departments and agencies.

Statistical Resouces on the Web. http://www.lib.umich.edu/government-documents center/explore/browse/statistics+economics/929/search/

Links to business, industry, trade, and economic statistics sites, maintained by the Documents Center at the University of Michigan.

Stock Research

YAHOO! Stock Research Center. http://biz.yahoo.com/r/

Earnings dates, stock splits, stock screener, historical quotes (back to the '60s) and much more.

Appendix G

Finding Business Case Studies

Source	Information Provided
Online Catalog	Keyword search, e.g., oil and case study
Databases	Do a keyword search. E.g. "case studies and airlines" Or Use the subject heading "case studies" in ABI/INFORM and Business Source Complete/Premier
Harvard Business School Case Studies http://web.hbr.org/store/index.php	The **Harvard Business Review** publishes one case study per issue. Generally the topic is fictitious. **HBS** case studies are not available for purchase by libraries, but students/faculty can buy them from http://web.hbr.org/store/index.php. Cases from several other schools are also available from this web site.
Darden School of Business (University of Virginia) https://store.darden.virginia.edu/	Searchable collection of case studies online. Abstracts and video previews are available. Purchases may be made at https://store.darden.virginia.edu/
Stanford Graduate School of Business http://gsbapps.stanford.edu/cases/	Cases are searchable online at http://gsbapps.stanford.edu/cases/. A few cases are available free but most are available for purchase through Harvard Business Publishing.
European Case Clearing House (ECCH) http://www.ecch.com/	Cases from European and some U.S. Schools. Some may be viewed free online, by educators, and purchase information is available at http://www.ecch.com/educators/ordering/buying/how.
IBS Case Development Center http://www.ibscdc.org/	Repository that covers the Asia Pacific Region. Searches and purchases can be made at http://www.ibscdc.org/.

Title List

IEBM Encyclopedia of Marketing, **140**

100 Questions & Answers about Buying a New Home, **351**

21st Century Economics: A Reference Handbook, **15**

A Dictionary of Statistical Terms, **118**

ABA Banking Journal, **216**

ABI/Inform (family of databases), **52**

About.Com Commodities, **298**

About.com Mutual Funds, **284**

Accountant's Business Manual, **179**

Accountant's Handbook of Formulas and Tables, **176**

Accounting Desk Book, **175**

Accounting for Dummies, **175**

Accounting Info.com, **174**

Accounting Reference Desktop, **175**

Accounting Review, **177**

AccountingWords, **174**

ACCRA Cost of Living Index. Louisville, **114**

Acronym Finder, **13**

Acronyms, Initialisms & Abbreviations Dictionary, **13**

Ad $ Summary, **155**

Ad$pender, **155**

Advertiser Red Books, **142**

Advertising Age Encyclopedia of Advertising, **140**

Advertising Age, **143**

Advertising Red Books. International Advertisers & Agencies, **142**

Agency Red Books, **142**

AICPA Online Professional Library, **179**

AICPA Professional Standards, **173**

Almanac of Business and Industrial Financial Ratios, **72**

Almanac: Business and Finance, **14**

American Banker Online. Glossary, **212**

American Banker, **217**

American Fact Finder, **125**

American Housing Survey, **357**

American Reference Books Annual, **10**

American Statistics Index, **119**

Annual Reports at Academic Business Libraries, **54**

Annual Survey of Manufactures (ASM), **61**

Arnold Encyclopedia of Real Estate, **348**

ASAE Trade Association Directory, **69**

Bank Directory, **213**

Banker, **216**

Bankers' Almanac, **213**

Banking Crisis Handbook, **212**

Bankscope, **50**

BankScope, **50, 213**

Barron's National Business and Financial Weekly, **40**

Barron's Real Estate Handbook, **348**

Beginners' Guide to Mutual Funds: Online Publications at the SEC, **283**

Best Business Books [Year]," Library Journal, **10**

Best's Aggregates & Averages: Property/Casualty, **333**

Best's Insurance Reports: Life/Health, **324**

Best's Insurance Reports: Property/Casualty, **324**

Best's Key Rating Guide: Life/Health, **326**

Best's Key Rating Guide: Property/Casualty, **326**

Best's Review, **327**

BestWeek, **327**

BizMiner, **68**

Blackwell Encyclopedic Dictionary of Accounting, **174**

Bloomberg Business Week, **28**

BNA Tax Management, **179**

BOMA Experience Exchange Report, **359**

Bond Buyer Full Text, **273**

Bond Guide, **272**

BondsOnline, **274**

Book of the States, **184**

Broadcasting & Cable Yearbook, **152**

Bulls, Bears, Boom, and Bust: A Historical Encyclopedia of American Business Concepts, **14**

Business & Company Resource Center, **52**

Business Books: Core Collections, **4**

Business Information Alert, **10**

Business Information Reports, **198**

Business Information. Needs and Strategies, **8**

Business Information: How to Find It, How to Use It, **6**

Business Rankings Annual, **148**

Business Serials of the U.S. Government, **32**

Business Source (family of databases), **51, 68**

Business Statistics of the United States: Patterns of Economic Change, **123**

Buying Your Home: Settlement Costs and Information, **351**

Capital IQ, **50**
Carroll's Federal Directory: Executive, Legislative, Judicial, **81**
Catalog of Federal Domestic Assistance, **99**
Catalog of Publications, 1790–1972, **105**
Catalog of U.S. Government Publications, **85**
CCH Internet Tax Research Network, **179**
Census Catalog and Guide, **105**
Census of Population and Housing, **357**
CEOExpress, **44**
Chicago Board of Trade Handbook of Futures and Options, **297**
Circulation, **150**
Class/Brand $, **155**
ClickZ, **154**
cnnmoney.com, **45**
Company/Brand $, **155**
Compete, **154**
Complete Book of Insurance: The Consumer's Guide to Insuring Your Life, Health, Property, and Income, **323**
Compustat, **51**
Concise Encyclopedia of Real Estate Business Terms, **348**
Conducting Market Research for International Business, **139**
Congressional Directory, **80**
Consensus, **299**
Consumer Americas, **146**
Consumer Guides (Insurance), **323**
Consumer Handbook on Adjustable Rate Mortgages, **351**
Corporate Affiliations, **54**
County and City Extra: Annual Metro, City, and County Data Book, **123**
County Business Patterns, **62**
CPA Examination Review, **166**
CRB Commodity Yearbook, **300**
CreditWeek, **273**
Cumulative List of Organizations Described in Section 170(c) of the Internal Revenue Code of 1986, Revised to 2006, **188**

Daily Stock Price Record, **241**
Data Sources for Business and Market Analysis, **138**
DATA.GOV, **125**

Datamonitor **68**, 360, **253**
DCAA Contract Audit Manual, **180**
Derivatives Demystified: A Step-by-Step Guide to Forwards, Futures, Swaps and Options, **287**
Derivatives, **290**
Dictionary of Accounting Terms, **174**
Dictionary of Derivatives, **290**
Dictionary of Economics, **118**
Dictionary of Insurance Terms, **320**
Dictionary of Marketing, **139**
Dictionary of Real Estate, **347**
Dictionary of Statistics & Methodology: A Nontechnical Guide for the Social Sciences, **118**
Direct Marketing List Source, **154**
Directory of Business Information Sources, **7**
Directory of Federally Insured Credit Unions, **214**
Directory of Obsolete Securities, **256**
DocuTicker DocuBase, **15**
Dollars & Cents of Shopping Centers/the SCORE, **359**
Dow Jones Averages, 1885–1995, **243**
DttP: Documents to the People, **97**

ECONData, **126**
Economagic.com, **126**
Economic Census, 61
Economic Census. Construction, **356**
Economic Indicators, **33**
Economic Report of the President, **124**
Economics & Finance FAQ, **18**
Editor & Publisher Market Guide, **144**
Encyclopedia of Accounting Systems, **175**
Encyclopedia of American Industries, **252**
Encyclopedia of Associations International Organizations, **69**
Encyclopedia of Associations: National Organizations of the U.S., **69**
Encyclopedia of Associations: Regional, State and Local Organizations, **70**
Encyclopedia of Busine$$ and Finance, **227**
Encyclopedia of Business Ethics and Society, **14**
Encyclopedia of Business in Today's World, **14**
Encyclopedia of Business Information Sources, **7**
Encyclopedia of Major Marketing Campaigns, **141**
Encyclopedia of Real Estate Terms, **348**
Ernst & Young Tax Guide, **187**

Essential Marketing and Advertising Dictionary, **139**

eurostat, **126**

ExecuComp, **51**

Factfinder for the Nation, **356**

FACTIVA, **42, 52, 241**

Facts & Figures, **237**

Facts and Figures on Government Finance, **193**

FDIC Quarterly, **217**

FDIC: Bank Data Guide, **211**

Federal Bulletin Board, **84**

Federal Data Base Finder, **96**

Federal Reserve Bulletin, **34**

Federal Tax Articles, **190**

Federal Tax Coordinator 2d, **190**

Federal Tax Handbook, **186**

Federal Yellow Book, **81**

FEDSTATS, **125**

Finance and Investment Handbook, **227**

Financial Accounting Research System (FARS), **172**

Fitch IBCA Ratings Delivery Service, **273**

Forbes, **30**

Fortune, **29**

FRED (Federal Reserve Economic Data), **126**

Frost & Sullivan, **64**

Fundamentals of Derivatives Markets, **290**

Fundamentals of Government Information: Mining, Finding, Evaluating, and Using Government Resources, **93**

Futures, **298**

GAAP Guide, **172**

GAAS Guide, **173**

Gale Directory of Databases, **45**

Gale Directory of Publications and Broadcast Media, **35**

Gartner.com Web Portal, **64**

Global Market Share Planner Market Share Tracker, **148**

Global Stock Markets Factbook, **238**

Glossary of Terms Used in the Federal Budget, **185**

Glossary of Terms, Acronyms and Abbreviations, **175**

Government Information Quarterly, **96**

Government Reference Books, **95**

Green Book: Worldwide Directory of Focus Group Companies and Services, **141**

Green Book: Worldwide Directory of Marketing Research Companies and Services, **141**

Guide for Buyers of Marketing Research Services, **141**

Guide to Economic Indicators, **116**

Guide to Insurance Research, **329**

Guide to Managing an Accounting Practice, **178**

Guide to Popular Government Publications, **95**

Guide to Reference, **10**

Guide to the 2007 Economic Censuses, **105**

Guidebook to North Carolina Taxes, **187**

Handbook of Common Stocks, **255**

Handbook of Insurance, **320**

Handbook of Loan Payment Tables, **340**

Handbook of Nasdaq Stocks, **255**

Handbook of U.S. Labor Statistics: Employment, Earnings, Prices, Productivity, and Other Labor Data, **123**

Handbook of United States Economic and Financial Indicators, **116**

Handbook of World Stock, Derivative and Commodity Exchanges, **297**

Harrap's Five Language Business Dictionary, **12**

Harvard Business Review, **31**

Historical Statistics of the United States, Colonial Times to the Present, **121**

Homes for Sale, **360**

How to Read the Financial Pages, **232**

HUD USER, **359**

Hulbert Financial Digest, **287**

I Want to . . . Buy a Home, **351**

I/B/E/S, **53**

IBISWorld Industry Reports, **63**

Income/Expense Analysis: Condominiums, Cooperatives, and Planned Unit Developments, **358**

Income/Expense Analysis: Conventional Apartments, **358**

Income/Expense Analysis: Federally Assisted Apartments, **358**

Income/Expense Analysis: Office Buildings, **358**

Income/Expense Analysis: Shopping Centers, **358**

Index to International Statistics, **119**

Index to U.S. Government Periodicals, **96**

Industry Norms and Key Business Ratios: Desktop Edition, **73**

Information for Uniform CPA Candidates, **165**

Insurance Almanac: Who, What, When, and Where in Insurance, An Annual of Insurance Facts, **323**
Insurance Fact Book, **333**
Insurance Marketplace, **326**
Insurance Periodicals Index, **329**
insurance.com, **323**
Interactive Advertising Source, **154**
Internal Revenue Bulletin, **191**
Internal Revenue Cumulative Bulletin, **191**
International Dictionary of Insurance and Finance, **320**
International Directory of Business Biographies, **54**
International Directory of Company Histories, **54**
International Handbook of Islamic Banking and Finance, **212**
International Historical Statistics: Africa, Asia & Oceania, 1750–2005, **121**
International Historical Statistics: Europe, 1750–2005, **121**
International Historical Statistics: the Americas, 1750–2005, **121**
International Macroeconomic Data Set, **127**
Internet Marketing Dictionary, **139**
Introduction to United States Government Information Sources, **94**
Investext Thomson Research, **53**
Investext, **253**
Investing in Bonds.com, **274**
Investing in Real Estate, **349**
Investment Statistics Locator, **243**
Investopedia, **227**
Investor's Business Daily, **37**
InvestorWords, **12, 229, 349**

Journal of Accountancy, **177**
Journal of Accounting & Economics, **177**
Journal of Accounting Research, **177**
Journal of Business and Finance Librarianship, **10**
Journal of Commerce, **40**
Journal of Financial Service Professionals, **328**
Journal of Futures Markets, **299**
Journal of Money, Credit, and Banking, **216**
Journal of Risk and Insurance, **328**
Journal of Taxation, **189**

Key Business Sources of the U.S. Government, **32**

Language of Real Estate Appraisal, **347**
LexisNexis Academic, **54**
LexisNexis Government Periodicals Index, **96**
LexisNexis, **42**
Life Insurance Fact Book, **332**
Lifestyle Market Analyst, **146**
List of Real Estate Terms, **348**

Major Marketing Campaigns Annual, **141**
Market Research Handbook, **139**
Market Research Toolbox: A Concise Guide for Beginners, **139**
Market Share Reporter, **148**
McGraw-Hill Real Estate Handbook, **348**
Medicare and You, **330**
Mergent Bank & Finance Manual, **213, 247, 286, 324**
Mergent Bond Record, **272**
Mergent Industrial Manual, **247**
Mergent International Manual, **248**
Mergent Manuals on Microfiche, **247**
Mergent Municipal & Government Manual, **248**
Mergent Online, **247**
Mergent OTC Industrial Manual, **248**
Mergent OTC Unlisted Manual, **248**
Mergent Public Utility Manual, **248**
Mergent Transportation Manual, **248**
Mergent WebReports, **52, 247**
Mergent's Industry Review, **252**
Metal Statistics, **300**
Mintel Reports, **67**
Mobile Marketing Handbook: A Step-by-Step Guide to Creating Dynamic Mobile Marketing Campaigns, **140**
Money, **32**
Moneyletter, **287**
Monthly & Annual Retail Trade Survey (ARTS), **61**
Monthly & Annual Wholesale Trade Survey (AWTS), **62**
Monthly Catalog of U.S. Government Publications, **86**
Monthly Labor Review, **34**
Monthly Product Announcement, **105**
Morningstar Investment Research Center, **286**
Morningstar, **274, 285**
Motley Fool Mutual Funds, **285**
Multistate Corporate Tax Guide, **184**
Mutual Fund Fact Book, **283**
Mutual Fund Investor's Center, **285**
Mutual Fund Prospector, **287**

National Bureau of Economic Research, **126**
National Real Estate Investor, **350**
National Tax Journal, **188**
National Technical Information Service (NTIS), **89**
National Underwriter: Life & Health, **327**
National Underwriter: P & C, **327**
NationMaster, **127**
Nelson's Directory of Institutional Real Estate, **349**
NetAdvantage, **51,247, 286**
New Products Catalog, **86**
New Trading Systems and Methods, **298**
Newspaper Advertising Source, **150**
North American Industry Classification System, **58**

OFFSTATS, **127**
Online Social Security Handbook: Your Basic Guide to the Social Security Programs, **321**
ORBIS, **49**
Osiris, **49**
Outstanding Business Reference Sources: Yearly Selection of Recent Titles. Annual Feature. Reference & Users Services Quarterly, **10**
Oxford Handbook of Banking, **212**

Palgrave Macmillan Dictionary of Finance, Investment and Banking, **229**
Passport GMID (Global Market Information Database), **65**
Penn World Tables, **128**
Places, Towns and Townships, **123**
Prentice Hall Dictionary of Real Estate, **347**
ProQuest Accounting & Tax Index, **176**
ProQuest Historical Annual Reports, **52**
ProQuest Statistical Insight, **119**

Questionnaire Design: How to Plan, Structure and Write Survey Material for Effective Market Research, **139**

Radio Advertising Source, **152**
RatingsDirect, **273**
Real Estate Dictionary, **348**
Real Estate Forum, **350**
Real Estate Investor's Deskbook, **349**
Real Estate Review, **350**
Real Time Marketing for Business Growth: How to Use Social Media, Measure Marketing and Create a Culture of Execution, **140**

Realty Trac, **359**
ReferenceUSA, **48**
Reproducible Federal Tax Forms for Use in Libraries, **183**
Resource Shelf, **15**
Review of Accounting Studies, **177**
RIA Checkpoint, **180**
RMA Annual Statement Studies Financial Ratio Benchmarks, **72**
Robert D. Fisher Manual of Valuable and Worthless Securities, **256**

S&P/Case-Shiller Home Price Indices, **359**
Sales & Marketing Management, **143**
SalesForce XP Xtra Performance for Sales Management, **143**
Schaeffer's Investment Research, **256**
SDC Platinum, **53**
SEC Accounting Rules, **178**
Service Annual Survey (SAS), **61**
Shepard's McGraw-Hill Tax Dictionary for Business, **185**
Silicon Investor, **241**
Smart and Simple Financial Strategies for Busy People, **226**
Social Security Bulletin, **329**
SOI (Statistics of Income) Bulletin, **192**
Sourcebook America, **145**
Sourcebook of County Demographics, **145**
Sourcebook of ZIP Code Demographics, **145**
SRDS Business Media Advertising Source, **151**
SRDS Consumer Media Advertising Source, **151**
SRDS Local Market Audience Analyst, **146**
Standard & Poor's Analyst's Handbook, **252**
Standard & Poor's Industry Surveys, **69**
Standard & Poor's Industry Surveys, **69, 252**
Standard & Poor's NetAdvantage, 51, 247, 286
Standard & Poor's Security Dealers of North America, **230**
Standard & Poor's Stock Reports, **254**
Standard Federal Tax Reporter, **190**
Standard Industrial Classification, **58**
Statistical Reference Index, **119**
Stock Options Trading, **306**
Subject Guide to U.S. Government Reference Sources, **95**
Survey of Current Business, **33**

TableBase, 69, **148**

Tapping the Government Grapevine: The User-Friendly Guide to U.S. Government Information Sources, **94**

Tax Features, **189**

Tax Notes, **189**

Tax Statistics, **193**

TAXSites.com, **184**

Technical Practice Aids, **178**

The Black Book of Economic Information: A Guide to Sources and Interpretation, **116**

The Business Library and How to Use It: A Guide to Sources and Research Strategies for Information on Business and Management, **8**

The Irwin Guide to Using the Wall Street Journal, **116**

The Street, **256**

The United States Government Internet Directory, **94**

Thomson Savings Directory, **214**

Thorndike Encyclopedia of Banking and Financial Tables, **222, 340**

Transnational Accounting (TRANSACC), **173**

TV and Cable Source, **152**

U.S. Housing Markets, **350**

U.S. Master Tax Guide, **186**

U.S. Real Estate Register, **349**

Ulrich's International Periodicals Directory, **35**

Ultimate Web Marketing Guide, **140**

Uniform CPA Examination: Official Questions and Unofficial Answers, **165**

Uniform CPA Examination: Selected Questions and Unofficial Answers Indexed to Content Specification Outlines 1900s–2000, **166**

United States Government Manual, **80**

United States Tax Reporter, **190**

UNSD Statistical Databases, **129**

US Banker, **216**

US Government on the Web Getting the Information You Need, **94**

Using Government Information Sources: Print and Electronic, **94**

Value Line Convertibles Securities File, **273**

Value Line Convertibles Survey, **273**

Value Line Investment Survey (Expanded Edition), **250**

Value Line Investment Survey, **250**

Value Line Mutual Fund Survey, **287**

Value Line Options, **307**

Wall Street Journal Complete Money and Investing Guidebook, **226**

Wall Street Journal, **37**

Wall Street Lingo: Thousands of Investment Terms Explained Simply, **229**

Wall Street Transcript, **40**

Who Audits America, **176**

Who Writes What in Life and Health Insurance, **326**

Who's Who in Insurance and Risk Management, **323**

Wiley CPA Examination Review, **166**

Wiley IFRS: Interpretation and Application of International Accounting and Financial Reporting Standards, **173**

World Currency Yearbook, **196**

World Development Indicators, **128**

World Directory of Marketing Information Sources, **138**

World Stock Exchange Fact Book, **238**

YAHOO! FINANCE, **44, 241, 256, 285**

Your Federal Income Tax, **186**

Zack's, **256**

Zephyr, **50**

Subject Index

Accounting, 163-180
  basic concepts, 167-172
    auditing standards, 172-173
    financial statements, 167-170
      auditor's report, 169
      balance sheet, 167-168
      income statement, 168-169
      tutorials, 170
    International, 173
    principles and standards, 170-172
      concepts, 171
      interpretations, 171
      statements, 171
  publications
    dictionaries, 174
    directories, 176
    electronic, 178-180
    encyclopedias, 175
    guides, 174
    government, 180
    handbooks, 175
    interpretations, 171
    loose-leaf, 178-180
    periodical indexes, 176
    periodicals, 177-178
    standards, 171
  types of 164-165
    government, 165
    private, 164
    public, 164
Accounting Firms
  Big 4, 164
  directories, 176
Accounting Principles and Standards, 170-172
  Accounting Principles Board (APB), 172
  American institute of Certified Public Accountants (AICPA), 165-167
  Financial Accounting Standards Board (FASB) 171-172
Acronyms, 361-364
Advertising, 149-156
  associations, 157-158
  audience measurement, 149-156
  costs, 149-154
  expenditures by companies, 155-156
  publications, 149-155

broadcast media, 151-153
direct mail media, 153-154
internet, 154-155
print media, 149-151
Adervtising Research Foundation, 158
Advisory Sentiment Index, 116
Advisory Srvices, Investment, 230-232
  bonds, 273
  futures, 302
  mutual funds, 287
  options, 307
AICPA see American institute of Certified Public Accountants (AICPA)
Almanacs, 14-15
American institute of Certified Public Accountants (AICPA), 165-167
American Marketing Association, 158
American stock exchange (AMEX)
amortization, 340-342
Annual percentage Rate (APR), 199-200
Annual report to Shareholders, 245
Annuities, 313
audience management, advertising, 149-156
Auditing standards, 172-173
Auditor's report, 169

Baby Bonds, 259
Balance sheet, 167-168
Banking Tables, 222
Banks and banking, 200-223
  commercial banks, 201-202
  credit unions, 203, 210, 214
  Federal Reserve System 204-209
  finance companies, 204
  investment banks, 204
  investment companies, 204
  mutual savings banks, 202
  Publications, 211-223
    government documents, 218-219
    guides, 211
    dictionaries, 212
    handbooks, 212
    manuals, 213-215
    newspapers, 217,
    online databases, 213-215
    periodicals, 216

Banks and banking (*cont.*)
    statistics, 219-222
  securities brokers, 204
  thrift institutions, 202-203
bearer bonds, 260
Bibliographies
  government, 85-88, 95-96
  general, 9-12
  marketing, 138
Big Mac index, 115
Boeckh, 353
Bond Market Association, 267, 272
Bond Tables, 270
Bonds, 259-275
  adjustable, 260
  bearer, 260
  call provisions, 261
  commercial paper, 263, 269
  convertible, 269-270, 272
  Corporate,
    sources of information 270-271
    types, 269-270
    trading, 270
  coupon, 260
  debenture, 269
  Federal Government,
    Treasury issues, 263-266
    Federal Agency issues, 266-267
  general obligation, 267
  Interest, 259-260
  Money market instruments, 263
  Municipal issues
    general obligation bonds, 267
    revenue bonds, 267-268
    sources of information, 268
  prices, 260
  ratings, 261-262
  registered, 260
  revenue, 267-268
  Secondary bond market, 262
  Sources of information, 271-274
    advisory sources, 273
    factual sources, 271-273
    for fee databases, 273-274
    web sites, 274
  Yield, 260-261
  zero coupon, 260
Boston Stock exchange, 237
Broadcast media advertising, 151-153
Bureau of National Affairs (BNA), 178, 361

Call provisions, Bonds, 261
Calls, Options, 304
Case Studies, 383
Census Bureau *See* U.S. Department
    Commerce. Bureau of the Census
Certified Public Accountant, 165-166
Chart Services, 255
Chicago board of Trade, 294, 297, 300, 361
Christmas Price Index, 115
Cincinnati Stock Exchange
Closed-end fund association, 285,288
Codes, 377
Commodity Research Bureau, 300
Common Stock, 233-234
Convertible preferred stock, 234
Commercial Banks, 201-202
Commerce Clearing House (CCH), 178
Commercial paper, 263, 269
Commodity futures trading commission, 295
Commodities, 292-293 see also Futures
  contracts, 295
  exchanges, 293-294
  information sources
    advisory services, 302-303
    databases, 303
    dictionaries, 298
    handbooks, manuals, guides 297-298
    periodicals, newspapers, newsletters,
      298-299
    statistics, 300-302
  prices, 295
  regulation, 295-296
  web sites, 378-379
Companies, 47-56
  annual reports, 245
  bonds, 269-270
  financial and performance ratios, 55-56
  Questions, 47
  types of information, 48
    contact, 48
    directory, 48
    descriptive, 48-56
    financial, 48-56
Compliance Exchanges, 238
construction statistics, 350-356, 358, 373
Consumer price index, 113-115, 373
Convertible bonds, 269-270, 271, 272, 273, 274
convertible preferred stock, 234
Corporate reports, 243-246
  Annual report to Shareholders, 245
  Form 10-K, 244

CPA *See* Certified Public Accountant
Credit, 198-200
Credit Reports, 198-199
Credit unions, 203, 210, 214
Creditworthiness, 198

Dealer quotations, 238
debenture bonds, 269
Demographic data, 68, 71, 104, 105, 124, 125, 127, 128, 129, 134-135, 143-147
Derivatives, 289-291 *See also* Futures
   guides, 290
   dictionaries, 290
Dictionaries, 12-13
   accounting, 174-
   acronyms and abbreviations, 13, 175
   banking, 212
   commodities, 298
   derivatives, 290
   financial, 306
   general business, 12
   insurance, 320
   investment, 229
   marketing, 138-139
   multilingual business, 12
   real estate, 347-348
   statistics, 118-119
   taxes, 185-186
Direct Mail Media Advertising, 153-154
Directories
   accounting, 176
   associations , 71
   company, 54
   insurance, 323
   marketing, 141
   mutual funds, 286
   periodical, 35
   real estate, 349
   subsidiaries
   taxes, 188
Discount rate bonds
Dividend Yield, 234
Dow Jones industrial Average, 242
Drinking Couple count, 116

Earnings per share, 234
Economic Census, 61, 105, 251-252, 339, 356, 379
Economic indicators, 33, 115-117, 373

Encyclopedias
   accounting, 175
   investment, 227
   marketing, 140-141
   real estate, 348
   statistics, 118-119
Exchanges Web sites
exposure drafts, 171-172

Fannie Mae (FNMA) *See* Federal National Mortgage Association
FASB *See* Financial Accounting Standards Board
Federal National Mortgage Association (FNMA or Fannie Mae) 343-344, 381
Federal Reserve System 204-209
   monetary policy, 208-209
   organizational structure, 205-207
   services, 207-208
Federal Agency bond Issues 266-267
Federal Deposit insurance Corporation *See* U.S. Federal Deposit insurance Corporation
Federal Depository Library Program, 82
Federal Farm Credit Bank *See* U.S. Federal Farm Credit Bank
Federal government *See also* names of federal agencies beginning with U.S.
   agencies, 80-81, 365-368
   branches, 77-80
   bibliographies and catalogs of federal documents, 83-88
   commercially published guides, bibliographies, periodicals , 93-97
   departments, 365-368
   experts, 98-99
   libraries, 82, 98
   periodicals, 87-88
   purchase of goods and services, 99
   services to business 97-98
   statistics, 103-106
   structure, 76,
Federal government agencies, 365-368
Federal government corporations, 369-370
Federal government departments, 365-368
Federal Home Loan Bank System *See* U.S. Federal Home Loan Bank System
Federal Home Loan Mortgage System *See* U.S. Federal Home Loan Mortgage System

Federal Housing Finance Board *See* U.S. Federal Housing Finance Board
Federal Insurance, 317-319
Federal National Mortgage Association (FNMA) *See* U.S. Federal National Mortgage Association
Federal Open Market Committee (FOMC) *See* U.S. Federal Open Market Committee (FOMC)
Federal Reserve System *See* U.S. Federal Reserve System
Federal Trade Commission *See* U.S. Federal Trade Commission
Finance Companies, 204
Financial Accounting Standards Board (FASB) 171-172
Financial and performance ratios, 72-74
Financial Statements
    annual reports, 245
    balance sheet, 167-168
    debt reports, 246
    income statement, 168-169
    form 10-K, 244
    other reports, 246
    security reports, 246
Food and Drug Administration *See* U.S. Food and Drug Administration
Forecasts and Projections, 112
Foreign Exchange, 196-197
Freddie Mac *See* U.S. Federal Home Loan Mortgage System
Futures, 291-303 *See also* Commodities
    contracts, 295
    exchanges, 293-294
    information sources
        advisory services, 302-303
        databases, 303
        handbooks, manuals, guides, 297-298
        periodicals, newspapers, newsletters, 298-299
        statistics, 300-302
    prices, 295
    regulation, 295-296
    types of
        commodities, 292
        financial, 295
    web sites, 378-379

GAAP *See* Generally Accepted Accounting Principles

GAAS *See* Generally Accepted Auditing Standards
GAO *See* U.S. Government Accountability Office
GDP *See* Gross Domestic Product
General obligation bonds
Generally Accepted Accounting Principles, 171
Generally Accepted Auditing Standards, 172
General Accounting Office (GAO) *See* U.S. Government Accountability Office
Government Accountability Office (GAO) *See* U.S. Government Accountability Office
Geographic Market Segmentation, 134
Ginnie Mae (GNMA) *See* U.S. Government National Mortgage Association
GNP *See* Gross National Product
Government National Mortgage Association (GNMA) *See* U.S. Government National Mortgage Association
Government Printing Office (GPO) *See* U.S. Government Printing Office
Gross Domestic Product, 115, 373
Guides
    accounting, 174
    banking, 211
    commodities
    derivatives, 290
    futures, 297
    government, 93-94
    insurance, 320
    marketing, 138
    mutual funds, 283
    options, 306
    statistics, 119
    taxes, 186-187
Guides types of, 4-8
    dictionary, 7-8
    for specific user group, 8-9
    general, 4-7

Handbooks, 15
    accounting, 175-176
    banking, 212
    economic indicators, 116
    futures, 297
    investment, 227, 230
    insurance, 320
    marketing, 139-140
    real estate, 347

stocks, 252, 255
taxes, 186
Handy Whitman Indexes, 353
Health Insurance, 313-314
Health Maintenance Organization (HMO), 313
Hedge Funds, 279
Households Using Television index, 152
HUD *See* U.S. Department of Housing and Urban Development
HUT *See* Households Using Television index

Income Statement, 168-169
Independent agencies relevant to business, 80, 369-370
index numbers, 112-113
Index of New One Family homes, 352
Industry Classification Codes, 57-59
Industry Information
   classification codes, 57-59
   ratios, 72-74
   reports, 63-71
   trade Groups and associations, 71-72
   U.S. Government surveys, 60-63
Insurance,
   associations, 319
   basics, 309
   characteristic, 309-310
   information sources, 324-333
      about insurance companies, 324-326
      directories, 324-325
      government, 329-332
      indexes, 329
      periodicals, 327-329
      policies, 326-327
      reports, 365-369
      statistics, 332-333
   private, 315-317
   public, 317
   regulation, 320, 326-327
   social, 317
   types of, 311
      health, 313-314
      life, 312-313
      property/casualty, 315
Insurance Information Institute, 319
Insurance policies, 369
Insurance reports, 365-69
Interest, 199-200
Interest only securities, 330
Intermountain Stock Exchange, 273

Internal revenue code, 183
International Advertising Association, 158
International Stock Exchanges, 238-239
Investment. *See also* Bonds; Commodities; Futures; Insurance; Mutual Funds; Options; Real Estate; Stocks
   background information, 225-226
   publications,
      dictionaries, 229
      directories, 230
      electronic, 50-53, 228
      encyclopedias and handbooks, 227-229
      guides, 226-227
      newspapers, 38-40
      periodicals, 30-32
      securities quotations, 232
Investment advisory services, 230-232
Investment banks, 204
Investment companies, 204, 277-281 *See also* Mutual Funds
   closed end, 280
   information sources, 283-288
      advisory newsletters, 287-288
      advisory services, 230-232
      directories, 286
      encyclopedias, guides, fact books, 283-285
   investment objective, 280
   load, 279-280
   no-load 279-280
   portfolio contents, 280-281
Investment Company Institute (ICI), 283
Investment Managers, 230

Kansas City Board of Trade, 292,297

Life insurance, 312-313
Lloyd's of London, 316-317
Loose-leaf services, 173, 174, electronic versions, 178-180
Loose leaf and electronic, 178-180

Marcive Company, 86
Market research, 135-137
Market research reports, 64-67, 160-61
Market share, 147-149
Market segmentation, 158-59
Marketing, 133-135
   activities, 157-58
   associations, 157-158

Marketing (*cont.*)
    basics of, 133-135
    publications, 138-157
        broadcast media, 151-153
        dictionaries, encyclopedias and guides,
            138-141
        directories, 131-142
        geographical information systems, 156
        internet, 154-155, 157
        periodicals, 142-143, 149-151
        regulation, 158-160
        reports, 64-67, 160-61
        research, 159-62
        segmentation, 134-136
        statistics, 144-147
Money, 195-197
    Banks, 200-203
    Credit, 198
    Credit reports, 198-199
    Federal Reserve System, 204-209
    Foreign exchange, 196-197
    Interest, 199-200
Monetary measures, 196
Monetary system, 196
Mortgage backed securities, 344
Mortgage bonds, 267
Mortgage Guaranty Insurance Corporation,
    344
Mortgages, 343-344
Municipal bonds, 267-269
Mutual Fund Education Alliance, 280, 289
Mutual fund information Web sites, 429
Mutual funds, 277-279 *See also* Investment
    companies
    information sources, 282-288
        advisory services, 287-288
        directories, 286
        encyclopedias, guides, factbooks, 283-284
        per share information, 281-282
        periodicals and newsletters, 286-288
        prospectuses, 282-283
        subscription databases, 286
        web sites, 284-285
    closed end, 282, 285
    current per-share, 281-282
    quotations, 281-282
    investment objectives, 280
    load, 279
    no-load, 279-280
    portfolio contents, 280-281

Mutual savings banks, 238,

NAICS (North American Industrial
    Classification System), 55, 58-59
NASDAQ (National Association of
    Securities Dealers Automated
    Quotations), 238
National Association of Insurance
    Commissioners, 319
New York Stock Exchange, 235-237
New York Stock Exchange Composite Index.
    242, 295
Newspaper advertising, 149-150
Newspaper price tables stocks, 240
Newspapers, 36-42
    advertising, 150
    aggregators, 42-43
    banking, 217
    business and financial, 37-40
    directories, 45
    employment, 69
    government, 68
    options, 299
    stock tables, 39
NTIS. *See* U.S. National Technical
    Information Service,
NYSE, 235-237

Office of the Comptroller of the Currency.
    See U.S. Office of the Comptroller of the
    Currency
Office of the U.S. Trade Representative, 78
OMB. *See* U.S. Office of Management and
    Budget
Online commercial databases
    background information, 22-27
    accounting, 178-180
    banking, 213-214
    bonds, 273-274
    commodities, futures, 303
    insurance, 326
    investment, 261, 262, 264
    mutual funds, 286
    producers, aggregators, vendors, 134-35
    real estate, 359-360
Options, 303-307
    basic features, 304
    exchanges, 304-305
    information sources advisory services,
        307

dictionaries and glossaries, 306
guides, 306
periodicals and newspapers, 306
statistics. 306
listed quotations, 305
Over-the-counter market (OTC), 237-238

Periodical indexes and abstracts, 24-27
Periodicals, 28-30
   accounting, 177-178
   advertising, 142-143
   banking, 216-217
   directories of, 35-36
   futures, 298-300
   insurance, 327-329
   marketing, 142-143
   options, 306
   real estate, 350-351
   taxes, 189-191
   types of, 49-57
      consumer, 31-32
      general,49-52
      government, 32-35
      regional, 35
      scholarly, 31
      trade, 30-31
Personal and commercial insurance, 315
Pipeline index, 353
Preferred stock, 233-234
Price-earnings ratio, 233-235
Private companies, 47
Producer Price Index, 115, 374
Property/Casualty insurance, 315
Psychographic market segmentation, 159
Public companies, 23
Public insurance, 359
Puts, options, 304
Radio advertising, 152-153
Ratio analysis, 55-56
Real estate
   basic concepts, 379-88
   categories, 336-337
   financing, 339-345
   government role, 345-347
   industry, 338-339
   information sources, 347-360
      dictionaries, encyclopedias and hand-
         books, 347-349
      directories, 348-350
      government documents, 351-352

      periodicals and periodical indexes, 350-351
      statistics, 352-360
Real estate investment trusts (REITs), 337
Regional reserve banks, 207
REITs. *See* Real estate investment trusts
Research Institute of America (RIA), 190, 191
Revenue bonds, 267-268
Russell 2000 Index, 242

S & P 500 Index. *See* Standard & Poor's 500
     Index
Sallie Mae, 267
Savings and loan associations, 200
SEC. *See* U.S. Securities and exchange
     commission
SEC filings, 243-246
Secondary bond market, 262-263
Securities brokers, 204
Short skirt index, 116
SIC (Standard Industrial Classification), 57-58
Sinking fund, 261
Social insurance, 317
Social Security Administration. *See*
     U.S. Department of Health and
     Human Services: Social Security
     Administration
Sociographic market segmentation, 136
Standard & Poor's 500 Index, 242
State governments, 100
   publications, 100, 102
Statistics, 103
   banking, 219-222
   basic concepts, 110-116
      economic indicators, 116
      forecasts and projections, 113-14
      index numbers, 112-115
      reliability, 118-19
      sampling, 110-11
      time series, 111-112
   commodities, 300-302
   federal agencies, 105-10
   insurance, 332-333
   international, 126-129
   marketing, 143-147
   options, 306
   publications
      compilations, 121-125
      dictionaries and encyclopedias, 118-119
      guides and indexes, 119-121
      selected web sites, 125-129

Statistics (*cont.*)
   real estate, 352-360
   taxes, 192-194
Stock exchanges, 235-239
   International Stock Exchanges, 238-239
   NASDAQ, 237
   New York Stock Exchange, 235-237
   Regional Stock Exchanges, 237
Stock price indexes, 242
   information, 242-243
Stock prices, 275, 278
Stock tables, 240-241
Stocks, 233-235
   common, 233-234
   dividend yield, 234
   indexes, 242
   investment services, 247-251
   preferred, 233-234
   price-earnings ratio, 234-235
   prices, 240
   publications
      annual reports, 245
      charting, 256
      corporate reports, 243-244
      debt reports, 246
      form 8-K reports, 282
      form 10-K reports, 244-245
      industry information, 251-254
      investment services, 246-247
      obsolete securities, 256
      other forms, 245
      prospectus, 243-244
      registration, 243-244
      security reports, 246
      stock exchanges, 235-239
      tables, 240-241
      warrants, 235
      web compilations, 257
Surly waiter index, 116
Swaps, 212, 289, 290

Tax code, 183-184
Taxes and taxation, 181-184
   basics of, 181
   Internal Revenue Service, 182-183
   kinds of taxes, 181-182
   other government agencies involved, 183
   publications, 183-194
      dictionaries, 185
      directories, 188

      government, 191
      guides, 186-188
      loose-leaf and online, 190-191
      periodicals, newspapers, indexes, 188-190
      statistics, 192-194
      states, 184-185
      tax law, 183-184
Television advertising, 147, 152-153
Treasury bills, 208, 260, 264-265
Treasury bonds, 265
Treasury notes, 265

Unit investment trusts, 278
U.S. Council of Economic Advisors, 78
U.S. Council on Environmental Quality, 78-79
U.S. Bureau of Alcohol, Tobacco, Firearms
   and Explosives, 367
U.S. Department of Agriculture, 300-301
U.S. Department of Commerce, 106
U.S. Department of Commerce. Bureau of
   the Census, 104-105, 144
U.S. Department of Health and Human
   Services. Social Security Administration,
   318, 321-323
U.S. Department of Housing and Urban
   Development, 344
U.S. Department of Labor. Bureau of Labor
   Statistics, 79, 107, 113-114
U.S. Federal Communication Commission,
   161-162
U.S. Federal Deposit Insurance Corporation, 210
U.S. Federal Farm Credit Bank, 267
U.S. Federal Home Loan Bank System, 210
U.S. Federal Home Loan Mortgage
   Corporation, 344
U.S. Federal Housing Finance Board, 346
U.S. Federal National Mortgage Association,
U.S. Federal Open Market Committee (FOMC),
U.S. Federal Reserve System, 196-197
   Board of Governors, 205-206
   monetary policy, 208-209
   reserve requirements, 208-209
   services, 207-208
   structure, 205-207
U.S. Food and Drug Administration, 161-162
U.S. General Accounting Office, 82, 191
U.S. Government National Mortgage
   Association, 343-344
U.S. Government Printing Office, 81-82
   bibliographies, catalogs, periodicals, 85-89

depository library program, 82-83
sales program, 83-84
U.S. Internal Revenue Service, 182-183
U.S. National Technical Information Service, 89-92
U.S. Office of the Comptroller of the Currency, 209
U.S. Office of Management and Budget, 79
U.S. Patent and Trademark Office, 92
U.S. Securities and Exchange Commission, 243-245

U.S. Small Business Administration, 97-98
U.S. Student Loan Marketing Association, 267

Warrants, 235
Wiltshire 5000 Equity Index, 243

Yield, 260-261
Yield to maturity, 261

Zero coupon bonds, 260

About the Authors

RITA W. MOSS is the Business/Economics Librarian and the team leader for Social Sciences at the University of North Carolina at Chapel Hill. She has been a librarian at UNC for twenty years and before that worked at Elon University.

In her current position she supervises subject librarians and works with them on developing and maintaining the collections in Davis Library. She also consults with faculty and students and provides essential information and classes.

Rita is also an adjunct lecturer in the School of Information and Library Science at the University of North Carolina at Chapel Hill where she co-teaches a class on business and economic resources.

Rita has a B.A. from the University College of North Wales, Bangor, U.K, with a double major in Social Theory and Institutions and History, an MA from the same institution, and an MLS from the University of North Carolina at Chapel Hill, received in 1988.

DAVID G. ERNSTHAUSEN is the Faculty Teaching and Research Support Librarian at the University of North Carolina at Chapel Hill's Kenan-Flagler Business School. He consults, instructs, and advises faculty and students in the selection and efficient use of resources that are most likely to provide useful information for their research and instruction needs. He also guest lectures for classes in the MBA and Bachelors degree programs on library and research resources available to students at UNC-Chapel Hill. Since 2006, David also is an adjunct lecturer in the School of Information and Library Science at the University of North Carolina at Chapel Hill where he co-teaches a class on business and economic resources. David has worked at the Kenan-Flagler Business School since 1997. Prior to 1997 he worked for 7 years as a reference librarian in the Z. Smith Reynolds Library at Wake Forest University. David has an MBA from the Babcock Graduate School of Management at Wake Forest University and a Master of Library Science degree from Indiana University.